URBAN
INEQUALITY

URBAN INEQUALITY

Evidence from Four Cities

ALICE O'CONNOR
CHRIS TILLY
LAWRENCE D. BOBO

EDITORS

A VOLUME IN THE MULTI-CITY STUDY OF
URBAN INEQUALITY

RUSSELL SAGE FOUNDATION / NEW YORK

The Russell Sage Foundation

The Russell Sage Foundation, one of the oldest of America's general purpose foundations, was established in 1907 by Mrs. Margaret Olivia Sage for "the improvement of social and living conditions in the United States." The Foundation seeks to fulfill this mandate by fostering the development and dissemination of knowledge about the country's political, social, and economic problems. While the Foundation endeavors to assure the accuracy and objectivity of each book it publishes, the conclusions and interpretations in Russell Sage Foundation publications are those of the authors and not of the Foundation, its Trustees, or its staff. Publication by Russell Sage, therefore, does not imply Foundation endorsement.

Library of Congress Cataloging-in-Publication Data

Urban inequality : evidence from four cities / Alice O'Connor, Chris Tilly, and Lawrence Bobo, editors.
    p. cm. — (A volume in the multi-city study of urban inequality)
   Includes bibliographical references and index.
   ISBN 0-87154-650-7 (cloth)   ISBN 0-87154-651-5 (paper)
    1. Sociology, Urban—United States.   2. Cities and towns—United States.
 3. Urban economics—United States. 4. Equality—United States.
 5. United States—Race relations. 6. United States—Social policy.
 7. United States—Economic policy. I. Bobo, Lawrence. II. O'Connor,
Alice. III. Tilly, Chris. IV. Multi-city study of urban inequality.

HT123.U7454 2001
307.760973—dc21   00-036618

RUSSELL SAGE FOUNDATION
112 East 64th Street, New York, New York 10021
10 9 8 7 6 5 4 3 2 1

The Multi-City Study of Urban Inequality

The Multi-City Study of Urban Inequality is a major social science research project designed to deepen the nation's understanding of the social and economic divisions that now beset America's cities. It is based on a uniquely linked set of surveys of employers and households in four major cities: Atlanta, Boston, Detroit, and Los Angeles. The Multi-City Study focuses on the effects of massive economic restructuring on racial and ethnic groups in the inner city, who must compete for increasingly limited opportunities in a shifting labor market while facing persistent discrimination in housing and hiring. Involving more than forty researchers at fifteen U.S. colleges and universities, the Multi-City Study has been jointly funded by the Ford Foundation and the Russell Sage Foundation. This volume is the seventh in a series of books reporting the results of the Multi-City Study to be published by the Russell Sage Foundation.

Contents

Contributors

ALICE O'CONNOR is associate professor of history at the University of California, Santa Barbara.

CHRIS TILLY is University Professor of Regional Economic and Social Development at the University of Massachusetts, Lowell.

LAWRENCE D. BOBO is professor of sociology and Afro-American studies at Harvard University.

IRENE BROWNE is associate professor of sociology and women's studies at Emory University.

CAMILLE ZUBRINSKY CHARLES is assistant professor of sociology at the University of Pennsylvania. She is also research associate at the University of Pennsylvania's Population Studies Center.

SHELDON DANZIGER is Henry J. Meyer Collegiate Professor of Social Work and Public Policy and director of the Center on Poverty Risk and Mental Health at the University of Michigan.

LUIS M. FALCÓN is associate professor of sociology and chair of the Department of Sociology and Anthropology at Northeastern University.

REYNOLDS FARLEY is Otis Dudley Duncan Collegiate Professor of Sociology, University of Michigan.

ROGER B. HAMMER is associate consultant and acting director of the Applied Population Laboratory at the University of Wisconsin, Madison.

TOM HERTZ is a doctoral candidate in economics at the University of Massachusetts, Amherst.

HARRY J. HOLZER is professor of public policy at Georgetown University and research fellow at the Urban Institute.

IVY KENNELLY is visiting assistant professor of sociology in the School of History, Technology, and Society at the Georgia Technological Institute.

JOLEEN KIRSCHENMAN is research associate of Distressed and High Yield Investments at Citadel Investment Group, LLC, in Chicago, Illinois.

JAMES R. KLUEGEL is professor of sociology at the University of Illinois at Urbana-Champaign.

MICHAEL P. MASSAGLI is research and development director at the Picker Institute.

EDWIN MELENDEZ is director of the Community Development Research Center and a professor of management and urban policy at the Milano Graduate School of Management and Urban Policy at the New School for Social Research.

PHILIP MOSS is professor in the Department of Regional Economic and Social Development at the University of Massachusetts, Lowell.

JULIE E. PRESS is assistant professor of sociology and women's studies at Temple University. She is also research fellow of the Temple University Center for Public Policy.

LEANN M. TIGGES is associate professor of rural sociology at the University of Wisconsin, Madison.

FRANKLIN D. WILSON is professor of Afro-American studies and sociology at the University of Wisconsin, Madison.

Acknowledgments

This volume, like the broader study on which it is based, is the product of close collaboration among a diverse, far-flung group of scholars. Thanks to generous support from the Russell Sage and Ford Foundations, we had the opportunity to meet on a regular basis for several years, in order to plan, design surveys, analyze, argue, and above all, review work-in-progress at each stage of this ambitious undertaking. Our heartfelt thanks to Eric Wanner, president of the Russell Sage Foundation, and Prudence Brown, program officer at the Ford Foundation at the time we started this project, for their all-important role in pushing us to articulate—and holding us to—both the broader vision and the detailed specifics of the Multi-City Study of Urban Inequality. We are especially appreciative of the way these foundations worked in partnership to support the goals of the project: conducting original new research; opening up opportunities for graduate students and early-career scholars; creating a unique public-use database and making it available to other scholars; and presenting what we have learned to a broad audience. The Social Science Research Council also played an important role in this institutional partnership, particularly in the early phases of project planning and development.

We are also grateful to the many people who have contributed to this project in the form of advice, review, technical support, constructive criticism, and research assistance. Our work benefited enormously from the contributions of our National Advisory Committee, Jorge Chapa, Mary Jackman, Arne Kalleberg, Frank Levy, Seymour Sudman, and Franklin D. Wilson. Special thanks to Robinson Hollister, chair of the committee, who offered careful scrutiny, invaluable advice, and detailed readings at each stage of the project. We were also most fortunate in being able to draw on the hard work and talents of a number of graduate students—many of whom have since gone on to complete their dissertations and start professional careers.

Finally, a word of thanks to Madge Spitaleri, Nancy Cunniff Casey, Cheryl Seleski, David Haproff, Suzanne Nichols, and other members of the professional, editorial, and support staff of the Russell Sage Foundation. Both literally and figuratively, they did wonders to provide the space where the work of the Multi-City Study could be completed.

ALICE O'CONNOR
CHRIS TILLY
LAWRENCE D. BOBO

UNDERSTANDING INEQUALITY IN THE LATE TWENTIETH-CENTURY METROPOLIS: NEW PERSPECTIVES ON THE ENDURING RACIAL DIVIDE

Alice O'Connor

T HE UNITED States enters the new millennium amidst widespread celebration of its vast prosperity. That prosperity is marred, however, by the same great problems with which the twentieth century began: growing inequality in the distribution of wealth, income, and opportunity; a rapidly restructuring "new economy" that is destabilizing older patterns of work and community; ethnic tensions sparked by the steady arrival of "new," racially "other" immigrants; and the endurance of what W. E. B. DuBois prophetically described one hundred years ago when he wrote that "the problem of the twentieth century is the problem of the color line; the relation of the darker to the lighter races of men in Asia and Africa, in America and the islands of the sea" (DuBois 1901, 354).

Nowhere are these intertwined problems more vividly captured than in the complex economic, gender-based, and racial and ethnic divisions of contemporary urban America. In major cities nationwide, overall economic growth is accompanied by higher than average rates of unemployment and poverty, concentrated especially in low-income, working-class minority neighborhoods that have only recently begun to show signs of recovery following decades of steady decline (U.S. Department of Housing and Urban Development 1999). Still, the low-skilled urban workforce, greatly expanded by the "end of welfare," has little access to local jobs that provide living wages, employment security, and adequate benefits. For the past several years job creation has been faster in the suburbs, where minority workers encounter greater racial discrimination in hiring (Holzer 1996). Meanwhile, despite gradually rising rates of nonwhite suburbanization, racial residential segregation remains the norm—laying the basis for racial and class segregation in education, transportation systems, access to public services, and political representation. Yet, the commitment to deliberate policies of integration, on the metropolitan as well as the national level, is in open retreat.

Explaining these economic, spatial, and racial divisions is the central purpose of the Multi-City Study of Urban Inequality, a unique inquiry launched in the early 1990s by an interdisciplinary team of social scientists with sponsorship from the Russell Sage and Ford foundations. Based on surveys of households and employers in the metropolitan areas of Atlanta, Boston, Detroit, and Los Angeles, the study affords a comprehensive and systematic look at the roots of inequality in labor markets, residential segregation, and racial attitudes.

Three long-range and far-reaching transformations in the post-World War II and especially the post-1970s urban landscape set the larger context for the Multi-City Study. One is the transformation of the urban economy, which for the past fifty years and with greater speed in the past two decades has become more decentralized, global, and heavily reliant on finance, services, and technology than on its once-larger and more powerful manufacturing base. Until recently, urban economies also manifested two deeply troubling and interrelated long-term trends in the broader U.S. economy. The first, the two-decade-long stagnation and decline in real wages for American workers, has only recently been reversed, thanks largely to the high-employment economy. The second, a trend toward growing inequality in the distribution of income, has not been significantly altered, while wealth inequality has continued to gain momentum during the current economic boom. Although cities have historically been associated with the extremes of concentrated wealth and concentrated poverty, the postindustrial urban economy has left a large segment of working- and middle-class families struggling to keep up as well (Danziger and Gottschalk 1995; Levy 1998; Mishel, Bernstein, and Schmitt 1999). Moreover, the consequences of economic restructuring and polarization have played out differently across racial lines. Nonwhites, historically disadvantaged in access to educational opportunity, have suffered disproportionately from the decline of high-wage, unionized manufacturing jobs for non-college educated workers. And although nonwhite college graduates have indeed benefited from the "premium" to education, far fewer minority households have been in a position to share in the gains that wealth generates in the "new economy" (Wilson 1987, 1996; Oliver and Shapiro 1995).

Accompanying economic restructuring and rising inequality has been a second, equally consequential transformation in the urban landscape, brought about by the metropolitanization of residential and industrial space. Spurred on by post–World War II public policies and government-subsidized infrastructure building, the long-term trend toward residential suburbanization and industrial deconcentration has profoundly altered the geographic map of opportunity, shifting jobs toward what for many remains an elusive periphery and away from the central cities and "inner-ring" suburbs that are often home to minority workers. While spatial restructuring varies physically across metropolitan areas, its racial significance does not: shaped by a long history of segregationist policies, institutional practices, and social attitudes, the metropolitanization of population and employment has meant diminished work opportunities and neighborhood decline for poor and working-class minorities, who remain barred by race as well as income from following the trajectory of metropolitan sprawl (Jackson 1985; Kasarda 1989; Massey and Denton 1993; Sugrue 1996).

The third transformation, and the most recent in origin, is the vast demographic change brought about by the post-1965 growth and changing nature of immigration to the United States. In contrast to the principally European origin of nineteenth and early twentieth-century migration, today's "new immigrants" have come from Asia, Latin America, and Africa, adding visibly to the racial, ethnic, and cultural diversity of their predominantly urban destinations (Portes and Rumbaut 1990). Especially in high-immigrant cities such as Los Angeles, New York, and Miami, this changing demographic profile has affected intraminority relations in complicated ways. On the one hand, groups once reviled as "newcomers" to the cities—African Americans, native-born Latinos, and other, more established ethnic communities—now picture themselves as threatened old-timers, vying with a new wave of immigrants for residential space, labor market position, and cultural recognition. Further heightened by years of urban deindustralization, physical deterioration, and political neglect, the resulting tensions set the stage for daily conflict as well as "multiethnic rebellion" during the 1980s and 90s in America's major immigrant destination points (Oliver, Johnson, and Farrell 1993; Waldinger and Bozorgmehr 1996; Mohl 1997 [1995]). On the other hand, in recent years these same transformations and interethnic conflicts have also fostered growing awareness of the need for cross-ethnic coalition building within and between urban neighborhoods, particularly around issues of economic, environmental, and racial justice, education and social services, and governing institutions that are more adequately representative of the multiethnic urban core.

Connected though they may be to economic and social forces that are taking place on a global level, these changes in urban America have been shaped by policy choices made within a political environment that over the past quarter-century has grown increasingly hostile to government activism in the areas of poverty and race, and that has looked more and more to individualized, free market forces as explanations for

and solutions to social problems. This shift in public philosophy, reflected most dramatically in manifestos such as the Republicans' 1994
Contract with America and the "end of welfare" in 1996, is part of a
broader ideological and political transformation that has challenged the
very underpinnings of the New Deal and post–World War II welfare
state—and has had important consequences for urban minority and
working-class communities. One is a retreat from public investment in
physical and social infrastructure in central cities, even in the face of
the industrial decentralization and metropolitan sprawl that have been
encouraged by government policies (Caraley 1992; O'Connor 1999). A
second is the erosion of the political coalitions that have given voice to
urban interests in national and regional politics (Dreier 1995, 2000; Wolman and Marckini 1998). Third has been a withdrawal from race-
targeted policies such as affirmative action and aggressive civil rights
enforcement (Days 1984; Williams 1998).

How, the Multi-City research team set out to ask in the early 1990s,
are contemporary patterns of inequality related to the transformations
that have made late twentieth-century cities at once more multiracial,
more metropolitan in orientation, and less traditionally industrial than
they have been since the century's start? How and why does the postindustrial metropolitan economy distribute opportunity unequally across
the overlapping lines of class, gender, and race? Do patterns of inequality
differ significantly across metropolitan areas, and if so, why? To answer
these and a host of related questions, the Multi-City Study team collabo-
rated on a series of linked household and employer surveys in the Atlanta,
Boston, Detroit, and Los Angeles metropolitan areas. These surveys were
designed to dig beneath the broad patterns discernible in census statistics,
to provide comprehensive and in-depth information on local labor markets, residential segregation, and racial attitudes. The breadth of the issues surveyed, the multi-city scope of the project, and the pairing of
household and employer interviews combine to give a uniquely comprehensive and detailed look at urban America at the turn of the millennium.

This volume of essays represents one of several products of the
Multi-City Study research, which include separate volumes on each of
the four metropolitan areas under study, plus two volumes based on
employer telephone and face-to-face (listed at the end of this volume)
interviews. In this book, researchers present results from *cross-city* analyses, selected to highlight both the special strengths of the surveys
and the complex and interrelated factors contributing to urban inequality. While the city-specific volumes draw out the unique historical,
structural, and political conditions that differentiate these metropolitan
areas from one another, the focus in this volume is on identifying more
broadly prevailing patterns.

These analyses tell us that ongoing economic, spatial, and demographic restructuring has heightened the advantages of education, technological skill, and suburban residence in the metropolitan opportunity structure, while deepening the disadvantages of less-educated and inner city residents. They also tell us that, while a visible part of the ethnic "niche" economy, recent immigrants constitute a growing segment of the broader low-wage labor pool, earning lower wages—and, frequently, higher praise—than their native-born counterparts from employers eager to maintain a cheap, cooperative workforce. And our analyses tell us that metropolitan job opportunities are segmented by gender, especially within industries and firms, leaving women at a disadvantage that is further compounded by the greater burden of child care and household responsibility they carry. But the disadvantages generated by changing skill demands, spatial "mismatch," immigration, gender, and family responsibility cannot fully account for the substantial and enduring racial disparities that mark social and economic outcomes in the contemporary American metropolis. Those disparities cannot be understood without confronting the complex, and cross-cutting, significance of race. A central theme in this book is that racial barriers, having in some ways diminished since the landmark civil rights legislation of the 1960s, remain a powerful, albeit not always readily visible, social and structural dimension of contemporary inequality.

The significance of race in urban inequality is to be found not in any single place but in various aspects, and at multiple levels, of social experience: in discriminatory behavior, policies, and institutional practices; in the structural segmentation of labor markets and residential space; and in the attitudes, stereotypes, and ideological belief systems through which people make sense of broader social conditions and determine their own policy preferences. Race has a deep and enduring historical significance as well, still visible in residential color lines constructed by years of racial exclusion, violence, and overtly discriminatory policies; in the persistent racial gaps in education, skills, and capital that stem from opportunity denied; and in the mistrust between minorities and local law-enforcement agencies that has once again erupted around the issue of racial profiling. And race has significance as the basis of a color-coded sense of social hierarchy that affects individual attitudes and behavior, and that is embedded in social structure as well as in shared cultural norms.

The significance of race as a factor in urban inequality, then, cannot fully be captured in a single social scientific variable or by considering social and economic outcomes in isolation from one another. Nor can its effects easily be separated out from those associated with economic restructuring and metropolitanization, which are often treated as non-racial, or race-neutral forces in the literature (Wilson 1999). Race, of course, is by no means the only fault line in urban America; it does, however, enter into, complicate, and form a context for understanding the divisions of class, gender, and space.

In light of their varied disciplinary backgrounds, it should come as no surprise that the authors contributing to this volume do not take a uniform approach to measuring and disentangling the significance of race. For some, indeed, the significance of race lies precisely in the entanglements—in the extent to which race relations and racialized perceptions shape market dynamics, residential settlement patterns, and a whole host of economic, social, and cultural processes that affect the distribution of opportunity and outcome. Analyses that purport to "explain" racial disparities in terms of human capital or other non-racial gaps miss an important aspect of how race affects social and economic outcomes: they do not adequately acknowledge the racial context within which these disparities are generated, judged, and maintained. Others, however, argue that it is not only possible but imperative to pinpoint race effects categorically, by first taking the full measure of disparities in education, skill, socioeconomic status, and other nonracial variables that can account for racial disparities in social and economic outcomes. In one view, the significance of race is pervasive and built into the social environment; in the other view, it is contained within what, after accounting for a host of other variables, can be attributed to racial discrimination. By either measure, according to Multi-City Study findings, race is a major force in generating economic and social inequality.

In what follows, I offer an overview of the Multi-City Study and its findings that seeks not so much to resolve as to recognize these differences of approach—acknowledging, at the outset, two things we continually encountered in the course of our collaboration. First, the complexities of measuring race are compounded not just by discipline and methodology but by the enduring political as well as fundamentally moral significance of race as America's central unresolved dilemma. Encountering that dilemma with the tools of social science does not, as Gunnar Myrdal long ago recognized, make it a "value-free" exercise. That, indeed, is why race remains such a deeply conflicted issue, in social science as in society at large. Second, while it did not produce universal consensus, this collaborative research did give us the common ground upon which we could come to important points of agreement, while continuing to air our differences of interpretation.

Project Origins

The Multi-City Study was motivated by a confluence of institutional as well as intellectual and policy concerns, all of which are important for understanding its scope and theoretical framework, as well as its unique contribution to the ongoing social scientific study of inequality. Indeed, the "story" of constructing the Multi-City Study necessarily brings together several sometimes divergent strands—and unresolved tensions—within the social science of race and inequality more generally. As such, it offers insights into the challenges as well as the importance of conducting this kind of collaborative multidisciplinary research.

The idea for the Multi-City Study was itself the product of a period of renewed intellectual vitality in urban studies, as foundations and social scientists in the late 1980s and early 1990s took stock of the vast structural changes affecting worldwide urban centers while lamenting the consequences of urban policy neglect. That vitality was evident in research that moved toward reconceptualizing urban prospects and urban problems by pointing to the rise of postindustrial "global" cities, as well as to the emergence of a postindustrial urban underclass (Sassen 1991; Wilson 1987). It was evident, as well, in an emerging network of institutions devoted to new urban research. Foundations played an important role in fostering this network, not only by providing direct funding for research and training, but also by creating intermediaries, such as the Social Science Research Council's Program for Research on the Urban Underclass, to steer research agendas toward problems of persistent, concentrated poverty (Gephart and Pearson 1988; Jencks and Peterson 1991). What was most important about these foundation-sponsored initiatives, however, was that they were committed to providing a venue for younger, and particularly for minority scholars, to get access to research and training opportunities and, ultimately, to forge new directions in urban research. Such was the case with University of California at Los Angeles's Center for the Study of Urban Poverty, established by a group of young minority scholars as an interdisciplinary research institute with strong ties to the local community at a time when many Los Angeles neighborhoods were reeling with the combined forces of demographic restructuring, political disfranchisement, and economic decline (Oliver and Johnson 1984; Johnson and Oliver 1989). By 1991, these intellectual and institutional resources had started to come together in the extended process of conceptualizing and planning the Multi-City Study.

The project originated when the social scientists at UCLA's Center for the Study of Urban Poverty joined forces with their counterparts at the University of Michigan, who since the late 1980s had been engaged in a parallel research and graduate training program funded as part of foundation efforts to reinvigorate the study of race and urban poverty. Their initial plan was to use an already-scheduled replication of the 1976 Detroit Area Survey of racial attitudes and residential segregation as an opportunity to conduct a much-expanded and comparative survey in Detroit and Los Angeles. The new survey would build on the well-established, albeit contested, sociological and social psychological literature linking segregation to race relations, and specifically to the strong degree of white resistance to residential integration with blacks (Farley et al. 1978). It would also look more closely and extensively at interracial attitudes, in the interest of incorporating more recent work documenting the enduring power of racial stereotypes (Bobo and Kluegel 1997). And by fielding the survey in Detroit's predominantly black-white as well as in Los Angeles's more multi-racial and ethnic setting, the collaborative project would provide insight into how racial attitudes and relations were affected by localized demographic trends.

Equally important, the contemplated Los Angeles-Detroit survey would broaden the scope of the inquiry even further, by surveying households about their employment and labor market as well as their residential experiences. In this way, it would take advantage of the revival of interest in research on urban labor markets, stimulated in part by William Julius Wilson's widely influential concept of the underclass, and subsequently cultivated in the fellowships and research planning networks sponsored by the SSRC Committee for Research on the Urban Underclass. That work had brought renewed prominence to a variety of structural explanations for persistent urban poverty, particularly to the idea that urban deindustrialization had devastated employment opportunities for the inner-city poor through a combination of skill and spatial mismatches between less educated workers and secure, decent-paying jobs.

More immediately relevant to the original survey planners, interest in the underclass had also generated a series of small but revealing employer surveys showing, among other things, employer prejudice and discriminatory practices toward the minority workforce (Kirschenman and Neckerman 1991; Fix and Struyk 1993). This research helped to stimulate wider attention to what was happening on the "demand" side of the labor market for low-skilled and minority workers, and became the basis of a series of meetings on employer surveys sponsored by the Russell Sage Foundation.

Finally, the Los Angeles-Detroit survey planners were also influenced by a then-burgeoning literature documenting the dramatic rise of inequality since the 1970s, evidenced for some in the polarization of income and wages (Levy and Murnane 1992) and for others in the emergence of a decidedly two-tiered economy, heralded by the decline of once-powerful unionized labor and divided between high-wage opportunities requiring education and credentials, and permanently low-wage, low-skilled, mostly service-sector jobs (Harrison and Bluestone 1988; Sassen 1990).

In hopes of drawing from each of these still-disparate strands in the literature, the UCLA-Michigan team secured funding from the SSRC Committee for Research on the Urban Underclass to sponsor a planning conference early in the summer of 1991. At that conference, the seeds were planted for what became the Multi-City Study of Urban Inequality, expanded from the originally contemplated two-city household survey to an even more ambitious series of linked household and employer surveys fielded in four widely divergent metropolitan areas. Discussions at the conference generated interest among researchers and funders alike, leading both groups to begin discussing, and then actively planning, a broader study.

The four cities incorporated in the final study represent a cross-section of the varied circumstances and fortunes of urban America. Detroit is the quintessential rust belt city, hit hard by decentralization and loss of heavy manufacturing and sharply divided between its heavily black urban core and the surrounding white suburban periphery. Atlanta combines a "new South," heavily service-based economy with persistent black-white segregation despite the presence of a substantial African American middle class. Boston stands at the hub of a declining New England manufacturing economy that in the 1980s began to transform itself into a rising high-technology center, with a history of majority white-minority black tension recently complicated by the arrival of substantial numbers of Asian and Latino immigrants. And Los Angeles is by far the most multiracial, economically diversified, and geographically sprawled of the study sites, with its recent emergence as a major destination point for a diverse array of Latin American and Asian immigrants and its now reduced manufacturing economy offset by the growth in high-tech, services, finance, and the long-present entertainment and tourist industries. In addition, the Multi-City Study added two major new components, designed to gather firsthand information on the structure of metropolitan job opportunities: a telephone survey of employers, focusing on jobs, skill requirements, and hiring and related practices; and a series of face-to-face interviews with a subset of these employers to explore their attitudes, perceptions, and employment policies in more depth.

The result, following several months of intensive planning, was a project that was at once larger and more interdisciplinary than even the original collaborators had envisioned, now constituting an extensive nationwide network of investigators that included economists, political scientists, and historians, as well as the geographers, sociologists, and social psychologists who had launched the initial planning effort. Indeed, in scope and interdisciplinarity it was reminiscent of the historic urban social surveys of the late nineteenth and early twentieth centuries: aiming, like DuBois's *The Philadelphia Negro* (1996 [1899]), to investigate the social structural underpinnings of racial inequality, while mapping labor market conditions with the comprehensiveness of the first major research undertaking of the newly founded Russell Sage Foundation, the 1909 Pittsburgh Survey. Over thirty academics took part in some stage of the design and execution of the Multi-City Study, along with a similar number of graduate students. The multiracial team, which encompassed African Americans, Latinos, Asians, and whites, roughly evenly split between men and women, mirrored the diversity of the urban areas under study.

As the project grew, it became far more complicated logistically, requiring the creation of a central research coordinating committee with representatives from each survey component and each metropolitan area research team. This committee was designated to make key, sometimes contested, decisions about the study design, in particular to determine the content of the core survey to be fielded in all locations while still allowing room for a battery of city-specific questions. The Social Science Research Council took on the role of helping coordinate and guide the planning effort, establishing an interdisciplinary committee of outside advisers who would review draft surveys, offer comments, and, on occasion, arbitrate among the various research interests, specializations, and disciplinary perspectives the Multi-City Study embraced—inevitably an issue in crafting a broad-gauged survey that could be conducted within reasonable time limits.[1]

The main work of planning, however, fell to the investigators, who, in sustaining their commitment to the multidisciplinary collaborative, opened themselves up to an intensive process of learning across disciplines as well as areas of specialization. As a result of this collaboration, analysts of spatial mismatch moved beyond measures of commuting time and physical distance to grapple with the social and symbolic meaning of place (Sjoquist 1996; Tilly et al., this volume). Students of social attitudes, in turn, grappled with the tensions between labor market theory and sociological theories of racial stratification in their investigations of the patterning of racial attitudes (Bobo, Johnson, and Suh 2000).

For all their diversity in terms of discipline and perspective, however, the multi-city investigators were in agreement about designing a study that would extend the boundaries of previous research in several specific ways. First, the planners sought to move beyond the predominant black-white biracial race relations paradigm by refining their surveys to accommodate an increasingly multiracial reality, in which relations among different racial and ethnic minorities could prove as consequential as those between white and nonwhite. Second, they sought to move beyond the standard national-sample survey by gathering original data at the metropolitan level, allowing for a more detailed picture of variation in local race relations, labor market, and residential processes, as well as an opportunity to conduct comparative research.

Third, the planners wanted to construct a more realistic and complete picture of labor market dynamics by gathering information from the demand as well as the supply side of the employment and earnings structure, adding the characteristics of jobs, employer practices, and attitudes to an inquiry hitherto focused on individual human capital traits. At the same time, they worked to overcome the relative absence of gender analysis in labor market research, by incorporating measures of gendered stereotypes, hiring and promotion practices, and family and child care responsibilities into the surveys. Fourth, they sought to overcome the bias toward single-variable explanations by exploring employment, residence, and attitudes as interacting processes in generating and shaping the class, gender, and racial dimensions of inequality. Finally, the planners sought to broaden a social scientific discourse that had thus far focused heavily on concentrated poverty, by exploring the forces driving the larger distribution of advantage as well as disadvantage for people of all income levels within metropolitan areas.

Of course, planning for the Multi-City Study did not take place in a vacuum. In important ways the project was influenced by, and certainly it drew a sense of purpose from, the visible deterioration of urban conditions and the absence of an affirmative policy response. At the same time, investigators took pains to look beyond the most immediate or extreme expressions of dislocation to answer questions that would be of long-range relevance to our understanding of urban inequality. Thus, while designed to uncover the roots of poverty and joblessness, which by the early 1990s had reached new heights, the multi-city surveys were also designed to situate those problems within an understanding of the changing conditions of work, neighborhood, and family, in particular for the low-wage, low-skilled workforce. Meanwhile, shortly after the first household surveys had been fielded in Detroit, the Multi-City Study was given new urgency by the 1992 uprising in South Central Los Angeles following the acquittal of four white police officers for the widely broadcast beating of African American motorist Rodney King. Still several months away from fielding their own survey, the Los Angeles-based investigators were in a position to assess the impact of the uprising in subsequent focus groups and in a series of questions included on the household survey (Bobo et al. 1994). Most important, however, with a large sample of white, black, Latino, and Asian respondents and an extensive set of questions ranging from residential and labor market experience to attitudes, they were in a position to explore the deeper and complex currents of interracial and ethnic tension that helped give shape to the uprising itself.

Planning for the Multi-City Study can also be seen as part of two related developments in the politics and in the ongoing public discourse about race and inequality, which played a role in shaping the project's research agenda and figured prominently in our own internal deliberations and debates.

One was an intensification of debate about the state of black-white relations in the United States, captured in a number of prominent books published throughout the 1990s as well as in sustained political controversy over affirmative action and other race-based anti-discrimination policies.[2] In some ways this heightened racial discourse was a continuation of older debates about the nature and degree of racism in American society, centered principally on the question of whether African American disadvantage should be traced to racial prejudice and discrimination or to some combination of class status, family structure, and culture (O'Connor 2001). But it was also grounded in more recent disputes about the changing nature of "the race problem" in post-civil rights America, and especially those over the question of whether race was declining as a source of disadvantage for the black working and "under" class (Wilson 1980; Willie 1979). Feeding into this debate was a growing emphasis on economic restructuring, human capital, limited access to jobs, family structure and other nonracial explanations for black-white inequality in wages, income, and employment (Kasarda 1989; O'Neill 1990; Holzer 1991). Equally important was a turn, especially within liberal and "new Democrat" circles, to a putatively race-neutral policy framework for addressing racial inequality (Wilson 1990; Williams 1998).

Originating, as it did, during a period when the emphasis on race had been muted in social science and social policy, the Multi-City Study helps to mark a new stage in the debate over race and its significance, when scholars, concerned that problems of racial discrimination, prejudice, and segregation were being neglected or marginalized in the literature, sought not just to put race back on the agenda but to understand it as a structurally-rooted phenomenon (Massey and Denton 1993). Thus, in bringing race to the forefront of measurement and analysis, the multi-city researchers sought not simply to substitute one kind of explanation for another, but to transcend the limitations of the either/or debate. At the same time, they sought to recognize the complexity of race as a social scientific variable, looking not only to measures of discriminatory behavior but to its structural and institutional expression in labor and residential markets, and in the patterning of racial stereotypes. Here the Multi-City Study joined with what has emerged as an ongoing rethinking of the measure and meaning of race as a sociological category, spurred not just by the fact of increasing racial and ethnic diversity but also by frustration with analyses that treat racial disadvantage as stemming from a collection of individual-level attributes, as opposed to institutional and structural processes (Bonilla-Silva 1996; Winant 2000). Notably, this effort to recognize the complexity of race also took multi-city investigators back to themes sounded in such pioneering sociological classics as DuBois's *The Philadelphia Negro* and St. Clair Drake and Horace Cayton's *Black Metropolis*, which long ago rejected the either/or framework by mapping the interlocking contours of the color line in employment, housing, social relations, and racial beliefs (DuBois 1996 [1899], Drake and Cayton 1993 [1945]). The issue then, as it became for the investigators, was not *whether* but *how* "race matters"—and on a more fundamental level, whether, in the highly racialized context of urban America, it makes sense to think about a racially progressive policy agenda in race-neutral terms.

That the investigators continue to differ in the way they answer these questions is itself testament to the complexity of race as a social and social scientific category. But the nature of their differences is also an indication of the complication and insights the Multi-City Study brings to the debate. Thus, analyses of the household and employer data confirm that there are considerable skill differences between white and nonwhite workers, and that nonwhites suffer in the labor market as a result (Holzer 1998). By some measures, including several reported in this volume, this skills gap can be said to explain most of the racial disparity in employment and wages. By other measures, also included in this volume, the meaning of the skills gap cannot be considered apart from the racial context within which skills acquisition and labor markets are formed and operate. Skills, that is, are not race-neutral variables—not only because they originate in racially unequal educational opportunities but because they are embedded in social structures and processes that the Multi-City Study investigates in some depth: the racially segregated networks that provide access to both jobs and skill acquisition, and the racialized perceptions through which employers filter workforce decisions.

A second political development also figured in deliberations about the study, and that was the successful effort—launched while the surveys were getting started and culminating not long after the final component of field research had been completed—to bring "welfare as we know it" to an end. The issue of welfare, like the continuing debate over affirmative action, does not at all capture the full policy or intellectual significance of the project. Nevertheless, their prominence has had an important impact, in creating a context of welfare-state retrenchment and polarized racial discourse to which this research can be addressed. Thus, the devolution and "work-first" emphasis of post-welfare policy has redoubled the need for the kind of analysis of local labor market opportunities available to disadvantaged workers that the Multi-City Study can provide (O'Connor 2000; Holzer and Danziger, this volume). Similarly, the intensified debate over affirmative action and other racially targeted policies calls more than ever for direct evidence and nuanced analysis of the extent and nature of racial disadvantage.

The Surveys

The single largest component of the Multi-City Study is the comprehensive Household Survey, administered to a total of 8,916 non-Hispanic white, African American, Hispanic and Asian adults (twenty-one years or older) across the four metropolitan areas.[3] Samples were drawn separately in each metropolitan area, and weighted to yield respondents representative of the prevailing local racial and ethnic mix (white-black in Atlanta and Detroit; white-black-Hispanic in Boston; white-black-Hispanic-Asian in Los Angeles). The sample was constructed to include equal numbers of each racial-ethnic group and a sizable number of low-income and below poverty-level households, to allow a detailed analysis of these groups; weighted results are representative of each metropolitan area as a whole. Interviews were conducted in person, generally lasting from ninety to a hundred minutes, in the respondent's native language (requiring English, Spanish, Mandarin, Cantonese, and Korean versions in Los Angeles), and in the majority of cases interviewers and respondents were of the same race, to assure candor and minimize tension or bias when covering questions about race and ethnicity (Johnson, Oliver, and Bobo 1994, 80). The Household Surveys took place over several months in each metropolitan area, starting in Detroit in the spring of 1992 and reaching completion with Boston and Los Angeles in the fall of 1994.[4]

Employer telephone surveys (numbering 3,510) were timed to coordinate with the household surveys in each area and were administered between 1992 and 1994, with a supplemental sample of about 300 firms added in 1995.[5] The Face-to-Face Employer Surveys, interviewing in greater depth 365 managers at 174 firms already contacted by the Telephone Survey, were conducted between the summers of 1994 and 1996.[6] In both employer surveys, cases were roughly equally divided across the four metropolitan areas. Of the Telephone Survey employers, almost 1,200 were the current or last employer identified by the household respondents. The remainder were drawn from business directories.

The household survey provides rich and unusually detailed data on intergroup attitudes, residential segregation, and labor market experience, offering a uniquely comprehensive look at processes that are often considered separately, while also allowing scholars to explore a wide range of more narrowly framed questions about specific dimensions of inequality. In the area of intergroup attitudes the survey documents several aspects of race and gender relations, including the strength and pervasiveness of stereotypes, the sense of competition or threat between groups, and the pattern of beliefs about the existence and nature of discrimination in local housing and labor markets. Moreover, taking advantage of its multiracial sample, the survey explores relations among different minority groups, while also recognizing gender as part of the configuration of attitudes and stereotypes. Data from the survey also offer insight into the social and ideological roots of racial and gender belief systems, how they relate to patterns of support for social policies, and how they affect various aspects of the urban opportunity structure.

One link between attitude and opportunity, extensively explored in the Multi-City Household Survey, is through the degree of preference and/or tolerance for racial residential integration and its impact on the range of residential choices available to different race and ethnic groups. Expanding on a series of show cards first developed in the 1976 Detroit Area Study, the Household Survey explores how respondents react to the prospect of living with varying proportions of groups other than their own, including the prospect of being racial "pioneers"—or distinct minorities in their own neighborhoods. The survey also gauges how metropolitan-area residents perceive the affordability and racial openness of actual neighborhoods, as well as the quality and desirability of their own residential communities. Here again the Multi-City Study goes beyond the black-white dichotomy characteristic of previous residential segregation research by exploring tolerance for a variety of racial and ethnic mixes. It also offers rare insight into the broader social meaning of racial and ethnic "succession" in urban neighborhoods, by probing how people think and talk about the appearance of "others" in their midst—and why, in some instances, it might lead to flight from the neighborhood (Farley et al. 1994). In another important experimental innovation, the survey asks respondents to construct their own ideal neighborhoods, allowing for a more finely grained picture of tolerance for integration and proximity to other racial groups.

Labor market questions gather extensive information on job search, including the use of networks, requirements regarding wage levels and commute times, and access to knowledge about job opportunities. The survey also draws out information about what previous research has found or hypothesized to be serious barriers to gainful employment, including education and skill levels, the availability of transportation, child care or related family obligations, and the actual experience or perception of employer bias. Parallel to questions asked about the housing market, the survey addresses how respondents vary in their cognitive "maps" of the metropolitan labor market—allowing researchers to explore how the perception of racial hostility in certain areas acts as a strong deterrent to minority job applicants (Sjoquist 1996). Equally important, the survey taps into such key but often unexamined aspects of actual labor market experience as the race and gender composition of the workplace and its supervisory structure, as well as the experience or perception of discrimination at the workplace.

What is perhaps most distinctive about the Multi-City Study labor market data is that it is linked to a set of surveys on employer demands, practices, attitudes, and perceptions with regard to the metropolitan labor force. The larger of these is the Employer Telephone Survey, administered to approximately eight hundred establishments in each metropolitan area. In order to yield as much information as possible on the prospects for disadvantaged workers, the sample was weighted toward larger firms (reflecting the greater numbers of jobs in those businesses), and designed with an emphasis on jobs that do not require a college degree (Holzer 1996). The telephone survey itself gathers information on a range of demand-side factors shaping local labor market opportunities, including the skill requirements, wage and benefit levels, location and related characteristics of available jobs; the demographic composition and degree of union representation within the firm; employer recruitment, screening, training, promotion, and affirmative action practices; and employer preferences with regard to race, gender, and other characteristics of employees. (See Holzer 1996 for a more complete description of the Employer Telephone Survey.)

Supplementing the statistical data generated by the Employer Telephone Survey is a more in-depth survey, based on longer, face-to-face interviews with 175 of the originally surveyed employers. Focusing again on the job characteristics, employer practices, and attitudes that shape opportunities for lower-wage workers, these open-ended interviews were structured to draw out the intentions, preferences, labor market perceptions, and attitudes behind the broader patterns indicated in the Telephone Surveys. What determines employer skill demands and preferences for certain categories of workers? Why do employers rely on certain kinds of recruitment and hiring methods, and with what effect? How do employers decide where to locate, and relocate, and why? What are their perceptions of the local workforce, and how do they affect hiring and recruitment practices? These interviews provided investigators with an opportunity to probe all these issues at greater length and in more depth than in the Telephone Survey. (See Moss and Tilly 2001 for a more complete description of the in-depth Employer Survey.)

Whether considered as part of a whole or separately, these interrelated components of the Multi-City Study provide a unique source of empirical data for enhancing and testing some of the principal findings and explanations that have emerged in recent literature on inequality. Thus, it brings new evidence, from both supply and demand sides of the labor market, to test hypotheses about skills and spatial mismatches, about the role of social networks, and about the impact of job search mechanisms on employment and wages. To the literature on discrimination, which has focused primarily on the experience of African Americans, the Multi-City Study adds an expanded set of questions as well as information for whites, Hispanics, and Asians across class and gender lines (Bobo and Suh 2000). It similarly expands on existing residential segregation literature, not only by exploring factors—racial prejudice, in-group preferences, class background, affordability—that have been offered as competing explanations but also by incorporating data from multiethnic settings, and by exploring the consequences of residential segregation.

Additional features of the Multi-City Study create an opportunity to complicate and move beyond the existing range of hypotheses as well. First is that the surveys were conducted at the metropolitan rather than the national level, allowing for a more detailed picture of the local dynamics of inequality in each metropolis, as well as analyses of how and why patterns may vary—or hold steady—in different social, economic, and political settings. Among the most important advantages of metropolitan-level analysis is that it allows investigators to refer to specific residential or employment areas by name, affording an opportunity to explore the social meaning of space and how it affects decisions about housing, job search, hiring, and firm location. It also allows for a more detailed picture of the institutional and compositional dimensions of the local labor market, revealing important features—such as the degree of occupational segregation and the immediate context of job opportunities for workers—that cannot be determined through relying on national-level data alone. By exploring these issues through a blend of qualitative and quantitative data, the Multi-City Study allows us to capture the racialization of key aspects of the metropolitan opportunity structure—in social perception as well as in social fact.

Second is the unusual breadth of issues covered in the linked surveys, which allows researchers to look at different places and mechanisms within the broader metropolitan context where inequality is generated, as well as their interactive effects. Indeed, the Multi-City Study was specifically designed not only with the understanding that no single-variable explanations would—or necessarily should—emerge but also as a way of appreciating how those variables intersect. And third, by paying attention to the institutions, practices, and attitudes that mediate the distribution of opportunity, the Multi-City Study expands the focus of analysis beyond individual-level variables and toward an appreciation of the structural underpinnings of inequality. Finally, the study is unusual in the extent and variety of measures it incorporates on race and gender attitudes, stereotypes, biases, and discrimination, allowing researchers to assess these sources of inequality in greater depth and more directly than in most social or labor market surveys.

Perspectives from Multi-City Analysis

In companion volumes published in the multi-city series, investigators from the city-based research teams trace the complex dynamics of inequality in each of the four metropolitan areas, drawing attention to what is historically distinctive about local patterns of segregation, labor market restructuring, and racial attitudes even as they parallel similar dynamics in other metropolitan areas. Thus, Detroit stands out as the most racially polarized of the four cities in terms of central city-suburban residential segregation, income inequality, and employment outcomes, a pattern that must be understood as part of a long history of racial conflict as well as the severe impact of industrial decline and deconcentration on the job prospects for African Americans (Farley, Danziger, and Holzer 2000).

In Atlanta, racial segregation and income disparities have persisted despite a greater degree of African American suburbanization and a rapidly growing economy, a situation described by the Atlanta-based investigators as the "Atlanta paradox" (Sjoquist 2000). The greater Boston metropolitan area, in contrast, witnessed income growth across racial lines after recovering from the decline of its manufacturing sector in the 1970s and restructuring its economic base toward finance, technology, and services. Still, amid the rapid demographic diversification that has accompanied the recent arrival of immigrants from Latin America, the Caribbean, Asia, and Africa, segregation and an ongoing history of interracial antagonism continue to sustain racialized patterns of inequality (Bluestone and Stevenson 2000). It is in Los Angeles, however, that the combination of industrial and demographic diversification has been largest, most visible, and spatially dispersed, dividing what the Los Angeles research team calls a "prismatic metropolis" along complex lines of class, race, ethnicity, immigration status, and geography (Bobo et al. 2000).

The chapters in this volume are based on cross-city analysis, and highlight not so much the distinctiveness as the common patterns shaping metropolitan inequality. At the same time, they draw attention to the unique strengths of the Multi-City Study as an opening toward a fuller and more integrated understanding of how race shapes and limits opportunity.

In chapter 1, Reynolds Farley uses census data to provide an overview of the four metropolitan areas, sketching the statistical outlines of a marked, if complicated, racial divide in residence, income, education, employment, and other key markers of socioeconomic status. Despite significant and important variations, all the metropolitan areas displayed broadly similar patterns on several indicators. First, Farley re-

ports high rates of black-white residential segregation, despite slight improvements over time, and lower but still significant Latino-non-
Latino segregation in Boston and Los Angeles. Second, there are large
disparities in the racial distribution of income, with blacks and Latinos
disproportionately represented among the poor and near-poor and underrepresented at the upper end of the income distribution. Third, despite
gains among all nonwhite minorities, especially among blacks and minority women, the racial gap in educational attainment persists, and in
some places has actually grown wider at the postsecondary level, which
economists point to as especially important for achieving success in the
changing labor market. Fourth, there are persistent racial disparities in
the distribution of employment and occupation, clustering minorities in
low-wage menial jobs and leaving white men and women more likely to
be employed and in higher-prestige positions than their nonwhite counterparts.

As Farley's analysis points out, the patterns displayed in census statistics are highly complicated, differing by gender, city, and immigration
status. In some instances, historical trend lines provide a measure of
progress toward racial parity; in others, they show stagnation or decline.
Certainly there is also inequality within racial categories, across class as
well as gender lines. Nevertheless, in the four socially and economically
diverse metropolitan areas, racial segregation and inequality stand out
as persistent and serious problems that can be understood as part of
broader national patterns.

The remaining chapters in this volume use data from the Multi-
City Study to examine the interlocking factors that sustain the racial
divide, focusing on the structural and institutional as well as the individual-level processes that generate inequality.

Racial Attitudes

We begin by considering the substance and determinants of racial attitudes and beliefs, and the extent to which they operate as important
sources of meaning and behavior for household survey respondents. The
chapters by Lawrence D. Bobo and Michael P. Massagli and by James R.
Kluegel and Lawrence D. Bobo map out the ideas and perceptions through
which people make judgments about one another, make sense of racial
and economic disparities, and form preferences about policies to promote racial equity. Together, these two chapters make a compelling case
for reintegrating attitudes and beliefs into social scientific accounts of
racial inequality. Though less likely to appear as overt expressions of
racial prejudice, the authors show, racial attitudes and beliefs continue
to operate in prejudicial ways: by forming the basis of negative stereo-

types that "color" social behavior and practices; by justifying existing racial inequities as a reflection of group characteristics; and by limiting the possibilities for cross-racial cooperation in matters of policy.

Chapter 2 focuses on one of the most widely recognized mechanisms of social prejudice by examining the composition, foundations, and extent of racial stereotyping. Racial stereotypes are widespread, the authors find, and arranged in a hierarchical order that makes distinctions among minorities as well as between minorities and whites, and that cuts across local context. While ranking whites and Asians highly on key traits related to socioeconomic status, achievement, and socially approved behavior, that hierarchy in turn places African Americans and Hispanics at the bottom, with the most stigmatized social attributes. As we shall see, the sense of racial hierarchy expressed in these rankings is replicated at several points within the urban opportunity structure.

In an especially effective use of the survey's multiracial sample and comparative framework, Bobo and Massagli also come to important conclusions about the nature of stereotypes. One is that they are drawn from a generalized, widely shared cultural repertoire of images and social perceptions rather than from the local specifics of race relations. Reflective though they may be of individual beliefs and attitudes, stereotypes operate more broadly in society as a common language and a cultural belief system that in turn shapes, gives order to, and to some degree operates independently of individual attitudes. Second is that this hierarchical system of stereotypes is at least partly grounded in the reality of racial stratification; this is not merely ethnocentrism at work. Thus, positive and negative stereotypes are influenced by who's on top and who's at the bottom of the earnings structure, even as they play a role in shaping, justifying, and perpetuating that status quo through their influence on housing and labor market practices. Nor are they simply imposed by dominant whites on racial "others"; stereotypes influence the way minorities view one another, and in some instances the way they view themselves. Clearly, these conclusions tell us, the importance of stereotypes is not merely incidental. They warrant further attention as one of the structural underpinnings of inequality.

In chapter 3, Kluegel and Bobo examine another aspect of how racial beliefs and attitudes act as a lens for interpreting social conditions, this time with important consequences for social policy. Here the central focus is on how the climate of racialized perception discussed in the previous chapter applies to the question of job discrimination. Taking advantage of the richness of the multi-city data, Kluegel and Bobo provide an unusually in-depth analysis of racial gaps in perceptions of the extent and seriousness of job discrimination, asking not only about underlying determinants but also about how this translates into racially divergent policy preferences.

While previous analyses have described a large white-black difference in perceived discrimination, Kluegel and Bobo are able to explore patterns for Hispanics and Asians as well, and to examine whether there is a comparable gap in perceptions of gender discrimination between women and men. Moreover, to a far greater degree than previous studies, they are able to explore what shapes these divergent perceptions of an issue that has taken center stage in recent policy debate. Reporting similar patterns across all four metropolitan areas, Kluegel and Bobo conclude that perceptions of discrimination are more heavily racialized than gendered: the gap between whites and both blacks and Hispanics with regard to racial discrimination is significantly larger than the male-female gap in perceived gender discrimination. Indeed, while white men and women both tend to diminish the extent of gender discrimination, black men and women are consistently more likely to see it as a serious problem.

Equally significant, perceptions of discrimination are racialized in other ways as well. First, Kluegel and Bobo report a racial gap in what *determines* perceptions of discrimination, with whites influenced chiefly by the abstractions of ideology and nonwhites by concrete experience. The most effective way of eliminating the gap in perception, they conclude, is to eliminate the discrimination itself. Second, however, Kluegel and Bobo show how these differences in perception complicate that task, linking them to a substantial racial division in support for anti-discrimination policy. Nevertheless, they express some hope for a more informed public discourse, based on the fact that most whites do acknowledge the existence of at least some racial discrimination.

Residence, Employment, and the Significance of Space

In turning to the racialized dimensions of metropolitan social geography, the volume begins to consider how racial beliefs, attitudes, and perceptions are implicated in and are in turn replicated by the urban infrastructure. Chapters 4 and 5 reveal how patterns of racialization are structured into urban housing markets, by examining the causes and the consequences of racial residential segregation. Chapter 6 investigates space as a component of the labor market that is similarly infused with perceptions and assumptions about race.

In chapter 4, Camille Zubrinsky Charles brings multi-city evidence to bear on what has long been a matter of contention in segregation research, by assessing the importance of race in sustaining residential segregation. Zubrinsky Charles takes several factors into consideration as possible explanations, including racial gaps in socioeconomic status, disparate knowledge or perceptions of the housing market, and racial attitudes, preferences, and prejudices. She also draws on a novel measure of racial residential preferences, known as the Ideal Neighborhood Experiment, which allows respondents to configure their own preferred living environment and to consider integration with several different out-groups. The evidence, she concludes, reveals a complex array of factors, all of which point to the central importance of race: racial discrimination, stereotypes, and economic disparities that originated in racial restrictions all contribute to maintaining segregation. In a pattern that varies across cities in specifics but not in its broad contours, Zubrinsky Charles finds a powerful connection between racial stereotypes and a widely shared hierarchical rank-ordering that rates whites, Asians, Hispanics, and blacks, in descending order, as preferred out-group neighbors. Thus, while blacks express the strongest preference for integrated neighborhoods, they are most likely to meet with resistance.

That these preferences can have far-reaching consequences is confirmed by the analysis in chapter 5, where Franklin Wilson and Roger Hammer focus on how ethnic homogeneity affects neighborhood quality. While most people express a preference for at least some degree of residential integration, Wilson and Hammer find that, for a small but statistically significant number of respondents, living in an ethnically homogeneous neighborhood can be attributed to a stated preference for living among co-ethnics. A more important factor for blacks (though not for Hispanics), however, is that the expectation of meeting with discriminatory barriers steers them toward more homogeneous neighborhoods. Taking advantage of the breadth of the Multi-City Study household data, Wilson and Hammer find that residence in homogeneous neighborhoods carries stark and racially disparate consequences in all four metropolitan areas—whether respondents "choose" homogeneity or not. For minorities, it means low neighborhood socioeconomic status, housing quality, and access to services, and, for blacks, more limited proximity to jobs. For whites, neighborhood ethnic homogeneity brings the opposite: higher status, better housing and services, and fewer reported neighborhood problems. Like Zubrinsky Charles, these authors conclude that racial restrictions, over and above other factors, play a powerful role in limiting residential opportunities for blacks and Hispanics, with implications that go beyond the immediate neighborhood environment.

Chapter 6, by Chris Tilly and others, provides a bridge to part III of the volume, by focusing on the significance of neighborhoods in metropolitan labor markets. It also features a distinctive component of the Multi-City Study, drawing on the Face-to-Face Employer Survey to explore how employers think about urban space, and in particular how race figures into the map of desirable locations for doing business and recruiting employees. Using the literature on spatial mismatch as their point of departure, the authors find evidence to support a conclusion reported in a substantial body of quantitative research that minority workers are disadvantaged by the physical distance between their neighborhoods of residence and the increasingly suburban location of jobs.

But the main thrust of their analysis is to emphasize how race and space are intertwined in employers' minds: certain neighborhoods, that is, act as racially charged "signals" that in turn affect employer decisions with regard to location, recruitment, and hiring. As the authors demonstrate in their richly textured discussion of the interview findings, employer perceptions are closely attuned to the local particularities of social geography and race relations: Detroit's starkly segregated city-suburban dividing line cannot be taken as the urban norm, particularly in a city like Los Angeles, where the urban "core" is itself diffuse. Moreover, in Boston and Los Angeles, the growth of "new immigrant" populations has complicated the racial significance of space, bringing greater diversity to still heavily minority neighborhoods and also, for some employers, a welcome source of low-wage labor. Nevertheless, and despite important geographic and demographic differences, the authors find that space acts as a racial signal in similar ways across all four metropolitan areas, "coloring" how employers view prospective location and the quality of the metropolitan workforce. "Inner city" emerges from these interviews as a highly pejorative blanket term, one uniformly associated not only with blacks and Latinos but with a cluster of attributes—high crime, low-quality workforce, family breakdown, welfare dependence—that parallels the racial stereotyping reported in the Multi-City Study Household Surveys. While acknowledging that employer concerns about inner-city crime and workforce skills do have basis in reality, the authors draw on the in-depth interviews to point out how these concerns are filtered and magnified through a racial lens that stigmatizes black neighborhoods and workers in particular.

Inequality and the Structure of Labor Market Opportunity

Chapters 7 through 9 begin to illuminate what the Multi-City Study can tell us about how metropolitan labor markets work, focusing particular attention on the variegated mechanisms through which minority and female workers are channeled into often segregated, lower-wage positions with limited opportunities for advance.

In chapter 7, Luis M. Falcón and Edwin Melendez delve into the extensive data on job search and social networks to look at a relatively unexamined aspect of labor market experience. How, they ask, do processes of labor market incorporation differ by race and ethnicity, and with what consequence? What they find points to three key dimensions of racial and ethnic segmentation in the labor market. First, across the metropolitan areas, job search methods are "bundled" differently by race and ethnicity. While all groups rely on a combination of networks, formal intermediaries (for example, agencies or unions), and open market techniques, whites have far greater access to a broader range of contacts and are more often in a position to use strategies leading to the credentialed sector of the labor force. Second, Falcón and Melendez report racial and ethnic differences in the way different groups of workers actually find jobs. Latinos and Asians, especially, connect to jobs through relatives and close friends, while whites are more likely to find work through distant contacts. Moreover, the social networks that produce jobs are themselves highly segregated; contacts for all groups remain substantially confined to co-ethnics. Third, the reliance on these segregated networks has strikingly disparate consequences for different groups, leading nonwhites to lower-status, lower-wage, racially segregated jobs, while showing no negative consequences for whites. Falcón and Melendez conclude by pointing to the need for job search mechanisms that help minorities connect to more stable opportunities. Ultimately, however, they view the racial segmentation of job search as more symptom than cause: a reflection of segregated neighborhoods and, as revealed in this and the next chapter, highly segregated workplaces as well.

While Falcón and Melendez use the Multi-City Household Survey to explore job search processes in depth, in chapter 8 Irene Browne, Leann Tigges, and Julie Press exploit its capacity to illuminate different dimensions of labor market experience to investigate the structural, institutional, and individual-level sources of racial and gender earnings inequality. Invoking the concept of "double" or what they term "multiple" jeopardy, they focus on how race and gender act as intersecting sources of labor market disadvantage for African American women and Latinas. They also examine how disadvantage is generated at multiple points within the labor market—through overall occupational segregation, within-firm segregation in jobs and authority hierarchies, and a variety of family arrangements, including single parenthood and/or a gendered division of household and child care responsibility—that have been linked to lower earnings among women. Their findings, which control for human capital characteristics, strongly parallel patterns reported elsewhere in this volume. There is a high degree of racial and ethnic segregation within the workplace, the authors report, reflected to some degree in metropolitan-wide occupational distribution but more prominently at the firm level, in the degree of segregation within jobs. This extends to supervision: workers are most often supervised by someone of the same race and gender. Like segregated neighborhoods and job search networks, working in a job dominated and supervised by co-ethnics carries a high price: lower earnings and more limited advancement opportunities for black women and Latinas—more so for minority women than minority men. Meanwhile, women of all racial and ethnic backgrounds suffer the consequences of lower earnings when they encounter child care constraints, although men do not. The authors conclude that it is the institutional factors of racial segmentation within firms and gender divisions within the family that create multiple jeopardy, operating together to push black women and Latinas to the bottom of the wage distribution.

Tom Hertz, Chris Tilly, and Michael P. Massagli continue the institutional focus in chapter 9, here taking advantage of the unique link between household and employer data in the Multi-City Study to examine the nature and extent of race and gender discrimination in the labor market. To a far greater degree than in most studies of labor market discrimination, they are able to take institutional context into account, drawing on household survey information about workplace composition as well as on employer descriptions of job requirements, hiring, and wage-setting practices. Equally important, they are able to compare employer reports of job qualifications and starting wages with the actual skills and wages of job holders, to see what factors beyond human capital attributes influence who gets hired and at what wage. Their findings point to the importance of persistent occupational segregation by race and gender, but also to the differences in pay rates for the same occupation *between* different firms. Higher-paying firms, they conclude, are least likely to hire women and minorities—adding to such firm-specific institutional features as suburban location and customer demographics that other literature has identified as sources of gender and racial wage disparities. In their consideration of employment outcomes, they also find that extending the analysis to include involuntary *under*employment as well as unemployment significantly widens the race and gender gaps.

The two remaining chapters offer a comprehensive overview of the structure of opportunity from the standpoint of what workers bring to the labor market as well as what barriers they face.

In chapter 10, Philip Moss and Chris Tilly build on the link between the qualitative and the Telephone Employer Surveys to provide an analysis of what they call the "jobscape" for low-skilled urban minority workers. Shifting the focus that prevails in labor market research, their objective in this chapter is to look at what disadvantages minority workers from the demand rather than the supply side. By drawing on both the Telephone and the In-Depth Employer Surveys, they also begin to elaborate some of the trends reported by Harry J. Holzer (1996) in his analysis of the Employer Telephone Survey, adding evidence from more detailed, Face-to-Face Interviews to help explain what lies behind the persistent, and for many years worsening, racial gap in earnings and employment. Keying their analysis to several factors identified in the literature, they find strong evidence to support the notion that changing skill demands, spatial mismatch, employer attitudes toward minority workers, and hiring-recruitment methods create disadvantages for minority workers. But they also bring important new insights to these findings. Thus, employer reports of changing skill demands emphasize the growing importance of "soft" (behavioral and interactive) skills as well as "hard" skills that require at least a high school education—both of which weigh especially heavily against minority males. Moreover, like the employer maps of desirable location and recruitment areas, qualitative evidence shows perceptions of skill to be highly racialized and riddled with stereotypes. Policies to assist minority workers, Moss and Tilly conclude, need to recognize that the effects of skill and spatial mismatches cannot easily be separated from the barriers of race, by investing in strong antidiscrimination enforcement as well as in programs to improve skills and access to jobs.

In chapter 11, Harry J. Holzer and Sheldon Danziger take a somewhat different angle on the question of job prospects for disadvantaged workers, providing estimates of the actual availability of jobs. In an innovative analysis using data from both the Household and the Employer Telephone Surveys, they link the supply with the demand side of the labor market by comparing what household respondents report about their own skill levels, residence, labor market experience, and other relevant characteristics to what employers report about the skill requirements, location, and racial composition of available jobs. Holzer and Danziger then conduct simulations that "match" workers to jobs based on both sets of reported characteristics, using the results to estimate the likelihood that disadvantaged workers will be able to find jobs. In findings that are of immediate relevance to the outcome of welfare reform, Holzer and Danziger report that a substantial number of job seekers— between 9 and 17 percent—will have difficulty finding work, even in a tight labor market. They also report that the rates of mismatch between jobs and job seekers are much higher for minorities, women, high school dropouts, and welfare recipients—principally, they argue, because these workers lack the skills that employers require for available jobs, but also due to spatial mismatch and racial discrimination. Even when successful in the job search, these workers face wages and benefit levels that are likely to leave large numbers in poverty. Clearly, these findings sound a strong note of caution amid the current celebration of declining welfare rolls. Holzer and Danziger conclude by emphasizing the ongoing importance of proactive public policies, including expanded investments in education and training, transportation and job placement, government job creation, and stronger antidiscrimination enforcement.

Conclusion: Race and the Structure of Urban Opportunity

The essays in this volume do not tell a simple story. They point to intergroup attitudes, residential and industrial location, discriminatory practices, and the declining prospects for low-skilled workers as important, interlocking sources of inequality across metropolitan America. But they also point to several conclusions about race, both as a shaping force in the distribution of opportunity and as a variable in social scientific analysis. While not offered as a statement of consensus, they do advance the ongoing debate about race and inequality in important ways.

First, and indeed a point all agree on, is that race continues to play a powerful role in shaping life chances, and to a far greater degree than those who call ours a color-blind society would admit. Race matters palpably in the composition of social attitudes and stereotypes, and in the persistence of housing and labor market discrimination.

Second, and related, is that race operates within the urban infrastructure in complex and varied ways that go beyond individual attitudes or acts of discrimination, leading all of us to recognize that its effects cannot easily be separated from economic or other nonracial factors, and some among us to urge a rethinking of standard distinctions made between "race" and socioeconomic background effects. To be sure, the data provide evidence that racial disadvantage continues to take the form of individual discrimination and prejudice. But these analyses also reveal that race operates even more pervasively at the institutional and structural level—especially in the form of highly segregated housing and labor markets, along with the practices that keep them that way. Surveys also provide evidence of a widespread, stereotypically defined sense of racial hierarchy that finds structural expression in patterns of residential segregation and in employer hiring and locational preferences. It is a hierarchy, that, with striking consistency across metropolitan areas of varied demographic composition, puts black at the very bottom of a color-coded scheme that ranks Hispanic and Asian in ascending order toward white at the top.

A third insight from the Multi-City Study, albeit one explored more fully in the separate Los Angeles and Boston volumes, is that recent immigration complicates without necessarily dismantling the racial hierarchy, on the one hand placing recent Hispanic and Asian immigrants at the bottom of earnings measures, and on the other generating a source of low-wage labor employers prefer over native-born blacks. A similar conclusion can be drawn with respect to gender, which does not operate separately so much as in conjunction with the racial hierarchy to put black and Hispanic women at the bottom of the wage structure even as employers express preferences for hiring minority women over minority men.

Fourth, by showing race to be both pervasive in influence and institutional and structural in nature, the Multi-City Study necessarily complicates and enhances social scientific understanding of skills and space as explanations for racial gaps in earnings and employment—without undermining the significance of either one. It provides powerful evidence that it is not only economics but racial attitudes and stratification that shape labor market relations and outcomes, much as race influences the configuration of residential and industrial space. It reminds us that policies to improve skills and access to jobs among minority workers are of great importance, but they must be part of a broader policy agenda that seeks direct and innovative ways to address the structural and institutional underpinnings of the racial divide.

A final insight from the analysis underscores the importance of making race a top and explicit policy priority, and that is the very high price of persistent racial segregation, whether in neighborhoods, social networks, or jobs—a price, as we have seen, that is borne most immediately by nonwhite minorities but that fundamentally undermines our capacity as a society to make genuine equality of opportunity a reality rather than a distant goal.

The message of this volume, then, is not simply that race continues to shape inequality in urban America. Race does indeed matter—as do gender, education and skill, and residential location. This research tells us more: that race and ethnicity matter in ways that are subtle and changing. Race is woven into the fabric of residential and industrial location choices, of hiring and wage determination, and of the human perceptions that underlie all these processes. It is critical to affirm the continuing import of race and ethnicity. But it is likewise critical to understand the ways—many newly emerging—in which racial divisions pervade, complement, and in some cases conflict with other dimensions of opportunity. Indeed, to ignore this dimension of urban inequality is to risk perpetuating the patterns that make race an enduring challenge as we enter the twenty-first century.

Thanks to Larry Bobo, Chris Tilly, Harry Holzer, Sheldon Danziger, Abel Valenzuela Jr. and the anonymous reviewers for their comments on earlier drafts of this chapter.

Notes

1. Members of the Multi-City Study of Urban Inequality advisory committee were Robin Hollister (chair), Swarthmore College; Jorge Chapa, University of Texas, Austin; Mary Jackman, University of California, Davis; Arne Kalleberg, University of North Carolina, Chapel Hill; Frank Levy, Massachusetts Institute of Technology; Seymour Sudman, University of Illinois, Champaign-Urbana; and Franklin Wilson, University of Wisconsin, Madison.

2. Among the most prominent of recent publications are Hacker (1992), West (1993), Cose (1993), Carnoy (1994), Steinberg (1995), Thernstrom and Thernstrom (1997), and Patterson (1997).

3. The actual number of households surveyed are as follows (unadjusted response rates for each metropolitan area are indicated in parentheses): Atlanta, 1528 (75 percent); Boston, 1820 (71 percent); Detroit, 1543 (78 percent); Los Angeles, 4025 (68 percent). The household surveys were face-to-face interviews, ranging from an average of fifty minutes in average interview length (Detroit) to ninety-five minutes (Boston). Detroit and Atlanta interviews were conducted in English; Boston in English and Spanish; Los Angeles in English, Spanish, Mandarin, Cantonese, and Korean. For non-English interviews, field materials were translated using independent forward-backward translation. The percentage of household respondents interviewed by someone of the same race or ethnicity are as follows: Atlanta: white 80 percent, black 94 percent; Boston: white 92 percent, black 49 percent, Hispanic 55 percent; Detroit: white 92.5 percent; black 89.6 percent; Los Angeles: white 53 percent, black 82 percent, Hispanic 74 percent, Asian 92 percent. Sample characteristics are described in more detail in the city volumes.

4. The combined four-city Household Survey file, along with data from the Employer Surveys described herein, is currently available through the Inter-University Consortium for Political and Social Research (ICPSR), located at the University of Michigan's Institute for Social Research in Ann Arbor.

5. The 297-Firm Supplemental Survey was drawn from the Household responses in Boston and Los Angeles. Due to the longer time frame for administering the Household Surveys in those metropolitan areas, the supplement was needed to raise the number of matched responses included in the Employer Telephone Survey.

6. Interviews were conducted at forty-five firms in Atlanta and Los Angeles, forty-six in Boston, and thirty-nine in Detroit. Up to three interviews were conducted per firm, depending upon size and firm structure, in an effort to incorporate perspectives at the level of CEO, personnel manager, and immediate supervisor. In a small number of firms with complex managerial structures (for example,

those using subcontractors), more than three interviews were conducted.

References

Bluestone, Barry, and Mary Stevenson. 2000. *Greater Boston in Transition: Race and Ethnicity in a Renaissance Region*. New York: Russell Sage Foundation.

Bobo, Lawrence D., Devon Johnson, and Susan A. Suh. 2000. "Racial Attitudes and Power in the Workplace: Do the Haves Differ from the Have-Nots?" In *Prismatic Metropolis: Race, Segregation, and Inequality in Los Angeles*, edited by Lawrence D. Bobo, Melvin L. Oliver, James H. Johnson Jr., and Abel Valenzuela Jr. New York: Russell Sage Foundation.

Bobo, Lawrence D., and James R. Kluegel. 1997. "Status, Ideology, and Dimensions of Whites' Racial Beliefs and Attitudes: Progress and Stagnation." In *Racial Attitudes in the 1990s: Continuity and Change*, edited by Steven A. Tuch and Jack K. Martin. Westport, Conn.: Praeger.

Bobo, Lawrence D., Melvin L. Oliver, James H. Johnson Jr., and Abel Valenzuela Jr. 2000. *Prismatic Metropolis: Race, Segregation, and Inequality in Los Angeles*. New York: Russell Sage Foundation.

Bobo, Lawrence D., and Susan A. Suh. 2000. "Surveying Racial Discrimination: Analyses from a Multiethnic Labor Market." In *Prismatic Metropolis: Race, Segregation, and Inequality in Los Angeles*, edited by Lawrence D. Bobo, Melvin L. Oliver, James H. Johnson Jr., and Abel Valenzuela Jr. New York: Russell Sage Foundation.

Bobo, Lawrence D., Camille L. Zubrinsky, James H. Johnson Jr., and Melvin L. Oliver. 1994. "Public Opinion Before and After a Spring of Discontent." In *The Los Angeles Riots: Lessons for the Urban Future*, edited by Mark Baldassare. Boulder, Colo.: Westview Press.

Bonilla-Silva, Eduardo. 1996. "Rethinking Racism: Toward a Structural Interpretation." *American Sociological Review* 62(3): 465–80.

Caraley, Demetrios. 1992. "Washington Abandons the Cities." *Political Science Quarterly* 107(1): 1–27.

Carnoy, Martin. 1994. *Faded Dreams: The Politics and Economics of Race in America*. New York: Cambridge University Press.

Cose, Ellis. 1993. *The Rage of a Privileged Class*. New York: HarperCollins.

Danziger, Sheldon, and Peter Gottschalk. 1995. *America Unequal*. New York and Cambridge, Mass.: Russell Sage Foundation and Harvard University Press.

Days, Drew S. 1984. "Turning Back the Clock: The Reagan Administration and Civil Rights." *Harvard Civil Rights-Civil Liberties Law Review* 19(2): 309–47.

Drake, St. Clair, and Horace Cayton. 1993 [1945]. *Black Metropolis: A Study of Negro Life in a Northern City*. Chicago: University of Chicago Press.

Dreier, Peter. 1995. "Putting Cities on the National Agenda." *Urban Affairs Review* 30(5): 645–56.

———. 2000. "Labor's Love Lost? Rebuilding Unions' Involvement in Federal Housing Policy." *Housing Policy Debate* 11(2): 327–92.

DuBois, W.E.B. 1996 [1899]. *The Philadelphia Negro*. Philadelphia: University of Pennsylvania Press.

———. 1901. "The Freedman's Bureau." *The Atlantic Monthly* 87(March): 354–65.

Farley, Reynolds, Sheldon D. Danziger, and Harry J. Holzer. 2000. *Detroit Divided: Racial and Spatial Inequalities in Employment and Housing*. New York: Russell Sage Foundation.

Farley, Reynolds, Howard Schumann, Suzanne Bianchi, Diane Colasanto, and Shirley Hatchett. 1978. "'Chocolate City, Vanilla Suburb': Will the Trend Toward Racially Separate Communities Continue?" *Social Science Research* 7(4): 319–44.

Farley, Reynolds, Charlotte Steeh, Tara Jackson, and Keith Reeves. 1994. "Stereotypes and Segregation: Neighborhoods in the Detroit Area." *American Journal of Sociology* 100(3): 750–80.

Fix, Michael, and R. Struyk, eds. 1993. *Clear and Convincing Evidence: Measurement of Discrimination in America*. Washington, D.C.: Urban Institute Press.

Gephart, Martha A., and Robert W. Pearson. 1988. "Contemporary Research on the Urban Underclass." *Items* 42 (June): 1–10. New York: Social Science Research Council.

Hacker, Andrew. 1992. *Two Nations: Black and White, Separate, Hostile, Unequal*. New York: Scribner's.

Harrison, Bennett, and Barry B. Bluestone. 1988. *The Great U-Turn: Corporate Restructuring and the Polarizing of America*. New York: Basic Books.

Holzer, Harry J. 1991. "The Spatial Mismatch Hypothesis: What has the Evidence Shown?" *Urban Studies* 28(1): 105–22.

———. 1996. *What Employers Want: Job Prospects for Less-Educated Workers*. New York: Russell Sage Foundation.

———. 1998. "Employer Skill Demands and Labor Market Outcomes of Blacks and Women." *Industrial and Labor Relations Review* 52(1): 82–98.

Jackson, Kenneth T. 1985. *Crabgrass Frontier: The Suburbanization of the United States*. New York: Oxford University Press.

Jencks, Christopher, and Paul E. Peterson, eds. 1991. *The Urban Underclass*. Washington, D.C.: Brookings Institution Press.

Johnson, James H., Jr., and Melvin L. Oliver. 1989. "Interethnic Minority Conflict in Urban America: The Effects of Economic and Social Dislocations." *Urban Geography* 10(5): 542–62.

Johnson, James H., Jr., Melvin L. Oliver, and Lawrence D. Bobo. 1994. "Understanding the Contours of Deepening Urban Inequality: Theoretical Underpinnings and Research Design of a Multi-City Study." *Urban Geography* 15(1): 77–89.

Kasarda, John D. 1989. "Urban Industrial Transition and the Underclass." *Annals of the American Academy of Political and Social Science* 501(January): 26–47.

Kirschenman Joleen, and Kathryn M. Neckerman. 1991. " 'We'd Love to Hire Them, But. . . ' : The Meaning of Race for Employers." In *The Urban Underclass,* edited by Christopher Jencks and Paul E. Peterson. Washington, D.C.: Brookings Institution Press.

Levy, Frank. 1998. *The New Dollars and Dreams: American Incomes and Economic Change.* New York: Russell Sage Foundation.

Levy, Frank, and Richard J. Murnane. 1992. "U.S. Earnings Levels and Earnings Inequality: A Review of Recent Trends and Proposed Explanations. *Journal of Economic Literature* 30: 1333–81.

Massey, Douglas S., and Nancy A. Denton. 1993. *American Apartheid: Segregation and the Making of the Underclass.* Cambridge, Mass.: Harvard University Press.

Mishel, Lawrence, Jared Bernstein, and John Schmitt. 1999. *The State of Working America, 1998–99.* Ithaca, N.Y.: Cornell University Press.

Mohl, Raymond. 1997 [1995]. "Blacks and Hispanics in Multicultural America: A Miami Case Study." Reprinted in *The Making of Urban America,* edited by Raymond Mohl, 2d ed. Wilmington, Del.: Scholarly Resources.

Moss, Philip, and Chris Tilly. 2001. *Stories Employers Tell: Race, Skill, and Hiring in America.* New York: Russell Sage Foundation.

O'Connor, Alice. 1999. "Swimming Against the Tide: A Brief History of Federal Policy in Poor Communities." In *Urban Problems and Community Development,* edited by Ronald F. Ferguson and William T. Dickens. Washington, D.C.: Brookings.

———. 2000. "Poverty Research for a Post-Welfare Era." *Annual Review of Sociology* 26: 547–62.

———. 2001. *Poverty Knowledge: Social Science, Social Policy, and the Poor in Twentieth Century U.S. History.* Princeton, N.J.: Princeton University Press.

Oliver, Melvin L., and James H. Johnson Jr. 1984. "Interethnic Conflict in an Urban Ghetto: The Case of Blacks and Latinos in Los Angeles." *Research in Social Movements, Conflicts and Change* 6: 57–94.

Oliver, Melvin L., James H. Johnson Jr., and Walter C. Farrell Jr. 1993. "Anatomy of a Rebellion: A Political-Economic Analysis." In *Reading Rodney King/Reading Urban Uprising,* edited by Robert Gooding-Williams. New York: Routledge.

Oliver, Melvin L., and Thomas M. Shapiro. 1995. *Black Wealth/White Wealth.* New York: Routledge.

O'Neill, June. 1990. "The Role of Human Capital in Earnings Differences Between Black and White Men." *The Journal of Economic Perspectives* 4(Autumn): 25–45.

Patterson, Orlando. 1997. *The Ordeal of Integration: Progress and Resentment in America's "Racial" Crisis.* Washington, D.C.: Civitas Counterpoint.

Portes, Alejandro, and Ruben G. Rumbaut. 1990. *Immigrant America: A Portrait*. Berkeley and Los Angeles: University of California Press.

Sassen, Saskia. 1990. "Economic Restructuring and the American City." *Annual Review of Sociology* 16: 465–90.

———. 1991. *The Global City: New York, London, Tokyo*. Princeton, N.J.: Princeton University Press.

Sjoquist, David L. 1996. "Spatial Mismatch and Social Acceptability." Paper presented at the Multi-City Study of Urban Inequality Conference, New York, April 1996.

Sjoquist, David L., ed. 2000. *The Atlanta Paradox*. New York: Russell Sage Foundation.

Steinberg, Stephen. 1995. *Turning Back: The Retreat from Racial Justice in American Thought and Policy*. Boston: Beacon Press.

Sugrue, Thomas J. 1996. *The Origins of the Urban Crisis: Race and Inequality in Postwar Detroit*. Princeton, N.J.: Princeton University Press.

Thernstrom, Stephan, and Abigail Thernstrom. 1997. *America in Black and White: One Nation, Indivisible*. New York: Simon & Schuster.

U.S. Department of Housing and Urban Development. 1999. *Now is the Time: Places Left Behind in the New Economy*. Washington: U.S. Government Printing Office.

Waldinger, Roger, and Mehdi Bozorgmehr, eds., 1996. *Ethnic Los Angeles*. New York: Russell Sage Foundation.

West, Cornel. 1993. *Race Matters*. Boston: Beacon Press.

Williams, Linda Faye. 1998. "Race and the Politics of Social Policy." In *The Social Divide: Political Parties and the Future of Activist Government*, edited by Margaret Weir. New York/Washington, D.C.: Russell Sage/Brookings.

Willie, Charles V., ed. 1979. *The Caste and Class Controversy*. New York: General Hall, Inc.

Wilson, William J. 1980. *The Declining Significance of Race: Blacks and Changing American Institutions*. Chicago: University of Chicago Press.

———. 1987. *The Truly Disadvantaged: The Inner City, the Underclass, and Public Policy*. Chicago: University of Chicago Press.

———. 1990. "Race-Neutral Programs and the Democratic Coalition." *The American Prospect* 1(Spring): 82–89.

———. 1996. *When Work Disappears: The World of the New Urban Poor*. New York: Knopf.

———. 1999. *The Bridge Over the Racial Divide: Rising Inequality and Coalition Politics*. Berkeley/New York: University of California/Russell Sage Foundation.

Winant, Howard. 2000. "Race and Race Theory." *Annual Review of Sociology* 26: 169–85.

Wolman, Harold, and Lisa Marckini. 1998. "Changes in Central City Representation and Influence in Congress Since the 1960s." *Urban Affairs Review* 34(2): 291–312.

METROPOLISES OF THE MULTI-CITY STUDY OF URBAN INEQUALITY: SOCIAL, ECONOMIC, DEMOGRAPHIC, AND RACIAL ISSUES IN ATLANTA, BOSTON, DETROIT, AND LOS ANGELES

Reynolds Farley

T HE MULTI-CITY Study of Urban Inequality investigated racial differences in social and economic status in four of the nation's largest metropolises in the 1990s. This study sought to answer questions about why African Americans remain disadvantaged on almost all economic indicators thirty years after the civil rights revolution altered not only the nation's laws but its values about the legitimacy of racial discrimination. Another important aim of this study was to describe the racial and economic change now occurring in major ports of entry as many Latinos and Asians migrate to the United States. This chapter provides an overview of the Multi-City Study sites, focusing on the social, economic, and demographic differences that distinguish the racial groups.

Population Composition in 1990 and Recent Growth in the Metropolises Studied

Three hundred and eighteen metropolitan areas were defined for the census of 1990. In terms of population size, the four Multi-City Study metropolises ranked first (Los Angeles), fifth (Detroit), seventh (Boston), and ninth (Atlanta) on this list. All had large populations, ranging from the 8.8 million residents of metropolitan Los Angeles to the 2.8 million in metropolitan Atlanta. Together, they comprised 8 percent of the nation's population in 1990.

Population Composition

This profile of the four Multi-City Study sites begins with information about their population composition in 1990. Figure 1.1 shows the distribution of population in each metropolis. In this figure and in most of the other figures in this chapter, we provide information for the metropolitan area defined for the 1990 count. In Detroit and Los Angeles, the Primary Metropolitan Statistical Area is used, thereby excluding outlying metropolitan areas.[1]

FIGURE 1.1   *Racial Composition of the Multi-City Study Sites in 1990*

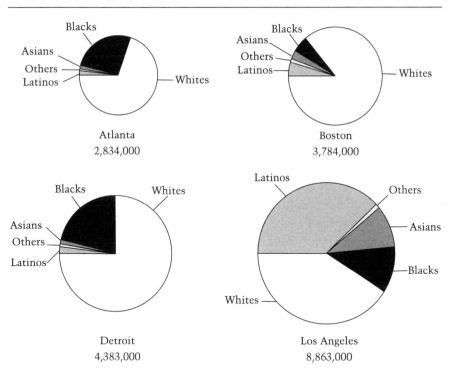

Source: U.S. Bureau of the Census, *Census of Population and Housing: 1990*, Public Use Microdata Sample.

Note: Data refer to the non-Hispanic black, non-Hispanic white, non-Hispanic Asian, and other populations. "Other" includes American Indians, as well as persons who identified their racial identity in a way that could not be classified.

Among these four locations, Boston was the most racially homogeneous: eighty-six out of every one hundred residents were white by race.
Los Angeles was the most heterogeneous and was the only major metropolitan area in the country in 1990 in which whites were a numerical
minority (41 percent).

It is not easy or unambiguous to classify the population by race.
The census asked everyone either to fill in one of fourteen circles to
indicate racial identity or to write in a term for their race. And every
person was asked whether or not their origin was Spanish. If so, they
could fill in a circle indicating Mexican, Puerto Rican, or Cuban or write
a term for their Spanish origin. Approximately 58 percent of those who
indicated they were Spanish in origin also reported a race—typically
white, although a few Hispanics said they were black, American Indian,
or Filipino. But 42 percent of those who said they were Spanish in origin
wrote in a phrase on the race question indicating their origin was Spanish. Should the white population include those whites who went on to
report that their origin was Spanish, or should it be limited to the non-
Hispanic whites? Because the 1980 and 1990 censuses asked distinct
questions about race and Spanish origin, it is possible to distinguish the
Hispanic population from other groups. However, previous censuses did
ask separate questions, so it is impossible to use a consistent procedure
for identifying the Spanish-origin population for censuses prior to 1980.[2]

In this chapter, the following mutually exclusive racial groups are
used when data are presented for 1980 and 1990:

non-Hispanic whites—that is, persons who said their race was white
and that they were not Spanish in origin

non-Hispanic blacks

non-Hispanic Asians

non-Hispanic Other Race—these are primarily American Indians,
Aleuts, and Eskimos

Hispanics

Returning to the topic of racial composition shown in figure 1.1, we
observe that Atlanta had the highest representation of blacks. About one
resident in four there was African American, while in metropolitan Detroit it was about one in five, and Boston had the lowest representation
of blacks. Los Angeles was the only site with numerous Hispanics;
three-eighths of the residents reported their origin as Spanish. (In this
chapter, we use *Latino, Hispanics,* and *Spanish origin* interchangeably
to refer to the same group.) About 5 percent did so in Boston, but Atlanta and Detroit were most similar to inland metropolises in that they
have hardly been affected by immigration from abroad and have a very

small representation of those of Spanish origin. Among the Multi-City Study sites, Asians were numerous only in Los Angeles; indeed, they were just about as numerous as African Americans there.

The origins of the Spanish population in Boston differ greatly from the origin of those living in Los Angeles. Table 1.1 shows the largest groups in both sites and reveals the uniqueness of Los Angeles in terms of its demographic composition. The Spanish-origin population of that metropolis—3.2 million in 1990—was greater than the total population of metropolitan Atlanta and about three-quarters as large as the population of metropolitan Detroit. One group—Mexicans—numerically dominated the Los Angeles Latino population; about two-thirds who claimed a Spanish origin were Mexican. Central Americans—Salvadorans, Guatemalans, and Nicaraguans—were also numerous, while there were few Cubans or Puerto Ricans.

This table also indicates one of the complexities of ethnic classification in an era when the immigration stream arrives from many different countries. The census question in 1990 asked people of Spanish origin to fill in a circle to indicate their origin as Mexican, Cuban, or Puerto Rican, or to write a phrase describing their origin. Some wrote a phrase indicating a specific country of origin, such as Colombia, while many others wrote a broader term such as Spanish or Hispanic.

Although the Spanish-origin population may now seem large to older Boston residents, it included only 120,000 persons, or 3 percent of the total metropolis, in 1990. It is a diverse population—Puerto Rican being the modal Spanish origin reported—while smaller numbers came from the Dominican Republic, Central American nations, and Mexico. No one group dominates the Latino population of Boston, the way Mexicans dominate Los Angeles.

Approximately one million Asians lived in metropolitan Los Angeles in 1990—the largest concentration of Asians in the country. This also is a diverse population, with just under one-quarter million Chinese residents, about the same number of Filipinos, and then smaller numbers of other groups—although the four largest groups—Chinese, Filipinos, Koreans, and Japanese—comprised three-quarters of the total.

One other dimension of the heterogeneity of population composition concerns immigration; that is, the proportion of foreign-born population. Here we turn to information for the groups interviewed in the Multi-City Study: blacks and whites in every site; Hispanics in Boston and Los Angeles; and Asians in the Pacific rim metropolis. Atlanta and Detroit are locations with few recent immigrants: only 3 percent of whites in Atlanta and 6 percent in Detroit had foreign birthplaces and, among blacks, the proportions of foreign-born were even smaller. Given the Latin American and Asian dominance of the recent immigration flow, it is no surprise that only a small proportion of non-Hispanic

TABLE 1.1   *Composition of the Spanish-Origin Population in 1990 in Boston, and Spanish-Origin and Asian Populations in Los Angeles*

Boston		Los Angeles			
Spanish-Origin Groups (000)		Spanish-Origin Groups (000)		Asian Groups (000)	
1. Puerto Rican	44	1. Mexican	2,497	1. Chinese	231
2. Dominican[a]	13	2. Salvadoran[a]	250	2. Filipino	225
3. Salvadoran[a]	8	3. Guatemalan[a]	127	3. Korean	145
4. Mexican	7	4. Cuban	46	4. Japanese	132
5. Colombian[a]	6	5. Hispanic[a]	43	5. Asian Indian	43
6. Cuban	5	6. Puerto Rican	40	6. Cambodian[a]	31
7. Guatemalan[a]	5	7. Nicaraguan[a]	32	7. Thai[a]	18
8. Spanish[a]	3	8. Spanish[a]	32	8. Taiwanese[a]	16
9. Spaniard[a]	3	9. Spaniard[a]	26	9. Samoan	11
10. Honduran[a]	3	10. Honduran	23	10. Indonesian[a]	8
Total[b]	121		3,299		958

Source: U.S. Bureau of the Census, *Census of Population and Housing: 1990*, Public Use Microdata Sample.
[a] These groups self-identified because a respondent wrote this phrase. Other groups were identified by respondents filling in a circle on the census schedule.
[b] This total includes persons in all the Spanish-origin or Asian groups represented in these metropolises.

whites in Los Angeles and Boston were born abroad. International migration is hardly contributing to the growth of the white population. As figure 1.2 reports, the majority of Latinos in Los Angeles and almost three out of four Asians there were immigrants to the United States. And many of these arrived recently. That is, more than 40 percent of Asians living in Los Angeles arrived in the 1980s, as did just under one-third of the Hispanic population. For purposes of this tabulation, individuals from Puerto Rico are considered immigrants, even though they are United States citizens at birth.

From the end of slavery to the Spanish-American War, there was almost no in-migration of blacks to this country. With the acquisition of Cuba and Puerto Rico, small flows of blacks began to arrive but this stream did not grow rapidly until new immigration laws took effect in 1968. The flow of black immigration is still modest compared to Latino or Asian immigrants, but now many arrive each year from the Dominican Republic, Haiti, Jamaica, other Caribbean isles, and, more recently, Africa. Black immigrants are distinctive for their geographic concentration in metropolitan New York, Miami, and Boston. That is, about one-quarter of the black population of Boston were immigrants to the United States, compared to less than 1 percent in Detroit, 3 percent in

FIGURE 1.2   *Nativity and Date of Arrival for Racial Groups in Multi-City Study Sites*

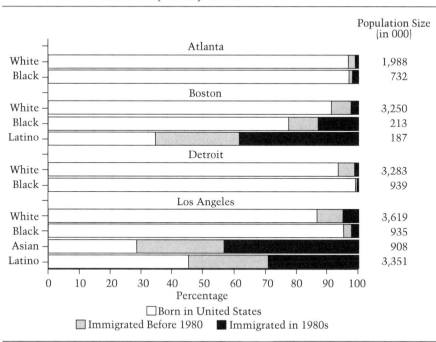

	Population Size (in 000)
Atlanta	
White	1,988
Black	732
Boston	
White	3,250
Black	213
Latino	187
Detroit	
White	3,283
Black	939
Los Angeles	
White	3,619
Black	935
Asian	908
Latino	3,351

□ Born in United States
▨ Immigrated Before 1980   ■ Immigrated in 1980s

Source: U.S. Bureau of the Census, *Census of Population and Housing: 1990*, Public Use Microdata Sample.
Note: Data refer to non-Hispanic whites, blacks, and Asians.

Atlanta, and 4 percent in Los Angeles. Nationally, 5.7 percent of African Americans were immigrants.

What are the origins of the foreign-born black population of Boston? Listed in table 1.2 are the most frequently reported places of birth:

TABLE 1.2   *Place of Birth of Foreign-Born Blacks in Metropolitan Boston, 1990*

	Number
Haiti	21,700
Jamaica	6,900
Trinidad	5,200
Barbados	3,100
Dominican Republic	2,500
Honduras	2,300
Puerto Rico	2,000
Total Born Outside the United States[a]	55,100

[a]This total includes all blacks born outside the United States.

Population Growth in the 1980s

The information presented thus far describes the four Multi-City Study sites in 1990, but their composition in that year was the outcome of differential growth rates for the groups. Figure 1.3 shows average annual rates of population changes in the 1980s for these locations. Information about population growth for the nation is also provided. Although the overall rate of national population growth in the 1980s was quite low—less than 1 percent per year—racial differences were great, with non-Hispanic whites increasing at less than half the national average. The black population grew at about the national rate, while the Asian population doubled and the Latino population was up by 60 percent. Recall that an average annual growth rate of 7 percent doubles a population in one decade.

Two of the areas—Boston and Detroit—were just about stagnant with regard to overall population growth. Boston, in the 1980s, added about 100,000 residents to its population of 3.8 million, while Detroit was the only major metropolis with a declining population—but the loss was a relatively small 100,000 compared with the base population of 4.4 million, or a rate of decline of less than 0.1 percent per year. Boston's population, however, experienced a modest racial shift, since there was rapid growth of the Spanish-origin and Asian population. And Detroit's population stagnated not only because it lost white population but also because it failed to attract many of the new immigrants arriving from Asia and Latin America. Although numerically small, the Asian population of Detroit is growing rapidly since its economic niche— world headquarters of the now booming motor vehicle industry—means Detroit attracts many Asian scientists and engineers.

In terms of their demographic trajectories in the 1980s, Atlanta and Los Angeles differed greatly. All the major groups grew in Atlanta. To be sure, the Latinos and Asian population in that location were small in 1980 so even their high growth rates—13 percent per year for Asians and 8 percent for Latinos—produced little change in the racial composition. Atlanta's black and white populations continue to grow at healthy rates so racial change will occur slowly. Demographic change is occurring in a different manner in Los Angeles. The black population there grew very slowly—at a much lower rate than Detroit's—while the white population just about stagnated during the 1980s. But growth of Asian and Latino population in the 1980s propelled the transition to even greater racial diversity.

Racial Segregation in the Four Metropolises

The Multi-City Study of Urban Inequality sought to analyze why racial residential segregation remains at a high level. In this section, we pro-

FIGURE 1.3   *Average Annual Rates of Population Change in the 1980s, Multi-City Study Sites*

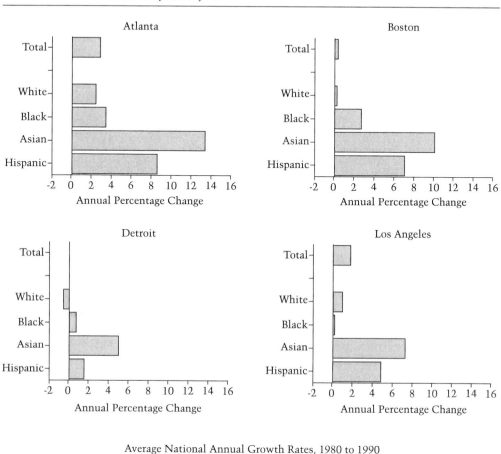

Average National Annual Growth Rates, 1980 to 1990

Total Population	+0.9%
Non-Hispanic	
White	+0.4
Black	+1.1
Asian	+6.6
Hispanic	+4.1

Source: U.S. Bureau of the Census, *Census of Population and Housing: 1990*, Public Use Microdata Sample.
Note: Growth rates refer to the non-Hispanic white, black, and Asian populations.

vide information about the extent of that segregation and compare 1980 and 1990 levels.

The Evenness of
Geographic Distributions

The most frequently used measure of residential segregation is the index of dissimilarity. This is calculated from census data showing the distribution of two groups across geographic units, such as block groups. Were every geographic unit to be racially homogeneous—that is, some block groups with only black residents and others with only white residents—the index of dissimilarity comparing the residential distributions of blacks and whites would equal its maximum value of 100, thereby describing a situation of complete racial apartheid. Were blacks and whites randomly distributed to their places of residence—and this, of course, does not happen either—the index would approach its minimum value of zero. The numerical value of the index of dissimilarity reports the percent of either racial group who would have to change their place of residence to eliminate segregation; that is, to bring about an index of dissimilarity of zero.

Figure 1.4 describes racial residential segregation in geographically comparable metropolises using information at the level of the block group. These are individual residential blocks or sets of contiguous blocks defined by the Census Bureau for tabulation purposes, and contained an average of 564 residents in 1990. They are, for our purposes, neighborhoods, since persons living within a block group will often greet their neighbors in local shops and fast food restaurants and, quite likely, will send their children to the same public schools.

The upper panel of the figure reveals a high level of black-white segregation in the Multi-City Study sites in both years. Over all metropolitan areas in the United States, the comparable index comparing those who said they were white by race to those who said they were black was 68 in 1980 and 64 in 1990. The Multi-City Study sites had segregation levels above the national average in both years, but the levels varied from one site to another. Detroit was the most segregated and the only site in which segregation failed to decline in the 1980s. In both years, it would have been necessary for 88 percent of either whites or blacks to shift their block group of residence to eliminate black-white residential segregation. By 1990, both Los Angeles and Boston had black-white indexes of dissimilarity of 71, considerably lower than Detroit, while Atlanta's score was just a bit higher than those for Boston and Los Angeles. In the typical metropolis across the nation, this index fell by 4 points—just about the change recorded in every Multi-City Study site except Detroit.

FIGURE 1.4   *Racial Residential Segregation as Measured by Indexes of Dissimilarity, Multi-City Study Sites, 1980 and 1990*

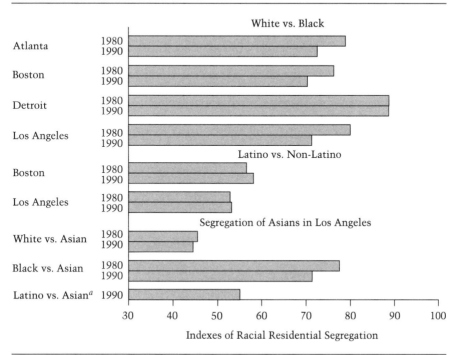

Source: U.S. Bureau of the Census, *Census of Population and Housing: 1990*, Summary Tape File 1.
Note: Latinos may be in any racial group.
[a]Similar score cannot be calculated from block group data in 1980.

Latinos and Asians are much less segregated than blacks, although the comparisons become more complicated as additional groups are considered. We considered the segregation of Latinos from all non-Latinos in Boston and Los Angeles. As figure 1.4 reports, there was moderate segregation, since 55 percent of Latinos or non-Latinos would have to move to eliminate it. However, blacks were much more segregated from whites in these metropolises than Latinos were segregated from non-Latinos.

For Los Angeles, Asians were compared to whites and blacks in both years, but data to measure Asian-Hispanic segregation were available only for 1990. As the figure reports, Asians were moderately segregated from whites—scores of about 45 in both years—but were quite highly segregated from blacks. Asians were as residentially segregated from blacks in Los Angeles at the beginning and end of the 1980s as whites were segregated from blacks. Even though most Asians arrived in Los Angeles recently, they have taken up residences that allow them to be as highly segregated from African Americans as whites are. Asians in Los Angeles in 1990 were more segregated from Latinos than from whites, but not at all as segregated from Latinos as from blacks.

Interracial Contact at the Neighborhood Level

The index of dissimilarity is widely used and easily understood because it is an ideal measure of the evenness with which two racial groups are distributed across the urban landscape. But it does not tell us a great deal about the racial composition of the typical neighborhood of a resident. When we examine the types of neighborhoods where people live, we find important differences among the Multi-City Study sites. For the most part, whites live in predominantly white areas, but the racial composition of the neighborhoods of blacks greatly varies from one location to another.

Figure 1.5 is also based on data from the census of 1990 showing the number of whites, African Americans, Asians, and Hispanics living in each block group. Some individuals live in neighborhoods numerically dominated by their group, while others live in neighborhoods where they may be one of a few people representing their racial group. The pie charts in figure 1.5 show the racial composition of the typical or average individual in a specific group. The index of dissimilarity is, statistically, independent of the population size of the two groups being compared, but these neighborhood composition measures are strongly affected by both the level of racial residential segregation as measured by the index of dissimilarity and the relative size of the two groups.[3]

The top panel shows the racial composition of neighborhoods occupied by the typical white resident. Given the high levels of residential segregation and the large size of the white population, it is no surprise to find that whites live in overwhelmingly white neighborhoods in three of the sites. Atlanta whites typically have a few more black neighbors than do whites in Detroit or Boston because of slightly lower segregation scores and because the black population is relatively larger. Whites in Los Angeles live in a different environment and experience much more heterogeneity as they do local shopping, meet their neighbors, or take their children to school since, in that metropolis, whites lived in neighborhoods where more than one-third were minorities. Their neighborhoods were about 20 percent Latino while the remaining 10 percent were Asians and blacks. Los Angeles whites presumably meet many La-tinos as they go about their neighborhood chores, but this occurs rarely in the other three metropolises. And Atlanta whites are distinctive for the potential frequency with which they see blacks in their neighbor-hoods.

Among blacks, those living in metropolitan Detroit and Los An-geles differ from those in Atlanta and Boston. The high levels of segrega-tion and the virtual absence of Hispanics and Asians means that Motor City blacks live in neighborhoods where five-sixths of the residents are black, a demographic phenomenon that limits opportunities for school integration or interracial political coalitions. In Boston—and more so in Los Angeles—blacks live in neighborhoods where their racial group is the numerical minority: the majority of their neighbors are not black. In Boston, 38 percent of the residents of a black's typical neighborhood are white, while more than 10 percent are Latinos. Heterogeneity is even greater for African Americans in Los Angeles, since there are quite a few whites, Asians, and Hispanics living in the block groups inhabited by blacks in that location.

Latinos in Boston live in majority-white neighborhoods but, as re-vealed by figure 1.5, this is not the case in Los Angeles. The segregation of Hispanics in Los Angeles was no higher than in Boston as measured by the index of dissimilarity, but the ratio of Hispanics to whites and Asians was very different. As a result, Latinos numerically dominate their neighborhoods in Los Angeles but have many white and Asian neighbors. The most heterogeneous neighborhoods of all were those of Asians in Los Angeles. They were, roughly, one-quarter Asian, one-third Latino, and three-eighths whites.

Whites and, even more so, the racial minorities, experience quite different racial compositions in their own neighborhoods. Presumably, as Latinos or Asians go about their daily lives or utilize the services provided at the neighborhood level by municipal governments, they come into contact with many individuals from the array of racial groups now repre-sented in this country. This will be much less the case for whites. In many ways, the most racially isolated groups are whites, reflecting, undoubt-edly, a traditional reluctance to live next door to most minorities. It is important to note that minority races have, presumably, many more op-portunities for neighborhood contacts with whites than whites do with minorities—except for those whites who live in Los Angeles.

City-Suburban Segregation

These metropolises differ with regard to a third dimension of racial resi-dential segregation: namely, the concentration of minorities in the cen-

FIGURE 1.5   *Racial Composition of the Neighborhood of a Typical*
Resident of Multi-City Study Sites, 1990

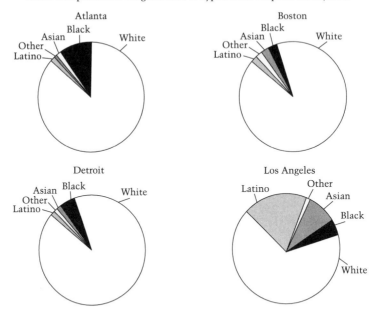

Racial Composition of Neighborhood of Typical Non-Hispanic White, 1990

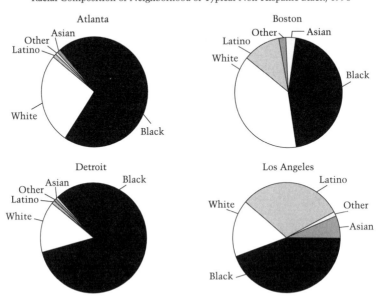

Racial Composition of Neighborhood of Typical Non-Hispanic Black, 1990

Source: U.S. Bureau of the Census, *Census of Population and Housing: 1990*, Summary
Tape File 1.

FIGURE 1.5   *Continued*

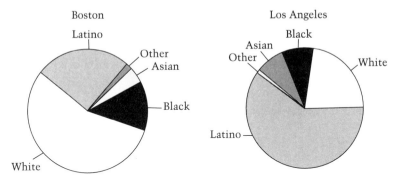

Racial Composition of Neighborhood of Typical Latino, 1990

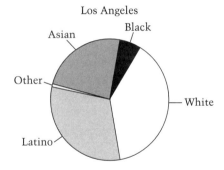

Racial Composition of Neighborhood of Typical Asian, 1990

tral city and whites in suburban rings. In its foreboding predictions of three decades ago, the Kerner Commission argued that if then current trends did not change, by the 1990s in many of the nation's larger metropolises, there would be a largely black and impoverished central city surrounded by a largely white and much more prosperous suburban ring. Fortunately that did not turn out to be an accurate prediction except in one of the Multi-City Study sites—Detroit.

Within each of these metropolises, there is a central city that once dominated a surrounding suburban and rural hinterland. In the case of Boston, the city's boundaries were set more than two centuries ago and, in Detroit, shortly after World War I. In Atlanta and Los Angeles, however, the annexation of suburban land occurred after World War II, so there is a major difference in the geography of these locations. Figure 1.6 shows the distribution of population by race in the Multi-City Study

FIGURE 1.6   *Population Composition of Central Cities and*
              Suburban Rings in Multi-City Study Sites, 1990

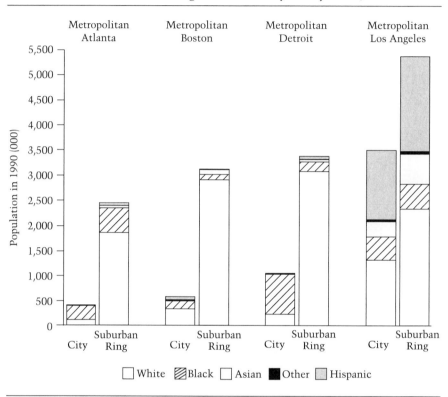

Source: U.S. Bureau of the Census, *Census of Population and Housing: 1990, Summary Tape File 1.*

locations, distinguishing central cities from suburbs. Recall that in Los Angeles and Detroit, we are using the Primary Metropolitan Statistical Area, not the much larger Consolidated Metropolitan Statistical Areas—areas that now include, in one case, a very large section of southeastern Michigan and, in the other, much of southern California.

In all the locations, suburban residents were much more numerous than those in the central city. In Boston and Atlanta, just one resident of the metropolis in seven had a home address in the city in 1990, reflecting rapid suburban growth and the dearth of space in the city for new housing. At the other extreme, about 40 percent of metropolitan Los Angeles residents were in the city.

A new pattern of suburban migration is very evident. Indeed, this

helps to explain why the Kerner Commission predictions did not come
to pass. African Americans are now leaving central cities for the suburbs. In Atlanta, more than two-thirds of the black residents lived in the
suburban ring, not the city, and in Los Angeles a majority also did. In
many ways, intrametropolitan migration streams among blacks in the
1980s and 1990s resemble those of whites in the 1960s: a substantial
movement of the more affluent population from the city to the ring.
Nevertheless, whites led this exodus, and in every comparison propor-
tionally fewer whites than blacks lived in the city. The most extreme
racial contrast was in metropolitan Detroit. In 1990, 82 percent of the
metropolitan black population lived within the city of Detroit, while
only 6 percent of whites did.

In all the sites except Los Angeles, central-city whites make up a
very small proportion of the total white population, so the political interests of whites are overwhelming those of suburbanites. Except in Detroit, there are many blacks living in both the central city and the suburban rings, implying that the city-suburban divide is no longer an
extreme black-white divide.

The Economic Welfare of Racial
Groups in the Four Sites in 1990

When we consider the racial groups and the Multi-City Study locations,
we find that whites were more prosperous than minorities in all four
places, but the magnitude of the racial difference varied. Indeed, the description of which groups are prospering and why and which groups are
disadvantaged is a complicated one. We begin by looking at summary
measures of economic status and then move on to look at key factors
determining the economic standing of a group: its educational attainment, its employment, the jobs workers hold, and their earnings.

Poverty and Prosperity

Using data from the census of 1990 reporting the number of persons in a
household and the household's pretax cash income, we classified all persons by the race of their household head and by the relationship of their
household's income to the poverty line for a household of their size. In
1989, the poverty line for a household of four was $12,674. Four eco-
nomic categories were used to describe levels of economic welfare:

(1) persons living in households with cash incomes below the poverty
     line, often termed *impoverished;*

(2) persons living in households with cash income between 100 percent and 199 percent of the poverty line, here termed *near poor;*

(3) persons living in households with cash incomes between 200 percent and 499 percent of the poverty line, here termed the *economic middle class;*

(4) persons living in households with cash incomes five or more times the poverty line for households of their size, here termed *comfortable.* A household of four needed an income greater than $63,000 in 1989 to be in this situation.

Figure 1.7 shows distributions by economic status. There are five dimensions of economic status summarized by the information in this figure. We start by focusing on one overall summary measure of the standing of each group: median household income in 1989. Not surprisingly, the median income of white households greatly exceeded that of blacks in every Multi-City Study site, with the maximum difference in Detroit, where the white median was double that for blacks. Latino households in both Boston and Los Angeles had median incomes quite close to those of black households. Asians in Los Angeles reported household incomes above those of whites. Restricting the comparisons to specific races, the census revealed that whites in Atlanta and Boston were somewhat more prosperous in terms of median household income than whites in the other two sites. Blacks in Detroit had the lowest median household incomes—about 25 percent below the income of blacks in Boston, where they were most prosperous.

Second, there is great interest in the proportion of population in a precarious economic status as indicated by the poverty rate. The lowest poverty rate for any of these groups was for whites living in Atlanta—just 5 percent were in households below the poverty line; the highest poverty rates for whites was in Detroit: 7 percent. Among blacks, those who resided in Detroit had a considerably higher poverty rate, 33 percent, than blacks in the other three sites. Blacks in Atlanta were more prosperous than those in other sites, but they still had a poverty rate of 22 percent, almost five times the poverty rate for Atlanta whites.

Third, we focus on the upper end of the income distribution as measured by the percent of households with incomes five or more times the poverty line. In every comparison, the relative size of the white upper-income class was much larger than those for minorities. Among whites, the percent comfortable in financial terms was greatest in Los Angeles—44 percent—and least in metropolitan Detroit, where only 35 percent were so prosperous. The share of blacks in this economic status was also

FIGURE 1.7   *Distribution of Population in Multi-City Study Sites by Economic Status, 1990*

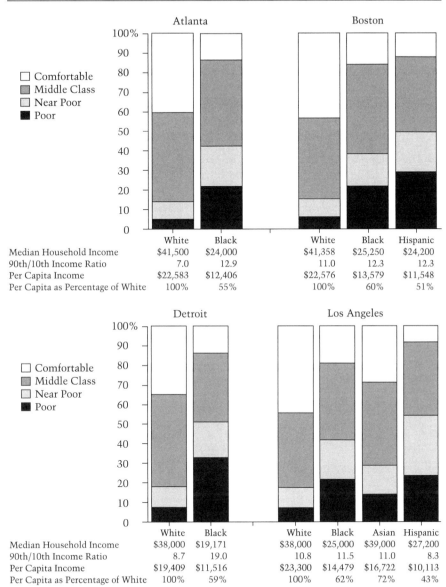

	White	Black		White	Black	Hispanic
Median Household Income	$41,500	$24,000		$41,358	$25,250	$24,200
90th/10th Income Ratio	7.0	12.9		11.0	12.3	12.3
Per Capita Income	$22,583	$12,406		$22,576	$13,579	$11,548
Per Capita as Percentage of White	100%	55%		100%	60%	51%

	White	Black		White	Black	Asian	Hispanic
Median Household Income	$38,000	$19,171		$38,000	$25,000	$39,000	$27,200
90th/10th Income Ratio	8.7	19.0		10.8	11.5	11.0	8.3
Per Capita Income	$19,409	$11,516		$23,300	$14,479	$16,722	$10,113
Per Capita as Percentage of White	100%	59%		100%	62%	72%	43%

Source: U.S. Bureau of the Census, *Census of Population and Housing: 1990*, Public Use Microdata Sample.

greatest in Los Angeles and smallest in Detroit, 19 percent comfortable for blacks in the Pacific Rim metropolis and 14 percent in the Motor City.

Fourth, figure 1.7 provides a measure of income inequality. It indexes this by reporting the ratio of the income of the household at the 90th percentile in the household income distribution to the income of the household at the 10th percentile. Among black households in Detroit, for example, the household at the 90th percentile reported an income of $60,700, while at the 10th percentile it was only $3,200, giving a 90/10 ratio of 19.0.

Looking at these ratios shows that income is more equitably distributed among whites than among minorities. In Atlanta, for example, the 90/10 ratio for whites was 7.0 but for blacks 12.9, revealing a much greater relative distance between the top and the bottom of the income distribution for African Americans. Latinos and Asians in Los Angeles were the racial minorities with household income distributions more equitable than whites. Especially interesting is the large degree of income inequality among African Americans in Detroit. The restructuring of employment in the automobile industry had the consequence of leaving many black households far down the income scale, but also created opportunities for many other blacks to prosper.

Finally, this figure reminds us that a complete picture of economic differences should take household composition into account. White households are typically smaller in size than those of other races, while Asian and Latino households, on average, are quite large. Comparisons of median household incomes provide useful information about the relative economic standing of races, but additional information is gathered by examining per capita income; that is, household income divided by household size. In all four sites, black per capita income averaged between 55 and 62 percent that of whites, with Atlanta at the low end and Los Angeles at the high end. That is, the purchasing power of blacks in Los Angeles, on a per capita basis, was only five-eighths that of whites. Latino income was strongly influenced by the large size of such households, so their per capita income fell far below that of blacks in both Boston and Los Angeles. Indeed, per capita income for Hispanics in Los Angeles was only two-thirds that of blacks. And Asians in Los Angeles present a seeming paradox, for their median household income was greater than that of whites, while their per capita income was much lower. Asians appear more prosperous than whites if we think about household income, but are closer to blacks than whites in terms of per capita income. This is explained by the large average size of Asian households, since extended families with numerous relatives and two or more generations are more common for Asians than for the other racial groups.

The average number of persons per household in Los Angeles at the time of the census of 1990 was:

Non-Hispanic white households	2.3
Non-Hispanic black households	2.7
Non-Hispanic Asian households	3.4
Hispanic households	4.2

Differences in
Educational Attainment

The following sections describe differences between the sites and between the racial groups in key indicators of status pertinent to economic welfare: educational attainment, labor force participation, occupational achievement, and earnings. Data are presented for whites and African Americans in every site, for Latinos in Boston and Los Angeles, and for Asians in Los Angeles. A similar format will be used for each of these statuses. A first figure will report differences in 1990, contrasting the sites and the racial groups. A second figure will present trends over time in the same indicator, utilizing information from the censuses of 1940 through 1990. Data are shown for both men and women since, on many indicators of educational attainment, labor force participation, and earnings, black-white differences are large among men but small among women. Indeed, for a few indicators of earnings, black women exceed white women. No distinction is made between native-born and immigrant Latinos and Hispanics, although there are large differences in their status—a topic discussed when we examine earnings. This section focuses exclusively on adults aged twenty-five to sixty-four.

The census provides dozens of indicators of each of the dimensions we are considering—educational, labor force, occupation, and earnings. I selected one or two of each. With regard to schooling, I considered the percent of adults who completed high school, including those who reported a General Educational Development (GED) certificate, and then those who reported four or more years of college. The educational question asked in the census of 1990 differed from that of earlier censuses, but the Integrated Public Use Microdata Sample files of 1940 to 1990 data recoded education so that the tabulations are comparable insofar as that is possible.

Figure 1.8 shows the percent of adults with high school diplomas or college degrees. Turning first to the left panel, you see small differences among whites in the percent with high school educations, although those in Detroit lag a bit behind those living in other sites. In every location, the percent was lower for blacks than for whites, but this

FIGURE 1.8　　*Percentage High School Graduates and Percentage College Graduates for Population Aged Twenty-Five to Sixty-Four by Race in Multi-City Study Sites, 1990*

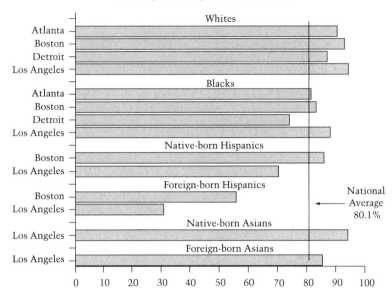

Percentage Male High School Graduates

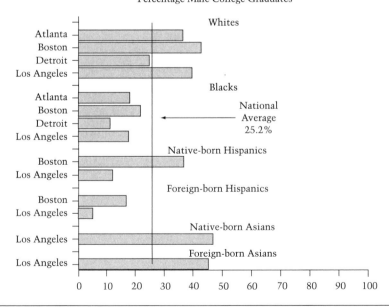

Percentage Male College Graduates

Source: U.S. Bureau of the Census, *Census of Population and Housing: 1990*, Public Use Microdata Sample.

FIGURE 1.8   *Continued*

Percentage Female High School Graduates

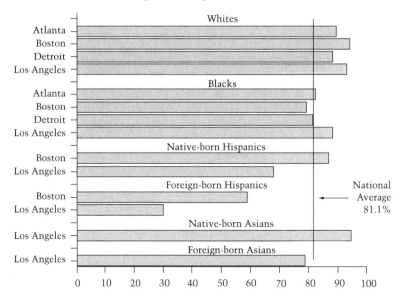

Percentage Female College Graduates

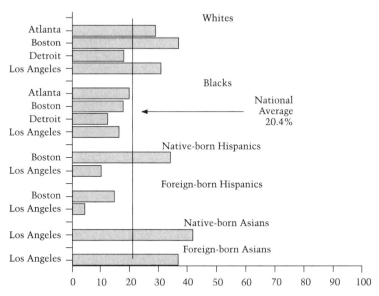

racial difference was smaller among women than among men. An unusually low percent of black men in Detroit had high school educations, while those in Los Angeles were most likely to have this attainment. In both Boston and Los Angeles, adult Hispanics were much less likely than whites or blacks to have high school educations, thereby clearly marking them as the population most disadvantaged with regard to educational credentials. Boston's Hispanic population, however, reported a much higher level of education than those in Los Angeles.

Racial and site differences in college completion are much greater than for secondary school completion. In every location, whites were more likely than blacks or Hispanics to have completed four years of college training, but there were important differences among the locations; most notably the low proportion of Detroit adults who were college-educated. This is linked to the industrial history of that metropolis and to the selective migration that is now reshaping all these places. Asian men in Los Angeles fell far behind white men in terms of the percent with college degrees, but Asian women there were the most extensively educated of the racial groups in that site. This is accounted for, in part, by the large Filipino immigration stream moving to Los Angeles, a predominantly female immigration stream that now includes an unusually large number of women who earned college degrees in nursing or accounting.

Information about trends over time in the educational attainment of racial groups in all four locations is shown in figure 1.9, with the dotted lines showing trends in high school completion and the solid lines, college completion. With regard to secondary school education, Atlanta stands out from the other locations. Given the educational traditions of the South and the selective migration to the North of those southern blacks who had more advanced educations, it is no surprise to find that, in 1940, the black-white difference was greater in Atlanta than in Boston, Detroit, or Los Angeles. In all these locations, the secular trend toward much greater educational attainment led to higher proportions of blacks and whites reporting high school educations and, quite clearly, there was much convergence in attainment, especially as the late baby boom birth cohorts completed their schooling. This convergence is occurring more rapidly among women than among men, both nationally and in these Multi-City Study locations. Nevertheless, the percent with secondary school diplomas in 1990 was about 10 percentage points less for blacks than for whites in these places. While there is a secular trend toward higher proportions of blacks and whites completing college, the racial gap is not closing either in relative or absolute terms. That is, a growing share of young blacks complete college by their mid-twenties, but the rise has been of approximately the same magnitude for whites, so the black-white gap in this important indicator remains basically unchanged.

Limited data are available for an analysis of changes over time in the educational attainment of Hispanics in Boston or Hispanics and Asians in Los Angeles. Asians, since 1970, have had a considerably higher proportion with college degrees than whites, while Hispanics, in both Los Angeles and Boston, lagged far behind whites and Asians. While the educational indicators moved up in the 1980s for blacks and whites, the rises in percentages with degrees were much smaller for Asians and Hispanics. This is explained by the high rate of migration, since many of the newly arrived immigrants—including those from South China coming to Los Angeles—report very low levels of attainment.

Differences in Labor Force Participation

The economic welfare of adults—and those they support—is primarily determined by whether they work, how many hours they spend on the job, and what they earn while at work. These are influenced by their own skills and abilities, by macroeconomic trends, by where people live, and, in many cases, by their gender and their race. Fortunately, it is possible to document current differences and past labor force trends in the Multi-City Study sites because censuses since 1940 have asked questions about labor force participation, hours of employment, and earnings.

Two measures of labor force status will be used. First, we consider the employment-to-population ratio for the population aged twenty-five to sixty-four. If half of the people in a group hold jobs, their employment-to-population ratio will be 500; that is, 500 at work per 1,000 persons. For purposes of these computations, no distinction is made between full- and part-time jobs, but only paying jobs are considered. Second, we present information about per capita hours of employment. Since 1940 censuses have inquired about how many weeks a person worked in the prior year and how many hours they typically spent working each week, allowing us to estimate per capita hours of employment. If a person works forty hours every week, he or she will work two thousand hours in the year.

Figure 1.10 shows employment-to-population ratios for the Multi-City Study sites in 1990, thereby revealing several important differences. Black men were much less likely to be employed than white

FIGURE 1.9   Trends in Percentage with High School or College Degree by Race for the Population Aged
Twenty-Five to Sixty-Four in Multi-City Study Sites, 1940 to 1990

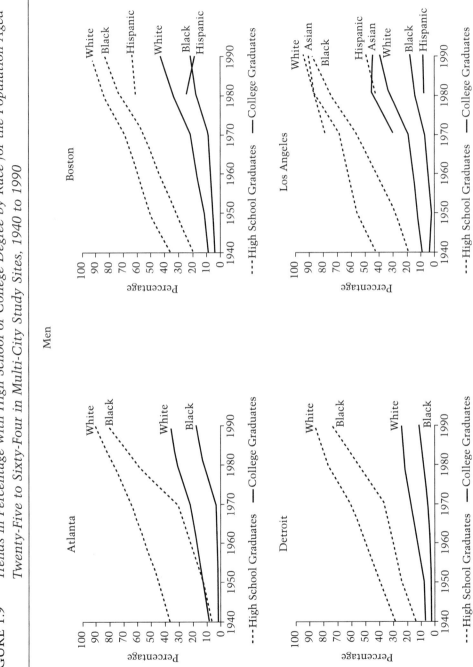

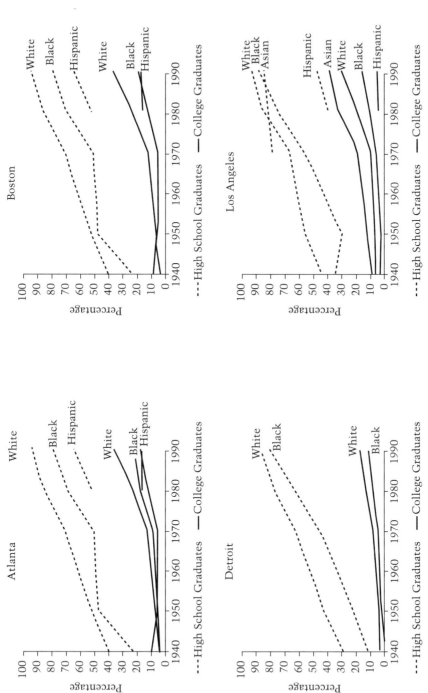

Women

Boston

Los Angeles

Atlanta

Detroit

- - - High School Graduates — College Graduates

Source: Ruggles and Sobek 1997.

FIGURE 1.10 Employment-to-Population Ratios for Persons Aged Twenty-Five to Sixty-Four by Race and Sex, Multi-City Study Sites, 1990

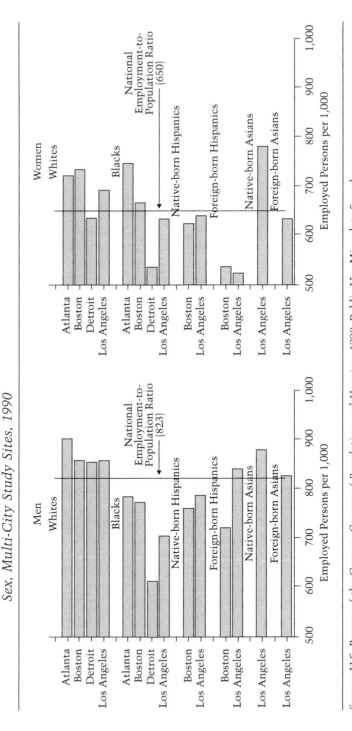

Source: U.S. Bureau of the Census, Census of Population and Housing: 1990, Public Use Microdata Sample.

men, with Detroit distinctive for the unusually low employment rate of blacks. At the time of the 1990 census, just 610 per 1,000 black men in the Motor City held jobs, compared with 850 per 1,000 white men. In every location, black men fell far behind white men in employment. Gender, however, interacts importantly with race. The gap in employment between black and white women was much smaller than among men and, in metropolitan Atlanta, a higher proportion of black than white women held jobs. Detroit was once again distinctive for the low percent of black women holding jobs.

Immigrant Latinos and Asians were less likely to hold jobs than the native-born in the same group, with the exception of foreign-born Hispanic men in Los Angeles. This may be accounted for by the proximity of Mexico and Central America. Immigrant men from nearby countries who fail to find a job in Los Angeles may return home, and this selective return migration may have raised the proportion employed when the census was taken. Native-born Asians were unusual for their high employment-to-population ratios.

Trends over time in employment to population ratios are shown in figure 1.11. The most dramatic change is the gender one. That is, the ratio among men has been basically constant or slightly declining, while, among women, it has risen steadily, although it is still the case that proportionately more men than women hold jobs nationally and in every Multi-City Study site. Looking more closely at trends since the end of the Depression, we find that black-white gaps have increased— substantially in Detroit, moderately in other locations. In 1970, employment-to-population ratios for men in each site were not greatly different from what they had been in 1940 but, after 1970, employment fell much more rapidly among adult black men than among white, leading to these much larger black-white differences. In Los Angeles in recent decades, Asian and Latino men have had employment-to-population ratios comparable to those of white men but, in Boston, relatively few Hispanic men were at work.

African American women in Atlanta in 1940 and 1950 had much higher rates of employment than white women; many of them worked as domestic servants. A different racial pattern was evident in Detroit, where black and white women had similar employment-to-population ratios. After 1960, white women increased their employment more rapidly than black women, leading first to an elimination of the black-white difference in jobholding and later to a situation in which a higher proportion of white than black women were employed. A continuation of recent trends implies even larger black-white gaps on this dimension, a gap that helps account for the economic advantage of whites. Hispanic women in Boston and Los Angeles trailed behind the other groups in employment.

FIGURE 1.11 Employment-to-Population Ratios for Persons Aged Twenty-Five to Sixty-Four in Multi-City Study Sites, 1940 to 1990

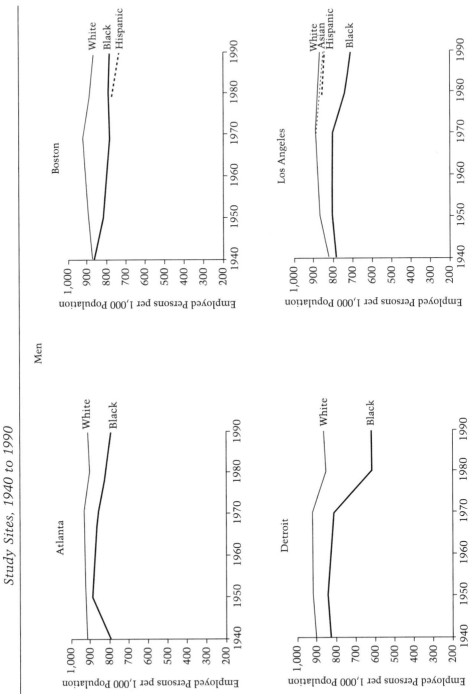

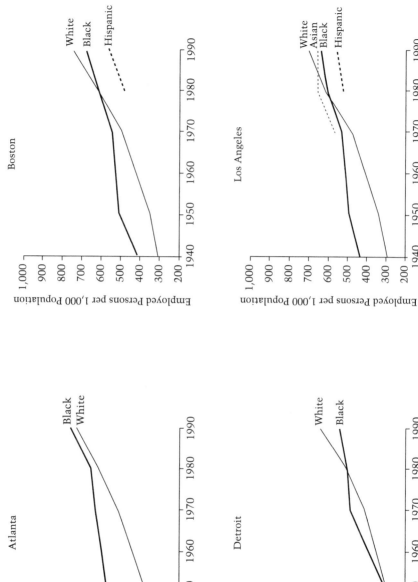

Women

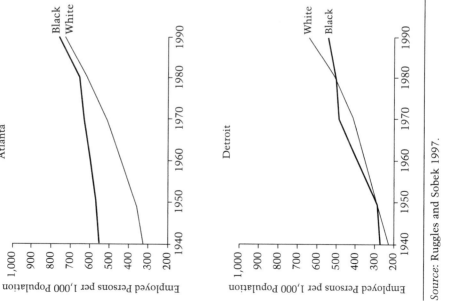

Source: Ruggles and Sobek 1997.

FIGURE 1.12   Per Capita Hours of Employment for the Population Aged Twenty-Five to Sixty-Four, by
Race and Sex, for Multi-City Study Sites, 1990

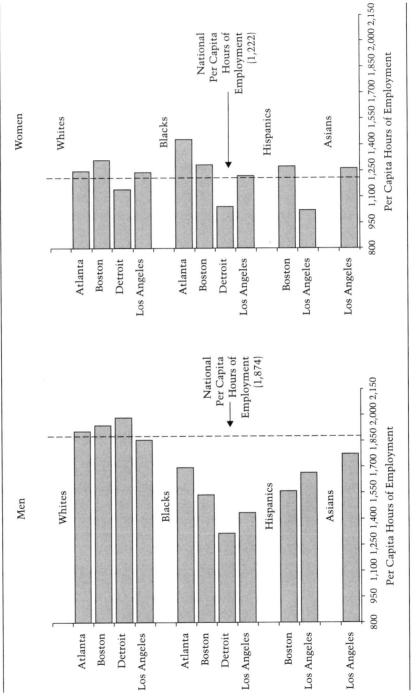

Source: Ruggles and Sobek 1997.

How much time the typical person spent working is the second indicator of employment. This analysis includes all persons aged twenty-five to sixty-four, not just those active in the labor force. Figure 1.12 shows these data for 1990. A glance at this figure reveals the large racial difference among men and the small difference among women, expect in Detroit, where black women fared poorly on this indicator of economic status. Looking at data for the specific locations reveals the distinctiveness of Atlanta for its high per capita hours of employment and Detroit for its low per capita hours, except for white men. Many of the differences were large. White men in Detroit averaged 1,990 hours of work in 1989, black men only 1,319, giving white men an advantage of 13 hours on the job every week. Even if there were racial parity in hourly earnings in Detroit, black men would cash paychecks only two-thirds as large as those of white men because of the fewer hours worked. Hispanics in Boston and Los Angeles worked many fewer hours than whites; indeed, their hours of employment were closer to those of blacks than whites. And among both Hispanics and Asians, the native-born worked more than the foreign-born, presumably reflecting the advantage an American birth and an American education give in the search for employment.

The final figure in this section reports trends over time in the per capita hours of employment of adults. Once again, the major story is the increasing employment of women and the persistent disadvantage of black men vis-à-vis white men. With the exception of Los Angeles, black men have always worked many fewer hours than white men, but that racial difference has grown larger in every location, further handicapping blacks with regard to economic achievement. Detroit is distinctive for the increasing disadvantage of blacks—a trend evident for both genders. Among women, blacks once worked more hours than whites, but that also has changed such that, by 1990, white women were putting in more hours at work than black women.

Differences in
Occupational Achievement

Most large cities have had a long history of racial contests over who would live in specific neighborhoods. As black population grew rapidly during and after this century's major wars, they sought improved housing, but usually faced strong opposition from whites, who wanted to keep their neighborhoods racially homogeneous. Eventually whites moved to the suburbs, producing the type of segregation shown in figures 1.5 and 1.6. Although they are less frequently described, there have been similar struggles—sometimes involving considerable violence—to preserve racial segregation in the occupational ranks. (For descriptions

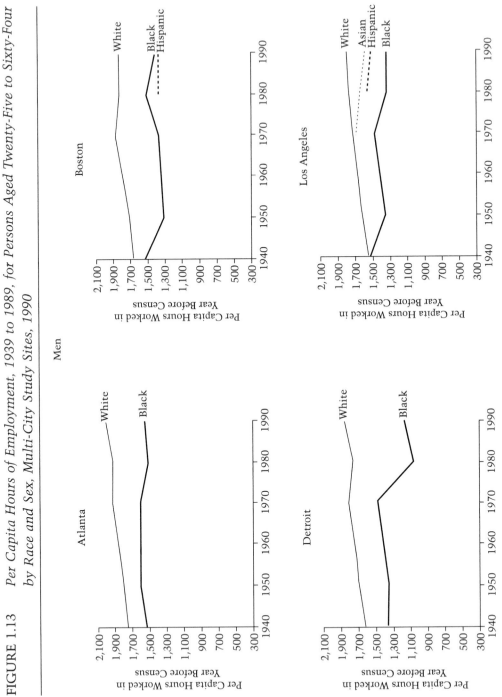

FIGURE 1.13   Per Capita Hours of Employment, 1939 to 1989, for Persons Aged Twenty-Five to Sixty-Four by Race and Sex, Multi-City Study Sites, 1990

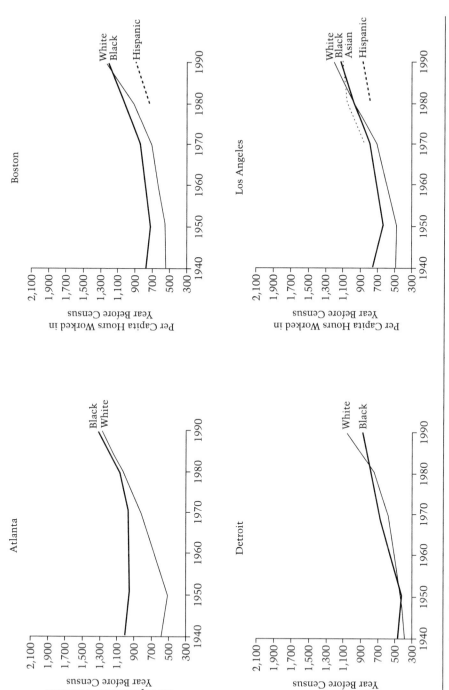

Women

Boston

Atlanta

Los Angeles

Detroit

Source: Ruggles and Sobek 1997.

and analyses of black-white conflicts over who could hold specific jobs, see Lieberson 1980, chaps. 10 and 11; Meier and Rudwick 1979; Waldinger 1996). Some unions—including the railway operating unions and many locals in the construction industry—established Jim Crow rules and maintained them until the 1960s. Sometimes management insisted on hiring only whites, as the owners of baseball teams did until Jackie Robinson played for the Brooklyn Dodgers in 1947. If one racial group can preserve a system of occupational stratification so that they get the high-paying jobs, while another racial group is targeted for discrimination, the result will be large differences in earnings, asset holdings, and homeownership.

Census data supply the information needed to analyze racial differences in occupational achievement. Since 1940, censuses have asked employed persons what they did when they worked. Those responses were then classified into specific occupational categories such as sheetmetal worker, grinding machine operator, nurse, or stevedore. At a later point, those specific categories were grouped into major occupational categories such as professionals, managers, or skilled crafts workers. Although a basically similar occupational question has been asked since 1940, a major change in the coding occurred with the enumeration of 1980. The creators of the Integrated Public Use Microdata Samples (IPUMS) of census data developed a systematic classification system to maximize comparability over time insofar as that was possible. Their coding of occupations is used in this chapter.

Figure 1.14 reports the distribution of employed adults by occupation for the Multi-City Study sites in 1990. It shows the proportion holding jobs in the professional and managerial ranks—typically the highest-paid jobs; the proportion working at clerical or sales jobs; the proportion in the skilled trades—that is, the percent with crafts jobs and the proportion in the unskilled category: machine operators, laborers, and domestic servants.

A look at this figure reveals that major differences continued to distinguish the races some twenty-five years after Title VII proscribed racial discrimination in the labor market. Even with the emphasis on labor productivity, there are still many unskilled tasks that must be performed: cleaning hotel rooms, working in kitchens, operating machines in factories, and preparing the processed foods we buy in supermarkets. Minorities were much more likely than whites to hold such jobs. At the other extreme, whites were much more highly represented than blacks or Hispanics in the jobs at the top of the occupational ladder: professional and managerial positions.

The layout of information in this figure allows us to readily grasp the advantage whites enjoy over minorities, but there are other efficient ways to quantify this. The IPUMS data provide an occupational prestige score for each detailed occupation, based on an investigation Dudley Duncan (1961) carried out several decades ago. A numerical score in the 0 to 100 range was assigned to every occupation based on surveys concerning how national samples evaluated the job and on census information about wage rates and educational prerequisites. Dentists received a prestige score of 96; janitors, only 9. Average occupational prestige scores are presented in figure 1.14.

The occupational prestige of whites—both men and women—was highest in Los Angeles and lowest in Detroit, reflecting the continued presence of many semiskilled jobs in the motor vehicle industry. Among blacks, those living in Los Angeles also had the most prestigious jobs, while those in Atlanta and Detroit were more likely to be holding jobs with low prestige scores. Hispanic employees in Los Angeles worked at even lower-ranked jobs than blacks. Asian men had occupational achievements falling only slightly below white men, but many Asian women in Los Angeles held jobs in the needlework trade, thereby lowering the average prestige score for the group.

Finally, the occupational distribution of each minority was compared to that of whites, using data for eleven broad occupational categories. If a minority group had an occupational distribution identical to that of whites, the index of occupational dissimilarity would equal its minimum value of zero, implying no racial difference in occupations. If segregation in the job market were so extreme that some broad occupational categories had only white incumbents while others were totally filled by minorities, this index would take on its maximum value of 100, implying that either 100 percent of white workers or 100 percent of black workers would have to shift from one broad occupational category to another to eliminate the racial segregation in the occupations.

When the occupational distributions of black men are compared to those of white men, we find that racial differences were smaller in Detroit and Los Angeles than in Boston or Atlanta. Among women, racial differences in occupations were smaller in every location than among men, but Detroit stood out for its low level of racial occupational segregation: just 11. That is, black and white women in Detroit were more similar in their jobs than in other sites. Asian men and women in Los Angeles had occupational distributions quite similar to those of white men and women, while Hispanics had occupational distributions very unlike those of whites. They were greatly overrepresented in the lower blue-collar jobs.

To describe changes over time, figure 1.15 shows the average occupational prestige scores of employed adults for the 1940 to 1990 span.

(Text continues on p. 74.)

FIGURE 1.14 *Distribution of Employed Population Aged Twenty-Five to Sixty-Four by Occupation, Multi-City Study Sites, 1990*

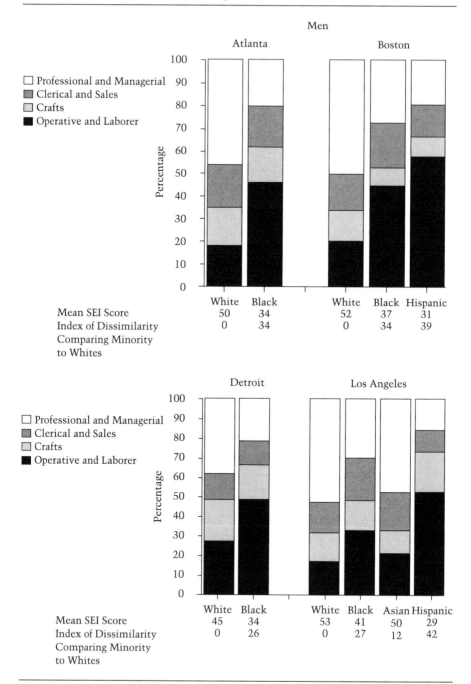

Source: U.S. Bureau of the Census, *Census of Population and Housing: 1990*, Public Use Microdata Sample.

FIGURE 1.14   *Continued*

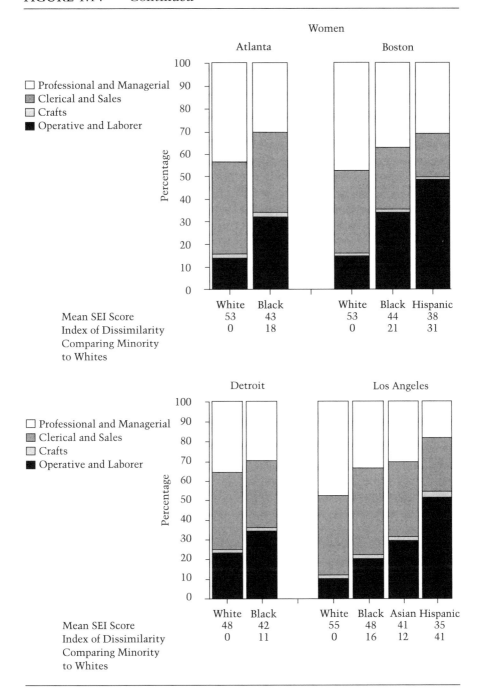

Women

Atlanta   Boston

| Professional and Managerial |
| Clerical and Sales |
| Crafts |
| Operative and Laborer |

	White	Black		White	Black	Hispanic
Mean SEI Score	53	43		53	44	38
Index of Dissimilarity Comparing Minority to Whites	0	18		0	21	31

Detroit   Los Angeles

| Professional and Managerial |
| Clerical and Sales |
| Crafts |
| Operative and Laborer |

	White	Black		White	Black	Asian	Hispanic
Mean SEI Score	48	42		55	48	41	35
Index of Dissimilarity Comparing Minority to Whites	0	11		0	16	12	41

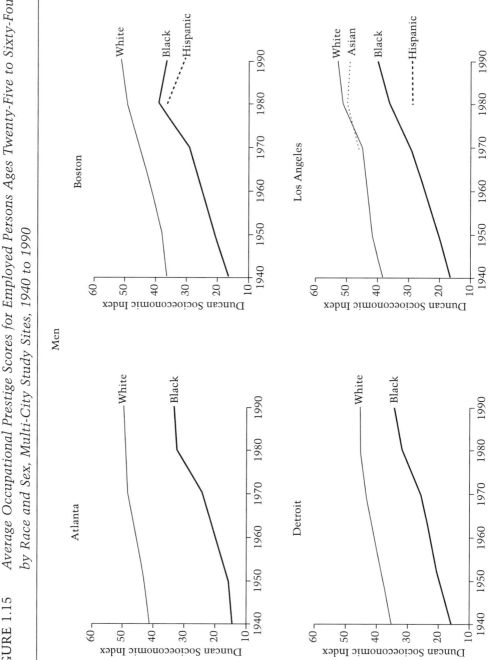

FIGURE 1.15   Average Occupational Prestige Scores for Employed Persons Ages Twenty-Five to Sixty-Four by Race and Sex, Multi-City Study Sites, 1940 to 1990

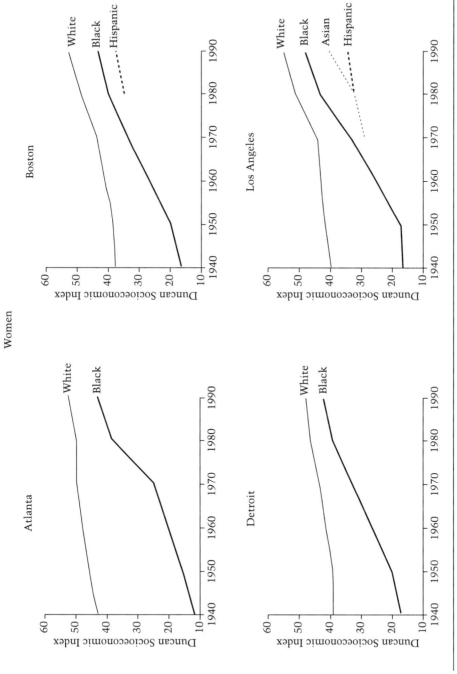

Women

Atlanta

Boston

Detroit

Los Angeles

Source: U.S. Bureau of the Census, *Census of Population and Housing: 1990*, Public Use Microdata Sample.

Two conclusions should be drawn from this figure. First, there is a persistent trend toward increases in occupational status resulting from the rapid growth of high-tech and white-collar jobs, along with the disappearance of manual labor. As we will see in the next section, wage rates for men peaked around 1970 but, with regard to occupational status, continued increases were the rule. Second, in every site and for both men and women, the jobs of blacks have been upgraded more rapidly than those of whites, leading to a narrowing of racial gaps. Blacks in 1990 in every site continued to hold less prestigious jobs than whites, but the differences were smaller than in the past, so there is an unambiguous trend toward a black-white convergence in occupational prestige.

The occupational prestige of black women rose especially rapidly as they moved away from domestic service, an occupational niche they once dominated. In 1940, black women who worked, with few exceptions, cooked meals, washed clothes, cleaned floors, and tended children in the homes of white women—white women who typically did not work. Shown here are the percentages of employed black women in domestic service on the eve of World War II:

Atlanta	85%
Los Angeles	80
Boston	72
Detroit	72

Black women born after the Depression have not gone into domestic service, helping to change the occupational distribution and bringing black women much closer to white women in terms of the jobs they hold.

Differences in Earnings

This concluding section describes the earning of employed adult workers. It is limited to those who actually reported wage or salary earnings for the year before the census. A question about earnings has been asked in every census since 1940, although the wording has changed. To target directly how much workers earned for time spent on the job, we eliminated those who said they were self-employed at the time of the census. The amounts reported in each year were converted into dollars with the purchasing power of those reported in the census of 1990, using the revised CPU-U consumer price index.[4]

Proceeding with the usual format, we first profile the median earnings of men and women in the four metropolises, in figure 1.16. Among employed men, earnings were considerably higher in Detroit and Los Angeles than in Atlanta or Boston, but for women, the highest wages

FIGURE 1.16   *Median Earnings for the Population Aged Twenty-Five to Sixty-Four Reporting Earnings in 1989 by Race, Multi-City Study Sites, 1990*

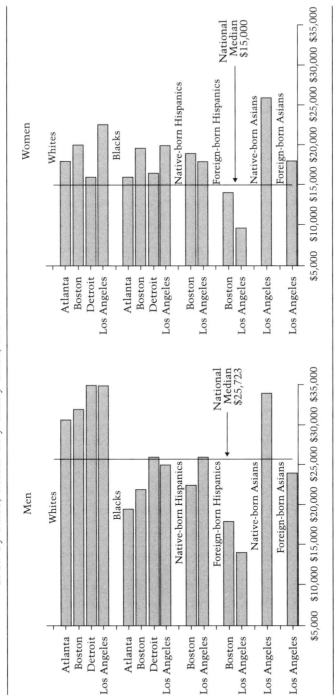

Source: U.S. Bureau of the Census, *Census of Population and Housing: 1990,* Public Use Microdata Sample.

were earned by those living in Boston and Los Angeles. When racial differences are examined, we see clearly that gender interacts with race. That is, black men had median earnings in every location that were far behind those of white men, ranging from a low of 46 percent as much as whites in Detroit to 64 percent as much in Los Angeles. But the median earnings of black women were much closer to those of white women, ranging from 63 percent as much in Detroit to 89 percent as much in Boston. No matter the indicator of earnings—median or mean; annual, weekly, or hourly—the racial gap was smaller among women than among men.

Trends in earning over time are shown in figure 1.17. These data reveal a straightforward story. For men, earnings rose rapidly and consistently from 1940 until 1970—more specifically, until the energy price crisis of 1973 triggered a restructuring of employment in the United States. (For a description of those events, see Levy 1987 and 1995.) Since then, the earnings of men have stagnated in Atlanta, risen slowly in Boston and Los Angeles, and declined in the Rustbelt metropolis of Detroit.

Trends in earnings of employed women followed a different pattern, since they have gone up consistently for the last half-century. This analysis, of course, is restricted to women who worked in the year prior to the census, so some of the rise in median female earnings is attributable to more weeks of work and more hours spent on the job. Black-white differences in earnings were smaller among women in 1940 than among men, but that difference was pretty much eradicated in every metropolis by 1970 or 1980.

The ratio of black-to-white medians readily summarizes changes over time in the racial difference. Such ratios are laid out in figure 1.18, and they reveal both the large gender gap and the unusually prosperous standing of black men in Detroit just after World War II. Turning to the left panel, presenting information about the relative status of black men, we see that back in 1940 Atlanta black men fell exceptionally far behind white men in earnings, reflecting the extreme Jim Crow employment practices of the South. Over time, the earnings of Atlanta black men rose more rapidly than those of white men but, even in 1990, the racial gap in male earnings was largest there. In Detroit, the employment boom generated by World War II and the sustained era of prosperity that followed meant that, by 1950, black men in that metropolis earned 82 percent as much as white men. Indeed, black men in Detroit in 1950 had median earnings just about equal to those for white men nationally: $14,854 for blacks in Detroit, $15,570 for the national white population. But that approach to earnings parity did not persist and, in the last four decades, the earnings of Detroit's black men have lagged far behind than those of white men.

Two generations ago, when black women typically worked as domestic servants, their wages fell far below those of white women, but after World War II, black women shifted rapidly into low-level service-sector jobs and later into pink-collar jobs. They entered the labor force more rapidly than white women, who, for several decades after World War II, generally worked only before they married or after their children were raised. As a result, the incomes of black women rose much more rapidly than those of white women. By 1980, black women in metropolitan Los Angeles had median earnings nearly equal to those of white women, while in Boston they earned 10 percent more than white women, and in metropolitan Detroit 18 percent more. However, as the baby boom cohorts of white women became adults, they greatly increased their investments in education and then adopted patterns of labor force participation resembling those of their brothers and fathers. (For descriptions of this, see Spain and Bianchi 1996.) As a consequence, the earnings of white women rose more rapidly than those of black women in the 1990s.

Returning to figure 1.17, we observe a seemingly dismal trend in the median earnings of Hispanic and Asian men. Their earnings have been falling, while those of whites and blacks have stagnated or increased a bit. Hispanics and Asians earned less in 1990 than previously, but this is largely accounted for by rapid immigration. Foreign-born persons typically have a struggle in the United States labor market shortly after arrival, so they may be unemployed or may take jobs for which they are overskilled and thus they earn little. If they remain here for a couple of decades, their employment situation will likely improve and their earnings may reach or exceed those of the native-born in their own group.

Table 1.3 describes Hispanics and Asians in 1990 in metropolitan Boston and Los Angeles, classifies them by nativity and the foreign-born by date of arrival, and then shows their per capita hours of work in 1989 and their mean hourly earnings. Looking at the columns to the left, we see that native-born white men in Boston averaged 1,962 hours on the job in 1989. Native-born Hispanic men fell far behind, with an average of only 1,700 hours on the job. But Hispanics who arrived in the United States in the five-year span before the census worked just 1,437 hours. Increased length of residence in this country was matched by a rise in the time spent at work. Indeed, those Hispanics who came to the United States more than three decades before 1990 worked more hours per year than native-born Hispanics.

(Text continues on p. 82.)

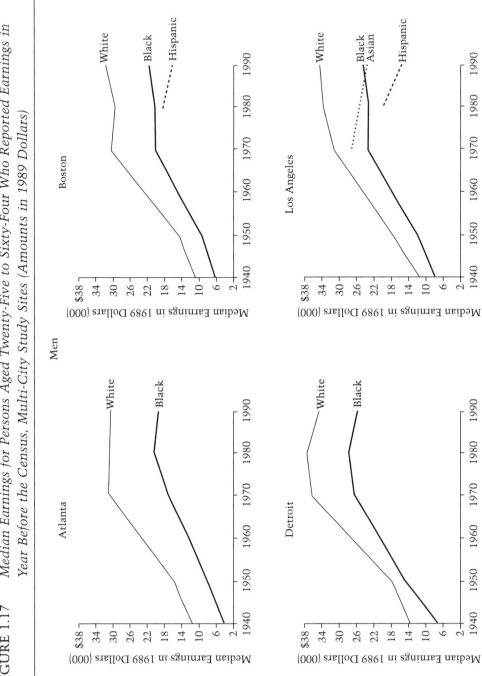

FIGURE 1.17   Median Earnings for Persons Aged Twenty-Five to Sixty-Four Who Reported Earnings in Year Before the Census, Multi-City Study Sites (Amounts in 1989 Dollars)

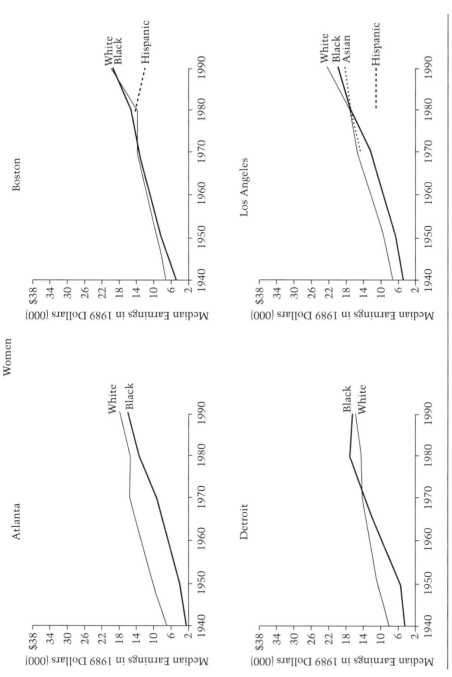

Women

Boston

Los Angeles

Atlanta

Detroit

Source: Ruggles and Sobek 1997.

FIGURE 1.18   Median Earnings of Blacks as a Percentage of Median Earnings of Whites for Persons Aged Twenty-Five to Sixty-Four Reporting Earnings in Year Prior to the Census, Multi-City Study Sites, 1940 to 1990

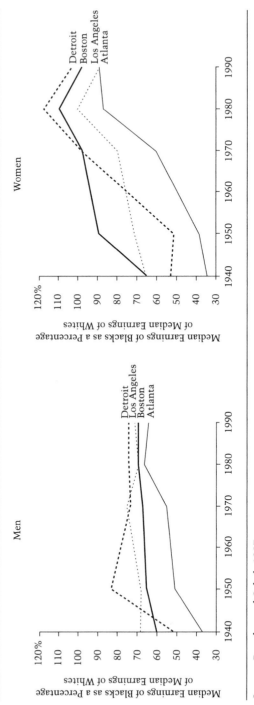

Source: Ruggles and Sobek 1997.

TABLE 1.3   *Information About Hours of Employment and Hourly Earnings for Persons Twenty-Five to Sixty-Four for Hispanics in Boston and Los Angeles and Asians in Los Angeles in 1990, by Nativity and Date of Arrival*

	Men			Women		
	Boston	Los Angeles		Boston	Los Angeles	
	Hispanics	Hispanics	Asians	Hispanics	Hispanics	Asians
Per Capita Hours Worked in 1989						
Native-born whites	1,962	1,934	1,934	1,333	1,354	1,354
Native-born minority	1,700	1,692	1,936	1,147	1,191	1,514
Foreign-born minority, by dates of arrival						
1985 to 1990	1,437	1,362	1,361	768	741	870
1980 to 1984	1,550	1,698	1,734	1,047	970	1,240
1975 to 1979	1,610	1,758	1,906	1,070	990	1,378
1970 to 1974	1,631	1,760	2,040	1,202	997	1,534
1965 to 1969	1,632	1,753	1,950	1,185	1,034	1,562
1960 to 1964	1,370	1,722	2,033	1,088	1,054	1,315
1950 to 1959	1,871	1,641	1,981	1,068	996	1,224
Mean Hourly Earnings in 1989 for Persons Reporting Earnings in That Year						
Native-born whites	$19.34	$21.90	$21.90	$13.57	$15.33	$15.33
Native-born minority	15.32	14.78	18.47	12.27	11.65	14.51
Foreign-born minority, by dates of arrival						
1985 to 1990	11.94	6.96	13.15	9.46	5.74	9.76
1980 to 1984	10.23	8.22	13.67	8.64	6.29	11.10
1975 to 1979	10.81	9.44	17.54	11.43	7.32	12.83
1970 to 1974	12.28	11.10	18.75	11.06	7.94	14.07
1965 to 1969	11.94	12.50	21.43	12.16	9.36	15.95
1960 to 1964	13.96	13.76	21.14	10.51	10.00	17.80
1950 to 1959	11.21	17.21	22.97	11.61	11.21	13.26

Source: U.S. Bureau of the Census, *Census of Population and Housing: 1990*, Public Use Microdata Sample.

The lower panel of the table shows information about hourly earnings. All date-of-arrival groups of Hispanics in Boston earned much less than the $19.34 of native-born white men, but among the foreign-born, increased duration of residence was generally matched by rising earnings.

Turning to data for Los Angeles, we see why figure 1.18 showed declining median earnings for Hispanics and Asians from 1980 to 1990: recent arrivals worked relatively few hours, and when they held jobs, they earned much less than the native-born in their own group. With regard to Asians and Hispanics, two processes occur simultaneously: the earnings of immigrants go up the longer they remain here, but these groups grow rapidly because of new arrivals who start at the bottom. At the present time, the latter effect outweighs the former, leading to lower earnings over time for these groups. Selective return migration also helps explain the increase in hours of work and earnings with length of residence in the United States. (For further analyses of these processes, see Chiswick 1978; Borjas 1994; National Research Council 1997, chap. 5.)

Data in table 1.2 report that Asian immigrants to Los Angeles approached parity with the native-born population much more rapidly than do Latino immigrants. After twenty-five years in this country, Asian immigrants work at least as many hours as native-born whites and earn as much.

This analysis of economic trends started with a focus on poverty. It ends with a similar focus. Throughout much of the post–World War II era, especially in the early years of the War on Poverty in the 1960s, there was consensus that with full employment and high wages for men, poverty rates would be low, since almost all men would marry and use their earnings to support their families. Welfare policies from the Depression decade through the 1960s focused on minimizing the unemployment of men and maximizing their earnings. Information about the pervasive economic growth stimulated by World War II and the boom that followed—as well as information about the reshaped labor market of recent decades—is provided in figure 1.19. This reports the percentage of men aged twenty-five to sixty-four whose earnings in the year prior to the census exceeded the poverty line for a family of four—that is, their earnings would lift a family of four above the poverty line.

Poverty was extensive in 1940. It is only a modest exaggeration to assert that, at the end of the Depression, almost all black men's earnings fell below the poverty line for a family of four. This was also the case for the majority of white men. Favorable changes in the next three decades improved the situation greatly. These trends, of course, helped encourage the early marriage and high fertility pattern of the baby boom era. At

FIGURE 1.19   *Percentage of Men Aged Twenty-Five to Sixty-Four with Earnings in Year Before Census Above the Poverty Line for a Family of Four, Multi-City Study Sites, 1940 to 1990*

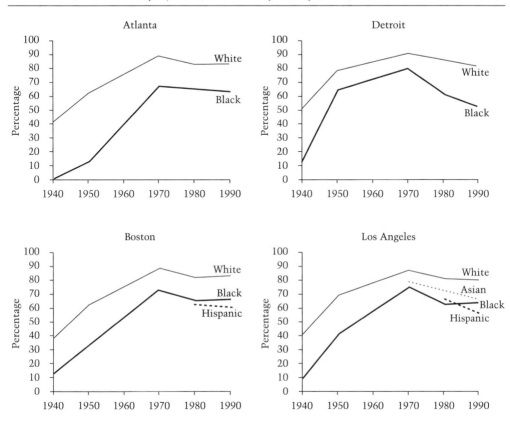

Source: Ruggles and Sobek 1997.
Note: This figure considers all men aged twenty-five to sixty-four, including those who had no earnings in the year before the census. It shows the percentage of men with earnings above the poverty line for a family of four.

the end of the civil rights decade, in 1969, 90 percent of white men and 70 percent of black men in the Multi-City Study had earnings sufficient to keep a family of four out of poverty. To be sure, there was a great racial difference in that year, but the modern American middle class was created by the beneficial trends of that era. And if the 1940-to-1970 trends had continued, almost all adult men would now cash paychecks large enough to keep their families far above the poverty line on the basis of their earnings alone. That trend did not continue. Since 1970, the proportion of men with earnings of this magnitude declined modestly, except for black men in Detroit, who saw a large change. In 1950, 65 percent of African American men there had earnings above the poverty line for a family of four; forty years later, that figure was just 48 percent.

The author thanks Judy Mullin for the preparation of this draft, including the figures, and also thanks Nancy Collins, who prepared data from the integrated public microdata samples of the 1940 through 1990 censuses.

Notes

1. The counties making up these metropolises in 1990 are as follows:

   Atlanta Metropolitan Statistical Area (eighteen counties)

Barrow	Cobb	Fayette	Henry	Spalding
Butts	Coweta	Forsyth	Newton	Walton
Cherokee	DeKalb	Fulton	Paulding	
Clayton	Douglas	Gwinnett	Rockdale	

   Boston New England County Metropolitan Area (five counties)

Essex	Plymouth
Middlesex	Suffolk
Norfolk	

   Detroit Primary Metropolitan Statistical Area (seven counties)

Lapeer	Oakland
Livingston	St. Clair
Macomb	Wayne
Monroe	

   Los Angeles Primary Metropolitan Statistical Area (one county)

   Los Angeles

   The Detroit and Los Angeles Primary Metropolitan Statistical Areas (PMSA) are components of larger Consolidated Metropolitan Statistical Areas (CMSA). The Detroit PMSA accounted for 94 percent of the population of the Detroit CMSA in 1990 but the Los Angeles PMSA made up only 61 percent of the population of the Los Angeles CMSA.

2. The censuses of 1980 and 1990 asked all respondents to answer one question identifying their race and another about whether their origin was Spanish. In 1970, the Spanish-origin question was asked of only a 5 percent sample, making it challenging to compare data

from that enumeration to those from the censuses of 1980 and 1990.

From 1950 through 1970, the Census Bureau identified a Spanish-origin population through use of Spanish surnames in the five southwestern states and by identifying those born in Puerto Rico or with at least one parent born in Puerto Rico in northeastern states. These data are hardly comparable to those derived from the enumerations of 1980 and 1990.

3. Data used to calculate the composition of the block group of the typical person in a group refer to the Hispanic population and to the non-Hispanic white, black, and Asian populations. There is a remaining small population of non-Hispanic Indians and non-Hispanic other races shown as "other" in figure 1.5.

4. The factors used to inflate dollars from earlier censuses to dollars having the purchasing power of dollars in the census of 1990 were:

Census of 1940	8.91
Census of 1950	5.21
Census of 1960	4.26
Census of 1970	3.39
Census of 1980	1.71
Census of 1990	1.00

References

Borjas, George J. 1994. "The Economics of Immigration." *Journal of Economic Literature* 32(4): 1667–1717.

Chiswick, Barry R. 1978. "The Effect of Americanization on the Earnings of Foreign-Born Men." *Journal of Political Economy* 86(5): 897–921.

Duncan, Otis Dudley. 1961. "A Socioeconomic Index for All Occupations." In *Occupations and Social Status*, edited by Albert J. Reiss, Jr. New York: Free Press of Glencoe.

Levy, Frank. 1987. *Dollars and Dreams: The Changing American Income Distribution.* New York: Russell Sage Foundation.

———. 1995. "Incomes and Income Inequality." In *State of the Union: America in the 1990s.* Vol. 1, edited by Reynolds Farley. New York: Russell Sage Foundation.

Lieberson, Stanley. 1980. *A Piece of the Pie: Black and White Immigrants Since 1880.* Berkeley: University of California Press.

Meier, August, and Elliott Rudwick. 1979. *Black Detroit and the Rise of the UAW.* New York: Oxford University Press.

National Research Council. 1997. *The New Americans: Economic, Demographic, and Fiscal Effects of Immigration.* Washington, D.C.: National Academy Press.

Ruggles, Steven, and Matthew Sobek. 1997. Integrated Public Use Microdata Series. Vers. 2.0. Mimeo. University of Minnesota, Department of History, Historical Census Projects.

Spain, Daphne, and Suzanne M. Bianchi. 1996. *Balancing Act: Motherhood, Marriage, and Employment Among American Women*. New York: Russell Sage Foundation.

Waldinger, Roger. 1996. *Still the Promised City? African-Americans and New Immigrants in Post-Industrial New York*. Cambridge, Mass.: Harvard University Press.

Part I

RACIAL ATTITUDES

2

STEREOTYPING AND
URBAN INEQUALITY

Lawrence D. Bobo and Michael P. Massagli

S OCIAL inequality is understood and studied as fundamentally involving a set of structural conditions and processes. Whether the
main analytical perspective emphasizes Marxian class dynamics,
distinct labor markets and sectors, major institutional actors, or key social policy decisions, supra-individual factors are typically the focus of
attention. Yet, according to the sociologists Katherine O'Sullivan See
and William Julius Wilson, "It is important to underline that different
types of ethnic stratification are not only structured by different arrangements of the economy and the polity, they are also shaped by the
participants in the intergroup arena" (1989, 238). To wit, the perceptions
and ideas that guide human behavior and interaction are likely to be
core elements in determining who gets a larger or smaller piece of the
pie (Reskin 2000). This is perhaps especially so when the issue is how
and why privilege or disadvantage is allocated among racial and ethnic
groups (Allport 1954; Jackman 1994; Sidanius and Pratto 1999).

In this chapter we are concerned mainly with the perceptions and
ideas commonly held about the characteristics of members of different
racial and ethnic groups. These beliefs, we submit, are a critical ingre-
dient in the creation and reproduction of patterns of racial and ethnic
labor market inequality, segregation of housing, and general intergroup
tension and misunderstanding. To be sure, stereotypes have long been
taken into account by serious students of racial and ethnic inequality.
For example, in his pioneering study *The Philadelphia Negro*, W. E. B.
DuBois (1996 [1899], esp. 323–24) wrote of how prevailing prejudices
closed the doors of opportunity for African Americans (see Bobo 2000b;
O'Connor 2000). Likewise, stereotypes and the rationalizing function they
often serve were critical elements in Gunnar Myrdal's (1944) classic assessment of why racial discrimination permeated all aspects of pre–

World War II American social life. And St. Clair Drake and Horace Cayton (1945, esp. 266–73) stressed that it was the many convenient "folk-beliefs" about race that sustained and perpetuated the "color line" in "Midwest Metropolis."

This classical foundation notwithstanding, there was a long period of relative disinterest in stereotyping—intergroup attitudes and prejudice—as a factor contributing to social inequality. In part, this reflected how the institutionalization of the social sciences occurred in major universities. Studies of stereotyping and prejudice became the province mainly of psychologists interested principally in cognitive functioning (not social stratification and inequality). In part, this reflected an explicit turn within sociology against microsocial theories of prejudice and toward macrosocial theories of historically emergent and structural forms of racism. In part, this reflected an interest in topical or controversial issues of the day (for example, opinions on school desegregation) among those survey researchers who might have been more expressly concerned with whether and how attitudes connected to social inequality (Kinder and Schuman, forthcoming).

The collective weight of a number of obdurate social facts, major demographic trends, and related intellectual developments served to redirect scholarly attention to questions of the extent, nature, and effects of racial and ethnic stereotypes. First, despite profound changes in the economic and political structure of racial inequality in the United States (Wilson 1978), there remained many forms of black-white inequality. In particular, a complex of social ills such as crime and welfare dependency grew from the intensification of ghetto poverty (Wilson 1987) and persistently high rates of racial residential segregation (Massey and Denton 1993). The black-white divide, in brief, remained an often bitterly divisive social cleavage. Second, steady waves of immigration to the United States from Asian and Latin American countries after 1965 greatly accelerated the extent and pace of racial and ethnic diversification of the urban population (Waldinger 1989; Harrison and Bennett 1995; Bean and Bell-Rose 1999). Nonetheless, many Latinos soon found themselves facing limited chances for upward mobility (Ortiz 1996; Valenzuela and Gonzalez 2000), and even upwardly mobile third-generation Asian-Americans often found that whites continued to assume they were foreigners (Tuan 1998). At the same time, anti-immigrant rhetoric, political movements, and legislation intensified (Chavez 1997; Sears et al. 1999).

Third, a social milieu reflecting the intersection of persistent, severe black disadvantage and rapid population change sometimes erupted into deadly violence, as seen in events like the Los Angeles uprisings of 1992 (Johnson, Farrell, and Oliver 1993; Bobo and Hutchings 1996).

Fourth, and most proximate to our concern, studies of social inequality that allowed for an explicit concern with racial and ethnic stereotypes began to find influences of these beliefs on key labor market outcomes (Kirschenman and Neckerman 1991) and residential sorting processes (Farley et al. 1994). The combined result of these developments is that lines of scholarship on critical dimensions of social inequality and on basic stereotyping processes that had become largely uncoupled and separate have increasingly been brought back together (see, for example, Reskin 2000 and the work of Tsui, Xin, and Egan 1995).

As the introduction to this volume explains, we expressly designed the Multi-City Study of Urban Inequality to improve our leverage on how stereotypes play into the dynamics of life in contemporary urban centers. Thus, the Household Surveys in Atlanta, Boston, Detroit, and Los Angeles contained explicit measures of racial stereotypes. Likewise, the Employer Telephone Surveys and the Employer In-depth Interviews sought to gauge the images that those with power in the workplace hold regarding members of different racial and ethnic groups. Each component of the project thus aimed to increase our capacity to assess when, how, and why stereotypes may contribute to residential sorting and segregation processes, unequal employment and earnings outcomes, or broad patterns of intergroup cooperation or conflict.

Using Multi-City Study Household Survey data from Atlanta, Boston, Detroit, and Los Angeles on the views of whites, blacks, and Hispanics, this chapter examines stereotyping in the modern urban context. We investigate a range of issues, including how salient and how negative (or positive) racial stereotypes are, how they are organized in individual cognition, whether they exhibit important contextual variation (for example, city-specific), and to the extent possible with cross-sectional survey data, the sources of stereotypes. In order to help clarify the fundamental nature of stereotypes, we organize the analysis that follows around two basic questions about stereotypes that, in some other research contexts, might be assumed to have well-known answers:

(1) Are racial and ethnic stereotypes reflective of a general, broad ethnocentric bias or are they group-specific? That is, do we find evidence of a general psychological tendency to denigrate any and all out-groups, or are stereotypes closely tailored to particular groups?

(2) Are racial and ethnic stereotypes highly contextually specific and variable or largely insensitive to context? By *context*, in this case, we mean metropolitan area (Atlanta versus Boston versus Detroit versus Los Angeles). We wish to know whether there are sharp differences across metropolitan areas in the organization and correlates of racial and ethnic stereotypes.

Clearer answers to these questions will better specify whether we should think of the operation of stereotypes as mainly reflecting powerful human psychological processes of perception or as mainly the product of unique historical and cultural sets of intergroup relationships (question 1); and whether stereotypes derive mainly from a broad common cultural environment and experience or derive mainly from local, directly experienced, and highly contingent social environments (question 2). We thus aim to better elucidate both the nature of racial stereotypes themselves and their role in urban inequality. In so doing, we hope to further the revitalization of a view of social psychological and stereotyping processes as organic and necessary factors in research on inequality.

We offer a few remarks here to presage our theoretical discussion, findings, and major conclusions. After measuring stereotypes aimed at tapping perceptions of both broad competence and sociability, we find that whites receive the most favorable ratings, and African Americans and Latinos the least favorable ratings, with perceptions of Asians falling close to those of whites. Specific group targets are essential to understanding the nature of stereotypes, yet the basic organization of the stereotypes does not differ sharply across respondent racial group, target group, or social context.

Consistent with prior research, we suggest that racial stereotypes are at once social products and social forces; they spring in part from the fact of social inequality among groups but also form constituent elements in the reproduction of inequality. Stereotypes are social products in the sense that they emerge from the history and context of particular relations among groups. They reflect the positioning of groups in physical space, work or occupational roles, and the overall economic hierarchy. Yet stereotypes are also social forces and highly generalized, durable cognitive constructs. They are bundles of ideas that directly influence individual expectations, perceptions, and social behavior in intergroup contact settings. Social psychological research shows that stereotypes influence what we see, what we believe to be true, what we expect, and therefore how we tend to behave toward members of groups other than our own. Thus, a white employer may expect Latinos to be more cooperative and hard-working employees than otherwise comparable blacks; an Asian American family seeking to buy its first home may search only in overwhelmingly white neighborhoods, even though many integrated communities contain the mix of homes and resources they are looking for; and an African American or perhaps a Latino shopper may anticipate and ultimately receive rude treatment from a Korean American store owner.

We begin with a full theoretical discussion of the concept and origins of stereotypes. We then clarify the role of stereotyping in the reproduction of social inequality. Next we develop the rationale for our core concern with the organization and structure of stereotypes (question 1) and contextual variation in stereotypes (question 2).

The Nature of Stereotypes

Walter Lippman's early discussion of stereotyping spoke of the "the pictures inside the head" (1922, 18)—an apt intuitive characterization. Subsequent generations of social scientists have attempted more formal statements. A stereotype is a "set of beliefs about the personal attributes of members of a particular social category" or a "set of cognitions that specify the personal qualities, especially personality traits, of members of an ethnic group" (Ashmore and Del Boca 1981, 13). As the social psychologists David Hamilton and Tina Trolier put it, stereotypes are "cognitive structures that contain the perceiver's knowledge, beliefs, and expectations about human groups" (1986, 133). Racial stereotyping thus involves assumptions and expectations about the likely characteristics, capacities, and behaviors of members of a particular racial or ethnic category.

In common sense usage, racial stereotyping is typically assumed to bring with it categorical or extreme judgments, clear negative valence, and resistance to new or contradictory information. It is precisely in response to this conception of stereotypes that "stereotyped" thinking is seen as a bad and usually inaccurate form of "prejudgment" that contributes to bias (Allport 1954). Modern social psychologists, however, tend to limit the meaning of the stereotype concept to the ideas or perceptions about groups, without making strong assumptions that these ideas are necessarily categorical, negative, rigid, or even bad (Ashmore and Del Boca 1981). Social categorization is an inevitable tool that we as perceivers rely on to simplify and impose coherence on the enormous flood of stimuli bombarding us at any given moment.

Social psychologists commonly distinguish between cultural stereotypes and personal beliefs. *Cultural stereotypes* refer to widely shared, quite possibly consensually held, ideas about members of a particular racial and ethnic category (Devine 1989; Devine and Elliot 1995). Any particular individual, while almost certainly aware of the broad cultural stereotype about a salient racial or ethnic group, may not personally accept or adhere to that stereotype. Some of the evidence from Patricia Devine and colleagues suggests, for example, that a growing fraction of the white population personally rejects the negative cultural stereotype of African Americans. However, social categories, such as racial distinctions, are often made salient in ways and under conditions that result in the *automatic* activation of the negative cultural stereotype. Even those who may personally resist the conventional negative image given a particular outgroup may succumb to negative and discriminatory behavior toward members of that group. Only in circumstances that facilitate inhibiting the otherwise routine activation of the negative cultural stereotype should one expect no biasing effect of the negative stereotype.

The impetus to accept or adhere to prevailing stereotypes has several potential sources or points of origin (Duckitt 1992; Brown 1995). Individuals may come to accept stereotypes through one of three principal avenues. The first mechanism is *social learning*. Socialization into a particular culture or other direct contact with members of particular racial or ethnic groups, or even vicarious learning experiences such as occurs through the media, may all be sources of stereotypes. These beliefs stem in part from the distribution of groups into particular structural locations. Stereotypes have long been found to respond to the geographic distribution (rural versus urban and large versus small community), work roles, and class standing of social groups (Stephan and Rosenfield 1982). Stereotypes may also have *motivational bases*, serving a rationalization function (Lippman 1922; Myrdal 1944; Clark 1965): that is, stereotypes may derive from some externality or instrumental consideration. It is easier to exploit and deny rights to those one perceives as inferior (Blumer 1958; Bobo 1999). A less instrumental but no less motivational basis for stereotypes may be found in personality attributes. Strongly ethnocentric (Sumner 1940 [1906]), intolerant and authoritarian (Adorno et al. 1950; Altemeyer 1988), or dominance-oriented individuals (Sidanius and Pratto 1999) may be particularly likely to hold negative views of outgroup members.

Lastly, stereotypes may result from *normal cognitive biases*. Many social psychologists might see this as the primary source of stereotypes (Stephan 1985). As perceivers, we employ categories to help impose order and meaning on the steady stream of social stimuli impinging upon us at any given moment. It is both necessary and natural for us to do so. However, once social categories exist, and given a principle of efficiency (the assumption that all else equal, we are "cognitive misers"—expending as little energy as possible in processing information), it is likely that we exaggerate the degree of between-group difference and underestimate the degree of within-group variation. This tendency can have pernicious effects in an interracial or interethnic context. Research suggests that rare or infrequently occurring phenomena, especially if linked to negative or unwanted outcomes, can assume exaggerated prominence in memory (such as the perception of minority group members as prone to crime and violence). Thus, there may develop highly salient and easily mobilized views, for instance, of blacks as criminals (Hurwitz and Peffley 1997) or welfare cheats (Gilens 1999), or of Latinos as docile people, well suited to low-skill, low-paying work (Bobo et al. 1995), or of Asians as forever foreign and unassimilable (Tuan 1998).

Stereotyping in Discrimination and Inequality

There was at one time a debate over whether attitudes influenced behavior or, more precisely, whether measured attitudes bore any relation to observed behavior (see discussions in Schuman et al. 1997; Krysan 2000). This debate has been, we believe, rather decisively resolved in favor of the view that well-measured attitudes and beliefs will, ordinarily, exhibit a clear relation to well-measured patterns of behavior (Schuman 1995). Prior attitudes are one causal input to behavior, along with important situational and normative factors and other individual attributes and experiences. Indeed, our interest in stereotypes rests on the assumption that these are ideas that matter for significant social behavior. In particular, there are good grounds to expect stereotypes to influence the dynamics of group inequality through their impact on perception and understanding in situations of intergroup contact generally, and to do so through a variety of job market– and housing market–specific mechanisms.

Perception and Understanding

The first and most important effect of a stereotype is that when a social category is made salient, it leads to the activation of an existing bundle of ideas and information, This existing cognitive structure or schema about "blacks," or "Hispanics," or "Asians," or even "whites" then tends to organize and direct the information taken in by the individual during any specific situation. That is, social psychologists have long assumed that the existing stereotype biases what one sees in any situation and the meaning one assigns to objects and events in the immediate situation. Accordingly:

> In keeping with this long-standing tradition, we believe that stereotypes affect overt responses producing discriminatory judgments and behaviors, via their impact on the construal of social targets and the immediate social situation. Once activated, stereotypes affect which stimuli people notice and how they interpret them, as well as whether and how they remember the information later. [Bodenhausen, Macrae, and Garst 1998, 318]

The clearest finding of research on stereotyping is that these are ideas that shape what we see and believe (Duckitt 1992; Brown 1995).

Stereotyped expectations influence perception, action, and the course of interaction (Bodenhausen, Macrae, and Garst 1998; Lieberson 1985). As Galen Bodenhausen and colleagues explained: "stereotypic expectations guide attention to the subset of available stimuli to which they are relevant. In so doing, they can bias the interpretation placed on a target and his or her behavior. It is these biased interpretations that give rise to discriminatory responses" (1998, 319). Critically these stereotypes can influence willingness to enter a situation of between-group contact, how warmly or coldly one engages a member of another group, and whether that interaction is positive or negative in overall quality. The nature of these dynamics is easy to apprehend. In the simplest case, one can envision a white person holding many of the prevalent negative images of African Americans. Any particular African American individual is likely to be aware of these images and monitor for signs of behavior that signal adherence to these beliefs among whites (Lieberson 1985). Bringing two such individuals from different groups together, in the light of these underlying expectations, is fraught with the potential for tension and interactional failure.

More specifically, Lee Sigelman and Steven Tuch (1997) showed that African Americans have clear ideas about how whites view them as a group and that these "meta-stereotypes" are reasonably correspondent to the actual distribution of whites' views. Bringing individuals with these perspectives into face-to-face contact is thus an opportunity for the interplay of stereotyped expectations, just as much of the literature on the often conflictual nature of black-white interaction emphasizes (Feagin and Sikes 1994; Hochschild 1995; Bobo 2000a).

The Job Market

There are good reasons to believe that stereotypes matter in one's prospects for employment, benefiting members of those groups held in positive regard and harming members of those groups held in negative regard (Neckerman and Kirschenman 1991; Reskin 2000). In an experimental study that simulated hiring decisions, John McConahay (1983) found that negative attitudes toward blacks reduced evaluations of a potential black job candidate. Carl Word, Mark Zanna, and Joel Cooper (1974) found that those with negative expectations for a black job candidate actually behaved in more negative ways in the course of an interview situation and actually elicited stereotype-confirming behaviors from the candidate. Joleen Kirschenman and Kathryn Neckerman (1991) found widespread negative views of African Americans and more positive views of other groups in their in-depth interviews with Chicago-area employers. Indeed, William Julius Wilson's general summary of results from the employer interviews done as part of his Urban Poverty and Family Life Study showed that:

Of the 170 employers who provided comments on one or more of these traits, 126 (or 74 percent) expressed views of inner city blacks that were coded as "negative"—that is, they expressed views (whether in terms of environmental or neighborhood influences, family influences, or personal characteristics) asserting that inner-city black workers—especially black males—bring to the workplace traits, including level of training and education, that negatively affect their job performance. [Wilson 1996, 112]

Both studies suggest that these perceptions affect whom employers interview and hire, as well as where they advertise and recruit for workers. These sorts of processes are by no means restricted to in-depth interviews performed in Chicago. Analyses from Atlanta (Browne and Kennelly 1999; Kennelly 1999) and Los Angeles (Waldinger 1996; Moss and Tilly 1995) identify many of the same patterns. Similarly, Harry Holzer's (1996) telephone surveys from four cities with employers pointed to clear preferences for particular groups over others.

The Housing Market

Stereotypes also play a part in creating and sustaining patterns of racial residential segregation. Douglas Massey and Nancy Denton (1993) hypothesized, consistent with a research tradition reaching back to DuBois (1996 [1899]) and Myrdal (1944), that racial prejudice was a key element in relegating blacks to "ghetto" communities. More recent studies of community racial turnover and transition (Cummings 1998) identify a central role for negative racial stereotypes as well.

Reynolds Farley and colleagues (1994) found that, indeed, a direct measure of antiblack stereotypes was a strong predictor of whites' willingness to share residential space with blacks among their sample of Detroit-area residents. This finding was extended by Lawrence Bobo and Camille Zubrinsky (1996), who found that the effect of negative stereotypes held whether one was looking at data on white, black, Latino, or Asian respondents. Their data from Los Angeles County showed negative stereotypes to influence willingness to live in integrated settings among all groups. Camille Zubrinsky Charles (2000a, 2000b, and this volume) has shown that this pattern holds true using far more sensitive measures of openness to residential integration than were available in any of the earlier studies.

Stereotypes as a Social Force

We tend to acquire stereotypes before we are called upon to act socially. We pick up the ideas about "them," members of other racial or ethnic groups, that our culture, inclinations, and perceptual biases give us, and only then engage the social world in which we live (rather than the other way around). This is why stereotypes are such an important element in the structuring and dynamics of urban inequality. This, too, is why the operation of stereotypes is a troubling factor in the social processes that create and maintain social inequality. As the eminent social commentator and analyst Walter Lippman once put it:

> A pattern of stereotypes is not neutral. It is not merely a way of substituting order for the great blooming, buzzing confusion of reality, It is not merely a short cut. It is all these things and something more. It is the guarantee of our self-respect; it is the projection upon the world of our own sense of our value, our own position and our own rights. The stereotypes are, therefore, highly charged with the feelings that are attached to them. They are the fortress of our tradition, and behind its defenses we can continue to feel ourselves safe in the positions we occupy. [1922, 63–64]

Stereotypes lead one to assume dissimilarity between the in-group and members of other groups, to overgeneralize and behave toward a social category rather than toward a particular individual, and therefore often to elicit behavior from out-group members that confirms the very biased perceptions with which the interaction began. In a context of historic and enduring inequality in life chances between members of different racial and ethnic groups, stereotypes become key elements in structuring and reconstituting differential chances in life depending upon one's race or ethnicity.

Possible Structures and Correlates

A handful of recent studies notwithstanding, most of the research on stereotypes derives from experiments conducted on college undergraduates, usually introductory psychology students (Katz and Braly 1933; Devine and Elliot 1995; Fiske 1998). The survey research literature has devoted far less attention to stereotypes until recently (Jackman 1994; Kinder and Sanders 1996; Bobo and Kluegel 1997; Sniderman and Carmines 1997; see Bobo 2000a for a review). As a result, we have a very limited base of knowledge about the basic structure and correlates of stereotypes among respondents to general population surveys. And most of this work focuses exclusively on the black-white divide and usually just the perceptions of white respondents (Bobo and Kluegel 1997; Peffley and Hurwitz 1998; Levine, Carmines, and Sniderman 1999; see Sigelman, Shockey, and Sigelman 1993 for one exception). We begin, then, by developing expectations for the basic organization of stereotypes.

Stereotypes may arise, be organized, and function in any of several ways. Our first major empirical question concerns how stereotypes are organized. We wish to know whether out-group stereotypes reflect a singular us-versus-them dichotomy, wherein members of any outgroup are seen as different and lesser, or whether out-group stereotypes follow a group-specific mapping of the social landscape. The former structure implies a heavily psychologically grounded, perceptual, cognitive, and individual motivational view of stereotyping. The latter structure implies a heavily socially grounded, historical, and cultural view of stereotyping. The two views constitute quite different understandings of the nature of stereotyping and prejudice. If stereotypes do *not* follow a group-specific pattern, instead reflecting derision of any and all out-groups, then the primary path to improvement is to eliminate the perception of any group boundaries. If, however, stereotypes *do* follow a more group-specific pattern, then the primary path to improvement is to address those aspects of culture and social organization that support negative views of particular groups. We do not presume that an either/or choice must be made between these approaches. Rather, for reasons of analytical clarity and because so little work on stereotyping involving large general population samples has been done, it is useful to start from this simplified set of alternatives.

There are ample substantive grounds for posing the question in this manner. Racial attitudes and behavior are often discussed as if, ultimately, they reflect a singular, general tendency to like or dislike members of a particular racial or ethnic group. Classical discussions emphasized a general pattern of in-group preference and general out-group derision. Thus, William Graham Sumner's pioneering discussion of ethnocentrism claimed that:

> Ethnocentrism is the technical name for this view of things in which one's own group is the center of everything, and all others are scaled and rated with reference to it. Folkways correspond to it to cover both the inner and the outer relation. Each group nourishes its own pride and vanity, boasts itself superior, exalts its own divinities, and looks with contempt on outsiders. Each group thinks its own folkways the only right ones, and if it observes that other groups have other folkways, these excite its scorn. (1940 [1906], 13)

Research on the authoritarian personality pointed to a powerful general tendency toward ethnocentrism and hostility to a range of outgroups (Adorno et al. 1950). This view, without the explicit psychoanalytic claims and methodological flaws that weakened the original analysis, has been revived in some important, more recent lines of work as well (Altemeyer 1988; Duckitt 1992). Although contemporary scholars usually adopt a multidimensional conceptualization of racial attitudes (Jackman 1977; Bobo 1983; Pettigrew and Meertens 1995), there are still a number of scholars who make a case for a strong general prejudice-to-tolerance continuum organizing racial attitudes (Kleinpenning and Hagendoorn 1993; Levine, Carmines, and Sniderman 1999).

Our second major empirical question asks whether stereotype structure is similar across different social contexts or whether stereotype structure is highly contingent on the immediate social context. In the extreme case, we would find that a single us-versus-them dichotomy, quite insensitive to specific out-groups, characterizes the stereotype measures in each of the four cities. A less extreme, but still heavily psychological process-oriented pattern would hold if we found the same group-specific (multidimensional) structure in each city. Alternatively, we might find important city differences in the structure of stereotypes. If so, this would begin to suggest that localized patterns of group interaction and experience do much to drive the nature of stereotypes.

Some basis for potentially expecting a highly uniform structure to intergroup attitudes has come from recent cross-national work by the social psychologist Thomas Pettigrew and others. This work has shown that concepts and theories of prejudice derived almost exclusively from studies of black-white relations in the United States translate very well to a wide range of Western European countries now dealing with a variety of different immigrant groups and associated conflicts (Meertens and Pettigrew 1997; Pettigrew et al. 1998). Despite enormous differences in national history, culture, language, institutions, and the specific groups in contention, the same core variables—though often indicating different average levels of hostility—worked effectively across national boundaries.

Alternatively, on at least four grounds, the extant body of research provides warrant to expect local context to matter for stereotypes. First, in general, stereotypes come to reflect the positioning of groups in the social structure and the types of social roles that group members are commonly observed to perform (Stephan and Rosenfield 1982). To the extent that there are important city differences in group size, economic status, and occupational and educational attainments of different groups, we should expect stereotypes to vary. Farley (this volume) has documented a number of across-city differences between groups on these dimensions. To cite just a few examples, at the time of the 1990 census the proportion black varies from a low of about 5 percent in Boston, to 12 percent in Los Angeles, 20 percent in Detroit, and a high of about 25 percent in Atlanta. There was even greater variation across cities in the representation of Latinos, Los Angeles being clearly at the top, with nearly half its population Latino, whereas Atlanta and Boston were each roughly 5 percent Latino and Detroit fell below even that mark. There were also important economic status differences between groups across cities. Los Angeles had the highest fraction of very affluent whites and very affluent blacks. Detroit had the highest black poverty rate, at 33 percent, with the other cities hovering around 20 percent. Latino poverty rates exceeded the black poverty rate in Boston and Los Angeles. Detroit was far more segregated by race than any of the other cities, though all exhibit significant levels of segregation (particularly black-white segregation).

Second, aspects of local demographic composition have been found to influence attitudes and beliefs. A spate of recent studies has shown that the overall negativity of attitudes toward blacks varies directly with the size of the local black population. As the proportion of the population that is black grows, so does the level of expressed racial prejudice by whites (Fossett and Kiecolt 1989; Glaser 1994; Quillian 1996; Taylor 1998). As Marylee Taylor recently argued: "traditional prejudice rises as the local black population share swells. The magnitude of this effect rivals those of the more powerful individual-level predictors of prejudice" (Taylor 2000, 134).

Third, Mary Jackman (1994) has very persuasively argued that stereotypes are part of ideological belief systems that are exchanged between groups. Under conditions of overt conflict and challenge from a subordinate group, she maintains, the character of group stereotypes is likely to change. In particular, members of a dominant group will find it more effective and appealing to mute and qualify the stereotypes they hold about members of a subordinate group if members of that group are openly resisting their disadvantaged status. The gist of her argument—and the data she presents in the three contexts of race, class, and gender relations—is that specific group contexts and dynamics shape the expression of stereotypes. Her argument helps make sense out of the empirical findings of the often small, qualified nature of whites' negative stereotypes of blacks, but more often categorical nature of class- and gender-based stereotypes expressed in surveys.

Fourth, the growing body of work on the racial beliefs and attitudes of employers often treats employers' expressed views as if they were arrived at through direct, localized workplace experiences and/or contained a substantial element of truth (Kirschenman and Neckerman 1991; Moss and Tilly 1995; Wilson 1996). For example, Philip Moss and Chris Tilly noted that "employers were acutely aware that black men lag behind their white counterparts in education. When asked to explain why black men have an especially hard time finding and keeping jobs, many cited deficits in education and related basic skills" (1995, 364). In a somewhat similar vein, Kirschenman and Neckerman wrote:

> whether or not the urban underclass is an objective social category, its subjective importance in the discourse of Chicago employers cannot be denied. Their characterizations of inner-city workers mirrored many de-

scriptions of the underclass by social scientists. Common among the traits listed were that workers were unskilled, uneducated, illiterate, dishonest, lacking initiative, unmotivated, involved with drugs and gangs, did not understand work, had no personal charm, were unstable, lacked a work ethic, and had no family life or role models. [1991, 208]

In sum, several different research traditions suggest that features of localized context and experience may drive observed stereotypes.

We examine two different types of correlates of stereotypes. First, there is a set of demographic characteristics that may influence the level of stereotyping. In the main (though not entirely), these demographic variables reflect or capture underlying socializing processes. Better-educated individuals usually express more positive intergroup attitudes and beliefs than those who are less well educated (Schuman et al. 1997). Likewise, younger individuals, presumably by virtue of socialization during a more tolerant and liberal time period (rather than aging per se), hold more enlightened views. Women are often found to express more positive intergroup attitudes than are men (Schuman et al. 1997; Sidanius and Pratto 1999). Those with higher incomes sometimes are found to express more negative attitudes, presumably out of a vested interest in preserving an advantage over others (Schuman et al. 1997). We also examine the effects of native versus foreign-born status. Prior research does not establish any clear baseline expectations in this case, however.

Second, there may be other social psychological correlates of stereotypes (Peffley and Hurwitz 1998). Two are of special interest to us. We treat the perception of group economic status as a determinant or cause of other, more personality-based trait beliefs. That is, all else equal, the more economically successful the members of a group are perceived to be (rich versus poor), the more favorable the other trait beliefs will be (intelligent, self-sufficient, easy to get along with, and speaking English well). This is consistent with the general finding that racial and ethnic stereotypes routinely correspond to the distribution of groups into particular roles and positions in the social structure (Stephan and Rosenfield 1982; Duckitt 1992; Brown 1995). It is also consistent with the emerging proposition that beliefs about social stratification and inequality powerfully influence more race-specific outlooks (Kluegel and Smith 1986; Bobo and Kluegel 1993). Both Farley et al. (1994) and Bobo and Zubrinsky (1996) found that the more dispositional or personality trait stereotypes were affected by perception of group economic status. In addition, individual susceptibility to stereotyping should vary with political ideology (Sears et al. 2000). More conservative individuals subscribe to more traditional outlooks, including a greater willingness to express negative views about members of out-groups (Sniderman and Carmines 1997; Peffley and Hurwitz 1998).

Measures

Using the Multi-City Study of Urban Inequality, we are able to compare out-group perceptions of non-Hispanic white and black respondents across the four cities, and of Hispanic respondents in Boston and Los Angeles.[1] Out-group perceptions are measured through responses to a series of survey questions asking respondents to characterize racial and ethnic groups as a whole with respect to several characteristics. The survey used a stereotype trait-rating measure to overcome potential limitations of traditional survey questions that only allow respondents stark yes/no or agree/disagree options. The method we employed allowed respondents to rate groups positively as well as negatively, or to opt not to characterize the group as a whole. The survey questions had been tested and evaluated to ensure that respondents were willing to perform the task, respondents did not consistently bias their answers in socially desirable ways, responses about individual traits related to one another in an internally consistent fashion, and the responses were related to variables usually understood to correlate with indicators of prejudice, such as education, age, and political ideology (Smith 1991; Bobo, Johnson, and Oliver 1992).

Respondents were given the following instructions:

> Now I have some questions about different groups in our (U.S.) society. I'm going to show you a seven-point scale on which the characteristics of people in a group can be rated. In the first statement a score of 1 means that you think almost all of the people in that group are "rich." A score of 7 means that you think almost everyone in the group is "poor." A score of 4 means you think that the group is not toward one end or the other, and of course you may choose any number in between that comes closest to where you think people in the group stand.

In addition to thinking of the groups as rich or poor, respondents were asked to place the groups on scales contrasting the following four additional traits:

unintelligent or intelligent,

prefer to be self-supporting or prefer to live off welfare,

easy to get along with or hard to get along with,

speak English well or speak English poorly.[2]

These traits include matters of competence and ability as well as general sociability. They were selected because collectively they tap attributes long considered important in our achievement-oriented society (intelligence), of relevance to likely successful performance in the workplace (easy to get along with, English-speaking ability), and capturing a core disparaging typification of stigmatized racial groups (prefer welfare dependency to self-reliance). We did not seek to create an exhaustive map or inventory of all widely held stereotypes. Rather, our goal was to develop a set of measures reflecting characteristics that drive judgments in the labor market and residential location choices, and yet of sufficient range to tap potentially important variation in the propensity to negatively characterize out-group members.

The scores for the ends of the scale were alternated to reduce respondent bias toward a particular scale value. For ease of interpretation, all scales were transformed so that positive ratings received positive scores (1, 2, or 3), negative ratings received negative scores (−3, −2, or −1), and neutral ratings were equal to 0. Interviewers also recorded whether respondents said they didn't know how to rate a group on a particular trait, or if they refused to answer. "Don't know" responses were scored as 0.[3]

The bipolar trait-rating method is a flexible and comparison-rich way of tapping stereotypes. We find that respondents specify clear and meaningful group differences, use the full range of response options, and are willing to give quite unflattering ratings of some out-groups on specific traits. Figures 2.1, 2.2, and 2.3 graphically depict these salient features of respondent behavior in the trait-rating portion of the interview. The first figure, which portrays whites' rich/poor ratings by race of target group, shows that all rating options are used for all groups, whites are most likely to characterize their own group as neither "rich" or "poor"—that is, they are more likely not to stereotype their own group than other groups, and extreme negative perceptions of blacks and Hispanics are relatively common. This approach taps substantial and, in this instance, sociologically sensible perceptions of group differences. Figure 2.2, depicting whites' welfare stereotypes of blacks in each city, shows that while there is remarkable similarity across cities in the distribution of response, the difference in mean rating is primarily a function of using the neutral option and options immediately adjacent—that is, average city differences do not stem from substantially varying tendencies in the use of extremely positive or extremely negative ratings. Yet, negative ratings, even the highest possible negative rating, occur with some frequency in each city. Finally, figure 2.3 shows Boston respondents' stereotypes of the English-speaking ability of out-groups.

(Text continues on p. 111.)

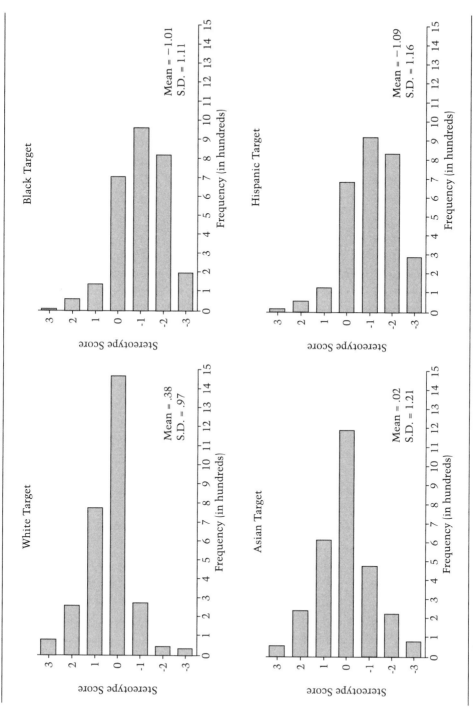

FIGURE 2.1   Whites' Rich/Poor Stereotype Rating by Race of Target

White Target

Mean = .38
S.D. = .97

Black Target

Mean = −1.01
S.D. = 1.11

Asian Target

Mean = .02
S.D. = 1.21

Hispanic Target

Mean = −1.09
S.D. = 1.16

Source: Multi-City Study of Urban Inequality.

FIGURE 2.2   Whites' Welfare Stereotype Rating of Blacks

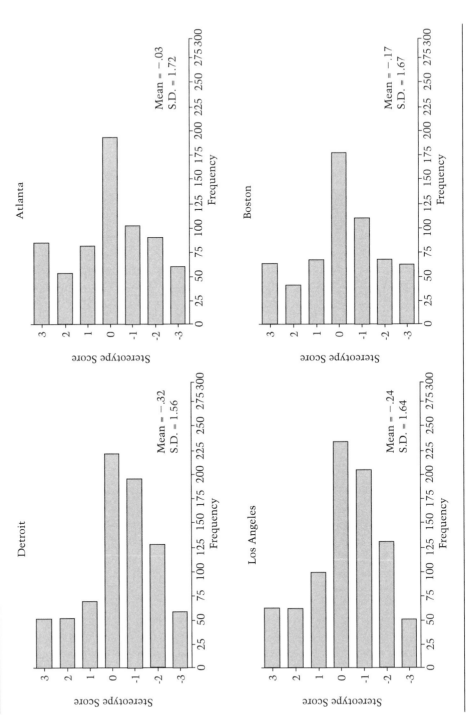

Source: Multi-City Study of Urban Inequality.

FIGURE 2.3   *Boston Respondents' Stereotype Rating of*
    English-speaking Ability, by Race

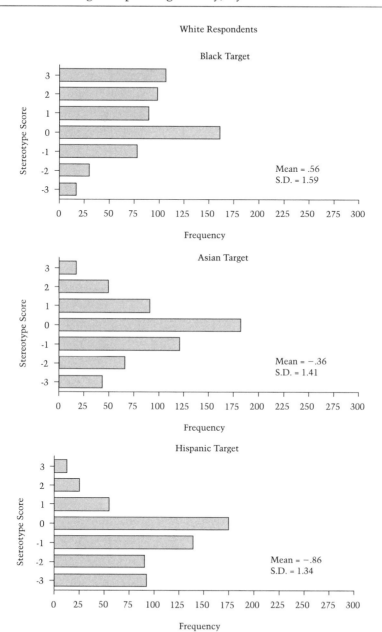

White Respondents

FIGURE 2.3   *Continued*

Black Respondents

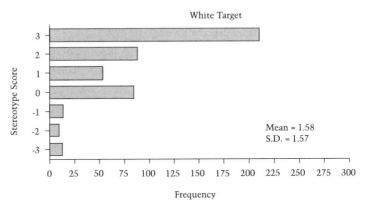

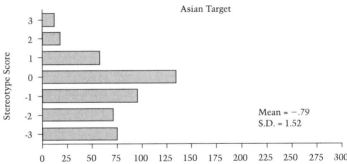

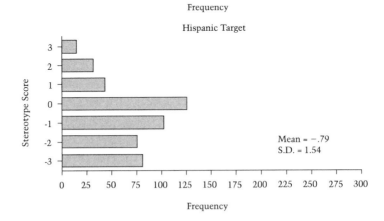

FIGURE 2.3   *Continued*

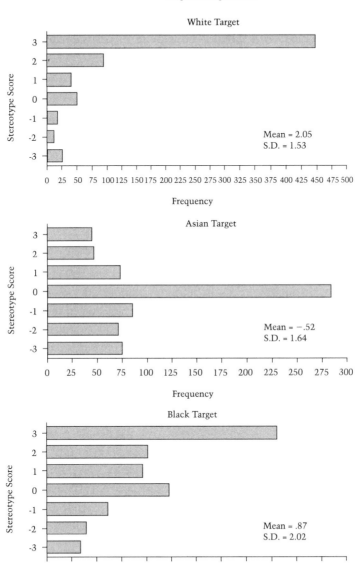

Source: Multi-City Study of Urban Inequality.

TABLE 2.1   Mean Stereotype Trait Ratings by City and Race

	White Respondents				Black Respondents				Hispanic Respondents	
	Detroit	Atlanta	Los Angeles	Boston	Detroit	Atlanta	Los Angeles	Boston	Los Angeles	Boston
N	765	662	854	579	696	786	1106	449	992	698
Tend to be rich										
White target	.50	.34	.37	.25	1.02	.97	1.04	.91	1.37	.52
Black target	-1.14	-.87	-1.15	-1.12	-.99	-.75	-1.02	-.98	-.96	-1.45
Asian target	-.01	-.17	.36	-.49	.19	-.00	.80	-.28	.96	-.83
Hispanic target	-1.09	-.98	-1.34	-1.31	-1.02	-.92	-1.18	-1.07	-1.25	-1.14
Intelligent										
White target	.85	1.09	.91	.82	.65	.46	.60	.60	.93	.93
Black target	-.01	.28	.16	.14	.56	.70	.64	.60	.08	.27
Asian target	.77	.83	1.08	.61	.56	.39	.71	.48	1.12	.84
Hispanic target	-.00	.15	-.01	.05	.02	.21	.14	.36	.37	.45
Easy to get along with										
White target	.92	1.31	.78	.95	-.12	-.10	.08	.25	.40	.11
Black target	.29	.42	.19	.24	.62	.72	.88	.33	-.28	-.22
Asian target	.55	.52	.34	.34	-.13	-.16	-.33	-.11	-.09	-.47
Hispanic target	.33	.33	.38	.09	.23	-.01	.62	.07	1.27	.70
Self-supporting										
White target	1.38	1.76	1.53	1.41	.88	1.31	1.04	.73	1.07	.21
Black target	-.32	-.03	-.24	-.17	.05	.68	.00	-.01	-1.39	-1.15
Asian target	1.31	1.37	1.67	.87	.83	.94	1.19	.44	1.16	-.08
Hispanic target	.18	.38	-.02	-.21	.06	.36	-.21	-.28	-.34	-1.06
Speak English well										
White target	1.58	1.97	2.03	1.87	1.59	1.56	2.01	1.58	2.44	2.05
Black target	.01	.44	.58	.56	.72	1.21	1.22	.66	1.19	.87
Asian target	.08	-.14	.14	-.36	-.45	-.72	-.76	-.79	-.09	-.52
Hispanic target	-.16	-.65	-.74	-.86	-.55	-.86	-.77	-.79	-.40	-.56

Source: Multi-City Study of Urban Inequality.

These data confirm that substantial numbers of each respondent group, even in this ostensibly liberal metropolitan area, view different targets in extreme and categorical terms. The trait-rating method of eliciting stereotypes in a standardized survey interview thus appears to be valid.

Analysis and Results

We conducted three types of analysis to produce descriptive statistics from the trait-ratings to address our research questions. First, we computed the mean rating and standard deviation of each trait by each group of respondents in each city, and the correlation between ratings, to determine whether out-groups are seen differently.[4] Second, we summarized the structure, or pattern, of correlations among trait ratings of target groups using a confirmatory factor model for each respondent group in each city, suggesting differing degrees among respondent groups of coherence in negative out-group perceptions. Last, using simple linear models, we examined the dependence of out-group perceptions on perceived group economic standing and the relative importance of this determinant compared to individual characteristics reflecting the respondent's background and social standing (such as level of education).

Basic Stereotype Distributions

Table 2.1 shows the mean rating of each target group by each group of respondents in each city. White respondents gave the most positive ratings to whites as a group on every trait in every city, almost without exception. This is consistent with the behavior of members of more powerful and high-status groups found in the social psychological literature generally (Sachdev and Bourhis 1987, 1991; Sidanius and Pratto 1999). In two instances, however, both observed in Los Angeles, Asians were assigned the highest ratings, on average, for the intelligent/unintelligent and self-supporting/welfare traits. In each city, the economic position of blacks and Hispanics as groups was perceived more negatively than that of Asians. For three of the remaining four traits— "intelligent," "easy to get along with," and "self-supporting"—blacks and Hispanics were always rated in more negative terms than Asians. For the last trait, "speak English well," Asians and Hispanics received more negative ratings than did blacks, except in Detroit, where Asians were rated more positively than blacks.

Among black respondents, ratings vary in interesting ways by trait, but not by city. Blacks rated themselves and Hispanics as a group much more negatively than they rated whites or Asians for the rich/poor and self-supporting welfare traits. On average, they rated themselves similarly to whites and Asians on the intelligent/unintelligent trait—all more positively than Hispanics. Blacks rated themselves and Hispanics most positively with respect to "easy to get along with," whites and Asians more negatively, with Asians rated most negatively by blacks in each city. Finally, blacks rated their group's ability to speak English more negatively than whites, but a good deal more positively than the ability of Asians and Hispanics.

Hispanic responses were similar to those of blacks with respect to the traits relating to economic life; they saw themselves and blacks in more negative terms than whites and Asians. Their average ratings of whites and Asians were higher on the intelligent/unintelligent trait, while blacks as a group received a lower average rating than Hispanics. Hispanics rated their own group most positively on "easy to get along with," while rating blacks and Asians most negatively. They rated whites and blacks positively on "speak English well" and rated themselves and Asians negatively.

Overall, in each city we find a pattern of ratings in which whites see themselves most favorably and in terms that might suggest that their achievement as a group (economic standing) is consistent with more frequent possession of characteristics associated with merit (intelligence, speak English well, easy to get along with) and motivation (self-supporting). In contrast, the other three groups, with reference to the same traits, also recognize whites' more favorable economic standing, but do not see the group as so different with respect to the other traits. At the same time, each group would place itself closer to whites than to another out-group.

The Underlying
Structure of Stereotypes

Viewed trait by trait, there appears to be little systematic difference among the four cities in each group's perceptions of members of other race-ethnic groups. We now turn to consideration of the traits jointly, to determine whether out-group stereotyping occurs in a generalized fashion or is highly nuanced with respect to its consequences and determinants.

Focusing first on white respondents, we wish to know whether the stereotypes reflect general out-group derogation or more group-specific patterns of response. Simple correlations among the out-group trait-rating measures for each respondent group by city are shown in the appendix to this chapter (tables 2A.1, 2A.2, and 2A.3). On average, the correlations among the trait ratings are modest—for example, they average 0.36 for whites in Boston. Upon inspection it is clear that there are really three levels of correlation: a relatively large correlation among the ratings of a single trait across different groups, a moderate correlation among the ratings of different traits within group, and almost no correlation among the ratings of different traits across different groups. This pattern suggests that the data cannot be accounted for either by a singular propensity to stereotype all out-groups or by independent out-group targeting. Furthermore, it is possible that the interview protocol and cognitive demands of the question-and-answer task may instill consistency of response because the respondent was asked to rate each group on a given trait—white, Asian, black, Hispanic—before being asked about another trait.

To explore the structure of out-group stereotypes across respondent groups, we estimated several (confirmatory factor) measurement models using Karl Jöreskog's general method for the analysis of covariance structures (Sörbom and Jöreskog 1981).[5] Table 2.2 displays goodness-of-fit tests for selected measurement models. The likelihood ratio test statistic (L^2) follows a chi-square distribution with degrees of freedom (df) equal to the difference between the number of variances and covariances in the observed data matrix and the number of independent parameters in a model. It contrasts the null hypothesis that the constraints imposed on the variance-covariance matrix by the parameters of the model are satisfied in the population with the alternative that the variance-covariance matrix is unrestricted. The difference in likelihood ratio statistics between two nested models—a general model and a constrained version of that model—provides a likelihood ratio test of the constraints. Because the size of the likelihood ratio is affected by sample size, we also present the adjusted goodness of fit index (AGFI) (Jöreskog and Sörbom 1989, 43–45), which compares the minimum of the fit function after the model has been fitted to the minimum of the fit function before any model has been fit, adjusted for the degrees of freedom. The AGFI should range between 0 and 1, although it is technically possible to obtain results outside this range.[6]

Our model fitting strategy involved fitting alternative models for white respondents, then using those models in confirmatory fashion for blacks and Hispanics. This approach allows us to gauge the consistency of the structure of stereotyping of out-groups. The results we present emphasize relative improvement in fit as the result of introducing broad classes of parameters (for example, correlated measurement errors within traits and between groups, similar in each city) rather than searching for a specification that is highly unique to a respondent group or city. Results for whites, blacks, and Hispanics are presented separately, by city, providing the maximum opportunity to evaluate the consistency of the structure of stereotypes.

TABLE 2.2 Measurement Model Goodness of Fit, by City and Race

White Respondents

Model	Model df	Atlanta (N = 662)		Boston (N = 579)		Detroit (N = 765)		Los Angeles (N = 854)	
		X²	AGFI	X²	AGFI	X²	AGFI	X²	AGFI
1 1 Factor	54	2030.71	.524	1991.58	.505	2016.24	.587	1815.05	.629
2 3 Factor, no c.e.	51	1929.70	.521	1906.55	.488	1917.29	.573	1663.65	.637
3 2 + B-H, c.e.	47	879.22	.731	689.97	.754	608.11	.825	458.14	.873
4 2 + A-H, c.e.	47	1218.14	.660	1415.23	.620	1401.37	.664	1406.76	.804
5 2 + A-B, c.e.	47	1661.25	.590	1489.92	.598	1610.48	.640	1455.59	.680
6 2 + B-H, A-H, A-B, c.e.	39	183.37	.911	113.39	.937	118.65	.950	153.10	.941

Contrasts

Model	Model df	Atlanta		Boston		Detroit		Los Angeles	
2 versus 1	3	101.01		85.03		98.95		151.40	
3 versus 2	4	1050.48		1216.58		1309.18		1205.51	
4 versus 2	4	711.56		491.32		515.92		256.89	
5 versus 2	4	268.45		416.63		306.81		208.06	
6 versus 2	12	1746.44		1793.16		1798.64		1510.55	

Black Respondents

Model	Model df	Atlanta (N = 786)		Boston (N = 449)		Detroit (N = 696)		Los Angeles (N = 1106)	
		X²	AGFI	X²	AGFI	X²	AGFI	X²	AGFI
1 1 Factor	54	1417.35	.678	774.73	.663	1084.17	.705	1963.00	.673
2 3 Factor, no c.e.	51	1303.58	.692	650.91	.694	1054.44	.698	1859.27	.670
3 2 + A-H, c.e.	47	488.13	.844	407.63	.800	705.10	.761	1503.31	.713
4 2 + W-H, c.e.	47	1183.50	.718	536.23	.747	1000.04	.699	1663.96	.693
5 2 + A-W, c.e.	47	1027.59	.749	449.23	.774	519.30	.829	717.90	.852
6 2 + A-H, W-H, A-W, c.e.	39	150.95	.937	126.74	.910	214.17	.900	342.04	.897

Source: Multi-City Study of Urban Inequality.
Note: A = Asians, B = Blacks, H = Hispanics, W = Whites, and c.e. = correlated error terms. Models 3 through 6 consist of Model 2, plus correlated errors in the trait rating sets specified.

Contrasts

2 versus 1	113.77	123.82	29.73	103.73
3 versus 2	1255.45	243.28	349.34	355.96
4 versus 2	120.08	114.68	54.40	195.31
5 versus 2	276.99	201.68	535.14	1141.37
6 versus 2	1152.63	524.17	840.27	1517.23

Hispanic Respondents

Model	Model df	N = 698		N = 992	
		X^2	AGFI	X^2	AGFI
1 1 Factor	54	1200.62	.671	1119.96	.785
2 3 Factor, no c.e.	51	1045.73	.709	1094.88	.778
3 2 + A-B	47	839.20	.741	958.45	.786
4 2 + W-B	47	756.18	.764	825.20	.818
5 2 + A-W	47	917.23	.722	472.71	.877
6 2 + A-B, W-B, A-W	39	444.87	.808	152.07	.950
Contrasts					
2 versus 1	3	154.89		25.08	
3 versus 2	4	206.53		136.43	
4 versus 2	4	289.55		269.68	
5 versus 2	4	128.50		622.17	
6 versus 2	12	600.86		942.81	

The first model specifies that the correlation among out-group trait ratings of intelligence, welfare use, ease of getting along, and ability to speak English is due to the regression of the observed ratings on a single latent variable (factor): the general tendency to stereotype members of other groups. We reject this model. The likelihood ratio (L^2) is large for all groups in all cities and the adjusted goodness of fit index also indicates relatively poor fit. This model also bears little intuitive relation to either the pattern of means in table 2.1, which suggests some tendency to order out-groups consistently across traits, or the simple correlations, which suggest a target group–specific structure. The second model specifies group-specific factors: for whites, we fit Asian, black, and Hispanic factors; for blacks, we fit white, Asian, and Hispanic factors; and for Hispanics, we fit white, Asian, and black factors. Comparison of L^2 indicates a better fit, but the AGFI is either a bit worse or substantially unchanged in most cases.

The individual group-specific factors are not sufficient to account for the correlation among the trait ratings. The simple correlations suggest that there are other linkages among the group images and between each trait across groups. The next three models show that the fit can be vastly improved by specifying within-trait, between-group correlated errors. These correlations between the specific variance terms in each trait rating for each outgroup could arise either as a consequence of respondents trying to inject consistency into their ratings that they view as consistent with the relative standing of the groups, or simply from the tendency to shift one's favored response category as the interview moved from trait to trait. For each respondent group in each city, some improvement accrues to the addition of a single type of correlated error (for example, between ratings of blacks and Hispanics), but the results for model 6 indicate that the best overall fit is obtained when all forms of within-trait, between-group error are included for all traits (see figure 2.4 for an illustration of the measurement model). Examination of all the estimated correlated errors shows that they are positive, indicating consistent bias between ratings of the different groups on each trait. These results are found for all respondent groups (whites, blacks, and Hispanics) and in all four cities.

It is unclear whether these patterns call for a substantive or a methodological interpretation. Substantively, these results may suggest that group images are not merely correlated, but are thoroughly interdependent in a manner reflective of social comparison processes (that is, all the racial groups exist in a perceptual gestalt, with ideas about one group always tested in relation to ideas about others). Methodologically, these results may suggest that the trait-rating task itself creates interdependence among the measures. (The results reported next incline us to favor the substantive interpretation, though both processes are probably operative.)

(Text continues on p. 122.)

FIGURE 2.4   Stereotype Measurement Model

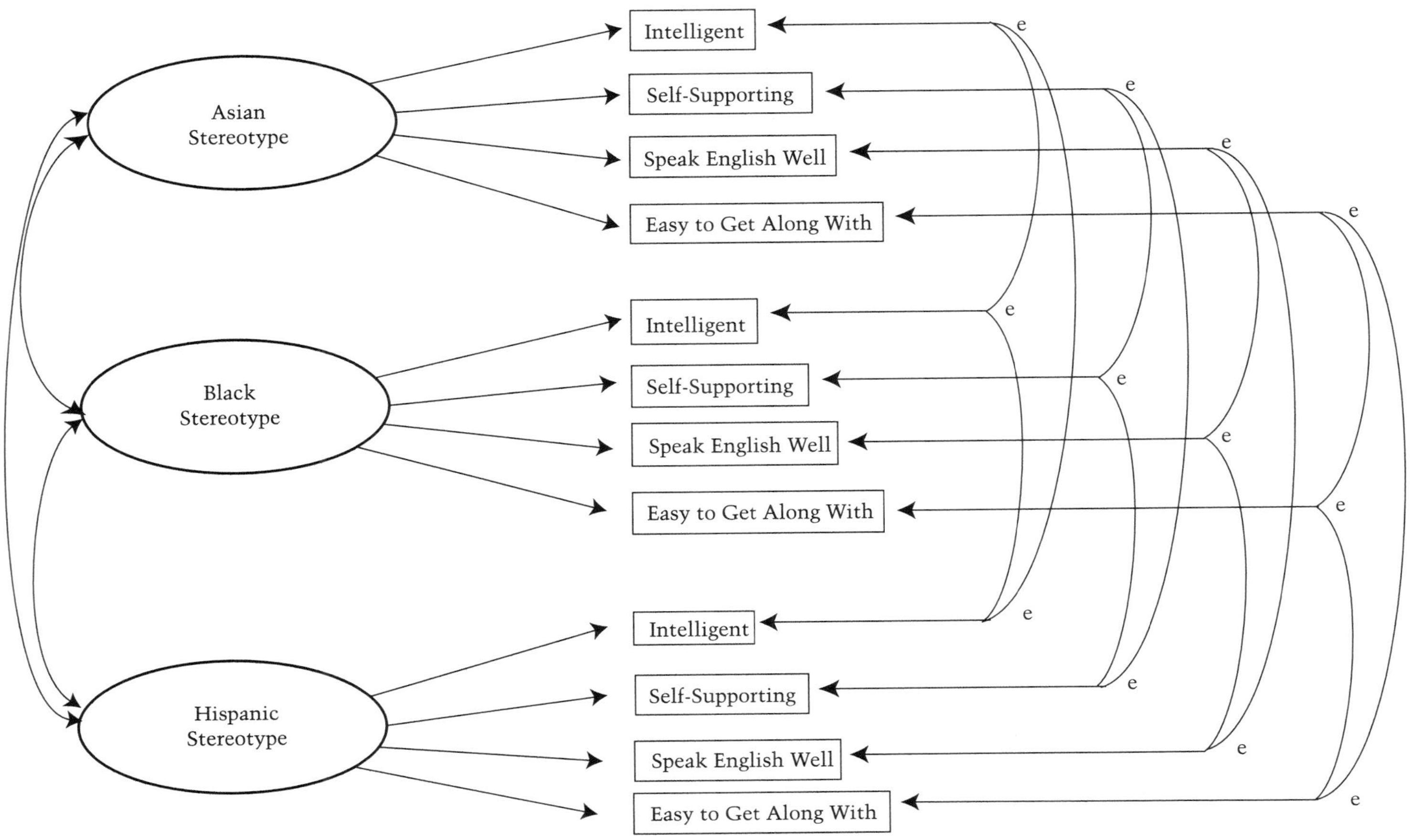

Source: Authors' compilation.

TABLE 2.3   *Measurement Model Parameter Estimates and Factor Loadings, by City and Race*

	Atlanta				Boston			
	W	A	B	H	W	A	B	H
White respondents								
Whites intelligent								
Asians intelligent		.456				.340		
Blacks intelligent			.488				.405	
Hispanics intelligent				.442				.390
Whites self-supporting								
Asians self-supporting		.576				.620		
Blacks self-supporting			.556				.511	
Hispanics self-supporting				.421				.569
Whites easy to get along with								
Asians easy to get along with		.200				.515		
Blacks easy to get along with			.649				.619	
Hispanics easy to get along with				.457				.659
Whites speak English well								
Asians speak English well		.230				.485		
Blacks speak English well			.615				.519	
Hispanics speak English well				.346				.514
Black respondents								
Whites intelligent	.317				.121			
Asians intelligent		.233				.030		
Blacks intelligent								
Hispanics intelligent				.294				.099
Whites self-supporting	.530				.622			
Asians self-supporting		.285				.331		
Blacks self-supporting								
Hispanics self-supporting				.500				.513
Whites easy to get along with	.457				.538			
Asians easy to get along with		.625				.469		
Blacks easy to get along with								
Hispanics easy to get along with				.542				.414

	Detroit				Los Angeles		
W	A	B	H	W	A	B	H
	.512				.372		
		.529				.618	
			.562				.631
	.644				.336		
		.527				.657	
			.498				.557
	.459				.488		
		.477				.476	
			.489				.345
	.362				.557		
		.422				.440	
			.348				.677
.277				.235			
	.399				.110		
			.350				.244
.507				.062			
	.594				.048		
			.677				.492
−.047				.804			
	−.080				.683		
			−.071				.352

(Table continues on p. 120.)

TABLE 2.3   *Continued*

	Atlanta				Boston			
	W	A	B	H	W	A	B	H
Whites speak English well	.592				.560			
Asians speak English well		.503				.703		
Blacks speak English well								
Hispanics speak English well				.249				.739
Hispanic respondents								
Whites intelligent					−.192			
Asians intelligent						.107		
Blacks intelligent							.776	
Hispanics intelligent								
Whites self-supporting					.868			
Asians self-supporting						.563		
Blacks self-supporting							−.080	
Hispanics self-supporting								
Whites easy to get along with					.659			
Asians easy to get along with						.567		
Blacks easy to get along with							.519	
Hispanics easy to get along with								
Whites speak English well					.158			
Asians speak English well						.702		
Blacks speak English well							.169	
Hispanics speak English well								
Measurement model factor correlation								
White respondents								
Asians		1.00				1.00		
Blacks		.179	1.00			.519	1.00	
Hispanics		.213	.780	1.00		.586	.787	1.00
Black respondents								
Whites	1.00				1.00			
Asians	.688	1.00			.204	1.00		
Hispanics	.524	.717		1.00	−.005	.674		1.00
Hispanic respondents								
Whites					1.00			
Asians					−.052	1.00		
Blacks					−.664	.218	1.00	

Source: Multi-City Study of Urban Inequality.
Note: W = Whites, A = Asians, B = Blacks, H = Hispanics.

	Detroit				Los Angeles		
W	A	B	H	W	A	B	H
.555				−.081			
	.195				.607		
			.283				.640
				.067			
					.111		
						.395	
				.306			
					.072		
						.417	
				.180			
					.973		
						−.330	
				.440			
					.249		
						−.010	
	1.00				1.00		
	.323	1.00			.289	1.00	
	.492	.738	1.00		.260	.838	1.00
1.00				1.00			
.471	1.00			.655	1.00		
−.271	.229		1.00	.255	.473		1.00
				1.00			
				.261	1.00		
				−.513	−.103	1.00	

Table 2.3 shows the factor loadings estimated under model 6. These represent the regression of each trait rating on its respective group factor. Both the observed variables and factors are scaled to have their variance equal 1.0, so the factor loadings provide a measure of the relative reliability of each trait rating as an indicator of the propensity to hold stereotypic attitudes of a group. For example, among white respondents in Detroit, the most reliable indicator of their view of Asians is their rating of Asians' preference to be self-supporting (the factor loading is .644, compared with .362 for the rating of Asians' ability to speak English well). The most reliable indicator of Detroit whites' views of Hispanics is their rating of Hispanics' intelligence. White views of Asians in Boston are also most reliably indicated by their rating of Asians' preference to be self-supporting, but their views of Hispanics are most reliably indicated by the rating of how easy Hispanics are to get along with (compare factor loadings of .620 and .659).

Comparison of the factor loadings by target group for whites generally shows the loadings to be more similar when the out-group rated is blacks than when it is Hispanics or Asians—that is, there is greater consistency in whites' use of the trait ratings to characterize blacks, compared to how these traits are used for rating Hispanics or Asians. Further, for white respondents, the overall variation in loadings is less than for black or Hispanic respondents (compare, for example, the factor loadings when Asians are the target of whites, blacks and Hispanics in Boston). This suggests a firmer cognitive grounding to views of blacks among white respondents, compared to their views of other groups.

Another aspect of the measurement model that is more consistent for whites than for blacks and Hispanics is shown in the estimated correlation of the factors. The correlation between the stereotyping of blacks and Hispanics by whites is above 0.7 in each city. The correlation between all the factors is positive for white respondents. But this is not the case for black or Hispanic respondents, and there is not a consistent pattern of positively and negatively signed correlations across cities. Any attempt to explain these results post hoc would be purely speculative. Nonetheless, all the factor loadings, correlations between factors, and correlated errors of measurement are large enough to achieve statistical significance using conventional tests, giving some plausibility to their magnitude and sign.[7]

Common Determinants of
Variation in Stereotyping

We are also concerned with understanding factors that would make stereotypic assessments more positive or negative. The variables considered in this analysis include perception of the group's economic standing (rich/poor trait rating), the respondent's sex (represented by an indicator variable coded 1 if the respondent was male, 0 if the respondent was female), the respondent's age, the respondent's level of education (represented by years of schooling completed: 0 to 17 or more), whether the respondent was born in the United States (an indicator variable coded 1 if born in the United States, 0 otherwise), the respondent's family income (with levels represented by the midpoint of 20 closed-response options, representing ranges from $0 to $5,000 to $150,000 or more), and self-report of political ideology, ranging from extremely liberal (1) to extremely conservative (7), with those saying "don't know" classified as moderate (4). Means and standard deviations for each of these variables are shown in table 2.4 for each group of respondents in each city. There are few notable differences across city for any given group, with the exception that white respondents in Los Angeles are more likely to be foreign-born than in the other cities, black respondents in Boston are more likely to be foreign-born, and Hispanic respondents in Los Angeles are much more likely to be foreign-born than in Boston.

Table 2.5 shows the results obtained by regressing the group-specific stereotype factors on the independent variables. Three regression models were estimated for each group. The first model specifies that the stereotype factor for each group depends only on the respondent's perception of the economic standing of the group. The second model builds on the first by allowing the other person's characteristics also to affect the stereotyping factors. The third and final model builds on the first and second by allowing the stereotyping factors to be influenced by perceptions of the economic standing of other out-groups. For example, perceptions of the economic standing of blacks are allowed to affect the Hispanic stereotyping factor. (Figure 2.5 provides a graphic illustration of the first-stage structural model.) Overall, while comparison of L^2 suggests that allowing personal characteristics and cross-group effects of perceptions of economic standing improves the model fit, the AGFI is virtually unchanged. This occurs for every group of respondents in each city.

Parameter estimates from model 3 for each group of respondents in each city are shown in table 2.6. The main conclusion to be drawn from examination of the parameter estimates is that more positive stereotypes are usually associated with positive perceptions of the target group's economic standing, net of personal characteristics usually associated with positive attitudes toward out-groups (education, liberal ideology, being female). This pattern is consistent with James Kluegel's argument about the centrality of stratification beliefs to intergroup

(Text continues on p. 127.)

TABLE 2.4 Descriptive Statistics, by City and Race

	Atlanta		Boston		Detroit		Los Angeles	
	Mean	S.D.	Mean	S.D.	Mean	S.D.	Mean	S.D.
White respondents								
Sex	.51	.50	.47	.50	.48	.50	.50	.50
Age	44.72	15.79	45.89	17.14	45.74	17.19	44.98	15.28
Education	13.99	2.49	13.83	2.40	13.30	2.40	14.21	2.11
Native-born	.94	.23	.96	.21	.90	.30	.85	.36
Family income	$56,024	$38,360	$53,639	$38,797	$49,693	$33,673	$56,754	$42,505
Liberal-conservative	4.47	1.47	4.07	1.42	4.15	1.31	4.00	1.41
Black respondents								
Sex	.43	.50	.47	.50	.43	.49	.49	.50
Age	41.67	14.16	40.42	15.45	44.12	16.45	41.12	15.41
Education	13.41	2.55	12.45	2.72	12.60	2.49	13.08	2.71
Native-born	.97	.17	.66	.47	.99	.10	.91	.28
Family income	$33,791	$23,028	$29,991	$24,626	$33,616	$31,948	$38,843	$35,134
Liberal-conservative	3.59	1.38	3.90	1.56	3.76	1.46	3.57	1.53
Hispanic respondents								
Sex			.47	.50			.50	.50
Age			37.02	13.31			37.10	12.83
Education			10.60	3.51			10.13	4.05
Native-born			.54	.50			.27	.44
Family income			$27,423	$17,729			$27,604	$22,543
Liberal-conservative			4.19	1.48			4.05	1.30

Source: Multi-City Study of Urban Inequality.

TABLE 2.5 Structural Equation Model Goodness of Fit Results, by City and Race

White Respondents

	Model df	Atlanta N = 662 X²	AGFI	Boston N = 579 X²	AGFI	Detroit N = 765 X²	AGFI	Los Angeles N = 854 X²	AGFI
Model									
1 Rich-poor	144	615.42	.874	603.99	.858	498.87	.911	645.27	.895
2 1 + all exs.	126	486.70	.884	457.90	.874	391.67	.917	483.56	.907
3 2 + cross R-P	120	476.04	.881	395.89	.886	347.07	.923	452.95	.909
Contrasts									
2 versus 1	18	128.72		146.09		107.20		161.71	
3 versus 2	6	10.66		62.01		44.60		30.61	

Black Respondents

	Model df	Atlanta N = 786 X²	AGFI	Boston N = 449 X²	AGFI	Detroit N = 696 X²	AGFI	Los Angeles N = 1106 X²	AGFI
Model									
1 Rich-poor	144	682.84	.880	491.16	.852	552.70	.888	1276.39	.842
2 1 + all exs.	126	576.40	.883	425.75	.851	451.13	.894	1079.43	.847
3 2 + cross R-P	120	541.93	.884	404.25	.851	426.33	.893	1035.26	.845
Contrasts									
2 versus 1	18	106.44		65.41		101.57		196.96	
3 versus 2	6	34.47		21.50		24.80		44.17	

Hispanic Respondents

	Model df	Boston N = 698 X²	AGFI	Los Angeles N = 992 X²	AGFI
Model					
1 Rich-poor	144	1677.75	.720	884.03	.882
2 1 + all exs.	126	1384.69	.729	739.83	.882
3 2 + cross R-P	120	1275.02	.737	691.59	.881
Contrasts					
2 versus 1	18	293.06		144.20	
3 versus 2	6	109.67		48.24	

Source: Multi-City Study of Urban Inequality.
Note: All exs. = all explanatory variables; cross R-P = both nontarget group rich-poor trait ratings allowed to influence.

FIGURE 2.5   *Full Structural Model for White Respondents*

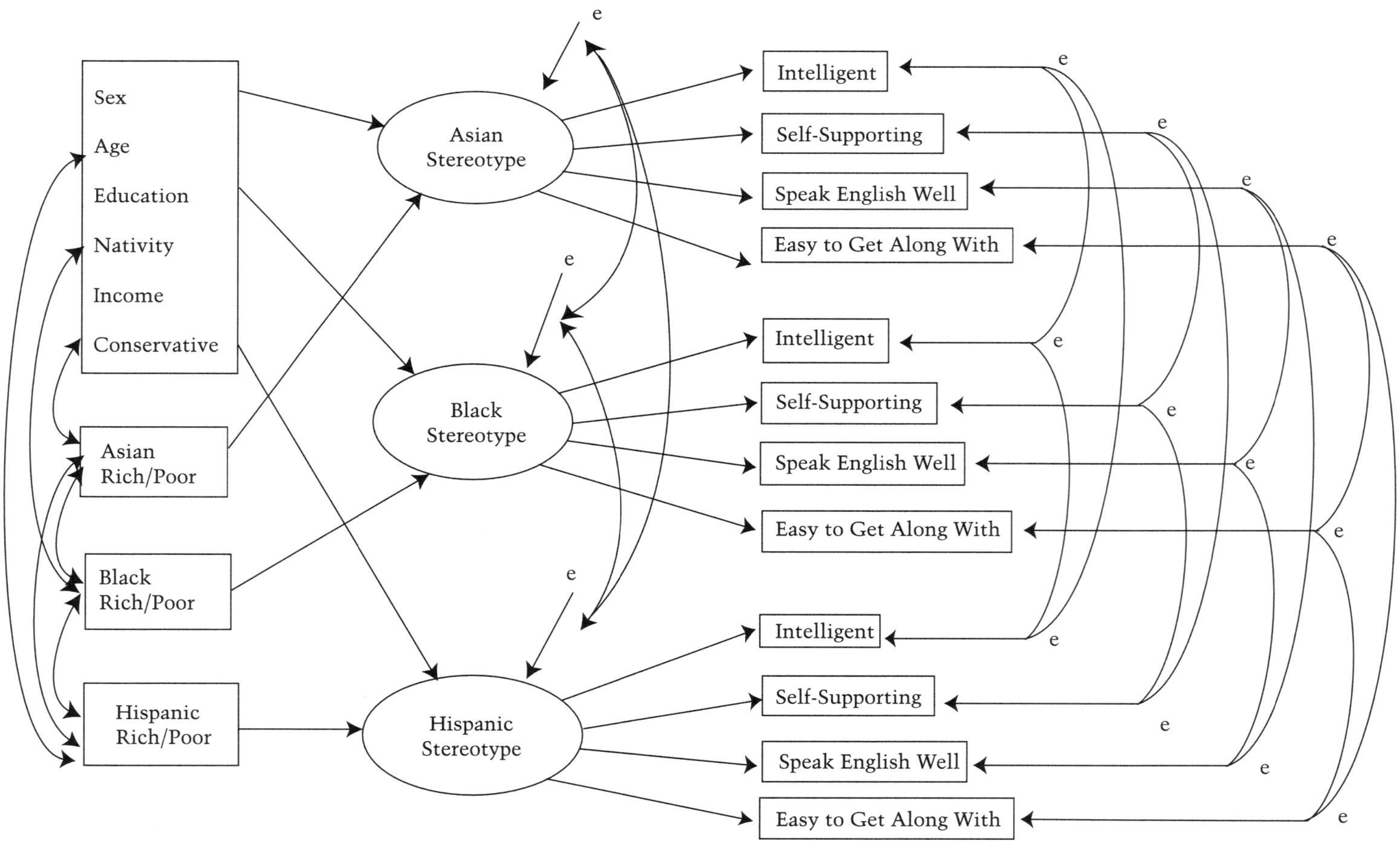

Source: Authors' compilation

attitudes (Kluegel and Smith 1986). There are a few interesting exceptions. Among whites in Boston, those who have more positive views of blacks' economic position are likely to express more negative stereotypes (the regression estimate is $-.191$). Among black respondents in Los Angeles and Hispanic respondents in Boston, those with more positive views of the economic position of whites and Asians are more likely to express more negative stereotypes of those groups.

The model allowing only the rating of group economic position to affect the out-group stereotype usually accounted for less than 10 percent of the estimated variation in the stereotype factor. Exceptions included whites' ratings of Hispanics in Los Angeles (11 percent), blacks' ratings of whites in Boston (15 percent) and Detroit (21 percent), blacks' ratings of Asians in Detroit (18 percent), Hispanics' ratings of blacks in Boston (34 percent), and Hispanics' ratings of whites (14 percent) and Asians (36 percent) in Los Angeles. The amount of variation explained increases two- to fourfold when the model includes effects of sex, age, education, native-born, family income, and political ideology, but the effects of these variables are not always consistent and are usually not as large as the effect of the perception of group economic position. The most consistent effect is due to education, which is nearly always positive, so that those with more education are more likely to express more positive stereotypes. The relative strength of the education effect often equals or exceeds the effect of the perception of group economic standing. The effect of sex tends to be negative, meaning that male respondents held more negative views than women did. The effect of age, income, and political ideology was inconsistent, both in sign and strength, varying by group and city. Native-born respondents in all groups usually held more positive views than did foreign-born respondents.

Adding cross-group effects of perception of economic position on the other stereotypes usually did little to improve the overall fit of the model, and in a few cases the estimate of variation explained was actually worse than when these effects were not included at all. Exceptional improvement by inclusion of these effects did occur in the models for Hispanic respondents. Statistically significant effects do emerge in a number of instances.

Some of the patterns are suggestive of potentially important metropolitan-area differences in effects. For example, among Los Angeles–area whites, the more economically successful that Asians are perceived to be, the less favorable are the images of blacks and Hispanics. This implies that in Los Angeles, the area with the largest and most affluent Asian population among our sites, a sort of "model minority" myth effect may be at work. Few of the differences, however, lend themselves to straightforward interpretation.

TABLE 2.6   *Full Structural Equation Model Parameter Estimates, by City and Race (Standardized Coefficients)*

	Atlanta				Boston			
	White	Asian	Black	Hispanic	White	Asian	Black	Hispanic
White respondents								
Sex		−.135*	−.067	−.019		−.006	−.109*	.097*
Age		.035	.018	.140*		.109*	−.160*	−.084
Education		.310*	.278*	.312*		.140*	.315*	.325*
Native		−.147*	.131*	.068		.030	.016	.000
Income		.138*	−.125*	−.094		.029	.028	.005
Liberal-conservative		−.045	−.157*	−.160*		.054	−.050	−.050
Rich-poor Asians		.298*	.009	−.030*		.394*	−.015	−.426*
Rich-poor blacks		.039	.183*	−.030		.055	−.191*	−.100
Rich-poor Hispanics		−.182	.007	.207*		.050	−.040	.166*
Variance explained								
Model 1		.09	.05	.05		.03	.05	.08
Model 2		.25	.16	.16		.12	.21	.23
Model 3		.26	.15	.15		.25	.19	.18
Black respondents								
Sex	−.302*	−.064		−.098	−.016	−.069		.161
Age	.128*	.135*		.168*	.067	.111		.118
Education	.059	.109		.256*	−.002	.060		.157
Native	−.096*	.017		.132*	.139	.207		.300
Income	−.061	−.086		−.083	−.064	.120		.056
Liberal-conservative	.069	.098*		−.034	−.037	−.062		.054
Rich-poor whites	.281*	.030		.031	.331	−.195		−.072
Rich-poor Asians	−.174*	.090		.086	−.053	.350		.188
Rich-poor Hispanics	−.096*	−.063		.213*	−.120	−.078		.107
Variance explained								
Model 1	.07	.01		.08	.15	.05		.03
Model 2	.19	.04		.16	.17	.17		.19
Model 3	.24	.04		.14	.16	.21		.21
Hispanic respondents								
Sex					−.330*	−.048	−.230*	
Age					−.058	.040	−.099*	
Education					−.071	−.187	−.054	
Native					.185*	.250	.222*	
Income					.084	.154	.053	
Liberal-conservative					.112*	.072	.302*	
Rich-poor whites					−.236*	.304	.071	
Rich-poor Asians					−.292*	−.479	−.158*	
Rich-poor blacks					.055	−.103	.110*	
Variance explained								
Model 1					.05	.34	.00	
Model 2					.21	.56	.27	
Model 3					.24	.65	.29	

Source: Multi-City Study of Urban Inequality.
*$t > 1.96$.

	Detroit				Los Angeles		
White	Asian	Black	Hispanic	White	Asian	Black	Hispanic
	.045	−.099*	−.033		−.112*	.072	.194*
	−.192*	−.258*	−.269*		.014	−.128*	−.046
	.137*	.225*	.163*		.123*	.046	.060
	.032	.109*	.038		.057	.080*	.069
	.009	−.024	−.054		.142*	.032	.095*
	.065	−.039	.017		.011	−.298*	−.199*
	.292*	−.080	.004		.056	−.149*	−.148*
	−.269*	.164*	−.055		−.019	.288*	.073*
	−.005	.055	.293*		.053*	.127	.374*
	.06	.05	.09		.01	.09	.11
	.17	.20	.19		.06	.20	.20
	.23	.19	.17		.05	.27	.28
−.136*	.076		−.050	−.048	.025		.105*
−.107	.044		−.003	.230*	.069		−.105*
.126	.206*		.096	.227*	.208		.160*
.097	.009		.039	−.239*	−.013		.094*
.016	.075		.190*	.110	.021		.078*
−.162*	−.089		−.101	−.014	−.143		−.112*
.455*	.036		−.059	−.383*	.097		−.117*
.031	.555*		.034	.006	−.297		−.002
−.201*	−.322*		.250*	.206*	.099		.207*
.21	.18		.08	.09	.09		.08
.36	.26		.15	.51	.19		.15
.41	.49		.12	.52	.18		.17
				−.090	−.138*	−.123	
				−.146*	.014	.357*	
				−.077	.308*	.264*	
				−.016	.147*	.448*	
				−.002	.019	.116	
				−.024	−.247*	.084	
				.209*	−.152*	−.296*	
				.154*	.716*	−.153	
				−.153*	−.194*	.205*	
				.14	.36	.07	
				.14	.61	.34	
				.17	.73	.89	

129

At least, the following caveats apply: (1) in most instances, a large amount of variation in the use of the trait ratings cannot be explained by the factors we included in the models, and (2) the relationship between perceived group economic standing and out-group ratings might well differ with a different underlying set of traits. Yet, given the scope of traits included here, we would expect, in any case, the impact of perception of group economic position to be a persistent driver of the group stereotype, independent of the impact of measures of the respondent's experience and social position usually associated with variation in racial attitudes, such as education and ideology.

Conclusion

Scholars such as DuBois (1996 [1899]), Myrdal (1944), and Drake and Cayton (1945) treated stereotypes as fundamental and organic factors in the dynamics of group inequality. No doubt this legacy contributed to the conclusion by See and Wilson that "persistent ethnic stereotypes and prejudicial attitudes are one of the major factors in limiting intergroup contact and preserving ethnic boundaries" (1989, 226). Our own analyses of the contemporary urban landscape renew and reinforce this view of the importance of stereotyping. Respondents rarely gave "don't know" or "refused" responses to the effort to measure stereotypes. Target-group differences emerge on specific traits and in terms of overall evaluative judgments, with African Americans and Latinos given the least favorable ratings and whites generally given the most favorable ratings (with Asians close behind). On the whole, we have found a sensible organization and pattern of correlates for the measured stereotypes. All these patterns point toward a view of stereotypes as socially consequential ideas.

First, in response to our opening core concern with the structure of stereotypes, we find for the Multi-City Study data that we can reject a view of stereotypes as organized around a simple, singular us-versus-them dichotomy. Specific racial-ethnic group targets matter. This is true in all four cities and for our white, black, and Latino respondents. But before we rush to reject a centrally psychological view of stereotypes, we find, second, in response to our other core concern with contextual variation in stereotypes, that a largely similar structure or organization to stereotypes exists in each city and, with the exception of Hispanics in Boston, for respondents from each racial group. Third, the social psychological variable of perceived group economic success is always an important influence on the other dispositional or personality stereotype trait ratings. Fourth, the social learning variable of level of education usually influences the degree of negative stereotyping, with the better educated expressing less negative views. There was less consistent evidence that an individual's age, gender, native versus foreign-born status, and political ideology shaped the degree of negative stereotyping

By implication, then, and following a broad legacy of previous stereotyping research, we conclude that stereotypes are grounded in social structure and shaped by direct social learning and the acquisition of group culture. They vary across individuals in acceptance and likely responsiveness to new information and experience. Racial stereotypes are multiply determined but also highly generalized ideational constructs. In all likelihood, they influence perception and understanding, individual action, and interpersonal interaction. They facilitate bias and discrimination in face-to-face encounters, in important workplace dynamics, and in the operation of housing market and neighborhood sorting processes.

Some of the basic descriptive patterns for our results confirm expectations of general theories of stereotypes (Jost and Banaji 1994). Whites, the dominant social group, are the most likely to rate themselves positively. Whites are also the group most likely to be seen in positive terms by members of other groups. The subordinate groups, particularly Hispanics but also African Americans to a degree, are the least likely to see members of their own groups in favorable terms. And these groups are least likely to be seen in a favorable light by members of other groups.

Since stereotypes flow from the structural placement of groups in society and the evolving group cultures and patterns of relationship, these beliefs contain a kernel of truth. Thus, social reality and the perceptions we measured point to the fact that blacks and Hispanics tend to be less affluent than Asians, who, in turn, are much closer in economic status to whites. Similarly, consistent with the stereotype perceptions, African Americans and Hispanics are disproportionately dependent on welfare. In addition, to the extent that group differences are perceived, our data suggest that for most people these differences are seen in muted terms (consistent with Jackman's argument [1994]). Despite a kernel of truth and qualified expression, there should be no doubt that we regard these stereotypes as highly problematic, as they tend to be applied categorically and to have self-reinforcing properties in the face of contradictory information (Bodenhausen, Macrae, and Garst 1998; Fiske 1998). Moreover, when made salient by the presence of members of an out-group, it is the broad cultural stereotype that is most readily—indeed, often automatically—activated (Devine 1989).

Consider for a moment the potential workplace influence of these stereotypes. We know that employers frequently must make decisions on the basis of partial information about potential employees and often are not good judges of future performance (Holzer 1996). Indeed, employers frequently ignore readily obtainable information on formal credentials in favor of their own "gut instincts" and input from what they regard as "trustworthy" ties (Miller and Rosenbaum 1997). These circumstances open the door for the biasing and discriminatory effects of stereotypes to operate (Reskin 2000 and forthcoming). A similar dynamic almost certainly enters into the difficult terrain that members of stigmatized racial groups must negotiate in order to rise to positions of power in workplace settings as well (Smith 1997, 1999).

In this regard, we would stress that the lack of sharp city-specific variation in the basic structure of stereotypes, and the lack of theoretically consistent differences across cities in the correlates of racial stereotypes, is telling. This pattern cautions against a view of stereotypes as highly localized and context-specific. Still, it would be inappropriate on the basis of these data to reject any role for local context. We know that under the right conditions (equal status, common goals, positive institutional support), close intergroup contact can improve some aspects of intergroup attitudes (Jackman 1994; Ellison and Powers 1994; Kinder and Mendelberg 1995), and that local normative conditions may exert effects as well (Oliver and Mendelberg 2000). But we speculate that much of the content and functioning of racial stereotypes derive from the joint effects of mutual embeddedness in both a larger national historical or cultural context and the contemporary social organization of race, and the general social psychological processes of stereotype formation. Thus, we find that whites' views of blacks are probably the most firmly rooted of the group stereotypes, that whites' views of blacks and of Hispanics are often closely correlated but still involve some target group–specific features (for example, extent of English language mastery), and that generally the group images exhibit a substantial element of interdependence or mutual relevance (that is, the factor correlations, correlated error structures, and across-target group effects of perceived economic status).

We think this multiply determined but highly generalized nature of stereotypes is also why in-depth employer interviews reveal employers making patently contradictory claims. For example, black women can be typified as "single mothers" in ways that make them either especially good or especially bad employees (Browne and Kennelly 1999; Kennelly 1999). There is clearly a general stereotype perception out there that employers appear to share with the mass of individuals not holding such workplace power (compare Bobo, Johnson, and Suh 2000). A general cultural stereotype does exist and is brought by individuals into a variety of social settings and encounters. As an aspect of learned group culture and experience, the cultural stereotype is a bundle of ideas that can be drawn upon to provide an account for one's actions, including those of an employer seeking to explain his or her actions. Walter Lippman perhaps said it best: "For the most part we do not first see, and then define, we define first and then see. In the great blooming, buzzing confusion of the outer world we pick out what our culture has already defined for us and we tend to perceive that which we have picked out in the form stereotyped for us by our culture" (1922, 54–55).

From our vantage point, what is important about the stereotype is not derived from the workplace setting or neighborhood context itself, but rather from the acquisition and functioning of the larger cultural belief. For example, it is clear that negative stereotypes of African Americans or Latinos as potential neighbors do not derive from direct personal experience in neighborhood settings; the extant patterns of residential segregation by race make this unlikely. The negative stereotypes matter, sadly, because larger patterns of social organization (overt historical racism, vast and durable inequalities in wealth, contemporary segregated communities, friendship and family networks) and the ideas conveyed by numerous cultural artifacts (such as Aunt Jemima, Uncle Ben, Willie Horton, Charlie Chan, Hop Sing, Speedy Gonzalez), institutions (the media, realtors), and leaders (that is, elite social discourse) reinforce these stereotypes (Entman and Rojecki 2000; Gilliam and Iyengar 2000).

The prevalence and effects of racial stereotypes carry a deeper implication for our thinking about studies of social inequality. If our own work and the enormous body of historical and social psychological research on stereotyping and prejudice are accurate, then we suspect that mainstream approaches to inequality are flawed. More precisely, there is something both ahistorical and asociological, we think, about recent research that proceeds on the basis of an under-racialized view of social dynamics. For example, we are doubtful of interpretations of labor and housing market dynamics that seek to explain away racial group inequality in terms, respectively, of the "skills variable" (for example, Farkas and Vicknair 1996) or of the "fear of crime variable" (for example, Harris 1999).[8] From our vantage point, such arguments substitute arid "variable analysis" for nuanced social analysis. To be sure, we too measure variables in order to test our ideas about processes operative in the social world. But the effects of significant variables in regression or other types of statistical models do not in and of themselves constitute *social* explanations or theories. Variables are lent meaning, and theories hold explanatory, predictive, and policy-relevant power, only when securely anchored in an appreciation of the full historical, cultural, social psychological, and individual processes that produce observed patterns of relationship. With the noteworthy exceptions of William Julius Wilson (1987, 1996), Douglas Massey and Nancy Denton (1993), and

Melvin Oliver and Thomas Shapiro (1995), too much of our research and knowledge about urban inequality proceed on the basis of an atomizing, socially uprooted analytical framework that seems to have forgotten this important lesson—a lesson we credit to the exemplary work of Du Bois, Myrdal, and Drake and Cayton (O'Connor 2000).

Given our data on stereotypes and a U.S. history and culture that the eminent historian George M. Fredrickson (1999) described as involving an unambiguous "ethnic hierarchy," it is fair to say that the disadvantages faced by African Americans, Latinos, and, to a lesser degree, Asian Americans continue to be linked to deeply racialized contemporary social conditions and processes (Sanjek 1994; Jankowski 1995; Zubrinsky and Bobo 1996; Bonilla-Silva 1997; Gans 1999; Dawson 2000). That is what the tilt of our analysis of racial stereotypes tells us. Again, we think Walter Lippman put it well when he observed nearly a century ago that:

> The subtlest and most pervasive of all influences are those which create and maintain the repertory of stereotypes. We are told about the world before we see it. We imagine most things before we experience them. And those preconceptions, unless education has made us acutely aware, govern deeply the whole process of perception. They mark out certain objects, as familiar or strange, emphasizing the difference, so that the slightly familiar is seen as very familiar, and the somewhat strange as sharply alien. [1922, 59]

Although not as extreme or potent as they once might have been, stereotypes of historically stigmatized and disadvantaged racial and ethnic groups remain alive today. Though almost never the only or the overdetermining input to behavior and social interaction, racial stereotypes are ideas that matter. Whether as omnipresent cultural backdrop or as the individual's tool kit of ideas for engaging a variety of social interactions, racial stereotypes envelop the relations and dynamics that bring about social inequality. Researchers and policymakers concerned with ameliorating urban inequality must attend to these facts as well.

We wish to thank several colleagues for helping us complete this paper. Reynolds Farley, Robinson Hollister, Harry Holzer, and Irene Browne gave us good advice in reaction to a preliminary draft of this paper presented during a Multi-City Study project conference held at the Russell Sage Foundation in October 1997. Alice O'Connor, Howard Schuman, Jim Sidanius, Abel Valenzuela, Camille Zubrinsky Charles, Devon Johnson, and Monica McDermott read and critiqued the substantially completed manuscript. We, of course, are responsible for any remaining shortcomings and errors. This research was partly supported by a National Science Foundation grant.

Appendix

(follows next page)

TABLE 2A.1   *Means, Standard Deviations and Correlation Matrices for White Respondents by City*

White Respondents
Atlanta (N = 662)

	Mean	S.D.	Correlation Matrix (Design Weighted)						
Sex	0.506	0.500	1.000						
Age	44.718	15.795	0.023	1.000					
Education	13.985	2.490	0.079	−0.264	1.000				
Native-born	0.942	0.233	0.031	0.077	0.039	1.000			
Family income	56024	38360	0.142	−0.114	0.335	0.110	1.000		
Liberal-conservative	4.467	1.475	0.059	0.141	0.010	−0.095	0.149	1.000	
Asian rich-poor	−0.184	1.251	−0.018	−0.104	0.079	−0.056	−0.024	−0.061	1.000
Black rich-poor	−0.854	1.041	−0.024	−0.060	−0.102	−0.064	−0.090	−0.099	0.162
Hispanic rich-poor	−0.962	1.173	−0.061	0.093	−0.068	−0.094	−0.099	−0.003	0.367
Asian intelligent	0.812	1.242	−0.062	−0.025	0.062	−0.129	−0.022	−0.011	0.108
Black intelligent	0.268	1.235	−0.114	0.043	0.020	−0.023	−0.113	−0.102	−0.072
Hispanic intelligent	0.142	1.131	−0.094	0.129	−0.005	−0.038	−0.090	−0.050	−0.072
Asian self-supporting	1.346	1.462	−0.072	−0.060	0.274	−0.065	0.184	−0.031	0.159
Black self-supporting	−0.041	1.716	−0.054	0.033	0.208	0.066	0.006	−0.167	0.061
Hispanic self-supporting	0.348	1.514	0.000	0.076	0.197	0.019	0.057	−0.085	0.022
Asian easy to get along with	0.527	1.408	0.129	−0.026	0.082	−0.077	0.092	0.059	−0.106
Black easy to get along with	0.423	1.460	0.002	−0.035	0.162	0.114	0.033	−0.049	0.011
Hispanic easy to get along with	0.327	1.344	0.061	0.005	0.157	0.046	0.009	−0.043	−0.016
Asian speak English well	−0.147	1.328	−0.013	−0.040	0.169	0.008	0.048	−0.040	0.161
Black speak English well	0.445	1.601	0.037	−0.164	0.097	0.061	−0.093	−0.141	0.047
Hispanic speak English well	−0.661	1.284	0.015	0.018	0.078	0.030	−0.028	−0.088	0.094

Boston (N = 579)

	Mean	S.D.	Correlation Matrix (Design Weighted)						
Sex	0.466	0.499	1.000						
Age	45.888	17.139	−0.105	1.000					
Education	13.832	2.396	0.180	−0.174	1.000				
Native-born	0.956	0.206	0.054	−0.082	0.081	1.000			
Family income	53639	38797	0.043	−0.068	0.364	0.054	1.000		
Liberal-conservative	4.068	1.421	0.063	0.143	−0.176	−0.037	−0.038	1.000	
Asian rich-poor	−0.501	1.057	−0.040	−0.130	0.141	0.010	−0.072	−0.098	1.000
Black rich-poor	−1.131	1.051	0.013	−0.068	−0.117	0.064	−0.204	0.026	0.350
Hispanic rich-poor	−1.318	1.119	−0.091	−0.021	−0.130	0.092	−0.250	−0.019	0.428
Asian intelligent	0.608	1.246	−0.008	−0.076	−0.055	0.029	0.040	0.151	−0.039
Black intelligent	0.142	1.177	−0.032	−0.135	0.060	0.045	0.021	0.050	−0.051
Hispanic intelligent	0.051	1.151	0.051	−0.146	0.045	0.061	0.032	0.040	−0.051

1.000												
0.584	1.000											
−0.045	−0.040	1.000										
0.120	0.032	0.341	1.000									
0.025	0.052	0.405	0.763	1.000								
−0.036	−0.079	0.254	0.016	0.023	1.000							
0.109	0.066	0.036	0.292	0.216	0.343	1.000						
0.038	0.023	0.002	0.130	0.137	0.495	0.738	1.000					
0.120	−0.003	−0.003	−0.065	−0.060	0.231	0.110	0.199	1.000				
0.134	0.038	0.112	0.324	0.270	0.105	0.386	0.303	0.416	1.000			
0.119	0.080	−0.033	0.098	0.132	0.181	0.289	0.363	0.589	0.650	1.000		
0.027	0.168	−0.001	−0.062	−0.044	0.098	0.117	0.083	0.271	0.148	0.277	1.000	
0.116	0.076	0.121	0.341	0.234	−0.034	0.291	0.105	0.060	0.422	0.217	0.184	1.000
0.025	0.244	−0.054	0.033	0.105	−0.011	0.236	0.203	0.117	0.199	0.266	0.577	0.293

1.000				
0.661	1.000			
−0.131	−0.084	1.000		
0.014	0.056	0.513	1.000	
0.054	0.101	0.486	0.818	1.000

(Table continues on p. 138.)

TABLE 2A.1   *Continued*

White Respondents
Boston (N = 579)

	Mean	S.D.	Correlation Matrix (Design Weighted)						
Asian self-supporting	0.872	1.490	0.055	0.055	0.227	−0.030	0.135	−0.015	0.112
Black self-supporting	−0.168	1.677	0.031	−0.053	0.289	−0.019	0.099	−0.145	0.037
Hispanic self-supporting	−0.210	1.639	0.139	−0.052	0.277	−0.025	0.059	−0.138	0.054
Asian easy to get along with	0.340	1.172	0.063	0.091	0.077	0.019	0.023	−0.020	0.151
Black easy to get along with	0.233	1.254	0.026	−0.167	0.128	0.058	0.101	−0.073	0.167
Hispanic easy to get along with	0.087	1.270	0.126	−0.090	0.217	0.073	0.104	−0.046	0.146
Asian speak English well	−0.367	1.412	−0.086	0.021	0.128	0.005	0.086	−0.048	0.183
Black speak English well	0.555	1.594	−0.003	−0.215	0.075	0.042	−0.013	−0.018	0.030
Hispanic speak English well	−0.871	1.344	−0.054	−0.002	0.247	0.026	0.034	−0.133	0.204

Detroit (N = 765)

	Mean	S.D.	Correlation Matrix (Design Weighted)						
Sex	0.481	0.500	1.000						
Age	45.739	17.190	−0.082	1.000					
Education	13.301	2.402	0.109	−0.302	1.000				
Native-born	0.899	0.302	0.061	−0.133	0.086	1.000			
Family income	49693	33673	0.036	−0.179	0.361	0.097	1.000		
Liberal-conservative	4.149	1.305	0.073	0.062	0.047	0.035	0.018	1.000	
Asian rich-poor	−0.009	1.111	0.034	−0.148	0.071	−0.021	0.016	−0.046	1.000
Black rich-poor	−1.152	1.074	−0.056	−0.003	−0.119	−0.002	−0.106	0.031	0.274
Hispanic rich-poor	−1.096	1.062	0.013	0.065	−0.169	−0.011	−0.141	0.046	0.276
Asian intelligent	0.786	1.102	0.043	−0.183	0.096	0.098	0.029	0.018	0.196
Black intelligent	−0.008	1.031	−0.106	−0.159	0.056	0.009	0.019	0.041	−0.036
Hispanic intelligent	−0.011	0.973	−0.032	−0.132	0.070	−0.026	0.005	0.024	0.043
Asian self-supporting	1.334	1.294	0.089	−0.139	0.243	0.024	0.143	0.017	0.126
Black self-supporting	−0.325	1.563	−0.007	−0.116	0.263	0.150	0.135	−0.061	0.007
Hispanic self-supporting	0.173	1.367	0.030	−0.121	0.187	0.089	0.074	0.001	0.043
Asian easy to get along with	0.557	1.186	0.085	−0.140	0.073	0.040	0.061	0.049	0.073
Black easy to get along with	0.287	1.296	0.048	−0.108	0.089	0.096	0.010	−0.019	0.029
Hispanic easy to get along with	0.339	1.160	0.061	−0.112	0.043	0.030	0.013	0.044	0.020
Asian speak English well	0.090	1.201	−0.009	−0.113	0.073	0.071	−0.005	0.011	0.144

−0.159	−0.271	0.191	0.067	0.104	1.000							
0.074	−0.065	0.059	0.175	0.161	0.518	1.000						
0.032	−0.015	0.107	0.162	0.220	0.531	0.858	1.000					
−0.048	−0.093	0.139	0.019	−0.006	0.331	0.163	0.207	1.000				
0.034	−0.003	0.088	0.272	0.190	0.192	0.313	0.279	0.542	1.000			
0.002	0.041	0.072	0.179	0.210	0.281	0.297	0.406	0.569	0.715	1.000		
0.011	−0.023	0.024	−0.012	−0.058	0.324	0.199	0.188	0.295	0.248	0.257	1.000	
0.098	−0.005	0.108	0.208	0.153	0.161	0.331	0.300	0.124	0.315	0.197	0.267	1.000
0.085	0.233	0.027	0.133	0.191	0.216	0.283	0.336	0.148	0.183	0.343	0.473	0.260

1.000											
0.716	1.000										
−0.099	−0.070	1.000									
0.054	0.020	0.225	1.000								
0.025	0.079	0.196	0.686	1.000							
−0.199	−0.161	0.329	0.018	0.142	1.000						
0.044	0.017	0.035	0.261	0.236	0.379	1.000					
0.054	0.096	0.021	0.151	0.255	0.468	0.778	1.000				
−0.077	−0.033	0.227	0.184	0.279	0.280	0.134	0.178	1.000			
0.074	0.052	0.101	0.288	0.215	0.054	0.225	0.161	0.480	1.000		
0.037	0.066	0.118	0.216	0.337	0.134	0.214	0.287	0.608	0.660	1.000	
0.079	0.078	0.142	0.137	0.129	0.228	0.132	0.120	0.211	0.153	0.174	1.000

(Table continues on p. 140.)

TABLE 2A.1 Continued

White Respondents
Detroit (N = 765)

	Mean	S.D.	Correlation Matrix (Design Weighted)						
Black speak English well	0.017	1.491	−0.048	−0.269	0.055	0.021	−0.026	0.007	0.045
Hispanic speak English well	−0.168	1.183	−0.048	−0.161	0.056	0.075	−0.035	−0.060	0.095

Los Angeles
(N = 854)

	Mean	S.D.	Correlation Matrix (Design Weighted)						
Sex	0.496	0.500	1.000						
Age	44.978	15.283	−0.040	1.000					
Education	14.212	2.109	0.173	−0.103	1.000				
Native-born	0.846	0.361	0.055	0.017	0.001	1.000			
Family income	56754	42505	0.062	−0.049	0.263	−0.057	1.000		
Liberal-conservative	4.002	1.411	0.027	0.081	−0.065	0.024	−0.042	1.000	
Asian rich-poor	0.370	1.064	0.017	−0.081	−0.048	−0.001	−0.049	0.044	1.000
Black rich-poor	−1.147	1.004	−0.065	−0.074	−0.104	−0.074	−0.154	0.060	0.128
Hispanic rich-poor	−1.335	1.037	0.021	0.033	−0.007	0.003	−0.157	0.030	0.094
Asian intelligent	1.075	1.224	−0.112	−0.043	0.041	−0.013	−0.024	−0.044	0.089
Black intelligent	0.161	1.169	0.012	−0.107	0.029	0.006	−0.058	−0.166	−0.061
Hispanic intelligent	−0.016	1.262	0.098	−0.040	0.069	0.037	−0.029	−0.111	−0.022
Asian self-supporting	1.679	1.245	0.018	−0.061	0.181	−0.015	0.088	−0.018	0.079
Black self-supporting	−0.226	1.639	0.069	−0.088	0.151	0.098	0.058	−0.241	−0.056
Hispanic self-supporting	−0.005	1.632	0.179	−0.028	0.207	0.063	0.118	−0.178	−0.104
Asian easy to get along with	0.343	1.505	0.039	−0.007	0.034	−0.006	0.076	−0.014	−0.044
Black easy to get along with	0.190	1.329	0.059	−0.034	0.058	−0.056	0.062	−0.163	−0.048
Hispanic easy to get along with	0.373	1.325	0.106	−0.039	0.001	−0.145	0.076	−0.078	0.012
Asian speak English well	0.145	1.373	−0.067	0.040	0.042	0.040	0.120	0.034	−0.003
Black speak English well	0.586	1.520	0.027	−0.210	−0.073	−0.044	−0.073	−0.123	−0.002
Hispanic speak English well	−0.729	1.388	0.119	−0.056	0.024	0.054	0.024	−0.081	−0.106

Source: Multi-City Study of Urban Inequality.

0.175   0.126   0.054   0.231   0.174   0.018 0.227 0.163 0.119 0.282 0.178 0.270 1.000

0.189   0.205   0.029   0.156   0.180   0.097 0.205 0.252 0.112 0.215 0.186 0.433 0.517

```
 1.000
 0.661   1.000
-0.027  -0.073   1.000
 0.167   0.116   0.235   1.000
 0.128   0.196   0.141   0.824   1.000
-0.087  -0.099   0.231   0.075   0.036   1.000
 0.190   0.173  -0.046   0.396   0.365   0.245  1.000

 0.108   0.190  -0.030   0.278   0.347   0.300  0.758  1.000

 0.023   0.102   0.219   0.137   0.159   0.103  0.101  0.118  1.000

 0.116   0.121   0.042   0.296   0.224   0.019  0.312  0.234  0.319  1.000

 0.111   0.073   0.002   0.247   0.239   0.035  0.186  0.233  0.331  0.519  1.000

 0.027   0.030   0.167   0.141   0.115   0.192  0.163  0.112  0.292  0.098  0.055  1.000

 0.233   0.194   0.000   0.232   0.176   0.016  0.262  0.142  0.054  0.314  0.132  0.169  1.000

 0.209   0.308  -0.060   0.329   0.422  -0.057  0.355  0.346  0.174  0.272  0.247  0.287  0.447
```

TABLE 2A.2   *Means, Standard Deviations, and Correlation Matrices for Black Respondents, by City*

Black Respondents
Atlanta (N = 786)

	Mean	S.D.	Correlation Matrix (Design Weighted)						
Sex	0.433	0.496	1.000						
Age	41.689	14.158	−0.033	1.000					
Education	13.408	2.553	−0.003	−0.369	1.000				
Native-born	0.969	0.174	−0.138	0.101	−0.192	1.000			
Family income	33791	23028	0.136	−0.076	0.380	−0.149	1.000		
Liberal-conservative	3.589	1.376	0.090	−0.119	−0.058	−0.059	−0.014	1.000	
White rich-poor	0.960	1.274	−0.070	0.019	−0.044	−0.018	−0.047	−0.037	1.000
Asian rich-poor	−0.009	1.430	−0.021	−0.093	0.012	−0.025	0.087	−0.025	0.239
Hispanic rich-poor	−0.930	1.287	−0.014	0.025	−0.174	0.040	−0.138	−0.070	−0.083
White intelligent	0.467	1.640	−0.119	0.046	−0.044	0.052	−0.096	0.029	0.036
Asian intelligent	0.389	1.397	−0.026	−0.047	0.092	−0.055	−0.059	0.057	−0.081
Hispanic intelligent	0.210	1.302	−0.089	0.008	0.088	0.053	−0.072	−0.011	0.059
White self-supporting	1.300	1.552	−0.183	0.135	−0.011	0.021	−0.055	0.017	0.202
Asian self-supporting	0.949	1.487	−0.146	0.011	0.105	0.064	0.069	−0.005	0.123
Hispanic self-supporting	0.359	1.533	−0.101	0.113	0.047	0.074	−0.030	−0.054	0.025
White easy to get along with	−0.095	1.857	−0.148	0.009	0.086	−0.094	0.009	0.030	−0.042
Asian easy to get along with	−0.169	1.608	−0.019	0.071	−0.025	−0.016	0.006	0.049	−0.042
Hispanic easy to get along with	−0.011	1.477	−0.065	−0.018	0.059	0.059	0.010	−0.076	0.006
White speak English well	1.586	1.522	−0.187	0.034	0.011	−0.078	−0.025	0.005	0.217
Asian speak English well	−0.720	1.597	−0.029	0.025	0.032	0.065	−0.044	0.041	0.014
Hispanic speak English well	−0.863	1.551	−0.048	0.000	0.070	0.092	0.062	−0.004	−0.041

Boston (N = 449)

	Mean	S.D.	Correlation Matrix (Design Weighted)						
Sex	0.469	0.499	1.000						
Age	40.424	15.451	−0.060	1.000					
Education	12.448	2.720	0.111	−0.361	1.000				
Native-born	0.657	0.475	−0.135	0.202	0.003	1.000			
Family income	29992	24627	0.121	−0.022	0.356	0.024	1.000		
Liberal-conservative	3.900	1.560	−0.032	−0.138	0.035	−0.157	0.076	1.000	
White rich-poor	0.899	1.385	0.043	−0.217	0.063	−0.055	−0.101	−0.185	1.000
Asian rich-poor	−0.280	1.222	−0.017	−0.110	0.061	−0.017	−0.073	−0.279	0.257
Hispanic rich-poor	−1.080	1.359	−0.122	0.164	−0.137	0.149	−0.028	0.058	−0.263
White intelligent	0.586	1.464	−0.008	0.026	−0.033	−0.120	0.007	0.089	−0.061
Asian intelligent	0.483	1.446	−0.006	−0.104	0.053	−0.032	−0.018	−0.070	0.010
Hispanic intelligent	0.352	1.305	−0.021	−0.035	−0.053	−0.005	−0.062	0.028	0.028
White self-supporting	0.742	1.730	−0.006	−0.032	0.160	0.097	−0.005	−0.049	0.333
Asian self-supporting	0.429	1.709	−0.048	−0.056	0.288	0.155	0.082	−0.043	0.056
Hispanic self-supporting	−0.276	1.883	0.079	0.033	0.210	0.167	0.123	−0.022	0.081

1.000													
0.311	1.000												
−0.020	−0.013	1.000											
0.080	−0.048	0.449	1.000										
0.096	0.057	0.357	0.543	1.000									
−0.069	−0.168	0.211	0.148	0.096	1.000								
0.243	−0.091	0.062	0.159	0.098	0.380	1.000							
0.092	0.110	0.112	0.049	0.147	0.310	0.582	1.000						
−0.142	−0.039	0.132	0.007	−0.016	0.233	0.154	0.195	1.000					
−0.146	−0.056	0.062	0.089	0.068	0.261	0.178	0.269	0.483	1.000				
0.064	0.045	0.076	0.115	0.161	0.189	0.200	0.297	0.234	0.545	1.000			
−0.071	−0.134	0.165	0.138	0.074	0.381	0.214	0.160	0.258	0.244	0.196	1.000		
0.123	0.100	0.085	0.058	0.100	0.064	0.078	0.204	0.190	0.302	0.163	0.006	1.000	
0.131	0.151	−0.034	−0.019	0.080	−0.011	−0.012	0.109	0.082	0.049	0.161	−0.054	0.608	

1.000							
0.249	1.000						
−0.184	0.035	1.000					
0.072	−0.020	0.415	1.000				
−0.008	−0.037	0.400	0.412	1.000			
0.028	−0.099	0.115	0.043	0.087	1.000		
0.091	0.068	0.089	0.191	0.189	0.433	1.000	
0.076	0.118	0.096	0.188	0.170	0.332	0.617	1.000

(Table continues on p. 144.)

143

TABLE 2A.2 *Continued*

Black Respondents
Boston (N = 449)

	Mean	S.D.	Correlation Matrix (Design Weighted)					
White easy to get along with	0.255	1.755	−0.013	0.096	−0.009	0.110	−0.033	−0.041	0.025
Asian easy to get along with	−0.103	1.609	−0.014	0.167	0.018	0.166	0.118	−0.096	−0.092
Hispanic easy to get along with	0.084	1.540	0.023	0.075	0.084	0.336	0.079	−0.124	−0.061
White speak English well	1.580	1.573	−0.008	−0.035	−0.127	0.084	−0.115	−0.184	0.247
Asian speak English well	−0.808	1.513	−0.068	0.080	−0.029	0.079	0.037	−0.043	−0.135
Hispanic speak English well	−0.795	1.542	0.075	0.069	0.091	0.109	0.059	0.082	−0.162

Detroit (N = 696)

	Mean	S.D.	Correlation Matrix (Design Weighted)					
Sex	0.426	0.494	1.000					
Age	44.122	16.453	−0.004	1.000				
Education	12.603	2.493	−0.020	−0.421	1.000			
Native-born	0.990	0.098	−0.056	0.019	−0.044	1.000		
Family income	33617	31949	0.021	−0.178	0.504	−0.009	1.000	
Liberal-conservative	3.760	1.460	0.013	0.054	−0.040	0.009	0.084	1.000
White rich-poor	1.011	1.240	0.030	−0.109	−0.019	−0.013	−0.039	−0.080	1.000
Asian rich-poor	0.201	1.174	−0.013	−0.009	−0.015	−0.056	−0.077	−0.185	0.331
Hispanic rich-poor	−1.053	1.244	−0.010	0.102	−0.208	0.044	−0.147	0.087	−0.085
White intelligent	0.653	1.412	−0.036	0.000	0.040	0.007	0.026	−0.010	0.090
Asian intelligent	0.547	1.329	0.008	0.013	0.112	0.000	0.040	−0.065	0.103
Hispanic intelligent	0.011	1.168	−0.107	0.009	0.071	0.026	−0.003	−0.100	0.025
White self-supporting	0.901	1.537	−0.063	−0.132	0.245	0.017	0.127	−0.143	0.208
Asian self-supporting	0.846	1.440	0.052	−0.109	0.236	−0.060	0.165	−0.138	0.051
Hispanic self-supporting	0.039	1.395	−0.030	−0.056	0.164	0.005	0.173	−0.040	−0.099
White easy to get along with	−0.147	1.531	−0.042	0.086	−0.029	−0.019	0.073	0.014	−0.155
Asian easy to get along with	−0.145	1.314	−0.001	−0.048	0.007	0.001	0.079	−0.020	−0.133
Hispanic easy to get along with	0.221	1.202	−0.058	−0.044	0.043	0.029	0.022	−0.128	0.052
White speak English well	1.598	1.518	−0.086	−0.136	0.004	0.056	0.004	−0.116	0.276
Asian speak English well	−0.455	1.290	−0.039	0.009	0.030	0.019	0.067	−0.022	−0.022
Hispanic speak English well	−0.567	1.271	0.032	−0.011	−0.010	0.038	0.104	−0.023	−0.003

Los Angeles
(N = 1,106)

	Mean	S.D.	Correlation Matrix (Design Weighted)	
Sex	0.492	0.500	1.000	
Age	41.119	15.408	−0.015	1.000

−0.103 −0.028 0.146 0.073 0.149 0.404 0.147 0.168 1.000

0.122 0.069 −0.016 −0.031 0.111 0.071 0.141 0.181 0.414 1.000

0.117 0.062 0.007 0.124 0.058 0.117 0.233 0.322 0.217 0.433 1.000

0.069 −0.205 0.050 0.060 0.050 0.318 −0.056 −0.086 0.336 0.104 0.099 1.000

0.139 0.081 0.059 0.019 0.141 0.028 0.182 0.183 0.119 0.376 0.197 0.022 1.000

0.078 0.186 0.024 0.084 0.076 −0.042 0.229 0.408 0.008 0.225 0.279 −0.140 0.503

1.000
0.145 1.000
0.083 −0.135 1.000
0.181 −0.210 0.517 1.000
0.058 0.035 0.229 0.369 1.000
0.082 −0.121 0.124 0.063 −0.029 1.000
0.239 −0.087 0.073 0.232 0.110 0.515 1.000

0.006 0.136 −0.031 0.011 0.234 0.143 0.366 1.000

−0.022 0.049 0.142 0.133 0.063 −0.043 0.000 0.078 1.000

−0.168 0.085 −0.054 −0.014 0.073 −0.074 −0.017 0.162 0.491 1.000

0.046 −0.049 0.141 0.121 0.063 0.086 0.014 −0.003 0.242 0.272 1.000

0.079 −0.137 0.131 0.098 0.015 0.271 0.166 −0.115 −0.145 −0.150 0.037 1.000

−0.044 0.042 0.154 0.253 0.177 0.031 0.079 0.106 0.183 0.195 0.228 0.056 1.000

0.012 0.119 0.136 0.161 0.204 −0.055 0.024 0.238 0.180 0.169 0.187 −0.030 0.598

(Table continues on p. 146.)

TABLE 2A.2 *Continued*

Black Respondents
Los Angeles (N = 1,106)

	Mean	S.D.	Correlation Matrix (Design Weighted)						
Education	13.080	2.712	0.104	−0.132	1.000				
Native-born	0.911	0.284	−0.231	0.181	−0.175	1.000			
Family income	38843	35134	0.227	−0.071	0.438	−0.367	1.000		
Liberal-conservative	3.567	1.533	−0.012	0.069	−0.091	0.265	−0.106	1.000	
White rich-poor	1.029	1.319	−0.143	−0.092	−0.056	0.210	−0.178	0.008	1.000
Asian rich-poor	0.801	1.367	−0.105	−0.127	−0.102	0.161	−0.179	−0.001	0.595
Hispanic rich-poor	−1.180	1.387	0.119	−0.052	0.054	−0.262	0.238	−0.059	−0.259
White intelligent	0.608	1.363	−0.036	0.036	0.042	−0.190	0.053	−0.053	−0.077
Asian intelligent	0.719	1.386	−0.011	−0.020	0.122	−0.111	0.116	−0.079	−0.061
Hispanic intelligent	0.143	1.249	0.027	−0.031	0.052	−0.234	0.155	−0.082	−0.118
White self-supporting	1.046	1.463	−0.075	0.032	0.028	0.084	−0.117	0.047	0.221
Asian self-supporting	1.192	1.453	−0.049	−0.063	0.169	0.087	−0.036	−0.034	0.238
Hispanic self-supporting	−0.209	1.600	−0.030	0.106	0.054	0.066	0.006	−0.077	0.024
White easy to get along with	0.082	1.770	0.070	0.060	0.129	−0.113	0.140	−0.025	−0.239
Asian easy to get along with	−0.320	1.762	0.019	0.083	0.122	0.089	0.012	−0.036	−0.111
Hispanic easy to get along with	0.620	1.573	0.023	−0.087	0.013	−0.056	0.006	−0.073	0.000
White speak English well	2.016	1.254	0.014	−0.188	−0.130	0.056	−0.082	0.023	0.226
Asian speak English well	−0.750	1.448	0.090	−0.007	0.206	−0.169	0.185	−0.153	−0.086
Hispanic speak English well	−0.764	1.601	0.165	−0.134	0.225	−0.120	0.228	−0.130	−0.173

Source: Multi-City Study of Urban Inequality.

1.000													
−0.199	1.000												
−0.090	0.109	1.000											
−0.015	0.075	0.635	1.000										
−0.131	0.201	0.305	0.383	1.000									
0.080	−0.123	0.152	0.089	−0.071	1.000								
0.260	−0.110	0.060	0.108	−0.054	0.600	1.000							
0.022	−0.007	−0.034	−0.001	0.070	0.230	0.300	1.000						
−0.149	0.101	0.220	0.095	0.036	0.038	−0.016	0.137	1.000					
−0.184	−0.059	0.104	0.070	0.053	0.117	0.079	0.229	0.617	1.000				
0.085	−0.047	0.151	0.172	0.149	0.077	0.112	0.179	0.304	0.287	1.000			
0.216	−0.051	0.111	0.095	0.004	0.245	0.233	−0.033	−0.034	−0.007	0.180	1.000		
−0.210	0.174	0.122	0.102	0.161	0.019	0.063	0.148	0.300	0.399	0.060	−0.028	1.000	
−0.115	0.268	0.033	0.032	0.165	0.041	0.131	0.334	0.116	0.183	0.245	0.028	0.375	

TABLE 2A.3 *Means, Standard Deviations, and Correlation Matrices for Hispanic Respondents, by City*

Hispanic Respondents
Boston (N = 678)

	Mean	S.D.	Correlation Matrix (Design Weighted)						
Sex	0.472	0.499	1.000						
Age	37.02	13.31	−0.009	1.000					
Education	10.60	3.51	−0.221	−0.257	1.000				
Native-born	0.539	0.498	−0.022	−0.064	−0.056	1.000			
Family income	27423	17730		−0.129	0.161	−0.029	1.000		
Liberal-conservative	4.185	1.481	−0.144	−0.047	0.011	0.011	−0.017	1.000	
White rich-poor	0.551	1.389	−0.220	−0.085	−0.118	0.109	0.053	0.292	1.000
Asian rich-poor	−0.868	1.413	−0.066	0.041	−0.011	−0.178	−0.215	−0.084	−0.033
Black rich-poor	−1.477	1.300	0.046	0.094	−0.204	−0.045	−0.241	−0.067	−0.036
White intelligent	0.830	1.666	−0.109	−0.184	0.065	0.179	0.097	0.172	0.089
Asian intelligent	0.795	1.575	−0.179	0.030	0.143	−0.019	0.026	0.212	−0.053
Black intelligent	0.236	1.466	−0.177	−0.049	−0.003	0.111	0.053	0.245	0.066
White self-supporting	0.370	1.952	0.185	0.041	−0.048	−0.153	−0.093	−0.083	0.058
Asian self-supporting	−0.040	1.813	0.010	0.114	0.144	−0.251	−0.268	−0.247	−0.314
Black self-supporting	−1.216	1.599	0.024	0.226	0.000	0.033	−0.218	−0.085	−0.076
White easy to get along with	−0.042	2.027	0.159	0.058	0.049	−0.153	−0.040	−0.069	0.098
Asian easy to get along with	−0.357	1.478	−0.064	−0.027	0.221	−0.141	−0.022	−0.069	−0.148
Black easy to get along with	−0.195	1.890	−0.212	−0.056	0.087	0.229	0.014	0.331	0.229
White speak English well	2.019	1.538	0.109	−0.240	−0.015	0.277	−0.028	0.085	0.195
Asian speak English well	−0.395	1.588	0.138	−0.184	0.034	−0.257	−0.118	0.037	−0.225
Black speak English well	1.020	1.973	−0.070	−0.227	−0.039	0.195	−0.075	0.048	0.202

Los Angeles
(N = 992)

	Mean	S.D.	Correlation Matrix (Design Weighted)						
Sex	0.503	0.500	1.000						
Age	37.10	12.83	−0.082	1.000					
Education	10.13	4.05	0.067	−0.189	1.000				
Native-born	0.269	0.444	0.042	0.064	0.355	1.000			
Family income	27604	22543	0.065	−0.051	0.396	0.368	1.000		
Liberal-conservative	4.055	1.300	−0.037	0.093	−0.020	−0.043	0.042	1.000	
White rich-poor	1.368	1.325	0.007	−0.146	−0.179	−0.204	−0.175	−0.104	1.000
Asian rich-poor	0.964	1.349	−0.033	−0.174	−0.013	−0.052	−0.032	−0.023	0.456
Black rich-poor	−0.956	1.257	−0.085	−0.054	−0.144	−0.035	−0.047	−0.044	−0.025
White intelligent	0.925	1.534	−0.079	0.049	−0.125	−0.168	−0.092	0.011	0.114
Asian intelligent	1.114	1.553	−0.070	−0.023	0.072	−0.072	0.022	−0.068	0.018
Black intelligent	0.074	1.325	−0.061	0.036	0.033	−0.024	−0.036	−0.006	−0.062
White self-supporting	1.068	1.678	−0.024	0.018	0.008	0.061	0.060	0.085	0.169
Asian self-supporting	1.155	1.578	0.005	−0.018	0.083	0.076	0.057	0.045	0.126
Black self-supporting	−1.393	1.490	−0.041	0.111	0.050	0.201	0.093	0.027	−0.118

1.000												
0.525	1.000											
−0.144	−0.035	1.000										
−0.109	−0.181	0.397	1.000									
−0.175	−0.126	0.348	0.530	1.000								
0.332	0.202	−0.260	−0.247	−0.424	1.000							
0.513	0.352	−0.084	−0.090	−0.059	0.193	1.000						
0.319	0.421	−0.215	−0.120	−0.096	0.274	0.303	1.000					
0.117	0.053	−0.250	−0.237	−0.394	0.586	0.035	0.221	1.000				
0.208	0.145	−0.089	−0.133	−0.159	0.132	0.341	0.158	0.252	1.000			
−0.075	0.048	0.211	0.263	0.486	−0.179	−0.056	−0.019	−0.079	0.033	1.000		
−0.181	−0.068	0.139	−0.053	0.045	0.125	−0.194	−0.129	0.162	−0.205	0.195	1.000	
0.362	0.206	−0.089	−0.002	0.046	0.234	0.398	0.108	0.073	0.350	0.012	0.016	1.000
−0.101	0.001	−0.017	0.109	0.228	−0.103	−0.147	−0.080	−0.027	−0.076	0.293	0.533	0.108

1.000							
−0.029	1.000						
−0.086	0.016	1.000					
0.132	−0.054	0.497	1.000				
−0.037	0.101	0.281	0.231	1.000			
0.119	−0.091	0.067	0.076	−0.101	1.000		
0.244	−0.017	−0.002	0.118	0.028	0.463	1.000	
−0.146	0.137	0.066	−0.043	0.147	0.071	0.072	1.000

(Table continues on p. 150.)

TABLE 2A.3   *Continued*

Hispanic Respondents
Los Angeles
(N = 992)

	Mean	S.D.	Correlation Matrix (Design Weighted)						
White easy to get along with	0.393	1.950	0.020	0.019	0.071	0.026	0.065	0.120	−0.099
Asian easy to get along with	−0.097	1.660	0.069	−0.022	0.108	0.026	0.113	0.108	−0.178
Black easy to get along with	−0.284	1.711	0.086	0.059	0.152	0.216	0.152	0.030	−0.122
White speak English well	2.441	1.209	−0.031	−0.170	−0.072	−0.085	−0.074	−0.073	0.235
Asian speak English well	−0.090	1.555	0.054	−0.020	−0.139	−0.212	−0.070	0.104	0.006
Black speak English well	1.195	1.700	0.076	−0.157	−0.161	−0.160	−0.146	−0.091	0.201

Source: Multi-City Study of Urban Inequality.

−0.077	0.072	0.066	0.049	0.012	0.060	0.021	−0.077	1.000				
−0.076	0.030	0.059	0.161	0.173	0.020	0.093	0.038	0.416	1.000			
−0.002	0.032	0.019	0.074	0.165	−0.032	0.022	0.156	0.133	0.323	1.000		
0.242	−0.039	0.134	0.137	−0.023	0.168	0.108	−0.192	0.096	−0.038	−0.048	1.000	
−0.031	0.146	0.083	0.046	0.105	0.015	−0.035	0.113	−0.020	0.226	0.019	0.011	1.000
0.139	0.124	0.074	0.094	0.090	0.047	0.074	−0.026	0.020	−0.028	0.027	0.427	0.205

Notes

1. Since our interest is to compare stereotypes across cities, we do not examine the data for the Multi-City Study Asian respondents. Only one city, Los Angeles, had enough Asian respondents to perform meaningful multivariate analyses. Lawrence Bobo and Devon Johnson (2000) provide a comprehensive analysis of these data.

2. The additional traits of "involved in drugs and gangs/not involved in drugs and gangs" and "treat members of other groups equally/discriminate against members of other groups" were also asked in three of the cities (Atlanta, Boston, and Los Angeles). Since we are interested in maximizing across city comparisons, we restrict attention to those trait-rating items available in all four cities.

3. Very few respondents refused to perform the rating task and offered judgments quite readily. We examined the relative frequency of "don't know" responses for each trait by each target group in each city (eighty trials each for the black and white respondent groups). Among blacks and whites we found the relative frequency of "don't know" response was 5 percent or lower in sixty trials. "Don't-know" responses occurred at a rate of 10 percent or higher in only five trials among whites, never exceeding 11 percent, and at a rate of 10 percent or higher in nine trials among blacks, never exceeding 15 percent. Hispanic respondents in Boston and Los Angeles also rarely used the "don't know" option. The relative frequency of this response was 5 percent or less in thirty-six out of forty trials and never exceeded 11 percent. Whites, blacks, and Hispanics alike most readily rated their own group; the rates of "don't know" responses were slightly higher when these groups were asked to rate other groups. Whites, blacks, and Hispanics all were most reluctant to judge Asians. Based on these results, we assigned "don't know" responses the same score (0) as a neutral rating. We also sought to determine whether images of the groups were associated with gender. Images common in today's media and mass culture frequently portray gang members as young black males and welfare recipients as black females (Entman and Rojecki 2000; Gilens 1999). To do this, we randomly assigned respondents, via a survey-based experimental manipulation (Schuman and Bobo 1988), the task of rating the group as a whole (whites, blacks, Hispanics, and Asians), rating males in each group, or rating females in each group. Analysis of variance in the experimental groups showed no strong or consistent differences in ratings due to gender of the target group, so we combined responses from the experimental forms for the analysis that follows.

4. Other analyses of these data (for example, Bobo and Johnson 2000; Charles 2000a, 2000b; Massagli 2000) rely on computing differences

between respondent's rating of own group and each outgroup. These measures of relative differences do not yield substantially different conclusions regarding the relative ranking of out-groups or the relationship among out-group ratings within a city, but lend themselves less well to a straightforward description of group and city differences in respondents' use of stereotypes.

5. This analysis method yields maximum likelihood estimates when the data are multivariate normal, an assumption that is most unlikely to hold given the complex sample design used in the Multi-City Study surveys. However, we use design-wrighted correlations which yield unbiased estimates of the covariation among trait ratings.

6. The L^2 statistic is affected by the sample size, which is somewhat problematic in the analysis of data obtained under complex sample designs. The correlations have been estimated using design-based weights, which take account of differential probabilities of selection and reproduce the estimated population size. For the production of likelihood ratio statistics we assume the observed sample size, or else we would seriously overestimate the importance of deviations between the fitted and observed correlations which could be reduced only by fitting relatively complex models. However, because the sampling scheme involved clustering of interviews by residential area, the observed sample is likely to be somewhat less efficient than a random sample of the same size. Effectively, standard errors of estimates that assume the observed sample size are likely too small (and t-tests are too large). Estimates of standard errors may effectively be inflated (t-tests deflated) by decreasing the effective sample size consistent with the assumed design effect. However, there is no simple correction that can be applied to the test statistics, as the design effect will vary by variable and by sampled stratum (Kish 1987). But the same action (decreasing the sample size) that reduces the potential bias in standard errors also increases the likelihood of acceptable goodness of fit with more degrees of freedom. Under the circumstances, we thought it best to assume the observed sample size in the calculation of goodness of fit and other test statistics, and to emphasize relative improvement in fit through the introduction of classes of parameters rather than specific parameters.

7. It is possible with structural equation models to perform a formal statistical test, using multiple group comparisons, for the equivalence of factor structures As a result of the very large sample sizes we are working with here, we decided to rely on more substantive assessment of the patterns (rather than purely statistical grounds) for judging similarity of the underlying factor structures.

8. In terms of the labor market, A. Silvia Cancio, T. David Evans, and David Maume (1996), Maume, Cancio, and Evans (1996), and perhaps especially Kenneth Arrow (1998) and William Darity and Patrick Mason (1998) make clear the empirical and conceptual weaknesses of a socially uprooted, "variable analysis" version of the "skills" argument. In terms of the housing market and fear of crime hypothesis, Camille Zubrinsky Charles (2000a and this volume) provides an equally trenchant rejoinder.

References

Adorno, Theodore, Elsie Frenkel-Brunswick, Daniel J. Levinson, and R. Nevitt Sanford. 1950. *The Authoritarian Personality.* New York: Norton.

Allport, Gordon W. 1954. *The Nature of Prejudice.* Garden City, N.Y.: Doubleday.

Altemeyer, Bob. 1988. *Enemies of Freedom: Understanding Right-Wing Authoritarianism.* San Francisco, Calif.: Jossey-Bass.

Arrow, Kenneth J. 1998. "What Has Economics to Say About Racial Discrimination?" *Journal of Economic Perspectives* 12: 91–100.

Ashmore, Richard D., and Frances K. Del Boca. 1981. "Conceptual Approaches to Stereotypes and Stereotyping." In *Cognitive Processes in Stereotyping and Intergroup Behavior*, edited by D. L. Hamilton. Hillsdale, N.J.: Lawrence Erlbaum.

Bean, Frank D., and Stephanie Bell-Rose. 1999. "Immigration and Its Relation to Race and Ethnicity in the United States." In *Immigration and Opportunity: Race, Ethnicity, and Employment in the United States*, edited by Frank D. Bean and Stephanie Bell-Rose. New York: Russell Sage Foundation.

Blumer, Herbert. 1958. "Race Prejudice as a Sense of Group Position." *Pacific Sociological Review* 1: 3–7.

Bobo, Lawrence. 1983. "Whites' Opposition to Busing: Symbolic Racism or Realistic Group Conflict?" *Journal of Personality and Social Psychology* 45(6): 1196–1210.

Bobo, Lawrence D. 1999. "Prejudice as Group Position: Microfoundations of a Sociological Approach to Racism and Race Relations." *Journal of Social Issues* 55: 445–72.

———. 2000a. "Racial Attitudes and Relations at the Close of the Twentieth Century." In *America Becoming: Racial Trends and Their Implications*, vol. 1, edited by Neil Smelser, William J. Wilson, and Faith N. Mitchell. Washington, D.C.: National Academy Press.

———. 2000b. "Reclaiming a Du Boisian Perspective on Racial Attitudes." *Annals of the American Academy of Political and Social Science* 568: 186–202.

Bobo, Lawrence D., and Vincent L. Hutchings. 1996. "Perceptions of Racial Group Competition: Extending Blumer's Theory of Group Position to a Multiracial Social Context." *American Sociological Review* 61: 951–72.

Bobo, Lawrence D., and Devon Johnson. 2000 "Racial Attitudes in a Prismatic Metropolis: Mapping Identity, Stereotypes, Competition, and Views on Affirmative Action." In *Prismatic Metropolis: Inequality in Los Angeles*, edited by Lawrence D. Bobo, Melvin L. Oliver, James H. Johnson, and Abel Valenzuela. New York: Russell Sage Foundation.

Bobo, Lawrence, James H. Johnson, and Melvin L. Oliver. 1992. "Stereotyping and the Multicity Survey: Notes on Measurement, Determinants, and Effects." Occasional working paper, vol. 2, no. 8 (July) Center for the Study of Urban Poverty, University of California, Los Angeles.

Bobo, Lawrence, Devon Johnson, and Susan A. Suh. 2000. "Racial Attitudes and Power in the Workplace: Do the 'Haves' Differ from the 'Have-Nots?'" In *Prismatic Metropolis: Inequality in Los Angeles*, edited by Lawrence D. Bobo, Melvin L. Oliver, James H. Johnson, and Abel Valenzuela. New York: Russell Sage Foundation.

Bobo, Lawrence D., and James R. Kluegel. 1993. "Opposition to Race-Targeting: Self-Interest, Stratification Ideology, or Racial Attitudes?" *American Sociological Review* 58: 443–64.

———. 1997. "Status, Ideology and Dimensions of Whites' Racial Beliefs and Attitudes: Progress and Stagnation." In *Racial Attitudes in the 1990s: Continuity and Change*, edited by Steven A. Tuch and Jack K. Martin. New York: Praeger.

Bobo, Lawrence D., and Camille L. Zubrinsky. 1996. "Attitudes on Residential Integration: Perceived Status Differences, Mere In-group Preference, or Racial Prejudice?" *Social Forces* 74: 883–909.

Bobo, Lawrence D., Camille L. Zubrinsky, James H. Johnson, and Melvin L. Oliver. 1995. "Work Orientation, Job Discrimination, and Ethnicity: A Focus Group Perspective." *Research in the Sociology of Work* 5: 45–86.

Bodenhausen, Galen C., Neil Macrae, and Jennifer Garst. 1998. "Stereotypes in Thought and Deed: Social Cognitive Origins of Intergroup Discrimination." In *Intergroup Cognition and Intergroup Behaviors*, edited by Constantine Sedikides, John Schopler, and Chester A. Insko. Mahwah, N.J.: Erlbaum.

Bonilla-Silva, Eduardo, 1997. "Re-Thinking Racism: Toward a Structural Interpretation." *American Sociological Review* 62: 465–80.

Brown, Rupert. 1995. *Prejudice: Its Social Psychology*. New York: Blackwell.

Browne, Irene, and Ivy Kennelly. 1999. "Stereotypes and Realities: Images of Black Women in the Labor Market." In *Latinas and African American Women at Work*, edited by Irene Browne. New York: Russell Sage Foundation.

Cancio, A. Silvia, T. David Evans, and David J. Maume. 1996. "Reconsidering the Declining Significance of Race: Racial Differences in Early Career Wages." *American Sociological Review* 61: 541–56.

Charles, Camille Zubrinsky. 2000a. "Neighborhood Racial-Composition Preferences: Evidence from a Multiethnic Metropolis." *Social Problems* 47: 379–407.

———. 2000b. "Residential Segregation in Los Angeles." In *Prismatic Metropolis: Inequality in Los Angeles*, edited by Lawrence D. Bobo, Melvin L. Oliver, James H. Johnson, and Abel Valenzuela. New York: Russell Sage Foundation.

Chavez, Leo. 1997. "Immigration Reform and Nativism: The Nationalist Response to Transnationalist Challenge." In *Immigrants Out: The New Nativism and the Anti-Immigrant Impulse in the United States*, edited by Jan F. Perea. New York: New York University Press.

Clark, Kenneth B. 1965. *Dark Ghetto: Dilemmas of Social Power*. New York: Harper & Row.

Cummings, Scott. 1998. *Left Behind in Rosedale: Race Relations and the Collapse of Community Institutions*. Boulder, Colo.: Westview Press.

Darity, William A., and Patrick L. Mason. 1998. "Evidence on Discrimination in Employment; Codes of Color, Codes of Gender." *Journal of Economic Perspectives* 12: 63–90.

Dawson, Michael C. 2000. "Slowly Coming to Grips with the Effects of the American Racial Order on American Policy Preferences." In *Racialized Politics: The Debate on Racism in America*, edited by David O. Sears, Jim Sidanius, and Lawrence Bobo. Chicago: University of Chicago Press.

Devine, Patricia G. 1989. "Stereotypes and Prejudice: Their Automatic and Controlled Components." *Journal of Personality and Social Psychology* 60: 817–30.

Devine, Patricia G., and Andrew J. Elliot. 1995. "Are Stereotypes Really Fading?: The Princeton Trilogy Revisited." *Personality and Social Psychology Bulletin* 21: 1139–50.

Drake, St. Clair, and Horace R. Cayton. 1945. *Black Metropolis: A Study of Negro Life in a Northern City*. Chicago: University of Chicago Press.

DuBois, W. E. B. 1996 (1899). *The Philadelphia Negro: A Social Study*. Philadelphia: University of Pennsylvania Press.

Duckitt, John. 1992. *The Social Psychology of Prejudice*. New York: Praeger.

Ellison, Christopher G., and Daniel A. Powers. 1994. "The Contact Hypothesis and Racial Attitudes Among Black Americans." *Social Science Quarterly* 75: 385–400.

Entman, Robert M., and Andrew Rojecki. 2000. *The Black Image in White Minds: Media and Race in America*. Chicago: University of Chicago Press.

Farkas, George, and Keven Vicknair. 1996. "Appropriate Tests of Racial Wage Discrimination Require Controls for Cognitive Skill: Comment on Cancio, Evans, and Maume." *American Sociological Review* 61: 557–60.

Farley, Reynolds, Charlotte G. Steeh, Maria Krysan, Tara Jackson, and

Keith Reeves, 1994. "Stereotypes and Segregation: Neighborhoods in the Detroit Area." *American Journal of Sociology* 100: 750–80.

Feagin, Joe R., and Melvin P. Sikes. 1994. *Living with Racism: The Black Middle Class Experience*. Boston: Beacon Press.

Fiske, Susan T. 1998. "Stereotyping, Prejudice, and Discrimination." In *Handbook of Social Psychology, 4th ed*, vol. 2, edited by Danel Gilbert, Susan T. Fiske, and Gardner Lindzey. New York: McGraw-Hill.

Fossett, Mark A., and K. Jill Kiecolt. 1989. "The Relative Size of Minority Populations and White Racial Attitudes." *Social Science Quarterly* 70: 820–35.

Fredrickson, George M. 1999. "Models of American Ethnic Relations: A Historical Perspective." In *Cultural Divides: Understanding and Overcoming Group Conflict*, edited by Deborah A. Prentice and Dale T. Miller. New York: Russell Sage Foundation.

Gans, Herbert J. 1999. "The Possibility of a New Racial Hierarchy in the Twenty-first Century United States." In *The Cultural Territories of Race: Black and White Boundaries*, edited by Michèle Lamont. New York and Cambridge: Russell Sage and Harvard University Press.

Gilens, Martin I. 1999. *Why Americans Hate Welfare: Race, Media, and the Politics of Antipoverty Policy*. Chicago: University of Chicago Press.

Gilliam, Franklin D., and Shanto Iyengar. 2000. "Prime Suspects: The Influence of Local Television News on the Viewing Public." *American Journal of Political Science* 44: 560–73.

Glaser, James M. 1994. "Back to the Black Belt: Racial Environment and White Racial Attitudes in the South." *Journal of Politics* 56: 21–41.

Hamilton, David, and Tina K. Trolier. 1986. "Stereotypes and Stereotyping: An Overview of the Cognitive Approach." In *Prejudice, Discrimination, and Racism*, edited by John Dovidio and Samuel Gaertner. New York: Academic Press.

Harris, David R. 1999. "'Property Values Drop When Blacks Move in Because . . .': Racial and Socioeconomic Determinants of Neighborhood Desirability." *American Sociological Review* 64: 461–79.

Harrison, Roderick J., and Claudine E. Bennett. 1995. "Racial and Ethnic Diversity." In *State of the Union, Social Trends: American in the 1990s*, vol. 2, edited by Reynolds Farley. New York: Russell Sage Foundation.

Hochschild, Jennifer L. 1995. *Facing Up the American Dream: Race, Class, and the Soul of the Nation*. Princeton, N.J.: Princeton University Press.

Holzer, Harry. 1996. *What Employers Want: Job Prospects for Less-Educated Workers*. New York: Russell Sage Foundation.

Hurwitz, Jon, and Mark Peffley. 1997. "Public Perceptions of Race and Crime: The Role of Racial Stereotypes." *American Journal of Political Science* 41: 375–401.

Jackman, Mary R. 1977. "Prejudice, Tolerance, and Attitudes Toward Ethnic Groups." *Social Science Research* 6: 145–69.

———. 1994. *The Velvet Glove: Paternalism and Conflict in Gender, Class, and Race Relations*. Berkeley: University of California Press.

Jankowski, Martin Sanchez. 1995. "The Rising Significance of Status in U.S. Race Relations. In *The Bubbling Cauldron: Race, Ethnicity, and the Urban Crisis*, edited by Michael P. Smith and Joe R. Feagin. Minneapolis: University of Minnesota Press.

Johnson, James H., Jr., Walter C. Farrell Jr., and Melvin L. Oliver. 1993. "Seeds of the Los Angeles Rebellion." *International Journal of Urban and Regional Research* 17(1): 115–19.

Johnson, James H., Jr., Melvin L. Oliver, and Walter C. Farrell. 1992. "The Los Angeles Rebellion: A Retrospective View." *Economic Development Quarterly* 6: 356–72.

Jöreskog, Karl G., and Dag Sörbom. 1989. *LISREL 7: A Guide to the Program and Applications, 2d ed.* Chicago: SPSS, Inc.

Jost, John T., and Mahzarin R. Banaji. 1994. "The Role of Stereotyping in System-Justification and the Production of False Consciousness." *British Journal of Social Psychology* 33: 1–27.

Katz, Daniel, and K. W. Braly. 1933. "Racial Stereotypes of 100 College Students." *Journal of Abnormal Social Psychology* 28: 280–90.

Kennelly, Ivy. 1999. "'That Single-Mother Element': How White Employers Typify Black Women." *Gender and Society* 13: 168–92.

Kinder, Donald R., and Tali Mendelberg. 1995. "Cracks in American Apartheid: The Political Impact of Prejudice Among Desegregated Whites." *Journal of Politics* 57: 402–24.

Kinder, Donald R., and Lynn M. Sanders. 1996. *Divided by Color: Racial Politics and Democratic Ideals*. Chicago: University of Chicago Press.

Kinder, Donald R., and Howard Schuman. Forthcoming. "Racial Attitudes: Developments and Divisions in Survey Research." In *A Telescope on Society: Survey Research and Social Science in the 20th and 21st Centuries*, edited by James House, F. Thomas Juster, Robert Kahn, Howard Schuman and Eleanor Singer. Ann Arbor: University of Michigan Survey Research Center, Institute for Social Research.

Kirschenman, Joleen, and Kathryn M. Neckerman. 1991. "'We'd Love to Hire Them, But . . . ': The Meaning of Race for Employers." In *The Urban Underclass*, edited by Christopher Jencks and Paul Peterson. Washington, D.C.: Brookings Institution.

Kish, Leslie. 1987. *Statistical Design for Research*. New York: Wiley.

Kleinpenning, Gerard, and Louk Hagendoorn. 1993. "Forms of Racism and the Cumulative Dimension of Ethnic Attitudes." *Social Psychology Quarterly* 56: 21–36.

Kluegel, James R., and Eliot R. Smith. 1986. *Beliefs About Inequality: American's Views of What Is and What Ought to Be*. New York: Aldine de Gruyter.

Krysan, Maria. 2000. "Prejudice, Politics and Public Opinion: Understanding the Sources of Racial Policy Attitudes." *Annual Review of Sociology* 26: 135–68.

Levine, Jeffrey, Edward G. Carmines, and Paul M. Sniderman. 1999.

"The Empirical Dimensionality of Racial Stereotypes." *Public Opinion Quarterly* 63: 371–84.

Lieberson, Stanley. 1985. "Stereotypes: Their Consequences for Race and Ethnic Interaction." *Research in Race and Ethnic Relations* 4: 113–37.

Lippman, Walter. 1922. *Public Opinion*. New York: Macmillan.

Massagli, Michael P. 2000. "What Do Boston Area Residents Think of One Another?" In *The Boston Renaissance: Race, Space, and Economic Change in an American Metropolis*, edited by Barry Bluestone and Mary Huff Stevenson. New York: Russell Sage Foundation.

Massey, Douglas S., and Nancy A. Denton. 1993. *American Apartheid: Segregation and the Making of the Underclass*. Cambridge, Mass.: Harvard University Press.

Maume, David J., A. Silvia Cancio, and T. David Evans. 1996. "Cognitive Skills and Racial Wage Inequality: Reply to Farkas and Vicknair." *American Sociological Review* 61: 561–64.

McConahay, John B. 1983. "Modern Racism and Modern Discrimination: The Effects of Race, Racial Attitudes, and Context on Simulated Hiring Decisions." *Personality and Social Psychology Bulletin* 9(4): 551–58.

Meertens, Roel W., and Thomas F. Pettigrew. 1997. "Is Subtle Prejudice Really Prejudice?" *Public Opinion Quarterly* 61: 54–71.

Miller, Shazia Rafiullah, and James E. Rosenbaum. 1997. "Hiring in a Hobbesian World: Social Infrastructure and Employers' Use of Information." *Work and Occupations* 24: 498–523.

Moss, Philip, and Chris Tilly. 1995. "Skills and Race in Hiring: Quantitative Findings from Face-to-Face Interviews." *Eastern Economic Journal* 21: 357–74.

———. 1996. "'Soft' Skills and Race: An Investigation of Black Men's Employment Problems." *Work and Occupations* 23: 252–76.

Myrdal, Gunnar. 1944. *An American Dilemma: The Negro Problem and Modern Democracy*. New York: Random House.

Neckerman, Kathryn M., and Joleen Kirschenman. 1993. "Hiring Strategies, Racial Bias, and Inner-City Workers." *Social Problems* 38: 433–47.

O'Connor, Alice. 2000. "Poverty Research and Policy for the Post-Welfare Era." *Annual Review of Sociology* 26: 547–62.

Oliver, J. Eric, and Tali Mendelberg. 2000. "Reconsidering the Environmental Determinants of White Racial Attitudes." *American Journal of Political Science* 44: 574–89.

Oliver, Melvin L., and Thomas M. Shapiro. 1995. *Black Wealth/White Wealth: A New Perspective on Racial Inequality*. New York: Routledge.

Ortiz, Vilma. 1996. "The Mexican-Origin Population: Permanent Working Class or Emerging Middle Class?" In *Ethnic Los Angeles*, edited by Rodger Waldinger and Mehdi Bozorgmehr. New York: Russell Sage Foundation.

Peffley, Mark, and Jon Hurwitz. 1998. "Whites' Stereotypes of Blacks: Sources and Political Consequences." In *Perception and Prejudice: Race and Politics in the United States*, edited by Jon Hurwitz and Mark Peffley. New Haven, Conn.: Yale University Press.

Pettigrew, Thomas F. 1998. "Reactions Toward the New Minorities of Western Europe." *Annual Review of Sociology* 24: 77–103.

Pettigrew, Thomas F., James S. Jackson, Jeanne Ben Brika, Gerar Lemaine, Roel W. Meertens, and Ulrich Wagner. 1998. "Outgroup Prejudice in Western Europe." *European Review of Social Psychology* 8: 241–73.

Pettigrew, Thomas F., and Roel W. Meertens. 1995. "Subtle and Blatant Prejudice in Western Europe." *European Journal of Social Psychology* 25: 57–75.

Quillian, Lincoln. 1996. "Group Threat and Regional Change in Attitudes Toward African Americans." *American Journal of Sociology* 102: 816–60.

Reskin, Barbara F. 2000. "The Proximate Causes of Employment Discrimination." *Contemporary Sociology* 29: 319–28.

———. Forthcoming. "Employment Discrimination and Its Remedies." In *Handbook on Labor Market Research*, edited by I. Berg and Arne Kalleberg. New York: Plenum.

Sachdev, Itesh, and Richard Y. Bourhis. 1987. "Status Differences and Intergroup Behavior." *European Journal of Social Psychology* 17: 277–93.

———. 1991. "Power and Status Differences in Minority and Majority Group Relations." *European Journal of Social Psychology* 21: 1–24.

Sanjek, Roger. 1994. "The Enduring Inequalities of Race." In *Race*, edited by Steven Gregory and Roger Sanjek. New Brunswick, N.J.: Rutgers University Press.

Schuman, Howard. 1995. "Attitudes, Beliefs, and Behavior." In *Sociological Perspectives on Social Psychology*, edited by Karen Cook, G. A. Fine, and James S. House. Boston; Allyn & Bacon.

Schuman, Howard, and Lawrence Bobo. 1988. "Survey-based Experiments on White Racial Attitudes Toward Residential Integration." *American Journal of Sociology* 94: 273–99.

Schuman, Howard, Charlotte Steeh, Lawrence D. Bobo, and Maria Krysan. 1997. *Racial Attitudes in America: Trends and Interpretations*. Cambridge, Mass.: Harvard University Press.

Sears, David O., Jack Citrin, Sharmaine V. Cheleden, and Collette van Laar. 1999. "Cultural Diversity and Multicultural Politics: Is Ethnic Balkanization Psychologically Inevitable?" In *Cultural Divides: Understanding and Overcoming Group Conflict*, edited by Deborah A. Prentice, and Dale T. Miller. New York: Russell Sage Foundation.

Sears, David O., John Hetts, Jim Sidanius, and Lawrence Bobo. 2000. "Race in American Politics: Framing the Debates." In *Racialized Politics: The Debate on Racism in America*. Chicago: University of Chicago Press.

See, Katherine O'Sullivan, and William Julius Wilson. 1989. "Race and Ethnicity." In *Handbook of Sociology*, edited by Neil J. Smelser. Beverly Hills, Calif.: Sage.

Sidanius, Jim, and Felicia Pratto. 1999. *Social Dominance: An Intergroup Theory of Social Hierarchy and Oppression*. New York: Cambridge University Press.

Sigelman, Lee, James W. Shockey, and Carol K. Sigelman. 1993. "Ethnic Stereotyping: A Black-White Comparison." In *Prejudice, Politics, and the American Dilemma*, edited by Paul M. Sniderman, Philip E. Tetlock, and Edward G. Carmines. Stanford, Calif.: Stanford University Press.

Sigelman, Lee, and Steven A. Tuch. 1997. "Metastereotypes: Blacks' Perceptions of Whites' Stereotypes of Blacks." *Public Opinion Quarterly* 61: 87–101.

Smith, Ryan A. 1997. "Race, Income, and Authority at Work: A Cross-Temporal Analysis of Black and White Men, 1972–1994." *Social Problems* 40: 328–42.

———. 1999. "Racial Differences in Access to Hierarchical Authority: An Analysis of Change over Time, 1972–1994." *Sociological Quarterly* 40: 367–95.

Smith, Tom W. 1991. *Ethnic Images*. General Social Survey technical report, no. 19. Chicago: University of Chicago, National Opinion Research Center.

Sniderman, Paul M., and Edward G. Carmines. 1997. *Reaching Beyond Race*. Cambridge, Mass.: Harvard University Press.

Sörbom, Dag, and Karl G. Jöreskog. 1981. "The Use of LISREL in Sociological Model Building." In *Factor Analysis and Measurement in Sociological Research*, edited by David J. Jackson and Edgar F. Borgatta. Beverly Hills, Calif. Sage Publications.

Stephan, Walter G. 1985. "Intergroup Relations." In *Handbook of Social Psychology, 3d ed.*, edited by Gardner A. Lindzey and Elliott Aronson. Hillsdale, N.J.: Erlbaum.

Stephan, Walter G., and David Rosenfield. 1982. "Racial and Ethnic Stereotypes." In *In the Eye of the Beholder: Contemporary Issues in Stereotyping*, edited by Arthur G. Miller. New York: Praeger.

Sumner, William Graham. 1940 (1906). *Folkways*. New York: Arno Press.

Taylor, Marylee C. 1998. "How White Attitudes Vary with the Racial Composition of Local Populations: Number Count." *American Sociological Review* 63: 512–35.

———. 2000. "The Significance of Racial Context." In *Racialized Politics: The Debate on Racism in America*, edited by David O. Sears, Jim Sidanius, and Lawrence Bobo. Chicago: University of Chicago Press.

Tsui, Anne S., Katherine R. Xin, and Terri D. Egan. 1995. "Relational Demography: The Missing Link in Vertical Dyad Linkage." In *Diversity in Work Teams*, edited by Susan E. Jackson and Mirian N. Ruderman. Washington, D.C.: American Psychological Association.

Tuan, Mia. 1998. *Forever Foreigners or Honorary Whites?: The Asian Ethnic Experience Today*. New Brunswick, N.J.: Rutgers University Press.

Valenzuela, Abel, and Elizabeth Gonzalez, 2000. "Latino Earnings Inequality: Immigrant and Native Born Differences." In *Prismatic Metropolis: Inequality in Los Angeles*, edited by Lawrence D. Bobo, Melvin L. Oliver, James H. Johnson, and Abel Valenzuela. New York: Russell Sage Foundation.

Waldinger, Roger. 1989. "Immigration and Urban Change." *Annual Review of Sociology* 15: 211–32.

———. 1996. "Who Makes the Beds? Who Washes the Dishes?: Black/ Immigrant Competition Reassessed." In *Immigrants and Immigration Policy: Individual Skills, Family Ties and Group Identities*, edited by H. O. Duleep and P. V. Wunnara. Greenwich, Conn.: JAI Press.

Wilson, William Julius. 1978. *The Declining Significance of Race: Blacks and Changing American Institutions*. Chicago: University of Chicago Press.

———. 1987. *The Truly Disadvantaged*. Chicago: University of Chicago Press.

———. 1996. *When Work Disappears: The World of the New Ghetto Poor*. New York: Knopf.

Word, Carl O., Mark P. Zanna, and Joel Cooper. 1974. "The Nonverbal Mediation of Self-Fulfilling Prophecies in Interracial Interaction." *Journal of Experimental Social Psychology* 10: 109–20.

Zubrinsky, Camille L., and Lawrence D. Bobo. 1996. "Prismatic Metropolis: Race and Residential Segregation in the City of Angels." *Social Science Research* 25: 335–74.

3

PERCEIVED GROUP DISCRIMINATION AND POLICY ATTITUDES: THE SOURCES AND CONSEQUENCES OF THE RACE AND GENDER GAPS

James R. Kluegel and Lawrence D. Bobo

S OCIAL science research gives a complex picture of factors shaping racial, ethnic, and gender inequalities. Yet, when the subject of inequality enters public discourse, and especially that involving social policy, the discussion often becomes simplified to assessments of whether or not a group is treated unfairly in the economic order. Is a group a victim of discrimination, and, if so, how much discrimination does it suffer?

The substantial gap between whites and African Americans in perceptions of how much discrimination is experienced by African Americans has been underscored by several scholars (Bobo and Kluegel 1997; Feagin and Vera 1995; Hochschild 1995; Jaynes and Williams 1989; Kluegel 1985; Kluegel and Smith 1986; Sigelman and Welch 1991; Sniderman and Hagen 1985). Whites, as has been well established, are far more sanguine about opportunity for blacks to get ahead than blacks are. Blacks see racial discrimination in the workplace as much more prevalent than do whites.

Some work—for example, a recent *Washington Post*-sponsored study (Morin 1995)—has begun to document differences among whites and other minorities as well. Research on this gap, however, has been largely descriptive, documenting the contours and size of the perception gap and examining some differences among basic demographic groups (by age, education, and gender) in their perceptions. More analytical research on minority group perceptions of discrimination is limited by its noncomparative quality. It focuses on single groups, with each study using unique sample designs and measures (Kuo 1995; Portes and Bach 1985; de la Garza et al. 1992).

Probing more deeply into what shapes perceptions of discrimination against different groups, and thus what produces the white-minority gaps in perception, is important for two reasons. First, gaps in perception in and of themselves are a source of tension and potential political conflict between groups. Minority groups react with frustration and anger at having the problem of discrimination they see as major taken as minor, or simply dismissed, by the white majority or other groups (Feagin and Vera 1995; Hochschild 1995). On the other side, the perception among many whites that minorities face a minor or nonexistent problem engenders anger toward minorities—that is, minorities are seen as making illegitimate demands for corrective action (Kinder and Sanders 1996).

The Multi-City Study of Urban Inequality permits us to provide both a more extensive and intensive analysis of perceptions of discrimination against different groups than achieved in prior research. The study is unique in posing *identical* questions about perceived discrimination and other factors to large samples of whites, blacks, Hispanics, and Asians in the same study. In this chapter we present a broadly comparative analysis of differences in perceived discrimination between blacks and whites, between the white majority and Hispanic and Asian minorities, and between men and women. As we shall see in the analysis that follows, there is a consistent gap across the four cities between whites, on the one hand, and blacks and Hispanics, on the other. Although whites and Asian Americans do not currently differ, we found evidence suggesting that differences in perceived discrimination paralleling the white-black and white-Hispanic gaps may develop in the future. We also found a racial gap in the determinants of perceived discrimination. Whites' perceptions are abstractly based, while nonwhites' perceptions are rooted in experience. The gender gap is much smaller, but it too is racialized.

Second, perceived discrimination affects support for policy to address economic inequality—in general and, of course, that targeted toward specific groups (Bobo and Kluegel 1993, 1997; Jacobsen 1985; Kluegel 1990; Tuch and Hughes 1996). Among the factors shaping the fate of policy in the political process, we certainly must attend to how the public responds to it (compare, Burstein 1985). Although supportive public opinion does not of itself lead to policy, as shown in the difficult history of affirmative action, opposing public opinion does make policy implementation difficult politically and in daily life.

The Multi-City Study data also allow us to construct a unique, broadly comparative perspective on white-minority differences as well as differences between men and women in support of such policy. Research has shown that perceptions of discrimination do play an important role in support for policy targeted toward African Americans. We lack such knowledge, however, concerning other minorities and women. In this chapter, we examine the effect of perceived discrimination on whites' attitudes toward policy targeted to blacks, Hispanics, Asians, and women. As our analyses will show, discrimination perceptions have real consequences, shaping attitudes toward opportunity-related policy targeted to each minority group and women, independent of their other major determinants.

Group Differences in Perceived Discrimination

The Multi-City Study respondents were asked the following question concerning job discrimination:

> In general, how much discrimination is there that hurts the chances of [*specific group*] to get good paying jobs? Do you think there is *a lot, some, only a little,* or *none at all*? [In this order, respondents were asked about discrimination affecting Hispanics, blacks, Asians, women, and whites.][1]

Accordingly, we may examine perceptions of job discrimination affecting the major minority groups, women, and indeed whites. The latter has come in popular treatment to be given the label of "reverse discrimination." Although the authors agree with many who see this term as a symbolically loaded misnomer, claims about reverse discrimination are now prevalent in political discourse. Understanding who holds and what shapes this sentiment is necessary to a complete appreciation of the public's comprehension of group-based inequality.

Perceived Discrimination Against Racial and Ethnic Groups

Table 3.1 arrays the percentage distributions of perceived job discrimination against minorities and whites by city and race. Results of Multi-City Study analyses for blacks and whites likely may be generalized to the broader urban United States. Because the Hispanic respondents are drawn primarily from only two cities, and virtually all the Asian respondents are from Los Angeles, we can offer only more limited generalizations about these groups.

Consistent with other research, we see in the table that the gap between blacks and whites in these four cities is large. It is not the case that most whites largely deny the existence of discrimination against

TABLE 3.1   Perceived Discrimination Against Blacks, Hispanics, Asians, and Whites, by City and Race-Ethnic Group

Perceived Discrimination Against Blacks

	None	A Little	Some	A Lot
Atlanta***				
Among whites	13.5	22.7	44.3	19.4
Among blacks	0.6	4.9	34.1	60.4
Boston***				
Among whites	5.7	16.3	44.6	30.1
Among blacks	2.1	6.4	34.5	57.0
Among Hispanics	3.4	12.4	33.3	48.9
Detroit***				
Among whites	8.8	14.6	43.6	33.1
Among blacks	1.5	6.5	30.4	61.5
Los Angeles***				
Among whites	8.5	16.6	46.2	23.1
Among blacks	1.3	4.7	24.7	69.3
Among Hispanics	7.2	15.3	37.2	40.3
Among Asians	9.5	34.4	42.0	14.1

Perceived Discrimination Against Hispanics

	None	A Little	Some	A Lot
Atlanta*				
Among whites	10.3	19.5	47.0	23.2
Among blacks	8.5	15.3	42.0	31.3
Boston***				
Among whites	9.7	16.3	45.7	28.3
Among Hispanics	4.0	13.7	33.2	49.0
Among blacks	5.1	15.7	43.2	36.0
Detroit***				
Among whites	8.1	16.4	56.0	19.9
Among blacks	4.5	15.8	46.4	33.2
Los Angeles***				
Among whites	9.3	19.5	48.9	22.3
Among Hispanics	3.6	9.6	27.4	59.3
Among blacks	10.0	17.1	36.1	36.8
Among Asians	10.7	38.9	39.6	10.8

Perceived Discrimination Against Asians

	None	A Little	Some	A Lot
Atlanta				
Among whites	14.7	31.7	40.6	13.0
Among blacks	14.0	24.0	44.7	17.3
Boston***				
Among whites	12.5	25.2	43.4	18.9
Among blacks	5.2	24.3	45.0	25.5
Among Hispanics	12.3	26.2	40.0	20.6
Detroit***				
Among whites	12.2	20.8	50.7	10.3
Among blacks	9.3	28.8	43.9	18.0
Los Angeles***				
Among whites	17.7	34.2	42.0	6.1
Among Asians	10.8	41.2	42.4	5.5
Among blacks	24.0	36.1	30.7	9.2
Among Hispanics	24.5	35.6	37.4	7.5

Perceived Discrimination Against Whites

	None	A Little	Some	A Lot
Atlanta***				
Among whites	26.8	38.5	29.4	5.2
Among blacks	60.1	25.2	12.2	2.5
Boston***				
Among whites	32.0	35.6	29.4	8.8
Among blacks	43.1	33.5	18.3	5.0
Among Hispanics	62.6	19.7	12.4	5.2
Detroit				
Among whites	—	—	—	—
Among blacks	—	—	—	—
Los Angeles***				
Among whites	30.2	37.4	28.0	4.4
Among blacks	65.5	24.5	8.2	1.8
Among Hispanics	73.8	15.8	8.1	2.2
Among Asians	74.1	19.8	9.3	0.9

Source: Multi-City Study of Urban Inequality.
* = p < .05. ** = p < .01. *** = p < .001.

blacks—although a substantial minority does, responding "a little" or "none." The modal perception among whites is that "some" job discrimination against blacks does exist. The contrast is found in the choice of "some" among 44 to 46 percent of whites and the choice of "a lot" by 60 to 70 percent of blacks. There exists among whites a perception of a middling or moderate level of job discrimination against blacks. The gap is best characterized as one between a somewhat halting recognition on the part of whites and a nearly consensual view among blacks that their group is the victim of prevalent job discrimination.

It is beyond the scope of this chapter to review research speaking to the amount of racial, ethnic, or gender discrimination that exists in fact. Nevertheless, we need make it clear at the outset that we believe that such research shows that job discrimination remains a serious problem. It is clear that respondents who claim that there is "only a little" discrimination or "none at all" do not see it as a problem, while those who choose "a lot" do. It is less clear what "some" implies for the perceived seriousness of discrimination. Our recent research (Bobo and Kluegel 1997) using national sample data, however, argues that most respondents who choose "some" stand closer to those choosing "only a little" than to those choosing "a lot" in their evaluated seriousness of discrimination. We found that two-thirds of white respondents choosing "some" when asked about the *amount* of discrimination deny that the black-white socioeconomic gap is "mainly due to discrimination" when asked to *explain it*.[2] Most whites, then, do not see the problem of discrimination against blacks as very serious, and clearly do not see it to be as serious as blacks do.

The black-white gap in the perceived seriousness of discrimination is strong in all four cities. It is somewhat smaller in Boston and Detroit than in Atlanta or Los Angeles. Nevertheless, the distributions of perceived discrimination against blacks among whites and blacks, respectively, quite closely match those found in a 1990 national survey (Bobo and Kluegel 1991, 1997). Do parallel white-minority gaps exist for Hispanics and Asians?

The white-Hispanic gap in perceived discrimination is somewhat smaller than the white-black gap, but nevertheless substantial. In Boston and Los Angeles the modal response among whites regarding job discrimination against Hispanics is "some." As in the case of blacks, the modal response among Hispanics is that members of their own group face "a lot" of job discrimination.

There is no gap in perceptions between whites and Asian Americans. Whites in Los Angeles are a bit more likely than Asian Americans to say "none" in response to a question about the prevalence of discrimination against Asians. Otherwise, the distribution of perceived discrimination against Asians is essentially the same for whites and Asian Americans. In light of the "success image" and "model minority" labels attached to Asian Americans (Chen and Hune 1995; Kuo 1995; Lee 1989) and the often subtle and hidden nature of discrimination against them (Duleep and Sanders 1992; Tang 1993), the tendency of whites to downplay discrimination against Asians is perhaps unsurprising. That Asian Americans share whites' views, however, perhaps is surprising.

Whites in three of the cities (perceived discrimination against whites was not measured in Detroit) share the same distribution of perceived "reverse discrimination." Whites do not see discrimination against their own group as pronounced. Only about 5 percent say "a lot"; five times this number say "none." The modal white response is somewhere between "a little" and "some." Yet there is a strong white-minority gap here. All three minority groups strongly deny that whites are the victims of discrimination. "None" is the majority response among each group in each of the three cities, with the sole exception of blacks in Boston.

The distributions of minorities' perceptions of discrimination against other minority groups show a shared sense of victimization between blacks and Hispanics, but there is an apparent fissure involving Asian Americans. Blacks and Hispanics each see more discrimination against their own respective group than they perceive against the other. But both also see more discrimination against blacks or Hispanics, respectively, than whites perceive against either one. Asian Americans in Los Angeles, however, are less likely than whites to perceive that blacks or Hispanics suffer from job discrimination. Blacks and Hispanics in Los Angeles are more likely to deny that Asians experience discrimination at all than are whites. In other cities, however, blacks and Hispanics perceive somewhat more extensive discrimination against Asians than do whites. This suggests that the interethnic tension in Los Angeles between blacks and Hispanics, on the one hand, and Asian Americans, on the other, documented in several studies (Bobo et al. 1995; Chang and Leong 1994; Jackson, Gerber, and Cain 1994; Johnson and Oliver 1994; Thornton and Taylor 1988), shapes mutual perceptions of discrimination against other minorities.

Perceived Discrimination Against Women

There is little research on perceived discrimination against women based on national-scope data (Kluegel and Smith 1986; Kane 1992, 1995; Kane and Sanchez 1994).[3] Multi-City Study data permit us to look not only at contemporary gender differences in perceived discrimination against women, but these perceptions within racial groups and to compare features of perceived discrimination against women to perceived discrimination against racial groups.[4] Table 3.2 gives the distribution of perceived discrimination against women separately by race and gender, within each of the four cities.

Three patterns in this table merit note. First, there is a significant gap in perception between white men and white women, such that white women see more discrimination against women than do white men. Only among Hispanics do we see a parallel gender gap for minority group respondents.

Second, the gap between white men and white women is markedly smaller than parallel white-black and white-Hispanic gaps. In general, white men are much more likely to deny discrimination against women than against blacks or Hispanics. Across the four cities, roughly 45 percent of white men characterize the extent of discrimination against women by the responses "a little" or "none." Contrasting percents for perceived discrimination against blacks and Hispanics are in the 25 percent range. The gender gap is smaller than the race gap because white women are substantially more likely than blacks or Hispanics (males or females) to downplay the extent of discrimination against their own group. Roughly a third of the white women deny any significant discrimination against women, and only about 9 percent on average perceive "a lot" of discrimination against women. This compares to parallel figures for blacks in the range of about 7 and 60 percent, respectively.[5]

Third, across the four cities blacks see more discrimination against women than is perceived by white women themselves.[6] Hispanics and whites have a similar profile in Boston, but Hispanic men and women in Los Angeles see somewhat more extensive discrimination against women than do their white counterparts. Asian American men and women share the same distribution of the perceived extent of discrimination against women, and they each perceive substantially less discrimination against women than do whites and other minorities.

In Sum

These comparisons show that perceived discrimination is much more "racialized" than "gendered." The gaps in perceived discrimination between whites, on the one hand, and blacks and Hispanics, on the other, are truly large. In contrast, although women are more likely than men to see discrimination against women as a serious problem, the gender gap in perceived discrimination is much smaller than the parallel race gap.

In each of the four cities, black women perceive somewhat more discrimination against women than do black men, but both black men and black women see substantially more discrimination against women than do white men. It appears that the consciousness of race discrimination prevalent among blacks increases sensitivity to gender discrimination among black women *and* men. Such sensitivity is less strong among Hispanics. Hispanic women do see discrimination against women as more serious than do Hispanic men. Whereas consciousness of discrimination against Hispanics seems to increase sensitivity to gender discrimination among Hispanic women, it does not seem to have this effect on Hispanic men. The distribution of perceived discrimination against women among Hispanic men is similar to that of white men.

The views of Asian Americans in Los Angeles in one respect are an exception to this racialized pattern. There is no gap in perceived race-ethnic discrimination between Asian Americans and whites. However, they are racialized in a within-minority group gap found in Los Angeles. Here the views of blacks and Hispanics about discrimination against Asian Americans are pitted against Asian Americans' views of discrimination against Hispanics and blacks—such that each downplays the extent of discrimination against the other. In another aspect of the racialization of discrimination perceptions, Asian Americans do stand with other minorities: all minority groups are united in the perception that whites are not the victims of "reverse discrimination."

Explaining Perceived Discrimination Against Racial Groups

How are we to explain this racialized pattern of discrimination perceptions? There is a small body of empirical research literature on factors shaping perceptions of opportunity for different groups (Bobo and Kluegel 1991, 1997; Sigelman and Welch 1991). It is especially small in contrast to the literature on "traditional prejudice"—overt bigotry and support for Jim Crow–style segregation. Research on perceptions of group opportunity, however, has quite clearly established that the factors shaping traditional prejudice relate much more weakly, if at all, to perceived discrimination against blacks (Bobo and Kluegel 1997). The college-educated, for example, are only slightly more likely to attribute the black-white gap to discrimination than are others, and there are no age group differences in opportunity perceptions. There are marked differences by age and education, however, in traditional prejudice (Bobo and Kluegel 1997).

Prior research on discrimination perceptions has gone little beyond examining the influence of sociodemographic variables. Thus it provides

TABLE 3.2   Perceived Discrimination Against Women by City, Race-Ethnic Group, and Sex

Atlanta

	None	A Little	Some	A Lot
Whites***				
Among men	19.5	32.3	40.2	7.9
Among women	12.9	23.2	51.5	12.4
Blacks**				
Among men	6.8	16.0	50.0	27.2
Among women	2.0	12.1	56.7	29.3

Boston

	None	A Little	Some	A Lot
Whites***				
Among men	16.5	30.8	41.0	11.7
Among women	10.2	22.0	45.7	20.0
Blacks				
Among men	8.7	19.5	43.6	28.2
Among women	4.8	15.6	47.4	32.2
Hispanics*				
Among men	20.7	24.4	38.9	16.1
Among women	17.4	25.8	32.1	24.7

Detroit

	None	A Little	Some	A Lot
Whites***				
Among men	17.1	29.4	44.3	9.2
Among women	11.3	18.1	50.6	19.9
Blacks				
Among men	4.6	20.5	49.0	25.9
Among women	3.9	16.3	46.3	33.6

Los Angeles

	None	A Little	Some	A Lot
Whites**				
Among men	13.2	30.4	47.9	8.5
Among women	11.8	22.2	50.7	15.4
Blacks***				
Among men	8.5	20.5	50.3	20.7
Among women	4.3	15.2	50.8	29.7
Hispanics***				
Among men	19.9	23.8	37.7	18.6
Among women	14.3	18.1	40.5	27.2
Asians				
Among men	28.6	38.3	29.7	3.4
Among women	26.4	41.0	29.9	2.7

Source: Multi-City Study of Urban Inequality.
* = $p < .05$. ** = $p < .01$. *** = $p < .001$.

little answer to our question about the racialized quality of perceived discrimination. It simply implies that group differences in perceived discrimination *cannot* be explained by differences among groups in their distributions of certain sociodemographic characteristics. The inability to explain perceived discrimination may stem from the failure to consider factors other than those known to shape prejudice.

Perceived discrimination may be the product of what might be labeled "social learning" variables. Many persons may downplay the importance or deny the influence of discrimination altogether because they live their lives in homogeneous circumstances that preclude firsthand experience with discriminatory acts taken against minorities or women. Some scholars have suggested that it is the segregation between blacks and whites, residentially and in the workplace, that supports a worldview downplaying or denying discrimination (Sniderman and Hagen 1985). One potentially important social learning factor is intergroup contact. Although the historical record of research seeking to find "contact effects" has been largely negative (compare, Jackman and Crane 1986), several recent studies have come to more positive conclusions (Bobo and Zubrinsky 1996; Ellison and Powers 1994; Powers and Ellison 1995; Sigelman and Welch 1993; Sigelman et al. 1996). However, the effects of contact demonstrated in this work have been limited to interpersonal relations, showing that contact reduces stereotyping and racial hostility. The question of whether contact affects perceived discrimination—against one's own or other groups—remains open.

A second "social learning" factor that may account for the gap is the personal experience of discrimination. Minority group members may perceive greater discrimination against their own group because they have greater experience with discrimination directed toward them as individuals.

A line of research developed by the authors of this chapter stresses what may be termed the "social theory"–driven nature of perceived discrimination (Bobo and Kluegel 1997; Bobo, Kluegel, and Smith 1997). In this perspective, among whites perceived discrimination derives more from social and political beliefs and ideology than from individual interests or experiences. One facet of popular "social theory" is general socioeconomic ideology. Denial of discrimination is substantially rooted in the ideological defense of the economic status quo in general. Societal and individual-blame explanations of poverty shape whites' perceived discrimination against blacks and other groups (Bobo and Kluegel 1991, 1997).

Another potentially important source of discrimination perceptions is group-based economic interest or threat. Individual-level self-interest, as defined by a person's place in the economic order and likely *individ-*

ual loss or benefit from social policy, has been shown to play little role in shaping intergroup beliefs and attitudes (Kinder and Sanders 1996). Following upon insights offered forty years ago by Herbert Blumer (1958), several recent studies have underscored that *perceived* group-based interests or threats to same, however, do have powerful effects on racial attitudes (Bobo and Hutchings 1996; Bobo and Kluegel 1993; Kinder and Sanders 1996; Quillian 1995, 1996). White denial that a minority group suffers from discrimination may serve to defend a sense of relative group privilege. That is, accepting that another group has suffered from discrimination gives legitimacy to efforts to promote increased opportunity for that group—opportunity that will be bought at the cost of reduced privilege for one's own group.

Finally, we also need to acknowledge simple naïveté. Recent research (Morin 1995) has shown, perhaps a bit astonishingly, that a substantial minority of white Americans sees no difference between whites and blacks or Hispanics in their relative economic standing. Whites see substantially more progress in blacks' economic conditions than do blacks (Hochschild 1995). In part, this perception may itself be theory-driven (Kluegel 1985). Such a belief serves to defend the economic status quo. However, naïveté may be the result of misinformation and lack of information about the history and current status of minority groups provided in American primary and secondary schooling (Loewen 1995) or through the media (Campbell 1995). To the extent that perceived equality of economic condition in and of itself leads people to deny discrimination, the white-minority gap in perceived discrimination may rest in social ignorance.

The Multi-City Study data contain direct or indirect measures of each of the factors discussed here. In subsequent sections of this chapter, we consider how they combine to influence perceived discrimination against racial groups. We contrast how whites' views of discrimination against each of the three minority groups (and their own group) are shaped by these forces with how each minority's view of discrimination *against its own group* is influenced by them. In so doing, we can evaluate how important each factor is in producing the white-minority gaps in perceived discrimination we have observed.

Sociodemographic Factors

We begin with an examination of how perceived discrimination differs along major sociodemographic lines. Table 3.3 gives a series of regressions for perceived discrimination on age group, education, family income, gender, and city.[7] In analyses estimated within the Hispanic and Asian American groups, we examine the influence of two other factors.

TABLE 3.3 *Regression Coefficients for the Effects of Sociodemographic Characteristics and City of Residence on Perceived Discrimination*

	Whites' Perceived Discrimination Against			
	Asians	Blacks	Hispanics	Whites
Age twenty-one to twenty-nine	.027	−.038	−.045	−.139*
Age thirty to thirty-nine	.015	−.049	−.087	−.017
Age forty to forty-nine	.050	−.072	−.106*	.009
Age sixty-five +	−.062	−.111*	−.137***	−.196***
Education	.061***	.139***	.121***	−.085***
Income	−.002	−.002	−.001	−.011**
Male	−.062*	−.014	−.101**	−.075*
Atlanta	−.083*	−.359***	−.067	.067
Boston	.092*	−.055	.054	−.011
Los Angeles	−.248***	−.111*	−.070	
R^2	.03	.05	.03	.03

	Perceived Discrimination Against		
	Asians Among Asians	Blacks Among Blacks	Hispanics Among Hispanics
Age twenty-one to twenty-nine	.075	.038	.063
Age thirty to thirty-nine	−.022	−.025	.036
Age forty to forty-nine	.099	.074	.080
Age sixty-five +	−.127	−.223**	−.231**
Education	.108***	.020	.018
Income	−.015	−.011	−.011
Male	−.032	−.046	−.054
Atlanta	—	.005	—
Boston	—	−.078*	—
Los Angeles	—	.082**	—
Japanese	.032	—	—
Korean	−.136*	—	—
Central American	—	—	.142
Dominican	—	—	−.054
Mexican	—	—	.255***
Puerto Rican	—	—	.069

(Table continues on p. 176.)

TABLE 3.3   *Continued*

	Perceived Discrimination Against		
	Asians Among Asians	Blacks Among Blacks	Hispanics Among Hispanics
Foreign-born English	−.044		−.035
Foreign-born non-English	−.233**		.262***
R^2	.08	.02	.06

Source: Multi-City Study of Urban Inequality.
Notes: Entries are metric OLS regression coefficients. The reference (excluded) group for age categories is ages fifty to sixty-four. The reference (excluded) group for nativity-language use is native-born English speakers. The reference (excluded) group for city of residence is Detroit. The reference (excluded) groups for ethnicity are Chinese and Mexican American, respectively.
* = $p < .05$. ** = $p < .01$. *** = $p < .001$.

First, we consider the impact of specific Hispanic and Asian American group origin. As Douglas Massey (1993) underscores, there are important differences among Hispanic groups in their respective social and economic circumstances, conditions of immigration, and incorporation into American society. Similar differences are present among Asian American groups as well (Espiritu 1997). Second, we employ a three-category variable to capture potential effects of nativity and English-language facility. We distinguish among respondents born in the United States, respondents not born in the United States but interviewed in English, and respondents not born in the United States and interviewed in a non-English language. Analyzing the effect of this variable on perceived discrimination permits us to address issues concerning acculturation among Hispanic (de la Garza, Falcon, and Garcia 1996; Portes and Bach 1985) and Asian American groups (Hein 1994).

The results in the table match findings from other research using national sample data looking at the influence of sociodemographic variables on whites' and blacks' perceptions of job discrimination against blacks (Bobo and Kluegel 1997; Kluegel and Smith 1986; Sigelman and Welch 1991), showing a rather weak pattern of effects. Here we see that this pattern extends to perceived job discrimination against Asians, Hispanics, and whites. Because our results for sociodemographic differences in whites' perceptions of discrimination against minorities and for blacks' perceived discrimination against blacks replicate prior findings, we will not comment on them in any detail.

Instead, we focus on the sociodemographic patterning of perceived discrimination among Hispanics and Asian Americans. This patterning sheds light on a key question posed in the study of Hispanics and Asian Americans concerning the consequences of increasing acculturation within each group. How does increasing exposure to American culture by virtue of increasing experience with the American educational system, through increasing facility with English, or simply through the succession of generations shape how Hispanics and Asian Americans view economic opportunity?

Some scholars have suggested that younger generations of minority groups may be socialized such that they perceive greater discrimination against their own group than do older ones. Alejandro Portes and Min Zhou (1993) discuss a potential increasing awareness of discrimination among second- and third-generation youth of Mexican descent. Jeremy Hein's (1994) analysis of Hmong refugees suggests that younger generations of Asian Americans and Hispanics may more frequently adopt a "minority" as opposed to an "migrant" identification, resulting in increased consciousness of racial discrimination.

We see little evidence that younger Asian Americans or Hispanics see more extensive discrimination than their elders. There is but one statistically significant age group difference. Hispanic respondents sixty-five or older see less discrimination than all other groups. However, it is among the groups aged eighteen to twenty-nine and thirty to thirty-nine that we are most likely to find second- and third-generation Hispanics or Asian Americans, and they do not differ from persons ages forty to sixty-four.[8]

Alejandro Portes and Robert Bach (1985) have advanced two competing hypotheses about the effects of acculturation among recent immigrant minorities. The "conflict hypothesis" proposes that as groups become more integrated in U.S. society, they become more aware of racial and ethnic prejudice and discrimination. The "assimilationist hypothesis" proposes that increased integration brings with it *decreased* perceived discrimination against one's own group. In their analyses of Cuban and Mexican immigrants, Portes and Bach (1985) found most support for the latter hypothesis.

Our results for Hispanics, however, do not support the conflict hypothesis. Among Hispanics, certain aspects of greater acculturation seem to produce less perceived discrimination. Hispanics who are foreign-born and were not interviewed in English see *more* discrimination than the other two Hispanic native-language groups. Mexican origin Hispanics see more discrimination than those who identify themselves as "Mexican Americans." Perceived discrimination among Hispanics does not increase with an increasing level of education, as the conflict hypothesis implies.

It is among Asian Americans that we find patterns fitting the conflict hypothesis. Among Asian Americans, the perceived prevalence of discrimination against Asians increases with years of education. Korean-origin respondents, on average the most recent arrivals among the immigrant groups in our study, see less extensive discrimination than do Chinese- or Japanese-origin groups. Asian Americans who are foreign-born and were not interviewed in English see *less* discrimination than the other two Asian American native-language groups.[9]

Fully explaining these findings requires a more dynamic analysis than is possible with our cross-sectional snapshot. However, viewing the seemingly contradictory patterns together suggests a possible unifying explanation: the patterns for each group correspond to findings concerning the objective "risk factors" of discrimination. Research on the "glass ceiling" points to higher discrimination against Asian Americans at higher levels of occupational status (Duleep and Sanders 1992; Tang 1993; U.S. Commission on Civil Rights 1992). Asian Americans with higher levels of education and greater English-language facility are more likely to hold jobs at higher status levels, and thereby to be at greater risk of job discrimination. Research also underscores the importance of English-language facility to the socioeconomic attainments of Hispanics (Massey 1993; Morales and Ong 1993; Stolzenberg 1990). Among Hispanics, the Mexican-origin group has the lowest average income, highest rates of poverty, and poorest rates of high school and college graduation (Reimers 1992). Lack of English facility and poor economic circumstances increase one's vulnerability to exploitation and discrimination.

Social Learning

Tables 3.4 and 3.5 array the results for two classes of social learning variables (information regarding the measurement of these variables is given in the appendix to this chapter). Table 3.4 gives coefficients for the effects of personal and workplace contact. Table 3.5 looks at the influence of authority position and perceived *personal* discrimination. In each case, the coefficients presented are from regressions including the sociodemographic variables in table 3.3.[10]

Results in table 3.4 show little consistent effect of personal or workplace contact. There are only two statistically significant effects of personal contact: whites who have a black person in their network are somewhat more likely to perceive discrimination against blacks, and Hispanics who have a white person in their networks perceive a little less discrimination against Hispanics.

Race of coworker has no significant effects at all. Whites who have a white supervisor, counter to our expectation, report *more* perceived discrimination against blacks and Hispanics. Social learning does seem

TABLE 3.4   *Regression Coefficients for the Effects of Personal and Workplace Contact on Perceived Discrimination*

	Whites' Perceived Discrimination Against			
	Asians	Blacks	Hispanics	Whites
Have Asian in network	−.109	—	—	—
Have black in network	—	.220*	—	—
Have Hispanic in network	—	—	−.096	—
Have nonwhite in network	—	—	—	.082
White versus nonwhite coworkers	.085	.023	.065	−.046
White versus nonwhite supervisor	.062	.148*	.135*	.033
R^2	.03	.06	.04	.03

	Perceived Discrimination Against		
	Asians Among Asians	Blacks Among Blacks	Hispanics Among Hispanics
Have white in network	−.034	−.035	−.170*
Have other minorities in network	−.022	.030	.137
White coworkers	−.078	.039	.141*
Other minority coworkers	−.016	−.020	.039
White supervisor	.080	−.009	.024
Other minority supervisor	.065	.098	−.020
R^2	.08	.02	.08

Source: Multi-City Study of Urban Inequality.
Notes: Entries are metric OLS regression coefficients from equations that also include the sociodemographic variables in table 3.2. See text for discussion of reference (excluded) groups for contact categories.
* = $p < .05$. ** = $p < .01$. *** = $p < .001$.

to take place, but not of the type expected. That is, some whites appear to take the simple presence of a nonwhite supervisor as evidence that discrimination against blacks or Hispanics is not widespread.

We measure job authority by two categorical variables. The first distinguishes between the self-employed and those who work for others. The second distinguishes those who do not have supervisory authority (workers) from those who do. From a social learning perspective, perhaps whites who are in authority positions are typically more knowledgeable about broader patterns in hiring and promotion, and accordingly in a better position to perceive discrimination. "Personal Race Discrimination" is a two-category variable distinguishing those who

TABLE 3.5   *Regression Coefficients for the Effects of Work-Related Characteristics on Perceived Discrimination*

| | Whites' Perceived Discrimination Against | | | |
	Asians	Blacks	Hispanics	Whites
Worker	−.024	−.015	−.065	−.047
Self-employed	−.003	.150*	.079	−.165*
Personal race discrimination	−.142*	−.274***	−.179***	.483***
R^2	.03	.06	.04	.06

| | Perceived Discrimination Against | | |
	Asians Among Asians	Blacks Among Blacks	Hispanics Among Hispanics
Worker	.058	−.050	−.043
Self-employed	.085	−.141*	−.140
Personal race discrimination	.272***	.190***	.278***
R^2	.10	.05	.09

Source: Multi-City Study of Urban Inequality.
Notes: Entries are metric OLS regression coefficients from equations that also include the sociodemographic variables in table 3.2. The reference (excluded) category for job authority is the category "supervisor" (persons who work for others and have supervisory authority).
* = $p < .05$. ** = $p < .01$. *** = $p < .001$.

perceive they have ever been discriminated against personally because of their race in either hiring or promotions (1) from those who report no personal experience of race discrimination at all (0).

Table 3.5 shows a small effect of organizational context. Whites who work for others (that is, are not self-employed) see less discrimination against blacks and more against whites. Blacks and Hispanics working for others show a slightly greater perception of discrimination against their own groups than do the self-employed. Holding a supervisory position, however, is of no consequence for discrimination perceptions.

The direction of causal relationship between perceived personal discrimination and perceived discrimination against one's own group is a matter of some dispute. In one view, perceived personal discrimination is the product, *not* the cause, of perceived group discrimination. In this view, perceived group discrimination is not rooted in real or experienced personal discrimination so much as in the incorrect or "overgeneralized" application of beliefs about group discrimination to personal circumstances.

We, however, assume that primary direction of cause is from the personal experience of discrimination to perceived discrimination against one's group. While no doubt some influence flows in the direction from perceived group discrimination to the perception of personal discrimination, we assume that the preponderant influence is from personal to group perceptions. We so assume because of strong evidence for the phenomenon of "denial of victimization" in general, and "denial of discrimination" in particular (Clayton and Crosby 1992; Major 1994). Among both minorities and women, a substantially larger fraction see their respective group as suffering discrimination than report that they as individuals have experienced personal discrimination. This may be the result of cognitive bias and emotional costs. It is difficult to infer discrimination in individual cases because most people do not have ready access to the kind of comparative data needed to support such a claim. In addition, the circumstances of each potential individual instance of discrimination are often unique and the causal forces involved are complex or ambiguous (Clayton and Crosby 1992; Major 1994).

These circumstances of "attributional ambiguity" (Major 1994) also may dispose persons who perceive a high level of discrimination against their own group to infer personal discrimination when evidence is unclear. However, the high psychological and social costs of acknowledging personal discrimination much favor denial and exempting oneself as an individual from group outcomes. We live in a culture of individualism, where the prevalent assumption is that individuals are responsible for their own success or failure (Kluegel and Smith 1986). To see oneself as a victim of external factors violates "just world" beliefs and the desire to be personally in control of one's circumstances. To see oneself as a victim also implies that one must take action against the source of personal discrimination. Often this involves action against those in authority positions, who may impose psychological or economic costs. For minorities, who also face a large numerical disadvantage, such costs can be especially high. Regarding personal gender discrimination, Susan Clayton and Faye Crosby (1992, 84) note: "To give up the belief that one has escaped the pitfalls of sexism, that one can play by her own rules but win at their game, that one is in charge of her own destiny and exempt from the society forces that limit other people is to forfeit a great deal."

For many persons, the recognition of personal discrimination comes only after a steady accumulation of discriminatory events that are initially denied. Or, it may come as the result of a particularly dramatic event (Clayton and Crosby 1992). Such personal experience often leads people to broader identification with their own group and to be more accepting of claims of group-based discrimination.

Findings from our survey are consistent with other evidence showing a bias against seeing oneself as a victim of discrimination (Bobo and Suh 1995). One might well imagine that the impersonal and transitory nature of the survey interview would facilitate reporting personal discrimination. Yet in all groups, the majority of respondents deny that they have ever experienced personal discrimination in being hired for a job or in promotion: 85 percent of whites, 82 percent of Asian Americans, 72 percent of Hispanics, and 55 percent of blacks.

A marked and clear pattern of effects is shown for the personal experience of race discrimination. We see in table 3.5 that whites who perceive that they have personally been the victim of reverse discrimination are more likely to *deny* that each minority group experiences discrimination, and especially more likely to see that whites as a group experience job discrimination. Asians, blacks, and Hispanics respectively, who report a personal experience with workplace discrimination are significantly more likely to perceive greater job discrimination against their own minority group.

Ideology, Interests, and Ignorance

To examine the impact of popular social theory, group self-interest, and social ignorance, we employ four variables. The first is self-assessed liberalism-conservatism on a 7-point scale. This measure is substantially correlated with general socioeconomic ideology (Kluegel and Smith 1986; Sidanius, Pratto, and Bobo 1996). Self-placed liberals are more likely than conservatives to attribute inequality in general to social causes and less likely to invoke individual blame (Feldman 1988; Fine 1992a; Griffin and Oheneba-Sakyi 1993; Zucker and Weiner 1993). We do not have measures of general socioeconomic ideology available in the Multi-City Study data, so we employ self-assessed political ideology as a reasonable proxy.

Two items concern group threat. (See appendix 3A to this chapter for measurement details.) The first measures a more general sense of threat due to immigration, and the second concerns perceived direct economic threats to one's own racial group.

The final measure concerns the perceived difference between whites and each minority group in their economic position. A high score on this measure indicates whites are seen to be more affluent than members of a given minority group. It permits us to assess the effect of simple social ignorance. Do people who perceive that whites and blacks have equal incomes downplay or deny the prevalence of job discrimination? The results in table 3.6 are from regressions that also contain the

TABLE 3.6   *Regression Coefficients for the Effects of Liberalism, Perceived Group Threat and Perceived Group Trait Differences on Perceived Discrimination*

	Whites' Perceived Discrimination Against			
	Asians	Blacks	Hispanics	Whites
Liberalism	.074***	.104***	.105***	−.024
Competition with immigrants	−.100***	−.096**	−.104***	.034
Job competition with GROUP	−.042	−.085**	−.023	.039
White versus GROUP wealth	.120***	.109***	.082***	−.074***
R^2	.09	.14	.11	.08

	Perceived Discrimination Against		
	Asians Among Asians	Blacks Among Blacks	Hispanics Among Hispanics
Liberalism	.008	.041**	.046
Competition with immigrants	−.002	.049**	.013
White versus GROUP wealth	.053**	.061***	.048***
R^2	.10	.07	.10

Source: Multi-City Study of Urban Inequality.
Notes: Entries are metric OLS regression coefficients from equations that also include the sociodemographic variables in table 3.2 and perceived personal discrimination. "GROUP" refers to the target group for perceived discrimination (Asians, then blacks, then Hispanics). For perceived discrimination against whites, however, *GROUP* refers to blacks.
* = $p < .05$. ** = $p < .01$. *** = $p < .001$.

sociodemographic variables arrayed in table 3.3 and perceived personal discrimination.

Table 3.6 shows that, among whites, perceived discrimination against minorities is very much the product of ideology, interest, and ignorance. Net of sociodemographic and other variables, white liberals perceive more discrimination against each minority group than do conservatives. Controlling for the influence of other variables, the perceived threat to whites as a group posed by immigration reduces the amount of perceived discrimination against each minority group. The amount of perceived discrimination against blacks is affected by perceived direct job competition with blacks, but only the threat associated with immigration has an effect among Asians and Hispanics. We also see that social ignorance plays a role. We see from the table that, independent of the influence of other factors, the smaller the perceived income gap between whites and minorities, the less the perceived discrimination against each minority group.

In contrast, perceptions of discrimination against one's own group—including the perception of discrimination against whites among whites—are little based in self-assessed liberalism-conservatism. It has a statistically significant effect only among Hispanics, and it is roughly half as strong as the effect among whites. Only among blacks do we see an effect of perceived group competition with immigrants. It also is weaker than the parallel effect among whites, and it is *opposite* in sign. A perception that continued immigration will hurt blacks' economic standing as a group somewhat encourages more extensive perceived discrimination against blacks among blacks. The perceived income gap between one's own group and whites does consistently affect perceived discrimination against one's group. Its effect is statistically significant in each of the three minority groups, and as for whites, the larger the perceived income gap, the greater the assessed prevalence of discrimination.

A Note on "City Effects"

Prior research on discrimination perceptions has for the most part been done with national-scope survey data. But cities are the arenas in which current multigroup relations are played out. The design of the Multi-City Study of Urban Inequality allows us to see if the city context makes a difference in beliefs about discrimination against minority groups. In particular, we can assess such effects among white and black respondents. For Asian American respondents we have but one city, and the confounding of Hispanic groups with city that we noted earlier does not permit us to separate the two.

Potential city effects may be of two kinds. They may be one of several factors that add up in determining beliefs (that is, as one of the "main effects"). The influence of a city may reflect the history of intergroup relations in a given city or region of the country. It also may capture a group salience effect due to the relative size of different racial or ethnic groups in a city or region. Other groups may view a given minority group as more of a competitive threat or simply be more aware of its social and economic circumstances when it constitutes a substantial fraction of the population. Simple differences in the distribution of beliefs, though, such as we observed in table 3.1, may be due to city differences in the levels of other variables that shape discrimination perceptions—that is, to what are commonly called "composition effects."

Table 3.3 gives the main effects for city net of sociodemographic composition. In addition, the regression analyses reported in table 3.6 include terms for the effects of city net of sociodemographic, personal discrimination, liberalism, group threat, and perceived income-gap composition. We do not report these coefficients here, but they point to two city main effects of note. Net of all the potential determinants of discrimination perceptions we have considered, white respondents in Atlanta perceive less extensive discrimination against blacks, and white respondents in Los Angeles perceive less extensive discrimination against Asians. The "Atlanta effect" matches other well-known findings showing that white beliefs and attitudes in the South are more negative than in other regions. The "Los Angeles effect" among whites requires a different explanation. The Asian American population, of course, is much larger in Los Angeles than in the other three cities, suggesting a group salience interpretation. The tendency among whites to downplay the perceived extent of discrimination against blacks in Atlanta and Asians in Los Angeles may have a common origin in the threat presented by relative group size (Quillian 1996).[11]

City effects may also take the form of differences among cities in the way factors shape perceived discrimination (that is, interactions of determinants with city). It may reasonably be assumed that certain variables, such as political liberalism-conservatism, affect perceived discrimination in the same manner in each city. One may well question, however, whether the effect of group threat variables is the same in different cities. Immigration arguably is more salient to the average Los Angeles resident than Atlantan, and hence perceived competition with immigrants may have a stronger effect in Los Angeles. Similarly, one might argue that Asian Americans and Hispanics present more salient direct group economic threat to whites in Los Angeles than in the other three surveyed cities.

To test the general possibility that the effect of any of our determinants differs among cities, we estimated the regression models that underlie the results in table 3.6 among white and black respondents separately in each of the four cities. Strikingly, they are nearly identical in each city. In Atlanta, for example, among whites, the perceived threat from competition with immigrants just as strongly reduces the perceived prevalence of discrimination against each minority group as it does in Los Angeles.

We also estimated the regressions presented subsequently in this chapter separately by city. Again, we found no evidence of city differences in how factors shape perceived discrimination or policy attitudes. Our results argue that discrimination perceptions and policy attitudes are largely shaped by a general or national regime.

In Sum

These results show that, among whites, beliefs about discrimination against minority groups are determined largely abstractly, following a national regime. They are not influenced by intergroup contact or by work circumstances that may make discrimination against blacks more visible to whites. Rather, they are shaped by liberal-conservative ideology and by perceived zero-sum competition between whites and other groups. The exception to the abstract determination of perceived group discrimination is the effect of personal race discrimination among whites on perceived group discrimination against whites. The effect of seeing oneself as a victim of "reverse discrimination" on perceived group discrimination against whites is even stronger than parallel effects for minorities who see themselves as personal victims of race discrimination. Whites also react to this experience with increased denial of discrimination against minorities.

In contrast, minorities' perceptions of discrimination against their respective groups are more concretely or experientially shaped. Political ideology has little to no effect. Perceived group discrimination among Asian Americans and Hispanics follows patterns by sociodemographic groups that reflect differences in the real-world risks of discrimination. Among all minority respondents, perceived personal race discrimination consistently results in increased perceived discrimination against one's own group.[12]

The white-black and white-Hispanic gaps in perceived discrimination are due in part to the propensity among whites to base beliefs about minorities on deduction from abstract principle. Hispanics and blacks are not so inclined. Black and Hispanic self-rated conservatives are little or no less likely than self-rated liberals to see prevalent discrimination against their own group.

These gaps also stem from a white-minority gulf in respective views of group differences in income. The tendency to see more discrimination against a minority group when one sees a larger perceived income gap between whites and a given minority group is shared by whites and minorities alike. Whites, however, have a substantially more optimistic assessment of the size of the income gap than do either blacks or Hispanics. The Multi-City Study data show that in each case, whites on average do see fellow whites as economically better off (mean = 1.42 for blacks and 1.54 for Hispanics). But blacks and Hispanics see the income gap between whites and minorities as much larger (mean = 2.07 for blacks and 2.53 for Hispanics).

Explaining Perceived Discrimination
Against Women

Tables 3.7 and 3.8 present regressions for perceived discrimination against women paralleling those in tables 3.3 through 3.5 for perceived discrimination against racial groups. To the sociodemographic variables examined in table 3.3, we add marital status as a potential predictor of perceived discrimination against women—a two-category variable differentiating persons currently married (1) from persons not currently married (0). We include this variable to examine the potential effect of dependence on men (for women) on women's attitudes toward gender inequality (Kane and Sanchez 1994).

Sociodemographic Factors

Table 3.7 shows little differentiation in perceived discrimination against women along sociodemographic lines among white, black, or Hispanic men or women. The only consistent effect is a slight tendency among the more highly educated to see more discrimination against women. Origin group has no effect among Hispanic respondents, but Koreans perceive less discrimination against women than do respondents from other Asian-origin groups. The strongest effect of a sociodemographic variable is found among Asian Americans, where combined nativity and English-language facility have a substantial influence. Men and women Asian Americans who were born in the United States perceive markedly more discrimination against women than the foreign-born and especially more than the foreign-born who do not speak English. This well may reflect patriarchal norms often held by Asian immigrants (Espiritu 1997). Interestingly, if this is so, our results suggest that acculturation reduces the influence of patriarchy equally among Asian American men and women.

As for perceived racial discrimination, results for perceived sex discrimination seem to support the conflict hypothesis for Asian Americans. Furthermore, the conflict hypothesis applies equally to Asian American men and women. Among Hispanics, however, we find little support for either the conflict or assimilationist hypotheses as applied to perceived gender discrimination. These findings, viewed together with those concerning acculturation and perceived racial discrimination, point to the role of isolation from the dominant culture in shaping the low level of perceived discrimination against women found among Asian Americans. Patriarchal norms, or simply a lack of comparative standards among Asian Americans who remain isolated by virtue of language or other factors, inhibit perceived group discrimination. The partial regression coefficient in table 3.7 does not convey just how large the apparent effect of isolation is. Seventy-eight percent of Asian American men and 80 percent of Asian-American women who are foreign-born and do not speak English chose "a little" or "none" to characterize the extent of discrimination against women. In contrast, 64 percent of Asian

TABLE 3.7   *Regression Coefficients for the Effects of Sociodemographic Characteristics and City of Residence on Perceived Discrimination Against Women*

| | Perceived Discrimination Against Women Among | | | |
| | White | | Black | |
	Men	Women	Men	Women
Age twenty-one to twenty-nine	−.095	−.027	−.084	.014
Age thirty to thirty-nine	−.024	.065	.023	.066
Age forty to forty-nine	.089	.024	−.015	.165***
Age sixty-five +	−.262**	−.236**	.035	−.090
Married	−.002	−.108*	.074	−.013
Education	.065***	.078***	.051***	.050*
Income	−.007	−.005	.026***	.001
Atlanta	−.134*	−.235***	.001	.031
Boston	.019	−.045	−.109	−.046
Los Angeles	.015	−.140*	−.138	−.068
R^2	.03	.04	.04	.02

| | Perceived Discrimination Against Women Among | | | |
| | Hispanic | | Asian | |
	Men	Women	Men	Women
Age twenty-one to twenty-nine	−.039	−.173	.006	.020
Age thirty to thirty-nine	−.165	−.300**	.058	−.065
Age forty to forty-nine	−.101	−.062	.032	−.012
Age sixty-five +	−.422*	−.248	−.034	−.127
Married	.075	−.024	.022	−.115
Education	−.012	.068*	.080**	.091*
Income	.008	.004	−.004	−.013
Japanese			−.174	−.088
Korean			−.347***	−.235**
Central American	.005	−.062		
Dominican	−.107	−.275		
Mexican	−.103	−.054		
Puerto Rican	−.019	−.083		
Foreign-born English	−.162	−.051	−.474***	−.296*

(Table continues on p. 189.)

TABLE 3.7   *Continued*

	Perceived Discrimination Against Women Among			
	Hispanic		Asian	
	Men	Women	Men	Women
Foreign-born non-English	−.117	−.101	−.811***	−.791***
R^2	.02	.03	.17	.20

Source: Multi-City Study of Urban Inequality.
Notes: Entries are metric OLS regression coefficients. The reference (excluded) group for age categories is ages fifty to sixty-four. The reference (excluded) group for nativity-language use is native-born English speakers. The reference (excluded) group for city of residence is Detroit. The reference (excluded) groups for ethnicity are Chinese and Mexican American, respectively.
* = $p < .05$. ** = $p < .01$. *** = $p < .001$.

American men and 68 percent of Asian American women who were born in the U.S. chose "some" or "a lot" to characterize discrimination against women.

Social Learning and Ideology

A more limited set of variables is available in the Multi-City Study data to examine how social learning and popular social ideology influence perceptions of discrimination against women. We do not have parallels for women to the measures of perceived group competition or group differences in income used to analyze racial and ethnic differences in perceived discrimination. Table 3.8 presents regressions involving the parallel measures of potential determinants of perceived discrimination present in the Multi-City Study data.

Neither having a male supervisor nor one's authority position was shown to influence perceived discrimination against women. The only statistically significant effects of either variable are found among self-employed white women, who see less prevalent discrimination than do other white women, and workers among Asian American men, who see more discrimination against women than Asian American men in authority positions.

There is a statistically significant and substantial effect among women, except Asian American women, of the experience of personal gender discrimination in the workplace.[13] Paralleling findings for minority groups, women who have experienced discrimination based on gender are more likely to perceive that their own group in general experiences job discrimination. In contrast to the case of whites' perceived

TABLE 3.8   *Regression Coefficients for the Effects of Work-Related Characteristics and Liberalism on Perceived Discrimination Against Women*

	Perceived Discrimination Against Women Among			
	White		Black	
	Men	Women	Men	Women
Supervisor is male	.023	−.049	−.135	.077
Worker	.036	−.032	−.024	.001
Self-employed	−.074	−.244*	—	−.019
Personal gender discrimination	−.005	.402***	.061	.215**
Liberal	.092***	.119***	.012	.016
R²	.05	.13	.04	.03

	Perceived Discrimination Against Women Among			
	Hispanic		Asian	
	Men	Women	Men	Women
Supervisor is male	−.116	−.104	−.039	.006
Worker	−.030	−.057	.130	−.012
Self-employed	—	—	—	—
Personal gender discrimination	.251	.340***	−.317	.259
Liberal	.084**	.044	.002	−.006
R²	.04	.05	.18	.21

Source: Multi-City Study of Urban Inequality.
Notes: Entries are metric OLS regression coefficients from equations that also include the sociodemographic variables in table 3.7. The reference (excluded) category for job authority is the category "supervisor" (persons who work for others and have supervisory authority). Too few black men, Asian men and women, and Hispanic men and women are self-employed to estimate its effects reliably.
* = $p < .05$. ** = $p < .01$. *** = $p < .001$.

discrimination against minorities, men who report that they have experienced gender discrimination do not significantly differ from other men in their perceived level of discrimination against women.

Among whites, both men and women, perceived discrimination is linked to self-assessed political ideology. This essentially is not the case among minorities, where we see an effect of political ideology on perceived discrimination against women among Hispanic men only.

In Sum

Our results show that the perceived personal experience with gender discrimination in the workplace plays largely the same role in producing the gender gap in perceived discrimination against women as a group as perceived race-ethnic discrimination does in producing the white-minority gap in perceived discrimination against racial groups. As for personal racial discrimination, the majority of persons do not report that they have ever been the victim of gender discrimination. The percent who report that they have ever personally experienced gender discrimination varies from a low of 9 percent among Asian American women to a high of 26 percent among white women. The parallel figures for men are 3 percent among Asian Americans to 15 percent among blacks.

We see, however, that a difference exists in the effect of personal discrimination on perceived discrimination against minorities and on perceived discrimination against women. Why do whites who see themselves as personal victims of race discrimination more often deny that minorities in general are the victims of race discrimination, while white men who see themselves as the victim of gender discrimination *do not* more often deny discrimination against women? We cannot answer this question directly with the data at hand. However, we suggest that it well may stem from who is held responsible by whites for their perceived personal experience of race discrimination versus who men see as responsible for personally experienced gender discrimination. Many white males may hold minorities as a group responsible for promoting affirmative action or other such programs. Men do not, however, seem to hold women as a group responsible for their perceived personal experience of gender-based discrimination. The anger whites feel from perceived race discrimination may be more readily targeted toward minority groups, increasing the likelihood that such whites will deny that minorities in general experience job discrimination. Anger among men based on perceived discrimination due to gender, however, is not readily displaced against women as a group. The merit of this explanation, of course, awaits further research.[14]

Policy Attitudes

We now examine how perceived discrimination combines with other major forces in the climate of intergroup relations to shape public support for policy to promote intergroup economic inequality. In so doing, we return to one of the issues with which this chapter began: How does the public's comprehension of intergroup inequality shape the political prospects for the successful implementation of policy?

We employ two items in the analyses that follow. Prior research has shown that attitudes toward racial policy are strongly influenced by "framing" (Bobo and Kluegel 1993; Fine 1992b; Kinder and Sanders 1996; Nelson and Kinder 1996; Sniderman and Piazza 1993). Support for racial policy differs according to how a question is worded. The type of policy—whether it refers to quotas or programs to help minorities acquire skills and training—the agency for carrying out policy—the federal government or private-sector organizations—and the rationale for implementing policy invoked in a question all shape the public's response. It is important to know the wording of questions employed to measure policy attitudes. Ours are as follows:

> Training Help: Now I have some questions about what you think about the fairness of certain policies. Some people feel that because of past disadvantages there are some groups in society that should receive special *job training and educational assistance*. Others say that it is unfair to give these groups special job training and educational assistance. What about you? Do you strongly favor, favor, neither favor nor oppose, oppose, or strongly oppose special job training and educational assistance for [*group*]?

> Job Preference: Some people feel that because of past disadvantages there are some groups in society that should be *given preferences in hiring and promotion*. Others say that it is unfair to give these groups special preferences. What about you? Do you strongly favor, favor, neither favor nor oppose, oppose, or strongly oppose giving special preferences in hiring and promotion to [*group*]?

Both questions employ a "past disadvantages" referent that is in one sense rather neutral, in that it does not invoke imagery of slavery or other emotionally laden characterizations of the history of racism and discrimination. It importantly does not reference "discrimination" itself, so we avoid a possible definitional link between perceived discrimination and answers to this question. The questions differ in referent to simple training and education assistance versus preferences. The wording of the latter question importantly avoids use of the term *quotas*, which has become highly symbolically loaded and will confound responses to the preferences per se with the range of emotional reactions it invokes. Finally, these questions do not invoke a role for the federal government, and thus do not make antigovernment sentiment highly salient.

There is a substantial literature on attitudes toward affirmative action, specifically, and equal opportunity policy in general. It has focused primarily on policy directed toward African Americans, but there is a growing literature on attitudes toward policy addressing gender inequality (Clayton and Crosby 1992; Kane 1992, 1995; Kane and Sanchez 1994; Major 1994; Matheson et al. 1994; Steeh and Krysan 1996; Tougas and Veilleux 1988). We are unaware of published research, however, that examines attitudes toward policy for Hispanics or Asian Americans.[15] Because prior studies often differ in the wording of questions or the time and design of samples employed, and most often involve attitudes toward a program targeted at a single group, we lack truly comparative analyses of policy attitudes across groups. The Multi-City Study data allow such comparative analyses, and we present them here.

Group Gaps in Policy Support

Table 3.9 gives mean levels for each of the questions mentioned about policy support by city and race, and separately by gender as well for policy directed toward women. We see initially that, as has been demonstrated repeatedly in prior research, in all four cities there is less public support for job preferences than for training or educational assistance programs. This holds whether the target of policy is a race or ethnic group or women. It holds as well among all racial groups, and among men and women.

In general, the gaps in policy support seen in the table follow the same contours of the group gaps in perceived discrimination. The gaps are largest between whites and blacks and between whites and Hispanics over support for policy targeted to blacks and Hispanics, respectively. To illustrate what the differences in means imply, it is useful to note a few percentage differences. In Atlanta, for example, 38 percent of whites "favor" and an additional 17 percent "strongly favor" training or educational assistance for blacks. In contrast, the same figures for blacks are, respectively, 35 and 52 percent. The gap is even starker for job preference. Among white Atlantans, 10 percent "favor" and an additional 6 percent "strongly favor" job preferences for blacks. In contrast, the same figures for black Atlantans are, respectively, 32 and 34 percent.

We see, then, a 30-percentage-point gap between white and African American Atlantans in support for what may be termed relatively minimalist or "weak" policy and a 50-percentage-point gap in support for stronger policy. The gaps are somewhat smaller in the other three cities, but even in the most liberal of the four cities, Boston, the gap in support for job preference policy is nearly 40 percentage points. Differences of this magnitude between groups are rare in any survey data, and represent a real chasm in opinion. As in perceptions of discrimination, the gaps between Asian Americans and whites and between women and men are substantially smaller than those between whites and blacks and between whites and Hispanics.

TABLE 3.9   Mean Level of Support for Training Programs to Help Minorities or Women and Support for Job Preference for Minorities or Women, by City and Race-Ethnic Group

| | Support Training Help For | | | | | Support Job Preference For | | | | |
| | | | | Women | | | | | Women | |
	Asians	Blacks	Hispanics	Men	Women	Asians	Blacks	Hispanics	Men	Women
Atlanta										
Whites	—	3.32	3.26	3.13	3.16	2.34	2.40	2.34	2.28	2.60
Blacks	3.62	4.34	3.78	4.09	4.26	3.16	3.81	3.27	3.47	3.80
Boston										
Whites	3.68	3.79	3.73	3.59	4.02	2.61	2.67	2.64	2.62	2.96
Blacks	4.05	4.34	4.24	4.20	4.31	3.42	3.65	3.56	3.56	3.62
Hispanics	4.03	4.08	4.16	4.15	4.22	3.52	3.52	3.62	3.46	3.73
Detroit										
Whites	—	3.62	—	3.30	3.83	—	2.49	—	2.44	2.73
Blacks	—	4.43	—	4.24	4.30	—	3.78	—	3.66	3.67
Los Angeles										
Whites	3.34	3.58	3.51	3.41	3.71	2.56	2.66	2.61	2.65	2.81
Asians	3.57	3.88	3.51	3.60	3.75	3.07	3.15	2.96	3.04	3.12
Blacks	3.64	4.34	4.06	4.21	4.43	3.27	3.65	3.61	3.81	4.05
Hispanics	3.71	4.08	4.08	4.00	4.12	3.20	3.52	3.50	3.37	3.62

Source: Multi-City Study of Urban Inequality.

Perceived Discrimination and Policy Support

Gaps in policy support mirror gaps in perceived discrimination, suggesting that perceived discrimination has a substantial effect on policy support. But does this correlation imply that beliefs about discrimination *determine* policy attitudes? This question has been debated in a symposium centering on research by Steven Tuch and Michael Hughes (1996) arguing that perceived discrimination against blacks (among other factors) does importantly shape racial policy support among whites.

One point of debate involves causal direction. Mary Jackman (1996) argues that racial policy attitudes should be seen as the cause rather than the consequence of discrimination beliefs. Tuch and Hughes—in our view, compellingly—argue on logical grounds against the extreme position that causation runs solely from policy attitudes to discrimination. We may accept the premise that some or many whites justify opposition to racial policy based solely on self-interest by denying that blacks are the victims of job discrimination. But, ask Tuch and Hughes (1996, 785), what racial interests lead whites to support racial policy? Furthermore, they ask: "Do whites who acknowledge the existence of pervasive discrimination against blacks do so *because* they support affirmative action?" (emphasis added).

In addition, we have seen in our analysis of the determinants of perceived discrimination that net of sociodemographic position, liberal-conservative ideology, and group interests, whites who see a larger income gap between themselves and minorities are more likely to see prevalent job discrimination against minorities. This implies, counter to Jackman's critique of Tuch and Hughes, that educating whites about the pervasiveness of discrimination can lead to greater policy support. We concur with Tuch and Hughes that it is wholly reasonable to assume a causal relationship from perceived discrimination to racial policy attitudes.

A second point of debate involves the multicausal basis of policy attitudes (Davis 1996; Sears and Jessor 1996). The breadth of the Multi-City Study coverage allows us to control for the influence of several competing explanatory factors, which we do in the regressions presented in table 3.10. They substantiate that, net of other factors, perceived discrimination does have an independent and important influence on white support of policy targeted toward all minority groups and toward women.

Because whites' views carry the most political force at present, and because policy support among blacks and Hispanics for policy to help their own groups is so high, we restrict analyses of support for policy

TABLE 3.10　Regression Coefficients for the Determinants of Policy Support Attitudes, White Respondents Only

| | Support Training Help For | | | | | Support Job Preference For | | | | |
| | | | | Women | | | | | Women | |
	Asians	Blacks	Hispanics	Men	Women	Asians	Blacks	Hispanics	Men	Women
Age twenty-one to twenty-nine	−.061	−.084	−.005	−.050	−.191*	−.097	−.127	−.017	−.174	−.134
Age thirty to thirty-nine	.011	−.061	.031	.057	−.007	−.006	−.057	.041	−.105	−.097
Age forty to forty-nine	−.019	−.074	−.022	.012	.068	.037	−.036	.052	−.092	−.026
Age sixty-five +	−.058	.020	−.061	.188	−.082	.021	.067	.034	.199	.005
Married	—	—	—	−.050	−.135*	—	—	—	−.077	−.059
Education	.022	.018	.036	−.072*	−.055*	−.025	−.041*	−.044*	−.028	−.066*
Income	−.032***	−.028***	−.035***	−.025***	−.022***	−.032***	−.032***	−.032**	−.030***	−.038***
Male	−.241***	−.231***	−.199***	—	—	−.110**	−.129**	−.096*	—	—
Atlanta	−.324***	−.206**	−.360***	−.116	−.144	−.182**	−.006	−.221**	−.018	−.075
Boston	—	.092	—	.225*	.097	—	.103	—	.087	.146
Los Angeles	−.171**	−.070	−.111*	.078	−.113	.043	.148**	.049	.138	.084

Competition with immigrants	-.155***	-.145***	-.156***	-.143***	-.110***	-.228***	-.214***	-.229***	-.189***	-.182***
Liberalism	.116***	.114***	.112***	.088***	.126***	.103***	.110***	.101***	.118***	.078***
Discrimination against group	.176***	.231***	.199***	.194***	.239***	.137***	.159***	.178***	.197***	.162***
White versus group welfare dependence	.020	-.036**	-.047***	—	—	-.004	-.039**	-.034**	—	—
R^2	.13	.15	.15	.11	.16	.13	.14	.15	.13	.11

Source: Multi-City Study of Urban Inequality.

Notes: Entries are metric OLS regression coefficients. The reference (excluded) group for age categories is ages fifty to sixty-four. Questions concerning Training Help and Job Preference for Asians and Hispanics, respectively, were not asked in Detroit. The reference (excluded) category for city of residence is Boston for policy support questions concerning Asians and Hispanics, and Detroit for policy support questions concerning blacks and women.

* = $p < .05$. ** = $p < .01$. *** = $p < .001$.

targeted to minorities to our white sample. For policy targeted to women, however, we do separate analyses among men and women.

The results in table 3.10 replicate for policy targeted to Asians and Hispanics several findings of research using national-level data on support of policy targeted to blacks. Here we see no statistically significant age group differences in support for either type of policy or for policy targeted to any of the three minority groups. Net of other factors, education does not effect support of training or educational assistance, but does have a negative effect on support for job preferences. Higher-income whites and white males consistently are more opposed to policy of both types across all groups. Married women oppose training help for women more than the nonmarried, but these two groups do not differ in support for job preferences. Our white Atlantan respondents oppose training help policy for all minorities more than do white respondents from the other three cities. Net of other variables, white Angelenos oppose policy to provide training assistance for Asians more so than do respondents from Boston (questions about policy targeted to Asians and Hispanics were not asked in Detroit). Although the greater policy opposition of Atlantans carries forward to job preference for Asians and Hispanics, they do not differ from whites in Boston or Detroit regarding support for job preferences for blacks. Angelenos show stronger support for job preferences for blacks than do white respondents from the other three cities.

There are no significant city differences in support for training assistance to women, other than a tendency for men in Boston to be more supportive. Otherwise the socioeconomic patterning of support for policy targeted to women is the same for white men and white women, and is essentially the same as that found for whites' attitudes toward policy targeted to minorities.

We include three measures to control for the influence of factors proposed in the debate over the determinants of policy attitudes to influence racial policy, and whose influence is potentially confounded with that of perceived discrimination. We include the previously used measure of perceived competition with immigrants to tap the influence of group self-interest. We also include our measure of self-assessed liberalism-conservatism to control for the argued political determination of policy attitudes (Davis 1996). Finally, we include a measure of perceived welfare dependency among minorities (see appendix 3A for wording and construction of this measure). It indicates the extent to which whites are perceived to be less "prone" to live off welfare (that is, to give more value to self-sufficiency) than are members of a particular racial group. We include this measure to tap the potential influence of a key component of symbolic racism (Sears 1988): blaming blacks for social ills, especially welfare. According to the symbolic racism perspective, many whites have come to recognize that overt expression of bigotry or Jim Crow racism is unacceptable. Thus, "safe" avenues for expressing hostility toward blacks are sought—such as labeling blacks welfare-dependent.

Factors other than perceived group discrimination do affect policy attitudes. Liberals support each type of policy for each group more than conservatives do, controlling for perceived discrimination and other factors. Self-assessed placement on the liberal-conservative dimension, of course, reflects more than socioeconomic ideology alone, and these dimensions (for example, anti–big government sentiment) also shape support for policy. Some whites who see blacks or Hispanics as more welfare-dependent than whites oppose policy to help them, even if they perceive that black or Hispanic groups suffer from discrimination.

The direct effect of perceived competition with immigrants on policy support underscores the basis of policy support in self-interest. There is an individual component of self-interest in the direct effect of income on support for training assistance, and of both income and education on support for job preferences. Support for policy of any kind is paid for by taxes that, in turn, are higher for the more well-to-do. Job preferences bring a challenge to the advantage that higher education provides in competition for jobs and promotions. The direct effect of perceived competition shows an effect of group self-interest as well.

We have demonstrated the effect of group self-interest on support of policy targeted toward blacks in other research (Bobo and Kluegel 1993). This research highlights how strong the influence of group self-interest is and shows its effect on policy targeted to other minorities and to women. Independent of their education, income, political leanings, and beliefs about minorities and women, white males as a group consistently more strongly oppose policies targeted to any minority or to women than do white women. This no doubt reflects simple defense of white male privilege and the "anti–white male" label often attached to affirmative action and other equal opportunity programs. Whites who see the world as a competition between or among groups over a zero-sum good oppose any efforts that will advantage some other group. (Interestingly, women who hold to this worldview also are more likely than other women to oppose policy helping *women*.) Note as well that perceived competition with immigrants has a stronger effect on support for job preference than on support for training help. This seems best interpreted as a result of the greater group-threat quality of job preferences than of training assistance. The latter, of course, involves a more individualistic approach and is a more diffuse threat than direct job preference.

Perceived discrimination has a substantial and statistically significant net effect on policy support across the board. Its effect is essentially equal for men or women. Furthermore, perceived discrimination completely mediates the effect of two factors we considered in analyzing its own determinants on support for policy targeted to minorities. Regressions (not shown) demonstrate that neither the perceived personal experience of race discrimination nor the perceived white-minority gap in income have statistically significant direct effects on whites' support for either training help or job preference for minority groups. Thus it appears that perceived group discrimination channels the influence of "data"—in the form of individual experience or societal knowledge—potentially relevant to supporting racial inequality policy.

Conclusion

We set out in this chapter to use the unique strengths of the Multi-City Study of Urban Inequality data to provide a broader picture of racial and gender gaps in perceived discrimination. We also sought to probe more deeply into the sources of these gaps and their consequences for opportunity-related policy.

We found a picture of a limited gender gap, but an extensive and multifaceted race gap in perceived discrimination. We have seen that the large white-black and white-Hispanic gaps in perceived discrimination against these respective minority groups is found in each of the four surveyed cities. These gaps in perceived discrimination are paralleled by large white-black and white-Hispanic gaps in support for policy to reduce racial inequality. At present there is no such white–Asian American gap in perceived discrimination against Asians in Los Angeles, but this may be temporary. We found evidence that increased acculturation among Asian Americans brings with it increased perceived discrimination—against Asians as a group and against women.

Our comparative analysis by race and gender shows that the racialization of discrimination perceptions involves two facets beyond whites' and minorities' beliefs about discrimination against minorities. It includes a substantial minority-white gap in perceived reverse discrimination. The majority of whites perceive "a little" or "some" race-based job discrimination against whites, but the large majority of each minority categorically says "none" exists. This itself may be a source of frustration and anger, as is the white-minority gap in perceptions about discrimination against minorities. In addition, the racialized quality of discrimination perceptions extends to beliefs about discrimination against women. As we have seen, the gap between blacks' greater and whites' lesser perceived gender discrimination is larger than the same gap between women and men.

We found that there is a large white-minority gap in the determinants of perceived group discrimination as well. Whites' beliefs do not reflect potential social learning from personal or workplace contact, but rest more in deduction from social ideology, perceived group interest, and social ignorance. In contrast, perceived discrimination among minority groups is a function of the actual risk and perceived personal experience with job discrimination. This suggests that one direct and straightforward way to reduce the white-minority gap in perceived discrimination is to eliminate actual discrimination.

The subject of eliminating discrimination leads us back to a consideration of inequality-related policy. We found that, net of other important determinants, perceived discrimination against minorities and women does shape policy attitudes. What, accordingly, are the implications of our findings about perceived discrimination for future public support of policy to reduce race-ethnic or gender inequality?

Our findings give some reason to be optimistic about increased public support for racial policy in response to research on "objective" group-based economic inequalities presented in this book and elsewhere. White acknowledgment of discrimination may be halting, but it is there. Only a minority of whites deny it altogether. Even for perceptions of discrimination against Asians, at least half of whites in each city say there is "some" or "a lot" of discrimination. That whites do acknowledge job discrimination against minorities results in at least moderate levels of support for minimalist interventions to promote equal economic opportunity.

White anger over "reverse discrimination" is one source of opposition to racial policy. Contrary to the impressions given by one line of questioning, whites in our cities do not see prevalent reverse discrimination against their own group. Questions such as those posed in the National Election Survey that ask whites to rate the likelihood that a white family member will be the victim show a high percentage rating such a chance as likely (compare, Kinder and Sanders 1996). Yet when the referent is fellow whites collectively, a very small percent of whites perceive a lot of reverse discrimination and the substantial majority see little or none. Perhaps there is a grain of realism shaping perceptions here, and recognition that numbers and segregation determine that the potential for whites as a group to suffer extensive discrimination due to being white is quite limited.

Viewed in one light, we have reason to be optimistic at the percentage of whites who see no income difference on average between whites and minorities: 59 percent see Asians as having income equal to or greater than whites, 23 percent and 20 percent share the same belief in equality, respectively, between whites and blacks or Hispanics. It holds out the promise that continued efforts to describe and interpret the stagnant or worsening economic gap between whites and minority groups may pay off in terms of an increased perception among whites that there are structural limitations to opportunity for minorities. The challenge is to understand who in particular holds this view and how best to educate them.

Other findings are not so sanguine. The white-minority gap involving blacks and Hispanics is just as strong among the young and the old. Age group differences may derive from social or biological aging per se, as well as reflect larger societal trends. Yet we know that age group differences in traditional prejudice shown with cross-sectional data do clearly parallel trend data. The young led the way in the decline of traditional prejudice, but we can make no such statement at present about perceived discrimination against minority groups.

We have found little to no evidence that personal or workplace contact leads to a greater recognition of discrimination against minorities. Although recent research demonstrates that such contact may have effects on interpersonal relations, our findings argue against such effects on beliefs about discrimination. Contact then may reduce hostility or, more positively, increase good feelings between whites and minorities *as individuals*. It does not appear to teach any lessons about the circumstances and treatment of minorities *as a group*.

Our results show this to be a consequence of the strongly abstract determination among whites of perceived discrimination against minority groups. Although, as we noted earlier, the social naïveté basis of perceived discrimination against minorities perhaps is malleable, other components are much more resistant to change. Liberal-conservative political ideology and the white sense of group entitlement are deeply rooted in American history and culture. Simple intergroup contact faces an uphill battle in overcoming them.

Our research also shows that perceiving prevalent job discrimination among minority groups or women in and of itself is not sufficient to produce support for policy. The visible political attention to opportunity-related social policy is frequently reduced to a debate over the fairness of "quotas." As we have seen, the simple mention of the word *preference* in the context of racial or gender policy was sufficient to produce widespread opposition among whites in each of the four cities. In addition, we have seen that attitudes toward inequality-related policy addressed to minorities or women are the product of several entrenched forces, including social-political ideology, negative racial effect in the guise of such characterizations as welfare dependency, and group interests.

Support for policy addressing gender inequality in the four cities rests on a rather uncertain base in opinion about job discrimination against women. As in the case of whites' perceptions of discrimination against minorities, at least half the male respondents in each city acknowledge "some" (the modal response) or "a lot" of job discrimination against women. In contrast to the case of blacks and Hispanics, however, women are much more divided in their opinion about the pervasiveness of discrimination against their own group. This implies, as we have seen empirically, that women are less strong advocates for programs targeted toward reducing gender inequality than blacks and Hispanics are for programs targeted toward their respective groups. Indeed, as we have seen, the greater denial of discrimination against women found among white women than among black men leads black men to support gender-related policy more strongly than do white women.

Recently, we have seen an increasing call for dialogue on matters of race by the president and other political figures. (Indeed, one might consider such a dialogue on matters of gender as well.) Often, the kind of dialogue that is envisioned includes only issues of racial prejudice and stereotyping. Yet we have shown in this research that the basis for intergroup anger and conflict over beliefs about discrimination is wide-ranging and even stronger than has been underscored in other research on whites and blacks (Feagin and Sikes 1994; Hochschild 1995). The results of this and other research show that there is potentially much to be gained by including racial and ethnic discrimination as a topic in this dialogue. The basis of minority group views in actual risk and personal experience of discrimination, however, argues that dialogue alone will not be sufficient to bridge the white-minority gap in perceived discrimination. It must be accompanied by action to end discrimination in the workplace.

Appendix: Measures
Sociodemographic Variables

Education is measured in five categories: (1) zero to eleven years, (2) twelve years, (3) thirteen to fifteen years, (4) sixteen years, and (5) seventeen or more years. *Income* is total family income for 1992 in twenty categories, ranging from (1) 0 to $4,999 to (2) $150,000 or more. It is measured in $5,000 intervals up to $69,999, $10,000 intervals up to $99,999, and $25,000 intervals up to $149,999.

Personal and Workplace Contact

To measure personal contact, we used the following question:

> From time to time, most people discuss important matters with other people. Looking back over the last six months, who are the people, *other than people living in your own household*, with whom you have discussed matters important to you?

Personal contact has been measured in different ways in prior research, but the restriction to contact involving important matters focuses attention on nontrivial engagement across race or ethnic lines. Thus, any potential effect of personal contact on perceived discrimination is allowed full opportunity to show itself in this research.

We employ two measures of workplace contact. Respondents were asked to indicate the race/ethnicity of their immediate supervisor at work. They also reported on the race/ethnicity of coworkers, indicating whether "most of the employees doing the kind of work you do/did at this location are non-Hispanic white, non-Hispanic black, Hispanic, Asian, or other."

These measures in principle permit one to look at the effects of personal contact viewed in many different configurations. In practice, however, because of the prevalence of white-minority segregation, we are limited to examining more simple operationalizations when analyzing the effects of contact on whites' perceptions. We analyze the effects of having one or more persons of a specific minority group in one's personal network on perceived discrimination against that minority group. In looking at how contact shapes perceived "reverse discrimination," we broaden the scope a bit, examining the effect of having any nonwhite member among one's personal network. We restrict our attention to whether or not whites work where their coworkers are predominantly white versus nonwhite (330 whites work with predominantly nonwhite coworkers), and to whether they have a white or nonwhite immediate supervisor (182 whites have a nonwhite supervisor).

Among minorities, we include two dimensions of personal contact: a variable distinguishing persons who number one or more whites in their personal network, and persons who number one or more other minorities in their network. Each workplace contact measure now has three categories among minority group members. Coworker race-ethnicity is composed of those who work with coworkers primarily of their own race-ethnicity, those who work with primarily white coworkers, and those who work primarily with coworkers from other minority groups. Supervisor race-ethnicity is composed of those who are supervised by a member of their own race-ethnicity, those who have a white supervisor, and those who are supervised by someone from another minority group than their own. The first category of each of these two variables is excluded in the regressions of table 3.4.

Personal Experience of Discrimination

The perceived personal experience of job discrimination due to race or gender, respectively, is measured by the combined response to the following questions:

> Have you felt that at any time in the past you were refused a job because of your race or ethnicity (your gender)?
> Have you ever felt at any time in the past that others at your place of employment got promotions or pay raises faster than you because of your race or ethnicity (your gender)?

A respondent is given a score of 1 if she or he answers yes to either one of these two questions, and a score of 0 if she or he answers no to both of them. Measures of personal race and gender discrimination were constructed for respondents who had ever worked for pay and who had complete data for each of the two questions.

Liberalism-Conservatism

Answers to this question were coded such that a high score indicates greater self-assessed political liberalism. Respondents were asked:

> We hear a lot of talk these days about liberals and conservatives. Here is a seven-point scale on which the political views that people might hold are arranged, from extremely liberal to extremely conservative. Where would you place yourself on this scale?
> [Responses are "extremely liberal," "liberal," "slightly liberal," "moderate," "slightly conservative," "conservative," and "extremely conservative."]

Group Threat

> *Competition with Immigrants:* If immigration to this country continues, do you believe people like you will probably have: much more opportunity than now, some but not a lot more, no more or less than now, less than now, or a lot less than now?
> *Job Competition with GROUP:* More good jobs for blacks-Hispanics or Asians mean fewer good jobs for R'S RACIAL/ETHNIC GROUP.
> [The response scale ranges from 5 ("strongly agree") to 1 ("strongly disagree.")]

White Versus GROUP Traits

To measure *White vs. GROUP Wealth* and *White vs. GROUP Welfare Dependence*, we asked respondents to rate "whites," "Asians," "blacks," and "Hispanics or Latinos" on 7-point scales. We used difference scores in our analyses, obtained by subtracting the rating for a particular minority group from that for whites. The items were recoded so that a higher value of a difference score indicates, respectively, that whites are perceived to be more affluent than a minority group or that whites are considered to be less "welfare-dependent." The specific questions used are as follows:

> *Wealth:* In the first statement a score of 1 means that you think almost all of the people in that group are "rich." A score of 7 means that you think almost everyone in the group is "poor." A score of 4 means that you think that a group is not toward one end or the other, and of course you may choose any number in between that comes closest to where you think people in the group stand.

> *Welfare Dependence:* Next, for each group I want to know whether you think they tend to be self-supporting or tend to prefer to live off welfare. A score of 1 means that you think almost all of the people in that group "prefer to be self-supporting." A score of 7 means that you think that almost everyone in the group "prefers to live off welfare." A score of 4 means that you think that a group is not toward one end or the other, and of course you may choose any number in between that comes closest to where you think people in the group stand.

Notes

1. Because questions about discrimination against different groups were placed together in the questionnaire, the possibility of "even-handedness" or a response consistency effect must be recognized (Schuman and Presser 1981). Correspondingly, we give more attention to the relative difference in perceptions of discrimination against different groups than to their absolute values.

2. In contrast, nearly two-thirds of those choosing "a lot" *affirm* that the black-white socioeconomic gap is "mainly due to discrimination."

3. Emily Kane (1992) examines attitudes toward gender stratification, including perceptions of discrimination and support for inequality-related policy—by gender and race. However, her analysis is based on small samples of black men (62) and black women (80), and does not include comparisons with Hispanics or Asian Americans.

4. For convenience of exposition only, we use the term *racial* in referring to Hispanics as well as blacks and Asians.

5. Results from a 1980 national survey (Kluegel and Smith 1986) showed slightly more perceived discrimination against women than blacks, and a smaller gap between men and women in the extent of perceived discrimination against women than we find in the Multi-City Study data.

6. Emily Kane (1992) found the same pattern for attitudes toward gender stratification in general.

7. We do not include variables to represent city of residence in analyses of Asian American and Hispanic perceptions of discrimination against their own respective groups. In the Asian American case, virtually all respondents, of course, are from Los Angeles. There is essentially no overlap in the distribution of Hispanic origin groups between Boston and Los Angeles. Hispanics from Boston are either Dominican or Puerto Rican in origin. Hispanics from Los Angeles originate from Central America or Mexico or are Mexican Americans. City and origin group thus are completely confounded, and we cannot include variables for both of them simultaneously in regression equations.

8. To more closely "capture" second- and third-generation persons, we analyzed age group differences among Hispanic and Asian American respondents born in the United States. These results differ from the results in table 3.2 in only one respect. Hispanic respondents sixty-five or older do not differ on average from other age groups in perceived discrimination against Hispanics. That is, there are no statistically significant differences in perceived discrimination at all among either Asian Americans or Hispanics born in the United States.

9. We also tested for possible differences among the respective Hispanic and Asian American origin subgroups in how sociodemographic variables affect perceived group discrimination. The smaller numbers of respondents in each subgroup limit how strong a test we can realize from these data. Nevertheless, the results show that the findings in table 3.3 for the respective Hispanic and Asian American origin groups combined are the same in each of the separate origin groups.

10. Questions about contact and work experiences were asked of partial subsets of respondents. To accommodate this problem of varying n's, we employed pairwise deletion of missing data. This effectively made use of all available information when we tested for the statistical significance of relationships between variables.

11. Consistent with this interpretation, Lawrence Bobo and Vincent Hutchings (1996) found that whites in Los Angeles perceive greater job and economic competition with Asians and Latinos than with blacks. In the Multi-City Study data, we find that white Atlantans

perceive more direct job competition on average with blacks than do whites in the other three cities, and white Angelenos perceive more direct job competition with Asians than with either blacks or Hispanics (the latter two groups have roughly equal means for perceived job competition).

12. In addition to its contemporaneous effect, the personal experience of race discrimination contributes to a historical and collective determination of perceived group discrimination through "racial alienation" (Bobo and Hutchings 1996). *Racial alienation* is shaped over time by a group's cumulative and collectively shared experience with racial disenfranchisement and unequal treatment (Bobo and Hutchings 1996; Feagin 1991). Forty-five percent of blacks and 28 percent of Hispanics report having ever personally been the victim of job discrimination, and it is substantially more likely that they will know a fellow member of their group who perceives having been so victimized than it is for whites or Asian Americans. The collectively derived knowledge of job discrimination against members of one's own group meets with the collective experience of discrimination in other areas to reinforce the sense that job discrimination is a serious problem faced by one's group (Feagin 1991).

13. The lack of a statistically significant effect for personal gender discrimination among Asian women reflects the small number reporting such experience. Of the 284 Asian women who were asked to report on experience with personal discrimination, 26 responded that they had ever experienced any gender discrimination in hiring or promotion. It is best to conclude that our data do not permit a reliable estimate of the effect of personal gender discrimination among Asian American women.

14. Social distance also may play a role. There, of course, is much greater social distance between whites and minorities than between white men and white women. It is correspondingly psychologically easier for white men to express anger toward minorities than toward women.

15. A review of poll and other survey data on affirmative action (Steeh and Krysan 1996) identifies only one unpublished study that examined attitudes toward programs targeting Asians and Latinos.

References

Blumer, Herbert. 1958. "Racial Prejudice as a Sense of Group Position." *Pacific Sociological Review* 1: 1–7.

Bobo, Lawrence, and Vincent L. Hutchings. 1996. "Perceptions of Racial Group Competition: Extending Blumer's Theory of Group Position to a Multiracial Social Context." *American Sociological Review* 61: 951–72.

Bobo, Lawrence, and James R. Kluegel. 1991. "Whites' Stereotypes, Social Distance and Perceived Discrimination Toward Blacks, Hispanics, and Asians: Toward a Multiethnic Framework." Paper presented at the 86th Annual Meeting of the American Sociological Association. Cincinnati, Ohio (August 23–27, 1991).

———. 1993. "Opposition to Race-Targeting: Self-Interest, Stratification Ideology or Racial Attitudes?" *American Sociological Review* 58: 443–64.

———. 1997. "Status, Ideology and Dimensions of Whites' Racial Beliefs and Attitudes: Progress and Stagnation." In *Racial Attitudes in the 1990s: Continuity and Change*, edited by Jack Martin and Steven Tuch. Westport, Conn.: Praeger.

Bobo, Lawrence, James R. Kluegel, and Ryan A. Smith. 1997. "Laissez Faire Racism: The Crystallization of 'Kinder, Gentler' Anti-Black Ideology." In *Racial Attitudes in the 1990s: Continuity and Change*, edited by Jack Martin and Steven Tuch. Westport, Conn.: Praeger.

Bobo, Lawrence, and Susan A. Suh. 1995. "Surveying Racial Discrimination: Analyses from a Multiethnic Labor Market." Working paper 75. New York: Russell Sage Foundation.

Bobo, Lawrence, and Camille L. Zubrinsky. 1996. "Attitudes on Residential Integration: Perceived Status Differences, Mere In-Group Preference, or Racial Prejudice." *Social Forces* 74: 883–909.

Bobo, Lawrence, Camille L. Zubrinsky, James H. Johnson, Jr., and Melvin L. Oliver. 1995. "Work Orientation, Job Discrimination and Ethnicity: A Focus Group Perspective." *Research in the Sociology of Work* 5: 45–85.

Burstein, Paul. 1985. *Discrimination, Jobs and Politics*. Chicago. University of Chicago Press.

Campbell, Christopher R. 1995. *Race, Myth and the News*. Thousand Oaks, Calif.: Sage.

Chang, Edward T., and Russell C. Leong. 1994. *Los Angeles: Struggles Toward Multi-Ethnic Community*. Seattle: University of Washington Press.

Chen, Kenyon S., and Shirley Hune. 1995. "Racialization and Pan-Ethnicity: From Asians in America to Asian-Americans." In *Toward a Common Destiny*, edited by Willis D. Hawley and Anthony W. Jackson. San Francisco: Jossey-Bass.

Clayton, Susan D., and Faye J. Crosby. 1992. *Justice, Gender, and Affirmative Action*. Ann Arbor: University of Michigan Press.

Davis, Darren W. 1996. "White Americans' Opposition to Racial Policies: Where Are the Political Explanations?" *Social Science Quarterly* 77: 747–50.

de la Garza, Rodolfo O., Louis DeSipio, F. Chris Garcia, John Garcia, and Angelo Falcon. 1992. *Latino Voices: Mexican, Puerto Rican, and Cuban Perspectives on American Politics*. Boulder, Colo.: Westview.

de la Garza, Rodolfo O., Angelo Falcon, and F. Chris Garcia. 1996. "Will the Real Americans Please Stand Up?: Anglo and Mexican-American Political Values." *American Journal of Political Science* 40: 335–51.

Duleep, Harriet Orcutt, and Seth Sanders. 1992. "Discrimination at the Top: American-Born Asian and White Men." *Industrial Relations* 31: 416–32.

Eberhardt, Jennifer, and Susan T. Fiske. 1994. "Affirmative Action in Theory and Practice: Issues of Power, Ambiguity, and Gender versus Race." *Basic and Applied Social Psychology* 15: 201–20.

Ellison, Christopher, and Daniel Powers. 1994. "The Contact Hypothesis and Racial Attitudes Among Black Americans." *Social Science Quarterly* 75: 385–400.

Espiritu, Yen Le. 1997. *Asian American Women and Men*. Thousand Oaks, Calif.: Sage.

Feagin, Joe R. 1991. "The Continuing Significance of Race: Antiblack Discrimination in Public Places." *American Sociological Review* 56: 101–16.

Feagin, Joe R., and Melvin P. Sikes. 1994. *Living with Racism: The Black Middle-Class Experience*. Boston: Beacon.

Feagin, Joe R., and Hernan Vera. 1995. *White Racism*. New York: Routledge.

Feldman, Stanley. 1988. "Structure and Consistency in Public Opinion: The Role of Core Beliefs and Values." *American Journal of Political Science* 19: 393–417.

Fine, Terri Susan. 1992a. "Individualism and Liberalism/Conservatism: Broadening Dimensions of Policy Support." *Polity* 25: 315–27.

———. 1992b. "The Impact of Issue Framing on Public Opinion Toward Affirmative Action Programs." *Social Science Journal* 29: 323–34.

Griffin, William E., and Yaw Oheneba-Sakyi. 1993. "Sociodemographic and Political Correlates of University Students' Causal Attributions for Poverty." *Psychological Reports* 73: 795–800.

Hein, Jeremy. 1994. "From Migrant to Minority: Hmong Refugees and the Social Construction of Identity in the United States." *Sociological Inquiry* 64: 281–306.

Hochschild, Jennifer L. 1995. *Facing Up to the American Dream*. Princeton, N.J.: Princeton University Press.

Jackman, Mary. 1996. "Individualism, Self-Interest, and White Racism." *Social Science Quarterly* 77: 760–67.

Jackman, Mary, and Marie Crane. 1986. "'Some of My Best Friends Are Black': Interracial Friendship and White Racial Attitudes." *Public Opinion Quarterly* 50: 459–86.

Jackson, Bryan O., Elisabeth R. Gerber, and Bruce E. Cain. 1994. "Coalitional Prospects in a Multi-racial Society: African-American Attitudes Toward Other Minority Groups." *Political Research Quarterly* 47: 277–94.

Jacobsen, Cardell K. 1985. "Resistance to Affirmative Action: Self-Interest or Racism?" *Journal of Conflict Resolution* 29: 306–29.

Jaynes, Gerald David, and Robin M. Williams, Jr. 1989. *A Common Destiny: Blacks and American Society*. Washington, D.C.: National Academy Press.

Johnson, James H., Jr., and Melvin Oliver. 1994. "Interethnic Minority Conflict in America: The Effects of Economic and Social Dislocations." In *Race and Ethnic Conflict*, edited by Fred L. Pincus and Howard J. Ehrlich. Boulder, Colo.: Westview.

Kane, Emily. 1992. "Race, Gender, and Attitudes Toward Gender Stratification." *Social Psychology Quarterly* 55: 311–20.

———. 1995. "Education and Beliefs About Gender Inequality." *Social Problems* 42: 74–90.

Kane, Emily, and Laura Sanchez. 1994. "Family Status and Criticism of Gender Inequality at Home and at Work." *Social Forces* 72: 1079–1102.

Kinder, Donald R., and Lynn M. Sanders. 1996. *Divided by Color*. Chicago: University of Chicago Press.

Kluegel, James R. 1985. "'If There Isn't a Problem, You Don't Need a Solution': The Bases of Contemporary Affirmative Action Attitudes." *American Behavioral Scientist* 28: 761–84.

———. 1990. "Trends in Whites' Explanations of the Gap in Black-White Socioeconomic Status, 1977–1989." *American Sociological Review* 55: 512–25.

Kluegel, James R., and Eliot R. Smith. 1986. *Beliefs About Inequality: Americans' Views of What Is and What Ought to Be*. Hawthorne, N.Y.: Aldine de Gruyter.

Kuo, Wen H. 1995. "Coping with Racial Discrimination: The Case of Asian Americans." *Ethnic and Racial Studies* 18: 109–27.

Lee, Sharon M. 1989. "Asian Immigration and American Race-Relations: From Exclusion to Acceptance." *Ethnic and Racial Studies* 12: 368–90.

Loewen, James W. 1995. *Lies My Teacher Told Me: Everything Your American History Textbook Got Wrong*. New York: New Press.

Major, Brenda. 1994. "From Social Inequality to Personal Entitlement: The Role of Social Comparisons, Legitimacy Appraisals, and Group Membership." *Advances in Experimental Social Psychology* 26: 293–355.

Massey, Douglas S. 1993. "Latinos, Poverty, and the Underclass: A New Agenda for Research." *Hispanic Journal of Behavioral Sciences* 15: 449–75.

Matheson, Kimberley, Alan Echenberg, Donald Taylor, Darlene Rivers, and Ivy Chow. 1994. "Women's Attitudes Toward Affirmative Action: Putting Actions in Context." *Journal of Applied Social Psychology* 24: 2075–96.

Morales, Rebecca, and Paul M. Ong. 1993. "The Illusion of Progress: Latinos in Los Angeles." In *Latinos in a Changing U.S. Economy*, edited by Rebecca Morales and Frank Bonilla. Newbury Park, Calif.: Sage.

Morin, Richard. 1995. "Across the Racial Divide." *Washington Post Weekly Edition*, October 16–22, 1995, 6–10.

Nelson, Thomas E., and Donald R. Kinder. 1996. "Issue Frames and Group-Centrism in American Public Opinion." *Journal of Politics* 58: 1055–78.

Portes, Alejandro, and Robert L. Bach. 1985. *Latin Journey: Cuban and Mexican Immigrants in the United States.* Berkeley: University of California Press.

Portes, Alejandro, and Min Zhou. 1993. "The New Second Generation: Segmented Assimilation and Its Variants." *Annals of the American Academy of Political and Social Science* 530: 74–96.

Powers, Daniel A., and Christopher G. Ellison. 1995. "Interracial Contact and Black Racial Attitudes: The Contact Hypothesis and Selectivity Bias." *Social Forces* 74: 205–26.

Quillian, Lincoln. 1995. "Prejudice as a Response to Perceived Group Threat." *American Sociological Review* 60: 586–611.

———. 1996. "Group Threat and Regional Change in Attitudes Toward African Americans." *American Journal of Sociology* 102: 816–60.

Reimers, Cordelia W. 1992. "Hispanic Earnings and Employment in the 1980s." In *Hispanics in the Workplace,* edited by Stephen B. Knouse, Paul Rosenfeld, and Amy L. Culbertson. Newbury Park, Calif.: Sage.

Schuman, Howard, and Stanley Presser. 1981. *Questions and Answers in Attitude Surveys: Experiments on Question Form, Wording and Context.* New York: Academic Press.

Sears, David O. 1988. "Symbolic Racism." In *Eliminating Racism,* edited by Phyllis A. Katz and Dalmas A. Taylor. New York: Plenum.

Sears, David O., and Tom Jessor. 1996. "Whites' Racial Policy Attitudes: The Role of White Racism." *Social Science Quarterly* 77: 747–50.

Sidanius, Jim, Felicia Pratto, and Lawrence Bobo. 1996. "Racism, Conservatism, Affirmative Action and Intellectual Sophistication: A Matter of Principled Conservatism or Group Dominance?" *Journal of Personality and Social Psychology* 70: 476–90.

Sigelman, Lee, Timothy Bledsoe, Susan Welch, and Michael W. Combs. 1996. "Making Contact: Black-White Social Interaction in an Urban Setting." *American Journal of Sociology* 101: 1306–32.

Sigelman, Lee, and Susan Welch. 1991. *Black Americans' Views of Racial Inequality: The Dream Deferred.* New York: Cambridge University Press.

———. 1993. "The Contact Hypothesis Revisited: Interracial Contact and Positive Racial Attitudes." *Social Forces* 71: 781–95.

Sniderman, Paul M., and Michael Gray Hagen. 1985. *Race and Inequality: A Study in American Values.* Chatham, N.J.: Chatham House.

Sniderman, Paul M., and Thomas Piazza. 1993. *The Scar of Race.* Cambridge, Mass.: Harvard University Press.

Steeh, Charlotte, and Maria Krysan. 1996. "The Polls-Trends: Affirmative Action and the Public, 1970–1995." *Public Opinion Quarterly* 60: 128–58.

Stolzenberg, Rafe M. 1990. "Ethnicity, Geography and Occupational

Achievement of Hispanic Men in the United States." *American Sociological Review* 55: 143–54.

Tang, Joyce. 1993. "The Career Attainment of Caucasian and Asian Engineers." *Sociological Quarterly* 34: 467–96.

Thornton, Michael C., and Robert J. Taylor. 1988. "Intergroup Attitudes: Black American Perceptions of Asian Americans." *Ethnic and Racial Studies* 11: 474–88.

Tougas, Francine, and France Veilleux. 1988. "The Influence of Identification, Collective Relative Deprivation and Procedure of Implementation on Women's Response to Affirmative Action: A Causal Modeling Approach." *Canadian Journal of Behavioral Science* 20: 15–28.

Tuch, Steven A., and Michael Hughes. 1996. "Whites' Racial Policy Attitudes." *Social Science Quarterly* 77: 723–45.

U.S. Commission on Civil Rights. 1992. *Civil Rights Issues Facing Asian Americans in the 1990s*. Washington, D.C.: Commission on Civil Rights.

Zucker, Gail Sahar, and Bernard Weiner. 1993. "Conservatism and Perceptions of Poverty: An Attributional Analysis." *Journal of Applied Psychology* 23: 925–43.

Part II

RESIDENCE,
EMPLOYMENT, AND THE
SIGNIFICANCE OF SPACE

4

PROCESSES OF RACIAL RESIDENTIAL SEGREGATION

Camille Zubrinsky Charles

R ACIAL residential segregation is the result of a complex set of in-
dividual- and institutional-level processes whose relative importance researchers continue to debate. The discussion is impaired
by the fact that the vast majority of segregation studies are limited in
focus to a single metropolitan area and/or a black-white paradigm (Farley et al. 1978, 1993; Kain 1986; Massey and Denton 1989, 1993; Clark
1986, 1992; Galster 1988, 1989, 1991; Galster and Keeney 1988). That
segregation research typically fails to include both individual- and aggregate-level measures and a multiethnic sample often causes researchers
and policy analysts to hesitate in extending findings beyond the single
area under study or discussing implications in multiethnic environments; and questions of the relative importance of individual and aggregate factors remain unresolved.

As a study of four major metropolitan areas, the Multi-City Study of
Urban Inequality begins to confront these limitations. The cities represent all four regions of the country and have racial-ethnic compositions
that vary from mainly black-white (Detroit and Atlanta) to the arche-
type of multiethnicity (Los Angeles [Wood and Lee 1991]). Each city has
its own history of economic and political development and of race relations, and its own experience of segregation. And each city varies in
experiences of economic restructuring, responses to racial-ethnic tension, neighborhood context, and racial residential segregation.

Traditionally, individual-level research on racial residential segregation has emphasized one or more of the following factors: socioeconomic
status; housing-market information and perceptions; neighborhood racial-composition preferences; and racial prejudice and stereotypes. Of
these factors, neighborhood racial-composition preferences and racial

prejudice and stereotypes have emerged as important indicators, due in large part to analyses of Detroit (Farley et al. 1978, 1993, 1994) and, more recently, Los Angeles (Clark 1992; Bobo and Zubrinsky 1996; Zubrinsky and Bobo 1996). Aggregate-level analyses by Douglas Massey and Nancy Denton (1989, 1993) also point to the importance of prejudice. This chapter represents an effort to understand how individual-level processes contribute, both independently and in conjunction with neighborhood context, to persisting racial residential segregation in the United States. And because these data are from four cities with varying racial-ethnic compositions, the analyses that follow also allow an examination of whether and how these dynamics vary across cities, which speaks to the legitimacy of generalizing from single-city and/or black-white studies. The results of the analyses that follow consistently point to the enduring salience of race as we approach the twenty-first century.

Socioeconomic Status Explanations

It has been argued that racial groups tend to reside in separate locations because of objective differences in their economic status (Muth 1986; Leven et al. 1976; Clark 1988). Simply put, members of minority groups—particularly blacks and Hispanics—cannot afford to live in the same types of neighborhoods that whites can. These differences in available economic resources are the result of both past and present structural inequality and labor market discrimination (Bound and Freeman 1992; Braddock and McPartland 1987; Kirschenman and Neckerman 1991; Holzer 1996). Group differences in median household incomes presented earlier in this volume lend credence to the economic-difference perspective. Across the four surveyed cities, black and Hispanic median incomes are substantially lower than those of either whites or Asians.

Nevertheless, and despite evidence of increasing economic residential segregation *within* racial groups (Jargowsky 1996), blacks continue to be more residentially segregated than other racial-ethnic groups. To date, however, most research suggests that economic differences are not an adequate explanation of the extreme and persistent levels of racial residential segregation they experience (Kain 1986; Galster 1988; Massey and Denton 1993).[1] Expenditures associated with housing are among the largest that a family has. The very real income differences among groups make it plausible that minority group members simply cannot pay as much for housing as whites and that this disparity explains actual residential patterns. One way to explore the relationship between group economic differences and actual residential patterns is to compare housing expenditures across racial-ethnic categories. Figure 4.1 presents the monthly housing expenditures of homeowners and renters by racial-ethnic group for the combined Multi-City Study sample.

FIGURE 4.1   Comparison of Monthly Housing Expenditures, Multi-City Study Respondents

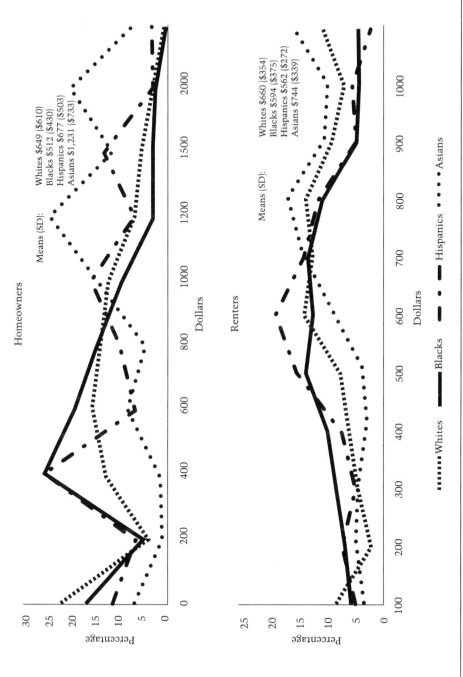

Source: Multi-City Study of Urban Inequality.
Notes: Missing homeowners = 803; missing renters = 114.
For means, $p < .001$.

Overall, there is a great deal of overlap in the housing expenditures of all groups. On average, white homeowners spend $649 per month on housing. This average mortgage payment is lower than that of both Hispanic ($677) and Asian ($1,231) homeowners, but higher than the mean for blacks ($512). Still, just over 40 percent of both whites and blacks report mortgage payments between $400 and $1,000 per month, as do nearly one-third of Hispanics. The majority of Asians report mortgages of well over $1,000 per month (57.4 percent spend between $1,000 and $2,000 per month). A similar pattern is evident in the monthly housing expenditures of renters: the average white renter spends $660 per month, slightly more than black ($594) and Hispanic ($562) renters, but less than the average Asian renter ($744).[2] Forty-seven percent of blacks, more than 55 percent of whites and Hispanics, and 62 percent of Asians report monthly rents between $500 and $1,000 a month. The overall similarities in monthly housing expenditures described here are also evident across racial-ethnic categories within each city. This suggests that large numbers of all groups can afford housing in a wide variety of neighborhoods.

While differences in median earnings across groups are sizable (see chapter 7), even more striking are the enormous differences in accumulated wealth among whites, blacks, Hispanics, and Asians in this country (Oliver and Shapiro 1989, 1995). The importance of these differences to current residential patterns is illustrated by their correlation with differences in rates of homeownership across racial-ethnic groups. A consideration of how these differences might impact residential location is therefore appropriate.

Table 4.1 presents rates of homeownership by race, both within and across the four cities. Notice that, within cities, the rate of homeownership always exceeds 50 percent among whites, reaching a high of roughly 71 percent among whites in Atlanta. The lower rates of white homeownership in Los Angeles (52.8 percent) and, to a lesser degree, Boston (65.0 percent) are likely a consequence of higher housing costs in these cities. Fifty-five percent of blacks in Detroit and 49 percent of blacks in Atlanta own their homes; however, these rates are still between 15 percent and 22 percent lower than whites in these cities. Differences in homeownership are most striking in Boston, where fewer than 30 percent of blacks own their homes, compared to nearly two-thirds of whites. Asian homeownership rates resemble those of whites in Los Angeles; the rate of Hispanic homeownership never exceeds 32 percent.

The rates of homeownership by race-ethnicity for the four surveyed cities mirror national rates (Yinger 1995; U.S. Bureau of the Census 1990). The low rates of minority homeownership reflect their differen-

TABLE 4.1   *Rates of Homeownership by Race and City*

	Whites	Blacks	Hispanics	Asians	Total
Detroit	70.2%	55.2%	NA	NA	62.9%
Atlanta	71.0	49.0	NA	NA	59.0
Los Angeles	52.8	33.5	27.2%	46.1%	39.4
Boston	65.0	26.5	31.2	NA	41.3
All cities	64.3	41.7	28.8	46.1	47.2
Nationally	69.1	43.4	42.4	52.2	65.0

Source: Multi-City Study of Urban Inequality and U.S. Bureau of the Census File STF3A.
Note: p < .001.

tial access to the accumulated wealth needed to either inherit a house or to afford a down payment and access to credit (Oliver and Shapiro 1995; Yinger 1995). How might the group differences therein affect current residential patterns? For most Americans, a home is our biggest investment and largest single source of wealth (Oliver and Shapiro 1995). Having home equity is associated with upward social mobility, allowing us to purchase additional units as investments and to sell a current home for a profit and move into one of greater value in a better neighborhood, with presumably better schools. Variations in homeownership rates therefore translate into different rates of upward social mobility and access to increased wealth.

Not only do fewer blacks and Hispanics own their homes, but the homes that they own tend to be of lesser value than those of whites, even when other socioeconomic status indicators are equal (Yinger 1995). This is potentially relevant in explaining racial residential segregation. White homeowners are overwhelmingly suburbanites who have left the city for newer housing stock and better services and amenities. It has been argued that these whites actively avoid residential contact with minorities because they associate increased minority concentration with neighborhood deterioration and declining property values, not race per se (Clark 1986; Harris 1997). Minority homeowners, on the other hand, are likely to live in the neighborhoods that whites have left behind—within city limits, in older housing stock, with lower-quality services and amenities (Massey and Denton 1993; Yinger 1995). Property values in these neighborhoods are usually lower, making them more easily accessible to those with insufficient savings for a large down payment but sufficient income to cover the resulting larger monthly mortgage payment. The lower property values and higher concentrations of minorities make these neighborhoods less desirable to whites, who not only continue to leave but avoid such neighborhoods. Equally important, stagnant or declining property values make it difficult for home-owners to "move up" to better housing as other indicators of social status improve (such as income and occupational status).

That minorities are overwhelmingly renters may have important implications, also. Newer suburban communities may have less rental housing, and that which does exist is more likely to be concentrated into apartment "communities." At the same time, the older neighbor-hoods occupied by minorities may have more rental housing. Histori-cally, as blacks moved into central cities, single- and double-family dwellings were converted to multiple-family units to increase landlords' profits. Additionally, public housing has traditionally been high-rise apartment buildings located in central cities (Massey and Denton 1993). The disadvantaged economic position of minorities translates into an inability to reap the benefits of homeownership and a greater need for rental housing. That housing may be more likely to be located in neigh-borhoods that have been largely deserted by whites.

Analysis of housing data challenges the adequacy of a race-neutral, socioeconomic explanation of racial residential segregation. In spite of objective differences in socioeconomic status, blacks, Hispanics, and Asians pay rents and mortgages in amounts comparable to those paid by whites. Furthermore, lower rates of homeownership among blacks and Hispanics are, to a great extent, the product of decidedly racist behavior on the part of whites (Massey and Denton 1993; Oliver and Shapiro 1995; Yinger 1995). There is clearly a need for new and innovative anal-yses that carefully consider the role of group differences in wealth accumulation. Whether judging from monthly housing expenditures or wealth, these results clearly indicate that economics, considered as a race-neutral factor, cannot explain racially segregated neighborhoods. Another category of factors, however, may shed additional light on the social class explanation.

Cognitive Explanations

Cognitive explanations deal with potential differences across racial/eth-nic categories in housing market information and perceptions thereof. Such factors as the accuracy of information regarding housing costs and minority perceptions of their own ability to afford housing might also be categorized as pertaining to perceived social class differences. This per-spective holds that minority group members (particularly blacks and Hispanics) live separately from whites because they *believe* they cannot afford housing in desirable suburban areas and therefore do not search for it there (Farley et al. 1978, 1993; Zubrinsky and Bobo 1996).

Accurate Housing-Cost Information

To ascertain the accuracy of housing market information, all Multi-City Study respondents were asked to estimate the cost of housing for a selected set of communities within each city. The first panel of table 4.2 summarizes mean housing-cost estimates by race for each city; the second provides mean home values for each community, based on 1990 Census of Housing information. Ratios of estimated to actual home values by respondent category are presented in the third panel. In all cases, a ratio of 1.00 indicates perfect knowledge, ratios below 1.00 reflect underestimates, and ratios above 1.00 express overestimates.

In general, racial-ethnic groups in the four cities have similar knowledge of housing prices. Since no minority group is shown to have distinctively inferior knowledge of housing costs, we must conclude that inaccurate information does not explain current residential patterns. That this has been demonstrated previously for both Detroit (Farley et al. 1978, 1993) and Los Angeles (Zubrinsky and Bobo 1996)—and is now confirmed in Boston and Atlanta—suggests that single-city analyses of the accuracy of housing market information are likely to be broadly generalizable.

Still, it is noteworthy that, across the four cities, whites tend to be the most consistently accurate in their estimates. This may be due to their higher rates of homeownership, if owners have a vested interest in knowing about home prices. The estimates of minority group members, especially those of blacks and Hispanics, tend to be most accurate for areas with the least expensive housing in a particular city (for example, Brockton in Boston, Palmdale and Pico Rivera in Los Angeles). The exception is Detroit, where blacks' most accurate estimate is of the most expensive housing. Finally, previous analysis of housing market information in Los Angeles found that blacks there tend to overestimate the cost of housing in the predominantly black affluent suburb of Baldwin Hills (Zubrinsky and Bobo 1996). The only similar finding to emerge from the other cities is from the Tri-Cities area of Atlanta, which is about 64 percent black.

Minority Affordability   Another possibility is that, despite comparatively accurate knowledge of the housing market, a substantial number of minority group members perceive housing in desirable, predominantly white areas as beyond the financial capacity of most "people like them."

To gauge the likelihood of this possibility, minority respondents were asked their perceptions of housing affordability in the selected communities of each city. Figure 4.2 presents the percentage of each

TABLE 4.2 Estimated and Actual Housing Costs for Selected Areas

	Cost of Homes Estimated by Survey Respondents				Mean Value 1990 Census	Ratio of Multi-City Study Estimates to Actual Costs			
	Whites	Blacks	Hispanics	Asians		Whites	Blacks	Hispanics	Asians
Detroit									
Southfield***	$102,062	$111,831	—	—	$ 90,100	1.13	1.24	—	—
Taylor***	69,453	83,977	—	—	52,200	1.33	1.61	—	—
Dearborn*	105,003	110,871	—	—	79,800	1.31	1.39	—	—
Troy***	148,537	134,832	—	—	141,500	1.05	0.95	—	—
Warren	82,936	83,873	—	—	69,000	1.20	1.21	—	—
Atlanta									
Decatur***	98,834	85,191	—	—	117,950	0.84	0.72	—	—
Midtown***	146,620	123,495	—	—	178,000	0.82	0.69	—	—
Tri-Cities**	87,392	96,179	—	—	75,000	1.16	1.28	—	—
Marietta-Smyrna	142,465	143,939	—	—	108,850	1.31	1.32	—	—
Roswell-Alpharetta	188,903	185,076	—	—	182,700	1.03	1.01	—	—
Norcross***	142,933	159,649	—	—	153,200	0.93	1.04	—	—
Los Angeles									
Alhambra***	197,257	202,180	$210,095	$219,909	227,900	0.86	0.89	0.92	0.96
Baldwin Hills***	222,888	300,389	243,434	214,417	218,619	1.02	1.37	1.11	0.98
Canoga Park***	206,674	207,998	187,486	218,656	257,600	0.80	0.81	0.73	0.85
Culver City**	211,664	230,093	202,720	220,924	329,400	0.64	0.70	0.61	0.67
Glendale***	256,752	256,075	236,595	254,604	341,700	0.75	0.75	0.69	0.74
Palmdale***	136,717	158,052	151,561	169,455	150,200	0.91	1.05	1.01	1.13
Pico Rivera***	161,956	163,833	169,197	173,672	163,800	0.99	1.00	1.03	1.06
Boston									
Cambridge***	190,923	160,997	147,520	—	263,800	0.72	0.61	0.56	—
Newton**	251,878	232,936	192,507	—	293,400	0.86	0.79	0.66	—
South Boston***	136,439	141,182	120,961	—	137,500	0.99	1.03	0.88	—
Lowell***	121,423	148,354	119,695	—	131,100	0.93	1.13	0.91	—
Brockton***	128,488	133,401	117,641	—	131,700	0.97	1.01	0.89	—

Source: Multi-City Study of Urban Inequality and 1990 U.S. Census.
*p < .05. **p < .01. ***p < .001.

FIGURE 4.2 Minority Respondents' Perceptions That "About Half," "Many," or "Almost All" Members of Their Group Can Afford Housing in Selected Areas

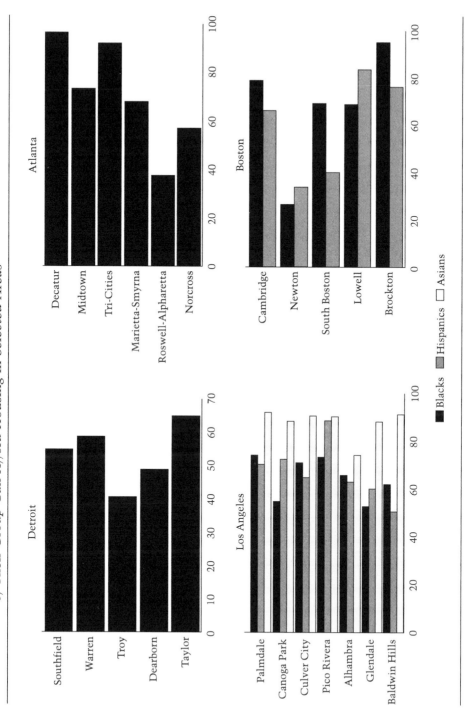

Source: Multi-City Study of Urban Inequality.

group asserting that "almost all," "many," or "about half" of their group can afford to buy housing in each area. In most instances, minority respondents believe that a substantial portion of their group can afford housing in a wide variety of areas, including the most expensive ones; this is particularly true of Asian and black respondents. In all instances, at least 70 percent of Asians believe that at least half of them can afford to live in the seven Los Angeles communities studied. Except for the most expensive communities of Detroit (Troy) and Boston (Newton), a majority of blacks also believe they can afford housing in large numbers. Confidence in group purchasing power is a bit lower among Hispanics in both Los Angeles and Boston. Still, in eleven of twelve instances, Hispanics believe at least half of their group can afford housing in these areas.

If minority group members were to think that housing in desirable, predominantly white areas were beyond their financial reach, they might disregard these communities when searching for housing. It appears, however, that blacks, Hispanics, and Asians all believe that significant portions of their respective groups can afford housing in a wide range of communities. Even with respect to the most expensive neighborhoods, at least one-quarter of blacks and Hispanics believe that at least half of each's own group can afford to live there. It does not appear, therefore, that minority housing-search behavior is affected by a belief that housing in predominantly white areas is financially out of reach.

General Desirability and Perceptions of Discrimination   While we may conclude that housing costs—real or perceived—do not effectively explain persistent racial residential segregation, there are other types of perceptions that might influence the housing-search behavior of minority-group members. For various reasons, racial-ethnic groups may differ in the types of communities they perceive as desirable places to live. We may reasonably suppose, for example, that minority-group members' perceptions of racial animus and housing market discrimination might alter their search for housing: if particular areas are perceived as hostile, they are more likely to be avoided. If minority-group members believe they are likely to face institutional barriers (such as reluctant lenders and realtors), they might hesitate to enter the homebuyer's market at all. Minimally, these home seekers might limit their search to areas with higher minority concentrations, where they know they are welcome and where they are less likely to encounter discrimination.

To examine these elements of housing-market perceptions, we first explore group similarities and differences in the view of the general desirability of selected communities in Detroit, Atlanta, Los Angeles, and Boston. Figure 4.3 summarizes the percentage of each racial group that

FIGURE 4.3   General Desirability of Selected Areas Across Cities, by Race

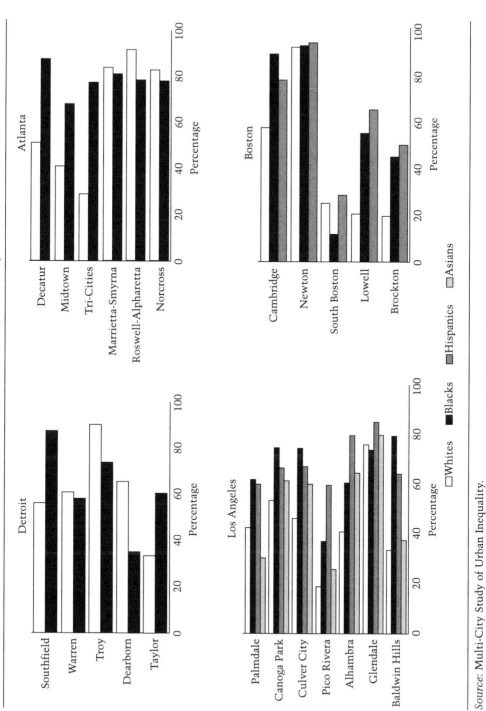

Source: Multi-City Study of Urban Inequality.
Note: p < .001, except Marietta/Smyrna and Norcross (p < .01) and Newton (ns).

perceives selected areas in each city to be "somewhat" or "very" desirable places to live. It may first appear that groups generally agree across cities on the desirability of the selected areas. Note, however, that areas characterized by high minority concentrations or perceived as open to minorities are more desirable to minority respondents and less so to whites. For example, Southfield, in Detroit, has a growing black population and a reputation for openness; it is among the least desirable areas to Detroit whites. Baldwin Hills—a predominantly black but affluent Los Angeles suburb—is one of the communities most poorly regarded by whites. The same is true with respect to Alhambra, a community with high-priced housing but growing Hispanic and Asian populations. In Boston, Brockton is the least desirable area to whites, with its growing black, Hispanic, and Asian populations, affordable housing, and reputation for openness toward blacks. Finally, the Atlanta communities of Decatur, Midtown, and Tri-Cities all have disproportionate numbers of black residents; Decatur and Midtown also have above-average housing prices. These three communities are less desirable to whites, relative both to blacks and to other communities.

These same areas are often the most attractive to minority-group members. Baldwin Hills is most desirable to blacks in Los Angeles, but they also view Glendale positively, despite its reputation for hostility toward them. The latter phenomenon is also true of blacks' perceptions of Warren and Dearborn in Detroit: a substantial number regard these communities as desirable, despite their reputations of antagonism toward blacks and their small black populations. A similar pattern emerges among Hispanic respondents: predominantly Hispanic Pico Rivera, in Los Angeles, is the most desirable to Hispanic respondents and the least so to other groups. Palmdale, a growing area outside the city of Los Angeles with affordable housing and a sizable Hispanic population, is far more attractive to blacks and Hispanics than to whites and Asians. (Overall, the perceptions of Asians in Los Angeles mirror those of whites there.) Finally, the Boston communities of Cambridge and Brockton are more desirable to Hispanics and blacks than to Whites.

The perceptions of general desirability described here shed little light on current residential patterns. Although respondents show some sensitivity to minority populations and reputation for integration, there is overall agreement regarding the general desirability of the selected communities. This suggests that segregation is not the result of group differences in "taste." To further examine the role of housing market perceptions, Multi-City Study respondents were also asked how they thought residents of the selected communities would respond to a new black, Hispanic, or Asian neighbor: Would residents welcome a new minority neighbor, or would they be upset? Figure 4.4 illustrates the per-

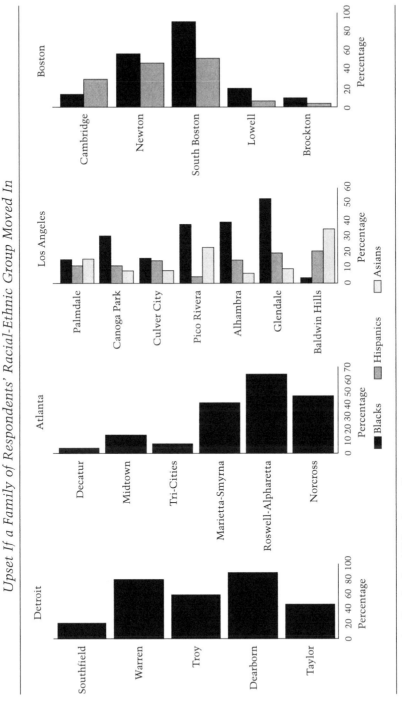

FIGURE 4.4   Percentage of Minority Respondents Reporting That Residents of Selected Areas Would Be Upset If a Family of Respondents' Racial-Ethnic Group Moved In

Source: Multi-City Study of Urban Inequality.

centage of black, Hispanic, and Asian respondents who believe that residents in the selected communities would be upset by a new neighbor of their respective racial-ethnic groups.

Generally speaking, blacks perceive more hostility toward members of their group than either Hispanics or Asians do. In three of five cases in Detroit (for Warren, Troy, and Dearborn), at least 60 percent of black respondents believe that area residents would be upset by a new black neighbor. In Atlanta, a clear split exists: for Decatur, Midtown, and Tri-Cities, blacks perceive little hostility toward their group; however, more than 40 percent of blacks believe that residents of Marietta-Smyrna, Roswell-Alpharetta, and Norcross would be upset by a new black neighbor. The three Atlanta communities perceived as most welcoming of blacks are also among blacks' most desirable areas.

Among Boston blacks, Newton and South Boston residents are the most likely to be perceived as upset by a new black neighbor (57.9 percent and 89.9 percent, respectively). Recall that South Boston was also generally least desirable to black respondents. Hispanics in Boston also perceive these communities, along with Cambridge, as the most hostile toward members of their group. In all cases except Cambridge, however, blacks in Boston perceive more hostility toward them than Hispanics do. In Los Angeles, perceptions of hostility also exist, particularly among blacks. Nevertheless, they are less likely overall to perceive themselves as unwelcome than are blacks in other cities. A similar pattern appears when Hispanics in Los Angeles and Boston are compared. Finally, Asian respondents are least likely to believe that area residents would be upset by a new Asian neighbor; this is especially true of predominantly white communities.

These results suggest that minority-group members have very clear ideas about which communities are welcoming of "people like us" and which are not. If blacks and Hispanics act on their perceptions and avoid searching for and/or securing housing in areas perceived as unwelcoming of them, the behavior will influence actual residential patterns. First found in Detroit (Farley et al. 1978, 1993) and later in Los Angeles (Zubrinsky and Bobo 1996), this dynamic now appears to be true of minority-group members in all four cities and may thus be broadly generalizable.

Finally, minority groups may alter their housing-search behavior based on their perceptions of institutional discrimination, as shown in figure 4.5. If minority-group members believe that white landlords and homeowners will not rent or sell to their group, that real estate agents will not show or sell homes to people like them, or that banks and lenders are likely to turn down mortgage loan applications from members of their group, these beliefs—real or perceived—could negatively affect housing search and settlement behavior. We asked survey respondents their perceptions of institutional barriers that cause members of their group to "miss out on good housing."

As has been the case throughout this section, blacks are the group most likely to perceive institutional barriers in the housing market. At least 80 percent of blacks believe that members of their group miss out on good housing "very often" or "sometimes" as a result of all three sources of discrimination just mentioned. Hispanics perceive less discrimination than blacks, but more than Asians. Roughly three-quarters of Hispanics believe whites "very often" or "sometimes" refuse to rent or sell to them, and well over half accept that discrimination by real estate agents, banks, and lenders is common. These beliefs are consistent with results of audit studies (Yinger 1995) and could negatively affect the search behavior of blacks and Hispanics by limiting the range of possible search locations and/or curbing efforts to buy.

Asians perceive the least amount of discrimination in the housing market. Fewer than 25 percent believe that they miss out on good housing because individual whites "very often" or "sometimes" refuse to rent or sell to them; less than 10 percent view discrimination by real estate agents and lenders as common problems. That Asians do not believe they confront significant institutional barriers that might positively impact their search behavior by expanding the range of possible search locations and encouraging homeownership.

The pattern of housing market perceptions coincides with actual patterns of minority residential segregation from whites. Blacks are the most segregated group, the most likely to perceive particular communities as upset by a new black neighbor, and the most likely to believe that members of their group commonly confront institutional barriers in the housing market. Hispanics are less segregated from whites than are blacks but more so than Asians; they perceive less hostility toward themselves from various communities and view institutional discrimination with less concern than blacks do. Finally, Asians are the least segregated from whites, perceive the least hostility from others, and are least likely to see institutional barriers.

Minority groups generally regard themselves as able to afford housing in a variety of locations, they substantially resemble whites in their evaluations of various communities, and their perceptions of prejudice and discrimination levels correlate with the degree of residential segregation they experience. While not conclusive, these patterns suggest a potential connection between minority-group members' housing market perceptions and their search behavior.

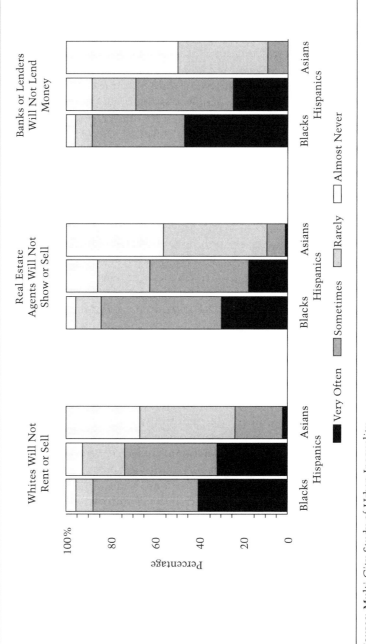

FIGURE 4.5   Perceptions of the Frequency with Which Co-Ethnics Confront Institutional Barriers in the Housing Market, by Respondent Race

Source: Multi-City Study of Urban Inequality.
Note: $p < .001$.

Race-Based Explanations

The factors examined to this point are typically described as race-neutral. Now we shift our attention to factors that are decidedly race-based: neighborhood racial-composition preferences. Some argue that preferences for neighborhoods with particular racial compositions—particularly for large numbers of same-race neighbors—are simply expressions of ethnocentrism that cross racial-ethnic boundaries (for example, Clark 1986, 1992). Alternatively, a growing body of research suggests that, while ethnocentrism does play a small role, preferences are more indicative of racial prejudice (Farley et al. 1994; Bobo and Zubrinsky 1996; Zubrinsky and Bobo 1996).

This portion of the analysis proceeds in two parts, beginning with an examination of preferences for neighborhoods with varying degrees of integration. This is followed by an analysis of the variation in preferences across the four cities, and the extent to which racial stereotypes, actual neighborhood racial composition, and social class concerns predict preferences. Group differences in neighborhood racial-composition preferences are examined using the Farley-Schuman show card procedure originally designed for the 1976 Detroit Area Study. A split-ballot format in Los Angeles and Boston allows expansion of the original experiment to include Hispanics and Asians in addition to blacks and whites.[3] The series of questions asked of white respondents differs slightly from that presented to nonwhite respondents. Each respondent category is treated in turn.

White Preferences

To explore the preferences of whites, respondents were shown a series of cards similar to those in figure 4.6. Each card depicts fifteen houses with varying degrees of integration with blacks, Hispanics, or Asians. The respondent's home is represented by the house in the middle of the card. The experiment begins with respondents being asked to imagine that they live in an all-white neighborhood. They are then shown the second card, with one minority home and fourteen white homes. Respondents are asked if they would feel "very comfortable," "somewhat comfortable," "somewhat uncomfortable," or "very uncomfortable" in this marginally integrated setting. Respondents indicating some degree of comfort are then shown cards with increasing levels of integration until they indicate discomfort or reach the end of the series: a neighborhood that is majority out-group. The first panel of figure 4.7 summarizes whites' responses by target group.

It is reassuring that a sizable majority of whites express comfort in

FIGURE 4.6   *White Respondents' Neighborhood Show Cards*

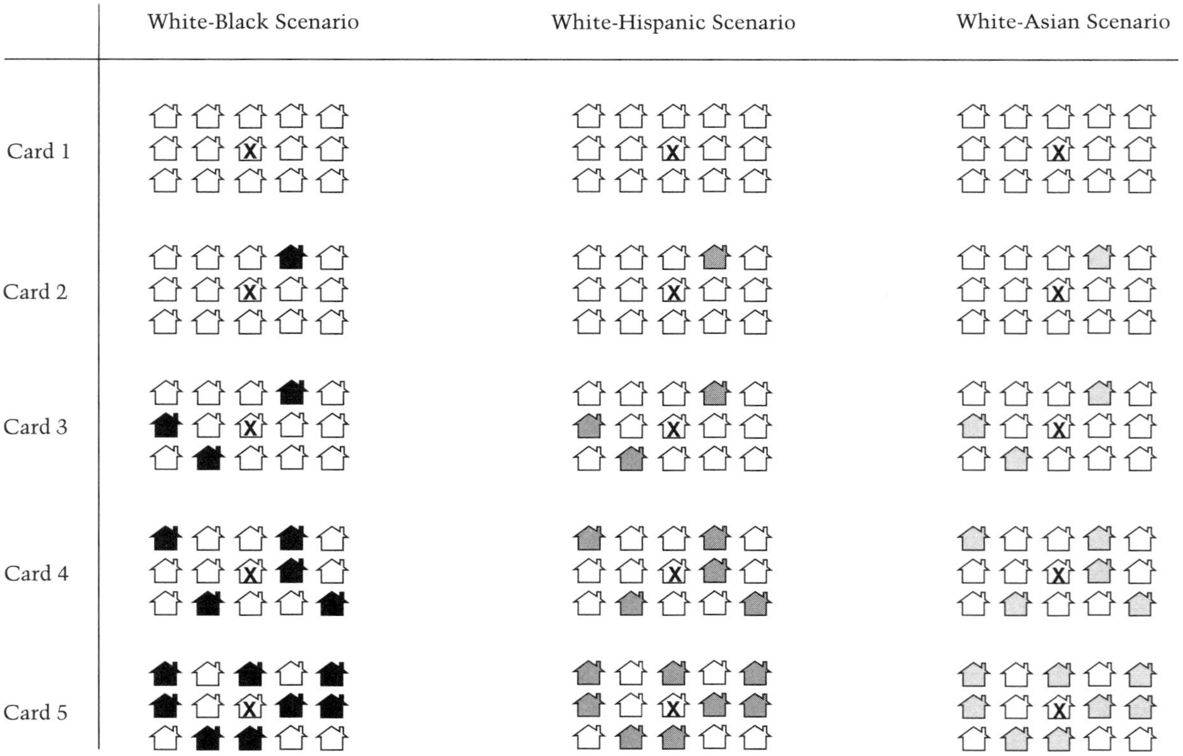

	White-Black Scenario	White-Hispanic Scenario	White-Asian Scenario
Card 1			
Card 2			
Card 3			
Card 4			
Card 5			

Source: Multi-City Study of Urban Inequality.
Note: White-Hispanic and white-Asian scenarios used in Los Angeles and Boston only.

FIGURE 4.7

Attractiveness of Neighborhoods with Varying Degrees of Integration with Blacks, Hispanics, and Asians

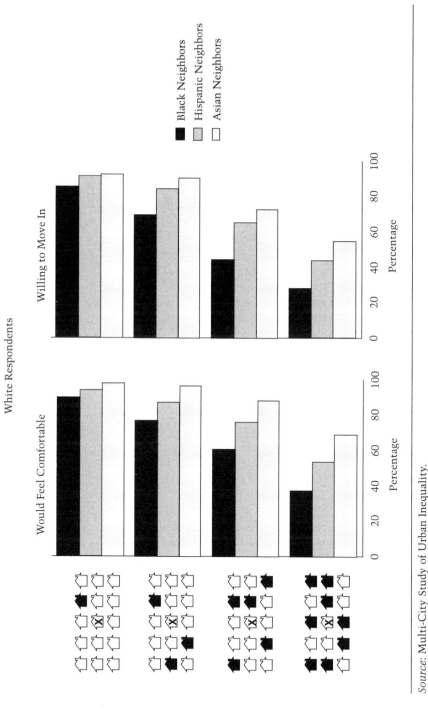

White Respondents

Would Feel Comfortable

Willing to Move In

Black Neighbors
Hispanic Neighbors
Asian Neighbors

Percentage

Percentage

Source: Multi-City Study of Urban Inequality.
Notes: Dark houses represent target group.
p < .001.

most of the neighborhoods: at least 60 percent express comfort in a neighborhood that is one-third minority. Still, a rank-ordering of out-group neighbors is apparent. Irrespective of the degree of integration, white respondents feel most comfortable with Asian neighbors and least comfortable with black neighbors; comfort with Hispanic neighbors falls in between. When whites are presented with the card depicting the majority-nonwhite neighborhood, their comfort level declines considerably. While the majority of whites are still comfortable with Hispanic and Asian neighbors, their ease in a majority-black neighborhood falls to less than 40 percent—a decline of more than 20 percent from the immediately preceding scenario. In fact, declines in whites comfort—from one hypothetical housing pattern to the next, more integrated one—are typically the largest with respect to black neighbors.

The set of questions about comfort levels assumes that white respondents live in an originally all-white neighborhood and tests their degree of comfort with racial change there. This relates to a long-standing explanation of residential segregation involving a tipping point, where the proportion of black neighbors reaches a level at which growing white unease leads to white flight and, ultimately, resegregation. A fuller understanding of residential segregation, however, requires that we also examine the extent of whites' willingness to move *into* neighborhoods containing more than token numbers of nonwhites. To measure this aspect of comfort, white respondents were also asked if they would consider moving into any of the neighborhoods shown on the cards:

> Suppose you have been looking for a house and have found a nice one you can afford. This house could be located in several different types of neighborhoods, as shown on these cards. Would you consider moving into any of these neighborhoods?

The split-ballot used in Los Angeles and Boston for the previous experiment applies here also: therefore, whites previously indicating comfort with increasing numbers of Hispanic neighbors, for example, are then asked to consider moving into neighborhoods with varying degrees of white-Hispanic integration. The second panel of figure 4.7 summarizes responses to this scenario.

The two panels' data are very similar, except that the decline in willingness to move into neighborhoods begins earlier and is never as high as comfort with neighborhood transition. This is especially true with respect to potential black neighbors: 60 percent of whites express comfort with a neighborhood that is one-third black; however, only 45 percent of whites are willing to move into that same neighborhood. Similarly, tolerance of a majority-minority neighborhood is substantially lower when whites contemplate the purchase of a new residence, rather than consider racial transition in their current neighborhood. Less than 30 percent of whites would enter a neighborhood that is majority-black; slightly over 40 percent would enter a majority-Hispanic neighborhood. Despite some decline from the comfort-with-racial-transition responses (panel 1), just over half of whites say they would move into a majority-Asian neighborhood.

Whites' acceptance of residential integration is conditioned by the race of potential neighbors. They are substantially more likely to express comfort living in, and willingness to move into, neighborhoods where their potential neighbors are Asian and, to a lesser extent, Hispanic. Integration with blacks is always seen as least desirable. This flies in the face of social class explanations, since blacks' socioeconomic status is better than that of Hispanics: if race were simply a proxy for social class, Hispanics would be the least desirable neighbors. This race-specific rank-ordering of out-groups as neighbors, therefore, supports a race-based explanation of racial residential segregation.

Black Preferences

A slightly different experiment tests the neighborhood racial-composition preferences of blacks. Instead of being asked about comfort levels in a neighborhood undergoing racial transition, black respondents are to imagine that they had been looking for a house and found a nice one they could afford. They are told that the house could be located in several different types of neighborhoods and are shown a series of five cards, illustrated in figure 4.8. These five neighborhood cards differ in composition from the white respondents' cards, ranging from an all-black neighborhood in card 1 to one that is entirely white, Hispanic, or Asian, save for the black respondent's home in the middle.

Respondents are instructed to arrange the five neighborhoods from most to least attractive. The split-ballot method described previously is employed: one-third of blacks in Los Angeles and Boston considered integration with whites, a third with Hispanics, and the remaining third with Asians. The left panel of figure 4.9 presents the percentage of black respondents selecting each of the five cards as either their first or second choice.

Blacks appear to want a sizable population of co-ethnics and, at the same time, substantial integration. The two most popular neighborhoods across target groups are cards 2 and 3 (the former is roughly 27 percent out-group; the latter, with seven out-group neighbors, closely approximates a 50/50 neighborhood). It is noteworthy, however, that the attractiveness of the all-same-race neighborhood varies by target group race. Blacks are least likely to rate the all-black neighborhood as most

FIGURE 4.8 *Black Respondents' Neighborhood Show Cards*

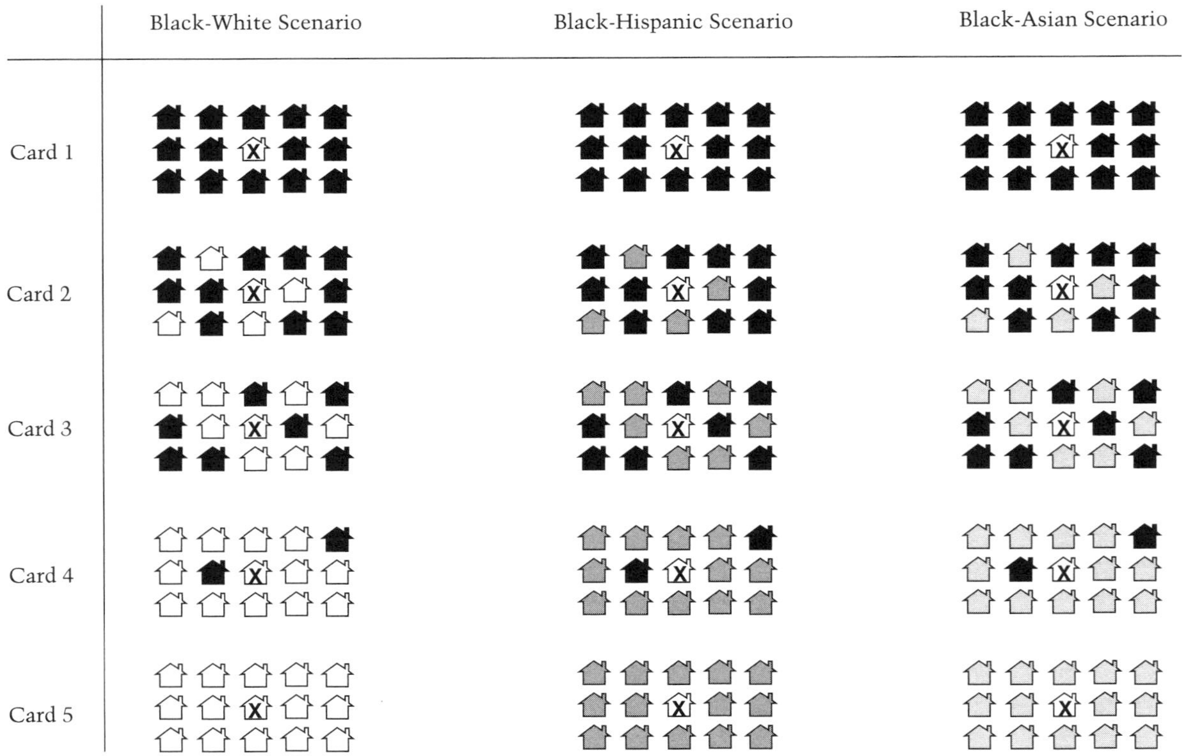

Source: Multi-City Study of Urban Inequality.
Note: Black-Hispanic and black-Asian scenarios used in Los Angeles and Boston only.

FIGURE 4.9   *Attractiveness of Neighborhoods with Varying Degrees of Integration with Whites, Hispanics, and Asians*

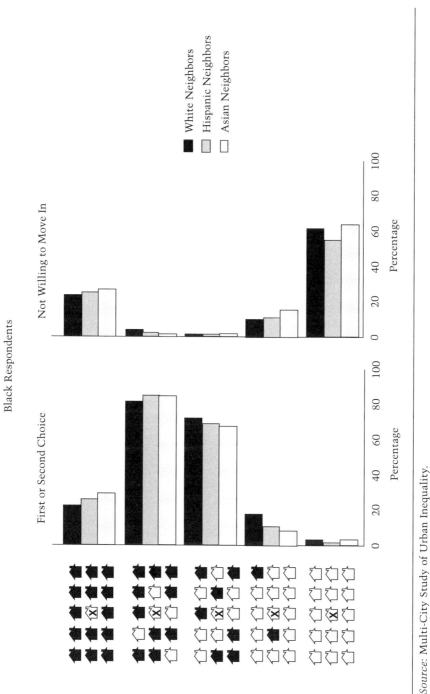

Black Respondents

Source: Multi-City Study of Urban Inequality.
Notes: Lighter houses represent target group. For Attractiveness, $p < .001$; for Unwilling-to-move cards 1, 2, and 5, $p < .01$; for Unwilling-to-move card 4, $p < .05$; for Unwilling-to-move card 3, p is ns.

attractive when integration is with whites (23.6 percent), compared with integration with Hispanics (26.8 percent) or Asians (29.5 percent). This pattern continues as numbers of out-group neighbors increase: a neighborhood with only two same-race neighbors is twice as attractive when the rest are white (17.5 percent), as opposed to Asian (8.7 percent); potential Hispanic neighbors (11 percent) fall in between. Finally, the percentage of blacks who find the single-black-on-the-block scenario to be the most attractive is always less than 5 percent.

A related question is whether or not there were any neighborhoods into which blacks simply would not consider moving. Like the follow-up question to white respondents, this second question is intended to assess blacks' willingness to move into a neighborhood, rather than simply reveal what they find attractive. The pattern of responses, summarized in the second panel of figure 4.9, mirrors that for neighborhood attractiveness. The neighborhood that black respondents are least willing to enter is one in which they would be the pioneer black family: roughly 60 percent are unwilling to enter such a neighborhood, regardless of the race of potential neighbors. A substantial minority of blacks are also unwilling to enter an entirely same-race neighborhood.

The pattern of responses for black respondents is consistent with historical desires for substantial integration (Pettigrew 1973; Bobo, Schuman, and Steeh 1986; Farley et al. 1978, 1993). In contrast to previously more distinct preferences for 50/50 neighborhoods, however, is black respondents' growing preference for neighborhoods that are majority same-race. This shift in preferences may reflect blacks' perceptions of persisting prejudice and discrimination and dwindling faith in the likelihood of racial equality, reported earlier in this chapter and discussed at greater length elsewhere (Cose 1993; Feagin and Sikes 1994). This may also explain why as many blacks select the all-black neighborhood as most attractive as say they are unwilling to move into such a neighborhood. Finally, though to a lesser extent than was true of whites, there is a rank-ordering of out-groups with respect to the top position: blacks appear most comfortable being a numerical minority when the out-group neighbors are white.

Hispanic Preferences

The measure of Hispanics' neighborhood preferences employs the same series of questions used for blacks. Hispanics are first asked to arrange the five neighborhood cards from most to least attractive and then to comment on their willingness to move into each of the increasingly out-group–occupied neighborhoods. Using the split-ballot format and cards similar to those in figure 4.10, researchers in Los Angeles and Boston

FIGURE 4.10   Hispanic Respondents' Neighborhood Show Cards

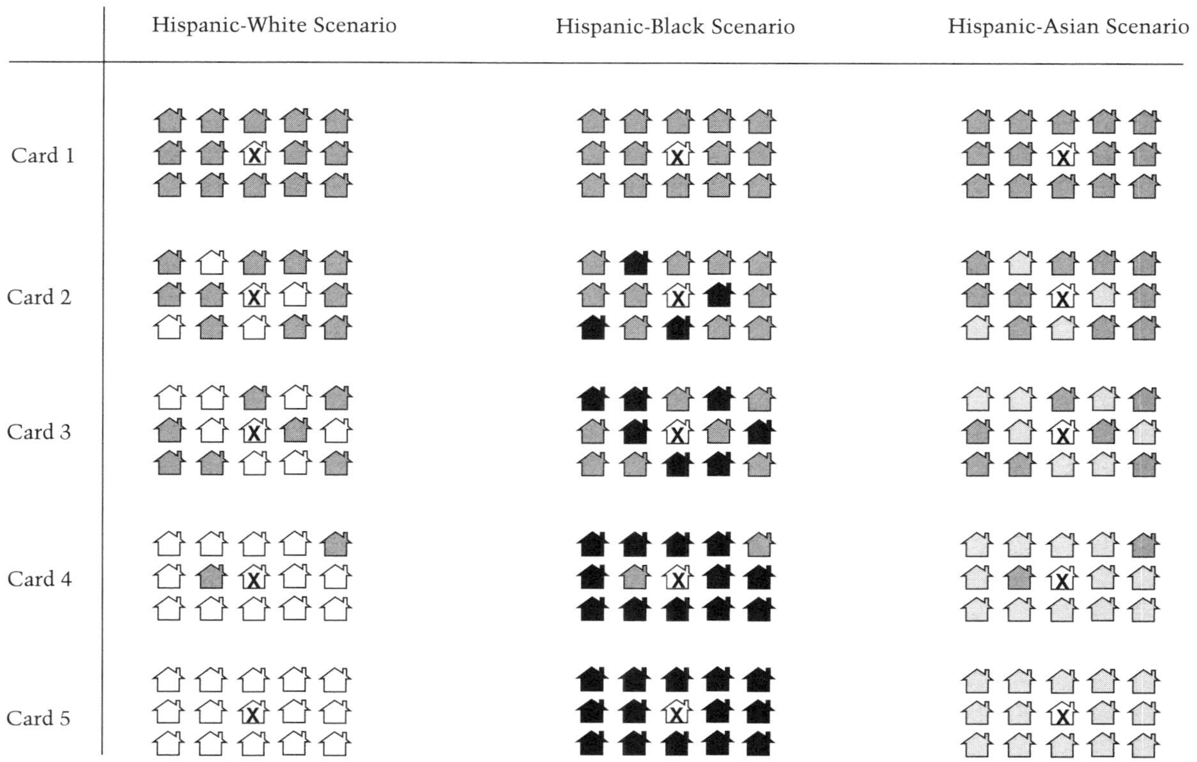

Source: Multi-City Study of Urban Inequality.
Note: Hispanic scenarios used in Los Angeles and Boston only.

asked one-third of Hispanics to contemplate integration with whites, a third to do so with blacks, and the remainder with Asians.

The left panel of figure 4.11 presents the percentage of Hispanics rating each of the five neighborhoods as the most or second most attractive for each of the target groups. (To distinguish Hispanic homes from those of the target group, the former are more lightly shaded.) As has been the case thus far, neighborhood attractiveness among Hispanic respondents appears to depend on the race of potential neighbors. An all-Hispanic neighborhood is most attractive when the alternative is integration with blacks and least attractive when potential neighbors are white: with blacks as the target group, 60 percent of Hispanics chose the all-Hispanic neighborhood first or second; this compares with 40 percent and 20 percent of Hispanics, when considering integration with Asians and whites, respectively.

The most attractive neighborhood overall depends on the race of potential neighbors. A neighborhood with four out-group homes is most attractive when the target group is either black (91 percent) or Asian (76.4 percent); however, when the neighbors are white, Hispanics are most likely to identify the neighborhood approaching half-Hispanic and half-white as most attractive (70.8 percent). Similarly, Hispanics evaluating neighborhoods that, except for themselves, are all-white or all-Asian are about five times more likely to find them attractive than they are comparably black neighborhoods (12.4 percent, 10.7 percent, and 2.2 percent, respectively). The idea of occupying the single Hispanic home or one of only two in a neighborhood that is not predominantly white is about as unappealing to Hispanics as to blacks contemplating a comparable situation.

When Hispanic respondents were asked if there were any neighborhoods into which they were unwilling to move, the pattern of responses was similar to that of blacks. As the number of co-ethnics in a neighborhood declines, Hispanics become increasingly unwilling to move into it. Once again, this is most often the case when potential neighbors are black and least so when they are white. Thus, to some degree, Hispanics seem to resemble blacks in wanting a sizable co-ethnic presence as well as fairly substantial integration. The relative strength of these desires ebbs and flows with the race of potential neighbors and, once again, a clear rank-ordering of out-groups emerges, in which whites are most preferred as neighbors and blacks least so. Finally, Hispanics are much more likely than black respondents to indicate that the all-same-race neighborhood is most attractive. This greater desire for entirely co-ethnic neighborhoods may reflect the high proportion among Hispanics of recent immigrants, the language barrier they face, and an initial need to rely on ethnic cultural institutions (Ong, Lawrence, and Davidson 1992).

FIGURE 4.11   *Attractiveness of Neighborhoods with Varying Degrees of Integration with Whites, Blacks, and Asians*

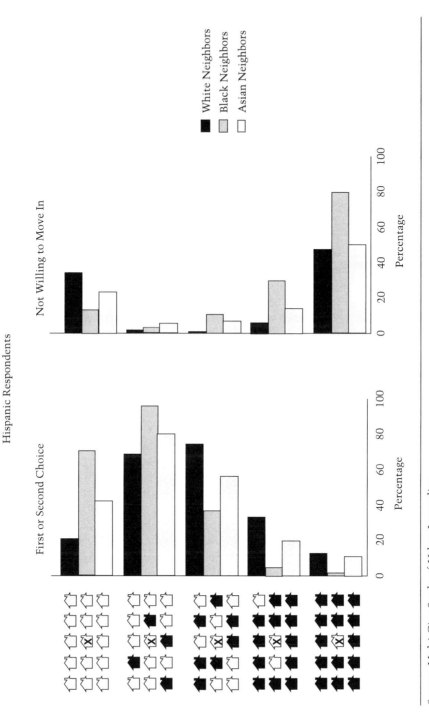

Hispanic Respondents

Source: Multi-City Study of Urban Inequality.
Notes: Darker houses represent target group.
$p < .001$.

Consistent with this view, first- and second-generation immigrants express strong desires for co-ethnic neighborhoods, while later generations find the perceived improvement in social class status and quality of life associated with predominantly white neighborhoods to be more attractive.[4]

Asian Preferences

Using neighborhood cards like the ones in figure 4.12, the experiment used to measure the neighborhood racial-composition preferences of Asians is the same as that used for blacks and Hispanics. Asian respondents' selections of the two most attractive neighborhoods are summarized in figure 4.13.

Asians share preferences with the other nonwhite groups but to such an extreme, in some cases, as to resemble whites more closely. For example, while an entirely same-race neighborhood is least attractive to Asians when potential neighbors are white and most attractive when they are black, the magnitude of the difference is striking: 16.7 percent of Asians selected an all-co-ethnic neighborhood in the Asian-white scenario, while 56.4 percent did so in the Asian-Hispanic housing pattern and 78.5 percent in the Asian-black arrangement. Asian respondents also resemble blacks and Hispanics in their evaluations of cards 2 and 3. Virtually all Asians selected card 2 (the nearly two-thirds same-race neighborhood) as most attractive when the target group was either blacks or Hispanics. When the potential neighbors were white, however, the neighborhood approximating 50/50 is seen as the most attractive (80 percent). Of the nonwhite groups, Asian respondents are least likely to select majority out-group neighborhoods as among the most attractive.

The recurrent, vivid contrast between whites and blacks as most and least desirable neighbors, respectively, appears again in Asians' degree of willingness to move into each of the five increasingly out-group neighborhoods (see the second panel of figure 4.13). Consistent with their ratings of neighborhood attractiveness, Asian respondents' willingness to move into modestly to moderately integrated areas (cards 2 and 3) is far greater than their enthusiasm for all out-group neighbors (card 5); the disparity is especially large between white and black target groups. Asians are less likely than blacks and Hispanics to shun the all-same-race neighborhood (card 1).

Like the other groups surveyed, the neighborhood racial-composition preferences of Asians appear to be driven by the race of potential neighbors. Asians are much more open to integration with whites than with other nonwhites and find integration with blacks least appealing. Also like blacks and Hispanics, Asian respondents show strong preferences for same-race neighbors, at the same time that they express a desire for

FIGURE 4.12   Asian Respondents' Neighborhood Show Cards

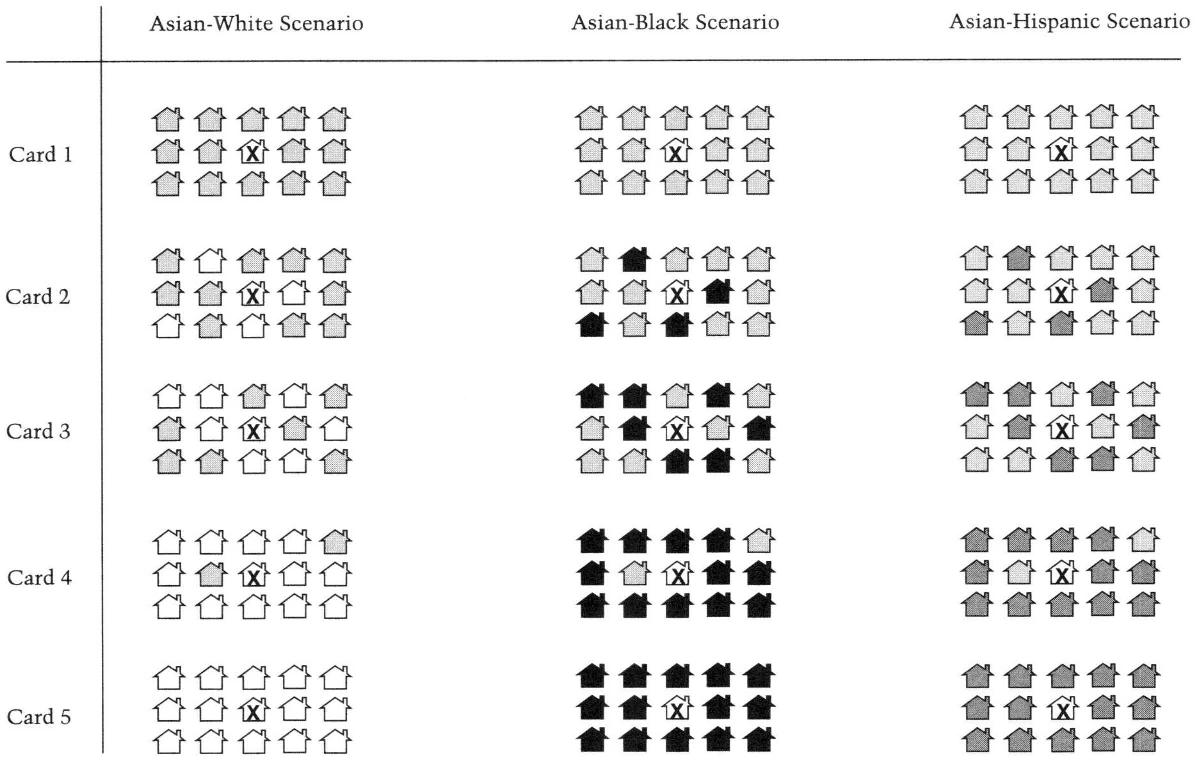

Asian-White Scenario   Asian-Black Scenario   Asian-Hispanic Scenario

Card 1

Card 2

Card 3

Card 4

Card 5

Source: Multi-City Study of Urban Inequality.
Note: Asian scenarios used in Los Angeles only.

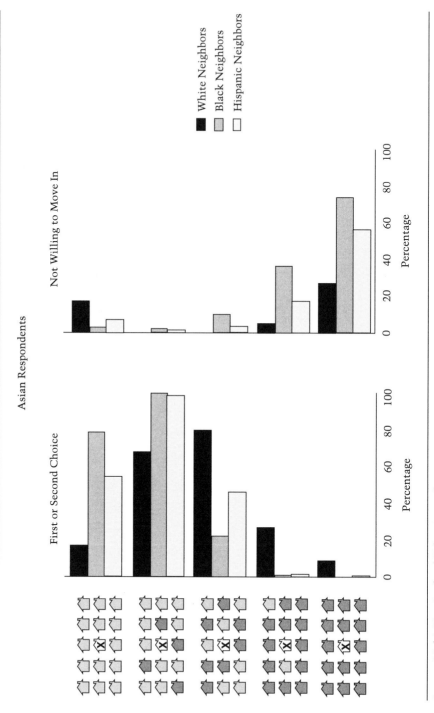

FIGURE 4.13   Attractiveness of Neighborhoods with Varying Degrees of Integration with Whites, Blacks, and Hispanics

Asian Respondents

First or Second Choice

Not Willing to Move In

White Neighbors
Black Neighbors
Hispanic Neighbors

Percentage

Percentage

Source: Multi-City Study of Urban Inequality.
Notes: Darker houses represent target group.
p < .001.

integration. Finally, as is true of Hispanics' preferences for co-ethnic neighborhoods, that of Asians could be related to the large numbers of recent immigrants among them and concomitant needs for parallel cultural institutions during the transitional period.[5]

These findings do not support the notion that preferences for same-race neighborhoods are due mainly to race-neutral, ethnocentric tendencies. If ethnocentrism were the primary cause, it would be strongest in the most segregated group (blacks) and its effect would be consistent across target groups. But, in fact, blacks stand out as the group most open to substantial integration with all other groups and most likely to reject individual or collective racial isolation. More likely is that the barrier to increased integration is located in the lower tolerance for black neighbors expressed by members of other groups.

This pooled analysis of four cities and four racial groups shows similarities with previous individual-city analyses (Farley et al. 1993, 1994; Bobo and Zubrinsky 1996; Zubrinsky and Bobo 1996). To inquire into potential city and/or regional differences in neighborhood racial-composition preferences and examine the importance of additional racial and nonracial factors, we now turn our attention to multivariate analysis.

Predicting Neighborhood
Racial-Composition Preferences

In accounting for variation in attitudes toward integration, both within and across racial groups, it is standard to consider respondents' race, education, and income. Another factor likely to influence such attitudes is city of residence. City-specific differences in neighborhood preferences are no doubt related to regional variations in patterns of race relations, both historically and currently. Therefore, each model in the following multivariate analysis includes dummy variables for the four surveyed cities.[6]

Another important consideration in understanding attitudes toward integration is the extent to which racial stereotypes and perceived group differences in socioeconomic status influence neighborhood racial-composition preferences. While previous research has examined this relationship, the Multi-City Study data provide the opportunity to examine the interactive relationship between metropolitan location and racial stereotypes. Thus, each model includes both a Stereotype Difference score[7] and a Perceived Socioeconomic Status (SES) Difference score.[8] These difference measures explore whether or not group members evaluate others as inferior to themselves and reveal the size of any perceived difference between the two groups (Bobo and Kluegel 1997; Jackman and Senter 1983). The Stereotype and SES Difference measures are summarized in table 4.3.

TABLE 4.3   Summary Statistics, Stereotyping Measures

Target Race	Respondent Race			
	Whites	Blacks	Hispanics	Asians
Whites				
Hard to get along	16.52	24.87	22.60	22.51
Prefer welfare	11.87	16.09	18.79	13.90
Unintelligent	17.01	20.00	16.92	17.40
Poor English	8.98	10.20	5.61	3.33
Stereotype rating	13.51	17.86	16.04	14.45
Difference score	—	−1.79	−8.23	−1.36
Poor	21.80	16.49	16.27	16.77
SES difference score	—	−16.50	−18.93	−4.65
Blacks				
Hard to get along	22.55	19.04	27.19	26.67
Prefer welfare	26.72	23.35	36.23	33.93
Unintelligent	23.77	19.56	23.62	27.80
Poor English	21.65	16.33	15.93	9.47
Stereotype rating	23.67	19.64	25.77	24.28
Difference score	10.06	—	1.43	8.46
Poor	34.29	32.98	35.00	36.26
SES difference score	12.52	—	−0.26	14.80
Hispanics				
Hard to get along	22.31	22.45	16.19	22.34
Prefer welfare	24.18	25.05	30.47	33.66
Unintelligent	24.64	23.51	21.50	28.91
Poor English	30.16	31.53	28.96	29.02
Stereotype rating	25.30	25.58	24.23	28.45
Difference score	11.64	5.80	—	12.66
Poor	35.42	34.34	35.29	37.35
SES difference score	13.67	1.30	—	15.86
Asians				
Hard to get along	20.95	26.89	27.25	15.80
Prefer welfare	13.10	16.58	19.13	10.74
Unintelligent	17.45	19.95	16.14	14.93
Poor English	25.37	31.03	27.36	21.97
Stereotype rating	19.09	23.48	22.59	15.80
Difference score	5.43	3.73	−1.93	—
Poor	25.32	22.46	23.01	21.48
SES difference score	3.63	−10.59	−12.10	—

Source: Multi-City Study of Urban Inequality.
Notes: Figures for individual traits and stereotype ratings are means on a 0 to 50 scale, where 50 is the negative end of a bipolar rating continuum. Figures for the Stereotype Difference SES Difference scores are means on a scale of −50 to +50, where high (positive) scores indicate more favorable perceptions of in-group members, relative to out-groups; low (negative) scores indicate more favorable perceptions of out-groups, relative to in-groups; and a score of 0 indicates no perceived differences between in-group and out-group members.
$p < .001$.

Measuring racial attitudes in this fashion is consistent with theories of race prejudice emphasizing the development and maintenance of relative status advantage (Blumer 1958; Jankowski 1995), rather than simple out-group hostility (Allport 1954; Pettigrew 1982). A group perceiving little or no social class gap between itself and another will regard it more favorably than one it views as substantially different socioeconomically.

According to the contact hypothesis, increased exposure to members of out-groups should favorably affect attitudes toward them (Allport 1954; Jackman and Crane 1986; Sigelman and Welch 1993). Testing this requires that we examine the relationship between actual interracial contact and the interacting groups' expressed preferences for integration with each other. To ascertain the impact of interracial contact in the residential setting, all models include measures of the target-group composition of respondents' neighborhoods.[9] Homeownership and neighborhood socioeconomic status are additional factors that may affect preferences. These social-class characteristics are easily confounded with race. To avert such confusion, all models include measures of homeownership and the poverty rate of respondents' block groups.[10]

To examine these relationships, Racial Preference Indexes (RPIs), similar to one developed by Reynolds Farley and colleagues (1978), were constructed as dependent variables for multivariate analyses. White respondents' RPI has a range of 0 to 100, where higher scores indicate greater acceptance of racial residential integration. For each of the four neighborhoods, a score of 25 is given to whites saying they would feel "very comfortable" there; a score of 20 is given for feeling "somewhat comfortable." Whites feeling "somewhat uncomfortable" or "very uncomfortable" in a neighborhood into which they are nevertheless willing to move receive a score of 12.5. Whites who are both "somewhat" or "very uncomfortable" *and* unwilling to move into a neighborhood receive a score of 0. Scores for responses to all four neighborhoods are summed for each respondent.

The RPI constructed for nonwhite respondents is slightly different: it is based on the series of neighborhood-preference questions and related show cards described in the previous section for each nonwhite respondent group. In this variant, scores range from 12.5 to 100 (low to high acceptance, respectively). Nonwhite respondents were asked to arrange the five neighborhood cards from most to least attractive. To compute the RPI, scores were given to each of the neighborhood cards; as with the overall scale, high values indicate acceptance of integration and low ones the opposite. These scores are then weighted according to respondents' willingness or unwillingness to move into each neighborhood. To arrive at the final RPI score, the five weighted values are

TABLE 4.4   *Summary Statistics, Racial Preference Index (RPI), by Respondent and Target Group Race*

Target Race	Respondent Race			
	Whites	Blacks	Hispanics	Asians
Whites	—	39.27	49.66	50.50
Blacks	66.89	—	29.36	26.46
Hispanics	75.71	41.35	—	30.30
Asians	84.99	38.99	39.25	—
N	2935	3167	1695	1057
F	101.636**	3.52*	148.37**	325.87**
Eta	.255	.047	.386	.618
Eta^2	.065	.002	.149	.382

Source: Multi-City Study of Urban Inequality.
Notes: The white RPI is a scale based on responses to cards depicting varying degrees of integration. Scores range from 0 (low acceptance of racial residential integration) to 100 (high acceptance). The nonwhite RPI is a scale based on responses to cards portraying varying degrees of integration that are slightly different from those used to compute whites' RPI. Nonwhite RPI scores range from 12.5 (low acceptance) to 100 (high acceptance). For details on scale construction, see Zubrinsky (1996).
Hispanic respondents in Los Angeles and Boston only; Asian respondents in Los Angeles only.
*$p < .05$. **$p < .001$.

summed for each respondent. Table 4.4 presents mean scores for the RPI measures by respondent- and target-group race, using pooled data.

Since the white RPI score is based on a different set of questions from those used to calculate minority-respondent RPI scores, we cannot conclude that the high mean preference scores of whites indicate greater openness to integration than is true of minority respondents. In fact, the foregoing analysis of neighborhood racial-composition preferences suggests the opposite.[11] It is nevertheless encouraging that whites' mean RPI scores indicate fairly high acceptance of integration across target-group categories. Less promising, however, is the recurrence of the racial-preference hierarchy observed throughout this analysis: whites are again significantly less tolerant of integration with blacks (66.89) than with Hispanics (75.71) or Asians (84.99). Hispanic and Asian respondents exhibit a similar pattern with respect to most and least preferred neighbors.

Deviating somewhat from this pattern, black respondents give Hispanics the highest average RPI score (41.35); slightly lower are their scores for whites (39.27) and Asians (38.99). Blacks score white neighbors roughly 10 points lower than do Hispanics or Asians. While this contradicts to some degree the image of blacks as the group most open to integration, it comports with their perception of whites as hostile toward them and with an aversion to potentially uncomfortable situations (Cose 1993). Consistent with their image as the group most open to integration, however, differences between black respondents' mean RPI scores for the various target groups are the smallest of all respondent groups; they barely reach the most lenient degree of statistical significance ($f = 3.52$, $p = .030$). Target-group race also explains the least amount of variance in RPI for black respondents ($Eta^2 = .002$).

Turning now to more complete multivariate analysis, recall that, for each racial respondent category, the target-group-appropriate Racial Preference Index is the dependent variable. For control purposes only, all models include measures of sex, age, education, income, and political ideology. The explanatory measures of interest in each model are as follows: city of residence; homeownership, neighborhood poverty rate, and SES Difference score; the target-group proportion of respondents' current neighborhood; and the Stereotype Difference score. Models for Hispanic and Asian respondents also include measures of immigrant status and national origin.[12] Where appropriate, models include significant interaction effects among stereotyping, city of residence, immigrant status, and national orgin.[13] Results are shown in table 4.5.

Earlier in this chapter, we explored the possibility that current residential patterns are the result of real and/or perceived differences in social class status across racial groups. The analysis in this table, which examines whether these same differences influence neighborhood racial-composition preferences, addresses the argument that rational, nonracial, class concerns about property values and neighborhood services and safety are primary influences—not race per se (Leven et al. 1976; Harris 1997). Of forty-eight coefficients related to social class concerns, only eight reach statistical significance. No clear pattern of relationships emerges. Homeownership—white homeowners prefer black neighbors less than other white respondents do (-3.04, $p < .05$)—is the only social class factor that significantly influences white acceptance of integration with blacks. But since whites, generally, regard Hispanics as poorer than blacks, this lesser preference of white homeowners for black neighbors seems to reflect race-based attitudes associated with the historical notion that the entry of blacks into white areas marks the beginning of neighborhood decline.

The socioeconomic makeup of white respondents' neighborhoods has no significant impact on their attitudes toward integration. Minority attitudes, on the other hand, are more consistently influenced by neighborhood poverty rates. Black and Asian respondents residing in neighborhoods with poverty rates below 10 percent express greater acceptance of integration with Asians and whites, respectively, compared

TABLE 4.5   *Multivariate Regression Coefficients Examining the Effects of Immigrant Status and Nationality, Social Class Concerns, Interracial Contact, City of Residence, and Stereotyping on Acceptance of Racial Residential Integration*

	White Respondents			Black Respondents		
	Black RPI	Hispanic RPI	Asian RPI	White RPI	Hispanic RPI	Asian RPI
Constant	92.01***	95.71***	91.38***	31.98***	34.81***	42.65***
Immigrant Status and nationality						
U.S.-born	—	—	—	—	—	—
Mexican	—	—	—	—	—	—
Puerto Rican	—	—	—	—	—	—
Chinese	—	—	—	—	—	—
Korean	—	—	—	—	—	—
Social class concerns						
Homeowner	−3.04***	−2.93	2.49	−0.94	3.85	−3.10
10 to 20 percent Poverty block group	−1.96	2.52	−0.15	−2.34	−0.20	−7.15***
+20 percent poverty block group	−3.24	2.96	−5.09	−0.43	0.31	−1.08
SES difference	−0.03	0.08	−0.43***	0.04	−0.06	−0.03
Interracial contact						
< 10 percent target block group	−9.03***	−1.20	−4.16***	0.37	−3.85	3.51
10 to 20 percent target block group	−3.03	0.61	−3.37	6.65***	−1.58	3.56
City of residence						
Atlanta	0.54	—	—	−0.61	—	—
Boston	6.60***	−4.79	1.95	6.05***	7.87***	−1.26
Los Angeles	4.21	—	—	2.86***	—	—
Stereotyping						
Stereotype Difference score	−1.10***	−0.72***	−0.21***	−0.33***	0.16	−0.47***
Interactions						
Atlanta × stereotype	0.33***	—	—	—	—	—
Boston × stereotype	—	—	−1.08***	—	—	—
U.S. Born × Stereotype	—	—	—	—	—	—
Puerto Rican × stereotype	—	—	—	—	—	—
R^2	.25***	.13***	.28***	.08***	.10	.21***
N	1904	409	410	1829	449	450

Source: Multi-City Study of Urban Inequality.
Note: Hispanics interviewed in Boston and Los Angeles only; Asians in Los Angeles only.
*$p < .05$. **$p < .01$. ***$p < .001$.

252

	Hispanic Respondents			Asian Respondents	
White RPI	Black RPI	Asian RPI	White RPI	Black RPI	Hispanic RPI
23.75***	32.33***	17.11***	44.67***	26.56***	39.36***
−10.62	−0.40	−3.67	4.16	3.51	0.39
−7.55	−0.18	−2.02	—	—	—
−21.14	−7.07***	−9.26***	—	—	—
—	—	—	0.74	1.14	2.71***
—	—	—	1.10	0.55	−0.31
1.56	10.39***	−2.32	−1.41	−0.41	−0.82
−5.81	6.52***	3.06	−13.75***	−2.31	1.00
−0.75	2.22	2.55	−10.24***	0.81	−1.57
−0.07	0.01	0.01	0.09	−0.10***	0.04
−15.50***	−1.64	−2.25	−11.22***	−1.40	4.08***
0.04	−1.16	−4.50	−6.00	5.88	−1.79
—	—	—	—	—	—
0.34	4.95	6.74***	—	—	—
—	—	—	—	—	—
−0.23	−0.61***	−0.42***	−0.38	0.19***	0.06
—	—	—	—	—	—
1.56***	—	2.22***	—	—	—
−0.66***	—	—	—	−0.37***	—
−2.20***	—	−2.56***	—	—	—
.34***	.24***	.31***	.35***	.14	.25***
436	416	422	289	296	284

253

to blacks and Asians living in medium- or high-poverty neighborhoods. The direction of effect is the opposite among Hispanic respondents: increased neighborhood poverty has a positive effect on tolerance for integration with blacks. This result is counter to expectations and may well reflect indirect evidence of the contact hypothesis. Hispanics are much more likely to share residential space with blacks, in neighborhoods that are disproportionately poor (Alba et al. 1995). Perhaps occupying common space and perceiving a common fate positively influence racial attitudes.

Among social class concerns, perceived differences in socioeconomic status appear to have the smallest impact on RPI scores. Noteworthy, however, is that the only significant effects are found among the two respondent groups at the top of the economic and social hierarchy: whites and Asians. The multivariate results relating to the entire category of social class concerns lead to a single conclusion: social class differences, real or imagined, do not play a major role in understanding neighborhood racial-composition preferences.

Another hypothesis tested was that increased residential contact with a particular target group would positively affect respondents' tolerance for integration with that group. This is one of many types of interracial contact thought to impact racial attitudes positively (Jackman and Crane 1986; Kinder and Mendelberg 1995; Sigelman and Welch 1993; Sigelman et al. 1996; Ellison and Powers 1994). The relationship between target-group neighborhood racial composition and attitudes toward integration is ambiguous but shows more promise than that between social class factors and attitudes. White respondents' acceptance of integration with blacks and Asians grows as interracial contact with these groups increases. When minority respondents have greater neighborhood interracial contact with whites, their attitudes toward integration with whites are more positive; under comparable conditions, however, Asian acceptance of integration with blacks declines. This latter effect may be understood in terms of the greater likelihood of poverty among the blacks with whom Asians share residential space than among neighboring whites (Alba et al. 1995), and Asians' concomitant desire to improve and/or maintain relative status advantage (Bobo and Zubrinsky 1996; Jankowski 1995).

Of the various types of interracial contact, that at the neighborhood level has shown the smallest and most inconsistent effect on racial attitudes. Interracial friendships and recurrent contact through employment and voluntary associations show larger, more consistent effects (Jackman and Crane 1986; Ellison and Powers 1994; Sigelman et al. 1996). Still, these results suggest that increased interracial contact improves racial attitudes and that the former is more influential in that respect than are social class concerns.

City of residence reveals some interesting patterns, suggesting subtle differences that single-city analyses cannot capture but that are nonetheless important. These patterns are generally consistent with objective levels of segregation and racial composition in the four cities: two aggregate-level factors thought to influence racial attitudes generally, and neighborhood racial-composition preferences specifically (Farley et al. 1978; Farley and Frey 1994). Note, first, that acceptance of integration across respondent categories is lower in Detroit than in the other three cities. Detroit is the most segregated metropolitan area in the country. It has a large black population (21.5 percent), but almost no Hispanic or Asian residents (less than 1 percent). Boston, on the other hand, is less segregated than both Detroit and Los Angeles. Boston's minority populations are small (6.2 percent black, 4.9 percent Hispanic, and 3.1 percent Asian) relative to a city like Los Angeles, but large enough to offer widespread visibility (Harrison and Weinberg 1992). And living in Boston appears to have the most favorable impact on white, black, and Hispanic respondents' acceptance of integration. In many instances, however, the interaction of city and stereotyping is of greater interest than the direct effect of city is.[14]

The Stereotype Difference score shows the most consistent effect on acceptance of integration, reaching significance in eight of twelve tests, always in the anticipated direction. But contrary to images of white southern bigotry, the effect of stereotyping on acceptance of integration with blacks is *smaller* among Atlanta whites $(-1.10 + 0.33 = -0.77, p < .001)$ than among whites in the other cities $(-1.10, p < .01)$. Of the four cities, Atlanta is the smallest (approximately 2.8 million people) and is tied with Boston for the lowest black-white segregation score (.677). Perhaps an oversensitivity to Atlanta's racial history, combined with its relatively smaller size and lower objective segregation help explain this counterintuitive finding. The effect of stereotyping on whites' acceptance of integration with Asians, moreover, is larger among Boston whites $(-0.21 - 1.08 = -1.29, p < .001)$ than among their counterparts in Los Angeles $(-0.21, p < .01)$. Whites in these two cities do not differ significantly, however, with respect to the effect of stereotypes on preferences for Hispanic neighbors $(-0.72, p < .05)$.

That there are no significant interactions among black respondents makes the interpretation of city and stereotyping effects straightforward: black Bostonians express significantly more favorable attitudes toward integration with whites (6.05, $p < .001$) and Hispanics (7.87, $p < .001$) than do blacks in the other cities. The effect of stereotyping is almost always smaller among black respondents than for whites and is nonsignificant with respect to attitudes toward integration with Hispanics.

Similarly uncomplicated is the effect of stereotyping among Asians: it is not a significant predictor of their preferences for integration with whites, either directly or interactively with city, national origin, or immigrant status. The effect of stereotyping on Asians' preferences for black neighbors is tied to immigrant status: stereotypes have a negative effect on preferences for black neighbors only among native-born Asians $(0.19 - 0.37 = -0.18, p < .001)$. Finally, Chinese Asians express greater tolerance for Hispanic neighbors than do non-Chinese $(2.71, p < .001)$; however, neither immigrant status nor stereotyping significantly influences these attitudes.

The effect of stereotyping on integration attitudes among Hispanic respondents is often mediated by city of residence, immigrant status, and nationality, but is still usually negative.[15] Hispanics' attitudes toward integration with blacks are not significantly different between the two cities in which Hispanics were sampled, nor are there any significant interaction effects. In this instance the effect of stereotyping is simple: negative stereotypes decrease Hispanics' preferences for black neighbors $(-0.61, p < .05)$. Hispanics of Puerto Rican descent express less acceptance of integration with blacks than do other Hispanic groups $(-7.07, p < .05)$, but no significant immigrant-status effect emerges. Relationships among city of residence, nationality, immigrant status, and stereotyping are more complicated, however, with respect to Hispanics' acceptance of integration with both whites and Asians. For example, the effect of stereotyping on acceptance of integration with whites is positive among Hispanics living in Boston $(-0.23 + 1.56 = 1.33, p < .05)$ but negative among Hispanics born in the United States $(-0.23 - 0.66 = -.89, p < .05)$ and those of Puerto Rican descent $(-0.23 - 2.20 = -2.43, p < .001)$. A similar pattern is evident with respect to Hispanics' acceptance of integration with Asians: the effect of stereotypes is positive for Hispanics from Boston $(-0.42 + 2.22 = 1.8, p < .001)$ but negative for Hispanics from Los Angeles $(-0.42, p < .05)$; the negative stereotype effect is seven times larger among Puerto Ricans $(-0.42 - 2.56 = -2.98, p < .001)$ than non–Puerto Ricans $(-0.42, p < .05)$; and the effect of stereotypes on Hispanics' preferences for Asian neighbors is not significantly different between the native- and foreign-born.

As a whole, these results lend strong support to race-based explanations of residential segregation. Racial stereotypes have the most consistent impact on acceptance of integration and these effects, along with others, vary by the race of both the respondent and potential neighbors.

Still, there are several limitations to the Racial Preference Index that deserve consideration. Respondents are limited to two-group scenarios in an increasingly multiethnic society; levels of integration are predetermined by the questionnaire; and the series of questions asked of white respondents differs from that asked of nonwhite respondents.

To address these limitations, the Multi-City Study introduced a major modification to the Farley-Schuman show card methodology. All the Los Angeles respondents and half the Boston respondents were given a blank neighborhood show card (illustrated in figure 4.14) and asked to specify the racial makeup of their ideal neighborhood. Specifically, these respondents were instructed as follows:

> Now I'd like you to imagine an ideal neighborhood that had the ethnic and racial mix you personally would feel most comfortable in. Here is a blank neighborhood card like those we have been using. Using the letters A for Asian, B for Black, H for Hispanic, and W for White, please put a letter in each of these houses to represent your ideal neighborhood, where you would most like to live. Please be sure to fill in all of the houses.

This measure allows respondents to consider integration with several out-groups at once and to have complete control over the degree and configuration of integration. It is also less reactive, thereby reducing the likelihood of false, socially desirable responses.[16] And unlike the original DAS experiment, the "ideal neighborhood" provides the same stimulus to all respondents, making results comparable across racial categories.[17]

Summary statistics for the Ideal Neighborhood Experiment are presented in table 4.6. The first column of each racial respondent-group category includes all respondents participating in the experiment, while the second column includes only those with moderately negative stereotypes of the out-groups.[18] Results are consistent with those of the original experiment and strengthen race-based explanations of residential segregation. Again, all groups prefer both substantial numbers of co-ethnic neighbors and considerable integration. Another recurring pattern is the rank-ordering of out-groups: whites are always the out-group with the highest representation in minority respondents' "ideal" multi-ethnic neighborhoods, and blacks are always the out-group with the lowest representation in those of nonblacks. On average, whites express the strongest preference for same-race neighbors (52.2 percent), and blacks the weakest (39.9 percent).

This table also presents the percentage of respondents who either create entirely same-race ideal neighborhoods or exclude particular target groups. Note that whites, the most likely to create entirely same-race neighborhoods (11.1 percent), do so at more than four times the rate

FIGURE 4.14   *"Ideal Neighborhood" Show Card*

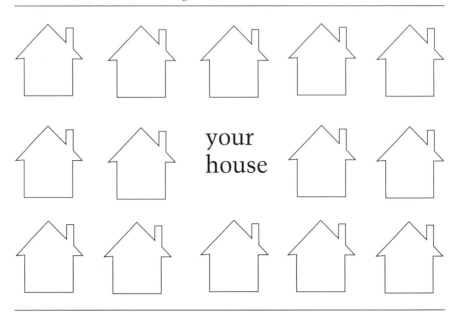

your
house

Source: Multi-City Study of Urban Inequality.
Note: Used in Los Angeles and on a split-ballot basis in Boston.

of blacks (2.5 percent), the least exclusionary group. Moreover, blacks are the group most often excluded from the ideal neighborhoods of others: about one-fifth of whites omit them, as do one-quarter of Hispanics and two-fifths of Asians. Whites, by comparison, are least often excluded from the ideal neighborhoods of nonwhite respondents.

This contrast is even more striking when we examine the ideal-neighborhood preferences of respondents expressing negative stereotypes of out-groups. Among whites, the mean percentage of each out-group falls below 10 percent, and rates of exclusion nearly double, reaching roughly 40 percent. Patterns are less extreme and more inconsistent among black, Hispanic, and Asian respondents, partly due to the small numbers expressing clearly negative stereotypes of other groups. Interestingly, negative stereotypes of whites often accompany their increased inclusion in the ideal neighborhoods of Asians and Hispanics. This might reflect desires for upward social mobility, which, as indicated earlier, is often symbolized by greater proximity to whites. A clear association between negative stereotypes and exclusion does show up among Asian respondents but is less apparent among Hispanics and blacks.

Deceptively simple, the Ideal Neighborhood experiment elicits highly

TABLE 4.6 Summary Statistics for All Respondents, and for Respondents with Moderately Negative Stereotypes of Out-Groups, Multiethnic Show Card Experiment

	Respondent Race							
	Whites		Blacks		Hispanics		Asians	
Target Group	All	Negative Stereotype	All	Negative Stereotype	All	Negative Stereotype	All	Negative Stereotype
Whites								
Mean percentage	52.2	—	21.7	17.0	26.0	30.9	29.6	31.1
No whites	0	—	10.2	19.8	11.8	5.3	8.7	3.7
All whites	11.1	—	0	0	0	0	0	0
N	1143	—	1316	118	1296	59	1052	41
Blacks								
Mean percentage	14.6	9.4	39.9	—	14.3	14.0	10.1	7.0
No blacks	21.9	39.9	0	—	26.9	24.9	41.2	54.2
All blacks	0	0	2.5	—	0	0	0	0
N	1143	235	1316	—	1296	88	1052	130
Hispanics								
Mean percentage	14.2	9.6	19.4	19.0	42.6	—	14.3	12.0
No Hispanics	23.9	40.0	11.9	12.9	0	—	27.6	32.4
All Hispanics	0	0	0	0	5.7	—	0	0
N	1143	349	1316	126	1296	—	1052	285
Asians								
Mean percentage	15.5	9.8	16.3	13.1	15.9	16.9	44.6	—
No Asians	19.9	41.2	17.5	27.9	21.2	17.0	0	—
All Asians	0	0	0	0	0	0	7.0	—
N	1143	206	1316	278	1296	85	1052	—

Source: Multi-City Study of Urban Inequality.
Notes: The percentage of each racial group in a respondent's "ideal" neighborhood is the sum of each group included in the experiment depicted in figure 4.1, divided by the sum of all houses. For negative stereotypes of blacks and Hispanics, Stereotype Difference scores are greater than or equal to 15. For negative stereotypes of whites and Asians, Stereotype Difference scores are greater than or equal to 10.
p < .001.

candid, easy-to-interpret responses across multiple racial categories. It is thereby capable of providing the most accurate picture to date of the role of race in neighborhood-composition preferences. In so doing, it demonstrates that substantially increased interracial residential contact is unlikely. We have shown, for example, that there remain a sizable number of Americans who, given the choice, would completely avoid residential contact with blacks.

The Ideal Neighborhood experiment also allows researchers to examine issues related to proximity, which prior studies of preferences have been unable to address. The original show card experiment provides predetermined degrees of integration and positioning of out-group neighbors, relative to the respondent's house, in the center of the card. The Ideal Neighborhood experiment, however, gives the respondent complete control over the placement of out-group neighbors. Figure 4.15 presents the distribution of out-groups for the four houses immediately surrounding the respondent's home. Conceptually, the houses to the right and left of center reflect next-door neighbors; those located above and below might be seen as across-the-street neighbors.

For the most part, the distribution of out-groups for these four houses is consistent with the pattern of mean responses presented in table 4.6: all groups want both diversity and substantial co-ethnic representation; whites are always the most desirable out-group neighbors; and blacks are always the least desirable. When rates fall short of the overall patterns, it is generally for the houses that represent next-door neighbors; this is particularly true of potential black and, to a lesser extent, Hispanic neighbors. This suggests that attitudes toward integration may be linked to the degree of proximity of particular out-groups to their in-group neighbors.

Figure 4.16 repeats the format of figure 4.15 but limits respondents to those with at least moderately unfavorable stereotypes of out-groups. It is again evident that stereotypes influence neighborhood racial-composition preferences, both overall and in terms of the specific location of out-group neighbors. Whites, Hispanics, and Asians who negatively stereotype blacks distribute them among the four houses with frequencies almost always well below the mean. This is also true among whites and Asians with regard to Hispanic neighbors. In contrast, negatively stereotyped whites are often overrepresented in the four houses surrounding Hispanic and Asian respondents. For these respondents, desires for upward social mobility and improved relative status advantage may outweigh their unfavorable perceptions of whites. The relationship between stereotypes and selection of surrounding out-group neighbors is least clear for blacks. While the phrase "not in my neighborhood" may no longer appropriately represent racial attitudes, "not next door to me" still rings true.

FIGURE 4.15 "Ideal" Racial Composition of Houses Immediately Around Respondents'

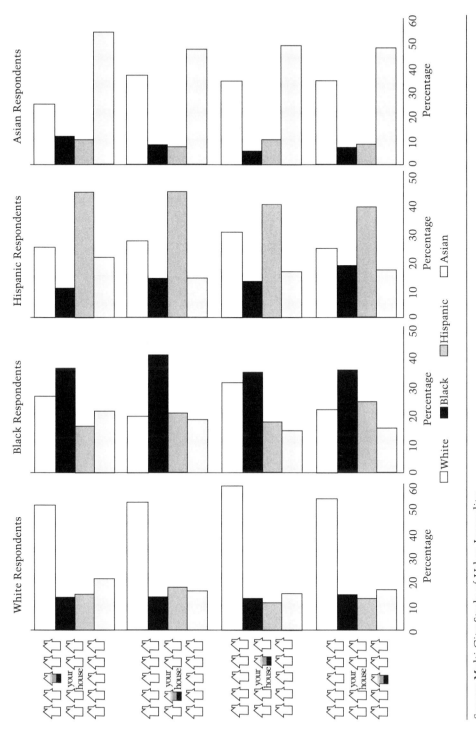

Source: Multi-City Study of Urban Inequality.
Note: p < .001.

FIGURE 4.16   "Ideal" Racial Composition of Houses Immediately Around Respondents' When Out-Group Stereotypes are Moderately Unfavorable

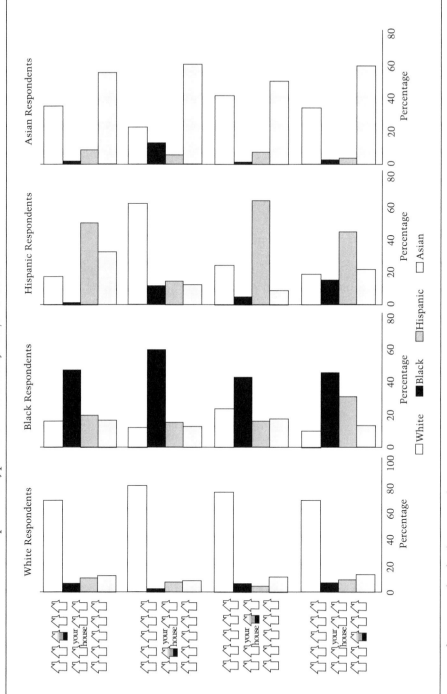

Source: Multi-City Study of Urban Inequality.
Notes: For percentage black or Hispanic, stereotype difference scores are greater than or equal to 15; for percentage white or Asian, scores are greater than or equal to 10.
p ≤ .001

Conclusion

The assertion that opened this chapter—that racial residential segregation results from a complex set of factors—is no less accurate at its close. The evidence presented here offers varying levels of support for each of the factors under study. We must nevertheless also conclude that "all roads lead to race." Economic disparities, for example, are often regarded as nonracial (Leven et al. 1976; Muth 1986; Clark 1989). An examination of economic differences, however, found considerable overlap in the monthly housing expenditures of all groups but substantial differences in rates of homeownership. The latter are inextricably tied to differences in wealth accumulation and access to credit that follow racial lines. These differences are not an accident of history but result from centuries of racial oppression (Oliver and Shapiro 1995) and continuing racial discrimination in all areas of American life (Kirschenman and Neckerman 1991; Cose 1993, 1997; Feagin and Sikes 1995; Yinger 1995; Collins 1997). Addressing these disparities is important and could reduce segregation, but requires different policy measures (for example, antidiscrimination efforts in employment, improvements in education and training, or policies directed specifically at wealth accumulation, such as reparations for slavery).

This study of housing market perceptions and information indicates that all groups have comparably accurate information about housing costs and similar perceptions of the general desirability of specific communities. Where differences exist, they are clearly racial. Communities with high minority concentrations are least desirable to whites, even when those communities are affluent. And, understandably, minority-group members tend to rate as less desirable communities they perceive as hostile toward them.

Minority-group members also express perceptions that institutional discrimination "causes members of their group to miss out on good housing," which are fairly consistent with reality (Yinger 1995). Taken together, these perceptions may cause minority-group members, particularly blacks, to limit their housing searches to areas where they feel welcome and where prospects of being turned down are low.

Neighborhood racial-composition preferences reveal a clear and consistent racial rank-ordering of out-groups as potential neighbors. Whites are always the most preferred out-group neighbors but are most likely to prefer all-same-race neighborhoods. Blacks are always the least preferred out-group neighbors, while being most open to substantial integration with all other groups. Moreover, blacks—the most segregated group in society—are least likely to prefer all-same-race neighborhoods.

All groups express desires for both substantial integration and a strong representation of co-ethnics. Nonblacks' desire for racial homogeneity increases, however, when potential neighbors are black. These patterns weaken ethnocentrism arguments. If current residential patterns were due mainly to ethnocentric tendencies that cut across racial lines, the observed preferences would be distributed more equally across groups. Perhaps more important, preferred rates of same-race neighbors would not be altered by the race of potential out-group neighbors.

Racial stereotypes seem to play a particularly important role in neighborhood racial-composition preferences. As out-group stereotypes become increasingly negative, preferences for integration with members of those groups decline. This relationship is strongest among whites, the group at the top of the status hierarchy. Negative stereotypes affect not only rates of inclusion but also preferred proximity. The effect of stereotypes is always stronger and more consistent than that of social class concerns or residential interracial contact.

The complicated relationship found among immigrant status, nationality, and stereotypes illustrates the importance of Hispanic and Asian heterogeneity in understanding their neighborhood racial-composition preferences. Also, respondents' city of residence appears to influence attitudes toward integration. These findings imply that generalizing from crudely drawn distinctions and city-specific studies carries some risk. Overall, however, the results of this analysis suggest a pattern of processes that can be generalized across metropolitan areas. Illuminating the complex interplay of factors influencing attitudes toward residential integration, they demonstrate the importance of these attitudes in producing and perpetuating actual residential patterns.

Taken together, these results offer strong evidence of the persistent influence of racial prejudice—not as simple out-group antipathy (that is, ethnocentrism) but as a sense of group position (Blumer 1958; Bobo and Hutchings 1996; Bobo and Zubrinsky 1996). With whites clearly dominating the economic, political, and prestige hierarchies in American society, nonwhites have traditionally associated upward social mobility with proximity to them. That many nonwhites holding negative attitudes toward whites nevertheless prefer them as neighbors indicates the persistence of this orientation (Jaynes and Williams 1989; Massey and Denton 1993; Jankowski 1995).

Conversely, whites' maintenance of status advantage and privilege requires a certain amount of social distance from nonwhites—particularly blacks and Hispanics, occupying the bottom of the aforementioned hierarchies. More than token integration with these groups signals an unwelcome change in status relationships. This is undoubtedly why the Stereotype Difference measure (emphasizing the size of perceived differences, in addition to the differences themselves) is a stronger predictor of whites' than of nonwhites' neighborhood preferences. The racial pecking order is so widely known that Hispanics and Asians— many of them unassimilated immigrants—mirror it in their preferences of out-group neighbors.

Achieving stable, integrated neighborhoods is not as simple as Rodney King's plea that "we all just get along." As the nation becomes increasingly diverse, the gap between haves and have-nots grows; this division is clearly color-coded. Whether voluntary or not, our living in a particular neighborhood has a substantial effect on our overall life chances, including opportunities for upward social mobility (Massey and Gross 1991). Residential segregation is thus a central component of racial inequality; we must confront it if we are serious in our commitment to a color-blind society.

Notes

1. This explanation seems to make more sense in explaining Hispanic and Asian segregation, since analyses of these groups find that Hispanic and Asian segregation from whites declines as SES improves (Denton and Massey 1988, 1991; Massey and Denton 1987; White 1986). Still, recent analysis of Los Angeles (Zubrinsky 1996) indicates that economic differences play only a small part in understanding Hispanic and Asian segregation in Los Angeles.

2. That Asian respondents report such high monthly housing expenditures is due in part to their having being sampled only in Los Angeles, a city with a very high cost of living. Another possible explanation is their status as recent immigrants and, therefore, more recent purchasers of homes with inflated prices.

3. One-third of each respondent racial category in Los Angeles (whites, blacks, Hispanics, and Asians) and Boston (whites, blacks, and Hispanics) was assigned to consider varying degrees of integration with one of three out-groups. For details, see Zubrinsky 1996.

4. A comparison of preferences by national-origin among Hispanics in Los Angeles finds statistically significant differences that support this argument.

5. As was true of Hispanics, there are statistically significant differences in the residential preferences of native-born and foreign-born Asians. The latter are more likely than the former to find the all-Asian neighborhood most attractive when responding to the Asian-white scenario (21 percent and 3 percent, respectively). The percentage of foreign-born Asians preferring an all co-ethnic neighborhood increases to 54 percent when the alternative involves integration with Hispanics. But irrespective of immigrant status, the importance of the race of potential neighbors is clear: 76 percent of

foreign-born and 85 percent of native-born Asians prefer the all-Asian neighborhood when the alternative is integration with blacks.

6. For models predicting white and black preferences for integration, the reference city is Detroit. For models predicting Hispanic preferences, the reference city is Los Angeles (only Boston and Los Angeles sampled Hispanics). Since Los Angeles was the only city to sample Asians, there are no city variables.

7. The original format of the stereotyping questions is a 1-to-7 scale taken directly from the 1990 General Social Survey (Bobo and Kluegel 1991; Smith 1991), which included a series of bipolar trait-rating items. This format has been shown to increase respondent comfort in expressing racial-ethnic stereotyping more than do older, forced-choice formats and thereby yield reasonable, reliable, and valid measures of prejudice (compare, Schuman, Steeh, and Bobo [1985] to Bobo and Kluegel [1991] and Smith [1991] as to reported levels of perceiving blacks as less intelligent; Bobo and Kluegel 1993; Farley et al. 1994). The Stereotype Difference score ranges from -50 to $+50$ and is computed by subtracting a respondent's rating of an out-group from his or her rating of his or her in-group. Positive scores indicate favorable in-group ratings relative to out-groups; negative scores indicate favorable out-group ratings relative to in-groups; and a score of 0 indicates no perceived difference between the two groups. The traits used for the Stereotype Difference score are the following: difficulty to get along with socially; preference for welfare dependency; intelligence; and English-language ability. For a detailed discussion of the trait-selection process, see Bobo and Zubrinsky (1996) or Zubrinsky (1996).

8. The SES Difference score uses a single bipolar-trait rating scale that asks whether members of each group "tend to be rich" or "tend to be poor." The range and meaning of scores are identical to those of the Stereotype Difference score; however, the rich-poor dimension is treated separately because it is not a personality or dispositional trait, as are those used in the Stereotype Difference score (see Farley et al. 1994).

9. This is measured at the block-group level using data from the 1990 Census STF3 file.

10. Block-level poverty is obtained from the 1990 Census STF3 file.

11. The structure of neighborhood-preference questions presented to whites imposes a linearity not present in that of comparable questions posed to minorities. More important, whites and nonwhites are asked to evaluate different degrees of integration. The neighborhood cards for white respondents range from all-white to just over 50 percent other-race, whereas nonwhites' cards range from all-

same-race to all-other-race neighborhoods. Whites' apparently high acceptance of integration thus could be attributed to the fact that they are not asked to imagine a situation in which they are the only white family in the neighborhood (Colasanto 1977, 100).

12. The Hispanic sample consists largely of individuals of Mexican and Puerto Rican descent. The reference category is anyone not of Mexican or Puerto Rican descent. The Asian sample includes only those of Chinese, Korean, and Japanese descent. In that Chinese and Korean respondents are largely recent immigrants, Japanese respondents are the reference category.

13. Regression estimates use STATA, which includes a survey-regression procedure to correct for the multistage cluster sampling used in the Multi-City Study. This produces accurate, design-based standard errors and confidence intervals (Stata Press 1997).

14. All models were estimated including interaction terms; however, only those with statistically significant coefficients are reported here.

15. Since Los Angeles and Boston were the only two sites with Hispanic samples, Los Angeles is the reference category.

16. Pretest respondents exhibited heightened engagement in this task. Self-completion tasks of this kind typically reduce social-desirability pressures (Jackman 1994, 184; Krysan 1995, 34–36).

17. The author wishes to thank Mary Jackman for her assistance in the development of this measure.

18. Negative stereotypes of blacks and Hispanics are represented by Stereotype Difference scores greater than or equal to 15. Negative stereotypes of whites and Asians are represented by Stereotype Difference scores greater than or equal to 10. Recall that a score of +50 represents the most unfavorable rating of an out-group. These cutoffs are based on mean stereotype scores presented in table 4.3 and include only those with unfavorable attitudes toward out-groups.

References

Alba, Richard D., Nancy A. Denton, Shu-yin J. Leung, and John R. Logan. 1995. "Neighborhood Change Under Conditions of Mass Immigration: The New York City Region, 1970–1990." *International Migration Review* 29: 625–56.

Allport, Gordon W. 1954. *The Nature of Prejudice.* New York: Doubleday Anchor.

Blumer, Herbert. 1958. "Race Prejudice as a Sense of Group Position." *Pacific Sociological Review* 1: 3–7.

Bobo, Lawrence, and Vincent L. Hutchings. 1996. "Perceptions of Racial

Group Competition: Extending Blumer's Theory of Group Position to a Multiracial Social Context." *American Sociological Review* 61(December): 951–72.

Bobo, Lawrence, and James R. Kluegel. 1991. "Modern American Prejudice: Stereotypes, Social Distance, and Perceptions of Discrimination Toward Blacks, Hispanics, and Asians." Presented at the Meeting of the American Sociological Association. Cincinnati, Ohio (August 23–27, 1991).

———. 1993. "Opposition to Race-Targeting: Self-Interest, Stratification Ideology, or Racial Attitudes?" *American Sociological Review* 58(1): 443–64.

———. 1997. "Status, Ideology, and Dimensions of Whites' Racial Beliefs and Attitudes." In *Racial Attitudes in the 1990s: Continuity and Change*, edited by S. A. Tuch and J. K. Martin. Westport, Conn.: Praeger.

Bobo, Lawrence, Howard Schuman, and Charlotte Steeh. 1986. "Changing Attitudes Toward Residential Integration." In *Housing Desegregation and Federal Policy*, edited by John M. Goering. Chapel Hill: University of North Carolina Press.

Bobo, Lawrence, and Camille L. Zubrinsky. 1996. "Attitudes Toward Residential Integration: Perceived Status Differences, Mere In-Group Preference, or Racial Prejudice?" *Social Forces* 74(3): 883–909.

Bound, John, and Richard B. Freeman. 1992. "What Went Wrong? The Erosion of Relative Earnings and Employment Among Young Black Men in the 1980s." *Quarterly Journal of Economics* 107: 201–32.

Braddock, JoHenry M., II, and J. M. McPartland. 1987. "How Minorities Continue to Be Excluded from Equal Employment Opportunities: Research on Labor Markets and Institutional Barriers." *Journal of Social Issues* 43: 5–39.

Clark, W. A. V. 1986. "Residential Segregation in American Cities: A Review and Interpretation." *Population Research and Policy Review* 5: 95–127.

———. 1988. "Understanding Residential Segregation in American Cities: Interpreting the Evidence, a Reply to Galster." *Population Research and Policy Review* 7: 113–21.

———. 1989. "Residential Segregation in American Cities: Common Ground and Differences in Interpretation." *Population Research and Policy Review* 8: 193–97.

———. 1992. "Residential Preferences and Residential Choices in a Multiethnic Context." *Demography* 29(3): 451–66.

Colasanto, Diane Lee. 1977. "The Prospects for Racial Integration in Neighborhoods: An Analysis of Residential Preferences in the Detroit Metropolitan Area." Ph.D. diss., University of Michigan.

Collins, Sharon M. 1997. *Black Corporate Executives: The Making and Breaking of a Black Middle Class*. Philadelphia, Pa.: Temple University Press.

Cose, Ellis. 1993. *The Rage of a Privileged Class: Why Are Middle Class*

Blacks So Angry? Why Should America Care? New York: Harper-Collins.

——. 1997. *Color-Blind: Seeing Beyond Race in a Race-Obsessed World*. New York: HarperCollins.

Denton, Nancy A., and Douglas S. Massey. 1988. "Residential Segregation of Blacks, Hispanics, and Asians by Socioeconomic Status and Generation." *Social Science Quarterly* 69: 797–817.

——. 1991. "Patterns of Neighborhood Transition in a Multiethnic World: U.S. Metropolitan Areas, 1970–1980." *Demography* 28(1): 41–63.

Ellison, Christopher G., and Daniel A. Powers. 1994. "The Contact Hypothesis and Racial Attitudes Among Black Americans." *Social Science Quarterly* 75(2): 385–400.

Farley, Reynolds, and William H. Frey. 1994. "Changes in the Segregation of Whites from Blacks During the 1980's: Small Steps Toward a More Integrated Society." *American Sociological Review* 59(1): 23–45.

Farley, Reynolds, Maria Krysan, Tara Jackson, Charlotte Steeh, and Keith Reeves. 1993. "Causes of Continued Racial Residential Segregation in Detroit: 'Chocolate City, Vanilla Suburbs' Revisited." *Journal of Housing Research* 4(1): 1–38.

Farley, Reynolds, Howard Schuman, Suzanne Bianchi, Diane Colasanto, and Shirley Hatchett. 1978. "'Chocolate City, Vanilla Suburbs': Will the Trend Toward Racially Separate Communities Continue?" *Social Science Research* 7: 319–44.

Farley, Reynolds, Charlotte Steeh, Maria Krysan, Tara Jackson, and Keith Reeves. 1994. "Stereotypes and Segregation: Neighborhoods in the Detroit Area." *American Journal of Sociology* 100(3): 750–80.

Feagin, Joe R., and Melvin P. Sikes. 1994. *Living with Racism: The Black Middle-Class Experience*. Boston: Beacon Press.

Galster, George C. 1988. "Residential Segregation in American Cities: A Contrary Review." *Population Research and Policy Review* 7: 93–112.

——. 1989. "Residential Segregation in American Cities: A Further Response to Clark." *Population Research and Policy Review* 8: 181–92.

——. 1991. "Housing Discrimination and Urban Poverty of African-Americans." *Journal of Housing Research* 2(2): 87–122.

Galster, George C., and Mark W. Keeney. 1988. "Race, Residence, Discrimination, and Economic Opportunity: Modeling the Nexus of Urban Racial Phenomena." *Urban Affairs Quarterly* 24: 87–117.

Harris, David R. 1997. "Racial and Nonracial Determinants of Neighborhood Satisfaction Among Whites, 1975–1993." *University of Michigan Population Studies Center Research Report No. 97–388*. Ann Arbor: University of Michigan Population Studies Center.

Harrison, Roderick J., and Daniel H. Weinberg. 1992. "Racial and Ethnic Residential Segregation in 1990." Washington: U.S. Bureau of the Census.

Holzer, Harry J. 1996. *What Employers Want*. New York: Russell Sage Foundation.

Jackman, Mary R. 1994. *The Velvet Glove: Paternalism and Conflict in*

Gender, Class and Race Relations. Berkeley and Los Angeles: University of California Press.

Jackman, Mary R., and Marie Crane. 1986. "'Some of My Best Friends Are Black . . .' : Interracial Friendship and Whites' Racial Attitudes." *Public Opinion Quarterly* 50: 459–86.

Jackman, Mary R., and Mary Scheuer Senter. 1983. "Different Therefore Unequal: Beliefs About Groups of Unequal Status." *Research in Social Stratification and Mobility* 2: 309–35.

Jankowski, Martin Sanchez. 1995. "The Rising Significance of Status in U.S. Race Relations." In *The Bubbling Cauldron: Race, Ethnicity, and the Urban Crisis*, edited by Michael Peter Smith and Joe R. Feagin. Minneapolis: University of Minnesota Press.

Jargowsky, Paul A. 1996. "Take the Money and Run: Economic Segregation in U.S. Metropolitan Areas." *American Sociological Review* 61(December): 984–98.

Jaynes, Gerald David, and Robin M. Williams, Jr. 1989. *A Common Destiny: Blacks in American Society.* Washington, D.C.: National Academy Press.

Kain, John F. 1986. "The Influence of Race and Income on Racial Segregation and Housing Policy." In *Housing Desegregation and Federal Policy*, edited by John M. Goering. Chapel Hill: University of North Carolina Press.

Kinder, Donald R., and Tali Mendelberg. 1995. "Cracks in American Apartheid: The Political Impact of Prejudice Among Desegregated Whites." *Journal of Politics* 57: 402–24.

Kirschenman, Joleen, and Kathryn Neckerman. 1991. "'We'd Love to Hire Them, But . . .' : The Meaning of Race for Employers." In *The Urban Underclass*, edited by Christopher Jencks and Paul Peterson. Washington, D.C.: Brookings Institute.

Krysan, Maria. 1995. "White Racial Attitudes: Does It Matter How We Ask?" Ph.D. diss., University of Michigan.

Leven, Charles, James T. Little, Hugh O. Nourse, and R. Read. 1976. *Neighborhood Change: Lessons in the Dynamics of Urban Decay.* Cambridge, Mass.: Ballinger.

Massey, Douglas S., and Nancy A. Denton. 1987. "Trends in the Residential Segregation of Blacks, Hispanics, and Asians." *American Sociological Review* 52: 802–25.

———. 1989. "Hypersegregation in U.S. Metropolitan Areas: Black and Hispanic Segregation Along Five Dimensions." *Demography* 26(3): 373–92.

———. 1993. *American Apartheid.* Cambridge, Mass.: Harvard University Press.

Massey, Douglas S., and Andrew B. Gross. 1991. "Segregation, the Concentration of Poverty, and the Life Chances of Individuals." *Social Science Research* 20: 397–420.

Muth, Richard F. 1986. "The Causes of Housing Segregation." *Issues in Housing Discrimination: A Consultation/Hearing of the United*

States Commission on Civil Rights 1: 3–13. Washington, D.C. (November 12–13, 1986).

Oliver, Melvin L., and Thomas M. Shapiro. 1989. "Race and Wealth." *Review of Black Political Economy*, 17: 5–25.

———. 1995. *Black Wealth/White Wealth: A New Perspective on Racial Inequality*. New York and London: Routledge.

Ong, Paul M., and Janette R. Lawrence, with Kevin Davidson. 1992. "Pluralism and Residential Patterns in Los Angeles." Unpublished paper. School of Architecture and Urban Planning, University of California, Los Angeles.

Pettigrew, T. F. 1973. "Attitudes on Race and Housing: A Social Psychological View." In *Segregation in Residential Areas*, edited by A. H. Hawley and V. P. Rock. Washington, D.C.: National Academy of Sciences Press.

———. 1982. "Prejudice." In *Dimensions of Ethnicity: Prejudice*, edited by S. Thernstrom, A. Orlov, and O. Handlin. Cambridge, Mass.: Belknap.

Schuman, Howard, Charlotte Steeh, and Lawrence Bobo. 1985. Racial Attitudes in America: Trends and Interpretations. Cambridge, Mass.: Harvard University Press.

Sigelman, Lee, Timothy Bledsoe, Susan Welch, and Michael W. Combs. 1996. "Making Contact? Black-White Social Interaction in an Urban Setting." *American Journal of Sociology* 101(5): 1306–32.

Sigelman, Lee, and Susan Welch. 1993. "The Contact Hypothesis Revisited: Black-White Interaction and Positive Racial Attitudes." *Social Forces* 71(3): 781–95.

Smith, Tom W. 1991. "Ethnic Images." *GSS Technical Report No. 19*. Chicago: National Opinion Research Center.

Stata Press. 1997. STATA Statistical Software Reference Guide. College Station, Tex.: Stata Press.

U.S. Department of Commerce. U.S. Bureau of the Census. 1990. *The 1990 Census of Population and Housing*. Washington: U.S. Government Printing Office.

White, Clay. 1986. "Residential Segregation Among Asians in Long Beach: Japanese, Chinese, Filipino, Korean, Indian, Vietnamese, Hawaiian, Guamanian and Samoan." *Social Science Research* 70(4): 266–67.

Wood, Peter B., and Barret A. Lee. 1991. "Is Neighborhood Racial Succession Inevitable?: Forty Years of Evidence." *Urban Affairs Quarterly* 26: 610–20.

Yinger, John. 1995. *Closed Doors, Opportunities Lost: The Continuing Cost of Housing Discrimination*. New York: Russell Sage Foundation.

Zubrinsky, Camille L. 1996. " 'I Have Always Wanted to Have a Neighbor Just Like You . . . ' " Ph.D. diss., University of California, Los Angeles.

Zubrinsky, Camille L., and Lawrence Bobo. 1996. "Prismatic Metropolis: Race and Residential Segregation in the City of Angels." *Social Science Research* 24(4): 335–74.

5

ETHNIC RESIDENTIAL SEGREGATION AND ITS CONSEQUENCES

Franklin D. Wilson and Roger B. Hammer

T HE LITERATURE on the extent, causes, and consequences of ethnic residential segregation is extensive and continues to increase (Clark 1986; Zubrinsky and Bobo 1996; Farley and Frey 1996; Massey and Denton 1993; Farley et al. 1994; White 1987). This is hardly surprising, considering that residential segregation is dynamic and is responsive to changes in the ethnic composition of cities, market forces that affect the supply and demand for housing, and intergroup dynamics that substantially affect residence decisions. In this chapter, we will analyze the association of attitudes and perceptions with the ethnic (racial) composition of residential neighborhoods and, in turn, the association of both with observed and perceived measures of neighborhood quality.

The availability of data from the Multi-City Study of Urban Inequality surveys provides the opportunity to estimate a comprehensive model that includes indicators for most of the major factors believed to be associated with the differential sorting of ethnic populations into neighborhoods. We focus primarily on the determinants and consequences of residential location for blacks and Hispanics, though we also present model results for non-Hispanic whites as a reference for assessing the substantive significance of the results for the former groups.

Three central questions guide our analysis. *First, what is the association between individuals' expressed preferences for living in ethnically homogeneous neighborhoods and the ethnic composition of the neighborhood in which they currently reside?* While previous research suggests that as many as a quarter of minority urban residents express preferences for living predominantly among co-ethnics, our objective is to assess the fit of preferences to the actual ethnic composition of the neighborhood in which they live. We evaluate the association of preferences with neighborhood ethnic composition, taking into account other known correlates of the latter. Our analysis points to a statistically significant association between preference and actual neighborhood homogeneity for blacks, Hispanics, and whites alike. The impact of preferences is modest, however, and does not fully explain the patterns of racial and ethnic segregation that characterize the metropolitan areas we studied.

Second, what is the association of perceived housing market discrimination against co-ethnic group members and the ethnic composition of the neighborhoods of current residence? We believe this association could provide important insight into how individuals link the ethnic-based milieu in which co-ethnic members reside and their own expectation of encountering barriers if they decide to seek residence in an area in which members of their group traditionally have not resided. We expect that minority households' perception of barriers in the housing market will influence their residential choices and where in the metropolis they are likely to search for housing. Here we find that perceived discrimination indeed has a statistically significant impact on residential choice for blacks, and is more important than preference for homogeny in explaining segregation patterns. Perceived discrimination does not figure as prominently in residential choice for Hispanics.

Finally, do residential preferences, perceived discrimination, and the actual ethnic composition of neighborhoods have consequences for the quality of individuals' neighborhood environment? In addressing this question, we focus on the association of preferences, perceptions, and neighborhood ethnic composition with observed and perceived measures of neighborhood quality. When living among co-ethnics, minorities tend to reside in residential areas consisting of aging housing stock of poor quality, few residential amenities (such as parks and recreational facilities), crime and vandalism, poor-quality school facilities and police and fire protection, and limited availability of retail and financial establishments. Predominantly white neighborhoods, in contrast, are linked to better-quality housing and services. Thus, our analysis highlights the racially disparate consequences of segregated residential patterns: whether by preference or out of perceived discrimination, blacks and Hispanics pay a price for living in ethnically homogeneous neighborhoods.

Literature Review

In this section, we seek to identify factors that tend to promote neighborhood ethnic homogeny; that is, factors that increase the likelihood of co-ethnic group members residing in the same neighborhood, segregated from members of other groups. Considerable debate in the segregation literature has centered on the degree to which prejudice and discrimination influence homogeny, relative to other economic and social factors (see Yinger 1995; Clark 1986, 1988, 1989, 1991, 1992; Galster 1988, 1989, 1992; Massey 1985). Our general framework for understanding the forces shaping neighborhood ethnic homogeny includes an analysis of its relations with other components of residential packages, including housing unit characteristics and neighborhood factors such as the socio-economic status of residents, amenities, accessibility, and public services (Wilson 1979). Ethnic group differences in residential consumption have little to do with "tastes" for residential packages that include components of a particular size, dimension, and quality. As far as current research has been able to determine, there are no intrinsic differences among ethnic groups with respect to preferences for residential consumption (see Wilson 1979; Myers 1990).

However, an obvious factor affecting residential choices in general, and neighborhood ethnic homogeny in particular, is the fact that an appreciable proportion of the members of an ethnic population may find it advantageous or desirable to live among co-ethnics for a number of reasons. First, and subject to the most debate and contention in the literature, individuals who share a common ethnic identity may express a preference for living in neighborhoods that are homogeneous with respect to ethnicity. Results from surveys suggest that as many as a quarter of minority populations, including African Americans, Asians, and Hispanics, indicate a desire to live among co-ethnics; another 20 to 25 percent would find residence in a neighborhood dominated by co-ethnics acceptable (Zubrinsky and Bobo 1996; Zubrinsky Charles, chapter 4 this volume; Clark 1992). The literature points to a complex and differentiated array of factors, however, in interpreting the significance of those preferences. On the one hand, scholars point to what pulls co-ethnics to live together. The sharing of cultural traditions and customs, community institutions and establishments, and similar labor market experiences may all act to facilitate the concentration of the members of an ethnic group. In addition, the level of comfort, the sense of security, well-being, safety, trust, and the ease of social interaction that ethnic neighborhoods engender are important for the development of a group identity and a collective sense of place (Suttles 1972; Clark 1991, 1992; Portes 1995). Furthermore, the establishment of immigrant communities at a destination, based on chain migration and institutionalization, often represents the initial stage in the development of ethnic communities (Massey 1985; Portes and Rumbaut 1996). On the other hand, scholars also point to interethnic prejudice, stereotypes, racial tensions, and out-group avoidance as important factors motivating the preference to live among co-ethnics—or to avoid mixing with racial "others." As reported in chapter 4, racial perceptions, attitudes, and stereotypes can have a decisive effect on residence decisions and on notions of what constitutes a desirable neighborhood, as indicated in the persistent conflation of race with an imagery of continuing neighborhood decline. For example, whites, when asked why they would move out of a neighborhood with a particular percentage of African American residents, expressed concerns about crime, personal safety, declining property values, and the general deterioration of the area (see Farley et al. 1994; Zubrinsky and Bobo 1996; chapter 4, this volume).

By the same token, the significance of ethnic preferences in determining residential choice is complicated by the reality that, in comparison to whites, nonwhites are far more circumscribed in their ability to act on those preferences. For example, African Americans, on average, express a preference for ethnically mixed black and white neighborhoods, while whites express a preference for neighborhoods in which a much smaller percentage of the population of the neighborhood is African American. Since whites are in the majority in practically all metropolitan areas in which African Americans are also residents, and given that whites have a much lower tolerance for living in neighborhoods with African Americans, their residential preferences would be expected to have a more decisive effect on prevailing levels of residential segregation.

A second, related reason why nonwhites might express preference for living among co-ethnics is the expectation that they will encounter discrimination as the minority in more integrated neighborhoods. Moreover, when attitudes and preferences influence individuals and groups to erect barriers to restrict access, then housing market discrimination becomes a relevant factor in promoting neighborhood ethnic homogeny. Although there is not a direct correspondence between attitude (residential preferences and attitudes) and behavior (discrimination), the former surely provides motivation and justification for the latter, depending on the situational context (see Galster 1992; Turner 1992; Yinger 1995). Housing market discrimination can be viewed as a behavioral response to threats of invasion by members of other ethnic groups. Discrimination occurs because group members perceive the presence of nongroup members as threatening their lifestyle, the socialization of their children, their lives, and their property. Although such threats may be based on stereotype and prejudices, it is group members' perception of threat that matters. Historically, housing discrimination against minorities has been effective because all major players in local housing markets have played an active role in channeling minority demand for housing to particular sections of the city, away from predominantly white areas. This includes existing owners, property managers, realtors, financial institutions, insurance companies, and, at one time, units of government (Massey and Denton 1993; Yinger 1995).

Of course, both discrimination and preferences for homogeny act on actual neighborhood ethnic composition in the context of many other influences, including social networks, labor market opportunities, and commuting patterns. Similarly, observed differences in ethnic mix have been found to be associated with household composition, particularly age of head; marital status and the presence of children; socioeconomic status, including education and the availability of financial resources; neighborhood social network relations; nativity, particularly as it relates to duration of residence; racial attitudes; and discrimination (see Wilson 1979; Myers 1990).

Finally, neighborhood ethnic composition must also be assessed within the context of affordability. Housing is distributed in metropolises not only with respect to type and features, but, more important with respect to price. Households are spatially distributed according to their ability to pay for housing at the price offered in the market, whether renting or owning. While income acts as a constraint, in view of other expenditures incurred by households, price acts as a filter, in which some areas are inaccessible because of housing costs. This filtering produces clustering of households according to their ability to pay for housing. Substantial disparities between ethnic populations in income and wealth can have a substantial effect on ethnic segregation (Clark 1986; Massey 1985; Guest 1977). For example, if a metropolis includes equal shares of whites and African Americans, but whites are disproportionately affluent and African Americans are disproportionately poor, then the level of residential segregation between the two groups is likely to range from low to modest (between twenty-five to fifty points), since most African Americans would not be able to afford to live in the same area as the average white.

Current Analysis

The analytic model we estimate focuses on three main sets of relationships. First, we examine how stated preferences for neighborhood racial or ethnic homogeny are associated with the actual homogeny of one's neighborhood. Second, we consider links between perceived discrimination, on the one hand, and preferred and actual neighborhood homogeny, on the other. Third, we probe the association between neighborhood homogeny and a variety of measures of neighborhood quality.

In estimating these relationships, we embed them in a more complete model that takes into account many other factors likely to be associated with homogeny and neighborhood quality. Thus, we also examine the extent to which all these variables are associated with family structure, nativity, education, age, labor force participation, household income, homeownership, length of residence, and involvement in neighborhood social networks.

Figure 5.1 graphically summarizes the model we estimate for black and Hispanic households. In this model, demographic factors (number of children and so on) and household income and labor market status influence perceptions of housing market discrimination, ethnic residential preferences, and a set of "rootedness" indicators such as homeownership. All these variables then combine in influencing neighborhood homogeny, and homogeny joins the rest of these variables in predicting neighborhood attributes and quality. The oval box framing perceived discrimination signals a latent variable with two or more observed (measured) indicator variables.[1] The model for whites differs from figure 5.1 only in that perceived discrimination is dropped from the estimation (since it is not measured for whites in our data). Our interest, then, is in determining whether survey data can provide evidence of these hypothesized neighborhood dynamics.[2]

In the following section, we discuss the key variables and hypothesized relations in more detail. Later sections then present and discuss results. To forecast the key results, we find that there is a small but statistically significant association between preference for ethnic homogeneity and actual neighborhood homogeneity for blacks, Hispanics, and whites alike. Perceived discrimination is also linked to high concentrations of co-ethnics for blacks, but not Hispanics. Finally, residence with large numbers of co-ethnics is associated with negative neighborhood characteristics for blacks and Hispanics, but positive ones for whites.

Ethnic Residential Preferences and Housing Market Discrimination

A first, critical set of relationships encompasses the effect of homogeny preferences and perceived discrimination on the actual homogeny of a respondent's neighborhood. Our measure of preference for residence in an ethnically homogeneous neighborhood was constructed in the same manner as the integration preference indices used in previous research, except the scale was reversed, assigning a higher value to preferences for homogeny and a lower value to preferences for integration (see Zubrinsky and Bobo 1996; Colasanto 1977). Specifically, we assigned scores, varying from zero to twenty, to the ranking respondents assigned to five different neighborhood configurations representing the neighbor-

FIGURE 5.1   *A Structural Equation Model of the Determinants and Consequences of Residence in Ethnically Homogeneous Neighborhoods for Black and Hispanic Households*

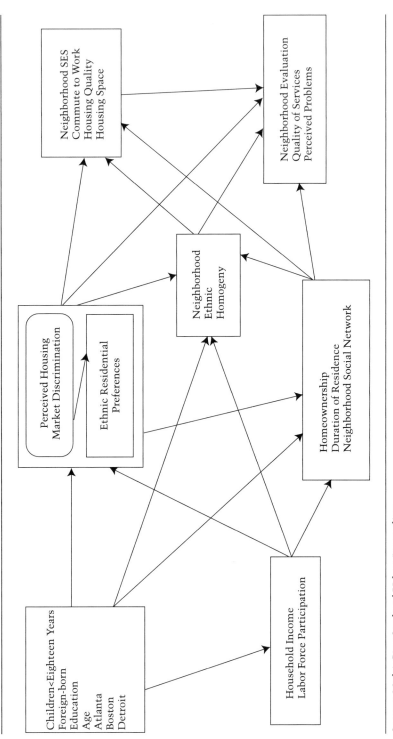

Source: Multi-City Study of Urban Inequality.

hood ethnic composition they most to least prefer as an area in which to live and their willingness to move into such a neighborhood.[3]

Housing discrimination often has the effect of channeling minority group members' demand for housing to particular sections of the city, resulting in the concentration of group members and their segregation from members of the dominant group.[4] We do not have a direct measure of housing market discrimination; rather, we use the respondent's perceptions of discrimination confronted by members of the respondent's group. The questions on discrimination included in the survey encompass the respondent's belief about discriminatory behavior on the part of individual property owners, real estate agents, and financial institutions in the rental and ownership housing markets. We hypothesize that perceived discrimination is inversely associated with housing and neighborhood socioeconomic status, but positively associated with neighborhood ethnic homogeny.

In the case of African Americans and Hispanics, ethnic preferences for neighborhood homogeny may not necessarily have a negative effect on housing and neighborhood quality, while it is generally assumed that housing discrimination does adversely affect the quality of the housing and neighborhood environment in which minority households reside, as well as the quality of the services, public and private, available to them. In addition, residential preferences and perceived discrimination are directly related, particularly in this instance, because our measured indicators of the latter are self-reported. Ethnic group members who perceive or expect to encounter hostility and discrimination from members of other groups may come to view residence among co-ethnics as the only viable option. Other individuals may infer the existence of discriminatory barriers based on secondhand accounts or the simple fact that a large proportion of co-ethnics living in the same neighborhood provides prima facie evidence for discrimination as the cause of this concentration. We hypothesize that minority group members who perceive high levels of discrimination against members of their ethnic group in a local housing market are more likely to express strong preferences for ethnically homogeneous neighborhoods, anticipating that they will be similarly treated.

In estimating these relationships, we control for a number of intermediate variables hypothesized to affect ethnic composition and other neighborhood characteristics: the extent of homeownership, number of years at current residence, and participation in neighborhood social networks.[5] In addition to the direct effects that ethnic residential preferences and perceived discrimination will have on neighborhood ethnic homogeny and the other components of respondents' residential packages, we expect that preferences and perceived discrimination will have indirect effects through the intermediate variables.[6]

Determinants of
Neighborhood Quality

In our model (figure 5.1), the housing quality and neighborhood SES (socioeconomic status) variables appear as outcomes of neighborhood homogeny, as well as of preferences and perceived discrimination. We expect homogeny to lead to poorer housing quality and lower SES among blacks and Hispanics, and the opposite among whites. We also expect perceived discrimination to be associated with lower housing quality and SES, even after controlling for neighborhood homogeny.

However, we treat the net associations among the housing and neighborhood attributes as being jointly determined by factors not included in the model, meaning that error terms in these models will be correlated (see figure 5.2). The most important of these excluded factors is the spatial distribution of housing, which reflects the cumulative impact of decisions made by developers, real estate agencies, governments, financial institutions, and individual households regarding the disposition of land for residential purposes relative to other usages.[7]

Finally, we turn to respondents' perceptions of the adequacy of neighborhood services and of the existence of neighborhood problems, as a final set of outcome variables. Estimates of the determinants of these perceptions will control for the basic measures of neighborhood quality, socioeconomic status, and housing quality. We expect that perceived discrimination and neighborhood homogeny will have indirect effects on these perceptions through the basic neighborhood quality measures, and hypothesize that these variables will exert added direct effects.[8]

Data

The data for this analysis are taken from the Multi-City Study of Urban Inequality surveys, with contextual information from the 1990 Census of Population and Housing at the block group level appended to individuals' records. In this analysis, we focus on blacks (n = 3,150) in Atlanta, Boston, Detroit, and Los Angeles and Hispanics (n = 1,727) in Boston and Los Angeles, although we also report results for whites (n = 2,251) in all four cities. In calculating weights, we divided the person weight for individual respondents by an average weight calculated separately for blacks, Hispanics, and non-Hispanic whites. Thus, the weights for each ethnic group are proportional to the population of each group across the cities in which respondents in each group were surveyed. Dummy variables for metropolitan areas are included in the model to control for the variation in associations related to city of residence.

FIGURE 5.2   Latent-Indicator Variable Relationships and Error Structure of Model Presented in Figure 5.1

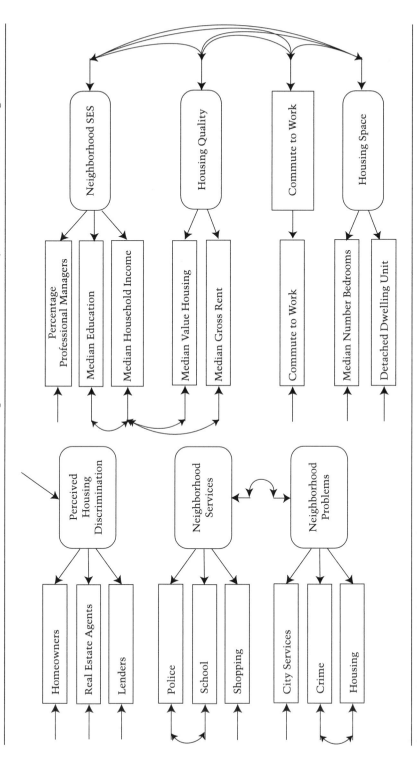

Source: Multi-City Study of Urban Inequality.

We estimated separate models for blacks, Hispanics, and whites, as displayed in figures 5.1 and 5.2. Figure 5.1 provides a schematic representation of the determinants and consequences of living in ethnically homogeneous neighborhoods, while figure 5.2 represents latent-indicator variable associations and the error structure of the model present in figure 5.1. As noted previously, variables encased in ovals are latent variables with two or more observed (measured) indicator variables. The definitions of all variables are reported in the appendix. Associated means and standard deviations are reported in table 5.10. We use an SPSS-compatible software package referred to as "AMOS" to estimate the structural equations associated with the path diagram presented in figures 5.1 and 5.2. Although the specification of relations among variables in the model presented in figure 5.1 is identical for blacks and Hispanics (and for whites, except that perceptions of housing discrimination are excluded as a variable), the relations among the error terms, as represented in figure 5.2, are not the same. This is because we were unable to estimate a model for each ethnic group with identical specifications of relations among error terms for the variables. We incorporate the findings for whites mainly to illuminate further the interpretation of results for blacks and Hispanics. For example, we would expect that the association of ethnic residential preferences with the actual ethnic composition of respondents' neighborhoods would be positive for all three ethnic groups, but we expect the association of ethnic composition of neighborhood with residence in neighborhoods and housing of high quality would be strongly positive for whites and negative for blacks and Hispanics. Finally, in discussing results, emphasis is given to variable relationships with associated coefficients that are approximately twice the size of their standard error (that is, $P \leq 0.05$).

Results

Consistent with the three questions posed at the beginning of the chapter, the key variable associations of interest derived from estimating the structural equation model are the relations among homogeny preference and perceived discrimination, actual neighborhood homogeny, and actual and perceived neighborhood quality outcomes. We give particular attention to the effects of residential preferences, perceived housing discrimination, and neighborhood ethnic composition on the other neighborhood-based variables. The estimated associations among background and intermediate variables will not be discussed. (The coefficients for these associations are available from the authors upon request.)

The discussion begins with the association of ethnic residential preferences and perceived housing discrimination with neighborhood ethnic homogeny. The coefficients for these associations are reported in table 5.1 for blacks, table 5.2 for Hispanics, and table 5.3 for non-Hispanic whites. Consistent with expectations, preference for living in an ethnically homogeneous neighborhood is positively associated with neighborhood ethnic homogeny. Specifically, the stronger the preference for living among co-ethnics, the greater the percentage of persons living in one's neighborhood who are co-ethnic group members. The standardized values of .061 estimated for blacks, .146 for Hispanics, and .074 for whites indicate that about two-thirds of the total association (as represented by the bivariate correlation coefficient) between ethnic residential preferences and neighborhood ethnic homogeny represents the direct effect of the former on the latter. (Correlation coefficients are not shown, but are available from the authors upon request.) Although this relationship is statistically significant, the coefficients are small, particularly for blacks and whites. The marginal size of the coefficients for the total association between residential preferences and neighborhood ethnic homogeny could be the result of a number of factors. First, there is probably a discrepancy between the neighborhood configurations respondents used to represent their preferences and the census block group configuration used to measure the ethnic composition of their neighborhoods. Second, continuous residence in a neighborhood in the face of changes in its ethnic composition could attenuate the relationship between preference and neighborhood ethnic composition. Third, residential preferences may simply be a weak predictor of neighborhood ethnic composition. On the other hand, a belief that one will encounter barriers to residence in one's preferred neighborhood could raise the share of blacks living among co-ethnics above what would be expected based on preferences alone.

A higher percentage of blacks than Hispanics (or Asians) express the opinion that co-ethnic members miss out on good housing because of housing market discrimination (see Zubrinsky and Bobo 1996; chapter 4, this volume). But a key issue is whether, as we hypothesize, the expectation of discrimination influences minority group members' evaluation of the options they face in making a residential location decision (see chapter 4, this volume). The coefficients for the association between perceived discrimination and neighborhood ethnic homogeny support this possibility. Blacks who perceive that members of their group experience various forms of housing discrimination are more likely to live in neighborhoods with a higher percentage of black residents. The relationship is also positive for Hispanics, but not statistically significant.

The association of other variables with neighborhood ethnic homogeny is also of interest. Black homeowners, those who have lived in

TABLE 5.1   *Determinants of Homogeny for Blacks*

| | Neighborhood Homogeny | | |
	Estimate	Standard Error	Standardized Coefficient
Number of children	0.169	0.435	0.006
Foreign-born	−8.054***	2.115	−0.061
Years of education	−1.001***	0.237	−0.072
Age	−0.008	0.043	−0.003
Atlanta (L.A. omitted)	27.478***	1.390	0.322
Boston (L.A. omitted)	20.760***	2.021	0.162
Detroit (L.A. omitted)	37.290***	1.377	0.466
Labor force status	−0.514	1.208	−0.007
Household income (000s)	−0.168***	0.019	−0.150
Housing discrimination	6.213***	1.475	0.074
Homogeny preference	0.111***	0.027	0.061
Homeowner	3.000*	1.275	0.041
Length of residence	0.675***	0.058	0.203
Neighbor social network	0.035*	0.017	0.032

Source: Multi-City Study of Urban Inequality.
*$p \leq 0.05$. **$p \leq 0.01$. ***$p \leq 0.001$.

TABLE 5.2   *Determinants of Homogeny for Hispanics*

| | Neighborhood Homogeny | | |
	Estimate	Standard Error	Standardized Coefficient
Number of children	1.096*	0.450	0.054
Foreign-born	6.971***	1.576	0.108
Years of education	−0.904***	0.187	−0.125
Age	−0.291***	0.056	−0.132
Boston (L.A. omitted)	−29.713***	2.852	−0.224
Labor force status	4.918***	1.356	0.083
Household income (000s)	−0.222***	0.029	−0.189
Housing discrimination	1.706	1.523	0.031
Homogeny preference	0.189***	0.029	0.146
Homeowner	−2.455	1.618	−0.038
Length of residence	0.791***	0.086	0.236
Neighbor social network	0.012	0.015	0.016

Source: Multi-City Study of Urban Inequality.
*$p \leq 0.05$. **$p \leq 0.01$. ***$p \leq 0.001$.

TABLE 5.3   *Determinants of Homogeny for Whites*

| | Neighborhood Homogeny | | |
	Estimate	Standard Error	Standardized Coefficient
Number of children	0.221	0.342	0.011
Foreign-born	−1.105	1.296	−0.014
Years of education	0.100	0.156	0.012
Age	0.009	0.027	0.007
Atlanta (L.A. omitted)	20.944***	1.063	0.365
Boston (L.A. omitted)	27.178***	0.838	0.622
Detroit (L.A. omitted)	27.099***	1.006	0.555
Labor force status	−0.210	0.785	−0.005
Financial (000s)	0.082***	0.009	0.156
Homogeny preference	0.128***	0.028	0.074
Homeowner	3.874***	0.800	0.092
Length of residence	−0.041	0.034	−0.025
Neighbor social network	0.016	0.010	0.027

Source: Multi-City Study of Urban Inequality.
*$p \leq 0.05$. **$p \leq 0.01$. ***$p \leq 0.001$.

their neighborhoods for a long time, and those who are involved in neighborhood social networks are more likely to live in neighborhoods with a high percentage of black residents. Of these three "rootedness" variables, only duration of residence is positively associated with the ethnic neighborhood composition for Hispanics, as is homeownership for whites. Among blacks, foreign birth, education, and household income are inversely associated with residence in neighborhoods with a high percentage of black residents; while for Hispanics, number of children, foreign birth, and labor force participation are positively associated, and education, age, and household income are inversely associated with residence in neighborhoods with a high percentage of Hispanics. Interestingly, while higher-income blacks and Hispanics are less likely to reside with co-ethnics, wealthier whites are *more* likely to do so. The association of the background demographic and economic variables with neighborhood ethnic homogeny are some of the strongest among all the variables, suggesting that their influence on neighborhood-level variables is not limited to indirect effects through intermediate variables such as residential preferences, perceived discrimination, and rootedness. The results do not imply that these background variables explain residential segregation. However, within ethnic groups the demographic and economic variables are important in determining the level of neighborhood ethnic homogeny an individual will experience.[9]

Tables 5.4 through 5.6 present the association of neighborhood quality (neighborhood SES and housing quality) with perception of discrimination, preference for living among co-ethnics, and ethnic composition of neighborhood, as well as background variables, homeownership, and length of residence. As expected, the relationship between the ethnic composition of the respondent's neighborhood and housing quality and neighborhood SES is strongly negative for blacks and particularly for Hispanics, whereas it is strongly positive for non-Hispanic whites. Specifically, the greater the percentage of black or Hispanic co-ethnics living in the respondent's neighborhood, the lower the quality of the housing and neighborhood environment; the opposite relation holds for whites. These relationships are highly statistically significant and quite large.

After controlling for actual neighborhood racial or ethnic composition, residential (homogeny) preferences are negatively associated with both neighborhood quality indicators for blacks, but only the housing quality component for Hispanics and only the neighborhood SES indicator for whites. All these measured associations are small. Measured associations between perceived discrimination and neighborhood quality, after controlling for neighborhood composition, are small and inconsistent. Thus, perceived discrimination predicts lower SES for blacks but higher SES for Hispanics; it is associated with higher housing quality for blacks but lower quality for Hispanics (though in each case, only the Hispanic effect achieves statistical significance). It appears that both homogeny preference and discrimination act on blacks' and Hispanics' neighborhood quality primarily by sorting them into homogeneous neighborhoods.

The direct associations of some of the background variables with objective neighborhood outcomes are substantial, after controlling for intermediate variables. Such associations include the positive link of education and household income with the neighborhood SES and housing quality indicators; the positive association of foreign birth with neighborhood quality for blacks and whites, and contrasting effects of the neighborhood quality components for Hispanics; and the positive association of household income with housing quality. Apparently, education and household income matter a great deal with respect to the quality of the housing and neighborhood environment inhabited by households, net of their influence through the intermediate variables. The contrasting influence of foreign birth probably captures the different residential experiences of native- and foreign-born blacks; while for Hispanics, it probably reflects the strong influences of the concentrating effect of recent immigration.

Tables 5.7 through 5.9 report the association of perceptions of the

TABLE 5.4   *Determinants of Neighborhood Quality for Blacks*

	Neighborhood SES			Housing Quality		
	Estimate	Standard Error	Standardized Coefficient	Estimate	Standard Error	Standardized Coefficient
Number of children	−0.344*	0.134	−0.042	−1.117	0.793	−0.018
Foreign-born	3.150***	0.655	0.084	42.138***	3.871	0.152
Years of education	0.827***	0.074	0.211	0.301	0.434	0.010
Age	0.035**	0.013	0.054	−0.155*	0.078	−0.032
Atlanta (L.A. omitted)	0.816	0.455	0.034	−75.931***	2.726	−0.425
Boston (L.A. omitted	−1.036	0.634	−0.029	−43.099***	3.752	−0.161
Detroit (L.A. omitted)	−2.132***	0.473	−0.094	−96.066***	2.846	−0.574
Labor force status	1.746***	0.373	0.084	13.604***	2.202	0.089
Household income (000s)	0.077***	0.006	0.245	0.404***	0.035	0.173
Housing dis-crimination	−0.825	0.454	−0.035	4.434	2.680	0.025
Homogeny preference	−0.035***	0.008	−0.067	−0.283***	0.049	−0.074
Homeowner	1.766***	0.394	0.086	2.110	2.326	0.014
Length of residence	−0.104***	0.018	−0.110	−0.183	0.107	−0.026
Neighbor social network	−0.003	0.005	−0.010	0.048	0.031	0.021
Neighborhood homogeny	−0.071***	0.006	−0.251	−0.613***	0.033	−0.293

Source: Multi-City Study of Urban Inequality.
*$p \leq 0.05$. **$p \leq 0.01$. ***$p \leq 0.001$.

inadequacy of neighborhood services and the existence of neighborhood problems, the final outcomes in the model, with the background factors, neighborhood and housing characteristics, perception of discrimination, preferences for living among co-ethnics, and neighborhood attachment variables. The services considered include the quality of schools, police protection, and retail shopping and financial services; the neighborhood problem areas include crime and vandalism, deteriorating housing, and city services such as street cleaning or garbage collection. Not surprisingly, these perceptions are inversely related to neighborhood socioeconomic status, though the relationship is statistically significant only

TABLE 5.5   *Determinants of Neighborhood Quality for Hispanics*

	Neighborhood SES			Housing Quality		
	Estimate	Standard Error	Standardized Coefficient	Estimate	Standard Error	Standardized Coefficient
Number of children	−0.401***	0.099	−0.055	−4.195***	0.895	−0.117
Foreign-born	−1.101**	0.346	−0.048	9.728**	3.139	0.085
Years of education	0.332***	0.041	0.128	1.152**	0.372	0.090
Age	0.049***	0.012	0.062	0.034	0.112	0.009
Boston (L.A. omitted)	−5.740***	0.643	−0.120	−63.789***	5.954	−0.271
Labor force status	−0.892**	0.297	−0.042	−7.352**	2.692	−0.070
Household income (000s)	0.056***	0.007	0.132	0.377***	0.059	0.181
Housing dis- crimination	1.788***	0.341	0.090	−6.214*	3.025	−0.064
Homogeny preference	0.004	0.006	0.009	−0.142*	0.059	−0.062
Homeowner	0.244	0.354	0.011	−4.831	3.198	−0.042
Length of residence	0.010	0.019	0.009	0.218	0.174	0.037
Neighbor social network	−0.006	0.003	−0.023	−0.035	0.030	−0.027
Neighborhood homogeny	−0.291***	0.006	−0.808	−1.198***	0.055	−0.673

Source: Multi-City Study of Urban Inequality.
*$p \leq 0.05$. **$p \leq 0.01$. ***$p \leq 0.001$.

for blacks. We have already learned that homogeny preferences and discrimination act on neighborhood quality primarily through homogeny
itself. We now are controlling not only for homogeny but also for neighborhood quality, so we don't expect much residual association between
preferences or discrimination and neighborhood problems and services.
Nonetheless, perceived discrimination does predict neighborhood problems for blacks and Hispanics alike, and deficient services for blacks.
Homogeny preference shows only one statistically significant association: a small, negative association with deficient services among blacks.

Discussion

The results reported in the previous section are complex and varied with
respect to providing substantive insight into factors associated with the
character of the neighborhood environment inhabited by blacks and His-

TABLE 5.6   *Determinants of Neighborhood Quality for Whites*

	Neighborhood SES			Housing Quality		
	Estimate	Standard Error	Standardized Coefficient	Estimate	Standard Error	Standardized Coefficient
Number of children	−0.959***	0.239	−0.082	−6.168***	1.638	−0.069
Foreign-born	3.777***	0.905	0.081	36.256***	6.207	0.102
Years of education	1.244***	0.110	0.241	6.142***	0.752	0.156
Age	0.126***	0.019	0.172	0.727***	0.130	0.130
Atlanta (L.A. omitted)	−2.552**	0.804	−0.075	−149.142***	5.549	−0.574
Boston (L.A. omitted)	−4.533***	0.709	−0.175	−76.837***	4.873	−0.388
Detroit (L.A. omitted)	−7.229***	0.809	−0.249	−182.836***	5.604	−0.826
Labor force status	−0.541	0.548	−0.022	2.810	3.756	0.015
Financial (000s)	0.078***	0.007	0.252	0.460***	0.045	0.194
Homogeny preference	−0.054**	0.020	−0.052	−0.174	0.136	−0.022
Homeowner	−0.646	0.562	−0.026	−14.189***	3.850	−0.075
Length of residence	−0.076**	0.024	−0.078	−0.186	0.161	−0.025
Neighbor social network	−0.001	0.007	−0.003	−0.062	0.050	−0.023
Neighborhood homogeny	0.195***	0.015	0.328	0.786***	0.101	0.173

Source: Multi-City Study of Urban Inequality.
*$p \leq 0.05$. **$p \leq 0.01$. ***$p \leq 0.001$.

panics. A useful point of departure would be to summarize the results according to the three central questions posed as guiding the analysis. First, is there a correspondence between individuals' preferences for living in ethnically homogeneous neighborhoods and the ethnic composition of the neighborhood in which they do live? The results indicate that net of other factors, there is a relatively marginal, but statistically significant, association between ethnic residential preference and actual ethnic neighborhood composition. The association for Hispanics is twice as great as that for blacks and whites. Moreover, in all instances, the strength of this association is not as strong as the results reported by William Clark (1991, 1992). Although we speculated on a number of reasons for the weak association, in the end the complicated process of residential decision making, involving a host of considerations re-

TABLE 5.7   *Determinants of Neighborhood Problems and Services for Blacks*

	Neighborhood Problems			Neighborhood Services (Inadequacy)		
	Estimate	Standard Error	Standardized Coefficient	Estimate	Standard Error	Standardized Coefficient
Number of children	−0.010	0.008	−0.027	−0.041***	0.011	−0.101
Foreign-born	−0.048	0.060	−0.029	0.395***	0.103	0.213
Years of education	0.014*	0.006	0.081	0.000	0.009	0.001
Age	−0.005***	0.001	−0.165	−0.008***	0.001	−0.253
Atlanta (L.A. omitted)	0.126	0.128	0.116	−1.048***	0.245	−0.878
Boston (L.A. omitted)	0.218***	0.066	0.133	−0.226	0.117	−0.126
Detroit (L.A. omitted)	0.234	0.142	0.230	−1.003***	0.271	−0.895
Labor force status	−0.136***	0.025	−0.146	0.019	0.036	0.018
Household income (000s)	0.000	0.000	−0.006	0.002***	0.001	0.131
Housing discrimination	0.333***	0.033	0.311	0.228***	0.042	0.195
Homogeny preference	0.000	0.001	−0.007	−0.002**	0.001	−0.094
Homeowner	0.035	0.048	0.038	−0.142*	0.071	−0.140
Length of residence	0.004***	0.001	0.095	0.006***	0.002	0.128
Neighbor social network	0.000	0.000	0.015	0.000	0.000	0.005
Neighborhood SES	−0.016**	0.005	−0.352	0.002	0.010	0.048
Commuting time	0.001*	0.000	0.049	0.003***	0.001	0.138
Neighborhood homogeny	0.002*	0.001	0.132	−0.001	0.001	−0.036
Housing quality	0.001	0.001	0.195	−0.009**	0.003	−1.280
Housing space	−0.175*	0.068	−0.210	0.269**	0.099	0.295

Source: Multi-City Study of Urban Inequality.
*$p \leq 0.05$. **$p \leq 0.01$. ***$p \leq 0.001$.

lated to other housing and neighborhood factors, might be the most plausible explanation.

What role did perceived discrimination play in respondents' selection of a neighborhood in which a given percentage of residents were co-ethnic group members? Our findings indicate that among blacks, but not Hispanics, perception of discrimination was positively associated

TABLE 5.8 *Determinants of Neighborhood Problems and Services for Hispanics*

	Neighborhood Problems			Neighborhood Services (Inadequacy)		
	Estimate	Standard Error	Standardized Coefficient	Estimate	Standard Error	Standardized Coefficient
Number of children	0.001	0.011	0.003	−0.024	0.015	−0.056
Foreign-born	−0.068	0.043	−0.060	0.139*	0.067	0.104
Years of education	0.022***	0.005	0.171	0.014*	0.006	0.090
Age	−0.003	0.001	−0.065	−0.007***	0.002	−0.145
Boston (L.A. omitted)	−0.072	0.084	−0.031	−0.361**	0.138	−0.131
Labor force status	−0.034	0.030	−0.033	−0.053	0.041	−0.043
Household income (000s)	0.001	0.001	0.065	−0.001	0.001	−0.025
Housing discrimination	0.094*	0.045	0.097	0.004	0.071	0.003
Homogeny preference	0.001	0.001	0.032	0.002	0.001	0.063
Homeowner	0.117*	0.048	0.104	−0.083	0.064	−0.062
Length of residence	0.002	0.002	0.040	0.014***	0.003	0.199
Neighbor social network	0.000	0.000	−0.012	0.001**	0.000	0.088
Neighborhood SES	−0.017	0.010	−0.342	0.010	0.018	0.174
Commuting time	−0.001	0.001	−0.020	0.000	0.001	0.010
Neighborhood homogeny	−0.003	0.001	−0.150	−0.003	0.002	−0.160
Housing quality	−0.001	0.002	−0.141	−0.007*	0.003	−0.637
Housing space	−0.301***	0.053	−0.345	−0.076	0.069	−0.074

Source: Multi-City Study of Urban Inequality.
*$p \leq 0.05$. **$p \leq 0.01$. ***$p \leq 0.001$.

with homogeneous neighborhood ethnic composition. In view of the high degree of consensus among all respondents (blacks, whites, Asians, and Hispanics) that blacks and Hispanics encounter discrimination at least "sometimes," it is tempting to interpret these finding as if the indicators of perceived discrimination were proxies for actual discrimination. This would not be wise, because the questions asked of respondents were not specific with respect to acts leading respondents to establish their current residence. As noted previously, however, perceived discrimination may motivate households to pursue a course intended to

TABLE 5.9   *Determinants of Neighborhood Problems and Services for Whites*

	Neighborhood Problems			Neighborhood Services (Inadequacy)		
	Estimate	Standard Error	Standardized Coefficient	Estimate	Standard Error	Standardized Coefficient
Number of children	0.038**	0.011	0.153	0.036	0.025	0.075
Foreign-born	0.114	0.415	0.116	−0.122	1.099	−0.064
Years of education	0.008	0.008	0.075	0.014	0.021	0.066
Age	−0.001	0.001	−0.040	−0.002	0.002	−0.076
Atlanta (L.A. omitted)	−0.779	3.840	−1.085	2.172	10.180	1.556
Boston (L.A. omitted)	−0.306	1.646	−0.560	0.953	4.363	0.897
Detroit (L.A. omitted)	−0.799	4.181	−1.307	2.378	11.084	2.000
Labor force status	0.006	0.099	0.012	−0.053	0.259	−0.052
Financial (000s)	0.001	0.003	0.150	−0.002	0.009	−0.152
Homogeny preference	0.002	0.003	0.072	0.001	0.007	0.034
Homeowner	0.024	0.052	0.045	−0.091	0.130	−0.089
Length of residence	0.005	0.010	0.225	−0.003	0.025	−0.075
Neighbor social network	0.000	0.002	0.031	0.001	0.004	0.074
Neighborhood SES	0.029	0.144	1.367	−0.087	0.381	−2.121
Commuting time	0.000	0.002	−0.051	0.002	0.006	0.109
Neighborhood homogeny	−0.005**	0.002	−0.385	−0.005	0.004	−0.226
Housing quality	−0.006	0.029	−2.171	0.016	0.076	3.008
Housing space	−0.239	0.663	−0.479	0.264	1.754	0.272

Source: Multi-City Study of Urban Inequality.
*$p \leq 0.05$. **$p \leq 0.01$. ***$p \leq 0.001$.

avoid confrontations and barriers that they believe exist. Hence, we interpret the positive association to mean that black households tend to seek neighborhoods where they expect to encounter the least resistance, whether or not the ethnic composition of the neighborhood is in accord with their preferences. The presence of other blacks in an area provides a good indication of whether they will encounter certain types of barriers to entry. On the other hand, that perceived discrimination affects blacks' residential choices, but not Hispanics', may also explain why the influence of black residential preferences on neighborhood ethnic homogeny was less substantial than that observed for Hispanics. That is, if blacks have a stronger reason for believing that they will encounter barriers to residence in their preferred neighborhoods, then their residence

TABLE 5.10   *Descriptive Statistics for Blacks, Hispanics, and Whites*

	Non-Hispanic Black		Hispanic		Non-Hispanic White	
	Mean	Standard Deviation	Mean	Standard Deviation	Mean	Standard Deviation
Atlanta	0.23	0.42	—	—	0.14	0.35
Boston	0.09	0.28	0.05	0.22	0.31	0.46
Detroit	0.28	0.45	—	—	0.22	0.41
Number of children	0.83	1.24	1.45	1.42	0.62	1.03
Age	42.09	15.54	37.19	12.99	45.62	16.35
Years of education	13.12	2.58	10.77	3.98	14.18	2.32
Foreign-born	0.08	0.27	0.73	0.45	0.07	0.26
Labor force status	0.61	0.49	0.63	0.48	0.64	0.48
Household income (000s)	30.86	32.04	25.44	24.49	48.57	38.54
Homogeny preference	55.62	19.60	61.16	22.20	14.32	11.73
Homeowner	0.42	0.49	0.28	0.45	0.64	0.48
Length of residence	9.23	10.74	6.26	8.58	11.70	12.42
Neighbor social network	16.95	32.63	29.53	39.99	19.80	33.56
Neighborhood homogeny	59.23	35.81	55.93	28.71	82.34	20.20
Commuting time	29.05	25.88	25.33	20.06	25.44	30.91
Seller discrimination	3.25	0.76	2.94	0.90		
City services problems	1.51	0.79	1.51	0.82	1.31	0.58
Crime problems	1.95	0.90	2.17	1.02	1.72	0.66
Housing problems	1.75	0.84	1.75	0.95	1.51	0.69
Real estate discrimination	3.10	0.75	2.63	0.92		
Lender discrimination	3.30	0.78	2.83	0.93		
Median home value	106.47	88.21	174.50	76.87	175.66	108.29
Median rent	549.84	186.01	616.74	159.13	644.81	238.37
Percentage professional	21.61	11.99	16.77	11.14	31.85	12.91
Median income (000s)	28.33	13.13	29.37	11.69	45.49	18.21
Median education	3.28	0.86	2.70	1.00	3.92	0.94
Median bedrooms	3.29	0.75	2.83	0.80	3.61	0.70
Single-family unit	0.56	0.50	0.47	0.50	0.71	0.45
Police quality	2.52	0.87	2.38	0.82	1.93	0.77
School quality	2.59	0.85	2.34	0.79	2.16	0.86
Shopping quality	2.46	0.94	2.16	0.75	1.87	0.82

Source: Multi-City Study of Urban Inequality.

in predominantly black residential areas would be higher than their preferences would predict.

The third question was whether preferences, perceived discrimination, and ethnic composition of neighborhoods were associated with the quality of the neighborhood environment inhabited by blacks and Hispanics. First, for both blacks and Hispanics, residence in a neighborhood with a high percentage of co-ethnics is associated with living in a neighborhood of low socioeconomic status and poor-quality housing, and which black respondents view as having limited access to services and where various kinds of problems exist. Second, even after controlling for homogeny, black respondents who perceive that members of their group are discriminated against in the housing market are also likely to perceive their neighborhood as being plagued by problems and feel that they receive limited services from both the public and private sectors. In the case of Hispanics, only perception of the neighborhood as being plagued by problems is associated with perceived discrimination. Finally—again, after controlling for neighborhood homogeny—black households that expressed a preference for living among other blacks are likely to live in low-income neighborhoods and poor-quality housing, although they tend to perceive the services they receive from local units of government as marginally more adequate.

The negative association of ethnic composition of neighborhood with neighborhood SES and housing quality for blacks and Hispanics is at least partially a function of ethnicity, resulting, in part, from the restricted residential choices such status imposes on minorities (see Massey, Condran, and Denton 1987; Logan et al. 1996). Conversely, among whites, living with co-ethnics is positively associated with neighborhood SES and housing quality and negatively associated with whites' perceptions of neighborhood problems, which simply indicates that whites of high socioeconomic status are more likely to be concentrated in the same area, in part because of a greater ability to select residential areas consistent with their status. The overall implications of these associations is that wherever whites live, the neighborhood environment is not likely to be viewed as problematic by whites, blacks, or Hispanics.

Differences among blacks, Hispanics, and whites are clearly one major source of variation in these results. A larger number of the key variable associations were statistically significant and in the expected direction for blacks and whites but not for Hispanics, with the exception of the effects of background variables of age, education, foreign birth, and household income. We suspect that *Hispanic*, as a pan-ethnic category, conceals considerable within-ethnic-group heterogeneity with respect to variable associations. In Los Angeles, Mexican is the largest

Hispanic group, but there is a growing presence of Central and South American groups. In Boston, Puerto Rican is the largest Hispanic group. Thus, distinctions such as country of birth and level of education may be more decisive for Hispanics than a somewhat diffuse ethnic identity. Conversely, blacks living in Los Angeles, Atlanta, Boston, and Detroit are predominantly native African Americans, although we should note that the results clearly indicate that the residential experiences of foreign-born blacks are much more similar to whites than to native-born blacks.

The background variables—particularly age, foreign birth, education, and household income—were directly associated with several of the attitudinal measures and neighborhood characteristics. The observed positive association of age, education, and household income with homeownership, neighborhood SES, and housing quality for blacks, whites, and Hispanics are of particular interest. A key difference between whites and the two minority groups is the association of the background variables with neighborhood ethnic homogeny. The relationship of neighborhood ethnic homogeny with education and income is negative for blacks and Hispanics. For whites, income is the only background variable that had a statistically significant relationship with neighborhood ethnic homogeny, and this association is positive. On the other hand, blacks and Hispanics of advantaged background are less likely to live among co-ethnics in predominantly black or Hispanic neighborhoods, unlike their white counterparts. These relations suggest that housing and neighborhood outcomes are also influenced by taste for particular kinds of residential configurations, life cycle position, and ability to pay for residential consumption packages. Thus, even among blacks and Hispanics, individual socioeconomic status characteristics have substantial effects on one's residential area attributes.

In summary, the story told by the data largely corresponds to our expectations. Living in a more ethnically homogeneous neighborhood is associated with a preference for neighborhood homogeny, but also, in the case of blacks, with perceived discrimination. Residence in an area with high concentrations of one's own ethnic group is—for blacks and Hispanics—linked to a variety of undesirable neighborhood characteristics, both perceived and objectively measured, whereas for whites it is linked to positive ones. Both the apparent causes and the apparent consequences of residential segregation point to serious grounds for concern.

The reported results have several implications with regard to the causes and consequences of ethnic residential segregation. First, although preferences for living in ethnically homogeneous neighborhoods play a role in continued patterns of ethnic segregation, it is also clear that real and perceived barriers to residential selections, in toto, are probably more important. That the majority of respondents in the Multi-City Study expressed the view that the residential selections available to minority, particularly black, households are substantially affected by discrimination clearly points to the need for continued vigilance in reducing discriminatory barriers in local housing markets (see Yinger 1995). Second, the reluctance of minority households to select housing options in nontraditional areas of residence is also of some importance. An obvious solution would be for housing specialists both to publicize the availability of housing for occupancy by minority households in majority areas and proactively to encourage them to pursue these options.

Appendix: Description of Variables

Variable categories appear in uppercase, boldface type. Latent (unobserved) variables appear in boldface type followed by their indicator variables. Variable names appear in parentheses.

1. Children: Number of children under the age of 18 living in the respondent's household.
2. Nativity: Dummy variable coded 1 if respondent was born outside the U.S., 0 otherwise.
3. Education: Number of years of schooling completed by respondent or number of years of schooling completed by respondent's spouse, if greater.
4. Age: Respondent's age in years.
5. Detroit: Dummy variable coded 1 if respondent resided in Detroit, 0 otherwise.
6. Atlanta: Dummy variable coded 1 if respondent resided in Atlanta, 0 otherwise.
7. Boston: Dummy variable coded 1 if respondent resided in Boston, 0 otherwise.
8. **Housing Discrimination**
   1. Real Estate Discrimination: Real estate agents will not show, sell, or rent to members of specified ethnic group (4 = very often, 3 = sometimes, 2 = rarely, and 1 = almost never).
   2. Bank and Lender Discrimination: Banks and lenders will not loan money to purchase a home to members of specified ethnic group (4 = very often, 3 = sometimes, 2 = rarely, and 1 = almost never).
   3. Seller Discrimination: Whites will not sell to members of specified ethnic group (4 = very often, 3 = sometimes, 2 = rarely, and 1 = almost never).

9. Labor Force Participation: dummy variable coded 1 if respondent was employed at least part-time, 0 otherwise.

10. Family Household Income: Family income before taxes in 1991 plus 6 percent of net family assets, in 1,000's of dollars.

11. Residential Preference: Index of a respondent's preference for living with members of his or her own ethnic-racial groups, with a range from zero, for preference for integration, to one hundred, for preference for living exclusively among co-ethnics (See Zubrinsky and Bobo 1996; Colasanto 1977). We assigned weights, varying from zero to twenty, to the ranking respondents assigned to five different neighborhood configurations representing the neighborhood ethnic composition they most to least preferred as an area in which to live. In this scheme, individuals who selected all-black or all-Hispanic neighborhoods as their first choice as a place to live were assigned the highest score on the index we constructed. The value of the scale ranges from zero to one hundred.

12. Homeownership: Dummy variable coded 1 if respondent owns his/her home, 0 otherwise.

13. Residential Tenure: Number of years respondent lived at current address.

14. Neighborhood Social Network: Percentage of respondent's social network composed of neighbors. Respondents were asked to name up to three persons with whom they discussed important matters.

15. **Neighborhood Socioeconomic Status**
    1. Percentage Professional/Managerial: Percentage of residents in respondent's census block group of residence who are employed in professional and managerial occupations (Census Occupation Codes).
    2. Household Median Income: Median household income in respondent's census block group of residence in 1989 in 1,000's of dollars.
    3. Median Education: Median number of years of schooling completed by persons 25 years and over in respondent's census block group of residence.

16. Commuting Time: Time respondent spends traveling one way to work each day, in minutes.

17. Neighborhood Homogeny: Percent of residents in respondent's census block group of residence that belong to the respondent's ethnic-racial group.

18. **Housing Quality**
    1. Median Value: Median value of owner-occupied housing units in respondent's census block group of residence, in 1,000's of dollars.
    2. Median Rent: Median gross rent of renter-occupied housing units in respondent's census block group of residence.

19. **Housing Space**
    1. Median Number of Bedrooms: Median number of bedrooms per housing unit in respondent's census block group of residence.
    2. Single-Family Dwelling Unit: Dummy variable coded 1 if respondent lives in a detached single-family dwelling unit, 0 otherwise.
20. **Neighborhood Services:** Respondents rated the quality of each type of service in their neighborhood (4 = poor, 3 = fair, 2 = good, and 1 = excellent).
    1. Police Protection.
    2. Public Schools.
    3. Shopping: Neighborhood shopping, such as grocery stores and drugstores.
21. **Neighborhood Problems:** Respondents rated the frequency with which each area constitutes a problem in their neighborhood (4 = always, 3 = often, 2 = sometimes, and 1 = never).
    1. City Services: City services, such as street cleaning or garbage collection.
    2. Crime: Crime and vandalism.
    3. Housing Deterioration: Housing and property not kept up.

Notes

1. For ease of interpretation, figure 5.1 omits the relationships between latent variables (such as perceived housing discrimination) and their multiple indicator variables (such as perceived discrimination by homeowners, brokers, and lenders). It also omits error correlations among the variables. Figure 5.2 depicts these added relations, which complete the model.

2. Although we derived empirical estimates for all the relations specified in figure 5.1 (and figure 5.2), the discussion of results focuses only on the association of a limited number of variable relations. Specifically, the endogamous variables that are of primary interest include neighborhood ethnic homogeny, observed measures of neighborhood quality, and perceived measures of the existence of neighborhood problems and of the adequacy of neighborhood services provided by public and private agencies. Hence, we do not discuss results for the determinants of perceived discrimination, residential preferences, homeownership, neighborhood social network, commuting time, and housing space; nor do we present results for the latent-indicator variables relationships and associated error structure presented in figure 5.2. These omissions are necessary to limit the scope of the discussion to those variable-relations that bear directly on the three objectives previously enumerated. (Omitted results are available from the authors.)

3. In this scheme, individuals who selected all-black, all-Hispanic, or all-white neighborhoods as their first choice as a place to live are assigned the highest score, followed by those respondents receiving progressively lower scores for the remaining neighborhood configurations selected, as preferences move toward residence in neighborhoods in which the respondents' ethnic group is in the minority. Conversely, the lowest total score was assigned to respondents who selected as their first choice the neighborhood configuration in which fewer members of her or his group are present as the most preferred, and selected all-black, all-Hispanic, or all-white neighborhoods as their least desired choice. It is important to note here that while our coding scheme shifts the emphasis from a focus on preferences for living in integrated neighborhoods to living in segregated neighborhoods, this should not be interpreted as suggesting that the high level of segregation observed between individual minority and white populations reflects the former's primary preference orientation. Rather, it is our claim that respondents' preferences for living in an ethnically homogeneous neighborhood is only one of several factors associated with segregated neighborhoods.

4. Ethnic preferences for neighborhood homogeny are based on self-selection and involve households making choices presumably based on individuals sharing a common culture, lifestyle, and ethnic identity. Housing discrimination, on the other hand, represents others' attempts to exclude members of a given group from residing among members of another group.

5. First among the intermediate variables is the extent of homeownership among members of an ethnic group population. A respondent who is a homeowner will be more likely to occupy a single-unit structure, recently constructed, with more interior and exterior space, and situated in a more desirable neighborhood. For whites, homeownership may be associated with greater ethnic homogeny, while it may display the exact opposite association for ethnic minorities. The number of years at current residence can be expected to have effects similar to those of homeownership. However, length of residence is also an excellent indicator of residential stability and the respondent's commitment to remaining in her current neighborhood—which may itself be associated with ethnic homogeny. Participation in neighborhood social networks once more indicates a respondent's level of commitment to the area. We hypothesize that involvement in neighborhood-based social networks will be positively associated with ethnic homogeny, because given the segregated nature of most social networks, persons with an affinity for neighborhood-based networks will tend to locate in more homogeneous locations. As noted previously, ethnic group members may seek out neighborhoods in which co-ethnics are present, because sharing a common cultural tradition and involvement in local institutions facilitates social interaction.

6. In addition to direct effects, ethnic residential preferences and per-
    ceived discrimination are hypothesized to have indirect effects on
    neighborhood ethnic homogeny and the other components of re-
    spondents' residential packages. We hypothesize substantial indirect
    effects of residential preferences via years of residence in a neighbor-
    hood and social network, and a weak effect through homeowner-
    ship. We hypothesize that a preference for homogeny indicates an
    underlying desire for control over one's residential environment, and
    therefore is linked to residential stability, neighborhood-based net-
    works, and homeownership. These variables reflecting the quest for
    control will thus be associated with greater homogeny. Perceived
    discrimination, on the other hand, is hypothesized to have strong
    indirect effects via homeownership and years of residence. Again,
    consider homeownership. Discrimination (or the perception thereof)
    reduces access to homeownership and residential stability for blacks
    and Hispanics, while increasing it for whites. So in this case we
    would expect homeownership and residential longevity to be *in-
    versely* related with neighborhood uniformity for blacks and His-
    panics, though not for whites. The indirect effect of perceived dis-
    crimination through homeownership is of particular importance
    because barriers to homeownership, in turn, result in further restric-
    tions on the availability of desirable housing and high-quality neigh-
    borhoods. We cannot predict with certainty the balance between the
    offsetting positive and negative indirect effects acting through own-
    ership and the like.

7. Most current occupants of housing had little or no influence on the
    distribution of housing by type, design, and quality; nor would it be
    appropriate to suggest that they are primarily responsible for the
    physical and socioeconomic characteristics of their neighborhood.
    When they choose a residential location, all these attributes are a
    part of the package, and, although a specific type of house, neighbor-
    hood SES, and so on, may not be unique to a specific residential
    location, it may be impossible to find two or more locations where
    the components of the residential package are identical. This is not
    to suggest that households have limited choices, but merely to point
    out that the vast majority of households, in selecting a residence,
    must choose from the existing residential stock, where there may be
    great variety, but not necessarily in the combination that a particu-
    lar household desires at the time a residential search is initiated.

8. These hypothesized relations are consistent with the point of view
    that minority households live in the worst areas of the metropolis,
    with high crime rates, dilapidated and abandoned housing, and inad-
    equate services from the government. In addition, they are likely to
    live in areas in which the public schools are poorly managed and
    provide low-quality services; police services are inadequate, partly

because of the great demand; and residents have very limited access to retail and financial services, partly because business owners perceive such areas to be high risk with respect to property and persons, and not likely to generate sufficient sales to ensure profitability. For whites, on the other hand, we expect more positive perceptions of more homogeneous neighborhoods. If one were to substitute the housing and neighborhood characteristics for ethnic homogeny, the outcome would be the same, except the relationships would be uniformly negative. Specifically, respondents who live in upper- and middle-income neighborhoods, whether white, black, or Hispanic, are much less likely to perceive their area as being plagued by problems and inadequate services.

9. Much evidence, based on census data up to 1980, points to the invariance of racial residential segregation across SES categories (see Massey and Denton 1993), which is inconsistent with the negative association of the SES attributes of individuals with the ethnic composition of the neighborhood in which they live as reported in table 5.1. However, it should be noted that these results are not directly compatible because of differences in the unit of analysis. On the other hand, recent findings reported by Sims (1997) also indicate an inverse association between tract level SES and racial composition in four major metropolitan areas (Chicago, Los Angeles, Miami, and San Francisco) in 1980 and 1990. His results indicate that the gaps in segregation between low and high status blacks and whites were between 8 and 15 points using the dissimilarity index.

References

Bobo, Lawrence, and Susan A. Suh. 1995. "Surveying Racial Discrimination: Analyses from a Multiethnic Labor Market." Working paper 75. New York: Russell Sage Foundation.

Clark, William A.V. 1986. "Residential Segregation in American Cities: A Review and Interpretation." *Population Research and Policy Review* 5(2): 96–127.

———. 1988. "Understanding Residential Segregation in American Cities: Interpreting the Evidence." *Population Research and Policy Review* 7(2): 113–21.

———. 1989. "Residential Segregation in American Cities: Common Ground and Differences in Interpretation." *Population Research and Policy Review* 8(2): 193–97.

———. 1991. "Residential Preferences and Neighborhood Racial Segregation: A Test of the Schelling Segregation Model." *Demography* 28(1): 1–19.

———. 1992. "Residential Preferences and Residential Choices in a Multiethnic Context." *Demography* 29(3): 451–66.

Colasanto, Diane Lee. 1977. "The Prospects for Racial Integration in Neighborhoods: An Analysis of Residential Preferences in the Detroit Area Study." Ph.D. diss., University of Michigan.

Farley, Reynolds, and William H. Frey. 1996. "Latino, Asian and Black Segregation in Multiethnic Metro Areas." *Demography* 33(1): 35–50.

Farley, Reynolds, Charlotte Steeh, Maria Krysan, Tara Jackson, and Keith Reeves. 1994. "Stereotypes and Segregation: Neighborhoods in the Detroit Area." *American Journal of Sociology* 100(3): 750–80.

Fielding, Elaine. 1997. "How Low Can It Go?: Applying Survey Data to Schelling Model of Segregation." Paper presented at the Annual Meeting of the Population Association of America. Washington, D.C. (April 1997).

Galster, George. 1988. "Residential Segregation in American Cities: A Contrary Review." *Population Research and Policy Review* 7(2): 93–112.

———. 1989. "Residential Segregation in American Cities: A Further Response to Clark." *Population Research and Policy Review* 8(2): 181–92.

———. 1992. "Research on Discrimination in Housing and Mortgage Markets: Assessment and Future Directions." *Housing Policy Debate* 3(2): 639–84.

Guest, Avery M. 1977. "Residential Segregation in Urban Areas." In *Contemporary Topics in Urban Sociology*, edited by Kent P. Schwirian. Morristown, N.J.: General Learning Press.

Logan, John R., Richard Alba, Tom McNulty, and Brian Fisher. 1996. "Making a Place in the Metropolis: Locational Attainment in Cities and Suburbs." *Demography* 33(4): 443–53.

Massey, Douglas S. 1985. "Ethnic Residential Segregation: A Theoretical Synthesis and Empirical Review." *Sociology and Social Research* 69(3): 315–50.

Massey, Douglas S., G. Condran, and Nancy Denton. 1987. "The Effect of Residential Segregation on Black Social and Economic Well-being." *Social Forces* 66(1): 29–56.

Massey, Douglas S., and Nancy Denton. 1985. "Spatial Assimilation as a Socioeconomic Outcome." *American Sociological Review* 50(1): 94–106.

———. 1993. *American Apartheid*. Cambridge, Mass.: Harvard University Press.

Myers, Dowell. 1990. "Introduction: The Emerging Concept of Housing Demography." In *Housing Demography: Linking Demographic Structure and Housing Markets*, edited by Dowell Myers. Madison: University of Wisconsin Press.

Portes, Alejandro. 1995. "Economic Sociology and the Sociology of Immigration: A Conceptual Overview." In *The Economic Sociology of Immigration: Essays on Networks, Ethnicity, and Entrepreneurship*, edited by Alejandro Portes. New York: Russell Sage Foundation.

Portes, Alejandro, and Rubin G. Rumbaut. 1996. *Immigrant America: A Propriat*. Berkeley: University of California Press.

Schelling, Thomas. 1971. "Dynamic Models of Segregation." *Journal of Mathematical Sociology* 1(1): 143–86.

Sims, Mario. 1997. "High Status Segregation in a Multi-ethnic Context: A Five Metropolitan Area Study of Comparative Inequality, 1980–1990." Ph.D. diss., University of Wisconsin, Madison.

Suttles, Gerald. 1972. *The Social Construction of Communities*. Chicago: University of Chicago Press.

Turner, Margery A. 1992. "Discrimination in Urban Housing Markets: Lessons from Fair Housing Audits." *Housing Policy Debate* 3(2): 185–215.

White, Michael. 1987. *American Neighborhoods and Residential Differentiation*. New York: Russell Sage Foundation.

Wilson, Franklin D. 1979. *Residential Consumption, Economic Opportunity and Race*. New York: Academic Press.

Wilson, Franklin D., and Roger Hammer. 1998. "Ethnic Residential Segregation and Its Consequences." Center for Demography and Ecology Working Paper 97-18. University of Wisconsin, Madison.

Yinger, John. 1995. *Closed Doors, Opportunities Lost: The Continuing Cost of Housing Discrimination*. New York: Russell Sage Foundation.

Zubrinsky, Camille L., and Lawrence Bobo. 1996. "Prismatic Metropolis: Race and Residential Segregation in the City of Angels." *Social Science Research* 25(4): 335–74.

6

SPACE AS A SIGNAL:
HOW EMPLOYERS PERCEIVE
NEIGHBORHOODS IN FOUR
METROPOLITAN LABOR MARKETS

Chris Tilly, Philip Moss,
Joleen Kirschenman, and Ivy Kennelly

E MPLOYERS do not carry out their business in a geographic vacuum. They are surrounded by a spatial environment, and each manager forms his or her own mental map of that environment. Employers' maps, in turn, have important effects on the labor market. In this chapter, we use data from in-depth employer surveys in the four metropolitan areas of the Multi-City Study of Urban Inequality to examine employers' mental maps, and how these maps shape their actions in labor markets. We particularly emphasize how space is linked to race in employers' minds and the consequences of that racialization for black and Latino urban communities. We argue, in brief, that space disadvantages some job seekers by acting as a signal for a whole complex of attributes—many of which are infused by race—that employers try to avoid in their location and recruitment practices.

Our point of departure is the extensive literature on the spatial mismatch hypothesis. The theory of spatial mismatch holds that within metropolitan areas, the locations of businesses offering relatively low skill jobs have disproportionately shifted away from the inner city and toward the suburbs. However, due to residential segregation, communities of color—particularly black communities—have remained concentrated within inner cities far from the loci of job growth. As a result, inner-city minority—particularly African American—populations, who on average have relatively low skill levels, have suffered heightened joblessness (see, for example, Kasarda 1993; Wilson 1987). While there is growing evidence for the spatial mismatch (Ihlanfeldt 1999), most analyses simply consider the correlation between location and economic disadvantage, without exploring the causal links. Christopher Jencks and Susan Mayer (1990) posited four distinct mechanisms that could account for lower black employment in suburban than in urban businesses. In two of the mechanisms, distance forms a barrier to black labor supply. First, distance may increase the time and money costs of commuting. Second, information about job openings may diminish with distance. But distance can also be an indicator of racial discrimination, as spelled out in two additional mechanisms. Suburban clienteles, themselves disproportionately white and Anglo, may prefer to deal with workers who are white and Anglo, leading employers to tailor their workforces accordingly. And the employers with a preference for white Anglo workers may choose to locate in the suburbs.

The first two explanations target space (distance) as a barrier to employment, whereas the second two point to race, specifically to racial discrimination. Most research on the spatial mismatch has focused on space as a barrier—not surprisingly, since distance is far more readily measurable than discrimination, and policy solutions are more obvious. There is some evidence, particularly in more recent data, that distance and commuting-cost barriers contribute significantly to black labor market disadvantage, especially for younger workers (in addition to Jencks and Mayer 1990, see Holzer 1991, Ihlanfeldt 1999, and Moss and Tilly 1991). Recent findings from the Multi-City Study of Urban Inequality confirm the importance of space as a barrier (Holzer 1996; Holzer and Ihlanfeldt 1996; Ihlanfeldt 1995).

But a growing body of spatially oriented research spotlights discrimination. Joleen Kirschenman and Kathryn Neckerman (1991) discovered that some Chicago employers used city or suburban school attendance, neighborhood, and even address (for example, whether a person lived in a public housing project) as screening criteria. Employers, they found, used space to refine the category of race, distinguishing among black workers. Philip Moss and Chris Tilly (1996, 2000) found that in Los Angeles and Detroit, certain employers targeted a suburban workforce, and therefore either located in the suburbs to access that workforce, or recruited suburban workers to urban worksites. In both studies, the employer actions tended to disadvantage black job seekers. Philip Kasinitz and Jan Rosenberg's (1994) study of the Red Hook neighborhood of Brooklyn found that most businesses there did not hire local black workers, due to multifaceted discrimination (based on class and location as well as race) and to recruitment through social networks that tended to exclude blacks.

Recent results from the Multi-City Study of Urban Inequality also build a case for the importance of discrimination correlated with employer location. Harry Holzer (1996) reports that even after controlling for job skill requirements, suburban employers hire a smaller proportion of black applicants than do urban employers (see also chapter 10 in this volume). David Sjoquist (1996) finds that after controlling for distance, blacks in the Atlanta area are less likely to search for work in areas rated by all respondents as more hostile toward potential black residents—despite other evidence that urban black workers who gain jobs in the suburbs earn a wage premium over those employed in the city (Holzer 1996; Ihlanfeldt and Young 1994). And Susan Turner (1996), drawing in part on some of the same data we analyze in this chapter, documents incidents of white suspicion of or hostility toward blacks traveling through predominantly white Detroit suburbs. Turner also reports that despite distance from black populations, some suburban Detroit employers nonetheless hire substantial numbers of black workers.

These findings suggest not simply that racial discrimination by employers and customers affects spatial outcomes, but that race and space are thoroughly intertwined in employer perceptions, making it difficult to fully separate the effects of the two causes. Space is a *signal* to employers: they have well-formed perceptions of certain neighborhoods, and draw inferences about the quality of workers from those neighborhoods. These perceptions, in turn, are strongly colored by the actual or perceived racial (as well as class) composition of neighborhood residents.

In this chapter, we build on these earlier analyses, drawing on employer interview data from the four cities surveyed in the Multi-City Study. Our key interests are, first, the way that employers view inner-city and minority areas, and workers from those areas; and, second, how employers' location and recruiting and hiring decisions are affected by these perceptions. We argue that for employers, space is a signal associated with perceptions about race, class, and worker skills and attitudes. However, within this mix, racial composition—in particular, the location of concentrated black populations—plays a prominent role in employers' perceptions of different locations within their metropolitan area. In many employers' minds, white areas are linked to positive workforce and location attributes; black and Latino areas are linked to negative ones.

Including four metropolitan areas helps us move beyond the "Detroit" metaphor that has dominated much discussion of the spatial mismatch hypothesis. Detroit is a declining Rustbelt metropolitan area with a monocentric spatial pattern and a sharp black-white divide that corresponds substantially with the central city–suburb distinction; the spatial mismatch is often viewed as if all cities took this form. Atlanta, Boston, and Los Angeles contrast markedly with Detroit in history and current urban form, allowing us to examine space as a signal in varying contexts.

After describing our data and methods, we give a brief introduction to each of our four metropolitan areas to set the context for our findings, as well as reporting how employers see the overall maps of their metropolitan areas. In the next section, we present evidence on employers' views of the inner city and elsewhere as business locations and recruiting grounds for workers. Evidence on how these perceptions affect employer actions follows. The final section offers our conclusions.

Data and Methods

Our data consist of a unique, large set of in-depth interviews with employers at firms in the Atlanta, Boston, Detroit, and Los Angeles metropolitan areas conducted as part of the Multi-City In-Depth Employer Survey. Face-to-face interviews were conducted at 45 establishments in Atlanta and Los Angeles, 46 in Boston, and 38 in Detroit, for a total of 174. Firms were surveyed between the summer of 1994 and the summer of 1996.

The sample for the In-Depth Employer Survey was drawn from the list of firms that had been identified by household respondents holding jobs requiring no more than a high school education, and had successfully completed a telephone survey. The response rate for screened firms in this subset of the telephone survey was 69 percent; the response rate for the in-depth survey was also about two-thirds. Interviewers spoke face to face with up to three (and in a few cases more) respondents per firm: the chief executive officer at the site or another top manager; a personnel official involved in hiring for the sample job; and a line manager or supervisor who managed employees in the sample job category. This strategy gathers the differing knowledge and perceptions of these various categories of managers. In smaller firms, these functions were often performed by two people or even just one person, so fewer interviews were conducted. In total, 354 interviews were conducted with 365 respondents (with some interviews gathering multiple respondents).

The in-depth interview involved a series of structured questions and follow-up probes. All questions were open-ended, and interviewers were trained to encourage respondents to elaborate, telling the story of their business's relationship to the labor market. Respondents spoke to a wide range of spatial issues, mainly in response to two questions focused specifically on space: "How is [this community] as a place to do business?" and "We have heard that [central city], particularly the inner city, is a difficult place to do business; what do you think?" Depending on responses, there were a variety of follow-up probes, notably: "Do you see a difference between workers from [central city] and workers from the suburbs?" The varied discussions prompted by these questions form a rich database on how employers' perceptions and actions approach the maps of their metropolitan areas.

A Tale of Four Cities

Views of the business environment and workforce of the inner city, or of minority areas in general, vary in intensity across the four metropolitan areas. For Detroit-area employers the inner city is a crisply defined, ever-present part of the map, even when geographically distant. For most Los Angeles and Boston employers, the inner city is remote, in many cases poorly defined, and irrelevant to their business activities. These differences in employers' mental maps are shaped by the social history of each area. The 1967 riots in Detroit etched the city-suburb distinction in stone in the minds of employers, and to many white employers the etching is defined in terms of black and white. The Watts riots in 1965 and the 1992 Los Angeles disturbances sharply outlined the predominantly black community of South Central as dangerous and undesirable, but the highly multiethnic character of its recent immigration makes the outer boundaries of the inner city diffuse. There certainly is no clear city-suburb distinction in Los Angeles. In the Boston area, decades-old black-white conflicts over school desegregation still resonate in the city, and presumed deficient education has become a strong signal attached to city minorities. But in many suburbs the recent Latino and Asian migrations raise the most immediate spatial-racial issues for employers. And in Atlanta, the north-south, black-white division is an issue for many businesses, but there is not Detroit's degree of disjunction between black population centers and economic activity.

Detroit: The Black-White Line

Industrial suburbanization in Detroit was launched by Henry Ford in the early 1900s, accelerated during the 1940s, and surged again in 1967 with white flight following Detroit's riot. (See map 6.1 for a map of Detroit and the surrounding area.) The current map of industrial activity in the Detroit area shows concentrations of manufacturing and industrial parks along every major road or highway leading out of Detroit, but relatively few within the city itself (SEMCOG 1984).

Overlying the industrial landscape is a starkly segregated racial geography. Detroit, perhaps more than any other city in the United States, has the image of "chocolate city, vanilla suburbs," George Clinton's phrase (put to academic use by Farley et al. [1978])—an African Ameri-

MAP 6.1   In-Depth Survey Large MCDs in Detroit, Michigan

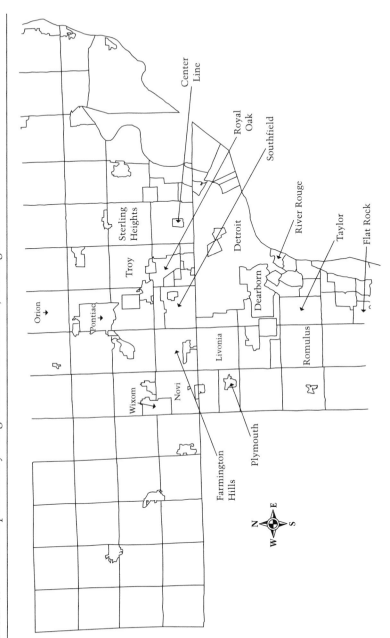

Source: Center for Industrial Competitiveness, University of Massachusetts Lowell.

can central city surrounded by nearly lily-white communities. The Detroit metropolitan area was the most segregated of the forty-seven U.S. metropolitan areas with populations of one million or more in 1990, and the only one to increase its level of segregation between 1980 and 1990 (Farley and Frey 1994). While 76 percent of Detroit residents were black, only 5 percent of the residents of the remainder of the three-county area of Wayne, Macomb, and Oakland were (Farley et al. 1993). Put another way, 83 percent of blacks in the metropolitan area lived in Detroit, and 93 percent of whites lived outside it. A long history of resistance to integration by white communities helps explain these dramatic contrasts. The racial differences are compounded with class: in 1990, Detroit poverty rates were four times as high as in the surrounding area, and median family income was less than half as great (Moss and Tilly 1993).

The three-county area is stitched together by a transportation system consisting primarily of freeways radiating from downtown Detroit. Public transit links between Detroit and surrounding areas are notoriously bad, reflecting many of the communities' history of resistance to black access.

In the hypersegregated metropolis of Detroit, dividing lines between black and white areas play an extraordinarily large role in employers' perceptions of space. More significantly, the line between black and white is closely linked in respondents' minds to other distinctions, such as the city-suburb boundary—particularly the frontiers of Detroit, but also the line between Pontiac and other northern suburbs of Detroit. Indeed, the Asian male manager of a fast food restaurant on the south side of 8 Mile Road, which forms Detroit's northern border, stated, "We are on the [south] side, on the other side, on the black side of the road," and his assistant manager added, "People [on this side] don't go [to] that side that often, and that side['s] people don't come here." Many respondents also implicitly identified the division between black and white turf with distinctions between "good" and "bad" neighborhoods, and (relatedly) between poor neighborhoods and those with working-class or wealthier residents.

Some suburban respondents were extremely concerned about the process of neighborhoods "turning" or "going downhill." Respondents spontaneously raised the subject at one-quarter of suburban sites. In many cases (though not all), their comments on the subject conflated race and class:

> I think [compared to Livonia, Southfield—an integrated community neighboring Detroit—is] a little less . . . a little more crime . . . a little dirtier out there. It's just kind of going downhill. Do you know what I'm

saying . . . ? I mean people are moving out to West Bloomfield, and Bir-mingham. You've, there's a big distinction between Birmingham and Southfield. . . . Because you're getting closer to Detroit, and I think it just gets a little yucky as you . . . [laughter].—White female office manager at the suburban regional HQ of a low-end retail chain

People are moving away [from the suburbs near Detroit]. You have a lot of blacks in the cities. It's very easy to make up your mind that you don't want to live in . . . those type of areas because you look around and you see things. I like nice things, I have a nice house, I take care of my yard. I go to areas maybe where there's a lot of blacks and I don't see what I want to see with respect to. . . . I wouldn't want to live there.—White male supervisor at a manufacturing plant located "downriver," in a primarily white area southeast of Detroit

In a few cases, respondents equated racial distance with physical distance. In a revealing comment, a white female suburban public-sector manager described her former home of Sterling Heights, which remains less than 1 percent black, as "thirty-five miles northeast of Detroit"; in fact, Sterling Heights is a rectangle extending from 6 to 12 miles above Detroit. Apparently, Sterling Heights feels far more distant from Detroit than it actually is.

Atlanta: The Line Moves North

The Atlanta metro area is markedly divided between majority-white areas in the northern suburbs and majority-black areas in the southern suburbs and inner city (see map 6.2). Jobs and population are growing at a rapid clip in the north, while growth in the southern suburbs has been spottier, and the inner city struggles to remain viable. As the population of the metro area has increased over the past three decades, the black-white dividing line has moved increasingly north, to where it now roughly separates the southern two-thirds of the city of Atlanta from the northern third and beyond (Bayor 1996; Rutheiser 1996). This bifurca-tion of space is facilitated by the sharp resistance of northern suburban homeowners to the extension of the mass transit system, MARTA, into their counties—a move that could provide African Americans from the city and the southern suburbs access to expanding job opportunities in the north.

Fulton County, which extends from the north of the Atlanta metro area through the bulk of the city down to the southwest corner, reflects some of the larger trends in the metro area because of its size and span. In the southern half of Fulton County, the African American population has grown from just over 15 percent in some areas in 1980 to at least 75

MAP 6.2   *In-Depth Survey Large MCDs in Atlanta, Georgia*

Source: Center for Industrial Competitiveness, University of Massachusetts Lowell.

percent in 1990 (Rutheiser 1996). In the northern half of that county, however, African Americans continue to comprise less than 15 percent of the population (Rutheiser 1996). This county includes the largest numbers of low-income and high-income households in the metro area, and class corresponds heavily with race (U.S. Census Bureau 1994). In true Southern spirit, north Fulton residents have even recently begun to push for secession from the county, claiming that their taxes are disproportionately being spent on the south side.

The population in the city of Atlanta itself has declined over 7 percent since 1980, although the racial balance has remained fairly constant, with African Americans consistently making up about two-thirds of the city's population from 1980 to 1992 (U.S. Bureau of the Census 1988, 1994). Outside the city all metro counties have experienced growth, especially in the northern suburbs of Gwinnett, Forsyth, and Cherokee—counties that are over 90 percent white. The counties experiencing the least growth since 1980, DeKalb and Fulton, also have among the highest population of African Americans. Interestingly, Cobb County, notorious for its conservative politics, has gone from almost 94 percent white in 1984 to over 42 percent African American in 1992, although its northernmost section is still almost all white (U.S. Bureau of the Census 1988, 1994).

Originally developed as a transportation center, Atlanta has always had a largely service-based economy. Thus the decline of manufacturing and the rise of services that occurred across much of this country's urban space did not have the same fallout here as in many northern cities. While the "center of Atlanta" has not emptied as it did in Detroit, Atlanta is no longer solely centered around its downtown. The airport anchors the south; government, education, and professional sports dominate the old downtown area; the new retail, restaurant, and nightspot epicenter lies largely in a predominantly white area called Buckhead in the northern part of the city; and the primary new center of industry, business growth, technological innovation, and economic expansion lies in the northern suburbs. This all points to Atlanta's multinodal, rather than simply inner-city-suburban, character.

Atlanta employers are keenly aware of the north-south division, which is in addition a black-white division. But the city-suburb distinction also enters their considerations. "We define [our stores] as inner city and within the perimeter and outside of the perimeter," said the manager of a fast food restaurant, "and I'm outside the perimeter but I'm probably more like an inside store [because the workforce is overwhelmingly black]."

Boston: Black Plus Latino-Asian
Inner Cities

The mix and geography of Boston-area jobs have changed markedly over the last several decades. Manufacturing has taken place well outside the city, either in satellite cities 15 to 40 miles from Boston, or dispersed along distant highways that circumscribe the city. Meanwhile, the economy of the city of Boston has been fueled by a growth in sectors such as legal services; finance, insurance, and real estate; and health care (Harrison and Kluver 1988; Porter 1994).

Beyond Boston is a set of residential suburbs, the most affluent of which are to the west and northwest, and a set of smaller, far less affluent industrial cities (see map 6.3). The residential suburbs supply the

MAP 6.3   *In-Depth Survey Large MCDs in Boston, Massachusetts*

Source: Center for Industrial Competitiveness, University of Massachusetts Lowell.
Note: Named cities and towns of 25,000 population or more in 1990.

commuters who dominate the job market in Boston (in 1989, 77 percent of jobs in the city were held by commuters [Dougherty 1993]). Other cities cut and fashioned by the Industrial Revolution of the nineteenth century, such as Lowell and Lawrence, 30 miles to the north of Boston, have struggled through most of this century. And in a ring around Boston, the well-known high-tech industrial complexes dot the landscape.

The public transportation system of Boston is quite extensive. The various parts of the city, the border cities and towns, and the inner residential suburbs are linked by subway and buses. Most of the outlying cities are on commuter rail lines. Travel from the subway and rail lines without a car becomes more difficult, of course, as one moves farther away from the city.

How does race map to the economic geography of greater Boston? In the decades prior to the 1980s, the nonwhite population of the greater Boston area was primarily black and living within the city of Boston. Further, blacks were concentrated in a few neighborhoods close to the central city, mainly Roxbury and the South End. In 1980, 8 percent of the population of the Boston Standard Consolidated Statistical Area (SCSA) was nonwhite, and blacks comprised half of that total. Within the city of Boston, however, blacks constituted 22 percent of the population and 75 percent of the nonwhite population. The segregation of blacks within the city of Boston, and the resistance to black access to white neighborhoods, were spotlighted in the mid-1970s by the difficult and at times violent course of court-ordered school desegregation (Lukas 1985).

During the 1980s, the overall picture of spatial demography changed significantly. By 1990, greater Boston had become much more racially diverse, with a pace and extent of change exceeding the nationwide average. The proportion of blacks did not change greatly, however. It was the inflow of Latinos and Asians that altered the terrain. Latinos almost doubled their population over the decade of the 1980s, reaching 4 percent of the Boston Consolidated Metropolitan Statistical Area (CSMA) in 1990, and the Asian population more than doubled, making up 3 percent of the CSMA in 1990. Latinos in Boston have settled particularly in areas that were primarily black, climbing from 6 to 11 percent of the city's population between 1980 and 1990. The most rapid growth among Latinos, however, occurred in Lowell, Chelsea, and Lawrence. Southeast Asian populations have expanded in some Boston neighborhoods, but the largest jump in the numbers of Asians took place in Lowell and surrounding areas. Overall, Boston-area Latinos and Asians have diffused more widely than have blacks.

The distinction between the city and the suburbs is not so sharp in the eyes of Boston's city and suburban employers as it is in Detroit and

Atlanta. Respondents often defined Boston's inner city with a list of neighborhoods: "Roxbury, Dorchester, Mattapan, Jamaica Plain . . . the most inner city of the neighborhoods." While this black-Latino core of the inner city was well defined in employers' minds, the boundaries were fuzzy—as indicated, for instance, by a respondent's inclusion of Cambridge (across the Charles River, predominantly middle class, but with a growing Caribbean population) in the inner city. Furthermore, employers' comments, while frequently negative, were not as racialized or pejorative, either about the inner city as a business location or about workers from the inner city, as were comments from Detroit and Atlanta employers. In contrast to Detroit and Atlanta, and more like Los Angeles, the substantial recent immigration and resulting racial and ethnic diversity in Boston and around the greater Boston area appears to have made the inner city, and black inner-city residents in particular, less important to Boston-area employers seeking low-wage labor. The old manufacturing cities such as Lowell and Lawrence, among others, have become important sources of labor for suburban Boston firms and have inner cities, and inner-city problems, of their own. It is useful to think of three geographic groups of firms in Greater Boston: the firms in the city of Boston, the firms in the suburbs of Boston, and the firms in cities such as Lawrence and Lowell, the particular satellite cities represented in our sample.

Los Angeles: What Is the Inner City?

The seemingly straightforward task of describing the objective contours of an urban space immediately bewilders when one arrives at Los Angeles (Waldinger and Bozorgmehr 1996). However, the characteristic urban sprawl and demographic diversity of Los Angeles are recent developments. The economy lacked a substantial industrial base until the early 1940s, when war in the Pacific motivated a defense-based economy, transforming the entire area into one of the most multiethnic, fastest-growing urban regions in the world.

Edward Soja, Rebecca Morales, and Goetz Wolff (1983) argue that in Los Angeles we see a combination of both Sunbelt and Frostbelt dynamics. The original "center" of industry, from South Central to San Pedro and Long Beach, echoes Detroit's decline, while the growth of high tech compares with Silicon Valley and the addition of low-skilled, exploitative manufacturing resembles Hong Kong and Singapore. This fragmented economic development contributes to the fragmented character of the region's physical space and to the socioeconomically polarized character of its population.

Los Angeles has never been very centralized, instead maintaining a

MAP 6.4   *In-Depth Survey Large MCDs in Los Angeles, California*

Source: Center for Industrial Competitiveness, University of Massachusetts Lowell.

low overall population density, distributed in socially distinct ways across space (see map 6.4). In recent shifts, the black population has stabilized (growing by only 1 percent between 1980 and 1990), the white population has declined (dropping by 8 percent), and the Latino and Asian populations have rapidly expanded (growing by 62 percent and 119 percent, respectively). In Los Angeles County an expanding Latino population has begun to overtake black majorities in South Central and challenged Anglo strongholds in the San Fernando Valley; Asian and Middle Eastern immigrants now inhabit the once all-white, middle-class neighborhoods in the San Gabriel Valley; some northern areas have experienced white growth; and Anglos maintain their exclusive enclaves along the coast: Santa Monica, Malibu, Brentwood (Clifford and Roark 1991). Segregation persists, but in a checkerboard pattern. The extensive freeway system links this multiethnic, geographically dispersed population with their places of work.

The complex geographic, industrial, and population differentiation of Los Angeles is reflected in employers' views of space. With the exception of South Central, the black-white, city-suburb, good-bad distinctions are not so vivid for Los Angeles employers. Areas that employers see as highly desirable and highly undesirable are scattered across the landscape. Employers tend to be concerned with their own current locations, not with areas that are both socially and physically distant. Respondents typically described the "inner city" by listing communities; those lists comprised low-income areas inhabited primarily by people of color—always black, sometimes Latino. Relatively few employers explicitly identified space with race, but many spoke readily about class markers such as housing costs and general levels of affluence. Some employers gave narrow definitions of the inner city as the black-Latino areas in and immediately adjacent to South Central. Broader definitions included downtown or extended the defined area west and/or east. Perhaps the most expansive definition came from the general manager of a LAX-based airport service company, who stated that his "inner city" janitorial workforce sweeps "from East LA, all the way through the South Central, the Watts . . . Carson, Culver City, Inglewood, Hawthorne, a little in the Torrance area." Some suburban employers expressed a more diffuse sense of the inner city's location, saying "it's just everywhere" or professing ignorance. Most respondents saw the inner city as socially and physically distant, and indeed their discourse about the inner city referred often to "what you see on the news" and "what you read in the papers." Despite their distance from it, most employers had opinions about the inner city and could describe what it connoted.

Employers' Perceptions: The "Signal" of Space

Employers in our four metropolitan areas are wary of the inner city as a business location and wary of the residents of the inner city as employees. This is true for a sizable fraction of employers across city, suburban, and other locations in each of the metropolitan areas.

Where employers locate and whom they hire are the ultimate concerns, but employers' views are important as well. The narratives of their attitudes give insight into *why* certain patterns of location and hiring outcomes, such as those we see in the Multi-City Study quantitative employer survey (see chapter 10), occur. The narratives help uncover the many reasons for employer decisions, more than the one or two that are measured and could be investigated in quantitative data. Finally, employers' discussions of their perceptions help explain why the location and hiring decisions that hurt urban minority workers occur more or less frequently in some areas or among some kinds of employers. Although we make some conjectures about the motives behind the perceptions employers voice, in particular, that attitudes about race—prejudices, stereotypes, and biases—are connected to some degree to employers' negative "business" views of the city and its residents, we cannot prove these conjectures. However, we have tried as much as possible to weigh the evidence.

How widespread are the negative attitudes toward an inner-city business location and toward workers from the inner city? Table 6.1 displays the views from the 354 interviews in our sample of 174 employers, broken down by the location of the employer—primary central city, other central city, or suburb. Although there are many other reasons employers gave for disliking the inner city as a business site, as we will discuss, we focus here on the issues of crime and the quality of the inner-city workforce.

Several patterns are apparent. Respondents at a majority of businesses noted crime and workforce problems in the inner city. Suburban employers were more concerned about the inner city as an unsafe place of business than were their counterparts in the central city. Conversely, employers in the central city were more critical of the quality of the inner-city workforce than were employers from areas outside the central city. The two issues listed in the table, quality of the workforce and crime, were expressed with similar overall frequency. It should be noted, however, that interviewers were asked to probe about workforce quality if the respondent did not bring the topic up spontaneously. This was not true about crime.

Our job now is to try to understand the story behind these outcomes.

Perceptions of the City as a Business Location

Employers voiced a number of factors when they expressed their hesitancy about the city as a place to do business. The most frequently ex-

TABLE 6.1   *Employers' Attitudes About Inner-City Business*
            Locations and Workers, by Respondent Business
            Location

	Primary Central City	Other Central City	Suburb	Total
Percentage of firms where respondents stated concerns about:				
Inner-city crime a problem for business				
At least one respondent	57%	65%	61%	60%
Half or more of firm respondents	43	50	55	50
Inner-city workforce worse				
At least one respondent	64	62	48	57
Half or more of firm respondents	40	53	37	41
Inner-city workforce better				
At least one respondent	15	15	30	21
Half or more of firm respondents	12	15	24	17

Source: Multi-City Study of Urban Inequality.
Note: "Other central city" also includes any municipality other than the primary central city that has a black population of 30 percent or more.

pressed concerns were those given in table 6.1: workforce quality and safety. Other issues raised were congestion, parking, traffic and commuting, taxes, unfriendly regulations, and government treatment of business (particularly salient in Detroit). These latter factors are part of the force pushing employers out of the cities, and creating a greater locational barrier for inner-city residents in search of work. Our concern in this chapter is with perceptions and factors tied to the *populations* living in the city, or in the inner city, the most important of which is the perception that the city is unsafe.

Employers in all cities expressed concerns about crime, violence, and safety, and the consequent fears of customers, employees, and proprietors. Employers located within the city complained of break-ins and gangs. In each metro area, several city employers described how they had secured parking areas and buildings for their employees. A number of city firms expressed concerns about being able to recruit employees who would fear working in rough areas of the city. The concern was voiced most frequently in regard to recruiting management-level employees, and much less when entry-level jobs were discussed. Several firms in Los Angeles spoke of the difficulty they faced getting employees to work in city areas after the disturbances following the 1992 Rodney King verdict.

Social service and public-sector agencies that served a variety of city neighborhoods frequently mentioned fear as a factor for some of their employees, as well as an influence on the public's image of the city. Detroit is "a place that suburban people don't want to go to," observed a manager at a Detroit-based nonprofit. "I have a hard time getting people to work in Roxbury if they are not a minority and they've been working other places," one public-sector manager noted. "Some people are very scared to go to Roxbury. They don't want to work there." Interestingly, the strongest racialized statement of concern for safety was voiced in the context of blacks traveling to work in South Boston, a primarily white area with a long history of animosity toward blacks.

However, several social service agency respondents moderated their comments with statements that the view of the inner city from the outside was exaggerated, and that the problem did not seriously compromise their ability to function. Indeed, employers located within the city in all four metro areas tried to counter the perception of their city as a scary place to be. Several Detroit employers decried the exaggerated negative views of others, using words such as "hysteria," "racism," and "overstated," and a few reported that they or colleagues were pleasantly surprised upon working in Detroit for the first time. Inner-city employers in Atlanta were quick to defend their turf from suburbanites' negative perceptions about issues like crime. "People have the idea that downtown is a more dangerous place than other parts of Atlanta," remarked the white general manager of an inner-city hotel, "which . . . people should be figuring out is probably not true anymore."

As table 6.1 suggests, the concerns about fear and safety were particularly strident among suburban employers. The perceptions varied somewhat across the metropolitan areas, reflecting the different pattern of city-suburb geography in the four areas. Most Atlanta employers in the southern suburbs remarked that crime is a problem in their locations. These responses show most poignantly how race is confounded with the desirability of particular locations. These employers explicitly linked crime with African Americans, and implicated areas where black populations are high as undesirable, both from customers' and employers' standpoints: "East Point and College Park area [two southern suburbs] has a fairly high crime rate . . . and the whole south side of Atlanta is fairly high on blacks, which makes a lot of whites nervous coming down in this area," said a white assistant director of a government agency.

Employers from the northern suburbs of Atlanta expressed concerns about crime in Atlanta itself, which they commonly defined as either the area encased in Atlanta's city limits or, more generally, the area inside the perimeter and south of them (including the inner city and the southern suburbs).

Boston employers in suburbs close to Boston certainly expressed concern with crime in Boston's inner city, which most often meant Roxbury (the largest concentration of blacks in Boston, but increasingly a Latino neighborhood as well). However, most firms in the suburbs closer to Boston were not as connected to the city as were firms in the suburbs of Detroit and Atlanta, and questions about the inner city of Boston as place to do business elicited less of a response. Firms in Boston's more distant suburbs think of the inner city of Boston very little, and the firms closer to or within the satellite cities, such as Lowell, Lawrence, and Brockton, view the inner city of those cities when they think of the inner city. These cities have concentrations of minority populations, and crime and drugs form an important part of the image of these populations.

Finally, many employers outside the city of Los Angeles spoke of a Los Angeles crime problem. Employers most frequently associated crime with the inner city with reference to the concentrations of blacks (and, increasingly, Latinos) in South Central Los Angeles. Such images of neighborhoods as crime-ridden may bear not just on their desirability as business locations but also on employers' views of workers from these areas. We turn now to these perceptions of the quality of the inner-city workforce.

Perceptions of the City Workforce

As table 6.1 demonstrates, negative views of inner-city workers are widespread. A range of concerns were common to employers in all four metropolitan areas. In many instances inner-city workers were seen as relatively lacking in hard skills such as reading and writing and soft skills such as communication and interaction with others, work motivation, and attitude in general. The response of a white supervisor at a suburban Detroit-area utility illustrated the concern with hard skills: "The more applicants we've been hiring from the Pontiac and Detroit area[s], the [more the] failure rate [on the company's exam] has increased." Skill deficits were only part of the list of criticisms, however. At times personal deficiencies of character were cited, along with educational background, family problems, and drug use. Respondents attributed causes that included class and culture in the inner city, single-parent and dysfunctional families, and inferior educational systems in the cities. Less often, they attributed workforce problems to inner-city residence itself, or to race, pure and simple. In these instances the racial group viewed negatively was most frequently black. This was true in Detroit and Atlanta, where minority status almost exclusively means black. But it was also true in Boston and Los Angeles, where there are other minorities as numerous or more numerous than blacks.

Consider first the views of suburban businesspeople. Unfortunately, as far as most suburban employers in the Detroit metropolitan area are concerned, Detroit workers carry with them much of the baggage of the city. Given Detroit's degree of segregation, an important issue is suburban customers' discomfort with black employees. Only a small number of managers commented on this, but their testimony was potent. Respondents told us about customers who don't want black workers at a laundry touching their clothes, retail customers who are uncomfortable with black employees, and a suburban school system that "get[s] real hysterical" about the hiring of one or two black custodians.

Suburban employers in Atlanta, though they complained about their local labor pool, ascribed much more serious problems to the inner-city workforce. A white store manager noted that "it's real difficult [finding enough qualified workers] in this area, when you're competing with the mall." But, he added: "I worked downtown in a [grocery chain] store, and it was . . . a nightmare. . . . It was so difficult working inner city to find anybody that's a pretty . . . a good person. Maybe one out of twenty people was a . . . was a halfway decent, moral person that you could . . . that would show up . . . that would, you know, do the job that they agreed to do."

In fact, over half of the northern suburban Atlanta employers expressed negative attitudes toward inner-city workers. They sometimes attributed the deficiencies of inner-city workers explicitly to the race of the area's residents, and other times blamed crime, drugs, housing projects, and "welfare mentality"—all racially loaded issues. Given this negative assessment, northern suburban employers expressed no desire to confront the barriers of distance and transportation to hire inner-city workers. That inner-city residents often need public transportation to get to the northern suburbs is often a barrier in the minds of northern suburban employers, but it is also a signal of other problems, including class, that they see with inner-city workers. A white woman general manager from a northern suburb said: "Your labor force [from the inner city] is comprised of a different education level and a different income level. . . . In the city of Atlanta, I have sometimes run ads in the Atlanta paper. And I find that all the employees . . . if you're not on the MARTA [the Atlanta public transit system] route . . . are not interested in working for you."

Boston-area employers spoke of similar problems with the inner-city workforce, but we heard the litany of race, class, and culture less often than we did from employers in other cities. Instead, several suburban employers, as well as Boston-based organizations, cited the schools as a key or the key difficulty with the inner-city workforce. Perceptions of the quality of Boston's inner-city workforce appeared to be closely connected to views about the quality of the Boston public schools. One public sector manager declared,

> I think we have a real problem. I think the problem is centered in the Boston public school system. Clearly, in my opinion, the school system in this city is not producing young people with the educational skills to get into the workforce, and in many cases, perform. . . . In most cases, the white . . . has gone either to private school or gone almost overwhelmingly to the Catholic parochial school system. . . . Minority kids either went to school in the deep South, where the per capita expenditure for education is as weak as you can imagine, or they graduated from the Boston public school system.

The Boston public schools have been a flash point for race relations in the city of Boston for many years, even before the confrontation over busing in the 1970s. The schools have become overwhelmingly minority, as white residents have left them for private schools or fled to the suburbs. Respondents drew a sharp contrast between the Catholic private schools and the public schools, where they alleged students get pushed through without receiving basic skills and without being given the sense that effort is required for achievement or reward. The purported crisis of the Boston public schools appeared to be a crucial way in which employers—including liberal ones—expressed negative views of inner-city workers. Given the evolved demography of the schools and the history of controversy, it is difficult to pull apart the issue of educational preparation from the issues of race, class, and space that the Boston public schools have come to symbolize.

Suburban firms farther from Boston paid little attention to the residents of Boston as a source of labor. When the employers near Lawrence or Lowell spoke of the inner city, it was their own inner cities they had in mind. Several employers in this group who sought soft skills (bank tellers, school bus drivers), voiced concerns about the poor skills of inner-city Latino residents and a reluctance to hire these residents.

Suburban employers in Los Angeles, for whom the notion of relocating to the inner city was an abstraction, generally expressed negative views of the inner-city workforce. A middle manager at a rehabilitation center thought an inner-city location would bring more black applicants, and commented that the center "get[s] a very low quality of work from black people." A supervisor at the same firm did not believe he could find the skills required for even a dishwasher job in the inner-city workforce.

In a few cases, suburban employers—and even some urban ones—dismissed the urban workforce altogether. From his standpoint in the northern suburbs of Detroit, one white lawyer implied that there simply is no clerical workforce living in Detroit, commenting that businesses in the city have a difficult time recruiting clerical workers because "economically, you have to offer something more to get people down there." A white female suburban retailer who has hired Detroiters for a store near Detroit with a largely black clientele described the young black women she hired as exceptions: "only a few [good] people out of a school of twenty-two hundred people." Even at one of the Detroit employers with a social commitment to remaining in the city, the human resource director admitted: "Our demographics don't come anywhere close to reflecting the Detroit workforce."

Quite a few urban employers echoed their suburban counterparts. In Atlanta, for instance, most inner-city employers remarked that they thought the quality of workers available in the inner city to be poor. Respondents related the poor quality of their labor supply with varying combinations of race, single motherhood, values, and education. But frequently it was explicitly linked to race, as in the case of this white male plant manager:

> When we get into the inner city, in my opinion, work values change, because you're talking about people that are primarily raised in a single [-parent] family. Very poor environment. . . . Now, I've not only got to teach them the job, but I've got to teach them values. And those type basic things that I don't want to teach. I want somebody that already has that, so all I've got to do is train him how to do my job the way I want it done. And if you're downtown, that's what you're faced with. . . . Just somebody just sitting there and listening to this will say, "You know what you're saying? You're talking about black people because that's primarily what's in the inner city." And unfortunately, that's true. I can't help it if they don't receive that type of upbringing.

And at a Los Angeles business that had moved from the inner city to a suburban location, a white human resources manager linked a workforce that "didn't care about their jobs" at the former site to "a predominantly black workforce" and "a lot, lot of single mothers."

Some respondents grounded their negative perceptions in concrete experiences. More often—especially in the case of suburban businesspeople commenting on the inner city—employers expressed views as opinions. The fact that the fraction that speaks disparagingly about inner-city workers is higher among employers located in the city than among suburban employers (see table 6.1) suggests that experience is likely to be important in forming opinions. Indeed, it suggests that employer encounters with real hard and soft skill gaps is likely to be an important contributor to the observed negative views and to differential hiring patterns as well. The types of expressions chosen, the association of inner-city residence with a litany of stereotypes, the at times seamless interchange between "inner-city" (in response to a direct query about the inner-city workforce) and race and class—most notably low-income black—suggest to us, however, that the negative attitudes about and reluctance to hire inner-city residents go beyond skill deficiencies.

Employers' spoken evaluations of the skills of urban and suburban workers were far from monolithic. In every city, substantial minorities denied that there was any difference between urban and suburban workers. Indeed, in quite a few cases respondents at the same business, and sometimes even the same respondents, gave apparently conflicting assessments. Why this mix? In many cases, managers volunteered negative views of urban workers, but when asked point-blank whether they saw a difference between city and suburban workers, answered no. We suspect, therefore, that many of these comments simply reflect respondents' attempts to provide socially desirable answers.

As table 6.1 indicates, a small minority of respondents even indicated that the inner-city workforce was better than the suburban workforce. The typical reason given for this ranking was that suburban workers—particularly young people—are more privileged and do not need to work as much as lower-income inner-city workers. The result was a lower work ethic and higher turnover among the suburban workers. Such responses occurred in all four metropolitan areas, particularly among businesses offering low paid or menial work. For instance, manufacturers based in Lawrence and Lowell were quite comfortable with inner-city residents—in these cases, immigrants and Latinos—as a low wage, hard-working labor force, despite making negative comments about inner-city life. The white male manager of a sporting goods store in a western suburb of Detroit, similarly, remarked: "[City workers] might be more motivated, they might be harder workers, more willing to do things for you. . . . They maybe do menial tasks, you know, take out the trash type of, physical labor type of things that some of our suburban employees might be against or, for instance, 'Oh, I don't cut the lawns at home, I'm not going to cut the lawns here,' type of thing."

However, quite a few employers attributed this superior work ethic to a desperate need for work derived from the financial exigencies of single parenthood, tying a positive evaluation of work ethic to a negative evaluation of city workers' character and family life. Moreover, these comments were largely limited to employers hiring for low-wage retail, service, and manufacturing jobs, meaning that the relevant suburban comparison group was primarily teens and very young adults.

In sum, employers in all four metropolitan areas viewed the inner-city workforce with a jaundiced eye. The incidence of such responses was higher among employers located in the city. Although skill deficits were frequently noted, the range of other attributes attached to the perception of inner-city workers, most notably whether or not they are black, suggests that inner-city residence broadcasts a negative signal over and above the actual skill level of the individuals involved.

How Perceptions Translate into Decisions: Location and Hiring

Employers' perceptions of space are particularly important to the extent that they shape their actions—chiefly, decisions about business location and recruiting or hiring. We do not observe behavior longitudinally, but we did gather information on the nature, rationale, and consequences of employer decisions. Our evidence for the relation between racially and class-tinged perceptions and actual location and hiring decisions remains primarily indirect.

Employer Perceptions and Location Decisions

How do employer perceptions of various localities color their location decisions? The In-Depth Employer Survey oversampled employers who reported a move in the last ten years, and asked them additional questions about a move. Thirty-six percent reported a past move (with four out of five of the moves after 1979), and 38 percent reported contemplating or planning a move; because of substantial overlap between the two categories, a total of 42 percent either had moved or were planning to do so.

However, most movers stayed within a particular type of area—for example, moving within the central city or from one suburban location to another. Table 6.2 examines the smaller 12 percent (twenty firms) that crossed from one type of location to another, organized by their point of origin. Confirming the results from the larger Telephone Survey analyzed by Moss and Tilly in chapter 10 of this volume, we find that firms that started out in the central city were almost twice as likely to leave as the average; suburban firms were one-third as likely to leave. Comparing movers' destinations with the original locational distribution of movers and nonmovers combined, we see that though 42 percent of firms started out in the central cities, only 10 percent of movers went

TABLE 6.2   *Firms That Moved, by Original Location and Destination*

| | As Percentage of Total | Percentage Who Moved | Of Those Who Moved, Percentage Who Moved to | | | |
			Primary Central City	Other Central City	Other Suburb	Row Totals
Original location						
Primary central city	42	22	—	6	94	72
Other central city	15	4	0	—	100	25
Other suburb	44	4	67	33	—	75
Total	100	12	10	10	80	172
Column totals	172	20	2	2	16	

Source: Multi-City Study of Urban Inequality 1994.
Note: "Other central city" also includes any municipality other than the primary central city that has a black population of 30 percent or more. In this table, "movers" include only those who moved from one type of locality to another (for example, from the primary central city to the suburbs). We include a small number of firms that have not moved but have an explicit plan to move in the near future.

there. Conversely, 80 percent of movers went to suburbs without high minority populations, even though only 44 percent of firms started in such suburbs. Table 6.2 documents the flow of firms from central city to suburbs, particularly to whiter suburbs.

So far the findings are familiar. The in-depth interviews also gave employers the opportunity to talk about their reasons for moving. Most movers gave standard business reasons that have little to do with perceptions of neighborhoods: needs for a larger space or lower rents or taxes; consolidation of scattered operations after downsizing; need for better access to transportation. But about one in seven of those moving or planning a move (eleven out of seventy-three) raised "inner city" issues in explaining the firm's decision to move or choice of destination. While this group represents a small minority of movers, their concerns are of interest as one contributor to location decisions.

At all firms in this small group, respondents raised issues of crime or related environmental issues of vandalism, trash, and economic class. For example, the white personnel director of a food processing firm that recently moved from one suburban location to another said that, although they looked at sites in Detroit, "We realized that we didn't want to move to Detroit. . . . For all the reasons about Detroit. I mean I know people myself that own businesses in Detroit. One in particular the guy was killed walking into his building."

Crime, class, and location quality were often linked together in ways that were objectively and subjectively correlated with race. In Atlanta, for instance, a white personnel officer at a household repair service that moved from the East Point area commented, "See, East Point was starting to get a more . . . higher crime rate. . . . The further south you go the worse it gets." Of course, the racial composition also becomes more black the farther south you go in the Atlanta metro area. In a statement we reported earlier in the chapter, a white supervisor at a Detroit-area retail administrative headquarters endorsed her firm's move from Southfield (adjacent to Detroit, 29 percent black and rising) to Livonia (0.3 percent black) by commenting that Southfield is "kind of going downhill." In the Los Angeles area, the Anglo owner of a bookkeeping and tax service explained that he had left Bell Gardens, a community that experienced a 61 percent decline in its white population and is now 88 percent Latino, to move to nearby Downey because "Downey is a nicer city than Bell Gardens is in my opinion. . . . Downey was pulling me because it had a higher economic standard than Bell Gardens did." None of these statements indicates that racial antipathy itself motivated a move, but all represent antipathy toward the *communities* in which blacks and Latinos reside.

In two cases, respondents raised workforce issues in addition to concerns about crime and class in general. The case of a financial research firm that relocated from the LAX airport area to Orange County, over 30 miles away, as told by an Asian American manager, is particularly interesting:

Respondent: [At the LAX office] a lot of them just kind of lived in the Inglewood area and that office mix was ninety-five percent black. . . . That work environment and that work attitude is night and day from this, this office. . . .

Interviewer: What do you mean?

Respondent: Just . . . you know coming to work, doing your work. There every rule, every policy was challenged. . . .

Interviewer: Why do you think it was different there from here?

Respondent: I think I . . . the employees I had, were, like I said were ninety-five percent black. It was their culture. I mean I really truly believe it was their culture.

When the company decided to move, the manager continued,

They narrowed it down here, this location, and there was a place in Glendale. . . . I said we need to like to [go to] a mall. . . . If I go to the mall, I will let you know, I can tell what kind of clientele shops there. Depending on what kind of clientele shops there, they have to live there and we'll figure out what kind of work source we're going to have. So . . . the senior vice president and my boss, the vice president, went to the [local] mall. I saw the second floor, so I said, "OK, I can hire from this place." 'Cause you know the people that were walking around . . . they were predominantly white but they still were a mixture of . . . other races. . . . And the way those people were dressed you could kind of tell they were educated. They weren't gang-related or street . . . you could just tell.

This narrative is quite dramatic, but it is also exceptional in our data. Paralleling the paucity of accounts of workforce-driven avoidance of the inner city as a business location, among businesses originally located in central cities the correlation between making or planning a move and expressing concern about the inner-city workforce is a scant 0.02. The correlation between moving and voicing concerns about crime is a slightly higher 0.04. The Anglo production manager of a manufacturing firm in Lawrence, predominantly Latino and the poorest community in Massachusetts, contrasted crime and workforce issues succinctly:

> *Respondent:* Right now [our location is] an issue . . . for us. It's all crack houses and prostitutes out here. You look out, right, . . . I'll guarantee you'll see somebody out there. And it's tough for us right now . . . bringing customers in . . .
>
> *Interviewer:* . . . What about in terms of getting qualified workers in the area . . . how is that?
>
> *Respondent:* Ahh . . . that hasn't been too, too difficult.

Indeed, this manufacturer, paying seven-dollar-an-hour entry wages, relies heavily on Lawrence's predominantly Latino workforce, who have few economic alternatives.

The eleven movers who attributed their moves (at least in part) to inner-city problems do not tell the full story. We asked about the most recent move, but some firms had an earlier history of multiple moves, branch plant closings, and/or shifts of production activity. Respondents at two large manufacturers in the Los Angeles area, for example, told of shutting down inner-city facilities. "It was never terribly efficient," the white manufacturing director at one of the companies remarked; "I think the work ethic was tough."

Moreover, for many firms the inner city was a nonissue because it simply was not on the map of possible locations. For instance, although Detroit is the geographic hub of southeastern Michigan, managers referred to Warren, Troy, and Livonia as "centrally located." The manufacturing human resource manager who called Warren central remarked, "We are probably as close to Detroit as you can get"; a law firm's senior partner called Troy "as close to everyone as we could be." The Latina controller of a West Los Angeles food manufacturer discussed plans to move to the southeast, near the city of Industry. When asked whether the company would consider South Central Los Angeles, located squarely between these two locations, she was clearly taken off guard:

> *Respondent:* No, I just know that it's, kind of like, not safe, safe area. That's all I know. And again, I don't think it's good for our industry or anything. If it's not safe for the employee . . . so you would be scared just to go to work. Just driving in those streets, so I think that is not a good idea at all.

> *Interviewer:* Do you think there would be hiring issues if you moved to, say, South Central?

> *Respondent:* Definitely. . . . Or maybe the people that would be in the area are not people that you want to work with you. You know what I am saying?

What of inner city–based businesses that choose not to move? We found three such groups. First, for smaller businesses and those tied to local clienteles (such as local merchants or banks), relocation is not an option. Second, a variety of employers, such as universities, government agencies, and nonprofits, have a strong commitment to their locations. The African American director of a Detroit social service agency stated, "Well, I suppose for our business, because it's a community service business and in part some of the stuff we do is to serve a distressed community, so it's probably a great . . . place to do business, yeah. I mean you're sitting right in the middle of your kind of customers." In fact, a federal agency had recently bucked the tide by relocating a suburban satellite office back into the city. "We'll never leave Detroit," an African American manager at the federal office stated flatly. "Congress doesn't like us to do that."

Third, some low-wage and/or environmentally deleterious industries found inner-city workforces and sites advantageous. This reminds us that business movement toward the inner cities does not necessarily represent a completely desirable trend: for example, a penal institution was one of the small number of firms moving to an inner-city location. The president of a manufacturing firm declared, "We will always be in Atlanta. . . . Our president was born and raised here in Atlanta"—but shortly afterward added, "In order to all of sudden decide you're going to manufacture somewhere else you run into a lot of legislative regulations, EPA issues, which now are more and more difficult." The CEO of a Detroit snack food manufacturer, who paid a black workforce from the neighborhood $5.63 an hour in 1994, summed up his situation by saying: "It's, like, I have this and it works, OK, and I'm able to make a profit at it, so why would I close that up? Even though there is some cost associated with being in Detroit that you may not have in another place."

To summarize our findings about firm relocations, in general our data reflect the well-known shift of low-end employment from central cities to suburbs. Only in a few cases did movers raise "inner city" issues to explain their move, and they primarily spoke of crime rather than workforce quality. But in other cases flight from the inner city predated the most recent move, or the inner city was simply overlooked in relocation decisions. Despite all this, a mixed group of businesses remain rooted in inner-city areas.

Employer Perceptions and Hiring

Modifications to employers' *hiring* strategies based on their perceptions of space were less visible than locational decisions in these data. While many employers' perceptual soliloquies included overt racism, few described active measures to avoid hiring workers from spaces they defined as less desirable. They may in fact have avoided taking such measures, since that would risk violating antidiscrimination laws. However, we suspect that some employers' silence amounts to the provision of socially acceptable answers. Striking evidence of this comes from the Telephone Employer Survey that served as the sampling frame for our in-depth interviews. When asked if they target particular neighborhoods for recruiting workers, 12 percent of employers replied "always," another 17 percent "sometimes," and 15 percent specified "rarely"; a slim majority of 55 percent said "never." But when asked if they *avoid* particular neighborhoods, 90 percent replied "never"—even though targeting some neighborhoods implies avoiding others.

One notable exception to the silence about spatially focused hiring was an employer in an organization in our sample that had sites across a county that reaches from the far north to the far south of Atlanta, encompassing most of the city itself. This employer presented an elaborate series of rationales for why he preferred to hire workers from the north, which he characterized as "wealthy," and is also predominantly white. Citing reasons primarily having to do with a higher rate of desperation "due to the socioeconomic background of south [county]" and lower skill level in applicants from the south (despite the fact that this organization had to train every worker they hired in the specialized skills required to do the job), he said that they weeded out fully 66 to 80 percent of the applicants from the south end, but they hired at least half of the north end applicants. His evaluation of southern applicants may have certainly been based on an objective appraisal of them compared to those from the north. Yet what was notable about his stance was that an applicant's address automatically determined her or his odds of passing the first screening: "So what we basically do is if we have forty applications from the south end, we'll try to screen them down to the best ten." Despite this selectivity in the south, he said, "We are always fighting in north [county] just to get the applications in." Consequently, applicants from the north got at least a stronger look, indicating that in the employment practices of this organization, space was a salient signal of employee desirability and a basis for hiring decisions.

Unlike this employer, who offered an above-market wage and was able to exercise a good deal of selectivity, most employers in every city drew their entry-level employees primarily from the immediate vicinity. Despite this, some employers did discuss their use of selective recruitment strategies that indirectly allowed them to avoid hiring employees from particular neighborhoods. Upon describing where they found workers to be most desirable, employers sometimes remarked that they relied on advertisements in the newspapers in those areas to recruit applicants. For example, a restaurant manager in College Park, a predominantly black southern suburb very close to Atlanta, complained about applicants from the local area. Since he was not impressed with these potential workers and was also uncomfortable with the amount of crime he said they attracted, this employer said he recently began to recruit workers from a white suburb about twenty miles farther south:

> I try now to run them [job advertisements] in a local paper instead of *Atlanta Journal Constitution* because you, you can actually select individual areas that you want to interview from. Like right now I have an ad running in the Newnan paper and I've got a really good turnout from it lately. You know, I ran an ad in the *Atlanta Journal Constitution* which is actually the most expensive paper you can run an ad in, I think [chuckle], and the turnout that you get may be minimal. And then again the turnout that you get may be from the other side of the city, and they just don't really know . . . "Why are you driving forty-five minutes to come to work for me?" You know, "Do you have" . . . you know . . . you're not really supposed to ask somebody if they have . . . you can ask them if they have reliable transportation or how they're going to get to work, but you're not really supposed to ask somebody if they have a car, blah blah blah and all that. "Are you on the bus line?"

Like this employer, who based some of his recruitment strategies and hiring decisions on the signals of space, many others in the suburbs sang the woes of public transportation in explaining why they advertised only in specific suburban newspapers rather than in the broader metropolitan dailies. Hiring practices that worked to change the racial balance of workplaces from minority to white, some suburban employers explained, were sometimes an unavoidable consequence of transportation problems for city residents. As one suburban Detroit employer with an all-white staff explained: "I think it's mainly geography. We advertise for our people mostly in the Macomb newspapers, because that's where we get the best results. We don't discriminate, but because of our distance from the city, where there's a larger black population, we hired from that area, but they find it difficult to get here." Eventually she discontinued any recruitment from majority-black areas, including the inner city. Unprompted, over one-third of Detroit employers—both suburban and urban—and many Atlanta employers alluded to city residents' difficulties with transportation. Since the need for transportation was so intertwined with the areas where workers lived, these perceived difficulties became a space-based signal to some employers about worker reliability.

Thus, by recruiting workers through newspapers in white suburban areas and counting out potential workers who relied on public transportation, some employers in all four cities in our sample acted on their perceptions of spatial patterns of race and class.

We must also note that in response to the ways they perceived space in its relationship to class and race, some employers took affirmative action in their hiring practices. A number of employers in each city remarked on how they actively attempted to recruit minority workers from various areas in an attempt to make their workforces reflect the demographic composition of their cities. Because of the substantial negativity imbued in employers' perceptions of workers from minority neighborhoods, we suspect that some proclamations of affirmative actions were, in part, simply more acceptable to make than admissions of discriminatory hiring practices. Yet the prevalence of these sentiments is still encouraging and reflects the fact that some employers use spatial targeting to attain diversity rather than avoid it.

Conclusion

In segregated urban America, race is a crucial factor determining people's conceptions of space—and employers are no exception to this generalization. For employers in Atlanta, Boston, Detroit, and Los Angeles, racial dividing lines, often closely correlated with class, are important perceptual demarcators. This is particularly true in Detroit, where the city-suburb line is paramount, and in Atlanta, where the north-south divide looms large. In Boston and Los Angeles, where concentrations of people of color and with low income are more dispersed and more multiethnic, employers have less crisp conceptions of what "inner city" means, and are more likely to simply ignore low-income, minority areas than to use them as a reference point.

Substantial minorities of employers across the metropolitan areas associate inner cities with crime and a lower quality workforce. Such conceptions surely have some objective basis—inner-city areas do have higher crime rates and lower average educational attainment—but other employers based in such communities criticize these views as overblown. Nonetheless, for many business decision-makers these negative views mark communities of color as undesirable places to locate and/or from which to recruit. For many business-based observers, these perceptions of the inner city are tied to race, class, and a variety of perceived urban ills, such as family breakdown, welfare dependency, and inadequate education.

Our evidence for actions flowing from such perceptions is considerably more limited. Perceived crime problems contribute to driving some employers away from black and Latino areas, and lead others to foreclose these communities as potential locations. However, the small number of respondents tying their moves to such concerns is overshadowed by a much larger (and overlapping) group citing traditional locational factors of cost and convenience. Examples of spatially selective hiring policies are even fewer in number. It seems likely that our data have captured only part of the actions driven by negative perceptions of black and Latino communities, and that some respondents are censoring or tailoring their responses toward greater social acceptability. Further research exploring the link between employer perceptions of space and employer actions within space would help determine whether the limited actions we have found accurately capture the true scope of this connection.

We gratefully acknowledge funding support from the Ford Foundation, Russell Sage Foundation, and Rockefeller Foundation. For research assistance, we thank Don Aldin, Tuck Bartholomew, Nancy Beale, Devon Johnson, Sherry Russ Lee, Michael Lichter, Julie Press, Cheryl Seleski, Bryan Snyder, and Susan Turner. We also thank Laurie Dougherty for research assistance and additional help in interpreting and offering key insights from the Boston data for this paper. Not least, we thank Larry Bobo, Sheldon Danziger, and Alice O'Connor for very helpful comments.

References

Bayor, Ronald H. 1996. *Race and the Shaping of Twentieth-Century Atlanta*. Chapel Hill: The University of North Carolina Press.

Clifford, Frank, and Anne C. Roark. 1991. "Racial Lines in County Blur But Could Return." *Los Angeles Times*, May 6, 1991, 1.

Darden, Joe T., Richard Child Hill, June Thomas, and Richard Thomas. 1987. *Detroit: Race and Uneven Development*. Philadelphia: Temple University Press.

Dougherty, Laurie. 1993. "Towards an Overview of the Economic History of the Greater Boston Consolidated Metropolitan Statistical Area Since World War II." Unpublished paper. University of Massachusetts, Boston, BUIRG Summer Project.

Farley, Reynolds, and William Frey. 1994. "Changes in the Segregation of Whites from Blacks During the 1980s: Small Steps Toward a More Racially Integrated Society." *American Sociological Review* 59(1): 23–45.

Farley, Reynolds, Howard Schuman, Suzanne Bianchi, Diane Colasanto, and Shirley Hatchett. 1978. "'Chocolate City, Vanilla Suburbs': Will the Trend Toward Racially Separate Communities Continue?" *Social Science Research* 7: 319–44.

Farley, Reynolds, Charlotte Steeh, Tara Jackson, Maria Krysan, and Keith Reeves. 1993. "Continued Racial Residential Segregation in Detroit: 'Chocolate City, Vanilla Suburbs' Revisited." *Journal of Housing Research* 4(1): 1–38.

Harrison, Bennett, and Jean Kluver. 1988. "Re-assessing the Massachusetts Miracle: An Analysis of Postindustrial Regional Restructuring." Department of Urban Studies and Planning, Massachusetts Institute of Technology. Unpublished paper.

Hill, Richard Child. 1984. "Economic Crisis and Political Response in the Motor City." In *Sunbelt/Snowbelt: Urban Development and Regional Restructuring*, edited by Larry Sawers and William K. Tabb. New York: Oxford University Press.

Holzer, Harry J. 1991. "The Spatial Mismatch Hypothesis: What Has the Evidence Shown?" *Urban Studies* 28(1): 105–22.

———. 1996. *What Employers Want: Job Prospects for Less-Educated Workers*. New York: Russell Sage Foundation.

Holzer, Harry J., and Keith Ihlanfeldt. 1996. "Spatial Factors and the Employment of Blacks at the Firm Level." Paper presented at the Multi-City Study of Urban Inequality conference on Residential Segregation, Social Capital, and Labor Markets. New York (February 8–9, 1996).

Ihlanfeldt, Keith. 1995. "Information on the Spatial Distribution of Job Opportunities Within Metropolitan Areas." Paper presented at Multi-City Study of Urban Inequality conference on Searching for Work, Searching for Workers. New York (September 28–29, 1995).

Ihlanfeldt, Keith. 1999. "The Geography of Economic and Social Opportunity Within Metropolitan Areas." In *Governance and Opportunity in Metropolitan America*, edited by Alan Altshuler, William Morrill, Harold Wolman, and Faith Mitchell. Washington, D.C.: National Academy Press.

lhlanfeldt, Keith, and Madelyn Young. 1994. "Intrametropolitan Variation in Wage Rates: The Case of Atlanta Fast Food Restaurant Workers." *Review of Economics and Statistics* 76: 425–33.

Jencks, Christopher, and Susan Mayer. 1990. "Residential Segregation, Job Proximity, and Black Job Opportunities." In *Inner City Poverty in the United States*, edited by Laurence E. Lind and Michael McGeary. Washington, D.C.: National Academy Press.

Kasarda, John D. 1993. "Inner-city Concentrated Poverty and Neighborhood Distress: 1970 to 1990." *Housing Policy Debate* 4(3): 253–302.

Kasinitz, Philip, and Jan Rosenberg. 1994. "Missing the Connection: Social Isolation and Employment on the Brooklyn Waterfront." Working Paper. Michael Harrington Center for Democratic Values and Social Change, Queens College, City University of New York.

Kirschenman, Joleen, and Kathryn M. Neckerman. 1991. "'We'd Love to Hire Them, But . . .': The Meaning of Race for Employers." In *The Urban Underclass*, edited by Christopher Jencks and Paul E. Peterson. Washington, D.C.: Brookings Institution.

Lukas, J. Anthony. 1985. *Common Ground: A Turbulent Decade in the Lives of Three American Families*. New York: Knopf.

Moss, Philip, and Chris Tilly. 1991. "Why Black Men Are Doing Worse in the Labor Market: A Review of Supply-Side and Demand-Side Explanations." Working paper. New York; Social Science Research Council Committee on the Urban Underclass.

———. 1993. "Why Aren't Employers Hiring More Black Men? Final Report." New York: Committee for Research on the Urban Underclass, Social Science Research Council.

———. 1996. "'Soft' Skills and Race: An Investigation of Black Men's Employment Problems." *Work and Occupations* 23(3): 252–76.

———. 2001. *Stories Employers Tell: Race, Skills, and Hiring in America*. New York: Russell Sage Foundation.

Neckerman, Katherine, and Joleen Kirschenman. 1991. "Hiring Strategies, Racial Bias, and Inner-City Workers." *Social Problems* 38(4): 801–15.

Porter, Michael E. 1994. "The Competitive Advantage of the Inner City." Unpublished paper. Harvard Business School.

Rutheiser, Charles. 1996. *Imagineering Atlanta. The Politics of Place in the City of Dreams*. London: Verso.

SEMCOG (Southeast Michigan Council of Governments). 1984. "Major Economic Activity in Southeast Michigan." Map. Detroit: SEMCOG.

Sjoquist, David. 1996. "Social Mismatch and Social Acceptability." Paper presented at the Multi-City Study on Urban Inequality conference. New York (May 30, 1996).

Soja, Edward, Rebecca Morales, and Goetz Wolff. 1983. "Urban Restructuring: An Analysis of Social and Spatial Change in Los Angeles." *Economic Geography* 59(2): 196–230.

Turner, Susan. 1996. "Barriers to a Better Break: Wages, Race, and Space in Metropolitan Detroit." Paper presented at the Multi-City Study of Urban Inequality conference on Residential Segregation, Social Capital, and Labor Markets. New York (February 8–9, 1996).

U.S. Department of Commerce. U.S. Bureau of the Census. 1988. *City and County Data Book*. Washington: U.S. Government Printing Office.

U.S. Department of Commerce. U.S. Bureau of the Census. 1994. *City and County Data Book*. Washington: U.S. Government Printing Office.

Waldinger, Roger, and Mehdi Bozorgmehr, eds. 1996. *Ethnic Los Angeles*. New York: Russell Sage Foundation.

Wayne State University (Center for Urban Studies/Michigan Metropolitan Information Center) and SEMCOG (Southeast Michigan Council of Governments). 1991. *1990 Census Community Profiles for Southeast Michigan*. Vol. 1: Macomb, Oakland, and Wayne Counties. Detroit: Wayne State University and SEMCOG.

Wilson, William Julius. 1987. *The Truly Disadvantaged: The Inner City, the Underclass, and Public Policy*. Chicago: University of Chicago Press.

Part III

7

RACIAL AND ETHNIC DIFFERENCES IN JOB SEARCHING IN URBAN CENTERS

Luis M. Falcón and Edwin Melendez

Most social and economic inequality across racial groups in American society is rooted in disparities in their position in the labor market. Labor market inequality has been a core concern of a large body of literature in sociology and economics. A substantial literature documents differences in labor market performance and rewards across racial and ethnic groups. These differences, it is argued, are largely due to differential human capital endowments across groups and/or to larger processes, such as shifts in the spatial distribution of jobs, and to discrimination (Baldwin and Johnson, 1996; Blackley 1990; Holzer 1994; Jencks 1991; Wilson 1983, 1988). A largely unexplored aspect of labor market inequality is how differences in job search patterns impact mobility opportunities for various racial and ethnic groups in urban areas. Assumptions, within the literature, on how the forces of supply and demand operate to allow workers and employers to connect tend to disregard social arrangements that may differ because of race and ethnicity. Because some of the most important aspects of the job-searching process are mediated by the social structure individuals participate in, these differences in the use of social structures may affect the way workers go about finding a job.

To the extent that the social forces shaping the labor market processes of various groups are embedded in racial and ethnic structures, it is important to understand their role. Social structures that are ethnically and racially bound may give shape to job search behavior and, in turn, provide varying opportunities to different groups (Marsden 1990). A potential outcome of differences in job search behavior could be differential opportunity that contributes to already existing labor market inequality. On the other hand, some of these differences in employment search patterns may not alter the overall distribution of labor market–based rewards across groups. As we will discuss later, the matching of workers to jobs is a complex process in which employers, and how they search for workers, also play a major part. Still, understanding the dynamics that surround labor market incorporation and how search patterns differ helps us understand how labor markets operate for the different racial and ethnic groups (Sassen 1995).

Analyses of post–labor market entry position of racial-ethnic minorities show labor market disadvantage, but to what extent is this related to factors other than labor market performance? Social dynamics induced by foreign birth, recent immigration, racial dynamics, lack of English-language skills, or social networks may well impact the path taken to enter the labor market or to search for a new job. Within groups, social bonds are established on the basis of ethnicity, race, and even social class, which may steer individuals to job slots otherwise inaccessible or even limit access to other sectors of the job market. These factors are typically disregarded when examining labor market position.

We know little about the dynamics surrounding employment searches among racial minorities, particularly among recent immigrants, and very few studies have made minority-majority comparisons. Many studies have shown that the use of social networks is the most common method used in an employment search (Green, Tigges, and Browne 1995; Granovetter 1973, 1983, 1995b; Montgomery 1991, 1992, 1994; Falcón 1995; Marsden and Hulbert 1988). More than half the jobs in the U.S. economy are found through personal contacts: family, friends, or acquaintances. Granovetter (1995b) assigns a major role to social contacts—in particular, having the right contact in the right place at the right time.

That is not to say that the search process that workers engage is the sole determinant of outcomes related to the search. The search to fill a job slot is a dual process involving both workers and employers. Workers engage in a series of activities, such as finding sources of information, securing needed references, figuring out where to search, and determining what resources may be available. Methods of job searching are not used uniformly across groups. If we conceive of search methods as mechanisms to access information about a job, then no method is without limitations. By their own nature, most methods of recruitment will tend to exclude some potentially eligible individuals. For example, workers employed in niche occupations will tend to draw other workers within their own network into available slots (Waldinger 1994, 1995). In many instances, ethnic ties permeate the social networks and work to the exclusion of nonethnic members. Workers who are disconnected from networks with access to that information will not be able to make use of the opportunity. Newspaper advertisements will tend to exclude those with low literacy or those who are unable to speak the language. Help-wanted ads posted on storefronts or community bulletins will exclude anyone not frequenting the area. Screening by formal intermediaries will select out anyone not meeting specific educational or experience criteria.

This is largely because employers recruit for workers in ways that are convenient and, in most cases, appropriate to the type of skills they are seeking (Melendez and Falcón 1998). To the extent that groups differ in socioeconomic characteristics and occupational distribution, we should expect differences to exist in the way they approach a job search. Accordingly, these seemingly separate processes—searching for a job and searching for workers—are but two sides of a process of matching workers to jobs.

Another important aspect in this process is the idea of social networks as a form of social capital (Coleman 1988; Waldinger 1994). It is not the social networks themselves that are a form of social capital, but the ability to mobilize those networks and their resources (Portes 1995). In this context, the use of different types of social networks by racial-ethnic groups may reflect varying levels of social resources. Social position as well as the strength of an individual's social ties to others affect access to information about occupations and, thus, the amount of social capital that individuals are able to mobilize.

The notion that the social capital associated with social networks can vary across individuals and groups is important. It is known that racial and ethnic groups in the U.S. labor market differ not only in labor market outcomes but also in the resources they bring to the market. We see the way individuals approach a job search as indicative of the resources available to them. Examining how labor market outcomes relate to job search processes may shed further light on how inequality gets structured within the labor market.

This chapter uses data from the Multi-City Study of Urban Inequality to examine racial and ethnic differences in the process of searching for and obtaining a job. We place emphasis on the emerging patterns across racial groups in the use of various job search strategies. Further, we examine how ethnic-racial differences in the job search process relates to the labor market disadvantage of minority groups. We begin by looking at the characteristics of job searchers in the four surveyed cities and how they carry out job searches. We examine search strategies in detail, highlighting differences across groups and cities. We focus on the role of social contacts and their characteristics, and how they play out in job searches for the various ethnic groups. The last section deals with the impact of various job search characteristics on a series of labor market outcomes. Among these are the effects of finding jobs through a social network contact, the effect of the type of social ties to the social network contact, and the effect of using a same-race network contact.[1]

Our findings suggest that there are significant and important differences in the way the various racial-ethnic groups organize job searches. Blacks, Latinos, and Asians differ from whites in the use of social networks, intermediaries, and direct contact with employers. Social networks, while an important job search method for all groups, are particularly important in helping Latinos and Asians find jobs. Social networks tend to be highly segregated by race.[2] Finding a job through social networks and some of the associated characteristics of these networks have negative implications for black and Latino workers in general. These findings are important in that they suggest the presence of entry-level mechanisms associated with the job search process that relate to the placement of minority workers in the labor market in a way that is different from that of whites.

Racial and Ethnic Differences in the Use of Search Methods

The Multi-City Study collected a considerable amount of data on the characteristics of the process of searching for a job. But the study design limited the data collection on job search patterns to those respondents who had searched for a job during the five years prior to data collection. Thus, the sample of job searchers in the study is really a sample of recent searchers. There are some differences between the subsample of recent searchers and the general Multi-City Study sample. Because the recent searchers tend to be younger, they are also better educated, but they also have less experience in the labor market and, for some, the recorded search is their first entry into the labor force. In addition, in Los Angeles and Boston, a noticeable number of the recent searchers are foreign-born, reflecting the rapidly growing immigrant population in these two cities.

The data across cities reflect, in general, a higher percentage of recent searchers among blacks and Latinos than among whites (see table 7.1). Within blacks, recent searchers ranged from 48 percent in Atlanta to as high as 67 percent in Boston. Around 60 percent of Latinos in Boston and in Los Angeles had searched for a job in the last five years. In contrast, among whites the percentage reporting having searched was lowest in Atlanta, at 41 percent, and highest in Los Angeles, at 49.2 percent.

TABLE 7.1   *Selected Characteristics of Job Searchers*

	Detroit	Atlanta	Boston	Los Angeles
Percentage of group that searched during previous five years				
Non-Hispanic white	45.4	41.7	47.2	49.2
Black	51.1	48.5	66.7	48.3
Latino			60.7	57.6
Asian				41.4
Percentage with access to car				
Non-Hispanic white	97.2	98.1	92.7	91.4
Black	77.9	74.2	41.1	83.6
Latino			61.9	68.1
Asian				78.8
Average longest commute in minutes				
Non-Hispanic white	45.1	46.7	45.1	44.6
Black	52.5	51.1	47.7	50.2
Latino			44.6	50.2
Asian				40.3
Reservation wage				
Non-Hispanic white	$10.50	$10.40	$12.70	$11.99
Black	7.92	8.09	9.00	11.21
Latino			9.30	7.00
Asian				15.34

Source: Multi-City Study of Urban Inequality.

The table presents additional information on selected characteristics of the respondents during their last search: whether they had access to a car while searching, the average longest commute they were willing to undertake, and the lowest hourly wage they were willing to accept. In all cities, blacks, Latinos, and Asians reported having less access to their own transportation than whites did. The percentage with access to a car while searching was particularly low in Boston (41 percent), where the black population is highly concentrated in a limited number of neighborhoods. Nonetheless, black job searchers across all four cities indicated a willingness to engage in a longer commute than whites, Latinos, or Asians. Minimum hourly wage expectations were fairly consistent across cities. Asians in Los Angeles reported the highest reservation wage, at about $15 per hour. The reservation hourly wage of blacks and Latinos was consistently below that of whites. Overall, blacks and Latinos showed a higher presence among those searching for jobs and a willingness to travel longer distances and to accept lower wages than did whites or Asians.

Is There a Pattern in the Way the Groups Search?

Most of the literature on the use of search methods by job seekers has focused on the use of friends and families as employment contacts. Such contacts, or "strong ties," are generally the preferred search methods because they are inexpensive and can provide access to jobs not yet open to other job seekers. However, job seekers use various methods to secure employment, including direct contact of employers or the use of formal intermediaries. The number of search methods used by job seekers and the combination of these methods vary by the labor market status of the person (employed or unemployed), their individual characteristics (sex, age, race), and other factors. A growing concern in the literature is that the quality of the personal networks and lack of access to the most effective intermediaries limit the opportunities of disadvantaged populations in securing adequate employment. (Portes and Sensenbrenner 1993; Menjivar 1997; Greenwell et al. 1997; Falcón 1995). Differences in access to social capital between whites and racial minorities may result in different outcomes of pursuing a particular search strategy. The objective of this section is to compare the search strategies used by different racial groups in Boston, Los Angeles, and Atlanta, and to identify distinctive patterns of searches.

We begin by proposing a categorization of search methods that is conceptually based on the strength of the relationship between the job seeker and the person or institution mediating the contact with the employer. Close friends and family social networks are generally regarded as "strong ties" in the sense that there is a close familiar relationship between the job seeker and the contact mediating access to either information or to the employer. Although well positioned, contacts or acquaintances in a firm who have a distant relationship to the job seeker ("weak ties") could be instrumental in securing better employment opportunities. Direct contact of employers or sending resumes responding to want ads or newspaper advertising can be regarded as an open-market search based on general information available to the public and embedding no direct ties to firm-specific contacts or to employers. The use of intermediaries—such as state, private, or temporary employment agencies, unions, and schools—falls somewhere between the use of social networks and the open-market strategies in the sense that these agents mediate employment information and access to employers in a way similar to social networks but the social ties may not be present. Intermediaries often provide other complementary activities to the search, such as referrals, screening through drug or skill testings, certification of competency, or needed references.

The effectiveness of search methods is directly related to how employers seek and recruit new workers. Friends and family contacts are more effective in providing information about job openings to the extent that employers use their workers to recruit new employees. Current employees can provide more reliable information and, in effect, screen out prospective employees better than other sources of recruitment can. Although recruitment through employees might be more effective for entry-level jobs or in some occupations (such as blue-collar jobs), more specialized personnel may require targeted recruitment or screening. "Headhunting" firms, specialized and targeted advertising, or college fairs are better sources for contacting experienced professionals or those with the necessary credentials. Available data from the Current Population Survey indicate that the number of job seekers using public employment agencies has declined, while the use of private and temporary employment agencies has increased. This trend is likely to be related to the employers' need to screen applicants for entry-level jobs more thoroughly. Some intermediaries are more effective than others in certifying or assessing occupational and social skills.

Respondents in the Multi-City Study were asked which out of a series of methods they had used to search for a job during their last job search. In every city except Detroit, this list included a total of eleven different search methods.[3] Table 7.2 presents data on the four cities showing the percentage within each racial group that used a specific search method during their last job search.

The various racial groups present clear differences in the way they approach the labor market when looking for work. These differences are consistent across all four cities. As suggested by research cited earlier, by far the most commonly used method of looking for work is to use friends and family as contacts. Consistently across cities and racial groups, about three out of every four respondents indicated having contacted friends in their last job search. In contrast, the use of relatives (or closer ties) is much lower than the use of friends—particularly among whites and blacks. Latinos, on the other hand, report the highest use of relatives as a job search method of any group in both Los Angeles and Boston: 62.5 percent and 53.3 percent, respectively.

While the use of newspaper ads as a search method is common across all groups, direct-contact methods, such as responding to want ads or walking in to inquire about job openings, are less common and vary noticeably across groups. When compared with blacks and Latinos, whites are less likely to use want ads or walk-ins as a search method. While these differences are important, they may have much to do with the type of job these groups are generally seeking and how these jobs are made available or recruited for.

347

TABLE 7.2   Methods Used During Last Search, by Race of Respondent and City

	Detroit		Atlanta		Boston			Los Angeles			
Method	Non-Hispanic White	Black	Non-Hispanic White	Black	Non-Hispanic White	Black	Latino	Non-Hispanic White	Black	Latino	Asian
Friends	64.8%	74.3%	74.0%	74.9%	70.1%	70.6%	64.3%	76.8%	74.3%	81.7%	74.2%
Relatives	—	—	34.5	47.5	49.3	50.9	54.2	46.1	46.0	58.6	47.8
Newspaper	70.8	71.0	66.5	72.0	75.8	81.7	58.2	69.1	67.7	60.7	74.6
Want ads	20.3	44.6	21.6	28.0	22.3	45.6	44.4	25.1	31.7	38.3	23.2
Walk-in	—	—	38.3	61.9	44.6	68.4	61.0	48.0	52.6	58.6	20.4
Union	4.3	9.4	2.8	6.5	3.8	9.8	3.4	4.5	4.8	5.5	0.7
State agency	9.2	33.3	12.3	32.6	20.7	29.2	21.5	18.0	21.2	13.9	4.2
Private service	—	—	14.3	15.2	20.6	15.8	14.2	24.8	21.7	5.7	8.8
Temp agency	—	—	18.5	28.1	10.9	25.4	12.7	21.0	30.2	16.5	3.2
School placement	11.8	18.3	15.9	17.4	14.0	16.7	5.3	12.3	12.3	7.5	13.7
Sent resume	—	—	61.8	59.4	68.9	68.8	35.5	70.0	59.9	32.7	37.8
Other	36.6	21.4	—	—	—	—	—	—	—	—	—

Source: Multi-City Study of Urban Inequality.

The next set of methods includes such formal mechanisms of employment searches as state agencies, private placement services, and unions. The latter are, by far, still used more frequently by blacks than any other group. Similarly, blacks also report the highest use of state employment agencies in all cities. Differences between whites and blacks in the use of private placement services are noticeable but not large. Temporary service agencies, however, show a much higher percentage of usage among blacks when compared with all other groups. Relative to blacks and to whites, Latinos and Asians tend to underutilize the employment agencies when looking for work.

The last two methods, school placement and sending a resume, are credential-based. Their pattern of use reflects the differences in education and the type of jobs sought by the different groups. Given the lower educational level of Latinos, they are not frequent users of either of these two methods. Among whites and even blacks, however, it is fairly common to send resumes as a method of seeking employment.

Most respondents used a variety of methods. Some methods, like newspapers, are available to most respondents; others, like placement services or sending resumes, require certain resources, and their use is more specific to the group. As suggested earlier, the deployment of a particular search strategy may correspond to the characteristics of both the searchers and the jobs being sought. The question we pose is whether this differential use of search methods converges into a consistent set of search strategies. In turn, are these search strategies used differently by the different groups?

The methods most frequently used by the survey respondents were related to direct contact and to social network–based strategies. However, there are some significant differences in the intensity of use of these strategies and the priorities assigned to them by the different groups. For example, use of direct contact or walk-in methods were much lower for whites in Atlanta, Boston, and Los Angeles than for blacks and Latinos in those cities. Latinos showed the least use of multiple search methods and were more dependent on social networks, particularly in Los Angeles. They also showed the lowest use of sending a resume to employers, a search method often used by technicians, office workers, and professionals. Intermediaries, unions, state and temporary employment agencies, and schools were most important for blacks in all cities, while whites had a relatively high use of private placement agencies. Latinos in Boston and Los Angeles and Asians in Los Angeles exhibited a relatively low use of intermediaries. Latinos, in particular, used significantly less school placement and unions in Boston and private services in Los Angeles. These methods were often used in conjunction with other methods or bundled into broader search strategies.

TABLE 7.3   *Grouping of Search Strategies*

	Atlanta		Boston		
Factor	Non-Hispanic White	Black	Non-Hispanic White	Black	Latino
One	State agencies Private services Temp agencies Send resume Newspapers	State agencies Private services Temp agencies Send resume Newspapers	Friends Relatives School referral Send resume	Unions State agencies Private services Temp agencies School referral	State agencies Send resume Want ads Walk-in Newspapers
Two	Walk-in Want ads	Friends Relatives	Want ads Walk-in	Send resume Want ads Walk-in Newspapers	Friends Relatives
Three	Friends Relatives School referral	Unions School referral	State agencies Private services Temp agencies Newspapers	Friends Relatives	Unions Private services Temp agencies
Four	Unions	Walk-in Want ads	Unions Newspapers School referral	Unions	School referral

Source: Multi-City Study of Urban Inequality.

This may include, for instance, direct contact and want ads, school placement and sending resumes, and searching through information and contacts provided by friends and relatives.

We used factor analysis to determine whether there was a consistent pattern to the use of different search methods by racial and ethnic groups.[4] A factor analysis model was estimated for each racial and ethnic group within cities, with no restrictions imposed on the number of factors to be produced by the procedure. Thus, the total number of factors and the combination of search methods for each group responded completely to the convergence of methods into factors representing search strategies for each group. The results of this exercise are reported in table 7.3, where the distribution of the various search methods within factors is presented in the order in which they entered. In some instances, a method is loaded high on more than one factor (.30 or higher). We have allowed, in such cases, for the method to be represented in more than one search strategy. In doing this exercise, we expect that the results would be consistent with our earlier argument as to the grouping of search methods into consistent patterns of search strategies.

The results of the factor analysis suggest important differences in the way these search strategies come together for the different racial-

Los Angeles			
Non-Hispanic White	Black	Latino	Asian
State agencies Private services Temp agencies	Want ads Walk-in Newspapers	State agencies Private services Temp agencies School referral	State agencies Private services Temp agencies School referral Send resume Walk-in
Want ads Walk-in	State agencies Private services Temp agencies Unions Send resume	Friends Relatives	Want ads Newspapers
Friends Relatives Send resume	Friends Relatives	Send resume Want ads Walk-in Newspapers	Friends Relatives
Unions Newspapers School referral	School referral	Unions	Unions

ethnic groups. The first search strategy for whites in Boston links social networks (the use of friends and relatives) to school referrals and sending resumes, which are associated with the credential-based segment of the labor market. The connection between these search methods suggests that, for whites, social networks may yield contacts to the college-educated or at least white-collar segment of the labor market. This association is also present for whites—with some variation—in Los Angeles and in Atlanta, but loads as a third factor in the model. In contrast, the social networks of blacks, Latinos, and Asians are not associated in any way with a strategy that includes schools or resume-based searches. For these groups, friends and relatives constitute a separate strategy in each of the three cities.

The second search strategy for whites in Los Angeles, Atlanta, and Boston establishes a relationship between the use of want ads and the direct contact of employers through walk-ins. This is clearly an open-market search strategy where there are no individuals or institutions mediating the relationship between the job seekers and employers. The last two factors for whites in Los Angeles, Atlanta, and Boston group together different sets of intermediaries, but there is no clear pattern across cities. In Los Angeles and Atlanta, friends and relatives enter with credential-based methods such as sending resumes and school re-

ferrals, just like in Boston. The use of unions appears by itself in Atlanta, and together with newspapers and school-referrals in Boston and
Los Angeles. This last grouping suggests that some of the school referrals are from trade schools, which is consistent with searching through
unions and newspaper ads. The search strategies for whites come together in a fairly consistent pattern to the one described earlier in the
chapter when examining the use of individual methods.

In general, the bundling of search strategies by racial minorities is
consistent with that of whites. For blacks, as for whites, the use of the
formal intermediaries—state agencies, private placement, and temporary agencies—appears as a well-defined strategy used consistently
across cities. This is also true for Latinos in Los Angeles, but not as
clear in Boston. In Boston, the use of state agencies by Latinos is associated with open-market search strategies, while private and temporary
agencies are associated with the use of unions. These associations suggest that for Latinos in Boston, state agencies provide information and
general employment referrals that are similar in quality to open-market
direct contact of employers or finding job listings in help-wanted ads
or newspapers. Considering all ethnic groups and cities, unions and
schools seem to be a different type of intermediary than private, state,
and temporary agencies. The major distinction between these sets of
intermediaries is that unions and schools may provide skill certifica-
tions and screening, while agencies may provide only the job placement.
Also, unions and schools may serve more specialized employment
niches than the employment agencies. Finally, in contrast to whites,
using social networks (friends and relatives) is a distinctly well defined
strategy for all the minority groups.

The results of the factor analysis are consistent with our theoretical
expectations regarding the combination of search methods into distinct
search strategies. The variations by ethnic group observed in the three
cities are consistent with differing patterns of access to social resources
(information, networks) and services (private and state agencies), with
differing qualities of social networks, and with corresponding differences in the economic sectors in which the groups search for employment.

To answer the question of how distinctive are the search strategies
of whites, blacks, Latinos, and Asians within cities, we re-estimated the
search strategy factors at the city level (rather than within racial groups),[5]
which allows us to contrast the groups to the general city pattern. The
factor analysis creates a set of factor variables (as many as there are
factors) (Kleimbaum, Kupper, and Muller 1988; StataCorp 1997). Each of
these factors were described earlier as representing a search strategy
(such as open market or direct contact). Each of these factors is a vari-

able with a value for each case in the sample, which is a weighted sum of the values of the variables used to create the factor (the actual search methods). Using this weighted variable, the factor procedure can then estimate regression-based scores for each search strategy within cities which indicate the magnitude of use of the strategy (StataCorp 1997). The four regression score variables—one for each search strategy—were then each transformed into an index to facilitate interpretation.[6] The resulting indexes have a mean of about 100 and a standard deviation of 10. We then compared the mean score for blacks, Latinos, and Asians to that of whites and noted any significant differences in means. Our interpretation of the scores is that values above the mean of 100 are suggestive of greater use of the particular strategy, while values below 100 indicate underutilization of the strategy. The overutilization or underutilization is relative to the general use of the strategy within the city as a whole. These results are presented in table 7.4, in which the minority groups are contrasted to whites and minority scores shown to be significantly different from that of whites are noted with asterisks.

The results are consistent with our earlier discussion. When compared to whites, black, Latino, and Asian job searchers are more likely to use open market–based search strategies in all three cities. The other significant differences between black and white searchers are in the use of friends and relatives in Atlanta and in the use of intermediaries in Los Angeles. Latinos, on the other hand, are very different from whites in their search strategies. When compared to whites in their respective cities, Latinos in Boston and in Los Angeles are more likely to rely on open-market strategies and friends and relatives and less likely to use intermediaries or credential-based strategies. Asians in Los Angeles are also significantly different from whites in Los Angeles in that they use every major strategy less than whites do.

Are There Differences in the Way They Find Jobs?

Differences across racial groups in the methods employed in a job search and in the frequency of use of the search methods are clearly important, but the actual job-producing methods present even more interesting results. In general, there are noticeable differences between blacks and whites in the methods that produced a job, and Latinos stand apart with a radically different pattern. As shown in figure 7.1, for most groups, the modal category for the method producing the last job was friends and relatives. Latinos present the extreme case, with 67.9 percent in Los Angeles and 76 percent in Boston indicating they found their last job through personal contacts. Only in a few instances did Latinos find jobs

TABLE 7.4   *Relative Use of Grouped Search Strategies, by Ethnic Group and City*

	Friends and Relatives	Open Market	Intermediaries	Credential-Based
Atlanta				
White	99.0	97.5	100.2	100.4
Black	100.7*	101.9*	99.9	100.1
Boston				
White	99.7	97.9	98.9	102.0
Black	98.7	101.3*	101.3*	101.1
Latino	101.5*	101.2*	100.1	97.5*
Los Angeles				
White	99.0	99.1	102.6	102.6
Black	99.9	101.8*	103.4	100.1*
Latino	103.3*	100.8*	97.7*	99.1*
Asian	96.0*	97.4*	97.1*	98.9*

Source: Multi-City Study of Urban Inequality.
*Significantly different at $p < .05$ from the score for whites.

through a personal contact other than a friend or a relative (3.7 percent in Los Angeles and 6.5 percent in Boston). Both whites and blacks report high use of personal contacts, but high percentages also report having used newspapers or other methods.

For two of the minority groups—Latinos and Asians—relatives or friends seem to provide a link to a job more frequently than other methods. For Latinos, between 60 and 70 percent of jobs came about through relatives or friends, and for Asians it was about 55 percent. For black workers, only about 40 percent of the jobs found by searchers came through a relative or friend, placing them at a level closer to that of whites. Moreover, for most minority searchers the person who produces the job tends to be a close personal contact rather than someone beyond the searcher's immediate circle of family and friends—in Granovetter's terms, a "strong social tie." In figure 7.2, the relationship to their contact for those respondents who found their last job through a personal contact is presented. Latinos, particularly those in Boston, stand out with a higher proportion than any other group of personal contacts who are relatives—35 percent in Los Angeles and 56 percent in Boston. Whites have the highest proportion of contacts outside the relative or friend categories. In contrast, very few of the racial minorities—blacks, Latinos, or Asians—reported finding a job through a contact beyond the acquaintance category. However, 12.5 percent of whites in Los Angeles, 8.8 percent in Boston, and 7.9 percent in Atlanta reported that access to the job was provided by someone other than a friend, relative,

FIGURE 7.1   *Method Used to Find Last Job, by City and Group*

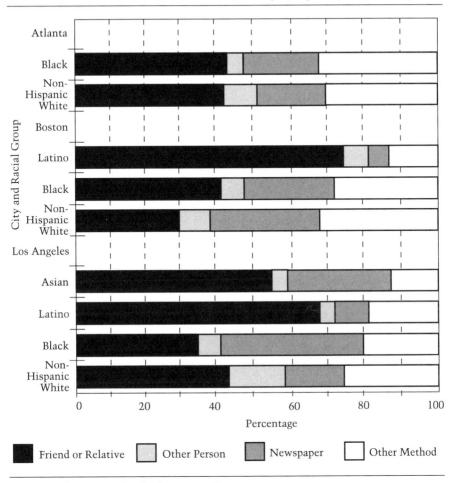

Source: Multi-City Study of Urban Inequality.

or acquaintance. In general, Latinos, Asians, and blacks (to some extent) are more likely than whites to find a job because of a "strong tie." Even though whites are less likely to enter a job through personal contacts, when they do, they seem to have a broader range of contacts—particularly beyond acquaintances—than the immediate circle of family and friends.

The importance of social networks to employment searches in this sample cannot be overemphasized. Networks matter in that they provide access to jobs for a substantial number of job searchers in every

FIGURE 7.2   *Relationship to Job Contact*

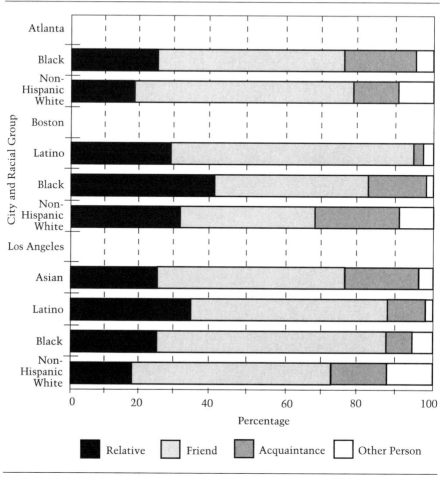

Source: Multi-City Study of Urban Inequality.

racial group. The groups, however, display important differences in their access to networks and how extensive these networks are. Groups with high numbers of recent immigrants, like Latinos, tend to rely heavily on networks of kinship and friends and seem to have limited access to anyone beyond this range. In a city like Boston, where half the Latino population arrived during the 1980s, we find an overwhelming use of personal ties in employment search and entry into a job. The question of what the ultimate impact of these differential patterns is on labor market outcomes still remains.

Do the Personal Contacts of Minority and Nonminority Workers Differ?

Finding jobs through personal contacts was the norm for Latinos and Asians in the Multi-City Study sample. While blacks and whites are also heavy users of personal contacts, they do not present as extreme a pattern as Latinos. Still, all three minority groups present a limited range of personal contacts when compared with whites. This point gets accentuated when we consider the type of assistance that was provided by the personal contact that led to the job. Figure 7.3 presents the type of help provided by the personal contact for those respondents who found their last job though a friend, relative, acquaintance, or other person. As can be seen, these personal contacts serve primarily as sources of information on the job or as intermediaries between the prospective employee and the employer. The former is particularly important for blacks—66 percent of blacks in Los Angeles, 56 percent in Boston, and 57 percent in Atlanta indicated that the contact had helped them by providing information on the job.

The other important result is the high proportion of Latinos who received help in the form of the contact intervening with the employer. About 35 percent of Latinos in Los Angeles and 63 percent of Latinos in Boston received help by having the contact talk to the employer about their availability to work in a particular job. This is consistent with the literature on immigrant employment that suggests the existence of immigrant-driven networks within occupational niches in the labor market (Waldinger 1994, 1995; Kasinitz and Rosenberg 1996). Employees sometimes bring new workers to the workplace on their own initiative and other times at the urging of the employer. A final point is the difference between whites and the racial minorities in the ability to reach out to contacts who can actually hire them. About 17 percent of whites in Los Angeles, 12.4 percent in Boston, and 15 percent in Atlanta reported that the contact had actually hired them for a job. These proportions are, in most cases, about twice as high as those reported by blacks and Latinos in their respective cities. The ability to employ someone else is predicated on ownership or some level of control over a workplace. Because the minority networks are segregated and there is a lower probability of self-employment for both Latinos and blacks in these cities, it is not surprising that their networks do not include access to those with the power to hire. Asians in Los Angeles are the only racial minority group reporting a proportion of contacts who hired them that is as high as that of whites. This may have to do with the existence of Asian ethnic-enclave economies in the Los Angeles area and the high rate of self-employment among Asians.

357

FIGURE 7.3   *Type of Help Provided by Contact*

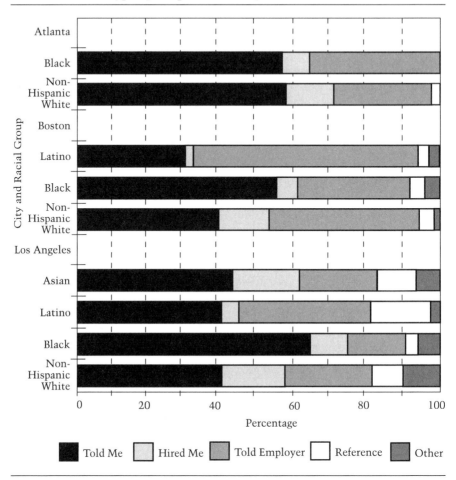

Source: Multi-City Study of Urban Inequality.

The social networks that produced jobs for the respondents in the Multi-City Study are also highly segregated. Table 7.5 shows the race of the contact who provided access to the last job by the race of the respondent. It also provides the racial composition of the labor market within the sample area as a benchmark. What is striking about these data is how little crossover there is from whites to the minority groups. About 96 percent of whites in Atlanta, 93 percent in Boston, and 85 percent in Los Angeles reported having used a white job contact. Minority respondents are also more likely to report a contact who is a member of their

TABLE 7.5   *Race of Contact, by Race of Respondent*

	Race of Contact				
City and Race of Respondent	Non-Hispanic White	Black	Latino	Asian	Other
Atlanta					
Non-Hispanic white	96.6%	3.4%	—	—	—
Black	13.5	85.7	—	—	—
Racial composition of market	69.1	25.4	0.025	0.031	—
Boston					
Non-Hispanic white	85.8	9.5	0.1	0.0	4.6
Black	25.6	72.7	1.0	0.4	0.4
Latino	12.8	4.5	79.2	0.0	3.5
Racial composition of market	85.2	5.1	4.1	5.0	—
Los Angeles					
Non-Hispanic white	84.8	3.5	5.6	3.4	2.8
Black	5.8	87.4	3.2	3.4	0.2
Latino	12.4	1.3	85.4	8.4	0.0
Asian	6.9	0.0	1.5	91.6	0.0
Racial composition of market	42.5	11.8	40.3	5.3	—

Source: Multi-City Study of Urban Inequality.

own minority group, and we find few instances of minority group respondents reporting a member of another minority group as their job contact. This is suggestive of both the extent to which there is little interaction between the members of these groups and the fact that many of the occupations that whites, blacks, and Latinos are seeking are, in fact, ethnically segregated. For members of racial minority groups, their social networks are so ethnically embedded within their own group that if the contact was not a co-ethnic he or she was more likely to be white than a member of another minority group.

This review of the job-seeking behavior of recent searchers in the sample leads to some important generalizations. First, social networks are important to all the groups examined; however, they seem to be far more significant for recent immigrants like Latinos. Social networks account for a large percentage of the jobs found by the job searchers in the sample. For two of the minority groups—Latinos and Asians—social networks led to the majority of jobs. Two of the most disadvantaged groups in the study—Latinos and blacks—exhibit very different patterns of search behavior. Latinos are more likely to use friends and relatives, but rely as much as blacks do on the use of open-market strategies. In addition, Latino job contacts are more likely to intercede with employers rather than just being conduits of information, as was largely the case with blacks.

Second, there are clear differentials across groups in the quality of their networks. Whites are able to mobilize networks with hiring ability, which is seldom the case with blacks and Latinos. Whites are also far more successful at tapping weak ties than any of the minority groups. Further, the networks are very segregated across racial lines. The little interaction across racial lines that takes place in the job search process seldom includes minority-to-minority contact.

Racial differences in search behavior and characteristics seem to be more important than differences across cities. With some exceptions in Atlanta, the various racial groups exhibit consistent patterns across the different cities. Given the persistence of racialized labor markets and residential segregation, it is important to determine whether the patterns of job search we have presented are also associated with differences in job conditions.

Are Network Jobs Different from Non-Network Jobs?

Because personal contacts are an important source of many of the jobs found by the respondents in the Multi-City Study sample, it is important to know whether the social network status of the job makes a difference. That is, do respondents who obtain a job through a personal contact differ in job characteristics from those who entered a job through other methods? The literature on job searches suggests that networks facilitate access to jobs but, in most cases, these do not affect the quality of the outcome. This is largely due to the embeddedness of social networks: individuals tend to interact more closely with others who share similar characteristics, so that network-based searches tend to produce jobs but have no other drawbacks.

Table 7.6 presents average scores for a series of job-related outcomes by racial group. Because the patterns described so far are fairly consistent within racial groups, the data has been aggregated across cities. The outcome variables are the socioeconomic index (SEI)[7] score of the job, the log of hourly wages, whether the respondent is currently employed, the log of firm size, whether the job is in a workplace where most workers are minorities, and whether the job is in a workplace where most workers are co-ethnic. The use of SEI, wages, and employability as outcomes is fairly standard. The firm size and the racial composition of the workplace are less commonly used outcomes. Our interpretation of the latter two outcomes is that larger firms, and firms where most of the workers are nonminority, will be more likely to provide better working conditions and opportunities for social mobility. We also see working with co-ethnics as akin to working in segregated work-places.

TABLE 7.6　Distributions and Average Score for Outcome Variables, by the Job's Network Status for Non-Hispanic Whites, Latinos, and Blacks

Variables	Non-Hispanic Whites		Blacks		Latinos		Asians	
	No Net[a]	Net Job	No Net	Net Job	No Net	Net Job	No Net	Net Job
Socioeconomic index of job	38.5*	36.3*	32.7*	28.9*	26.2*	22.9*	37.2*	29.1*
Hourly wages	$10.0	$10.3	$ 8.3	$ 8.0	$ 7.6*	$ 6.6*	$10.5*	$ 8.4*
Currently employed	72.0%	74.0%	63.0%	60.0%	63.0%	60.0%	84.0%	81.0%
Firm size	451	375	522	446	253*	139*	325	170
Works in minority workplace[b]	26.3%	22.2%	57.7%	73.6%*	74.2%*	84.9%*	79.4%	85.5%
Works with co-ethnics[c]	72.6%*	77.7%*	39.4%	56.3%*	61.7%*	71.4%*	64.7%	66.2%

Source: Multi-City Study of Urban Inequality.
[a] Job obtained by a method other than friends or relatives.
[b] Works in workplace where majority of workers are minorities.
[c] Works in workplace where majority of workers are same race-ethnic group as respondent.
* Scores are significantly different at $p < .10$.

The scores are presented by the method used to find the last job—network-based versus a non-network-based method. We want to determine whether jobs found through social networks are different from non-network jobs in their characteristics. Scores that are significantly different at $p < .10$ are indicated by an asterisk.

Two outcomes consistently seem associated with the network status of the job. Across all groups, those who entered their last job through a social network contact held jobs with a lower socioeconomic status than those who entered the job through other methods. In addition, entering a job through social networks seems associated with workplaces where the majority of workers belong to minority groups and are more likely to include co-ethnics. The results for hourly wages, employability, and firm size are less consistent. Network-found jobs are associated with lower hourly wages among Latinos and Asians, and with a smaller firm size only among Latinos.

The evidence so far is consistent with the notion that social contacts lead Latino and black workers to occupations that have lower socioeconomic status and are more likely to be segregated from white workers. It is likely, though, that some of the differences in the characteristics of network-found jobs when compared to non-network jobs are due to differences in the characteristics of those who end up in network jobs. One way to examine this question is to remove the effects of some of these characteristics and then examine the effect of the network-found job on the outcomes. Table 7.7 presents results from a set of twenty-four regression equations. The equations were calculated separately for each racial group in the study and included controls for years of education, sex, age, age square, city, nativity, and English-speaking ability (for Asians and Latinos only).[8] In addition, a dummy variable indicating whether the last job was obtained through a social network contact was included. For simplification, the table presents the coefficients only for the social network variable; coefficients that are significant at a p of .10 or less are presented, and nonsignificant coefficients are shown as a 0. In this table, the comparison frame is the group, within each racial category, that did not use social networks to find their last job. The SEI, log of hourly wages, and log of firm size are continuous variables, and the coefficients reflect the increase or decrease in the outcome if the respondent is in a social network–found job. The other three variables—employability, minority workplace, and co-ethnic workplace—are all dichotomous variables. The numbers presented are actually odds ratios of the impact a network-found job has on the event happening—namely, being employed, working with minorities, and working in a workplace with co-ethnics.

TABLE 7.7   *Effects of Entering Job Through Social Contacts on Job-Related Outcomes*

Outcome	Non-Hispanic White	Black	Latino	Asian
SEI				
Network job	0	−1.35	−1.2	−3.4
Log hourly wages				
Network job	0	0	−0.09	−1.44
Employed				
Network job	0	0	0	0
Log size of firm				
Network job	0	−2.99	−2.42	0
Minority workplace				
Network job	0	1.77	1.68	0
Co-ethnic workplace				
Network job	0	1.83	1.34	0

Source: Multi-City Study of Urban Inequality.
Note: Model includes controls for years of education, sex, age, age square, city, nativity, English-speaking ability (for Asians and Latinos only), marital status, and the presence of young children. Only significant effects shown.

Most of the negative effects associated with network-found jobs remain even after controlling for other characteristics. While for whites there are no negative effects in finding a job through a social contact, the effects for racial minorities are consistently negative. For Latinos and blacks, network-found jobs have a lower SEI, are in smaller firms, and are more likely to be in a minority workplace. We also found an association with lower wages for Latinos and Asian workers.

These results suggest that for minority workers in the Multi-City Study, networks matter in ways that go beyond providing access to a job. This is particularly important for blacks, who show the strongest effects of being in network-found jobs. Relative to blacks who did not enter their job through a network, blacks in network-found jobs have a lower-status job and work in more segregated workplaces. While there are similar effects for Latinos and Asians, the effects for black workers seem to be larger. For example, black workers who found jobs through a social network contact saw a decline in the log of the firm size of 2.99, while for Latinos it was 2.42. Similarly, black workers in network jobs were 1.83 times more likely to work with other blacks, while Latinos were only 1.34 times more likely. The latter is, perhaps, the most important of the effects for racial minorities of finding jobs through social networks: it leads them to workplaces that are disconnected from the majority workers.

Are There Any Advantages to Other Methods?

As shown earlier, Latinos, Asians, and blacks all rely heavily on friends and relatives in searching for and finding jobs. The previous analysis shows that this preferred strategy has some consequences for the characteristics of the jobs they find. We now contrast the use of friends and relatives to find employment with the use of acquaintances, newspapers, or other methods.[9] Table 7.8 presents the results from an analysis of the effects of the type of method that led to the job on labor market outcomes. The controls in these models are the same as in the previous table. Those respondents who found their job through a friend or a relative (strong ties) are used as the reference category. Indicators are used for having found the job through an acquaintance, newspaper, or another method. As suspected, relative to using friends or relatives to find a job, the use of other methods is consistently positive for blacks, Latinos, and Asians. Interestingly, the use of acquaintances by blacks and Latinos does not seem to have as much of an impact relative to using friends and relatives. (Only in two instances do we find significant and positive effects of the use of acquaintances by Latinos and blacks.) By using acquaintances, Latinos find jobs with an SEI higher by almost 2 points (1.8) and blacks are half as likely (.52) to end up in a workplace with other blacks. The strongest effect in using acquaintances relative to using friends and relatives is for Asians, who see an increase of 9.20 in SEI and .27 in the log of hourly wages. However, acquaintances do lead Asian workers to minority workplaces, albeit with higher salaries and better jobs. In general, the further removed black and Latino workers are from using friends and relatives (that is, using newspapers or other methods), the better their wages, the higher the quality of the job, and the less likely they are to work with other minority workers.

Our final analysis looks at one more aspect of the effect of social networks on the job outcomes of minority workers. We showed earlier that the social networks used by these workers are highly segregated and that there is little crossover among minority groups. The vast majority of minority workers used a co-ethnic as a contact. Those who did not were likely to have used a white contact. We replicated the analysis shown in tables 7.7 and 7.8, this time examining only the effect of the race of the social network contact. We entered in the models a dummy variable indicating whether the contact was a co-ethnic or not, and then

TABLE 7.8   *Effect of Method Used to Find Last Job on Job-Related Outcomes*

Outcome	Non-Hispanic Whites	Black	Latino	Asian
SEI				
Relatives or friends	—	—	—	—
Acquaintance	0	0	1.80	9.20
Newspapers	0	1.60	0	2.50
Other	0	1.90	0	8.80
Log hourly wages				
Relatives or friends	—	—	—	—
Acquaintance	0	0	0	0.27
Newspapers	0	0.11	0.12	0.16
Other	0	0	0.11	0
Employed				
Relatives or friends	—	—	—	—
Acquaintance	0	0	0	0
Newspapers	0	0	1.80	0
Other	0	0	0	0
Size of firm				
Relatives or friends	—	—	—	—
Acquaintance	0	−0.83	0	0
Newspapers	0	0	0	0
Other	0.43	0.42	0.52	0.95
Minority workplace				
Relatives or friends	—	—	—	—
Acquaintance	1.90	0	0	4.14
Newspapers	0	0.48	0	0
Other	1.60	0.59	0.58	0.38
Co-ethnic workplace				
Relatives or friends	—	—	—	—
Acquaintance	0.52	0.52	0	0
Newspapers	0	0.47	0	0
Other	0.61	0.56	0.62	0

Source: Multi-City Study of Urban Inequality.
Note: Model includes controls for years of education, sex, age, age square, city, nativity, English-speaking ability (for Asians and Latinos only), marital status, and the presence of young children.

controlled for all other relevant variables included in earlier models. These results are presented in table 7.9.

The results for a contact of the same race are consistent with the descriptive and multivariate results presented earlier. Co-ethnic contacts lower the SEI of black, Latinos, and Asian workers by about 2 to 3 points. Similarly, they lower the wages of Latino workers by a log of .11, but they have no effect on the wages of Asians or blacks. The greatest

TABLE 7.9   *Effects of Using a Contact of Similar Race on*
            Job-Related Outcomes

Outcome	Non-Hispanic White	Black	Latino	Asian
SEI				
Same-race contact	0	−1.77	−1.66	−3.12
Log hourly wages				
Same-race contact	0	0	−0.11	0
Employed				
Same-race contact	0	0	0.77	0
Size of firm				
Same-race contact	0	0	0	0
Minority workplace				
Same-race contact	0.67	1.86	2.02	1.82
Co-ethnic workplace				
Same-race contact	1.50	2.22	1.87	0

Source: Multi-City Study of Urban Inequality.
Note: Model includes controls for years of education, sex, age, age square, city, nativity, English-speaking ability (for Asians and Latinos only), marital status, and the presence of young children.

impact of a co-ethnic contact is, not surprisingly, on the racial composition of the workplace. It consistently leads minority workers to work with other minorities. For example, blacks who had a black contact were twice as likely to work with other blacks (2.22), while for Latinos it was 1.87 times.

Conclusion

In this chapter, we set out to describe the pattern of job searching for workers in the surveyed cities and to examine whether job search patterns are associated with labor market outcomes. We find, in this analysis, evidence of clear differences in the way racial-ethnic groups go about looking for employment, and even the way they eventually find a job. Within racial and ethnic groups, members do use a variety of methods while searching, but those who are racial minorities or with high proportions of immigrants seem to limit their search pattern to a narrower set of methods. For example, Latinos favor the use of social networks as a search method, with great emphasis on the use of relatives. While this may have something to do with the type of jobs being searched for, we find negative associations between some of the methods favored by racial minorities and labor market–related outcomes.

Social networks are terribly important and functional. They do provide access to information and they seem generally to lead to jobs. It has been suggested that the resources provided by social networks are not likely to affect every aspect of social mobility (Marsden and Hulbert 1988). As such, we did not expect the use of social networks as a method to relate negatively to every aspect of labor market outcomes. Our findings support that argument but also suggest that the character of job searching for Latinos and blacks does limit their opportunities, even though some of the effects may not just be on the traditional measures of attainment—such as wages—but on other, more pervasive aspects related to racial segregation and job security.

One of the important findings is the extent to which the job search process is segregated by race and by ethnicity. While it is noteworthy that minority groups are largely disconnected from the majority groups when searching for a job, there is also substantial segregation across minority groups. Searching through members of the same group increases the chances that a worker will end up in an occupation or firm that is predominantly minority, and for some groups this is associated with lower pay, smaller firms, and a lower-quality job. This may well speak to the lack of resources in many of the networks within which these minority group members operate. Nonetheless, this finding is one more aspect of the widespread segregation that appears throughout the labor market. The networks that members of minority groups have access to are so racially embedded that they tend to reproduce the same racial composition in their workplaces. To the extent that the social networks of minority workers remain segregated, for many of them, their participation in the labor market will also be limited to segregated workplaces.

We have underscored that some crucial mechanisms in the process of filling jobs are embedded into ethnic bonds and bounded by segregated arrangements. The reliance by minority group members on social networks and open-market search strategies works to their detriment, and any hope for changing these patterns requires changes in the way minority group members approach a job search. The issue, then, has to do with the connections established by Latinos and African Americans to workplaces and how the character of these can be improved. While it could be argued that improving the quality and heterogeneity of the social networks of minority group members would affect labor market outcomes in a positive way, that point of view is too simplistic. This would require changes not only in patterns of racial interaction between majority and minority groups but also in the social resources that members of minority social networks have access to. Changes in the level of racial interaction and of segregation—particularly between blacks and whites—have taken place at a very slow pace. Similarly, changes in the amount of social resources that members of minority groups have access to would require a reversal of processes that have been taking place in urban centers over the last several years. In fact, as documented by William Julius Wilson and others, the opposite has been happening (Wilson 1987, 1993, 1996; Wacquant and Wilson 1989). The poor and the working poor living in inner-city areas are increasingly isolated from interaction with members of other social classes. As a result, the social ties of these individuals seldom reach beyond their own social position.

What is needed is the creation of job search mechanisms to serve as alternatives to the reliance on strong social ties and open-market strategies as primary sources of job information and location. These job search mechanisms have to take the character of being both sources of information and overseers of how searchers package their search strategy, including interviewing skills and necessary references. Whatever form these intermediaries take, they have to enable racial minorities to reach out beyond the boundaries of their own friends and neighborhoods to reach for more stable work opportunities. This will require not only facilitating the connection to the jobs but also breaking down some of the structural barriers that keep neighborhoods and workplaces segregated.

Notes

1. The statistical results presented in this chapter were all produced using survey analysis procedures available in the STATA statistical software.

2. While there are also some differences in search patterns by gender, we have chosen to emphasize racial differences in this chapter. Our detailed analysis of the data suggests that the differences across racial groups are more important. Further, the analysis by gender substantially reduces the size of the sample, bringing into question the reliability of the findings.

3. Detroit included a total of seven search methods in its questionnaire, including friends and relatives in a single category and an "other" category. In addition, many of the search-specific questions included in Atlanta, Boston, and Los Angeles were not asked in Detroit, so respondents from Detroit are not included in the analyses presented beyond table 7.2.

4. Factor analysis is a technique used to identify patterns among a larger set of variables. The procedure allows for the reduction of the larger set of variables to a more manageable set of indicators that might conceptually represent "dimensions" of the interrelationships among the variables (Kleimbaum, Kupper, and Muller 1988).

5. It should be noted than when factor analysis is used, including all racial groups at the city level, the results differ slightly from results presented in table 7.3. The open market and the friends and relatives search strategies are very consistent. On the other hand, unions do not stand out as a distinctive search strategy but rather, as groups in Atlanta and Boston with the market intermediaries and as groups in Los Angeles with friends and relatives. In addition, credential-based methods, like sending resumes and school placement, tend to coalesce into a separate search strategy—in Atlanta and Boston, it includes the newspapers.

6. Since factor scores have a mean of 0 and a standard deviation, usually, of 1, the search strategy index is calculated by dividing the factor score over its standard deviation, multiplying the result by 10 and adding 100. The resulting index has a mean of 100 and a standard deviation of 10 (StataCorp 1997).

7. The socioeconomic index (SEI) scale is a commonly used measure in sociology to classify occupations on the basis of social status. The scale results from an equation in which income and education characteristics of occupational categories are the main predictors.

8. A similar analysis was conducted for racial groups within cities, but is not presented. Results were fairly consistent, but with fewer significant coefficients in some cities.

9. Unfortunately, the Multi-City Study did not collect information on the specific method that led to the job beyond friends, relatives, acquaintances, newspapers, or a catchall "other" category. This limitation does not allow us to explore in more detail the effects of intermediaries relative to that of social networks or other methods.

References

Baldwin, Marjorie L., and William G. Johnson. 1996. "The Employment Effects of Wage Discrimination Against Black Men." *Industrial and Labor Relations Review* 49: 302–16.

Blackley, Paul R. 1990. "Spatial Mismatch in Urban Labor Markets: Evidence from Large U.S. Metropolitan Areas." *Social Science Quarterly* 71: 39–52.

Coleman, James. 1988. "Social Capital in the Creation of Human Capital." *American Journal of Sociology* 94: S95–121.

Falcón, Luis M. 1995. "Social Networks and Employment for Latinos, Blacks, and Whites." *New England Journal of Public Policy* 11: 17–28.

Granovetter, Mark S. 1973. "The Strength of Weak Ties." *American Journal of Sociology* 78: 1360–80.

———. 1983. "The Strength of Weak Ties: A Network Theory Revisited." *Sociological Theory* 1: 201–33.

———. 1995a. "The Economic Sociology of Firms and Entrepreneurs." In *The Economic Sociology of Immigration: Essays on Networks, Ethnicity, and Entrepreneurship*, edited by Alejandro Portes. New York: Russell Sage Foundation.

———. 1995b. *Getting a Job: A Study of Contacts and Careers*. Chicago: University of Chicago Press.

Green, Gary P., Leann M. Tigges, and Irene Browne. 1995. "Social Resources, Job Search, and Poverty in Atlanta." *Research in Community Sociology* 5: 161–82.

Greenwell, Lisa, R. Burciaga Valdez, and Julie Da-Vanzo. 1997. "Social Ties, Wages, and Gender in a Study of Salvadorean and Filipino Immigrants in Los Angeles." *Social Science Quarterly* 78: 559–77.

Holzer, Harry J. 1994. "Black Employment Problems: New Evidence, Old Questions." *Journal of Policy Analysis and Management* 13: 699–722.

Jencks, Christopher, and Paul E. Peterson. 1991. *The Urban Underclass*. Washington, D.C.: Brookings Institution.

Kasinitz, Philip, and Jan Rosenberg. 1996. "Missing the Connection: Social Isolation and Employment on the Brooklyn Waterfront." Paper presented at the annual meeting of the American Sociological Association (1996).

Kleimbaum, David G., Lawrence Kupper, and Keith E. Muller. 1988. *Applied Regression Analysis and Other Multivariate Methods*. Boston: PWS-Kent.

Marsden, Peter V. 1990. "Network Data and Measurement." *Annual Review of Sociology* 16: 435–63.

Marsden, Peter V., and Jeanne S. Hulbert. 1988. "Social Resources and Mobility Outcomes: A Replication and Extension." *Social Forces* 66: 1038–59.

Melendez, Edwin, and Luis M. Falcón. 1998. "The Impact of Search Strategies on Labor Market Outcomes: A Comparison of Boston and Los Angeles Job Seekers." Unpublished manuscript. New School for Social Research.

Menjivar, Cecilia. 1997. "Immigrant Kinship Networks: Vietnamese, Salvadoreans and Mexicans in Comparative Perspective." *Journal of Comparative Family Studies* 28: 1–24.

Montgomery, James D. 1991. "Social Networks and Labor Market Outcomes: Toward an Economic Analysis." *American Economic Review* 81.

———. 1992. "Job Search and Network Composition: Implications of the Strength-of-Weak-Ties Hypothesis." *American Sociological Review* 57: 586–96.

———. 1994. "Weak Ties, Employment, and Inequality: An Equilibrium Analysis." *American Journal of Sociology* 99: 1212–36.

Portes, Alejandro, and Julia Sensenbrenner. 1993. "Embeddedness and Immigration: Notes on the Social Determinants of Economic Action." *American Journal of Sociology* 98: 1320–1350.

———. 1995. "Economic Sociology and the Sociology of Immigration: A

Conceptual Overview." In *The Economic Sociology of Immigration*, edited by Alejandro Portes. New York: Russell Sage Foundation.

Sassen, Saskia. 1995. "Immigration and Local Labor Markets." In *The Economic Sociology of Immigration: Essays on Networks, Ethnicity, and Entrepreneurship*, edited by Alejandro Portes. New York: Russell Sage Foundation.

StataCorp. 1997. *Stata Statistical Software: Release 5.0*, vol. 1. College Station, Tex.: Stata Corporation.

Wacquant, Loic, and William Julius Wilson. 1989. "The Cost of Racial and Class Exclusion in the Inner City." *Annals of the American Academy of Political and Social Sciences* 501: 8–26.

Waldinger, Roger. 1994. "The Making of an Immigrant Niche." *International Migration Review* 28: 3–30.

———. 1995. "The 'Other Side' of Embeddedness: A Case-Study of the Interplay of Economy and Ethnicity." *Ethnic and Racial Studies* 18: 555–80.

Wilson, William Julius. 1983. "Inner-City Dislocations." *Society* 1: 80–86.

———. 1987. *The Truly Disadvantaged: The Inner City, the Underclass, and Public Policy*. Chicago: University of Chicago Press.

———. 1988. "American Social Policy and the Ghetto Underclass." *Dissent* 1: 57–64.

———. 1993. "The Ghetto Underclass: Social Science Perspectives (Updated Edition)," edited by W. J. Wilson. Newbury Park, Calif.: Sage.

———. 1996. *When Work Disappears: The World of the New Urban Poor*. New York: Knopf.

8

INEQUALITY THROUGH LABOR MARKETS, FIRMS, AND FAMILIES: THE INTERSECTION OF GENDER AND RACE-ETHNICITY ACROSS THREE CITIES

Irene Browne, Leann Tigges, and Julie Press

M OST scholars recognize that investigations of race and ethnic inequality need to take gender into account. Women of color are described in the literature as experiencing "double" or even "multiple" jeopardy in the labor market, with the dual disadvantage of gender and race-ethnicity pushing African American and Latina women to the bottom of the wage hierarchy, and a dual privilege elevating white men to the top (King 1989). Feminist scholars, in particular, argue that race and gender cannot be studied separately, as if they were analytically independent "systems"; race and gender intersect within social institutions, creating unique conditions for various groups (Collins 1990). Women and men should therefore experience race differently in the labor market, with the disadvantages associated with race compounded for African American and Latina women by the disadvantages associated with gender (King 1989).

Yet the mechanisms that give rise to patterns of inequality by race, ethnicity, and gender continue to be the subject of debate. In particular, there is disagreement over whether the source of disadvantage is located in the structure of labor market opportunities, in the practices of firms, in the conflicting demands of family responsibilities, or in the attributes and attitudes that individuals bring to the labor market.

In this chapter, we investigate how race-ethnicity and gender intersect to create differences in wages in three of the metropolitan areas surveyed in the Multi-City Study of Urban Inequality, focusing on sources of earnings inequality among women. We posit that this inter-section occurs in at least three distinct arenas: the local labor market, the firm, and the family. Our inquiry is developed from combining economic and institutional theories of the labor market with insights from feminist theory about the intersection of gender and race.

To illustrate how race and gender converge within urban economies, we compare the cities of Atlanta, Boston, and Los Angeles. (We exclude Detroit, since many of the measures that we use in our analyses are not available in the Detroit sample.) Employment opportunities across the cities vary according to important local demand factors, particularly the social characteristics of the labor force and the occupational and industrial mix of the metropolitan economy. We show that race and gender also come into play inside the firm, where decisions about recruitment, hiring, and promotion are made. Finally, we demonstrate how child care obligations within the family become a salient factor in limiting economic rewards for women. Our research contributes to the debates about race and labor market inequality by expanding the conversation to include a systematic and multidimensional consideration of gender. Through looking at local labor market dynamics, institutional processes, and family responsibilities, we are able to see how labor market disadvantage occurs at different points. We are also able to show how these points converge to produce particular hardship for Latinas and black women. The analyses have important implications for current policy debates, as Latinas and black women are overrepresented among the long-term poor. Although previous research has investigated each of these arenas in part, we examine the intersection of race-ethnicity and gender in all three arenas (local labor market, firm, and family) with a multiethnic sample. We begin by laying out our general theoretical framework.

Race-Ethnicity, Gender, and Labor Market Processes
Queuing Theory and the Effect of Queuing on Wages

Institutional approaches to labor markets assume that wages are tied to positions within an organization, such as a "job," and that individuals are allocated into these positions through economic and social processes (Osterman 1988). Queuing theory provides an explanation of how gender and race become salient in the allocation process, so that women of color are relegated to the worst jobs. According to the version of queuing theory espoused by Barbara Reskin and Patricia Roos (1990), employers see the labor market in terms of "labor queues," in which job seekers are ranked hierarchically according to ascribed characteristics, particularly gender and race. White men are usually at the top of the queue, while African American women are often at the bottom (Reskin and Roos 1990; 33). There is also a "job queue" that arises from the ranking of jobs by workers and job seekers. Individuals at the top of the labor queue will be in the best position to obtain the most desirable job in the job queue. When a job loses its prime place in a queue through a downgrading of skills, a decline in wages, or a deterioration of working conditions, individuals at the top of the queue may seek another line of work. This opens jobs to individuals lower in the labor queue (Reskin and Roos 1990).

Myra Strober and Lisa Catanzarite (1988) posit that because some occupations are deemed more appropriate for one gender than another, the labor queue is diamond-shaped, with black women at the bottom of the diamond, white men at the top, and black men and white women across from each other at the two far sides of the diamond. When employers move down the queue from white men, their choice of whether to hire or promote black men or white women depends on the position that must be filled. White women will be preferred for typically "female" jobs such as clerical work. It is also conceivable that employers may favor women for jobs requiring an abundance of "soft skills," those interactional and communication skills most commonly associated with women (Moss and Tilly 1996). Thus, occupational segregation by gender expands the racial-ethnic labor queue horizontally as well as vertically.

From the perspective of queuing theory, employment opportunities are the most restricted for Latinas and African American women because occupations are segregated by both gender and race-ethnicity. Women of color are concentrated in relatively few female-dominated occupations, which are characterized by low wages, few benefits, and little room for upward mobility (Cunningham and Zalokar 1992; Gittleman and Howell 1995). For instance, Mary King (1998) created a matrix of 111 cells defined by the intersection of major industry and occupation categories. She found that black women were underrepresented in 49 occupational-industrial niches, while black men were underrepresented in 25. (Black women were overrepresented in 13 niches and black men in 35.) Although both groups were concentrated in the relatively lower paying occupational-industrial niches, the gender segregation of occupations presents black women with a narrower range of opportunities than black men.

Although Asians were located closer to the bottom of the labor queue until the 1950s to 1960s, they have since bifurcated, joining both whites at the top end of the queue and blacks and Latinos at the low end (Espiritu 1997). Part of the difficulty with understanding how gender and race-ethnicity affect Asians is the extreme heterogeneity of this group in terms of country of origin, education, and English-language ability. Groups from Southeast Asian countries, such as Vietnamese, Cambodian, Hmong, Laotian, and Thai tend to fare much worse than those originating in China, Japan, or Korea. The Multi-City Study sample of Asians in Los Angeles is limited to the northern Asian ethnic groups, and therefore we expect Asians in our study to be higher in the labor queue than African Americans and Latinos and Latinas.

When workers are crowded into a relatively few positions, wages should drop (Bergmann 1986). In addition to crowding, the lower wages in positions that are dominated by some minorities could be due to the human capital they bring to the labor market. African Americans, Mexicans, and Puerto Ricans tend to have less human capital than non-Hispanic whites and Asians, particularly in terms of the quality and quantity of schooling they are able to obtain (Corcoran, Heflin, and Reyes 1999; Farkas et al. 1997). Yet human capital differences do not explain why African American and Latina women earn lower wages than co-ethnic men. There is no schooling gap between African American women and men, for example, and there are few differences in years of experience (England, Christopher, and Reed 1999).

Local Labor Markets

Stanley Lieberson (1980) applies the queuing model to racial stratification in the labor market, and discusses the importance of population dynamics and local labor market structures in determining the shape of the labor queue. Opportunities for those at the bottom of the queue will depend on the size of the group at the top. In a tight labor market, where the number of qualified white applicants is relatively low, opportunities for Latinos, Latinas, and African Americans will be more plentiful, compared to a slack labor market where whites comprise a majority of the population. When there are multiple groups competing for employment, as in the case of Los Angeles, opportunities for those at the bottom will be more restricted than in less diverse settings.

In addition to the size and composition of the metropolitan population, a city's industrial and occupational mix also influences employment opportunities and wages. Therefore, the extent to which occupations contain high proportions of African American, Latina, or Asian women, the types of occupations in which these women are located, and the consequences of occupational segregation will depend on conditions within the local labor market.

In contrast to the research on occupational segregation by gender, most studies of race and labor market dynamics do not find an effect of the racial composition of occupations on wages (England 1992; Tomaskovic-Devey and Skaggs 1999). However, Jerry Jacobs and Mary Blair-Loy (1996) emphasize that studies based on national data are not sufficiently refined to capture the effects of racial/ethnic segregation of occupations. At the national level, there are no occupations that are predominantly African American or predominantly Hispanic, because these groups comprise such small proportions of the total employed U.S. population. The impact of the race-ethnic composition of occupations occurs only within particular local labor markets.

The presence of ethnic enclave economies also shapes the opportunities of Latinas and Asian women within local labor markets. Ethnic enclaves usually involve establishments within particular industries where the owners, workers, and clientele belong to the same ethnic group. These enclaves provide greater employment opportunities for co-ethnics, particularly those who recently immigrated to the U.S. (Portes and Bach 1985). For example, Tarry Hum and Melvin Oliver (1995) used the Multi-City Study data to estimate that, among immigrants, 57 percent of Chinese, 73 percent of Koreans, 45 percent of Mexicans, and 54 percent of Central Americans in Los Angeles participate in ethnic economies as either workers or employers. Korean immigrants are more likely to be employers, while the other three ethnic groups are more likely to be workers. Although employment rates may be higher, recent studies suggest that individuals who are employed within enclaves earn lower wages than they would in similar positions outside the enclave economy (Sanders and Nee 1996).

Firms and Jobs

Although the local labor market certainly provides an important context for the allocation of labor, actual decisions about recruitment, hiring, and promotion occur within firms. Indeed, the race-ethnic and gender segregation of jobs within particular establishments is much higher than the segregation of occupations in those labor markets (Bielby and Baron 1986; Reskin 1993). Even those occupations that appear to be gender-integrated are segregated at the job level (Bielby and Baron 1986).

Practices within firms that result in differential access to jobs by race-ethnicity and gender may not be discriminatory in intent. For instance, firms that hire through informal channels can unwittingly reproduce race and ethnic stratification of employment (Barron, Bishop, and Dunkelberg 1985; Corcoran, Datcher, and Duncan 1980; Holzer 1996;

Kluegel 1978). There is also some evidence that employers label jobs as appropriate or inappropriate for women or men, or a particular ethnic group (Epstein 1988), and invoke stereotypes about differences in the abilities and work commitments of men and women (Heilman 1995). When employers anticipate resistance from employees and customers, they are also more likely to channel workers into positions based on their race-ethnicity and/or gender (Becker 1985; Reskin and Roos 1990).

Gender and race-ethnicity also segregate people vertically within firms. Positions are often attached to job ladders within a firm, and promotion opportunities are distributed unequally. In predominantly female jobs, authority tends to be limited and job ladders relatively short (DiPrete and Soule 1988). Predominantly black jobs are also associated with relatively low authority and promotion possibilities (Kaufman 1986), so that the blocked paths to mobility among female-dominated jobs should also be compounded for minority women (McGuire and Reskin 1993). Theories of queuing and social closure would predict that jobs that are tied to mobility ladders inhabited by the dominant social groups would carry the greatest rewards.

Within firms, jobs are therefore segregated by gender and race in two ways: horizontally and vertically. *Horizontal* segregation puts race and sex groups in different kinds of occupations or different places within skill levels of an organization. *Vertical* segregation puts groups in different positions of authority, responsibility, or pay. For Latina and African American women, occupational segregation can impose a double risk associated with employment in a majority-female and predominantly co-ethnic job (Almquist 1975; McGuire and Reskin 1993; Reskin and Cassirer 1996). Asian women may also suffer from job segregation. Deborah Woo (1985) argues that Asian women receive lower returns to their years of education than comparable white women, due partially to gender and racial-ethnic occupational segregation. Asian women tend to work in female-dominated occupations like nursing and clerical work. But within those fields, they tend to be overrepresented as file clerks, cashiers, office machine operators, and typists—backstage jobs with lower levels of authority. This is particularly true of immigrants.[1]

The Family

In addition to the local labor market and the firm, the family represents a third institutional arena that can create disadvantage for women. Family roles not only differ for men and women; they produce opposite effects in the labor market: marriage and children tend to depress women's earnings while they raise the earnings of men (Witkowski and

Leicht 1995). Race-ethnic differences in the structuring of family relations occur within the context of a gendered division of labor in the
home, where women remain the primary caregivers (Hochschild 1989).

Theories of statistical and pure discrimination offer possible explanations for why marriage and children economically reward men and
disadvantage women. Statistical discrimination would occur if employers perceived that, on average, women with children had higher
turnover and were less productive because of family obligations. This
perception would lead them to favor men over women in hiring and
promotion. Employers might also favor married men over other groups
for training opportunities and higher wages if they perceived that, on
average, married men were more reliable and productive; presumably
marriage creates incentives and pressures for men to provide their families with long-term economic security.

Status-based, or "pure" discrimination explanations of the gender
differences in the effects of children and marital status on wages emphasize biases that (male) employers maintain to uphold the status quo and
the gender division of labor. In particular, allocating opportunities to
men and women based on their child care obligations and marital status
would represent an attempt at social closure.

It is also possible that child care responsibilities hinder women and
marriage rewards men in the labor market because these statuses are
connected to actual constraints and resources. Lack of adequate child
care is often cited by women as a reason for reducing hours or staying
out of the labor force altogether (Stolzenberg and Waite 1984). Child care
concerns are more often associated with decisions about whether to
seek employment, where to work, and the type of work rather than with
wages. However, if women are taking more sick days or leave time to
attend to a child's illness or to help elderly parents, these absences
might be reflected in lower earnings (Becker 1985; but see Bielby and
Bielby 1988). In contrast, the unpaid domestic labor from wives may
provide married men with greater flexibility and more time to devote to
their jobs.

Finally, a third line of argument used to explain the different effects
that children and marriage have on men's and women's wages involves
processes of self-selection. Scholars in the New Home Economics tradition contend that women select occupations that are most compatible
with their parental responsibilities, exchanging such amenities as flexible hours for lower wages (Mincer and Polachek 1974). However, research reveals that the wage gap is not offset by other amenities such as
flexibility (England 1992; Glass 1990). In fact, Jennifer Glass (1990) reports that as the concentration of women in jobs increases, flexibility
actually diminishes. Jobs such as nursing, teaching, and secretarial work

are especially rigid in their requirements, and do not allow women to interrupt their schedules easily to attend to a family emergency. In addition, never-married childless women are as likely to work in predominantly female jobs as are married mothers (Witkowski and Leicht 1995).[2]

There are important race and ethnic variations in family structure that could affect labor market outcomes. In households with married couples, Latinos, Latinas, and African Americans are often in greater need of income from two full-time earners than are whites or Asians because of Latino and African American men's average lower earnings and larger family sizes. Also, Latinas and African American women are more likely to be sole earners because they are more likely than white women to be single mothers. These racial and ethnic differences in family resources and family structure translate into greater exposure to the constraining effects of child care among women and fewer chances to reap the labor market rewards of marriage among men.

Hypotheses

The literature suggests that women of color can encounter multiple jeopardy through their dual statuses of female and African American, Latina, or Asian. (Social class represents a third source of jeopardy.) They can also encounter disadvantage in multiple arenas: the labor market, the firm, and the family. We have argued that local labor market processes are manifest through patterns of occupational segregation within the metropolitan area, that practices within the firm create jobs and the authority structures that are segregated by race-ethnicity and gender, and that family structure is important because women experience conflicts between their obligations to their employers and to their husbands and children. Specific hypotheses of the effects of each of these institutional sources of disadvantage are developed next.

Local Labor Markets: Demographic Composition of Occupations

We expect that gender and race-ethnicity will intersect at the level of local labor markets to affect women's wages through the demographic composition of the employed population. The proportion of an occupation that is black, Hispanic, and Asian varies by metropolitan area. For instance, Atlanta's population has the greatest percentage of African Americans, compared to Boston or Los Angeles; we should therefore find a higher concentration of African Americans in the occupations within the Atlanta economy. The differences across cities should emerge through variation in the mean levels of occupational composition by race/ethnicity. The cities should have similar effects of occupational composition on wages. In particular, we predict that jobs filled by the two highest groups in the labor queue (whites and Asians) will pay better wages than jobs filled by the two groups at the end of the queue (Latinos, Latinas, and blacks). If these effects are the result of restricted access to occupations—that is, queuing and crowding—then the results should hold even after controlling for individual human capital and the amount of skill required for the occupations.

Firms: Job and Authority Hierarchies

We expect that the race-ethnic composition of jobs should affect wages in the same direction as the occupation effects. If the sorting into particular positions actually occurs at the firm level, then the inclusion of job composition measures should diminish or eliminate the effects on wages of labor market occupational segregation.

Vertical segregation of jobs by race-ethnicity and gender should also affect wages. In particular, working under a supervisor who is white rather than black, Latinos, Latina, or Asian should indicate a more advantageous position on the mobility ladder, and should be accompanied by higher wages. Similarly, working under a supervisor who is a man rather than a woman should afford women greater opportunities and higher wages. The multiple jeopardy thesis also suggests an added wage bonus to jobs attached to supervisors who are white men.

Families

We predict that women's family obligations will restrict their labor market options and lower their wages. In particular, women who experience conflicts between their workplace and child care responsibilities will receive lower wages. Because they are not the primary caregivers, men will not see their wages affected by their family obligations. Marriage should bring labor market rewards to men but not to women.

Methods

We focus on one aspect of labor market outcomes: earnings. Our dependent variable is logged hourly earnings for individuals in the sample who reported wages within the past five years and were not self-employed.

Comparing four race-ethnic groups across three cities for both men and women presents an unwieldy number of contrasts. We simplify our presentation by focusing mainly on women in the labor market, making comparisons with men where they are most relevant. Even with the concentration on women, our quest to understand the intersection of race-ethnicity and gender posed certain challenges in designing the analyses. Atlanta has very few Latinas and Asians; Boston has few Asians. The only city with a large number of all four race-ethnic groups is Los Angeles. Thus, the effects of being Asian or working in a job that is predominantly Asian are compounded with the effects of living in Los Angeles in analyses that simply pool all cities or all race-ethnic groups.[3]

We therefore perform regressions on three overlapping subsamples: a pooled three-city Atlanta-Boston-Los Angeles sample that contains non-Hispanic whites and African Americans; a pooled two-city Boston-Los Angeles sample that contains non-Hispanic whites, African Americans, and Latinos, Latinas; and a Los Angeles sample that contains non-Hispanic whites, African Americans, Latinos, Latinas, and Asians.

Characteristics of Labor Market Institutions

We include a measure of the race-ethnic and gender composition of the respondent's occupation within the local labor market. Occupation is defined by the three-digit census code. The occupational composition variables are constructed from the 1990 Census Public Use Microsample (PUMS) files from the decennial census, and represent the percent of those employed in the respondent's occupation within his or her metropolitan area who are female, African American, Latino/a, or Asian. Thus, for respondents in Los Angeles, "percent black in the occupation" refers to the proportion of workers within an occupation who are black. This variable is designed to capture the racial and gender dimensions of local labor market competition from individuals with similar levels of education.

Some would argue that lower wages within an occupation that is predominantly female or predominantly black, Hispanic, or Asian are simply the result of fewer human capital requirements. For instance, since African Americans tend to have less education than non-Hispanic whites, earnings within the occupations in which they predominate would simply reflect the lower levels of skill required within these positions. To control for human capital requirements within an occupation that is relatively *independent* of its incumbents, we use two variables to measure skill requirements. The variables were created from the 1980 *Dictionary of Occupational Titles*, and modified by Paula England and Barbara Kilbourne (1988). The first skill variable, "training" (or "specific vocational preparation"), represents the number of weeks necessary for an individual to "learn the techniques, acquire the information, and develop the facility needed for average performance in a specific job-worker situation" (England and Kilbourne 1988, 9). The other skill variable, "general educational development" (GED), is a measure of the amount of formal and informal education necessary for "reasoning develop-ment and ability to follow instructions, and the acquisition of tool knowl-edges, such as language and mathematical skills" to successfully fulfill the tasks relevant to the occupation (England and Kilbourne 1988, 4).[4]

Our analyses control for the industry in which the respondent is employed to account for the difference in wages across industries. Indus-try is coded a set of dummy variables, defined by the Census Bureau's two-digit classification scheme.

Firm Characteristics

In order to investigate the dynamics associated with job segregation at the level of the firm, our models include a measure of the race-ethnic composition of the respondent's job. For the job segregation measure, respondents were asked about the race-ethnicity of "most of the em-ployees doing the kind of work" they do at their workplace. We include dummy variables for majority black coworkers, majority Hispanic, and majority Asian. Those who did not indicate black, Hispanic, or Asian are the excluded category in the regression equations; their cowork-ers may be majority-white or other race-ethnicity, or of mixed race-ethnicity.

Our models incorporate measures of the race-ethnic and gender seg-regation of authority hierarchies through a series of dummy variables indicating the race and gender of the respondent's supervisor. In particu-lar, we create dummy variables indicating whether the respondent's su-pervisor is white and whether the respondent's supervisor is a man.[5] A control variable indicating "no supervisor" is included in the analyses, so that the reference category is having a supervisor who is not a white man. To the extent that having a white male supervisor is an indicator of being relatively high in the organization, the included variables should be associated with higher wages for all groups.

Having power in the workplace through collective bargaining and working in large firms are both associated with higher earnings (England 1992). We thus incorporate measures into our analyses to capture these effects. Individuals who are either union members or whose jobs are covered by a collective bargaining agreement receive a code of 1 on the unionization variable. A measure of log of firm size is also included in the models.

Family Characteristics

Variables indicating family characteristics and responsibilities are mari-tal status, number of children in the household, and child care con-straints. Child care constraints is coded 1 if the respondent answered yes to any of the following questions:

In the past twelve months, has a concern about your child care needs caused you: (a) not to apply for work? (b) to turn down a job you were offered? (c) to not participate in school or a training program? (d) to quit or be fired from your job?

The variable is coded 0 if the respondent did not have a child younger than eighteen at home or if the respondent answered no to all of the questions.

To control for the presence of children, we include a measure of the number of children in the family. In addition, our models contain a dummy variable indicating whether the respondent is married.

Human Capital Characteristics

We incorporate standard measures of human capital characteristics in our analyses as control variables. For educational attainment, we use dummy variables for did not graduate from high school and high school graduate (or GED). Education beyond high school is the omitted category. Years of employment experience, years of experience squared, part-time work, and the respondent's age are also controlled.

In addition to these human capital characteristics, our models also account for the influence of English-language ability on wages. Among Hispanics and Asians, a lack of English proficiency can be an impediment to securing good jobs (Treiman and Lee 1996; Osterman 1993). Our measure is a dummy variable coded 1 if the interviewer perceived that the respondent spoke English "well" or "very well" and "0" otherwise. We used the interviewer's perception of English proficiency rather than the respondent's self-report because we wanted to approximate the perceptions of a potential employer.

Individual Characteristics

A measure of nativity status is also included, with 1 indicating "born outside the U.S. mainland." (This includes Puerto Ricans born on the island and respondents who are foreign-born.) Three dummy variables measure whether the respondent is black, Latino, or Asian. Non-Hispanic white is the excluded category for the race-ethnicity dummies.

Results

Descriptive Statistics: Comparisons Across Race-Ethnicity, Gender, and City

Is there a wage hierarchy by race-ethnicity and gender in our three cities? Does the group occupying the bottom vary by race-ethnicity and/

or gender across these cities? A comparison of median earnings reported in table 8.1 reveals that the answer to both of these questions is yes. Of the four race-gender groups present in Atlanta, black women have the lowest hourly earnings. In Boston and Los Angeles, in contrast, it is Latinas who are at the bottom of the wage distribution, followed by Latinos. The relative positions of white women and African American men in our sample also differ across cities in terms of magnitude, but not direction. White women in Atlanta, Boston, and Los Angeles earn more than black men, with the difference ranging from $1.87 per hour in Atlanta to $.80 per hour in Boston. The group at the top of the wage hierarchy also varies across cities. White men in our sample earn the highest wages in Atlanta and Boston. In Los Angeles, Asian women are the highest earners. We note that this finding should be interpreted with caution, as the Asian group is composed primarily of Japanese, Chinese, and Koreans and therefore represents a subset of all Asian groups.

From an inspection of the table, it appears that the way race-ethnicity and gender intersect depends on the local labor market. If we had collapsed race-ethnic groups and compared across gender, we would have concluded that men earn higher wages than women. This generalization holds only *within* race-ethnicity. In some contexts, women of one race-ethnic group earn more than men of another race-ethnic group. Similarly, if we had looked at race-ethnic differences in wages without taking gender into account, we would have missed the wage advantages that men of color hold over women in specific contexts. Our investigation of occupational and job segregation illustrate some of the factors generating the wage patterns that we uncover.

Do the cities differ in the gender and race-ethnic composition of occupations and jobs? We compare gender and race-ethnic segregation of occupations, jobs, and authority hierarchies for women of the race-ethnic groups in each city in table 8.2. We see that although gender segregation is constant across race, segregation by race-ethnicity is not. Within each city, the percent black in an occupation is higher for black women than for white women. In Boston, for example, white women are employed in occupations that are about 8 percent black, while African American women are in occupations that are 17 percent black.

Despite these differences, the majority of both black and white women in each city work in occupations where the majority of the incumbents from the local labor market are white. However, the occupational distributions actually mask substantial race-ethnic segregation in the workplace. Within *jobs*, segregation by race-ethnicity is striking. For over half of employed African American women in Atlanta, the majority of those who do their jobs in the firm are also black. Only 7 percent of white women in Atlanta are in majority-black jobs. In Boston and Los

TABLE 8.1   *Median Hourly Earnings by Gender and Race-Ethnicity in Atlanta, Boston, and Los Angeles*

	Atlanta	Boston	Los Angeles
Women			
White	$12.82	$10.80	$12.45
Black	$8.41	$9.84	$10.54
Latina	—	$8.67	$6.61
Asian	—	—	$15.92
N	336	519	977
Men			
White	$13.75	$14.74	$14.00
Black	$10.96	$10.00	$11.28
Latino	—	$8.98	$7.78
Asian	—	—	$12.50
N	179	335	864

Source: Multi-City Study of Urban Inequality.
Note: Estimate based on weighted samples of respondents with nonmissing values on all the variables used in the multivariate analyses (tables 8.6 and 8.7).

Angeles we find the same pattern: 25 percent of black women employed in Boston are in majority-black jobs, compared with 2 percent of white women. In Los Angeles, about 37 percent of employed black women are in majority-black jobs, compared with only 2 percent of employed white and Latina women and 8 percent of Asian women (table 8.2).

Not surprisingly, Latinas are the most likely to be working in jobs that are majority-Hispanic. Half of Latinas employed in Boston and 69 percent of Latinas employed in Los Angeles are working in majority-Hispanic jobs. Black women in Boston and Los Angeles are also more likely than white women to be working alongside Latinas, as table 8.2 shows. Asian women follow a similar pattern. Among women, 41 percent of Asians employed in Los Angeles are working in majority-Asian jobs, compared with 8 percent of whites, 12 percent of blacks, and 3 percent of Latinas.

The differences that we find in job segregation also emerge in the race-ethnic stratification of the authority structure. We examine who was being supervised by whom within each city, and present this information separately by gender of the respondent in three sets of figures. To examine the relative proportions of particular groups in authority positions, we based the numbers on those respondents who reported having a supervisor. Our data reveal two striking patterns across cities. First, women are often supervised by men, but men are much less often supervised by women. This can be seen by comparing figures 8.1, 8.2, and 8.3. For instance, in Atlanta, 42 percent of white women have a male super-

TABLE 8.2   *Gender and Race-Ethnic Composition of Occupations and Jobs Among Employed Women, by Race-Ethnicity and City*

	Atlanta		Boston			Los Angeles			
	White	Black	White	Black	Latina	White	Black	Latina	Asian
Occupation									
Mean									
Percentage female	68	70	62	67	49	67	69	66	67
Percentage black	36	46	08	17	12	14	17	11	14
Percentage Latino									
or Latina	—	—	06	08	12	30	36	55	31
Percentage Asian	—	—	—	—	—	18	16	14	19
Job									
Majority of									
coworkers									
Black	7%	50%	2%	25%	6%	2%	37%	2%	9%
Latino or									
Latina	—	—	1	5	53	8	12	69	11
Asian	—	—	—	—	—	5	8	3	41

Source: Multi-City Study of Urban Inequality.
Note: Composition variables are means computed from area data from the 1990 census. For instance, on average, white women employed in Atlanta were in occupations that were 68 percent female.

visor, but only 8 percent of white men have a female supervisor. In Boston, 38 percent of black women are supervised by a man, whereas only 28 percent of black men are overseen by a woman. In Los Angeles, about 51 percent of Latinas and 55 percent of Asian women have male supervisors, but less than 15 percent of Latino and Asian men have female supervisors. Another way of interpreting these figures is that male supervisors appear to have a wider range of opportunities to supervise—they can supervise women or men.

This is not the case for women, who are concentrated into positions where they hold authority over other women. The wider range of supervisory opportunities is partly due to the fact men are overrepresented in supervisory ranks compared to their share of total employment (see the last two bars in each panel of figures 8.1–8.3). But even after taking this overrepresentation into account, male supervisors are still more likely to supervise women than the other way around. The extent to which women have a male supervisor varies by race-ethnicity and by city. Asian women in Los Angeles are the most likely to be supervised by a man, and Latinas in Boston are the least likely. These city variations are likely the result of the types of industry and occupational opportunities available within the local labor markets.

Our second important finding is that despite the large variation in

FIGURE 8.1   *Percentage of Female and Male Respondents Supervised by Men, Atlanta*

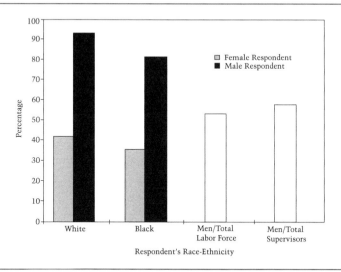

Source: Multi-City Study of Urban Inequality.

FIGURE 8.2   *Percentage of Female and Male Respondents Supervised by Men, Boston*

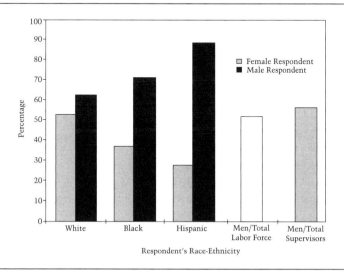

Source: Multi-City Study of Urban Inequality.

387

FIGURE 8.3   *Percentage of Female and Male Respondents Supervised by Men, Los Angeles*

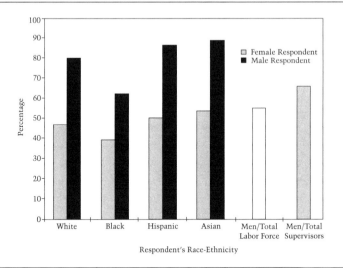

Source: Multi-City Study of Urban Inequality.

the race-ethnic composition of the population and occupations across the cities, there is some uniformity in the extent to which white women with supervisors are supervised by other whites (Atlanta, 95 percent; Boston, 96 percent; Los Angeles, 80 percent) (figures 8.4–8.6). Conversely, although African Americans, Latinas, and Asians are often supervised *by* whites, members of these groups seldom are supervisors *of* whites. Again, this is partly due to the fact that supervisors are disproportionately white, but goes beyond what one would expect based on the racial composition of supervisors alone. Consistent with theories of social closure, these patterns suggest that members of socially dominant groups (for example, men and whites) will have authority over each other and over subordinate groups (for example, women, African Americans, Latinos, Latinas, and Asians).

From a social closure perspective, job segregation both across firms and within the firm is a reflection of restricted opportunities for women of color. This perspective is buttressed through comparisons of the relative proportions of the race-ethnic groups among supervisors to the representation of these groups in the labor force within each city, as shown by the final bars in each panel of figures 8.7 through 8.9. For instance, black women comprise 13 percent of the labor force in Atlanta (U.S.

FIGURE 8.4   *Percentage of Female and Male Respondents*
              Supervised by Whites, Atlanta

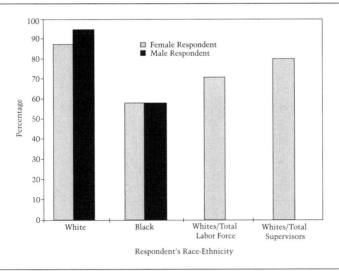

Source: Multi-City Study of Urban Inequality.

FIGURE 8.5   *Percentage of Female and Male Respondents*
              Supervised by Whites, Boston

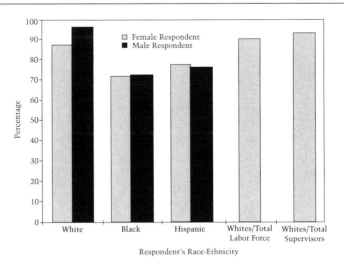

Source: Multi-City Study of Urban Inequality.

FIGURE 8.6   *Percentage of Female and Male Respondents*
             Supervised by Whites, Los Angeles

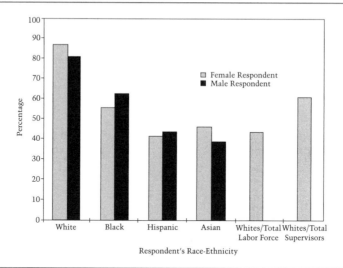

Source: Multi-City Study of Urban Inequality.

FIGURE 8.7   *Race-Ethnicity of Women Supervisors by Race-*
             Ethnicity of Respondent, Women in Atlanta

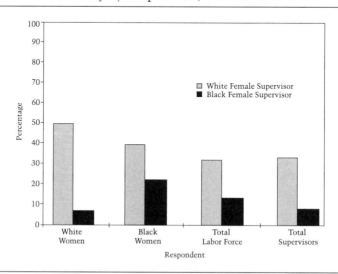

Source: Multi-City Study of Urban Inequality.

FIGURE 8.8   *Race-Ethnicity of Women Supervisors by Race-Ethnicity of Resondent, Women in Boston*

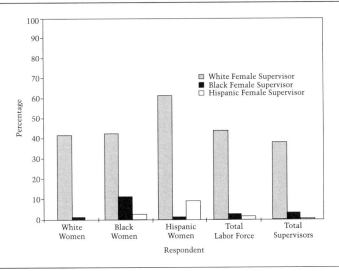

Source: Multi-City Study of Urban Inequality.

FIGURE 8.9   *Race-Ethnicity of Supervisor by Race-Ethnicity of Respondent, Women in Los Angeles*

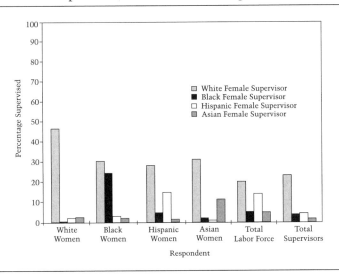

Source: Multi-City Study of Urban Inequality.

Bureau of the Census 1990), yet they are represented among the supervisors of our Atlanta respondents at much lower rates. Among all the respondents who had a supervisor, the proportion of supervisors who were black women is 8 percent in Atlanta. Hispanic women are 2 percent of Boston's labor force and 0.4 percent of the supervisors among the Boston respondents. In Los Angeles, Asian women represent 4 percent of the local labor force and only 1.5 percent of the supervisors for our sample.

Adherents of the multiple jeopardy perspective would emphasize that the *combination* of race and gender within occupations, jobs, and authority hierarchies is also important in shaping opportunities. In light of this thesis, we look at the race-ethnicity of female supervisors, by the race-ethnicity of the female respondents. We find that white women tend to supervise women of every race-ethnic group, while African American, Latina, and Asian women supervisors tend to hold authority only over members of their own race-ethnic and gender group (see figures 8.7–8.9). Once more, this asymmetry goes well beyond the results of white women's greater likelihood of holding a supervisory position.

The three sets of figures imply the existence of a tightly constricted set of promotion opportunities for African American, Latina, and Asian women that is grounded in the combination of gender and race-ethnicity. Those few women of color who occupy positions of authority are likely to be supervising women of the same race-ethnic background as themselves. White men have a "multiple advantage" in that they have the greatest opportunities to supervise all race-ethnic groups of men and women.

The descriptive findings in general illustrate that although the extent of race-ethnic segregation of occupations, jobs, and authority hierarchies differs widely across the cities, there are important similarities. Consistent with the expectations of queuing theory, Latinas and African American women tend to have the lowest wages in each city—particularly compared to white men, black men, and white women. Latinas and African American women are concentrated in jobs where the majority of their coworkers are also Latino, Latina or black.

Although the aim of the descriptive statistics is to chart the contours of the local labor markets as they pertain to the composition of occupations, jobs, and authority hierarchies, we also briefly consider race-ethnic differences in the other variables that are relevant to labor market outcomes among women (table 8.3). Compared to white and Asian women, black women and Latinas have less human capital and are employed in jobs requiring less skill. Reports of child care conflicts do not differ much between race-ethnic groups, or between working women in Atlanta and Boston. Child care constraints are more com-

TABLE 8.3   *Individual and Family Characteristics of Samples of Women in Atlanta, Boston, and Los Angeles, by Race-Ethnicity*

	Atlanta	Boston	Los Angeles
Family			
Percentage married			
White women	59.9	67.5	54.1
Black women	30.1	33.3	29.9
Latinas	—	70.8	50.6
Asian women		—	56.0
Percentage with child care constraints			
White women	17.3	16.5	27.1
Black women	16.4	15.7	20.8
Latinas	—	16.0	24.6
Asian women	—	—	18.4
Mean number of children			
White women	.69	.91	.75
Black women	.91	1.10	.78
Latinas	—	2.05	1.25
Asian women	—	—	.70
Individual			
Percentage with "good" English proficiency			
White women	96.5	97.8	100.0
Black women	100.0	100.0	100.0
Latinas	—	58.3	79.7
Asian women	—	—	92.0
Percentage with less than twelve years education			
White women	4.0	11.5	2.2
Black women	6.8	12.0	5.2
Latinas	—	66.7	45.2
Asian women	—	—	4.1
Percentage high school graduates			
White women	34.2	43.0	41.3
Black women	43.8	62.5	48.9
Latinas	—	20.8	20.0
Asian women	—	—	30.5

Source: Multi-City Study of Urban Inequality.

monly experienced in Los Angeles, with white women being most likely to report the conflict and Asian women least likely. Although employed Latinas have more children than other women in Boston and Los Angeles, they are not more likely to report child care constraints. Black women in all cities are the least likely to be married, but they are not more likely to report child care constraints.

Multivariate Analyses

Is there a relation between the relatively low wages of African American women and Latinas and their concentration in positions that are segregated by gender and race-ethnicity? Is this relation simply the result of human capital attributes, or does it belie more systematic disadvantage? If queuing and crowding processes are influencing wages, then compositional factors should remain salient even after human capital and skill requirements are taken into account.

We explore the intersection of race and gender and the question of multiple jeopardy with a reduced-form earnings model that controls for human capital and individual characteristics of education, experience age, number of children, part-time work, and industry of employment. Results of this model, shown in table 8.4, reveal a definite wage advantage for white men relative to the other race-ethnic-gender groups. Women of color and Latinos are disadvantaged in their earnings relative to white women (the reference group). Black and Asian men's wages do not differ significantly from white women's in this simple model. The disadvantage associated with being female is apparent within each racial-ethnic group, and women of color are generally disadvantaged by the combination of gender and race-ethnicity.

Individual human capital factors, as we have measured them, do not account for the differences in earnings among the race-ethnic-gender groups in our study. The occupational measures of human capital (average training and education) may be more relevant, since they are more specific indicators of the skills required to do the kind of work the respondent does. Our next model of hourly earnings includes these measures, as well as measures reflecting the segregation of occupations in local labor markets, the segregation of workers within firms, and the advantages and disadvantages associated with family life. This model is applied separately to the earnings of women and men so that we might fully capture the ways in which gender interacts with other labor market forces.

In table 8.5, we present results from the full model for women's earnings in each of the three subsamples. The analyses provide novel results for each institutional arena. The most striking finding relevant to the question of disadvantage among Latinas and African American women is that race-ethnic segregation affects wages at three different points: the occupation, the job, and the authority hierarchy. These points represent processes in the local labor market and the firm.

Local Labor Market Characteristics

Model 1 includes whites and blacks from Atlanta, Boston, and Los Angeles; model 2 encompasses whites, blacks, and Latinas in Boston and

TABLE 8.4   *Models Estimating Log Hourly Earnings, with Comparisons of Race-Ethnic and Gender Groups in Atlanta, Boston, and Los Angeles*

	Atlanta, Boston, Los Angeles		Boston, Los Angeles		Los Angeles	
	b	(S.E.)	b	(S.E.)	b	(S.E.)
Race-ethnicity and gender						
White men	.140**	(.033)	.160**	(.035)	.179**	(.046)
Black men	−.055	(.036)	−.012	(.046)	−.083	(.063)
Hispanic men	—	—	−.112*	(.044)	−.123*	(.060)
Asian men	—	—	—	—	.092	(.065)
Black women	−.171**	(.030)	−.155**	(.037)	−.198**	(.050)
Hispanic women	—	—	−.259**	(.032)	−.265**	(.043)
Asian women	—	—	—	—	−.134*	(.054)
Atlanta	−.102**	(.029)	—	—	—	—
Boston	−.054	(.030)	−.010	(.025)	—	—
Constant	2.221**	(.081)	2.174**	(.076)	2.112**	(.097)
N	2016		2420		1863	
R²	.433		.484		.497	

Source: Multi-City Study of Urban Inequality.
Note: Controls: high school dropout; high school graduate; experience; experience squared; age; number of children; industry dummies. S.E. = standard error. White women comprise the excluded category.
*$p < .05$. **$p < .01$.

Los Angeles; model 3 represents all four race-ethnic groups (whites, blacks, Latinas, and Asians) in Los Angeles only. Since these models contain overlapping samples, we look for predominant patterns in the three analyses.

The percent black and percent Hispanic in an occupation are statistically significant in the samples for model 2 even after the firm characteristics are included in the analyses. These results obtain over and above the effect of the measures of occupational skill. Contrary to our predictions, however, the percent black and percent Hispanic in the occupation are not significant in models 1 and 3. These results could indicate that local labor market effects are stronger in Boston than in Atlanta and Los Angeles. In the latter cases, the skill requirements of an occupation extinguish the effect of occupational race-ethnic segregation.

We include dummy variables for city in our models, and also test for interactions between city and a respondent's race-ethnicity. Since

TABLE 8.5 *Models Estimating Log Hourly Earnings Among Women in Atlanta, Boston, and Los Angeles*

	Atlanta, Boston, Los Angeles		Boston, Los Angeles		Los Angeles	
	b	(S.E.)	b	(S.E.)	b	(S.E.)
Race-ethnicity						
Black	−.050	(.026)	−.010	(.032)	−.050	(.045)
Hispanic	—		.014	(.037)	.041	(.050)
Asian	—		—		.069	(.058)
Atlanta	−.010	(.039)	—		—	
Boston	−.013	(.031)	−.127**	(.043)	—	
Occupation						
Percentage female	.055	(.059)	−.002	(.055)	.028	(.065)
Percentage black	−.158	(.107)	−.313*	(.141)	−.118	(.212)
Percentage Hispanic	—		−.355**	(.104)	−.201	(.150)
Percentage Asian	—		—		.404	(.236)
Average training	.002	(.001)	.004**	(.002)	.003	(.002)
Average education	.151*	(.029)	.065*	(.032)	.096*	(.042)
Job or firm						
Coworker black	−.078**	(.026)	−.118**	(.031)	−.115**	(.042)
Coworker Hispanic	—		−.119**	(.032)	−.107**	(.039)
Coworker Asian	—		—		.025	(.049)
Supervisor white	.073**	(.027)	.060*	(.025)	.054	(.032)
Supervisor male	.064**	(.024)	.030	(.023)	.054	(.029)
No supervisor	.130*	(.059)	.022	(.049)	.087	(.060)
Firm size (log)	.033**	(.006)	.035**	(.006)	.038**	(.007)
Unionized	.106**	(.029)	.102**	(.026)	.117**	(.033)
Family						
Married (1 = yes)	.005	(.022)	.026	(.020)	−.018	(.026)
Child care constraints	−.070*	(.032)	−.064*	(.028)	−.100*	(.039)
Individual						
Foreign-born	−.056	(.045)	−.075*	(.034)	.095*	(.048)
English proficiency (1 = excellent, good)	.097	(.082)	.041	(.036)	.087	(.046)
Constant	1.348**	(.154)	1.860**	(.168)	1.549**	(.227)
N	1222		1340		977	
R^2	.481		.507		.525	

Source: Multi-City Study of Urban Inequality.
Note: Controls: high school dropout; high school graduate; experience; experience squared; age; number of children; industry dummies. S.E. = standard error.
*$p < .05$. **$p < .01$.

none of the interactions is statistically significant, we have dropped them from the final model.

Job and Firm Characteristics

Results for the effects of firm and job characteristics on women's wages are consistent and strong across the models. Women's earnings fall when they are employed in a job where the majority of their coworkers are either black or Latino and Latina. In all the samples, working in a majority-black job lowers earnings. Working in a majority-Hispanic job in Boston or Los Angeles also reduces wages (models 2 and 3), but there is no effect in Los Angeles for jobs that were majority-Asian (model 3).

The race of the respondent's supervisor is another compositional factor within the establishment that is related to wages. Among those women who are supervised on their jobs, answering to a white supervisor rather than a nonwhite supervisor raises hourly wages.[6] In model 1, wages are also higher for women who are supervised by a man rather than by a woman.

Our results confirm the findings of previous studies that organizational factors affect wages. When women are employed in a job that is covered by a collective bargaining agreement or when women work in larger firms, they earn relatively higher wages (even controlling for industry).

Family-Related Characteristics

Women's family responsibilities appear to exert a direct impact on their earnings. In all our models, women who report conflicts with child care that led them to be late or absent from work, or that caused them to reduce their hours, receive lower wages than women who do not report such constraints.

The race-ethnic composition of the occupation, job, and authority hierarchy affect women's wages in our sample, but the gender composition of occupations does not. There is some evidence that the gender of supervisor is related to wages, but this finding appears in only one of our models. Some of the wage disadvantage of Latinas and African American women, shown in table 8.4, is reduced by race-ethnic segregation in the workplace. These women are more likely than their Asian and white counterparts to be employed in occupations and jobs that are predominantly black or predominantly Hispanic, and they are less likely to have a white supervisor. *Each* of these factors chips away at their wages, and pushes them to the bottom of the earnings distribution. For women of all race-ethnic backgrounds, gender roles within the family can further erode wages through the difficulties that many women encounter as they attempt to arrange care for their children.

The results from table 8.5 lead us to reinterpret how multiple jeopardy works. Among women, the direct effects of race on earnings disappear when local labor market, firm, and family characteristics are taken into account. In the multiethnic samples (models 2 and 3), the main effects of race disappear but the race-ethnic traits of occupations, jobs, and supervisors remain strong (or even strengthen). This suggests that the multiple jeopardy of minority women is produced through labor market processes that segregate them from whites within the firm.

Comparisons with Men

All organizational and family effects on women's wages are net of our controls for human capital, part-time or full-time work schedule, and industry. Although we expected part-time jobs to pay less than full-time ones (Tilly 1996), the variable is not significant in our models. The lack of significance is probably due to the other variables that differentiate part-time from full-time workers. These include industry, amount of training, firm size, collective bargaining, race and gender composition of occupations, and child care constraints. For example, very high levels of part-time work are found in the female and minority dominated occupations of sales, private household service work, other services, and laborers and in the trade and service industrial sectors (Tilly 1996, 92). The significance of the organizational and family variables, especially childcare constraints, for women's hourly wages does not suggest that part-time work is unimportant, but rather that it matters what leads people to part-time jobs. This affirms Tilly's (1996) argument that women managers and professionals who work part-time are relatively highly rewarded and should be considered as "retention" part-time workers. Women's wages are influenced more directly by the segregation of their job opportunities and by their inability to resolve work-family conflicts than by their holding part-time jobs.[7]

Additional support for a multiple jeopardy perspective emerges when we compare the earnings determination process for women to that of men, shown in table 8.6. Race-ethnicity influences wages somewhat differently for men and women. First, the effect of being African American or Latino remains consistently significant and negative in all three of the models for men.[8] In the sample of women, race produces no independent effect on wages. If this race-ethnic effect in the male sample is the result of human capital attributes, as some claim (Farkas and Vicknair 1996), then it is not clear why African American women would not exhibit similar patterns.[9]

Within the firm, men face similar disadvantages associated with the horizontal and vertical segregation of jobs. Similar to women's situation,

TABLE 8.6   *Models Estimating Log Hourly Earnings Among Men in Atlanta, Boston, and Los Angeles*

	Atlanta, Boston, Los Angeles		Boston, Los Angeles		Los Angeles	
	b	(S.E.)	b	(S.E.)	b	(S.E.)
Race-ethnicity						
Black	−.111**	(.030)	−.109**	(.036)	−.120*	(.050)
Hispanic	—		−.142**	(.040)	−.136*	(.052)
Asian	—		—		.044	(.056)
Atlanta	−.009	(.057)	—		—	
Boston	−.127**	(.038)	−.173**	(.053)	—	
Occupation						
Percentage female	.058	(.073)	−.028	(.061)	−.056	(.073)
Percentage black	−.133	(.146)	−.264	(.213)	−.162	(.268)
Percentage Hispanic	—		−.280*	(.116)	−.117	(.156)
Percentage Asian	—		—		−.045	(.234)
Average training	−.002	(.001)	.001	(.001)	−.001	(.002)
Average education	.199**	(.034)	.105**	(.036)	.158**	(.047)
Job or firm						
Coworker black	−.051	(.034)	−.095*	(.040)	−.111*	(.051)
Coworker Hispanic	—		−.125**	(.036)	−.129**	(.042)
Coworker Asian	—	—	—	—	−.094	(.065)
Supervisor white	.049	(.032)	.063*	(.027)	.073*	(.032)
Supervisor male	.028	(.037)	.022	(.033)	−.021	(.039)
No supervisor	.096	(.060)	.083	(.054)	.072	(.064)
Firm size (log)	.033**	(.008)	.035**	(.006)	.044**	(.008)
Unionized	.157**	(.040)	.189**	(.030)	.139**	(.036)
Family						
Married (1 = yes)	.146**	(.033)	.117**	(.029)	.099**	(.034)
Child care constraints	.004	(.067)	.002	(.051)	−.011	(.053)
Individual						
Foreign-born	.038	(.042)	−.019	(.035)	−.064	(.043)
English proficiency (1 = excellent, good)	.072	(.082)	.066	(.035)	.140**	(.041)
Constant	1.325**	(.167)	1.629**	(.184)	1.396**	(.253)
N	770		1055		864	
R^2	.483		.526		.562	

Source: Multi-City Study of Urban Inequality.
Note: Controls: high school dropout; high school graduate; experience; experience squared; age; number of children; industry dummies. S.E. = standard error.
*$p < .05$. **$p < .05$.

men's wages are diminished by working in a majority-black job and their wages are boosted if they report to a white supervisor (models 2 and 3). We also find a clear distinction in the way family structure influences labor market outcomes for men compared with women. Men do not suffer a wage penalty when they face child care constraints, as women do. In addition, matrimony provides an earnings boon to men but not to women, a result that is consistent with previous studies (England and Farkas 1986).

Conclusion

Latinas and African American women are situated in multiple contexts within the firm and the family that can lower their wages. These women are more likely than white or Asian women to work in jobs that are predominantly black or predominantly Hispanic, they are less likely to report to a white supervisor, and they face conflicts between job and child care responsibilities.

Our analyses did little to capture the unique labor market situation of Asian women. Research shows that some groups of Asian women face labor market conditions that are similar to white women (for example, native-born Asian ethnics and well-educated immigrant women from northeast Asian countries). However, the single category of "Asian" hides the great diversity among Asian women, and misses the disadvantages that some groups keenly feel (Espiritu 1997). Understanding the labor market experiences of Asian women and the disadvantages they confront may require more refined analyses of particular groups in particular settings.

The regression model for women in Los Angeles (table 8.5, model 3) shows that immigrant Asian women and Latinas have an additional burden in the labor market, disadvantaged by their newness (reflected in the coefficients for foreign-born and English proficiency), as well as by possible racial discrimination within the firm (coworker and supervisor effects) (see also Segura 1992; Woo 1985). Although some ethnic groups of immigrants greatly improve their position over time, the various groups do not progress at the same rate. Poorly educated immigrants are often severely exploited at the hands of co-ethnic employers. The Los Angeles garment factories are notorious for this practice. At the other end of the spectrum, there is downward mobility for many well-educated Asian immigrant women. Formerly professionals in their home country, these women cannot satisfy state licensing requirements and end up running small shops instead (Chai 1987). Self-employment is popular among many Asian immigrant groups because it provides them with independence, financial security, and the ability to hire relatives

(Gold 1988). As of 1983, 53 percent of Korean male workers in Los Angeles and 36 percent of women were self-employed (Espiritu 1997, 78).

Our data show that it is predominantly the processes within the firm and the family that generate race-ethnic earnings inequality among women. For women, much more than for men, the race-ethnicity of co-workers and the race of one's supervisor influence earnings. Women's earnings are diminished by child care constraints, but men feel no ill effects. For men, family roles can push wages upward through the earnings benefits of marriage. Employers may be using race-ethnicity and parental responsibilities to segregate women more than men into lower-paying jobs. (The Multi-City Study employer data allow us to understand how inner workings of the firm lead to inequality, and we refer the reader to the other chapters in this volume.)

Some may argue that the wage-dampening effects of job composition are really the result of the combined human capital attributes of the incumbents. Others would point to discriminatory practices associated with queuing. Our findings cannot directly arbitrate between the human capital and social structural explanations for the relation between earnings and the race-ethnicity of the individual, the workers in a job, and the supervisor. The finding of gender differences between the models raise questions about the adequacy of a strictly human capital interpretation of our results, however. That is, if human capital attributes were generating the lower wages associated with working in a majority-black or majority-Latino or -Latina job or with having a non-white supervisor, then we would expect similar effects among men and women. This is not the case.

Moving past these debates, our results are important for some issues addressed by other chapters in this volume. In particular, the descriptive statistics reveal that within firms, the labor market is segregated by race and ethnicity much like neighborhoods are segregated (although to a lesser degree). Sociologically, this creates different "social worlds" for individuals based on their race-ethnicity and their gender. For instance, a white man will almost always be supervised by other white men, and most often encounter women and men of color in subordinate positions. This may influence his perception of the leadership abilities of white men compared to other race-ethnic groups. At the very least, it will provide less information to him about the supervisory capabilities of anyone other than a white man.

Our results suggest that the growing diversity within U.S. cities is maintaining—rather than breaking down—economic hierarchies. Researchers concerned with questions of inequality need to attend more carefully to processes within the firm that lead to job segregation and the repercussions of that segregation. The feminist claim that gender and race-ethnicity "intersect" in the labor market provides a useful frame for approaching the complexity of labor market inequality, but this intersection occurs within particular institutional contexts. We must look beyond the general claim of "intersections" and begin to construct analyses that identify the *mechanisms* within local labor markets, firms, and families that give rise to unique experiences and opportunities for individuals based on their race, ethnicity, and gender.

The program to convert 1980 occupation codes to 1990 codes was provided by Barry Hirsch, Florida State University. We'd like to thank Solon Simmons, James Elliott, and Teresa Loftin for their assistance with the data analyses and manuscript preparation. We are also grateful to Luis Falcón, Edwin Melendez, Ren Farley, Chris Tilly, and the participants of the Emory Friday Sociology Seminar for their thoughtful comments on earlier drafts.

Notes

1. See Espiritu 1997 for an overview of studies about the progress of Asian ethnic groups in contemporary American labor markets from the perspective of the intersection of gender and race.

2. It has also been argued that the positive relation between marriage and earnings among men is spurious. Those personal characteristics that lead men into matrimony are considered to be the same characteristics that make good, productive workers (Nakosteen and Zimmer 1997).

3. While we have African American and white respondents in all three cities in our study, the numbers for separate analyses by city become too small to consider all the local labor market, firm, family, and control variables that are theoretically relevant.

4. Some argue that the measures of "skill" are endogenous to the gender composition of occupations, since the valuation of a "skill" is influenced by the cultural conceptions of whether the skill is the domain of women or men (Steinberg 1995).

5. We combine these variables into an interaction term that represents whether or not a supervisor is a white man. The interaction term is not statistically significant in any of the models, and is dropped from the final analyses.

6. It is possible that "male supervisor" is highly correlated with other aspects of the occupation and job, such as percent female. When we exclude these variables from the model, there is still no significant effect on wages of having a male supervisor.

7. There were an insufficient number of cases to separately analyze part-time workers, but we did obtain very similar results when the models included only full-time workers.

8. All differences in effects between men and women that we discuss are significant at the .05 level, using a t-test to compare coefficients across the female and male samples.

9. It is possible that the gender difference in the effect of race-ethnicity on wages is linked to soft skills. If soft skills are in greater demand, and if women of all backgrounds are generally considered to be more adept at the types of social interactions that soft skills imply, then Latinas and African American women may be shielded from the biases that accompany employers' assessments of the soft skills of race-ethnic minorities. There is currently insufficient information in the literature to test this proposition, since most of the publications regarding soft skills focus on men (Moss and Tilly 1996).

References

Almquist, Elizabeth. 1975. "Untangling the Effects of Race and Sex: The Disadvantaged Status of Black Women." *Social Science Quarterly* 56: 129–42.

Barron, John M., John Bishop, and William C. Dunkelberg. 1985. "Employer Search: The Interviewing and Hiring of New Employees." *Review of Economics and Statistics* 67(1): 43–52.

Becker, Gary. 1985. "Human Capital, Effort, and the Sexual Division of Labor." *Journal of Labor Economics* 3: S33–S58.

Bergmann, Barbara. 1986. *The Economic Emergence of Women*. New York: Basic Books.

Bielby, William, and James Baron. 1986. "Men and Women at Work: Sex Segregation and Statistical Discrimination." *American Journal of Sociology* 91(4): 759–99.

Bielby, William, and Denise Bielby. 1988. "She Works Hard for the Money: Household Responsibilities and the Allocation of Work Effort." *American Journal of Sociology* 93: 1031–59.

Catanzarite, Lisa M., and Myra H. Strober. 1988. "Occupational Attractiveness and Race-Gender Segregation, 1960–1980." Paper presented at the Annual Meeting of the American Sociological Association, Atlanta, August.

Chai, Alice Yun. 1983. "Sexual Division of Labor in the Contexts of Nuclear Family and Cultural Ideology Among Korean Student Couples in Hawaii." *Humboldt Journal of Social Relations* 10(2): 153–74.

———. 1987. "Freed from the Elders but Locked Into Labor: Korean Immigrant Women in Hawaii." *Women's Studies* 13: 223–34.

Collins, Patricia Hill. 1990. *Black Feminist Thought*. London: Harper-Collins.

Corcoran, Mary, Linda Datcher, and Greg Duncan. 1980. "Information and Influence Networks in Labor Markets." In *Five Thousand American Families*, vol. 8, edited by Greg Duncan and James Morgan. Ann Arbor, Mich.: Institute for Social Research.

Corcoran, Mary, Colleen Heflin, and Belinda Reyes. 1999. "The Economic Progress of Mexican and Puerto Rican Women." In *Latinas and African American Women at Work: Race, Gender, and Economic Inequality*, edited by Irene Browne. New York: Russell Sage Foundation.

Cunningham, James S., and Nadja Zalokar. 1992. "The Economic Progress of Black Women Since 1940: Occupational Distribution and Relative Wages." *Industrial and Labor Relations Review* 45(3): 540–55.

DiPrete, Thomas, and Whitman Soule. 1988. "Gender and Promotion in Segmented Job Ladder Systems." *American Sociological Review* 53: 26–40.

England, Paula. 1992. *Comparable Worth: Theories and Evidence*. Hawthorne, N.Y.: Aldine de Gruyter.

England, Paula, Karen Christopher, and Lori Reed. 1999. "Gender, Race, Ethnicity, and Wages." In *Latinas and African American Women at Work: Race, Gender, and Economic Inequality*, edited by Irene Browne. New York: Russell Sage Foundation.

England, Paula, and George Farkas. 1986. "Households, Employment, and Gender: A Social, Economic, and Demographic View." Hawthorne, N.Y.: Aldine de Gruyter.

England, Paula, and Barbara Kilbourne. 1988. "Occupational Measures from the Dictionary of Occupational Titles for 1980 Census Detailed Occupations." ICPSR 8942, machine-readable data file. Ann Arbor, Mich.: Inter-University Consortium for Political and Social Research.

Epstein, Cynthia Fuchs. 1988. *Deceptive Distinctions: Sex, Gender, and the Social Order*. New Haven, Conn.: Yale University Press.

Espiritu, Yen Le. 1997. *Asian American Women and Men: Labor, Laws and Love*. Thousand Oaks, Calif.: Sage.

Farkas, George, Paula England, Keven Vicknair, and Barbara Stanek Kilbourne. 1997. "Cognitive Skill, Skill Demands of Jobs, and Earnings Among Young European American, African American, and Mexican American Workers." *Social Forces* 75(3): 913–38.

Farkas, George, and Keven Vicknair. 1996. "Appropriate Tests of Racial Wage Discrimination Require Controls for Cognitive Skill: Comment on Cancio, Evans, and Maume." *American Sociological Review* 61(4): 557–60.

Gittleman, Maury, and David R. Howell. 1995. "Changes in the Structure and Quality of Jobs in the U.S.: Effects by Race and Gender, 1973–90." *Industrial and Labor Relations Review* 48(3): 420–40.

Glass, Jennifer. 1990. "The Impact of Occupational Segregation on Working Conditions." *Social Forces* 68(3): 779–96.

Gold, Steven J. 1988. "Refugees and Small Business: The Case of Soviet Jews and Vietnamese." *Ethnic and Racial Studies* 11(4): 411–38.

Heilman, Madeline E. 1995. "Sex Stereotypes and Their Effects in the Workplace: What We Know and What We Don't Know." *Journal of Social Behavior and Personality* 10(6): 3–26.

Hochschild, Arlie Russell. 1989. *The Second Shift: Working Parents and the Revolution at Home*. New York: Viking.

Holzer, Harry J. 1994. "Black Employment Problems: New Evidence, Old Questions." *Journal of Policy Analysis and Management* 13(4): 699–722.

———. 1996. *What Employers Want: Job Prospects for Less-Educated Workers*. New York: Russell Sage Foundation.

Hum, Tarry, and Melvin Oliver. 1995. "Immigrant Ethnic Economies in Los Angeles." Paper prepared for the Multi-City Study of Urban Inequality Conference on Searching for Work, Searching for Workers. New York (September 28–29, 1995).

Jacobs, Jerry A., and Mary Blair-Loy. 1996. "Gender, Race, Local Labor Markets and Occupational Devaluation." *Sociological Focus* 29(3): 209–30.

Kaufman, Robert. 1986. "Labor Structure and Black-White Employment." *American Sociological Review* 51(3): 310–22.

King, Deborah. 1989. "Multiple Jeopardy, Multiple Consciousness: The Context of a Black Feminist Ideology" *Signs* 14(1): 42–72.

King, Mary, 1998. "Are African Americans Losing Their Footholds in Better Jobs?" *Journal of Economic Issues* 32: 641–68.

Kluegel, James R. 1978. "The Causes and Cost of Racial Exclusion from Job Authority." *American Sociological Review* 43(3): 285–301.

Lieberson, Stanley. 1980. *A Piece of the Pie: Black and White Immigrants Since 1880*. Berkeley: University of California Press.

McGuire, Gail M., and Barbara F. Reskin. 1993. "Authority Hierarchies at Work: The Impacts of Race and Sex." *Gender and Society* 7(4): 487–506.

Milkman, Ruth, ed. 1985. *Women, Work, and Protest: A Century of U.S. Women's Labor History*. Boston: Routledge and Kegan Paul.

Mincer, Jacob, and Stanley Polachek. 1974. "Family Investments in Human Capital: Earnings of Women." *Journal of Political Economy* 82: S76–108.

Moss, Philip, and Chris Tilly. 1996. "'Soft' Skills and Race: An Investigation of Black Men's Employment Problems." *Work and Occupations* 23(3): 252–76.

Nakosteen, Robert A., and Michael A. Zimmer. 1997. "Men, Money, and Marriage: Are High Earners More Prone Than Low Earners to Marry?" *Social Science Quarterly* 78(1): 66–82.

Osterman, Paul. 1988. *Employment Futures: Reorganization, Dislocation, and Public Policy*. New York: Oxford University Press.

———. 1993. "Why Don't 'They' Work? Employment Patterns in a High Pressure Economy." *Social Science Research* 22(2): 115–30.

Portes, Alejandro, and Robert Bach. 1985. *Latin Journey: Cuban and Mexican Immigrants in the United States*. Berkeley: University of California Press.

Reskin, Barbara. 1993. "Sex Segregation in the Workplace." *Annual Review of Sociology* 19: 241–70.

Reskin, Barbara, and Naomi Cassirer. 1996. "Occupational Segregation by Gender, Race and Ethnicity." *Sociological Focus* 29(3): 231–43.

Reskin, Barbara, and Patricia Roos. 1990. *Job Queues, Gender Queues: Explaining Women's Inroads into Male Occupations*. Philadelphia: Pine Forge Press.

Romero, Mary, Pierrette Hondagneu-Sotelo, and Vilma Ortiz, eds. 1997. *Challenging Fronteras: Structuring Latina and Latino Lives in the U.S.: An Anthology of Readings*. New York: Routledge.

Sanders, Jimy, and Victor Nee. 1996. "Social Capital, Human Capital, and Immigrant Self-Employment." *American Sociological Review* 61(2): 231–49.

Segura, Denise. 1992. "Chicanas in White Collar Jobs: 'You Have to Prove Yourself More.'" *Sociological Perspectives* 35: 163–82.

Steinberg, Stephen. 1995. *Turning Back: The Retreat from Racial Justice in American Thought and Policy*. Boston: Beacon Press.

Stolzenberg, Ross, and Linda Waite. 1984. "Local Labor Markets, Children and Labor Force Participation of Wives." *Demography* 21(2): 157–70.

Tilly, Chris. 1996. *Half a Job: Bad and Good Jobs in a Changing Labor Market*. Philadelphia: Temple University Press.

Tomaskovic-Devey, Donald, and Sheryl Skaggs. 1999. "Gender and Racial Composition and Productivity: An Establishment Level Test of the Statistical Discrimination Hypothesis." *Work and Occupations* 26: 422–45.

Treiman, Donald J., and Hye-Kyung Lee. 1996. "Income Differences Among 31 Ethnic Groups in Los Angeles." In *Social Differentiation and Social Inequality: Essays in Honor of John Pock*, edited by James Baron, David B. Grusky, and Donald J. Treiman. Boulder, Colo.: Westview.

U.S. Department of Commerce. U.S. Bureau of the Census. 1990. *Census of Population and Housing: 1990*. Washington: U.S. Government Printing Office.

Witkowski, Kristine M., and Kevin T. Leicht. 1995. "The Effects of Gender Segregation, Labor Force Participation, and Family Roles on the Earnings of Young Adult Workers." *Work and Occupations* 22(1): 48–72.

Woo, Deborah. 1985. "The Socioeconomic Status of Asian American Women in the Labor Force: An Alternative View." *Sociological Perspectives* 28(3): 307–38.

9

LINKING THE MULTI-CITY STUDY'S HOUSEHOLD AND EMPLOYER SURVEYS TO TEST FOR RACE AND GENDER EFFECTS IN HIRING AND WAGE SETTING

Tom Hertz, Chris Tilly,
and Michael P. Massagli

O NE OF the main challenges in empirical research on race and gender discrimination in the labor market is that of measuring and controlling for the full range of factors *other* than discrimination that may explain observed differences in pay or employment rates between men and women, and between whites and people of color. The Multi-City Study of Urban Inequality and its cousin, the Multi-City Telephone Employer Survey, are particularly well suited to this task, for several reasons. First, the Household Survey contains questions on a number of attributes that fall under the general heading of human capital, including an informal assessment of the respondent's ability to understand the survey questions; questions on vocational education, military service, and length of job tenure; and a series of questions that allow for a good estimate of the actual amount of work experience accrued since leaving school.

Second, the survey asked about several noncognitive aspects of personality, some of which have been shown to have significant consequences in the labor market (Bowles, Gintis, and Osborne 2000). These include an interviewer's assessment that categorizes the respondent's attitude toward the survey process on a four-step scale (from "friendly and interested" to "hostile") and a variable that identifies the relatively small number of people who used derogatory racial epithets during the course of the interview. Employers interviewed by Philip Moss and

Chris Tilly (2000) sometimes asserted that an uncooperative or hostile attitude was a particularly important barrier to employment for people of color; these data allow us to test this hypothesis.

Third, both the Household and the Employer Surveys contain information on the frequency with which a number of specific tasks need be performed in any given job: talking to customers in person and on the phone, reading and writing, arithmetic, and using computers. These frequency estimates will be treated as indirect measures of the cognitive and social skills of the people who occupy those jobs, adding to our list of human capital controls. As we shall see, the task variables retain some explanatory power even after introducing detailed controls for occupation and industry.

However, like occupation and industry, these task variables are likely to be endogenous and thus may in part reflect the outcome of labor market discrimination. For example, if women are confined by gender discrimination to low-paying occupations or industries, or to jobs that are characterized by the frequent performance of poorly rewarded tasks and infrequent performance of higher-value tasks, then the inclusion of occupation, industry, and occupation-related variables such as our task measures should impart a downward bias to our estimates of the overall degree of labor market discrimination (Cain 1986).

A fourth advantage of the Multi-City Study is one that has thus far received little attention, namely, that some of the people interviewed as part of the Household Survey work at a firm, and in an occupation, that was sampled as part of the Employer Survey. For this subset, which we will refer to as the *linked dataset*, we may make use of the full list of Household Survey variables as well as the full list of Employer Survey questions. This allows us to control for an unusually broad range of variables that influence wages from both the supply and the demand sides of the labor market; if race and gender remain significant factors, this provides better-than-usual evidence for the presence of discrimination.

The link between the two surveys also enables us to compare pairs of workers who work for the same employers in the same occupations. This *paired dataset* allows us to control for all measured and unmeasured characteristics of the employer and the job, and to ask: Do differences in education, experience, and job tenure explain the wage differences among people in the same job at the same company, or do race and gender also matter?

Our findings may be summarized as follows. We observe that some, but not all, of the human capital and personality controls perform well in predicting employment. Their introduction serves to narrow the estimated employment gap between whites and people of color, but this gap remains statistically significant for black men and women and for Latinos. Asian American men appear to enjoy a positive employment effect compared to white men. These effects are not uniform across the four cities: for example, the employment penalty apparently experienced by blacks is disproportionately driven by the strong effect found in Detroit.

The estimated effect of gender on the probability of employment is actually somewhat larger in absolute value (more negative) after controlling for city, education, age, and the other human capital and personality controls. It is significant in three of the four cities as well as in the pooled four-city equation. We also note that both race and gender effects are larger when we take account of involuntary underemployment than when we do not.

We find that women experience an hourly wage penalty on the order of 14 percent relative to men, even after controlling for a number of human capital and personality indicators, tasks performed on the job, union status, occupation, industry, and employer characteristics. The wage gap falls to 10 percent, but retains its clear statistical significance, when we introduce over four hundred separate occupational indicator variables and over two hundred industry categories. The existence of a gender-related wage gap *within* detailed occupational categories is noteworthy, suggesting that occupational segregation is not the only problem women face.

The estimated black-white gap is 11 percent in the linked dataset and 5 percent in the full sample and is also robust to the inclusion of the full list of controls. For Latinos in the linked dataset the wage penalty is roughly 18 percent, while in the larger Household Survey dataset the effect is only 6 percent.

When we compare pairs of workers in the same occupations *at the same establishments*, we find no significant differences in wages by race and gender after adjusting for job tenure, experience, and education. The fact that comparing workers at the same establishments results in the reduction of wage gaps by race and gender suggests that employer-specific pay differentials are an important part of the story.

In the next section we describe the variables that figure in our analyses and explain our reasons for including them. We then present the regression results. A final section compares our findings to previous estimates, focusing on the question of what can and cannot be attributed to labor market discrimination, and briefly discusses some of the implications for public policy.

Estimation Strategy and
Variable Definitions

Employment

We first present a logistic regression analysis of the probability of employment for a sample of 5,727 labor force participants between the ages of twenty-one and seventy, using only the Household Survey. We examine both a strict and a broad definition of employment: under the broad definition, the dependent variable is set to 1 for both full-time and part-time workers, for those on temporary layoff, and for those on sick or maternity leave from their jobs.[1] Those who described themselves as unemployed were coded as 0. The strict definition modifies this procedure to account for the phenomenon of involuntary underemployment. First, those on temporary layoff were recoded to 0. (People on sick and maternity leave, however, were still counted as employed.) Second, for part-time workers we examined the response to the question: "What is the reason you usually work less than thirty-five hours a week?"[2] Those who chose the option "Not enough work. Could only find part-time work. Hours reduced" were deemed involuntarily underemployed and were recoded to 0. Table 9.1 presents the proportions employed under each definition, along with sample means for the other variables used in the analyses of employment and wages.

On the right-hand side of the employment equation we include indicator variables for women, blacks, Asian Americans, and Latinos or Latinas.[3] Thus negative coefficients for women indicate a disadvantage relative to men, and negative coefficients for people of color indicate a disadvantage relative to non-Hispanic whites. Initially men and women from all four cities are pooled; later men and women are analyzed separately and the cities are disaggregated. We then control for age and its square and for education using a set of indicator variables (high school, GED, or trade school graduates; two-year college graduates; four-year college graduates; and those with master's degrees or beyond).[4]

Next we consider the putative personality measures. The first is the interviewer's answer to the question: "In general, what was the respondent's attitude toward the interview?" The options were "friendly and interested," "cooperative but not particularly interested," "impatient and restless," and "hostile." Two coding schemes were considered: the first created an indicator variable for people in the latter two categories only. As noted in table 9.1, this amounts to just 5 percent of the labor force. In order to have a more broadly relevant variable, we also tried including the variable as a scalar measure from 1 to 4. Our prior assumption is that impatience, restlessness, and hostility are liabilities in the labor market; thus we would expect negative parameter estimates for this variable. We also expect a negative coefficient for the indicator variable that singles out those who used a derogatory term to refer to any racial or ethnic group.[5] We cannot control for the possibility that these personality attributes may themselves reflect past experience of discrimination in the labor market.

The final interviewer assessment we employ is taken from a question that reads: "How would you rate the respondent's understanding of the questions?" The options are "poor," "fair," "good," "very good," and "excellent." This is entered as an integer between 1 and 5, with higher values corresponding to a better perceived level of understanding; thus we expect a positive coefficient for this variable, which we interpret as a control for human capital.[6] It is possible that interviewers might have been influenced by their own racial biases in assigning both this score and the impatience variable, both of which are subjective. The survey team sought to minimize this problem by matching interviewers and respondents by race, and were successful in doing so for 77 percent of our sample of labor force participants.[7]

We next introduced a measure of the average number of years of education of the respondent's parents. This serves as a proxy for the quality of education received by the child, for two reasons: first, better-educated parents are typically able to afford a higher quality of education for their children; and, second, they should be able to make a more valuable direct contribution to the development of their child's verbal and other cognitive skills (Neal and Johnson 1996). We also include an indicator to identify those who had received formal vocational training after high school through employers or government programs, or in the form of specialized occupational training while in the military. Finally, we add indicators for those who ever served in the military on active duty (whether or not they received occupational training) and for married people.[8]

This last control is perhaps problematic. Because of the dramatic difference in marriage rates between blacks and whites (40 percent versus 62 percent in our weighted labor force sample), and because marriage enters positively in both wage and employment regressions, the inclusion of this variable resulted in a sharp reduction in the absolute value of the black coefficient in every specification we ran. If marital status is an exogenous indicator of human capital, motivation, or dependability, this outcome is as it should be. However, as noted by Glen Cain (1986), it is unlikely that marriage is exogenous to labor market outcomes. If a low marriage rate is due in part to a low employment rate, and the latter is due in part to discrimination in the labor market, then controlling for marriage will tend to cause us to underestimate the degree of labor market discrimination. It is also possible that the correlation between blacks' marital status and their employment outcomes is spurious: blacks may be less likely to marry for reasons that are unrelated to the labor market, and their poor labor market outcomes relative to whites may be unrelated to the marriage gap.[9]

All employment regressions use survey sampling weights and take account of the stratified and clustered nature of the survey in figuring standard errors. The usable sample that remains after dropping cases with missing data in any variable is 4 percent smaller than the full sample of labor force participants (5,727 versus 5,944 observations). We renormalized the sampling weights so that the distribution of usable cases across survey strata within each city under the revised weights is the same as the distribution of the full sample under the original weights.[10] We then adjusted the weights so that each of the four cities effectively contributed an equal number of cases; had we not done this, our four-city results would be dominated by data from Los Angeles, which contributed 45 percent of the raw number of cases. Our pooled four-city results should be viewed as statements about the average effect of race and gender across these four cities, without regard to their respective sizes, in the years 1992 to 1994. It is important to note that the Multi-City Study does *not* purport to be a nationally representative sample.

Wages in the Full Household Survey Dataset

The wage analyses use as their dependent variable the logarithm of the estimated hourly wage.[11] This information was collected both for the currently employed and for a smaller number of people who had worked during the last five years but were not currently employed, in which case all questions referred to the last job held. Wages were adjusted for inflation using the national Consumer Price Index and taking account of the date last worked and the interview date. We excluded the self-employed[12] and those whose race or ethnicity was given as Native American or other.

The coefficients on the indicators for gender and race or ethnicity may be interpreted as percentage wage differences between women and men, and between people of color and whites, holding all other factors equal.[13] Our control for years of work experience is constructed from information on current age and the age at which the person left school, the proportion of this interval for which the person was employed, and the proportion of this employment that was full-time.[14] This yields a more accurate estimate of accrued experience than the standard formula of age minus years of education minus six. This correction is especially important for the study of gender discrimination, given that women's work histories are often marked by periods of nonparticipation corresponding to the years spent raising children. Our measure demonstrates that in this dataset women with children had roughly half as much work experience as did men or women without children.[15]

Similarly, the higher unemployment rates for people of color imply that they often have lower levels of work experience than whites of similar ages. To ignore this fact is to run the risk of overstating the effect of race, while to acknowledge it is to run the risk of understating the significance of race, since a low level of work experience could in part reflect the effects of prior discrimination in the labor market.

We were able to supplement our measure of work experience with a control for the number of years of tenure in the current job (or the last job held), a variable that is nearly always associated with higher earnings.[16] The meaning of this association has been the subject of a lengthy debate, with some suggesting that it confirms the theory of specific human capital (Topel 1991), others pointing to the importance of internal labor markets (Bridges and Villemez 1994), and still others arguing that the observed relationship is driven by unobserved heterogeneity: more productive workers achieve longer job tenure (Altonji and Shakotko 1987). For our purposes, any of these explanations is sufficient grounds to motivate the inclusion of a tenure variable. However, because tenure, like experience in general, depends on prior labor market outcomes, to control for it is once again to run the risk of understating the importance of discrimination.[17]

Next we add measures of the frequency with which each job requires face-to-face contact with customers, telephone contact, reading and writing, and the use of math and computer skills.[18] Working with the employer dataset, Harry Holzer (1996) demonstrates that blacks and Latinos are less likely than whites to be found in jobs that require these tasks on a daily basis, and that several of these tasks are also correlated with higher wages. One interpretation is that the task measures reflect the skills of the people who occupy the jobs, and that, on average, people of color are less skilled. As already mentioned, another possibility is that occupational segregation limits access by people of color to those jobs that involve the frequent performance of better-paid tasks; this in turn could prevent people of color from acquiring these higher-value skills. Once again, the inclusion of this set of controls may tend to lead to an underestimate of the full effect of race discrimination in the labor market.

One quarter of our wage data comes from people who were previously employed but currently unemployed, or had withdrawn from the labor force. We elected to include a control for current employment status, which we treat as a measure of unobserved skills or other productive attributes, noting that it was strongly correlated with higher real wages. If there is discrimination in current employment, then the inclusion of this variable will also impart a downward bias to our estimated race and gender effects.

Our most detailed specification using the full Household Survey dataset controls for the variables just listed, the personality and human capital indicators used in the analysis of employment probabilities, a full set of occupation and industry indicators based on the three-digit Industrial and Occupational Classification Systems used in the 1990 census, and a flag for union members and those working in the public sector.[19] Survey weights were again renormalized to account for any changes in sample composition brought on by the nonrandom deletion of cases with missing values, and to assign equal weight to each of the four cities.

Wages in the Linked Household Survey–Employer Survey Dataset

During the course of the Household Survey, employed respondents were asked if they would be willing to provide the names of their employers. These names were passed along to the ongoing Employer Survey, and employers were then questioned about the occupation held by the household respondent; 1,179 linked employee-employer records were generated in this fashion. It is important to note that the employers were *not* asked to provide information about the household respondent, but rather to describe the job in question and its associated recruitment and hiring practices, and to provide basic information about the last person they hired into that job. This is why we have information on pairs of workers in the same job, which will be used in a later analysis.

In order to assure that the same occupation was in fact under discussion, we restricted the sample in three ways. First, we dropped 132 cases for which, although the survey organization contacted the employer of a given worker, it was not possible to interview someone who conducted hiring for that particular job, and therefore a different job was discussed. Second, in another 96 cases the employer claimed to be discussing the same job but we concluded that it was not actually the same because of substantial differences between the two occupational codes. Third, we included only household respondents who were currently employed, temporarily laid off, or temporarily on sick leave. Respondents who had worked in the previous five years but were not currently employed were asked to identify their last employer; these are included in the nonlinked wage analysis described here but are excluded from the linked analysis on the grounds that too much time had elapsed for us to be confident that the link was valid. Excluding these cases leaves us with 769 linked observations.

The subsequent deletion of cases with missing values for one or more covariates reduces the linked dataset to 597 records. Survey weights were once again renormalized so that the distribution of these 597 records across the sampling strata was the same as for the full set of employed household respondents, and to assign equal weight to each of the four cities. The weighted composition of this final linked dataset is described in table 9.1.

Our analysis of wages in the linked file is based on the (log) hourly wage reported by the household respondent, controlling for all the Household Survey variables already described, and augmented by the following variables from the Employer Survey:

(1) an indicator for seasonal or temporary jobs, which often pay less than permanent positions;[20]

(2) an estimate of the number of employees in the establishment, to control for firm size, which is generally positively correlated with wages;[21]

(3) indicator variables for firms located in primary central-city neighborhoods and for those located in other urban areas, compared to suburban employers: Holzer found that urban employers generally pay higher wages;[22]

(4) the employer's description of whether a high school degree, a college degree, general work experience, prior vocational training, job-specific work experience, or personal references were required for the job.[23]

The rationale behind including these latter variables deserves some explanation. We observe that the correlation between the job's stated requirements and the employee's credentials is imperfect. Thus it seems plausible that knowing whether or not the job requires a given degree, for example, should convey some information about wages beyond that captured by the employee's education variables. Holzer's analysis confirms that these requirements, particularly high school and prior experience in a related job, correlate positively with observed wages. It also seems likely that employers that screen on general experience, vocational training, job-specific work experience, and references will hire more productive workers than those that do not.

To continue the added variables:

(5) the employer's description of whether the position requires a job interview, a physical exam, a general aptitude test, a job knowledge test, or a test of personality or interests;[24]

(6) the employer's opinion of whether politeness, demonstrating motivation, and the ability to speak English well are particularly important during the job interview.[25]

For both the tests and the more subjective criteria, we again hypothesize that more selective employers are likely to hire more productive workers. However, Holzer's work suggests that these attributes need not always be positively associated with wages. For example, an emphasis on politeness may be associated with low-paying customer service jobs.

Comparing Wages of Workers in the Same Jobs and Establishments: The Paired Data

As noted, each linked record corresponds to two distinct employees: the household respondent and the last person hired into that occupation by the same employer. The composition of the dataset of worker pairs is described in the final column of table 9.1. The Household Survey human capital and personality variables are not available, since these were not collected for the last hires of the Employer Survey. In principle, this dataset should be twice as large as the linked dataset, but two problems serve to limit its size. First, current wages of the last person hired were not collected for a portion of the Boston and Los Angeles interviews. Second, whenever any data were missing for one worker in the pair, forcing their exclusion from the sample, the other worker was excluded as well. The final sample size was 634 (317 pairs), of which two-thirds are from Detroit and Atlanta and one-third come from Boston and Los Angeles.

For this dataset we present several specifications, including one similar to the full model run in the linked dataset. We then introduce employer-specific fixed effects. This is equivalent to examining the *difference* in wages between workers in the same job at the same establishment as a function of the *difference* in their individual attributes, including race and gender. The object is to control for all industry-specific, occupation-specific and employer-specific factors that may influence wages. Among these it is the ability to control for employer-specific effects that distinguishes the paired analysis, given that we already have other means of controlling for occupation and industry at a high level of detail.

TABLE 9.1   *Means of Variables Used in Analyses of Employment and Wages*

Variable	Employment Analysis	Wage Analyses		
		Full Sample	Linked Sample	Paired Sample
Currently employed: strict definition	0.85			
Currently employed: broad definition	0.91			
Log of hourly wage		2.44	2.44	2.28
Female	0.48	0.51	0.55	0.60
Black	0.16	0.17	0.18	0.34
Asian American	0.04	0.04	0.04	0.02
Latino or Latina	0.12	0.13	0.10	0.09
Age	38.7	37.5	37.2	34.3
High school, GED, or vocational	0.43	0.42	0.50	0.55
Two-year-college degree	0.14	0.14	0.14	0.11
Four-year-college degree	0.23	0.22	0.18	0.21
Master's degree or higher	0.11	0.10	0.13	0.08
Impatient, restless, or hostile	0.05	0.03	0.03	
Used derogatory racial term	0.03	0.03	0.02	
Understanding of questions[a]	4.26	4.27	4.35	
Parents' years of schooling	11.4	11.4	11.8	
Prior vocational training	0.43	0.43	0.44	
Military service	0.14	0.13	0.10	
Married	0.58	0.56	0.56	
Estimated years of work experience		14.7	14.1	14.6[f]
Years of job tenure		6.37	6.06	3.21
Talk face to face with customers[b]		2.97	2.96	3.14
Talk over phone with customers[b]		2.80	2.80	2.82
Read instructions, paragraphs[b]		3.05	3.06	3.02
Write paragraphs or memos[b]		2.55	2.53	2.43
Do arithmetic or computations[b]		3.16	3.22	3.06
Work with computer[b]		2.74	2.78	2.57
Government employer		0.15	0.22	
Union member		0.19	0.21	
Temporary or seasonal job			0.12	0.09
Log of number of employees			4.50	4.68
High school degree required[c]			0.80	0.78
College degree required[c]			0.30	0.24
General work experience required[c]			0.74	0.70
Specific experience in this job required[c]			0.70	0.63
Vocational training required[c]			0.50	0.41
References required[c]			0.77	0.78
Job application required[d]			0.87	0.91

(Table continues on p. 418.)

TABLE 9.1   *Continued*

| | | Wage Analyses | | |
Variable	Employment Analysis	Full Sample	Linked Sample	Paired Sample
Interview required[d]			0.88	0.90
Physical exam required[d]			0.18	0.21
General aptitude test required[d]			0.18	0.15
Job knowledge test required[d]			0.16	0.18
Test of personality or interests required[d]			0.09	0.05
Politeness important in interview[e]			2.75	2.77
Demonstrating motivation important[e]			2.80	2.77
Ability to speak English well important[e]			2.49	2.55
Unweighted sample size	5727	4474	597	634

Source: Authors' calculations from Multi-City Study data.

Note: For all but the paired analysis, means are calculated using sampling weights that have been renormalized to account for changes in sample composition due to omission of cases with incomplete information, and to give equal weight to each of the four cities. The paired analysis is unweighted. Blank cells imply the variable was not available or not applicable to that analysis. Occupation and industry indicators (not shown) are used in the regressions as described in the text.

[a] Understanding scores: 1 (poor), 2 (fair), 3 (good), 4 (very good), 5 (excellent).

[b] All variables are measured on a frequency scale of: 1 (almost never), 2 (monthly), 3 (weekly), 4 (daily).

[c] All variables are coded as 1 if the requirement was deemed absolutely necessary or strongly preferred and 0 otherwise, except for the college degree requirement, which was posed as a yes or no question and is coded accordingly.

[d] All variables are coded as 1 if the item was always required and 0 if sometimes or never required.

[e] All variables are coded on a scale of: 1 (not important), 2 (somewhat important), 3 (very important).

[f] In the paired sample, years of experience are estimated using the customary formula of age less years of education less six.

Findings
Employment

Table 9.2 reports the results of logistic regression analyses of the odds of employment under the two definitions of employment previously discussed. Negative coefficients represent an employment disadvantage for women relative to men and for people of color relative to whites. The first column reports the coefficients from a regression against the race and gender indicators alone; it demonstrates that there exist significant

TABLE 9.2   Logit Analysis of the Probability of Employment
             (Coefficients with Standard Errors in Parentheses)

Independent Variables	Strict Definition of Employment				Broad Definition
	[1]	[2]	[3]	[4]	[5]
Female	−0.459***	−0.491***	−0.503***	−0.519***	−0.302*
	(0.132)	(0.134)	(0.135)	(0.152)	(0.174)
Black	−0.671***	−0.528***	−0.520***	−0.341**	−0.241
	(0.130)	(0.128)	(0.128)	(0.133)	(0.163)
Asian American	0.333	0.441	0.422	0.364	0.296
	(0.378)	(0.357)	(0.359)	(0.352)	(0.463)
Latino or Latina	−1.030***	−0.361*	−0.364*	−0.389*	−0.062
	(0.152)	(0.209)	(0.211)	(0.231)	(0.273)
Education, age, city controls	No	Yes	Yes	Yes	Yes
Impatient, restless, or hostile			−0.495**	−0.411*	−0.627***
			(0.218)	(0.227)	(0.243)
Used derogatory racial term			−0.389	−0.300	−0.293
			(0.260)	(0.274)	(0.300)
Better understanding of questions				0.130**	0.123*
				(0.066)	(0.072)
Parents' years of schooling				−0.025	−0.028
				(0.021)	(0.025)
Prior vocational training				−0.036	0.111
				(0.148)	(0.180)
Military service				−0.262	−0.482**
				(0.227)	(0.241)
Married				0.747***	0.815***
				(0.137)	(0.169)
Constant	2.243***	0.570	0.636	1.670*	2.333*
	(0.127)	(0.888)	(0.892)	(1.006)	(1.355)
Pseudo-R^2	0.035	0.060	0.063	0.083	0.071

Source: Authors' calculations from Multi-City Study data.
Note: These are coefficients (with standard errors in parentheses) from logistic regressions of a binary employment status indicator against the variables listed. Sample size is 5,727 for all equations, and is defined by the set of labor force participants between the ages of twenty-one and seventy with complete information for all covariates. Under the *broad definition of employment*, the dependent variable is set to 1 for full- and part-time workers, for those on temporary layoff, and for those on sick leave or maternity leave. The unemployed are coded as 0. Under the *strict definition of employment*, the dependent variable is recoded to 0 for those on temporary layoff or who were working part-time because they could find only part-time work or their hours had been reduced. All regressions take account of survey design effects and use sampling weights that have been renormalized to account for changes in sample composition due to omission of cases with incomplete information, and to give equal weight to each of the four cities. The pseudo-R^2 expresses the goodness of fit on a scale from 0 (corresponding to a model with only the constant term as a regressor) to 1 (corresponding to perfect prediction). See notes to table 9.1 for variable coding details.
*Significantly different from 0 at 10 percent level of significance.
**Significantly different from 0 at 5 percent level of significance.
***Significantly different from 0 at 1 percent level of significance.

differences between the crude employment rates of men and women and of blacks and Latinos relative to whites. In the second column the introduction of controls for education, age (and its square), and city reduces the black and Latino coefficients but does not weaken the gender effect; all remain significantly different from zero.

The two putative personality measures, introduced in the third column, do display some explanatory power: those judged impatient, restless, or hostile pay a penalty that is comparable in size to the estimated effects of being black or female. Derogatory racial comments also enter with the expected negative coefficient; it is not significant at the conventional 10 percent threshold but is significant at the 15 percent level. (In table 9.3 we see that the effect of racist language varies by city and is particularly pronounced in Detroit.) We note that the race coefficients are not appreciably altered by the introduction of these personality controls, suggesting that the employment disadvantage experienced by people of color cannot be attributed to these elements of personality. The same holds true when the attitude variable is entered as a continuous measure or as a series of indicator variables (results not shown).

The fourth column adds the full range of available controls for human capital. Although the coefficient associated with blacks is reduced in absolute value by about one-third, it remains significantly negative, as do the coefficients for women and Latinos or Latinas, both of which are virtually unaffected by the change in specification. The interviewer's assessment of the respondent's degree of understanding of the survey questions also proves a clear predictor of employment. The effect of the difference between a rating of poor (1) and excellent (5) would be four times the reported coefficient, or 0.52, which is comparable in size to the effect of gender in that equation. Being married also increases the predicted probability of employment, while parental schooling, vocational training, and military service have insignificant effects.

To get a sense of the magnitude of these effects it is helpful to calculate the predicted probabilities of employment for various representative individuals.[26] Consider an unmarried, high school–educated white male, age 30, living in Boston, who displayed a good (but not excellent) understanding of the survey questions, whose parents also had high school educations, who was not judged impatient and did not use racial epithets, and who had no vocational training or record of military service. Using the specification of column 4, his predicted probability of employment would be 0.93. The same person with a hostile or impatient attitude would have a probability of employment of 0.89. If this same person were black (maintaining the impatience assumption), the probability falls to 0.86. If we change the gender to female, the estimated probability falls to 0.78.[27]

The final column demonstrates that both the race and gender effects are smaller when we define employment more broadly to include those who are working part-time but desire full-time work or who are temporarily laid off. The black coefficient is reduced in absolute value by about one-third; it remains significantly negative only at the 15 percent threshold. The effect for Latinos is virtually eliminated. The gender penalty is reduced by about two-fifths, but remains significant at the 10 percent level. Otherwise put, the unexplained gap in employment between men and women and between whites and people of color is larger when we count both unemployment and involuntary underemployment as negative outcomes than when we consider unemployment alone.

Table 9.3 disaggregates the results in column 4 of table 9.2 by gender and city. It shows that the apparent negative effect of race borne by blacks is of roughly the same size for men as for women; for Asian Americans the signs differ by gender, with Asian men apparently enjoying an employment advantage with respect to white men. The negative effect of Latino ancestry is much larger for men than for women. Looking across the cities we see that the female effect varies considerably, being particularly large in Boston and Detroit. The black effect is apparently driven largely by the results from Detroit, although its sign is negative in all cities. The personality variables display some peculiar sign reversals: impatience, restlessness, or hostility and racist language are apparent *advantages* in Boston.[28]

Hourly Wages

Table 9.4 reports the log wage equations for the full sample of 4,474 currently or recently employed men and women. The first column demonstrates that the crude difference between men's and women's wages, and between white and black wages, is on the order of 22 percent in this dataset. Latino and Latina workers earn 46 percent less per hour, on average, than do whites; average hourly wages of Asian Americans are not significantly below those of whites at conventional confidence levels.

The second column adds controls for city, education, and estimated years of work experience and its square. Education and experience are strongly significant, and will remain so as the number of control variables increases. The race and gender coefficients are noticeably attenuated, but all three of the previously significant effects are still significant. As is often observed, the gender coefficient falls by less than the black and Latino indicators because men and women are more similar in terms of education than are whites and people of color (Cain 1986).

The third column adds the human capital measures and the two

TABLE 9.3 Logit Analysis of the Probability of Employment, By Gender and City (Coefficients with Standard Errors in Parentheses)

Independent Variables	Women [1]	Men [2]	Atlanta [3]	Boston [4]	Detroit [5]	Los Angeles [6]
Female			-0.262 (0.248)	-1.046* (0.552)	-0.654** (0.295)	-0.427** (0.195)
Black	-0.368** (0.171)	-0.374* (0.214)	-0.244 (0.233)	-0.458 (0.419)	-0.770*** (0.202)	-0.117 (0.272)
Asian American	-0.030 (0.474)	1.051** (0.432)				0.575 (0.477)
Latino or Latina	-0.204 (0.294)	-0.729** (0.298)		-0.119 (0.681)		-0.331 (0.328)
Education, age, city controls	Yes	Yes	Yes	Yes	Yes	Yes
Impatient, restless, or hostile	-0.210 (0.292)	-0.534 (0.351)	-0.866* (0.450)	1.452** (0.665)	-0.533 (0.383)	-0.047 (0.330)
Used derogatory racial term	-0.490 (0.374)	-0.035 (0.431)	0.273 (0.843)	1.575 (1.022)	-1.094** (0.519)	-0.392 (0.360)
Better understanding of questions	0.098 (0.080)	0.164 (0.104)	0.422*** (0.147)	-0.159 (0.278)	-0.012 (0.111)	0.248*** (0.095)
Parents' years of schooling	0.000 (0.027)	-0.054* (0.030)	-0.120* (0.064)	0.097 (0.063)	-0.030 (0.036)	-0.035 (0.030)
Prior vocational training	-0.011 (0.190)	-0.036 (0.214)	0.104 (0.306)	-0.420 (0.536)	-0.030 (0.219)	0.064 (0.225)
Military service	-1.618*** (0.559)	0.092 (0.247)	0.163 (0.502)	-1.157** (0.566)	-0.599 (0.383)	0.351 (0.390)
Married	0.562*** (0.187)	1.028*** (0.221)	0.672** (0.265)	2.158*** (0.489)	0.391 (0.253)	0.379** (0.166)
Constant	1.142 (1.092)	1.601 (1.852)	3.310* (1.755)	-2.408 (4.029)	2.074 (1.455)	1.339 (1.251)
Pseudo-R²	0.087	0.094	0.090	0.268	0.104	0.057
Sample size	3086	2641	1022	1083	925	2697

Source: Authors' calculations from Multi-City Study data.
Note: the regression specification and weights are identical to that of table 9.2, column 4. See notes to table 9.1 for variable coding details.
*Significantly different from 0 at 10 percent level of significance.
**Significantly different from 0 at 5 percent level of significance.
***Significantly different from 0 at 1 percent level of significance.

TABLE 9.4   *Regression Analysis of Log Hourly Wages: Full Dataset (Coefficients with Standard Errors in Parentheses)*

	[1]	[2]	[3]	[4]	[5]
Female	−0.215***	−0.170***	−0.158***	−0.136***	−0.098***
	(0.031)	(0.025)	(0.024)	(0.024)	(0.023)
Black	−0.219***	−0.126***	−0.073***	−0.063***	−0.050**
	(0.036)	(0.027)	(0.026)	(0.022)	(0.022)
Asian American	−0.110	−0.046	0.054	0.067	0.075
	(0.113)	(0.079)	(0.070)	(0.056)	(0.060)
Latino or Latina	−0.463***	−0.222***	−0.107***	−0.095***	−0.056*
	(0.034)	(0.035)	(0.033)	(0.030)	(0.033)
Atlanta[a]		−0.097**	−0.099**	−0.086***	−0.118***
		(0.041)	(0.036)	(0.032)	(0.028)
Detroit[a]		−0.018	−0.031	−0.050*	−0.084***
		(0.037)	(0.032)	(0.029)	(0.029)
Los Angeles[a]		−0.018	0.000	−0.026	−0.043
		(0.036)	(0.031)	(0.028)	(0.027)
High school, vocational, GED[b]		0.310***	0.189***	0.126***	0.123***
		(0.031)	(0.033)	(0.029)	(0.031)
Two-year-college degree[b]		0.498***	0.320***	0.202***	0.220***
		(0.039)	(0.040)	(0.039)	(0.040)
Four-year-college degree[b]		0.701***	0.516***	0.335***	0.340***
		(0.038)	(0.046)	(0.046)	(0.044)
Master's degree or higher[b]		0.772***	0.573***	0.363***	0.388***
		(0.072)	(0.068)	(0.070)	(0.061)
Estimated years of work experience		0.034***	0.021***	0.018***	0.011***
		(0.004)	(0.004)	(0.004)	(0.004)
Squared years of experience		−0.0006***	−0.0004***	−0.0003***	−0.0002
		(0.0001)	(0.0001)	(0.0001)	(0.0001)
Years of tenure in job			0.021***	0.016***	0.014***
			(0.002)	(0.002)	(0.001)
Less cooperative, more impatient[c]			0.035*	0.043**	0.023
			(0.020)	(0.018)	(0.015)
Used derogatory racial term			−0.023	−0.026	0.018
			(0.053)	(0.051)	(0.059)
Better understanding of questions			0.073***	0.056***	0.038***
			(0.013)	(0.011)	(0.010)
Parents' years of schooling			0.016***	0.012***	0.005
			(0.005)	(0.004)	(0.004)
Prior vocational training			0.019	−0.004	0.017
			(0.024)	(0.022)	(0.019)
Military service			−0.040	−0.024	−0.007
			(0.046)	(0.040)	(0.034)
Married			0.088***	0.076***	0.068***
			(0.021)	(0.021)	(0.019)
Currently employed			0.117***	0.109***	0.132***
			(0.028)	(0.028)	(0.022)

(Table continues on p. 424.)

TABLE 9.4   *Continued*

	[1]	[2]	[3]	[4]	[5]
Number of occupation, industry variables	None	None	None	9,7	432,237
Talk face to face with customers[d]				−0.031*** (0.011)	−0.020** (0.009)
Talk over phone with customers[d]				0.044*** (0.011)	0.043*** (0.010)
Read instructions, paragraphs[d]				0.022** (0.010)	0.009 (0.010)
Write paragraphs or memos[d]				0.020 (0.013)	0.017** (0.008)
Do arithmetic or computations[d]				−0.007 (0.009)	0.007 (0.008)
Work with a computer[d]				0.040*** (0.011)	0.025*** (0.009)
Government employer				0.002 (0.033)	0.047 (0.039)
Union member				0.146*** (0.031)	0.158*** (0.026)
R^2	0.13	0.35	0.46	0.53	0.71

Source: Authors' calculations from Multi-City Study data.
Note: These are the estimated coefficients from regressions of log hourly wages against the variables listed, for Household Survey respondents with complete information on all covariates, omitting the self-employed. Those not currently employed reported wages and other attributes of the last job held within five years; wage data are adjusted for inflation. Sample size is 4,474. Standard errors (in parentheses) are estimated taking account of survey design effects. Sample weights were renormalized to account for changes in sample composition due to omission of cases with incomplete information, and to give equal weight to each of the four cities.
[a]Boston is the (arbitrary) reference category for the city indicator variables.
[b]Education effects are measured relative to those with no education.
[c]Measured on scale from 1 (friendly and interested) to 4 (hostile).
[d]Measured on scale from 1 (almost never) to 4 (daily).
*Significantly different from 0 at 10 percent level of significance.
**Significantly different from 0 at 5 percent level of significance.
***Significantly different from 0 at 1 percent level of significance.

personality indices. Longer job tenure, a better perceived understanding of the survey questions, better-educated parents, being married, and being currently (as opposed to recently) employed all make significant positive contributions to the wage. As before, we may multiply the coefficient associated with the understanding variable by 4 to arrive at an estimate of the difference in wages between someone with an excellent as opposed to a poor perceived understanding of the survey questions; in this case the result is a 29 percent change in the hourly wage. The positive effect of current employment (as opposed to having held a job in the past five years) is also large, at approximately 12 percent.

It appears that those who were judged less friendly and cooperative, and more impatient, restless, or hostile during their interviews (on a scale of 1 to 4) earn *higher* wages, all else equal, an effect that was far more pronounced for women than men. This finding runs counter to the negative *employment* effect observed for this variable. The effect of a proclivity toward using racist language appears to be small. Race and gender coefficients are further attenuated by the inclusion of these human capital and personality controls, but the wage penalties for women, blacks, and Latinos remain significant.

The fourth column adds nine occupation and seven industry indicators, the scalar indices of the frequency with which the six separate tasks are performed, and controls for public-sector workers and union members. Four of the six task variables are significant: those whose work involves more frequent face-to-face contact with customers receive *lower* wages, while telephone interaction, reading, and computer use are positively rewarded. If we multiply the reported coefficients by 3, we may estimate the predicted difference in wages between someone who almost never performs each task and someone who performs it daily. In the case of computer use, for example, this difference is 12 percent.

The estimated wage penalties for women (14 percent), blacks (6 percent), and Latinos or Latinas (10 percent) are all still significant at the 1 percent level. This is *not* because the variables we have added in columns 3 and 4 are poor controls; in fact, the additional variables perform quite well, raising the R^2 from 0.35 to 0.53.

In the final column we introduce the full set of 432 occupation and 237 industry indicators, which are able to explain another 18 percent of the variance in log wages, raising the R^2 to 0.71. The estimated wage penalties for women (10 percent), blacks (5 percent), and Latinos or Latinas (6 percent) remain significant: race and gender wage gaps exist between people in very similar jobs and after controlling for a wide array of other factors. Furthermore, despite the detailed control for occupation and industry, four of the six task variables remain significant predictors, confirming that job-specific information beyond occupational classification is important in understanding earnings.

Table 9.5 presents the results by gender and city. In the upper panel we use the minimal set of occupation and industry controls. We find that the black-white wage gap is significant for both women (6 percent) and men (7 percent), as are the gaps for Latinas (8 percent) and Latinos (10 percent) compared to non-Hispanic whites. Asian American women appear to enjoy a significant wage premium (15 percent). Looking across the cities we find that the gender effect varies between 10 and 15 percent; the black effect is strongest in Atlanta (10 percent); and the Latino effect is driven by the results from Los Angeles (14 percent).

TABLE 9.5   Race and Gender Coefficients from Regression Model of Log Hourly Wages: Full Dataset, By Gender and City (Standard Errors in Parentheses)

Independent Variables	Women [1]	Men [2]	Atlanta [3]	Boston [4]	Detroit [5]	Los Angeles [6]
Using nine occupation and seven industry categories						
Female			−0.123***	−0.098*	−0.134***	−0.151***
			(0.047)	(0.055)	(0.045)	(0.029)
Black	−0.060**	−0.069*	−0.103***	−0.047	−0.070	−0.070
	(0.030)	(0.036)	(0.037)	(0.044)	(0.043)	(0.043)
Asian American	0.150**	−0.056				0.092
	(0.061)	(0.067)				(0.060)
Latino or Latina	−0.077*	−0.102**		−0.034		−0.139***
	(0.041)	(0.046)		(0.070)		(0.034)
R²	0.55	0.54	0.54	0.58	0.61	0.57
Using eighty-six occupation and ninety-one industry categories						
Female			−0.092***	−0.034	−0.049	−0.151***
			(0.032)	(0.056)	(0.046)	(0.029)
Black	−0.058**	−0.091***	−0.071*	−0.003	−0.056	−0.080**
	(0.027)	(0.031)	(0.038)	(0.047)	(0.041)	(0.038)
Asian American	0.059	−0.178**				0.073
	(0.053)	(0.071)				(0.055)
Latino or Latina	−0.087**	−0.113**		0.012		−0.108***
	(0.039)	(0.048)		(0.072)		(0.033)
R²	0.64	0.66	0.77	0.80	0.73	0.66
Sample size, both	2548	1926	712	960	672	2130

Source: Authors' calculations from Multi-City Study data.
Note: The regression specification for the upper panel is that of table 9.4, column 4.
*Significantly different from 0 at 10 percent level of significance.
**Significantly different from 0 at 5 percent level of significance.
***Significantly different from 0 at 1 percent level of significance.

In the lower panel we introduce occupation and industry dummies at the two-digit level for the comparison across the sexes and the cities, where sample sizes do not permit the use of the more detailed set of indicator variables.[29] The black and the Latino effects are both larger for men than for women. A strong negative effect emerges for Asian men, but this should be viewed with some skepticism as we found it was not robust to minor changes of specification. The coefficient for Asian American women is now insignificant. In Boston and Detroit the gender coefficients are considerably attenuated by the use of the more detailed occupation and industry controls; Atlanta's coefficient is reduced by about one-quarter; but in Los Angeles, the largest sample, the estimated gender gap is unaffected by the change in specification. For these latter two cities it would thus appear that the unexplained gap between men's and women's wages is driven largely by something other than occupational and sectoral segregation.

Table 9.6 extends the analysis using the linked dataset. This reduces the sample size by an order of magnitude, to 597, but makes possible the inclusion of a host of job- and firm-specific variables. The first column reports the race and gender effects with no controls. The crude wage gaps for women and blacks are a few points higher in this subset than in the larger sample. The second column adds only the experience, education, and city controls; we note that the race and gender effects remain larger than the corresponding results from table 9.4, column 2, suggesting that the samples are not strictly comparable. Next we introduce the Employer Survey variables. With the exception of the high school degree, the employers' statements of educational requirements are not powerful predictors of the wage. The other requirements and screens also contribute relatively little, with the exception of a positive effect associated with tests of personality, However, several of these newly added variables will achieve statistical significance once we control for occupation and industry.

The final column reintroduces the other Household Survey variables relating to human capital, personality, tenure, occupation, industry, tasks, union status, and type of employer. The smaller sample size limits us to the two-digit level of occupational and industrial detail. The estimated penalties experienced by blacks (11 percent) and Latinos (18 percent) remain large and statistically significant. The effect for women is reduced to 6 percent; it is significantly different from 0 only at the 20 percent threshold.

Finally, in table 9.7, we demonstrate that if we extend the process of controlling for employer-specific factors to the fullest possible extent, by comparing workers at the same establishments (and in the same jobs), we do in fact see the elimination of significant race and gender

TABLE 9.6   *Regression Analysis of Log Hourly Wages: Linked Dataset (Coefficients with Standard Errors in Parentheses)*

	[1]	[2]	[3]	[4]
Female	−0.264***	−0.214***	−0.244***	−0.061
	(0.060)	(0.048)	(0.047)	(0.044)
Black	−0.258***	−0.155***	−0.192***	−0.114***
	(0.071)	(0.046)	(0.046)	(0.042)
Asian American	0.326	0.161*	0.060	0.027
	(0.222)	(0.085)	(0.111)	(0.102)
Latino or Latina	−0.444***	−0.319***	−0.315***	−0.175**
	(0.090)	(0.098)	(0.093)	(0.073)
City, education, experience controls	No	Yes	Yes	Yes
Controls for human capital, personality, tenure, occupation, industry, tasks, government, unions[a]	No	No	No	Yes
Central city			0.077	0.066
			(0.055)	(0.040)
Other urban area			−0.013	0.139**
			(0.081)	(0.065)
Temporary or seasonal job			−0.064	−0.142***
			(0.070)	(0.047)
Log of number of employees			0.018	−0.001
			(0.013)	(0.011)
High school degree required[b]			0.231***	0.033
			(0.063)	(0.055)
College degree required[b]			−0.002	−0.025
			(0.080)	(0.051)
General work experience required[b]			−0.064	−0.098**
			(0.063)	(0.043)
Specific experience in this job required[b]			0.043	−0.022
			(0.063)	(0.048)
Vocational training required[b]			−0.001	0.001
			(0.049)	(0.034)
References required[b]			−0.025	0.028
			(0.054)	(0.042)
Application required[c]			−0.057	−0.048
			(0.082)	(0.054)
Interview required[c]			0.019	−0.009
			(0.057)	(0.054)
Physical exam required[c]			0.003	−0.034
			(0.062)	(0.046)
General aptitude test[c] required			0.068	0.112**
			(0.071)	(0.045)
Job knowledge test[c] required			−0.083	−0.131***
			(0.058)	(0.040)

TABLE 9.6   *Continued*

	[1]	[2]	[3]	[4]
Test of personality or interests required[c]			0.201**	0.010*
			(0.082)	(0.057)
Politeness important in interview[d]			−0.022	−0.026
			(0.051)	(0.038)
Demonstrating motivation important[d]			−0.070	−0.049
			(0.051)	(0.038)
Ability to speak English well important[d]			0.036	0.064**
			(0.044)	(0.032)
R^2	0.17	0.45	0.50	0.84

Source: Authors' calculations from Multi-City Study data.

Note: Coefficients (and standard errors in parentheses) from regressions of log hourly wages against the variables listed, for the household-employer linked dataset. Sample size is 597. All equations take account of design effects and use sample weights that have been renormalized to account for changes in sample composition due to omission of cases with incomplete information, and to give equal weight to each of the four cities.

[a]Includes all Household Survey variables used in the full dataset regression of table 9.4, column 4, plus controls for occupation and industry at the two-digit level of detail (86 occupations and 91 industries).

[b]All variables in this section are coded as 1 if the requirement was deemed absolutely necessary or strongly preferred and 0 otherwise, except for the college degree requirement, which was posed as a yes or no question and is coded accordingly.

[c]All variables in this section are coded as 1 if the item was always required and 0 if sometimes or never required.

[d]All variables in this section are coded on a scale from 1 (not important) to 3 (very important).

*Significantly different from 0 at 10 percent level of significance.

**Significantly different from 0 at 5 percent level of significance.

***Significantly different from 0 at 1 percent level of significance.

differences in hourly wages. Prior to the inclusion of employer-specific fixed effects, the results are not dissimilar to those of the previous tables, with coefficients of 6.9 percent for women, 12.6 percent for blacks, and 9.3 percent for Latinos. Once the fixed effects terms are added in the final column, however, the race and gender coefficients are sharply attenuated: only education and tenure remain significant predictors of wages.

This suggests that if the previous findings were driven by race and gender discrimination, on average this discrimination is not of the most blatant variety that would create pay gaps between coworkers of similar seniority in the same jobs. Nor does occupational segregation tell the whole story, since in this dataset, as in the larger sample, significant race and gender effects persist even after controlling for occupation and industry in considerable detail. Instead, it appears that significant race and gender wage gaps emerge only when we compare employees of *different firms* within the same occupations and industries.

TABLE 9.7   *Regression Analysis of Log Hourly Wages: Paired Dataset (Coefficients with Standard Errors in Parentheses)*

	[1]	[2]	[3]	[4]
Female	−0.145***	−0.153***	−0.069*	−0.029
	(0.037)	(0.031)	(0.035)	(0.043)
Black	−0.235***	−0.125***	−0.126***	0.015
	(0.040)	(0.035)	(0.037)	(0.046)
Asian American	−0.017	−0.065	−0.180	0.042
	(0.120)	(0.104)	(0.110)	(0.140)
Latino or Latina	−0.233***	−0.146**	−0.093	−0.028
	(0.064)	(0.058)	(0.061)	(0.072)
Atlanta[a]		−0.139***	−0.154***	
		(0.046)	(0.047)	
Detroit[a]		−0.047	−0.114**	
		(0.044)	(0.050)	
Los Angeles[a]		0.090	0.070	
		(0.056)	(0.060)	
High school, vocational, GED[b]		0.211***	0.062	0.067
		(0.069)	(0.073)	(0.082)
Two-year-college degree[b]		0.430***	0.200**	0.169*
		(0.081)	(0.088)	(0.096)
Four-year-college degree[b]		0.613***	0.246***	0.226**
		(0.075)	(0.086)	(0.096)
Master's degree or higher[b]		0.831***	0.430***	0.332***
		(0.086)	(0.103)	(0.120)
Estimated years of work experience[c]		0.028***	0.012***	0.006
		(0.004)	(0.004)	(0.005)
Squared years of experience[c]		−0.0005***	−0.0002**	−0.0001
		(0.0001)	(0.0001)	(0.0001)
Years of tenure in job			0.015***	0.009***
			(0.003)	(0.003)
Controls for occupation, industry, tasks, hiring requirements and practices, interview factors, firm size, temporary jobs, urban locations[d]	No	No	Yes	
Employer-specific fixed effects	No	No	No	Yes
R^2	0.09	0.36	0.67	0.11[e]

Source: Authors' calculations from Multi-City Study data.

Note: These are the estimated coefficients (with standard errors in parentheses) from regressions of log hourly wages against the variables listed, in a dataset of 317 pairs of workers employed at the same firms and in the same jobs. No sampling weights were used.

[a]Boston is the (arbitrary) reference category for the city indicator variables.

[b]Education effects are measured relative to those with no education.

[c]Experience is measured using the customary formula of age less years of education less six.

[d]See table 9.1 for list of variables used. Note that the additional human capital and personality controls were not available in this dataset. Occupation and industry entered at two-digit level of detail.

[e]For the fixed effects equation, the R^2 pertains to the within-job variance in wages only.

*Significantly different from 0 at 10 percent level of significance.

**Significantly different from 0 at 5 percent level of significance.

***Significantly different from 0 at 1 percent level of significance.

Conclusion

Race and gender-based wage gaps in the United States have fallen over time, although not at a uniform rate and not for all cohorts. Peter Gottschalk (1997) reports the trend from 1963 to 1994 of the black and female coefficients from regressions of log weekly earnings against education, potential experience and its square, and region, using each year's March Current Population Survey. He finds that the coefficient on the black indicator variable fell steadily from 1963 to 1975 but has been relatively stable since then, at a value of between 10 and 13 percent. However, John Bound and Laura Dresser (1999) demonstrate that this apparent stability conceals a decline in the ratio of black male to white male wages, and a simultaneous decline in the ratio of black female to white female wages. (White women saw their wages rise steadily in relation to white men.)

Our results from a regression that is comparable (but not identical) in specification to Gottschalk's were similar (12.6 percent; see table 9.4, column 2). If we make our regression conform with his by analyzing weekly earnings and using the traditional experience measure, our black coefficient falls to 9.3 percent, a figure just slightly smaller than Gottschalk's nationwide estimates. Thus our sample does not appear to be unusual when judged by the size of the black-white wage gap.

The national average of the male-female earnings differential conditioned on education, experience, and region declined steadily from about 60 percent in the mid-1960s to about 33 percent in the early 1990s. This figure is roughly twice as high as we report in table 9.4, column 2, but this difference again reflects the fact that we consider hourly wages, not weekly earnings, and that we use the more accurate measure of experience. Both these choices of specification reduce the estimated gender penalty and both are recommended by Cain (1986), since men and women often work different numbers of hours per week and accumulate different amounts of lifetime work experience for reasons that may be largely independent of gender discrimination in the labor market. If our regression is recast in terms of weekly earnings and the traditional experience variable is used, the gender penalty rises to 43 percent. By this measure the gender effect in our four-city sample appears somewhat larger than in the nationwide sample, a caveat that should be borne in mind in the discussion that follows.

Citing the work of Gottschalk and others, William Darrity and Patrick Mason (1998) conclude that race discrimination in the labor market reduces the wages of African Americans by between 12 and 15 percent. James Heckman (1998) objects, arguing that the regression specifications upon which these results rest are often quite sparse, with few controls for quality of education and other factors that might explain the black-white earnings gap. In particular, analyses that control for measured cognitive skill attainment using the Armed Forces Qualifying Test (AFQT) tend to find a smaller unexplained black-white wage gap. Working with a sample of twenty-eight- to thirty-five-year-olds from the National Longitudinal Survey of Youth (NLSY), and controlling for a host of job-specific variables as well as the AFQT score, Paula England, Karen Christopher, and Lori L. Reid (1999) are able to explain 95 to 103 percent of the black-white wage gap for men, and 82 to 118 percent of the gap for women. Similarly, in a sample of men between the ages of twenty-two and twenty-nine, also drawn from the NLSY, O'Neill (1990) finds that black and white hourly wages differ by no more than 1 to 3 percentage points. Neal and Johnson (1996) use an equation that controls only for age, AFQT score, and its square. They find a significant black-white wage gap of 7 percent for men between the ages of twenty-six and twenty-nine, and an insignificant *positive* coefficient for black women of 3.5 percent. It is noteworthy, however, that all of these studies focus on relatively young workers, among whom black-white wage differences are smaller than for the general population (Cain 1986; O'Neill 1990).

The Multi-City Study lacks a test-based measure of cognitive skill. And while our informal, five-step interviewer's assessment of the respondent's apparent level of understanding performs well in both the wage and employment equations, it is not a particularly sophisticated measure. Its modal category is "excellent" implying that it is insensitive to differences at the upper end of the distribution of comprehension skills. Our strategy has been to increase the degree of control for unobserved skills in two ways. First, we included an array of person-specific variables, that should provide some information on qualities that are related to productivity. Second, we included a much larger array of controls for job- and firm-specific factors that influence wages, including occupation and industry indicators at the two- and three-digit level of detail. As already discussed, most of these additional variables are at least partially endogenous and may themselves reflect past experience of labor market discrimination; as a result, their inclusion should tend to lead us to underestimate the degree of discrimination. If more skilled individuals earn higher wages primarily because of their ability to find jobs in better-paying occupations and industries, it is plausible that our detailed occupation and industry controls (along with the other human capital proxies, personality variables, task variables, and other job-specific factors) will make up for the lack of an explicit measure of skill or productivity.

Some support for this proposition may be found in the fact that these variables collectively are able to reduce the effect of parental edu-cation, which is itself a robust predictor of the AFQT score (Neal and Johnson 1996), to insignificance in the final column of table 9.4. If this proposition is correct, then our residual black-white wage gap (5 percent in the largest sample, 11 percent in the linked subset) may be due to labor market discrimination against blacks. Consistent with previous research, for example that of Kimberly Bayard et al. (1999a), we find a larger gap for men than for women.

Our estimates of the gender effect (10 percent in the full sample, 6 percent in the linked dataset) probably understate the degree of discrimi-nation given that they do not capture the phenomenon of occupational segregation by sex, except insofar as this occurs *within* occupation cate-gories defined at the three-digit level of detail of the 1990 Census Occu-pational Classification System. Furthermore, it is unlikely that these effects are driven by unobserved differences in cognitive skills, since there are no systematic differences in parental education or local school quality between boys and girls, although there are between whites and people of color. This is confirmed by England, Christopher, and Reid (1999, 169) who note that "Differences in cognitive skills and years of education are important in explaining pay gaps between ethnic groups but irrelevant to gaps between men's and women's pay."

Although occupational segregation has also been studied in the con-text of race (for example, Mason 1999, Bayard et al. 1999a, Reskin and Cassirer 1996), it is in relation to gender and the debate over comparable worth that it has received the most attention. Paula England (1992) an-alyzes aggregate occupational data from the 1980 census and demon-strates the tendency of predominantly female occupations to pay less than predominantly male occupations that are similar in terms of skill demands, working conditions, and market conditions. We find that there also exists a male-female wage gap between similar people per-forming very similar jobs at different firms. This conclusion is consis-tent with the work of Francine Blau (1977), Erica Groshen (1991), and Kimberly Bayard et al. (1999a, 1999b) who find that women are concen-trated not only in low-wage occupations, but also in low-wage establish-ments holding occupation constant.

We reach the same conclusion for blacks and Latinos compared to whites, although the effects appear smaller (see table 9.4). However, un-like Bayard et al., we do not find evidence of gender or racial differences between people in the same job and the same establishment. This differ-ence in findings is not surprising given our small sample (317 cases). By contrast, the dataset assembled by Bayard et al. contains over 600,000 records, making it by far the largest employer-employee linked dataset currently available.[30]

It is noteworthy that the wage penalty experienced by Latinos and Latinas was less precisely estimated primarily because of their smaller numbers. In the linked dataset the effect remains quite large (18 percent) even after adding the two-digit occupational and industry variables; in the full dataset the addition of all variables including the three-digit occupation codes reduces the Latino coefficient to 6 percent. Table 9.5 demonstrates that the effect is larger for men than women. These findings provide some support to the argument made by Edwin Meléndez (1993) that the Latino-Anglo wage gap is in part due to persistent discrimination.

A study by Holzer and Keith Ihlanfeldt (1998) uses the Multi-City Study's Employer Survey to show that the racial makeup of the firm's customers can have an important effect on who gets hired, particularly in jobs that involve customer interaction. They also found that employees in establishments that have mostly black customers earn less than those working for firms serving a predominantly white clientele. Similarly, David Neumark (1996) found that customer discrimination partly explains the fact that female job applicants were significantly less likely to be hired to wait tables at better-paying restaurants than were comparably qualified male applicants. Mechanisms such as this could explain our finding of a race and gender pay gaps between otherwise similar people in very similar jobs at different firms.

Turning to the question of the probability of employment, we note that our estimates of the black-white employment gap are considerably smaller than those of John Bound and Richard Freeman (1992), even before we introduce our human capital and personality controls. They estimate the probability of employment for a black man with a high school education and five years of potential labor market experience in 1989 to be 0.74, compared with 0.89 for a white man. Using our results from table 9.2, column 2, the comparable estimates would be 0.83 and 0.89. Thus our sample does not appear to be characterized by an unusually large black-white employment gap.

After introducing our additional human capital proxies, we find a significant employment gap for women (in most cities), for black men and women (with the strongest effect in Detroit) and for Latino men. We find that an impatient or hostile attitude does serve as a barrier to employment, but that controlling for this effect makes no difference to our estimates of the employment gap by race or gender. In all cases race and gender effects are stronger when we consider both unemployment and involuntary underemployment as negative outcomes than when we look only at unemployment per se. This is consistent with a point made by Cain (1986) that discrimination can show up as a difference in hours of employment. One advantage of our estimates is that we are able to distinguish between voluntary and involuntary part-time work.

Several researchers have found that changes in the regional and industrial composition of employment contributed to the widening black-white employment gap in the 1970s and 1980s for men (Bound and Freeman 1992) and for women (Bound and Dresser 1999).[31] The results in tables 9.2 and 9.3 may reflect the continuing legacy of these economic changes. However, as Bound and Dresser note, employer discrimination could work to limit the ability of blacks who have been laid off to find work in new industries. It is also possible that the reemployment of blacks was impeded by unmeasured skill differences and the spatial mismatch between where blacks live and where jobs were being created (Holzer 1996). These latter factors, however, are unlikely to explain the significant gap in the employment rates of men and women.

Holzer's (1996) analysis of discrimination in hiring draws on information in the Employer Survey that relates the racial and gender composition of the job applicant pool to that of the set of new hires. He finds greater evidence of employment discrimination against blacks in suburban and smaller firms, in part due to the customer discrimination effect already mentioned. He suggests that an appropriate policy response might be to strengthen enforcement of federal equal employment opportunity regulations, targeting suburban firms that get significant numbers of minority applicants but hire an unusually small percentage of them. Our results suggest that it may be important to pay attention to the difference between full- and part-time job offers, given the much stronger race effects that obtain when involuntary underemployment is taken into consideration. Furthermore if better-paying firms are least likely to hire people of color, then addressing discrimination in hiring may have an effect not only on the black-white employment gap but on the wage gap as well.

Political pressure to address the problem of gender equity in the labor market appears to be on the rise. As of this writing, and for the first time since the 1970s, the Senate's Health, Education, Labor and Pension Committee is hearing testimony on gender equality in pay. New legislation, containing stronger sanctions than the rarely enforced Equity Pay Act of 1963, has been proposed. Support among women for such measures appears strong: a sample of working women recently polled by the AFL-CIO ranked equal pay at the top of their list of legislative priorities (United Auto Workers 2000).

Our results suggest that a nontrivial component of the gender wage gap is driven by differences in pay between firms, not between occupations or industries. Equalizing pay between traditionally male and female occupations within a given firm may address only part of the problem. The rest may be due to a bias against hiring women at the better-paying firms, and might best be addressed by means similar to those suggested by Holzer in relation to race.

To say that tighter enforcement of federal equal opportunity regulations may be warranted is not to claim that it is the only means, or even the most effective means, toward the goal of reducing the earnings gap between men and women or whites and people of color. For example, Holzer notes that the number of blacks who *apply* for work at suburban firms is small, suggesting that a strategy of combating suburban hiring discrimination, by itself, may not have a dramatic effect. It is also clear from our results that education has a large effect compared to race and gender: in table 9.4, column 5, the difference in predicted hourly wages for someone with a high school diploma versus a four-year-college degree is 22 percent, an estimate that is itself biased downward by the inclusion of occupation and task controls; in the same equation the gender penalty is 10 percent and the black coefficient is 5 percent.

Our aim has been to determine whether race- and gender-based wage and employment gaps persist after taking account of the wide range of factors made available to us in the Multi-City Study's Household and Employer Surveys; in most cases we find that they do. The link between the surveys made two aspects of the analysis possible. First, it enabled us to explore the effect on our race and gender estimates of including the employer's statements of job requirements, of hiring screens and tests, and of interview criteria. Second, the link made possible the fixed-effects comparison of pairs of workers in the same jobs in the same establishment. This allowed us to demonstrate that employer-specific factors beyond those captured by their size or economic sector play an important role in creating disparity in the labor market.

Notes

1. Employment status was ascertained from the Household Survey variable *fwkstat* (F6).

2. Variable *fwhyls35* (F21).

3. Race and ethnicity were collapsed into a set of mutually exclusive categories: black (not Hispanic), Asian American, Latino or Latina, and white (not Hispanic). Native Americans and members of all other ethnic categories were dropped for lack of sufficient sample sizes. The classification is based on the respondent's self-ascribed race and ethnicity, from the variables *crace* (C18) and *chispan* (C20). For 97 percent of household respondents this classification is the same as that made by the interviewer in the variable *gicrace* (G6), the main difference being that 106 out of 8,916 respondents

chose the category "other" but only 27 people were so designated by the interviewers. Note that Latinos were not systematically sampled in Detroit or Atlanta, although some do appear. A representative sample of Asian Americans was collected in Los Angeles only.

4. The level of education is taken from the variable *eedudeg* (E1), with eighteen cases recoded to resolve conflicts between this variable and *eeduyrs* (E4), which asked about the number of years of education completed. James Heckman (1998) notes that people with Graduate Equivalency Degrees earn less than people with traditional high school diplomas, and that the failure to distinguish between the two can lead to an overestimate of the effect of race discrimination. We find that GED-holders earn about 3 percent less than high school degree holders after controlling for all other factors, but that coding the GED as a separate variable does not alter the estimated impact of race.

5. Variables *lrattud* (L6) and *lrracist* (L13).

6. The variable is *lrundqs* (L8). (Note that our coding is opposite that of the survey instrument, which assigned higher numbers to lower levels of understanding.) The use of scalar measures for this variable and for the impatience variable has the drawback of imposing an arbitrary linearity but the virtue of enforcing monotonicity.

7. We may look for evidence of interviewer bias by comparing the scores assigned by same-race interviewers versus interviewers of different races than their subjects. In the case of the impatience variable, we find that blacks interviewed by nonblack interviewers received significantly *better* scores (more cooperative and less impatient) than did those interviewed by other blacks. This could occur for a number of reasons: white interviewers might have erred on the side of caution in judging their black respondents, or black respondents might have made more of an effort to cooperate with white than with nonwhite interviewers.

    Results for the understanding variable were similar: blacks (and Latinos) interviewed by nonblacks (non-Latinos) received better scores than did those interviewed by other blacks (other Latinos). For white respondents the reverse was true: same-race interviews produced higher scores. Possible interpretations are that nonblacks might have been reluctant to assign low scores to blacks, or blacks might have tended to judge other blacks too harshly. Similarly, nonwhites might have judged whites too harshly, or whites might have been too generous to fellow whites. Without further evidence it is difficult to tell which mechanism was at work and hard to predict how these apparent biases might affect our estimates of the race and gender coefficients.

8. Parental education was taken from the average of *emomeduc* (E18) and *edadeduc* (E16). These were missing for about 10 percent of

the labor force, with significantly higher rates of missing values for black and Latino respondents. In order to prevent this loss of sample size, own education, which is highly correlated with parental education, was substituted for parental education data when the latter were missing. Substituting this hybrid variable had no effect on race and gender parameter estimates in the subsample for which actual parental education was also available. Vocational training was indicated by a positive response to either *ejobtran* (E29) or *earmtran* (E35). Military service was taken from *earmactv* (E33). Marital status comes from *cmarrsta* (C1) and counts only those who were currently married.

9. England, Christopher, and Reid (1999, 169) note that the high rate of single-parenthood among African American women is "explained, in part, by their unique social location: the group of men who are their most probable marriage partners have the lowest employment and wage rates, and many are simply not present in the community because of death by homicide or because of imprisonment."

10. The original weights are taken from the variable *wpstpere*.

11. Hourly wages for household respondents are taken from *fhrwage* (F23a), which is constructed from earnings in *fernmain* (F22) and *fernunit* (F23) and hours per week in *fhrswkmn* (F20). This relates to the current or last job held, and is ostensibly a pretax wage, including tips and bonuses. Out-of-range values flagged by the variable *wageflag* (F23b) were dropped. The linked dataset gave us an opportunity to examine wage figures for another person in the same occupation at the same firm. This allowed us to clean the wage data by correcting apparent data entry errors in sixty-five cases where doing so would reconcile the two wage values, and was consistent with the reported occupation and with prior-year-earnings estimates. In the paired dataset the current hourly wage for the last person hired into the stated occupation is taken from the variable *cwage*.

12. Self-employment was taken from the variable *fselfemp* (F18).

13. The percentage difference between, for example, male and female predicted wages may be measured with either the male or the female wage as the denominator, yielding two estimates that differ in absolute value. Like most authors, we report instead the raw coefficient from the log wage equation, which is a third measure of this percentage difference, one that uses as its denominator the logarithmic mean of the predicted male (m) and female (f) wages, given by $(m-f)/\log_e(m/f)$ (Törnqvist, Vartia, and Vartia 1985). It has the advantage of being symmetric (the same for men versus women as for women versus men) and additive (so that the combined effect of, say, race and gender can be ascertained by adding their coefficients). Throughout this chapter we will refer to the percentage changes in wages associated with different attributes with this definition in mind.

An alternative approach to estimating the effect of race (or gender) is the decomposition technique used by the sociologist Otis Dudley Duncan (1968) and popularized among economists by Ronald Oaxaca (1973) and Alan Blinder (1973), which acknowledges that groups may differ not only in their attributes (such as education, experience, and so forth) but also in the realized marginal returns to these attributes. However, as noted by Glen Cain (1986), this method produces two separate estimates of the group effect, which may be quite different from one another in magnitude and even sign. Harry Holzer (1996) notes this difficulty in his analysis of the employer data. Paula England, Karen Christopher, and Lori L. Reid (1999) achieve an elegant compromise in their analysis of data from the *NLSY* by using pooled estimates of slopes where appropriate and race- and sex-specific estimates where necessary. The simpler approach we employ has the advantage of collapsing these two estimates into one, but only by forcing the parameter estimates for all right-hand-side variables into conformity across race (or gender) categories.

14. The necessary variables *faglvsch* (F1), *flvschwk* (F2), and *flvwkful* (F3) were not available for Detroit. There we applied the standard formula (age − education − 6), multiplied by a correction factor of 0.79 in order to account for the fact that the standard formula necessarily yields a higher estimate of experience than the more detailed approach that deducts for periods of nonemployment. The correction factor reflects the difference between the averages of the two measures, calculated for all those employed people for whom both measures were available.

15. Jane Waldfogel (1998) notes that correcting for actual work experience in this fashion typically reduces but does not eliminate the wage gap between women with children and women without. In our female wage equations, however, we find no significant penalty associated with having children after controlling for all other factors.

16. From the variables *fjobtenr* and *fjobtnun* (F38a,b).

17. England, Christopher, and Reid (1999, 142) note that work experience and job tenure together typically explain a quarter to half of the male-female wage gap. They further observe that differences in experience and seniority may also be increasingly important determinants of the black-white wage gap for both men and women. They caution, however, "Whether the employment and resulting experience gaps between ethnic groups result from labor market discrimination or other factors is not well understood, since few multivariate analyses have taken employment as a dependent variable."

18. The task measures are *ftasface*, *ftasphne*, *ftasread*, *ftaswrit*, *ftascomp*, and *ftasmath* (F50a–f). Unfortunately, the survey structure in Detroit called for skipping these questions when the job

under discussion was the last job held, not a current job. The inclusion of the task variables would thus result in a loss of 17 percent of the Detroit sample; furthermore, this is by no means a random deletion of cases, since it is defined in relation to current employment status. In order to prevent this change in sample composition from biasing our results, we took advantage of the fact that some of these jobs were also described in the Employer Survey, which asked an identical set of questions. This allowed us to reconstruct some missing values by inserting the Employer Survey response where available. For the remainder, we replaced the missing value by the mean of nonmissing values for that task for all jobs of the same three-digit census occupation code. Roughly 120 cases for each of the six task variables were imputed in this fashion, about 3 percent of the analysis sample.

19. Occupation codes were taken from the variable *foccup* (F16), industries from *findus* (F17). We used both the three-digit and the two-digit level of detail, depending on the sample size. We also defined a one-digit coding scheme as follows: managerial and professional, technical, sales, administrative and clerical, domestic, service occupations, skilled crafts, transport jobs, and farmers and laborers. For industry: agriculture and mining, construction, manufacturing, transport, wholesale and retail trade, finance, insurance and real estate, and the public and private service sectors. Union status was taken from *funncoll* (F31a); public sector from *femptype* (F19).

20. Employer Survey variable *c2e*.

21. Employer Survey variable *a6a*.

22. Variable *ccl*.

23. Variables *posl*, *c9a*, *c9b*, *c9d*, *c9e*, *a8a*.

24. Variables *c11a*, *c11b*, *c13a*, *c13b*, *c13c*, *c13e*. Questions that were not asked in Detroit were not used.

25. Variables *c14c*, *c14e*, *c32d*.

26. The predicted probability of employment is given by $\frac{e^{X\beta}}{1+e^{X\beta}}$, where $X\beta$ is the sum of the independent variables, including the constant, weighted by their estimated coefficients. Because this function is nonlinear, the effect on the probability of employment of a given change in one of the elements of X depends on all the other elements.

27. Note that the female effect is largest both because its coefficient is the largest in absolute value, but also because we have considered it last in the sequence, at a point where the slope of the logistic function is steeper. We also noted that the female coefficient was reduced from -0.519 to -0.440, but remained significantly negative at the 5 percent level, when the specification was altered to

include our measure of labor market experience (instead of age), and an indicator variable for women with children.

28. These sign reversals suggest that the personality variables should be allowed to interact with the Boston indicator variable. When the pooled equation is respecified in this way, the estimated coefficients for both of the personality variables become larger in absolute value, and both are significantly negative. However, the race and gender coefficients are unaffected. We conclude, as before, that although these personality measures do matter, they do not contribute to the race- and gender-based employment gaps.

29. For the three smaller cities, between 13 and 21 percent of the sample consisted of people who were alone in their three-digit occupational categories or were singletons in their three-digit industrial categories. Wages for such people can be perfectly predicted, and these cases thus have no influence on the other parameter estimates in the model. This changes the effective composition of the sample, making it difficult to compare across the specifications. At the two-digit level, the number of singletons never exceeded 3 percent.

30. Other research using linked datasets includes that of Arne Kalleberg and Mark Van Buren (1994) who use the National Organizations Study to examine within- and between-occupation wage dispersion as a function of the level of gender heterogeneity; but they do not consider race or gender difference in wages as outcome variables in their own right. James McPartland and colleagues surveyed employers of young workers who appeared in the National Longitudinal Survey of Youth, and Jomills Braddock and McPartland (1987) used this linked dataset to test for statistical discrimination.

31. Others have argued that the increase in black unemployment during this period, both absolutely and relative to whites, cannot be explained by the over-representation of blacks in declining industries and regions (Badgett 1990). Irene Browne (1997) makes a similar argument with respect to the decline in labor force participation by African American women.

We thank the Ford Foundation, Rockefeller Foundation, and Russell Sage Foundation for support for data collection, and the Russell Sage Foundation for support for analysis. All supporting tables, regression results, and Stata programs are available from the lead author upon request.

References

Altonji, Joseph G., and Robert A. Shakotko. 1987. "Do Wages Rise with Job Seniority?" *Review of Economic Studies* 54(3): 437–59.
Badgett, Mary Virginia Lee. 1990. "Racial Differences in Unemployment

Rates and Employment Opportunities." Ph.D. diss., University of California, Berkeley.

Bayard, Kimberly, Judith Hellerstein, David Neumark, and Kenneth Troske. 1999a. "Why are Racial and Ethnic Wage Gaps Larger for Men than for Women? Exploring the Role of Segregation Using the New Worker-Establishment Characteristics Database." Working paper 6997. Cambridge, Mass.: National Bureau of Economic Research.

Bayard, Kimberly, Judith Hellerstein, David Neumark, and Kenneth Troske. 1999b. "New Evidence on Sex Segregation and Sex Differences in Wages from Matched Employee-Employer Data." Working paper 7003. Cambridge, Mass.: National Bureau of Economic Research.

Blau, Francine D. 1977, *Equal Pay in the Office*. Lexington, Mass.: D.C. Heath.

Blinder, Alan. 1973. "Wage Discrimination: Reduced-Form and Structural Estimates." *Journal of Human Resources* 8(4): 436–55.

Bound, John, and Laura Dresser. 1999. "Losing Ground: The Erosion of the Relative Earnings of African-American Women in the 1980s." In *Latinas and African-American Women During the 1980s*, edited by Irene Browne. New York: Russell Sage Foundation.

Bound, John, and Richard B. Freeman. 1992, "What Went Wrong? The Erosion of Relative Earnings and Employment Among Young Black Men in the 1980s." *Quarterly Journal of Economics* 107(1): 201–32.

Bowles, Samuel, Herbert Gintis, and Melissa Osborne. 2000. "The Determinants of Earnings: Skills, Preferences, and Schooling." Unpublished paper. Department of Economics, University of Massachusetts at Amherst.

Braddock, Jomills Henry, II, and James McPartland. 1987. "How Minorities Continue to be Excluded from Equal Employment Opportunities: Research on Labor Market and Institutional Opportunities." *Journal of Social Issues* 43(1): 5–39.

Bridges, William P., and Wayne J. Villemez. 1994. *The Employment Relationship: Causes and Consequences of Modern Personnel Administration*. New York: Plenum Press.

Browne, Irene. 1997. "Explaining the Black-White Gap in Labor Force Participation Among Women Heading Households." *American Sociological Review* 62(2): 236–52.

Cain, Glen. 1986. "The Economic Analysis of Labor Market Discrimination: A Survey." In *Handbook of Labor Economics*, Vol. 1, edited by Orley Ashenfelter and Richard Layard. Amsterdam: Elsevier.

Christopher, Karen, 1996. "Explaining the Recent Employment Gap Between Black and White Women." *Sociological Focus* 29(3): 263–80.

Darrity, William A., and Patrick L. Mason. 1998. "Evidence on Discrimination in Employment: Codes of Color, Codes of Gender." *Journal of Economic Perspectives* 12(2): 63–90.

Duncan, Otis Dudley. 1968. "Inheritance of Poverty or Inheritance of Race?" In *On Understanding Poverty*, edited by Daniel Patrick Moynihan. New York: Basic Books.

England, Paula. 1992. *Comparable Worth: Theories and Evidence.* Hawthorne, N.Y.: Aldine de Gruyter.

England, Paula, Karen Christopher, and Lori L. Reid. 1999. "Gender, Race, Ethnicity, and Wages." In *Latinas and African American Women at Work*, edited by Irene Browne. New York: Russell Sage Foundation.

Gottschalk, Peter. 1997. "Inequality, Income Growth, and Mobility: The Basic Facts." *Journal of Economic Perspectives* 11(2): 21–40.

Groshen, Erica L. 1991. "The Structure of the Female/Male Wage Differential: Is It Who You Are, What You Do, or Where You Work?" *Journal of Human Resources* 26(3): 457–72.

Heckman, James. 1998. "Detecting Discrimination." *Journal of Economic Perspectives* 12(2): 101–16.

Holzer, Harry J. 1996. *What Employers Want: Job Prospects for Less Educated Workers.* New York: Russell Sage Foundation.

Holzer, Harry J., and Keith R. Ihlanfeldt. 1998. "Customer Discrimination and Employment Outcomes for Minority Workers." *Quarterly Journal of Economics* 133(3): 835–67.

Kalleberg, Arne L., and Mark E. Van Buren. 1994. "The Structure of Organizational Earnings Inequality." *American Behavioral Scientist* 37(7): 930–47.

Mason, Patrick L. 1999. "Male Interracial Wage Differentials: Competing Explanations." *Cambridge Journal of Economics* 23(3): 261–99.

Meléndez, Edwin. 1993. "Understanding Latino Poverty." *Sage Race Relations Abstracts* 18(2): 3–43.

Moss, Philip, and Chris Tilly. 2000. *Stories Employers Tell: Race, Skill, and Hiring in America.* New York: Russell Sage Foundation.

Neal, Derek A., and William R. Johnson. 1996. "The Role of Premarket Factors in Black-White Wage Differences." *Journal of Political Economy* 104(5): 869–95.

Neumark, David. 1996. "Sex Discrimination in Restaurant Hiring: An Audit Study." *Quarterly Journal of Economics* 111(3): 915–41.

Oaxaca, Ronald. 1973. "Male-Female Wage Differentials in Urban Labor Markets." *International Economic Review* 14(3): 693–709.

O'Neill, June. 1990. "The Role of Human Capital in Earnings Differences between Black and White Men," *Journal of Economic Perspectives* 4(4): 25–46.

Reskin, Barbara, and Naomi Cassirer. 1996. "Occupational Segregation by Gender, Race and Ethnicity." *Sociological Focus* 29(3): 231–43.

Topel, Robert. 1991. "Specific Capital, Mobility, and Wages: Wages Rise with Job Seniority," *Journal of Political Economy* 99(1): 145–76.

Törnqvist, Leo, Pentti Vartia, and Yrjö O. Vartia. 1985. "How Should Relative Changes Be Measured?" *American Statistician* 39(1): 43–46.

United Auto Workers. 2000. *Solidarity* (May): 9.

Waldfogel, Jane. 1998. "Understanding the 'Family Gap' in Pay for Women with Children." *Journal of Economic Perspectives* 12(1): 137–56.

10

WHY OPPORTUNITY ISN'T KNOCKING: RACIAL INEQUALITY AND THE DEMAND FOR LABOR

Philip Moss and Chris Tilly

O VER the last few years, the message the U.S. government has clearly sent is that, with few exceptions, poor people are expected to work their way out of poverty. The federal welfare reform passed in 1996 includes work requirements and time limits designed to push about one million women, most with limited education, into the workforce (Albelda and Tilly 1997). Other recent federal and state policies embody a similar philosophy. The notion behind these policies is that large numbers of poor people are failing to seize the available labor market opportunities; in order to prosper, they need stronger incentives to seek work. But a growing body of evidence shows that job opportunities are quite limited for job seekers with low educational attainment. Persistent and widening differences in employment outcomes by race and ethnicity have been documented. The Multi-City Study of Urban Inequality datasets offer a rare opportunity to look at these differences and the reasons for them from the demand side of the labor market. Adding the Employer Survey, we can learn both about patterns of labor demand and about some of the "why and how" behind these patterns.

To clarify what we mean by *labor demand*, let us briefly review the distinction between supply and demand. The supply side of the labor market consists of existing and potential workers. Supply-side explanations for the labor market difficulties of urban minority workers are based on levels and changes in the numbers of workers, their attributes, intentions, and decisions. Demand-side explanations, on the other hand, rest on levels and changes in the numbers, locations, characteristics, and behaviors of the employers in the labor market. The demand side, then, constitutes the *opportunities* available in the labor market.

Recent research on labor market outcomes of young black and white workers, male and female, finds widening racial gaps in *both* wages and employment since the mid-1970s (Bound and Freeman 1992; Bound and Dresser, 1999; Corcoran and Parrott, 1999; Moss and Tilly 1991, 1993). The fact that both disparities are expanding strongly suggests that shifts in demand are at play. Data on Latinos have not been as thoroughly analyzed, but there is some evidence that growing Latino-Anglo inequality results, at least in part, from labor demand movements (Corcoran, Heflin, and Reyes, 1999; Meléndez 1993).

Of course, the outcomes we observe in the Multi-City Study Employer Surveys result from the *interaction* of supply with demand, not from demand alone. Further, supply and demand play out in a highly structured institutional context. For these reasons, we cannot hope to observe "pure" demand effects. However, we can observe demand-side influences more directly than in the preponderance of labor market research, which is based on surveys of individuals and households.

We focus in this chapter on four demand side factors:

(1) the skills demanded by firms and changes in the skills sought, which can have important impacts, since African American and Latino workers, on average, have lower education and skill levels than other workers;

(2) business location and employers' locational shifts away from population concentrations of urban minority workers;

(3) the negative attitudes that employers hold about workers of color; and

(4) the disparate effects that various recruiting and screening methods have on such workers.

We find that all four appear to constitute important barriers to employment for black and Latino workers. Moreover, the four factors overlap in important ways. Both skill assessments by employers and perceptions of various locations as good places to do business or from which to recruit workers are confounded with racial attitudes and stereotypes. Racially disparate impacts of recruiting and screening methods appear to signal a combination of skill deficiencies and discriminatory practices.

The four demand-side factors, to the degree that they are the sources of labor market disadvantage for urban minority workers, call for different policy responses. Skill deficits imply a need for changes in education and training policies, both outside and inside firms. Increasing remoteness from the locus of job opportunities suggests that improvements to transportation systems and arrangements may help. Discrimination requires antidiscrimination enforcement and diversity training. To the degree that geography and skills are also connected to attitudes about race, working on training, transportation, or residential location alone cannot resolve the problems. In this case, antidiscrimination policy and diversity education and training should do triple duty in improving the labor market picture for urban workers of color.

In the next section of the chapter, we describe the two sets of Employer Survey data. Then we present quantitative and qualitative findings on skills, location, employer attitudes, and hiring procedures. Finally, we offer brief conclusions and some closing thoughts on public policy.

Data

The data we use in this chapter are drawn from two of the three coordinated Multi-City Study surveys: the large-scale, quantitative Telephone Survey and the qualitative, face-to-face, in-depth survey with employers in the Atlanta, Boston, Detroit, and Los Angeles metropolitan areas. The Telephone Survey of employers was administered by Professor Harry Holzer of Michigan State University. Roughly 800 employers in each of the four cities were interviewed between May 1992 and May 1994. The survey questions addressed the characteristics of the establishment of the last person hired in the firm and of the job that that person filled. Respondents were asked about frequency of performance of certain tasks, recruiting and screening procedures, other hiring requirements, the demographics of the worker hired, the demographics of the persons applying for the job, and the demographics of the firm's employees and customers. About a thousand of the firms interviewed were generated by respondents in the Household Surveys who reported their employer. (We administered 297 of these household-linked interviews with Joleen Kirschenman after Holzer's study was complete.) The rest of the firms were drawn from lists of firms from Survey Sampling, Inc., which, in turn, are generated from phone directories. The response rate for the Telephone Survey (including only firms that passed the screener) was about two-thirds. Holzer (1996b) has already reported many of the major findings from these data; our discussion covers much of the same ground but presents some new results as well. Results reported here differ from those reported by Holzer because they include responses from the 297 additional telephone interviews in the Boston and Los Angeles areas.

The sample for the in-depth Employer Survey was drawn from firms that had been identified by household respondents holding jobs requiring no more than a high school education, and that had successfully completed a Telephone Survey. Interviews were conducted at forty-five firms in Atlanta and Los Angeles, forty-six in Boston, and thirty-eight in Detroit. Firms were surveyed between the summer of 1994 and the summer of 1996. The response rate for the in-depth survey was about two-thirds.

The in-depth survey involves a series of structured questions and follow-up probes. Interviewers spoke face to face with up to three respondents per firm: the chief executive officer at the site or another top manager; a personnel official involved in hiring for the sample job; and a line manager or supervisor who manages employees in the sample job category. This strategy gathers the differing knowledge and perceptions of these various categories of managers. In smaller firms, these functions were often performed by two people or even just one person, so fewer interviews were conducted. Questions gather the details of the recruiting, screening, and hiring procedures used in filling the sample job, and what each procedure is designed to do. All questions are open-ended, and interviewers were trained to encourage respondents to elaborate, telling the story of their business's relationship to the labor market.

Findings from telephone and face-to-face surveys often have different focuses and may sometimes appear to be inconsistent. The purpose of this chapter is not to iron out or adjudicate any such differences, but to present results from both surveys and to point to potential conflicts or ambiguities as triggers for further research.

All the quantitative tabulations and qualitative evidence reported in this chapter refer only to jobs that require no more than a high school degree.[1] Given this limitation, the sampling and weighting schemes are designed to approximate an employment-weighted sample of the universe of businesses employing people who have no more than a high school education. The employment weighting means that a business's probability of appearing in the sample is roughly proportional to the number of people it employs; larger employers are more strongly represented.

Findings: The Shape of Employment Opportunities

Skill requirements, the changing geographic configuration of jobs, employer attitudes and stereotypes, and methods of recruiting and screening—all affect employment prospects for workers of color. We consider the evidence with regard to each of these factors, one at a time. In each case, quantitative and qualitative data provide complementary insights.

Because blacks and Latinos lag behind whites in average educational attainment and other measures of skill, we would expect skill requirements to constitute a significant barrier to job access for workers of color. Indeed, some researchers (Neal and Johnson 1996; Ferguson 1996; O'Neill 1990) find that expanded measures of skill such as the Armed Forces Qualifying Test can account for most or all the wage difference between black and white men (though with the AFQT, as with any standardized test, there is some question as to exactly what the exam is measuring). Similarly, George Borjas (1994) attributes declining earnings of successive cohorts of Latino immigrants to diminishing levels of education. Qualitative data, as well, indicate that skill requirements often screen out African American men (Moss and Tilly 2000). In addition, there is considerable evidence that demands for skill have risen over time (Bound and Johnson 1992; Cappelli 1993; Howell and Wolff 1991; Moss and Tilly 2000; Osterman 1995).

The Employer Surveys offer a more detailed look at what employers are demanding of entry-level hires: what tasks workers will perform, what skills they should possess, and what credentials the employers screen for in judging applicants. They confirm that skill requirements disproportionately exclude men of color—but not particularly women of color.

Job Tasks, Skills, and Credentials

Quantitative Evidence   What tasks do employers require entry-level workers to perform? The quantitative survey asked employers the frequency with which certain tasks—such as talking face to face or on the telephone to customers, reading instructions at least a paragraph long, writing paragraphs or memos, doing arithmetic, or working with computers—are done on the sample job.[2] The results are presented in table 10.1. All the tasks, except writing, are performed daily in at least half the jobs reported. The results also indicate how often a job requires these tasks.

Holzer breaks down the frequency of task performance by occupational category, and shows that while the top category of professional/managerial jobs has the greatest frequencies of daily task use, all occupation groups have substantial task requirements—with half or more jobs requiring each task in almost all cases. This is true even for the lowest-paid category, service workers, except in the case of computer use (see Holzer 1996b, 48–49, and table 3.2). He also shows that the frequency of task use is higher in the central city of the metropolitan area, in comparison to the suburbs and other areas (other central cities in the metropolitan area and municipalities with at least 30 percent of their population black). Clearly there appears to be a strong need for

TABLE 10.1   *Frequency of Task Performance*

	Daily	Weekly	Monthly	Almost Never
Talk face to face with customers	58.4%	7.2%	2.1%	32.0%
Talk on the phone with customers	53.1	7.2	2.4	37.1
Read instructions	54.1	20.8	6.8	17.8
Write paragraphs	30.6	16.8	9.6	42.8
Do arithmetic	64.6	11.8	4.1	19.0
Use computers	51.0	5.4	2.5	40.9

Source: Multi-City Study of Urban Inequality Telephone Employer Survey.

cognitive and personal skills to handle the daily tasks on entry-level noncollege jobs, particularly in central-city areas where the concentration of minority, less-educated workers reside.

Table 10.2 shows the credentials employers in the survey report they require. The level of required credentials is high. Most of the credentials are required for approximately two-thirds to three-quarters of the available jobs. The most frequently required credential is a high school diploma, while the least sought is prior vocational or other training (although even this certification is required by 30 to 40 percent of available jobs). The results also indicate that a higher fraction of employers in the primary central city require each of the hiring credentials, except for the case of vocational training. Holzer also shows that, except for the requirement of previous vocational or other training for sales, laborer, and operative jobs, which is relatively infrequent (25 to 35 percent of such jobs) in every job category, almost every credential is required by half or more of the employers (see Holzer 1996b, table 3.6). Table 10.2 also indicates that the pattern of hiring requirements and its geographic variation is quite consistent across the four metropolitan areas.

Taken together, these two tables tell a sobering story. The hurdle to qualify for entry-level jobs, especially in central cities, appears to be high. This indicates that less-educated minority workers, in particular, face a potential skills mismatch in their local labor markets.

To the degree that the trend of skill demands is a rising one, this mismatch is likely to worsen. The results in table 10.3 suggest that we should indeed expect a growing mismatch, at least for the near term.[3] Employers were asked to report whether the skills needed to perform the sample job were changing; if so, whether they were rising or declining; and, if rising, why they were rising. Less than half (40 percent) of all employers reported a change in the level of skills required on the sample

TABLE 10.2   *Hiring Requirements, by Primary Central City, Suburb, and Other Central Cities*

Requirements for Hiring	Primary Central City	Suburbs	Other Central Cities
All metropolitan areas			
High school diploma	74.5%	70.4%	68.1%
General experience	72.6	68.4	67.3
Specific experience	66.8	59.4	57.9
References	73.2	71.6	72.3
Vocational or other training	41.8	38.9	32.3
Los Angeles			
High school diploma	67.0	66.7	68.9
General experience	71.3	70.3	75.3
Specific experience	71.7	66.5	73.1
References	64.5	68.1	69.7
Vocational or other training	39.6	42.9	44.9
Boston			
High school diploma	80.3	74.6	61.4
General experience	77.5	71.0	72.0
Specific experience	68.9	57.9	60.4
References	81.3	80.7	80.2
Vocational or other training	43.4	43.6	29.3
Detroit			
High school diploma	73.2	70.6	71.6
General experience	75.7	62.3	59.3
Specific experience	66.1	51.4	47.8
References	61.2	64.4	63.2
Vocational or other training	38.5	28.3	27.4
Atlanta			
High school diploma	78.1	70.5	71.2
General experience	70.1	70.9	64.1
Specific experience	62.6	61.5	53.9
References	81.2	77.0	73.3
Vocational or other training	44.1	41.4	31.1

Source: Multi-City Study of Urban Inequality Telephone Employer Survey.

job. But among those who did report a change, essentially all reported a rise in skills. Basic reading, writing, and verbal skills—hard skills—are most frequently cited as the kind of skills that are rising. Very close behind are the social and verbal skills—soft skills—or a combination of both skills.

The greater need for basic skills appears to derive from the frequent reports of introducing new technology or use of computers. The heightened demand for social and verbal skills seems to originate from more

TABLE 10.3   *Proportion of Employers Reporting a Change in Skills Sought for the Sample Job*

	All Jobs	Clerical	Customer Service	Blue-Collar	Other
Report a change in skills	39.8%	52.3%	32.7%	34.1%	44.0%
Of those reporting a change					
Skills risen	96.3	97.1	96.1	95.3	96.4
Skills declined	3.1	2.5	3.0	4.3	2.9
Of those reporting a rise in skills					
What kind of skills					
Basic reading, writing, numeric	29.2	27.2	19.6	38.5	29.9
Social and verbal	26.6	20.4	44.6	20.0	24.3
Both	23.9	27.4	21.1	21.8	25.4
Other	17.8	24.2	13.2	16.1	16.8
Reasons for the rise					
New technology	83.1	94.3	70.3	78.8	85.6
Computers	71.7	92.3	63.2	48.2	79.6
New products	46.9	43.3	46.2	58.4	40.3
Higher product quality	62.5	57.7	51.8	73.9	64.4
New services provided	66.2	66.3	76.1	55.2	68.6
More customer contact	56.4	53.9	74.7	40.5	58.4
Organizational change	77.1	76.8	79.0	76.2	75.9

Source: Multi-City Study of Urban Inequality Telephone Employer Survey.

need for customer contact and, as our qualitative data suggest, from organizational change, which frequently involves more use of teams and, for most employees, a broader span of interaction across the organization.

The pattern of skill change across occupations is similar but with some notable differences. Employers report greater skill increases for clerical occupations, and this appears to be driven by the widespread introduction of computers into clerical work. As might be expected, blue-collar occupations are relatively more likely to require more basic skills, and customer service jobs are relatively more likely to demand greater social and verbal skills.

Table 10.4 displays for each source of skill change the fraction of employers that indicate each type of skill need that has increased. The pattern is fairly consistent across sources of skill change. Slightly more employers report basic skills rising as a result of the particular reason

TABLE 10.4   *Reasons for Skill Change, by Type of Skill Change*

	Basic	Social and Verbal	Both	Other	Total
Reason for skill change					
New technology	30.7%	22.6%	25.5%	21.2%	100.0%
Computers	30.5	22.1	25.9	21.5	100.0
New products	28.8	25.1	25.2	20.8	100.0
Higher product quality	30.3	23.6	26.6	19.4	100.0
New services provided	25.3	29.8	25.7	19.2	100.0
More customer contact	23.8	33.6	27.0	15.6	100.0
Organizational change	27.6	27.8	26.1	18.5	100.0

Source: Multi-City Study of Urban Inequality Telephone Employer Survey.

for skill change than report social and verbal skills rising or both rising as a result. This is particularly true when the reason for a skill change is technology, computers, or new products. More customer contact, not surprisingly, has caused a relative greater rise in the need for social and verbal skills.

Qualitative Data on Changing Skill Demands   Qualitative data from the face-to-face interviews tell us that there is often more to skill changes than meets the eye. For example, consistent with the Telephone Survey data, employers most commonly reported no change in skill requirements. But in some cases, employers stated that there had been no skill changes, but later described precisely such changes! Consider this interchange with the president of a small manufacturing company:

Interviewer: Have there been any changes in the kind of things you're looking for in a worker? Has that remained kind of constant?

Respondent: Yeah, we're still doing essentially the same thing we did thirty-one years ago. . . .

Interviewer: Has technology affected the way these people do business . . . work?

Respondent: Yeah, it's unbelievable. . . . Technology has changed our business. Technology has changed the way that we deal with our product. You know it's just unbelievable. Yeah, technology has had an unbelievable bearing on the way we service our customers, our customers' needs and the way that we do business.

Interviewer: Has it changed the kind of qualities that you're look-ing for in a worker? Has it affected what you need to look for?

Respondent: To a degree.

Interviewer: How so?

Respondent: Well . . . anybody that comes in here that if they were lucky enough at the time . . . that their school had computers and things of this type. . . . It's just an asset for them to have.

On the other hand, while numerous respondents described the com-puterization of various jobs, a substantial minority of them reported no resulting increase in the skills sought. "It takes about ten minutes" to train file clerks in how to use the computers, one Atlanta manager re-ported. A Boston construction supply wholesaler had just spent $250,000 on a new computer system, but was not looking for anything different among clerical hires, because "if it's not broke, don't fix it." Others commented that it has been easy to train people to use com-puters and other new automated equipment. In fact, the human re-sources director at a bank commented that she doesn't look for com-puter familiarity in new hires "because our computers are different. I mean all systems are different. They have to learn our, our system and that's what they're trained in." Similarly, some managers observed that general workforce skills had changed in step with the business's techni-cal requirements, or even ahead of them:

> We only got our computer system three years ago. . . . So we don't, by the time we get it everybody else has got it, you know, working someplace else, [so the employees] know more than we do.

> [Most applicants already know how to use a computer] because as an in-fant now they toddle up to the microwave, and press a few buttons, and cook their hot dog, right. So they have it . . . you know, they have all of those games they play on TV. It's not, it's not a problem for them. They learn it real fast.

In some cases, computerization has spelled deskilling. Most re-tailers commented that "smart" cash registers have actually made the cashier's job easier and diminished the need for mathematical skills. And the data entry supervisor at a consulting firm noted that computers have gotten easier to use.

Moreover, in some cases computerization has tremendous work-force impacts that have nothing to do with skill. In a fascinating sec-ondhand story, a Los Angeles mortgage company executive recounted:

> Two to three years ago the [name of bank], their mortgage company decided that they were going to convert all of their salespeople, or equip all of their sales people with laptop computers. And they were going to be required to, rather than fill out the loan application longhand and deliver it to the processor for closing, they were going to be required to enter the information. They had a 95 percent turnover in their sales force. They just quit. . . . It's because of the different attitudes about using the computer at that time. Typing, just the basic typing skills. Typing is women's work, and the loan officers, and the male loan officers considered it beneath them. Demeaning.

He went on to add that male attitudes had changed, and that now his sales force is "begging for us to buy them computers."

Despite these caveats, a growing need for computer skills was the most common skill change reported. We also heard repeatedly about three other kinds of rises in technical or hard skill requirements. First, some businesses have placed new emphasis on basic skills such as literacy, often in response to new equipment, new worker involvement in quality control processes such as statistical process control, or new standards for customer or worker safety, all of which may require reading written instructions or keeping written records. Second, employers told of a need for workers to handle a broader range of tasks, or to possess a more analytical overview of how their tasks fit into broader processes. Secretaries, for instance, are no longer typists but "information managers" at a small nonprofit organization in Detroit. Third, a variety of industry-specific changes call for added skill: home care aides need added technical knowledge because managed care is inducing hospitals to discharge sicker patients, the director of a Boston agency told us.

More frequent than any of the hard skill shifts except for computer literacy, however, were heightened demands for soft skills. Managers of retail, service, and clerical workers spoke of greater needs for the interaction skills involved in customer service—in some cases linked to a declining need for hard skills:

> [Computers have] taken a lot of the basic thinking process out of it. Y'know, a lot of it the computers do for you, so, a lot of those skills . . . probably communication skills [are what's needed].

> At one time we have more and more people what we consider operational functions. They unloaded trucks, they straightened up the stockroom, they worked in office areas but with the computer systems now in place that we have . . . our goal is to get more and more people on the selling floor to take care of our guests. And to be working in and around our guests. I guess that's what . . . our focus has been how to get people to get reports and let the computers do a lot of the things that once happened.

It's becoming more and more important that people have good communication skills and they're people-oriented, along with having your basic typing and word processing skills as well. There's not that many secretarial jobs anymore where you just sit in front of a computer and type all day.

As Philip Moss and Chris Tilly (1996) reported, employers related these new needs back to competitive pressure and to a competitive strategy designed to win over customers—to make these businesses "a fun place to shop and to work," in the words of one Detroit retailer. Less commonly, managers expressed a need for stronger interaction skills stemming from the adoption of "team" forms of organization.

Employers also talked about accentuated requirements for motivation. At a bakery, following automation "they actually need less skills to do the job, but I think they're a little more conscious of the quality of the work they do now." A car dealer says he looks more than before for workers who "give a damn about who's the customer"; a supervisor of equipment service people wants more of a "a can-do attitude, will-do, 'Let's go out there and knock those calls out.'" As these snippets suggest, businesses' push for more motivation is often tied to the same customer satisfaction goals as the drive for better interaction skills. Even in a consumer durable factory, the human resource director said he needs someone who is "more customer-oriented"—meaning someone who is motivated to think about the quality the customer seeks.

Skill Requirements Disadvantage Particular Groups

Race, Ethnicity, and Gender   Table 10.5 shows the association between the need for certain job tasks or the use of particular hiring credentials and the proportion of new hires in each of six race-ethnicity-gender groups (white, black, Hispanic, by male and female).[4] The results are striking. Looking at daily task use, white women are substantially more likely to be hired if *any* of the tasks are required daily. This is particularly so for the use of computers and talking on the phone, which, as Holzer notes, may reflect the concentration of white women in clerical and sales jobs (see Holzer 1996b, 81). This gender effect is also apparent for black women, but somewhat less so, and is not the case for doing math or reading instructions. Some daily task requirements increase the proportion of Hispanic women, but the differences are fairly small.

Black and Hispanic men are hit hard when any of these tasks must be performed daily. Talking face to face or on the phone particularly disadvantages Hispanic men, and one can speculate that this is due in part to lack of English-language proficiency. There is a large effect on Hispanic males when computers are used. Both black and Hispanic

TABLE 10.5   *Gender and Race of New Hires by Daily Task Use and Hiring Requirement*

	White Males	Black Males	Hispanic Males	White Females	Black Females	Hispanic Females
All jobs	26.0%	10.1%	10.4%	35.7%	10.9%	7.0%
Daily tasks						
Talk face to face with customers						
No	29.4	11.5	14.7	29.9	8.2	6.4
Yes	23.7	9.2	7.4	39.5	12.7	7.4
Talk on the phone with customers						
No	32.9	14.0	17.0	20.1	9.6	6.4
Yes	20.1	6.9	4.7	49.1	11.9	7.4
Read instructions						
No	24.9	11.7	12.3	33.1	11.2	6.9
Yes	27.0	8.8	8.8	37.7	10.5	7.2
Write paragraphs						
No	27.8	10.8	12.5	31.3	10.8	6.8
Yes	22.1	8.6	5.7	45.4	10.9	7.2
Do math						
No	21.8	13.5	14.7	28.2	13.2	8.7
Yes	28.3	8.3	8.0	39.9	9.5	6.1
Use computers						
No	32.6	13.6	16.4	21.6	9.3	6.5
Yes	19.4	6.7	4.5	49.6	12.3	6.5
Requirements for hiring						
High school diploma						
No	26.8	13.5	21.5	20.2	9.9	8.0
Yes	25.6	8.8	5.9	41.9	11.2	6.6
General experience						
No	24.2	12.7	13.3	28.7	12.7	8.4
Yes	26.7	9.0	9.1	38.7	10.1	6.4
Specific experience						
No	23.7	12.3	11.5	34.0	11.6	6.9
Yes	27.4	8.7	9.7	36.7	10.4	7.1
References						
No	25.6	10.6	12.5	31.2	12.1	8.0
Yes	26.1	10.0	9.6	37.3	10.4	6.6
Vocational or other training						
No	23.9	11.3	10.7	35.4	12.2	6.6
Yes	29.3	8.4	9.9	36.0	8.8	7.6

Source: Multi-City Study of Urban Inequality Telephone Employer Survey.

men's numbers plunge when writing or arithmetic is required. White men's proportion of the workforce tumbles noticeably when customer service and computer tasks are needed, but increases if reading or math is required.

Overall, in the entry-level jobs we are investigating women are considerably more likely than their male counterparts in the same race-ethnic groups to be the hired when any of these tasks are necessary on the job.

A similar, but not identical pattern of associations is evident for hiring credentials. White females boost their numbers when any of the hiring requirements are utilized, compared to when the credential is not necessary. Black and Hispanic males get clobbered when any of the hiring credentials are applied. Black females are less in evidence when general or specific experience or prior training is required, but are more likely to be hired if a high school diploma is necessary. As with job tasks, white and black females have a higher proportion of jobs than their male counterparts when any of the hiring credentials are applied. This pattern is not apparent for Hispanic men and women.

The results in this table clearly indicate that minority males are much less likely to obtain an entry-level job when any of the job tasks or hiring requirements are reported. White males show some of these effects as well. There is a strong gender effect, as females in each race-gender category are more likely to be hired than their male counterparts when the job tasks are necessary and, except for Hispanics, when the hiring credentials are utilized.

Education and Gender   In addition to asking about required credentials, the large-scale Employer Survey asked about the educational level of the person most recently hired, so that we can examine this directly. We expect high school dropouts to be at a disadvantage relative to high school graduates in general, and for this effect to be larger when jobs require more tasks or higher levels of credentials. Table 10.6 confirms this expectation and explores how the pattern varies by gender. For high school graduates and dropouts considered together, the gender difference mirrors the effects shown in the previous table. Men are less in evidence when any of the job tasks are necessary, and correspondingly women increase in numbers when this is the case. Women as a whole have higher representation when each of the credentials is applied, except for the vocational education requirement.

But the real story here is the contrast between high school graduates and dropouts. The situation for men who lack a high school degree is stark. Employers are two to three times as likely to hire male dropouts for jobs that do *not* require daily tasks of reading, writing, math,

TABLE 10.6   *Gender and Educational Level of New Hires by Daily Task Use and Hiring Requirements*

	Male High School Graduate	Female High School Graduate	Male Dropout	Female Dropout
All jobs	44.2%	50.9%	3.0%	1.9%
Daily tasks				
Talk face to face with customers				
No	51.8	43.5	3.3	1.4
Yes	39.4	55.5	2.8	2.3
Talk on the phone with customers				
No	56.0	36.7	5.2	2.1
Yes	35.8	61.0	1.3	1.8
Read instructions				
No	43.9	47.8	5.1	3.2
Yes	44.3	52.9	1.7	1.2
Write paragraphs				
No	47.4	45.5	4.6	2.5
Yes	40.1	57.8	0.1	1.2
Do math				
No	45.0	47.7	4.9	2.4
Yes	43.8	52.4	2.0	1.7
Use computers				
No	53.5	37.7	5.7	3.1
Yes	37.8	59.9	1.2	1.1
Requirements for hiring				
High school diploma				
No	50.4	31.5	11.4	6.7
Yes	39.5	58.0	1.4	1.2
General experience				
No	42.1	48.6	5.7	3.7
Yes	45.0	51.8	1.9	1.3
Specific experience				
No	42.2	49.1	5.4	3.3
Yes	45.2	51.8	1.7	1.2
References				
No	44.7	46.6	5.1	3.6
Yes	44.0	52.1	3.4	1.5
Vocational or other training				
No	41.8	51.6	4.3	2.3
Yes	47.3	49.9	1.2	1.5

Source: Multi-City Study of Urban Inequality Telephone Employer Survey.

computer use, or telephone conversation, as they are to hire dropouts for jobs that *do* require any of these tasks. Leaving aside the high school diploma requirement, credential requirements have a similar two- to threefold screening effect on male dropouts. In contrast, for male high school graduates many of the task and credential requirements have small to negligible negative effects, or even positive effects.

The contrast between female high school graduates and dropouts is also striking. All six task requirements increase the probability of hiring a female high school graduate. All except talking face to face with a customer and doing math *decrease* the chances of hiring a female high school dropout. Whereas every credential requirement screens *in* women with a high school diploma, every such prerequisite screens *out* women who lack the diploma—at rates similar to their male counterparts. In this particular comparison, educational differences overwhelm gender effects.

Counting Up the Available Jobs   How many jobs are available to workers with little experience or skill accumulation? The answer to this question gives us important information for assessing the likely impacts of the recently passed welfare reform legislation. Holzer has calculated the fraction of all jobs in the central cities, the suburbs, and in other places in the four metropolitan areas that require few or no job tasks and few or no hiring credentials (see Holzer 1996b, 62–66 and table 3.9; see also chapter 11 in this book). We replicate those calculations in table 10.7.

Very few of the jobs reported in this survey require none of the job tasks analyzed or none of the credentials. If the pool of jobs is expanded by adding the jobs that only require talking to customers, the situation improves somewhat but remains fairly bleak. The same is true when the stock of jobs is augmented to include those that require only a high school degree or, further, those that require only the high school degree and some general experience. More jobs become available, but the amount is still relatively small—increasing only from around 5 percent to around 10 percent of the jobs. (And recall that this set of jobs already excludes any jobs requiring college education.) Importantly, the fraction of available jobs is in all cases lower in the central cities than in their suburban areas, as less skilled workers, particularly minority workers and welfare recipients, are more likely to live in the central city. The pattern across cities indicates that low-educated workers in all of the four cities face difficult labor prospects. The availability of jobs without major tasks is relatively better in Los Angeles and much worse in Boston.

Jobs that require no or few tasks or credentials also pay poor wages and significantly less than the average for all entry jobs in this survey.

TABLE 10.7   *Percentage of Jobs and Wage Levels, by Number of Tasks and Requirements, by City and Suburb and Other Central Cities*

	All Four Metropolitan Areas		
	Primary Central City	Suburbs	Other Central Cities
Percentage of jobs			
Perform none of major tasks daily	5.8%	8.0%	8.6%
Perform none of major tasks except talking to customers	12.7	14.0	14.5
Requires no high school diploma, training, experience, or references	4.1	6.3	5.9
Requires only high school diploma	6.8	9.1	7.9
Requires only high school diploma and general experience	9.4	12.6	11.6
Wage levels			
All jobs	$8.72	$8.38	$8.31
Perform none of major tasks daily	6.88	7.02	8.33
Perform none of major tasks except talking to customers	7.54	7.06	7.37
Requires no high school diploma, training, experience, or references	5.87	6.14	7.14
Requires only high school diploma	6.59	6.17	6.68
Requires only high school diploma and general experience	6.74	6.27	6.84
Percentage of jobs (Los Angeles)			
Perform none of major tasks daily	8.6%	8.2%	4.8%
Perform none of major tasks except talking to customers	20.1	14.2	11.7
Requires no high school diploma, training, experience, or references	3.5	5.8	2.4
Requires only high school diploma	5.7	7.7	2.4
Requires only high school diploma and general experience	9.9	11.8	7.8
Wage levels (Los Angeles)			
All jobs	$8.74	$8.63	$9.32
Perform none of major tasks daily	6.70	6.68	*
Perform none of major tasks except talking to customers	7.94	7.94	8.07

	All Four Metropolitan Areas		
	Primary Central City	Suburbs	Other Central Cities
Requires no high school diploma, training, experience, or references	5.58	5.69	*
Requires only high school diploma	6.80	5.77	*
Requires only high school diploma and general experience	6.64	6.05	*
Percentage of jobs (Boston)			
Perform none of major tasks daily	2.2%	6.4%	16.0%
Perform none of major tasks except talking to customers	12.3	12.7	21.6
Requires no high school diploma, training, experience, or references	3.6	5.9	4.8
Requires only high school diploma	4.8	7.6	5.5
Requires only high school diploma and general experience	7.1	9.7	6.2
Wage levels (Boston)			
All jobs	$9.71	$9.18	$8.97
Perform none of major tasks daily	*	7.44	8.22
Perform none of major tasks except talking to customers	7.28	7.32	7.89
Requires no high school diploma, training, experience, or references	*	7.08	7.03
Requires only high school diploma	6.74	6.99	7.05
Requires only high school diploma and general experience	7.54	7.08	7.16
Percentage of jobs (Detroit)			
Perform none of major tasks daily	6.3%	8.9%	6.2%
Perform none of major tasks except talking to customers	11.3	16.4	17.3
Requires no high school diploma, training, experience, or references	80.0	8.2	8.6
Requires only high school diploma	11.6	13.5	11.1
Requires only high school diploma and general experience	13.8	18.0	18.2

(Table continues on p. 462.)

461

TABLE 10.7   *Continued*

	All Four Metropolitan Areas		
	Primary Central City	Suburbs	Other Central Cities
Wage levels (Detroit)			
All jobs	$8.16	$7.71	$7.47
Perform none of major tasks daily	6.49	7.17	*
Perform none of major tasks except talking to customers	7.18	6.95	6.78
Requires no high school diploma, training, experience, or references	6.30	5.99	5.72
Requires only high school diploma	6.53	6.02	5.55
Requires only high school diploma and general experience	6.29	6.06	5.72
Percentage of jobs (Atlanta)			
Perform none of major tasks daily	5.2%	9.1%	5.7%
Perform none of major tasks except talking to customers	8.1	11.1	7.3
Requires no high school diploma, training, experience, or references	3.1	4.3	6.9
Requires only high school diploma	6.3	6.4	11.2
Requires only high school diploma and general experience	8.1	9.4	14.1
Wage levels (Atlanta)			
All jobs	$8.48	$7.65	$7.59
Perform none of major tasks daily	7.64	6.83	6.22
Perform none of major tasks except talking to customers	7.17	7.06	5.95
Requires no high school diploma, training, experience, or references	5.94	5.83	6.57
Requires only high school diploma	6.45	6.17	6.03
Requires only high school diploma and general experience	6.86	6.20	6.10

Source: Multi-City Study of Urban Inequality Telephone Employer Survey.
*Very few observations.

The falloff in wages is largest for jobs in the central cities. This is important when considering the ability of former welfare recipients to support their families solely through earnings from the sorts of jobs they might get. Compared to all noncollege jobs reported in the central cities in this survey, jobs in the central cities that require no tasks pay 20 percent less (resulting in $13,800 for full-year, full-time annual income, compared with $17,120 for the average of all jobs in the central cities). Jobs in central cities that do not require a high school degree, training, experience, or references pay only $5.90, two-thirds the average for all jobs in the central cities (and resulting in a full-time annual income of only $11,800). In each of the four cities, the wages paid on jobs requiring no major tasks or few requirements are low compared to all jobs in that city. (A few of the cells in the individual tables have sample sizes of ten or less and should therefore be viewed with caution.)

Tables 10.4–10.7 complete a discouraging jobscape for less-educated workers, particularly those of color. The overwhelming majority of jobs require skilled tasks, educational or skill credentials, or both. Businesses are seeking higher levels of qualifications and abilities. Workers with limited education, and black and Latino men in particular, are disproportionately selected out of the jobs that have skill requirements. Further, the small number of jobs with few requirements pay quite poorly.

The qualitative findings reflect and contribute added detail to this discouraging picture. As the quantitative data indicate, higher hard-skill requirements may exclude people of color, who disproportionately lag in such skills. In one dramatic example, a Los Angeles-area hospital administered a new basic skills test to all its nursing assistants, and ended up laying off a large number of black aides as a result. Rising soft-skill requirements are also likely to reduce access for workers of color, as we have argued at length elsewhere (Moss and Tilly 1996). Here issues of objective skill levels are mingled with employer stereotypes about the interaction and motivation skills of particular groups, as well as customer and coworker racial and ethnic preferences. As we will discuss, employer, customer, and coworker biases are widespread, so augmented soft-skill demands inevitably leave a substantial opening for heightened discrimination.

Where the Jobs Are

Another impediment to employment for many workers of color is physical distance from the jobs for which they are qualified. The notion of a spatial mismatch between black communities and metropolitan-area jobs is an old one (Kain 1968). Recent research (Kasarda 1993) shows continuing shifts of employment from central city to suburbs, and there is growing evidence that distance and commuting cost barriers contribute significantly to black labor market disadvantage, particularly for younger workers and particularly in more recent data (Jencks and Mayer 1990; Holzer 1991; Ihlanfeldt 1999; Moss and Tilly 1991).

The Geographic Distribution of Jobs and Vacancies   Where are the jobs in Atlanta, Boston, Detroit, and Los Angeles? Table 10.8 shows the distribution of firms in the survey across the four metropolitan areas and, within those metropolitan areas, across central city, suburb, and other. Except in Atlanta, entry-level noncollege jobs are concentrated in the suburbs.[5] These findings raise the concern that the geography of jobs is a barrier to central-city minority workers. The potential mismatch between the location of jobs and the location of disadvantaged workers in need of jobs is treated in more detail in chapters 6 and 11 of this volume.

Although there are more jobs located in the suburbs, suburban firms are not more likely to report a current vacancy. In fact, a somewhat higher fraction of firms in the central cities report a current vacancy. Further, the mean number of vacancies in the firms that report having one is generally less among firms in the suburbs than either central-city firms or firms in other central-city areas.[6] Holzer reports the vacancy *rate*—the fraction of jobs in the firm that are currently unfilled—and finds that this rate does not vary substantially across city, suburb, and other (see Holzer 1996b, 25–37 and table 2.3).

The number of vacancies is higher in the central city, but the number of unemployed workers and their unemployment rate are higher as well and, further, suburban commuters take a significant number of the available jobs in central cities. Thus, as Holzer has shown, the *effective* level of unemployment, accounting for the size of the labor force and commuting patterns of suburban and city residents, is higher in the central cities (see Holzer 1996b, 32–37 and table 2.4). We replicate his results in table 10.9. In this table, we present the ratio of filled jobs, vacant jobs, and unemployed workers, respectively, to the resident labor force in the central city versus the suburbs plus other municipalities, for each metropolitan area. The effective unemployment and the gap between effective unemployment and the number of vacancies are shown as well, scaled by the size of the labor force in the area. Effective unemployment is calculated by assuming that unemployed residents will have the same commute patterns as employed residents, and apportioning the unemployed residents in each area to the central city or outside the central city using the commute pattern of the employed residents. The final line in the table gives the ratio of effective unemployment to job vacancies.

TABLE 10.8   *Jobs and Vacancies, by Primary Central City, Suburb, and Other Central Cities*

	Atlanta	Boston	Detroit	Los Angeles
Percentage of firms				
Primary central city	42.8	18.6	18.0	25.4
Suburbs	37.1	63.2	67.2	64.7
Other central cities	20.1	18.5	14.8	9.9
Percentage of firms reporting a vacancy				
Primary central city	45.0	56.6	49.9	38.9
Suburbs	40.1	39.8	44.5	41.4
Other central cities	45.1	44.7	40.2	49.9
Mean number of vacancies among firms reporting a vacancy (trimmed mean in parentheses)[a]				
Primary central city	21.7 (15.9)	26.2 (9.4)	38.4 (18.8)	36.4 (13.0)
Suburbs	4.4 (4.4)	21.6 (21.0)	6.7 (6.7)	26.4 (13.9)
Other central cities	8.6 (8.6)	7.4 (7.4)	12.0 (12.0)	7.3 (7.3)

Source: Multi-City Study of Urban Inequality Telephone Employer Survey.
[a]In many of the cells there was one (or two, in one case) firm that reported an anomalously high value for the number of current vacancies. The mean in parentheses was calculated after deleting the firms that reported a value of 200 or greater for the current number of vacancies. In almost all cells, there was only one such firm.

The results in the table show much more labor market distress in the central cities than in the suburbs and other areas. Effective unemployment is substantially higher in the central cities compared to outside the central city, as is the gap between effective unemployment and job vacancies. The difference is greatest in Detroit, where the central city-suburb distinction is sharpest, and smallest in Los Angeles, where the central city-suburb distinction is hardest to draw. (See chapter 6 in this book for a socioeconomic analysis of the city/suburb distinction in each of the cities, and chapter 11 for a fuller treatment of potential mismatches between available jobs and workers.)

The Process of Business Location

Quantitative Evidence Table 10.10 shows descriptive information from the quantitative survey on firms' current and past location, and whether they plan to move in the near future. (Recall that the "other" location category refers to central cities other than the primary one, and to other municipalities with a population that is at least 30 percent

TABLE 10.9   *Ratios of Filled Jobs, Vacancies, and Unemployed Workers*

	Primary Central City	Suburb and Other Central Cities
Atlanta		
Filled jobs/labor force	1.985	0.786
Vacancies/labor force	0.056	0.02
Unemployed, as percentage of labor force	9.2%	4.4%
Effective unemployment, as percentage of labor force	12.7%	3.9%
Effective unemployment – vacancies, as percent of labor force	7.1%	1.9%
Effective unemployed people per vacancy	2.27	1.95
Boston		
Filled jobs/labor force	1.472	0.816
Vacancies/labor force	0.037	0.021
Unemployed, as percentage of labor force	6.8%	6.5%
Effective unemployment, as percentage of labor force	10.8%	5.8%
Effective unemployment-vacancies, as percentage of labor force	7.1%	3.7%
Effective unemployed people per vacancy	2.92	2.76
Detroit		
Filled jobs/labor force	0.842	0.902
Vacancies/labor force	0.024	0.032
Unemployed, as percentage of labor force	19.7%	5.2%
Effective unemployment, as percentage of labor force	13.4%	7.0%
Effective unemployment-vacancies, as percentage of labor force	11.0%	3.8%
Effective unemployed people per vacancy	5.58	2.19
Los Angeles		
Filled jobs/labor force	0.938	0.88
Vacancies/labor force	0.022	0.019
Unemployed, as percentage of labor force	8.4%	6.8%
Effective unemployment, as percentage of labor force	8.2%	6.9%
Effective unemployment-vacancies, as percentage of labor force	6.0%	5.0%
Effective unemployed people per vacancy	3.73	3.63

Source: Multi-City Study of Urban Inequality Telephone Employer Survey.

black.) The results indicate that firms in all areas have an average tenure that is fairly high. Because the distribution is skewed upward by a relatively small number of values near one hundred years, we also present the median number of years in the present location. By either measure,

TABLE 10.10   *Location Characteristics of Firms, by City, Suburb, and Other Central Cities*

	Primary Central City	Suburb	Other Central Cities	All Firms
How long at the present location				
Mean number of years	23.8	19.2	21.0	20.6
Median number of years	14.6	12.0	13.3	12.7
Moved in the last ten years	40.8%	46.0%	40.7%	44.0%
A move is planned	8.2%	9.2%	9.1%	8.9%
Plan not to keep firm open indefinitely	1.5%	1.3%	1.9%	1.5%

	Did Not Move	Moved But Stayed in Category	Moved to Central City	Moved to Suburb	Moved to Other	Total
Started in Central city	66.0%	11.0%		17.0%	5.0%	100.0%
Rest of metro area	89.0%	10.0%	1.0%			100.0%

Source: Multi-City Study of Urban Inequality Telephone Employer Survey.

suburban firms have more recently moved to or opened in their present location. Despite substantial average tenures, the proportion of businesses that have moved in the past ten years is also strikingly high: 44 percent across all businesses and 46 percent for suburban firms in particular. Only about 8 percent of all firms are planning a move, and among those, there is not much difference across city, suburb, and other. Almost no firms in this survey report that they are likely to close in the foreseeable future.

The last panel of this table addresses the question: for firms that *started out* in a given part of the metropolitan area (primary central city, suburbs), how many moved elsewhere in the metro area, and to where? (Because this is based on a retrospective question of firms currently located in the metro area, it excludes businesses that moved out of the area altogether.) Moves out of the primary central city—to either suburbs or other cities in the metro area—totaled 22 percent of firms that started out there. This is far more common than the reverse move, undertaken by only 1 percent of businesses that started out outside the central city. Even taking into account that the primary central cities represent a minority of metro-area business sites (ranging from 20 percent of businesses in Boston to 45 percent in Atlanta, so that even businesses relocating at random would be more likely to move out than in), there is a strong net flow of relocating business away from these main cities. On the other hand, the most common moves kept businesses within the same category; such stayers combined with those who did not move at all add up to a substantial majority of businesses.

Qualitative Evidence   Employers are shifting to suburban areas, at greater distances from inner-city communities of color. But what can we learn about why they are doing so, and how they view such inner-city communities both as potential business locations and as potential sources of labor? Here we present a brief summary of our conceptual framework and our findings from the qualitative data from the four metropolitan areas. (We, along with Joleen Kirschenman and Ivy Kennelly, give a full treatment of our findings in chapter 6 of this book.)

The qualitative data reveal that racial composition features prominently in employers' cognitive maps of space. This information about race combines with other perceptions of an area to form signals about its desirability as a business location and the quality of its workforce. Most employers across the four cities do not view concentrated minority and/or low-income areas—particularly black neighborhoods—as desirable locations. The reasons for this view include crime, congestion, and access to desired labor supply, as well as, in some cases, outright racial antipathy. In addition, most employers have a negative assessment of the workforce available in concentrated minority and/or low-income areas—again, particularly predominantly black areas. Race, class, and location all contribute to this assessment of skills, typically with substantial overlap among the three. Racial stereotypes frequently enter these evaluations as well.

As employers carry out location decisions, recruiting, and screening, they act on this set of perceived signals. Given the highly segregated settlement patterns of these metropolitan areas (and, indeed, of most metropolitan areas in the United States), most people of color are in fact spatially concentrated, so in practice businesses' reservations about concentrated minority neighborhoods lead them to locate farther from most people of color. Such location decisions impose barriers of distance from jobs for some communities of color. The signal and barrier effects both contribute to the disadvantages suffered by people of color, particularly blacks, in the labor market.

Employers' cognitive maps differ across the four metropolitan areas. The differences in these maps appear to correspond to differences in the cities' current spatial and demographic configurations, as well as their histories. For example, in the Detroit area, where overwhelmingly white suburbs surround an overwhelmingly black and poor city, the urban-suburban, black-white, and working-poor distinctions run together in many employers' minds. In contrast, in multiethnic, polycentric Los Angeles, perceptions of the connections between race and space are far more diffuse. But in all four cities, elements of racial bias contribute to employers' views of space and to the actions stemming from these views.

Recruiting and Screening Methods

A key dimension of recruiting and hiring procedures is their degree of formality. Formality in hiring may affect the probability of employment of people of color in several ways. Formal hiring procedures may be more objective, reducing the ambit for biases, stereotypes, or social networks to drive recruitment and selection processes. Businesses may use formal procedures when they require higher levels of skill, or seek to reduce variation in skill levels of new hires. (Since, on average, black and Latino workers have lower levels of skill than others, this—unlike the other elements of this list—should cut *against* black and Latino employment.) Greater formality in screening may actually be a reaction to higher levels of black or Latino applicants, given many employers' perceptions of black and Latino skill levels. Alternatively, and somewhat more benignly, highly formal screening processes may be adopted by highly visible, well-paying employers, who must select from very large applicant pools; such employers may also attract disproportionate numbers of black applicants. Higher levels of public scrutiny and political pressure, and/or higher levels of intrinsic commitment to diversity, are likely to result in more formal procedures.

A long literature documents that the quintessential informal screening device, the pre-employment interview, incorporates the racial predilections of the interviewer (Dipboye 1982; Word, Zanna, and Cooper 1974). In an earlier study, we found a strong, negative statistical link between the importance of the interview as a screening device and the level of black male employment in a given firm (Moss and Tilly 1995a); our qualitative findings reinforced this connection (Moss and Tilly 2000). Kathryn Neckerman and Joleen Kirschenman (1991) reported that use of tests was positively associated with black employment.

If followed and enforced, affirmative action policies introduce greater formality into recruiting and screening. Most recent studies indicate that affirmative action policies have increased the employment and earnings opportunities of blacks and other minorities (Leonard 1990; Holzer 1996a; Holzer and Neumark 1999; the last two using the same data we analyze in this chapter). Although affirmative action policy may increase employment opportunities for minorities through a number of channels, one of them certainly may be through encouraging greater use of formal means of recruiting and screening workers.

As we will show, several recruiting and screening methods do have disparate impacts by race or ethnicity. Some part of the explanation may be discrimination, some part may be a confounding of cultural differences and stereotypes with perceptions of difference in certain types of skills (notably interaction and motivation skills), and some may be the effect of lower skills and lower access to important job networks on the part of workers of color. The quantitative results we report directly observe the outcomes but cannot easily disentangle these different sources of the outcomes. The qualitative evidence is more suggestive about how employer subjectivity can confound skills assessment with stereotyping of different groups.

Quantitative Evidence   Table 10.11 shows the recruiting and screening method that generated the last hire in the surveyed firms. There is not a great deal of variation across city, suburb, or other central cities in the use of recruiting or screening methods. More formal recruiting procedures, such as use of newspaper ads or referrals from employment agencies, community agencies, schools, or unions are less likely to be open to social network hiring that could have disparate effects on workers of color. Together, they generated roughly 40 percent of the hires, with newspaper ads accounting for over half that total. The other 60 percent were generated by more informal recruiting procedures, with employee referrals yielding nearly half of this group. For screening applicants, most firms use a written application and an interview. About half use some form of testing.

How do the different recruiting and screening methods affect who gets hired? The race-ethnicity and gender of the latest hire by recruiting and screening method is shown in table 10.12. Compared to their rate of representation in all jobs, black men are substantially more likely to be the hire when employers have taken a referral from a state employment agency or community agency. Latino men enjoy a smaller employment boost from these referral sources. These two recruiting methods are used fairly rarely, however, as table 10.11 showed. Again, compared to their representation in all jobs, use of employee referral reduces the representation of white and black females and improves the representation of Hispanic males. Surprisingly, employee referrals also hurt white

TABLE 10.11   *Recruiting Method for the Last Employee Hired, by City, Suburb, Other Central Cities*

	Primary Central City	Suburb	Other Central Cities	Total
Recruiting method for the last employee hired				
Newspaper ad	23.9%	28.8%	29.2%	27.6%
Help-wanted signs	4.2	4.6	4.9	4.5
Walk-in	14.1	13.9	12.7	13.8
Referrals from				
Current employees	26.0	24.8	27.0	25.5
State employment service	1.8	3.1	4.8	3.0
Private employment service	9.6	4.3	4.3	5.7
Community agency	2.2	1.2	1.0	1.4
Schools	3.4	4.6	2.4	3.9
Union	1.2	0.8	0.8	0.9
Other (such as acquaintances)	13.5	13.7	11.9	13.4
Used affirmative action in recruiting	56.0	48.5	54.8	51.5
Screening method used				
Written application	78.9	81.6	84.1	81.3
Interview	87.6	87.1	84.6	86.8
Physical and/or drug test	16.4	10.5	11.8	12.2
Other tests	49.9	40.2	42.5	43.3
Verify education	34.6	25.4	26.5	28.0
Check criminal record	32.3	29.1	38.9	31.6
Used affirmative action in hiring	36.5	32.6	37.4	34.4

Source: Multi-City Study of Urban Inequality Telephone Employer Survey.

males and have only a small negative effect on black males. Use of affirmative action in recruiting cuts against white men, as expected, but also, to a much smaller extent, against Latino men. Conversely, affirmative action recruiting increases the rate of hire for black men and women and, to a lesser extent, for white and Latina women.

Use of interviews and tests, except for physical tests, is associated with lower rates of hiring of white, black, and Latino men. Interviewing is also associated with lower rates of hiring of black women, while testing raises their rate of hire. (The use of a physical or drug test may be proxying for certain types of jobs, since it reduces rates of hiring most for white men, and secondarily for black men, while increasing the probability of hire for all other groups, especially Latina women.) Use of

TABLE 10.12 *Race and Gender of Last Employee Hired, by Recruiting Method and By Use of Hiring Screens*

	White Males	Black Males	Hispanic Males	White Females	Black Females	Hispanic Females
All jobs	25.5%	10.1%	10.7%	35.9%	10.6%	7.2%
Recruiting method						
Newspaper ad	23.2	10.0	7.2	45.5	9.3	4.9
Help-wanted signs	21.3	8.0	11.9	30.7	15.4	12.8
Walk-in	21.7	13.5	13.3	28.2	15.8	7.5
Referrals from Current employees	25.7	9.4	15.6	33.1	9.7	7.6
State employ- ment service	25.0	23.2	15.2	19.9	11.6	5.1
Private employ- ment service	16.3	10.2	4.5	48.6	11.6	8.8
Community agency	28.2	22.2	17.9	10.3	12.1	9.5
Schools	35.8	6.6	1.2	29.1	15.9	11.3
Union	32.7	3.9	31.1	20.1	8.2	4.1
Other (such as acquaintances)	35.5	6.6	9.8	34.9	6.4	6.9
Used affirmative action in recruiting						
Yes	30.7	9.3	11.2	33.1	9.3	6.4
No	21.3	11.0	9.8	37.5	12.6	7.8
Hiring screens						
Written application						
Yes	24.3	11.0	10.1	35.3	11.8	7.4
No	32.6	6.3	11.5	37.3	7.1	5.1
Interview						
Yes	25.6	9.5	9.5	37.7	10.6	7.2
No	28.3	15.0	16.7	21.2	12.9	5.9
Physical and/or drug test						
Yes	19.3	9.3	11.0	39.3	12.4	8.8
No	26.8	10.3	10.3	35.1	10.7	6.8
Other tests						
Yes	19.3	9.3	11.0	39.3	12.4	8.8
No	26.8	10.3	10.3	35.1	10.7	6.8
Verify education						
Yes	23.7	10.3	7.6	36.7	12.7	9.0
No	28.4	10.1	10.0	35.1	10.3	6.1
Check criminal record						
Yes	24.7	12.5	7.8	33.5	14.0	7.6
No	27.9	9.1	10.1	36.4	9.8	6.7

	White Males	Black Males	Hispanic Males	White Females	Black Females	Hispanic Females
Used affirmative action in hiring						
Yes	21.1	11.2	11.0	38.1	11.7	7.0
No	28.3	9.7	10.2	34.2	10.6	7.1

Source: Multi-City Study of Urban Inequality Telephone Employer Survey.

a written application as well as background checks on education and criminal record are associated with higher employment of black, Latina, and white women. Where employers use affirmative action in making the hiring decision, each group except white men and Hispanic men shows a higher rate of employment. The effects of affirmative action are largest for white and black men (negative and positive employment effects, respectively).

Based on these results, the relationship between procedural formality and the racial composition of the workforce is not simple. Consider black men in particular. Certain formal methods (written application, physical test, verification of education and criminal record, use of affirmative action) increase the chances that a black man will be hired; certain less formal or more subjective procedures (pre-employment interview) dampen those chances. But other formal steps are associated with *lower* black male employment. In our book (Moss and Tilly 2000 ch. 6), we examine the data with multiple regression, and find the same mixed pattern.

On the face of it, these mixed results appear to reflect mixed causes. It seems likely, for example, that:

- Interviews reduce black male employment because they offer an opening for biases, whereas written applications provide more objective information;

- Skill tests are more common in higher-skill jobs, for which fewer blacks are likely to qualify, and are particularly common in "female" clerical jobs;

- Physicals, drug tests, and checks of education and criminal record are more widely used to choose among applicants for low-skill jobs, who are disproportionately black.

But correlations in the quantitative data cannot establish causality. Qualitative data can offer important additional insights about why and how formality matters for the racial composition of hiring.

Qualitative Evidence   We have emphasized *why* formal hiring is associated with particular racial mixes of employment.[7] *How* formality plays out can vary greatly. Formality in hiring procedures varies widely in terms of content, implementation, context, and hence implications. Apparently formal procedures can conceal substantial loopholes; apparently informal procedures can actually be highly structured. A highly formal procedure such as a test can—by design or otherwise—strongly favor one group over another. Our qualitative data provide illustrations of both why and how formality is associated with racial representation. We examine the role of formality in recruiting and screening, and then turn to employers' discussion of the impact of affirmative action laws.

Informal recruiting, particularly recruiting driven by current employee referrals, privileges employer and incumbent employee networks. For example, a supervisor at a Boston-area manufacturer explained the high number of Asian workers in the plant as follows: "I think a lot of internal references . . . so that may have a lot to do with it. I see amongst that group a lot of people trying to help, help members of their family, friends. Get them a job, get them in the company."

But such informal recruiting does not always cut against black employment. For instance, a Boston home care provider serving low-income, largely minority neighborhoods historically recruited mainly via referrals from clients (who suggested neighbors or friends to provide care to them), and consequently has a workforce weighted toward black women. In fact, in this case, rising skill and certification demands have since shifted recruiting toward training programs—but this more formal recruiting is yielding *fewer* black employees.

Changing the racial composition of a workforce may require supplementing informal channels with more formal ones. A human resource specialist from a Los Angeles–area location of a large national retail chain indicated that informal recruiting, which makes up the bulk of their recruiting, does not generate sufficient black applicants for their company goals. They adopt formal advertising to increase the flow of black applicants: "It's not cost-efficient, actually, to advertise in the newspaper. We really don't need it for recruitment. The reason we advertise in the black newspaper is because I have a hard time drawing in people that are qualified from that area. That's actually the only reason that we invest in that."

However, there are typically loopholes in nominally formal recruiting. Consider a uniformed public service agency that advertises in major dailies as well as community newspapers from communities of color, sends notices to community organizations, and posts jobs with the state employment agency. Nonetheless, a manager commented that candidates for the dispatcher job—our sample job—are typically found by informal means: "[W]e'll get calls from . . . somebody who is a [current employee in this job] who'll say, 'Gee, I worked with, I know this kid.' . . . We find that that, the informal public safety network is quite often the best, the best way to go."

Our data amply document the subjectivity of the pre-employment interviews. As the director of human resources for an Atlanta-area manufacturing plant indicated in response to the question of how you gauge an applicant's soft skills: "Right now it's truly a personal evaluation. We are looking into getting testing application where we can measure that more effectively. But right now it's truly a gut feeling." The percent of workers who were black in this plant was also well below average for the entire sample and for this subgroup of firms. And at a public agency grappling with issues of affirmative action,

> We don't place a great deal of emphasis on interviews. . . . We do not have an interview board or panel because the consent decree requires that we have very detailed reasons for rejecting a candidate, so we have to be on sound footing, and the results of an interview really aren't that . . . in my opinion . . . it's too. . . . You know, it's too subjective. We need individuals that we . . . we want to really document why someone's not suitable.

Our own earlier research and other literature argue that particular reliance on the interview disadvantages black applicants because of the subjectivity involved. An Atlanta greeting card store manager offered an interesting perspective on this. He started by stating that black applicants do not know how to apply for a job:

> Blacks, from what I see, do not have the knowledge for seeking a job. They've not been trained in high school. . . . They just don't seem to know how to apply for a job. . . . They don't know how to dress. They simply [answer] questions yes and no. They don't ask about the job. They don't seem interested. They don't show up on a timely basis. . . . That just seems like a bad way to apply for a job.

But moments later, he added that, in fact, many of these "poor" applicants are actually qualified for the job: "They're fine once they get the training. In fact, I . . . you know, I maybe sound like I'm putting the young black kids down, but the group we have right here—they were all greenhorns then, and they're very good right now."

Of course, formality in screening does not altogether eliminate subjectivity. Even in civil service environments constrained by consent decrees, there are loopholes to be found. A black employees' leader in uniformed public service claimed:

As a matter of fact we found out that they skipped over a guy. . . . They skipped over a guy last time, and what they had to do is hire an extra guy to make up for what they did on the previous list . . . skipping over people. There's still a lot of nepotism. Still getting away with it, you know.

In the worst case, the formality of the process is simply subverted. A large Detroit manufacturer has been administering a skills test aimed at eleventh-grade proficiency in math and language. A supervisor admitted (off the record—when the tape recorder had been shut off) that sometime previously, when mostly white men were hired, they would give test answers to people they wanted to hire.

Moreover, formal selection methods can be adopted to screen blacks and other people of color in, but also to screen them out. A large manufacturing facility outside Boston, which had never tested applicants for blue-collar jobs, began aptitude testing when the surrounding area's population tilted toward people of color. Other changes surely contributed to this shift: there was a growing labor surplus, and skill requirements were being upgraded. Nonetheless, the timing is suggestive, especially in connection with comments like this one from a plant operations executive:

I mean, these people come from a very different background. We have a strong welfare system. You know, coming into a factory every day and building and assembling things, they're not necessarily fun jobs all the time. And so, when people can maintain a certain standard of living, and they don't have to do that, then what kind of work ethic would people come here with? So, we have to be very careful in our screening to be sure that people are motivated.

Affirmative action typically contributes to formality in recruiting and screening, and is most developed in large firms and in the public sector. The firm size effect captures the size and federal contracting thresholds in affirmative action/EEO regulations. In addition, it reflects the visibility of large firms. But it also reflects management approaches that differ according to scale. At one Boston-area federal agency, for example, the division chief remarked (in comments that also touched on the strong diversity objectives of many government agencies): "We have to be very conscious and cognizant as a federal employer that we have guidelines and mandates that we have to follow and therefore, . . . I mean, I have a full-time EEO officer and she has two or three people who work for her."

Employer attitudes toward affirmative action vary widely. Some employers openly opposed affirmative action, at least in its present form. Such respondents were typically white males, and the complaint, as might be expected, was reverse discrimination. This opinion was voiced in both the private and the public sector, particularly the public-sector agencies we spoke with that were under consent decrees. In another twist, a number of firms indicated that while they try to abide by their affirmative action goals, affirmative action has a chilling effect on the willingness to hire minorities because firing a minority is so difficult. The response of a branch manager for a mortgage sales company in Los Angeles typified this attitude:

> *Respondent:* I think one of the things as an employer that we kind of . . . under our breath, saying it's much more difficult to fire a black person than it is to fire a female person. I think at this company, if we're going to do that we take extra care that we're documenting and following the laws that we have to.

> *Interviewer:* Do you think that kind of worry puts some people off from hiring them in the first place?

> *Respondent:* Absolutely, absolutely. But I think at the same time there's the other side of it, where there are people that are looking to hire, so that they may have better numbers, and look like they're hiring more black people. The labor board does look at those kinds of things.

But other managers, including some white males, spoke in support of affirmative action. As with other types of formal hiring, the qualitative evidence shows how affirmative action can aid minority employment, but also reveals the complexity of employer motivations and actions that mediate the effects of any particular type of hiring procedure.

Employer Attitudes

Employer perceptions of and attitudes toward racial and ethnic groups ineluctably infiltrate hiring decisions. Earlier work done by our colleague Joleen Kirschenman, based on in-depth face-to-face interviews with employers in Chicago (Kirschenman 1991; Kirschenman and Neckerman 1991; Neckerman and Kirschenman 1991) and by us based on comparable interviews in Detroit and Los Angeles (Moss and Tilly 2000), documents this. These researchers found that many employers rate black workers worse than others in terms of soft and hard skills and few, if any, rate them better, and that some employers voice negative, stereotypical views of blacks. Roger Waldinger (1997) reported similar results from a Los Angeles study. While some of these negative perceptions surely stem from actual average skill differences, bias clearly plays a part as well. Audit studies that sent out job applicants with identical qualifications found that employers chose white and Anglo applicants more often than black and Latino ones (Bendick, Jackson, and Reinoso 1994; Fix and Struyk 1993). The Employer Surveys provide added leverage for understanding employers' views of various racial and ethnic groups.

Quantitative Measures of Ethnocentrism An employer might lower her demand for minority workers if she herself had negative attitudes toward minority workers. But she might also lower her demand if she thought her customers or her employees held these negative views (Becker 1957). The quantitative survey asked employers about each of these three sources of negative attitude by asking whether customers, employees, or other employers in the industry prefer to deal with people of their own race or ethnicity. Employers were also asked directly whether they felt that inner-city residents made poorer job applicants or employees than residents of other areas. The results are reported in table 10.13. Overall, about 20 to 23 percent of employers reported ethnocentric preferences by customers, employees, or other employers. Sixteen percent held a negative view of inner-city residents. About a third of employers report at least one of the forms of ethnocentric preferences. These results are fairly similar across cities. Los Angeles employers and Detroit employers were more likely to report ethnocentric preferences among employees, however. In Los Angeles, this may be due to the tendency of the workforces of many firms to develop into ethnic enclaves. The employee ethnocentrism in Los Angeles is most pronounced in the city, where the ethnic diversity is greatest.

Somewhat surprisingly, central-city employers in all cities except Atlanta were more likely to report ethnocentricity of customers, employees, or employers, and were more likely to voice a negative view of inner-city residents, than their counterparts in the suburbs or other areas. Of particular note, the contrast between city and suburb is most pronounced for Los Angeles and Boston. One might have expected the difference between city and suburb to be sharpest in Detroit and then in Atlanta, given the qualitative findings on space reported in chapter 6.

A second panel of table 10.13 shows the racial composition of customers, comparing businesses that reported customer racial preferences with those that did not. The main finding is that customer ethnocentrism is primarily white, non-Latino ethnocentrism: non-Hispanic whites account for more than half the customers from both groups. Businesses that reported customer ethnocentrism have higher than average representation of black and Latino customers. One potential interpretation is that white, Anglo consumers and employers are most sensitive to workers' race in businesses located in "transitional" or "border" neighbor-

TABLE 10.13   *Proportion of Employers Reporting Ethnocentrism, by Customers, Employees, Other Employers*

	All Employers	Central City	Suburbs	Other Central Cities
Employers reporting Customers prefer to deal with employees of their own race or ethnic group	19.7%	23.0%	19.0%	16.6%
Employees prefer other employees of their own race or ethnic group	23.2	28.0	21.8	20.0
Other employers in your business prefer employees of their own race or ethnic group	21.4	24.6	20.6	19.4
Any of the types of ethnocentrism	31.6	36.7	29.9	29.8
Inner-city residents are weaker job applicants or employees	16.1	16.6	15.3	17.8

Racial composition of customers of employers reporting ethnocentric customer preferences versus employers who do not	Customer Ethnocentrism	No Customer Ethnocentrism		
Black	19.6%	18.7%		
Hispanic	15.4	11.8		
Asian	9.2	8.3		

	All Employers	Central City	Suburbs	Other Central Cities
Los Angeles employers reporting Customers prefer to deal with employees of their own race or ethnic group	20.9%	26.0%	20.2%	12.1%

(Table continues on p. 480.)

TABLE 10.13   *Continued*

	All Employers	Central City	Suburbs	Other Central Cities
Employees prefer other employees of their own race or ethnic group	25.3	34.3	23.2	15.8
Other employers in your business prefer employees of their own race or ethnic group	21.3	21.9	21.2	20.6
Any of the types of ethnocentrism	39.7	46.0	38.7	30.0
Inner-city residents are weaker job applicants or employees	15.1	15.6	14.9	15.2
Boston employers reporting				
Customers prefer to deal with employees of their own race or ethnic group	17.7	21.3	17.8	13.9
Employees prefer other employees of their own race or ethnic group	19.1	27.0	18.0	15.6
Other employers in your business prefer employees of their own race or ethnic group	19.8	23.8	19.6	16.9
Any of the types of ethnocentrism	29.6	38.4	27.7	27.4
Inner-city residents are weaker job applicants or employees	13.1	11.9	14.1	11.2
Detroit employers reporting				
Customers prefer to deal with employees of their own race or ethnic group	21.0	27.6	19.2	22.4

TABLE 10.13   *Continued*

	All Employers	Central City	Suburbs	Other Central Cities
Employees prefer other employees of their own race or ethnic group	25.8	31.3	24.8	24.5
Other employers in your business prefer employees of their own race or ethnic group	22.4	31.0	20.7	20.9
Any of the types of ethnocentrism	21.9	26.2	20.5	23.1
Inner-city residents are weaker job applicants or employees	16.9	15.3	16.2	22.2
Atlanta employers reporting				
Customers prefer to deal with employees of their own race or ethnic group	19.5	20.4	18.5	19.4
Employees prefer other employees of their own race or ethnic group	23.0	22.7	22.2	24.9
Other employers in your business prefer employees of their own race or ethnic group	22.7	25.3	20.1	20.6
Any of the types of ethnocentrism	33.7	33.5	32.2	36.9
Inner-city residents are weaker job applicants or employees	19.7	19.7	17.3	23.7

Source: Multi-City Study of Urban Inequality Telephone Employer Survey.

hoods, where a broader mixture of racial groups mingle. For whites in segregated suburbs, the issue simply may not be salient.

Another, less direct indicator of employer attitudes is the ratio of employees and new hires to applicants by racial, ethnic, and gender group. Table 10.14 presents the ratio of the percent of current employees

TABLE 10.14   *Employment Levels and Hiring, by Race and Gender in Proportion to Application Rates*

	Primary Central City	Suburbs	Other Central Cities
All metro areas			
Ratio of firm's employees to applicants for			
Black males	0.61	0.52	0.59
Black females	0.88	0.61	0.67
Hispanic	0.87	0.87	0.71
White and other	1.29	1.22	1.34
Ratio of firm's latest hires to applicants for			
Black males	0.62	0.51	0.60
Black females	0.89	0.68	0.74
Hispanic	1.01	1.12	1.02
White and other	1.18	1.09	1.00
Los Angeles			
Ratio of firm's employees to applicants for			
Black males	0.55	0.50	0.31
Black females	0.94	0.57	0.42
Hispanic	0.95	0.92	0.89
Asians	1.12	0.79	0.84
White and other	1.32	1.41	1.34
Ratio of firm's latest hires to applicants for			
Black males	0.53	0.40	0.77
Black females	0.80	0.65	0.51
Hispanic	1.11	1.12	0.95
Asians	1.05	0.94	1.00
White and other	0.93	1.19	0.64
Boston			
Ratio of firm's employees to applicants for			
Black males	0.58	0.56	0.50
Black females	0.72	0.61	0.50
Hispanic	0.81	0.73	0.53
Asians	0.71	0.72	0.47
White and other	1.17	1.11	1.37
Ratio of firm's latest hires to applicants for			
Black males	0.55	0.58	0.54
Black females	0.59	0.41	0.68
Hispanic	1.12	1.09	1.07
Asians	0.62	0.60	0.60
White and other	1.15	1.00	0.97

TABLE 10.14   *Continued*

	Primary Central City	Suburbs	Other Central Cities
Detroit			
Ratio of firm's employees to applicants for			
Black males	0.66	0.40	0.46
Black females	0.86	0.51	0.59
Hispanic	0.54	0.82	0.93
White and other	1.41	1.21	1.72
Ratio of firm's latest hires to applicants for			
Black males	0.63	0.41	0.45
Black females	0.97	0.70	0.67
Hispanic	0.42	0.87	1.38
White and other	1.39	1.07	1.34
Atlanta			
Ratio of firm's employees to applicants for			
Black males	0.59	0.65	0.70
Black females	0.82	0.71	0.75
Hispanic	0.98	0.97	0.86
White and other	1.31	1.12	1.18
Ratio of firm's latest hires to applicants for			
Black males	0.65	0.74	0.65
Black females	0.89	0.82	0.83
Hispanic	0.89	0.85	0.82
White and other	1.25	1.08	1.08

Source: Multi-City Study of Urban Inequality Telephone Employer Survey.

and the percent of latest hires by race, ethnicity, and gender (for blacks) to the corresponding group's percentage of applicants. While both sets of ratios are interesting, we concentrate on the ratio of latest hires to applicants, as that better reflects current conditions. As the table shows, businesses hire a greater proportion of white and other applicants than of black male, black female, and Latino applicants. (We are not able to separate white applicants from "others" due to the questionnaire design, but "others" represent only 6 percent of the workforce and 2 percent of the most recent hires, so "white and other" is primarily white.) In almost every instance, the ratios are smallest for black males, and in several cases the difference between the ratio for black males and other groups is startling. Some of these differences no doubt result from differing qualifications in the applicant pools. But the divergence between central city and suburban ratios suggests that there is something more going on. Compared to their urban counterparts, suburban firms hire a smaller proportion of black male and female applicants. Again, the disparity is largest for black males. The contrast in the probability of hiring a black between city and suburban firms is even more striking because city jobs on average require higher levels of skill and set higher requirements than jobs in the suburbs (see tables 10.2 and 10.6). As blacks have lower levels of hiring credentials, education, and test scores, on average, than whites, we would expect the hiring ratios to be higher in the suburbs.

These hiring ratios differ across the four cities as well. Black males show the lowest ratios in Los Angeles and Boston, but the sharpest contrast between city and suburb in Detroit. Black females fare most poorly in Boston, and again the contrast of city to suburb is largest in Detroit. Latinos show much less distress on these indicators than do blacks, except in Detroit, where the Latino population is very small. Such contrasts between city and suburb, and among metropolitan areas, seem unlikely simply to reflect differing qualifications among applicant pools. Instead, suburban employers—and employers in general in Boston, Detroit, and Los Angeles—appear to be more likely to discriminate against black job seekers.

The quantitative data give another piece of suggestive evidence that attitudes as well as skills matter to employers. Other work with these data by us and by Holzer show that larger firms are much more likely to hire blacks, controlling for a large number of other factors (Moss and Tilly 2000; Holzer 1996b, 102, 1996c). But skill requirements are greater the larger the firm. If a skill gap were the primary reason for not hiring blacks, large firms would hire fewer blacks. It is likely that closer contact among employees and among employees and owners in small firms, as well as use of less formal hiring procedures, gives rise to a greater influence of attitudes in hiring.

Nature of Negative Employer Attitudes   In-depth interviews from the Multi-City Study of Urban Inequality add additional depth and context to this picture of employer attitude, confirming and extending previous literature based on such interviews. Interviewers asked managers whether they saw differences in skill or worker quality among whites, blacks, Latinos, and Asians. The questioning focused on differences between black and white workers, particularly in Atlanta and Detroit, where other racial-ethnic groups are relatively small.

Many employers did describe such differences. However, it is important to note that the largest group of respondents consisted of those who answered "I don't know" (sometimes citing the fact that their workforce is too segregated to assess different groups) or "I don't see any differences." Based on context, some of these answers appear to be sincere, whereas others were offered as the socially acceptable answer. Certainly a number of respondents were uncomfortable with the question, as in the case of this clerical supervisor at an Atlanta-area educational institution:

Interviewer: A number of the people that we have talked to in the area have commented on the differences between black and white workers. Would you . . . could you comment on that?

Respondent: [whispers inaudible words]

Interviewer: But it's confidential.

Respondent: I know, I know. I guess you hear me hedging a little. It just depends on the individuals. But this has been one of our problems. The . . . a lot of it is the . . . and it's not true, it's not true, blanket . . . definitely it's not but unfortunately in the majority of the cases we have problems that tend to be minority. . . . I am going to close my door in case anyone comes down the hall.

Moreover, many respondents gave mixed responses, at some points delineating racial differences and at other points denying them. Consider this Atlanta-area restaurateur, who offered a detailed indictment of black job applicants:

When you have white people come in the door . . . [they usually] are more qualified than some of the black people that come in off the street. . . . Because most of the time . . . black people that come in off the street are . . . They've had sixteen jobs in the last two months just because they're never satisfied with what they have. . . . You never know if they're telling you the truth. Whereas . . . white people . . . nine out of ten times theirs are pretty much what they write down. . . . A white person will come in dressed in a tie whereas, you know, a black person will come in dressed in . . . you know, rags. . . . Have four earrings in each ear and. . . . In this business you want someone that comes to the table that's not going to intimidate you. . . . You want somebody that's going to, you know, look presentable, have good communication skills.

But at the end of this diatribe, he insisted, "I love my black employees as much as I love my white employees. . . . They do just as much a job, you know."

When employers did note black-white differences, they often pointed to a black disadvantage in hard skills. Many attributed these skill differences to educational attainment or school quality. In Boston, very few employers openly acknowledged racial skill differences, but many complained about the quality of the inner-city workforce, and attributed these problems to the degeneration of the Boston public schools, which have become overwhelmingly minority. Quite a few respondents, especially in Detroit, argued that the skill differences are due to class, not race. As one Detroit manager put it, skill disparities are "more a reflection of . . . the people of that race might fit into this social-economic structure, and therefore they reflect the values of that social-economic structure."

Employers' criticisms of blacks' hard skills often shaded over into discussions of soft skills—for example, the claim that many African Americans do not know how to apply for a job. The human resource director of a Los Angeles-area department store, for example, complained that few black or Latino men "come in a suit, and look, and present that professional image that I need for [commission sales]. . . . They just don't know how to get a job." Quite a few managers also complained about black dialect, particularly in jobs involving customer contact.

In fact, most respondents who were negative about African Americans' skills turned at some point to the subject of soft skills. Standard stereotypes about black hostility or oversensitivity abounded. Many employers opined that black workers have "a chip on their shoulder," or "feel like they're owed"; these phrases came up recurrently. "It's that old adage, you know, 'The world owes me a living and here I am—give it to me,' type thing," remarked a supervisor of nursing aides in the Los Angeles area. "Even some of them don't want to be told what to do." Furthermore, some employers deplored blacks' tendency to congregate in cliques and share stories of perceived discrimination—"the grapevine gets going in the wrong direction," as one Atlanta manager put it. However, some employers viewed black workers' assertiveness as understandable or even positive. Said the African American director of a Detroit-area social service agency, "Because of things that . . . we've gone through that maybe people more in the mainstream or majority don't go through, um, we're just a little more testy and sometimes people in the majority take that to mean that we don't like them or we're aggressive or real pushy or mean or something."

Another recurrent soft-skill stereotype depicted blacks as lazy or unmotivated. Typical comments asserted that black workers "tend to work a little slower," "are not as dependable," "have more of an 'I don't care' attitude," "don't really want to work," "are lazy." But tipping the balance the other way are employers who see black workers as needing the job more, and therefore more willing to work hard, do menial tasks, and stay at a job longer. Reflecting back on his experience hiring at a department store in a previous job, a white manufacturing supervisor from Atlanta noted:

> Initially the people from the more affluent areas, whether they be white or black, but primarily they were white, from an interviewing and presentation standpoint they were much more polished. So [you would think], "Hey, this is a great person, let me put them on the floor." They can work in the designer area whatever and present themselves very well. Whereas the group from the lower income areas which were primarily black may not present themselves as well at first or may not be as polished or whatever. So you may think, "Well, for this particular position this [upper income] person presents better so we'll go with this person." But the lower income person may need the job more and may be the more solid employee. If you hire both of them, the lower income person, the black person or whatever may stick around longer and be a much more solid citizen than the upper income person, because [the upper income person is] always looking for something else to go to.

Employer views about the dependability of black workers varied by employee gender. Joleen Kirschenman (1991) and Ivy Kennelly (1999) have pointed out that managers have a schizophrenic perception of black women: on the one hand, they see black women as motivated workers because they tend to be single mothers supporting a family; on the other hand, they see single mothers as unreliable because of family demands—"baby and boyfriend problems," as one Atlanta employer put it. In our sample, the former view predominated. Black women are better workers due to "their desire to provide for their child," asserted the white male owner of a store in downtown Detroit. "I think they are willing to work harder at it than a black man." A number of respondents, especially in Detroit, also described African American women as better educated than their male counterparts.

As with their perceptions of gender differences among blacks, employers' assessment of immigrants was two-sided. In jobs where language and communication skills were paramount, respondents voiced concern about language barriers. (Of course, in a number of businesses serving immigrant communities, bilingualism, or even speaking the immigrant language alone, is instead a plus.) More commonly, however, employers saluted the immigrant work ethic, particularly among Latinos and Asians. Some employers compared immigrants favorably to native whites. The remarks of two Boston-area managers are striking in this regard:

> *Respondent:* [The Latinos] work pretty well. . . . They're trying to support . . . their family, or families, or whatever they have. . . .

487

Interviewer: Would you say you have more problems in getting the white people to work?

Respondent: Absolutely. . . . We won't . . . I mean, not that we won't hire them, but . . . we will look twice before we hire just a regular white guy for a floor job.

Respondent: The Cape Verdean guys back there [in the kitchen] are my hardest workers. These guys are absolutely fantastic workers. . . . When I was younger . . . in all restaurants, you always had young, white, American boys washing dishes. Now, you know, I almost try to stay away from them in a way because they're so lazy at times. . . . I get Cape Verdean kids in here and they bust their butt. You know, I get these white kids in here, they're young, sixteen, seventeen, eighteen years old, and they think they're just going to hang out and just be lazy all day.

However, in many cases whites are not applying for the jobs in question, so employers compared immigrants favorably to blacks alone. The personnel director of an Atlanta-area laundry had strong opinions on the subject:

[Hispanics] have a much higher work ethic [than blacks]. . . . Hispanics . . . while they are employed with you are very good employees. They're diligent. They do their job. . . . They don't complain as much. . . . [Blacks are] more vociferous than Hispanic people. . . . If we are going to have complaints or we're going to have . . . people not coming into work, it's going to be more predominantly black than it is Hispanic.

But while employers lauded the work ethic of new immigrants, some pointed out that succeeding generations did not necessarily inherit this attitude. "There is an issue of respect" with Hispanics, much as with African Americans, stated a manager at a Los Angeles–area utility.

Looking across the four cities, we find that each city contains the full cross-section of employer attitudes and perceptions described here. However, each city's mix is different. In Atlanta, white employers were more likely than elsewhere to simply voice casual stereotypes. Boston employers, on the other hand, appeared extremely cautious. A large majority stated that there were no racial or ethnic differences in workforce quality—although quite a few used public school quality as a coded way of talking about these differences. Detroit businesses divided between plain-spoken, often bigoted white manufacturing managers, and managers in public-sector or other white-collar organizations who were more apt to attribute workforce disparities to class rather than race. Los Angeles has considerably larger Latino and Asian communities, including immigrants, than the other three metro areas, so employers commented far more on these groups.

Unfortunately, it is difficult to separate three possible sources of observed variation in employer attitudes across cities. The source of most interest, of course, is the set of demographic, social, and historical differences among the four cities. But in addition, interviews were conducted by a different team of interviewers in each city, so interviewer effects may contribute. Moreover, the industrial compositions of the samples differ by city—for example, the Boston sample is strongly tilted toward public and nonprofit agencies—which could also affect observed employer attitudes. Separating out these three effects calls for additional analysis.

In summary, then, employers frequently describe negative views of people of color held by themselves or others. A substantial minority of respondents described ethnocentric preferences by customers, employees, or fellow employers. In addition, many employers voiced negative views of blacks as workers; their views of Latinos appear to be more ambivalent. Some of the expressed views clearly fall into the category of stereotypes. This suggests that we should view the data on skill and minority employment, discussed earlier in the chapter, with some caution. Though skill shortfalls in African American and Latino populations represent a real, serious problem, differential access to jobs requiring skills appears likely to be in part due to slanted employer perceptions of the hard and soft skills of different racial and ethnic groups. As we have argued elsewhere (Moss and Tilly 1996), it is particularly difficult to distinguish between legitimate, skill-based screening and discrimination when soft or social skills are involved.

Conclusion

This chapter has ranged over a lot of territory, but several unifying points emerge from the analysis of labor demand in these four metropolitan areas.

Skill requirements, location, and discrimination all pose significant barriers to workers of color and/or who are less-educated. Job tasks such as using computers, writing paragraphs, and interacting with customers knock down the likelihood that black and Latino job seekers will land the job. The situation is worst for black and Latino males. Hiring requirements such as high school diploma, experience, or references have the same effect. The difference in the rate of hire between high school graduates and dropouts is stark, and made worse by further job tasks or hiring requirements. Jobs not requiring college are more available relative to the labor pool in the suburbs. Employers in general express negative views of inner-city workers and of the inner city as a place to do business, and businesses are considerably more likely to move out of cities than to move in. Many managers explicitly state negative judgments of black and Latino workers' skills, and stereotypes often enter these judgments. Suburban employers appear to discriminate more in their hire rates of black job seekers than city employers. Employers also report ethnocentrism among customers and workers—attitudes likely to further curtail minority access to jobs.

Jobs with few requirements are spare in numbers and offer low wages. The fraction of noncollege jobs without major requirements is less than 10 percent throughout metropolitan areas and lowest in the city. Relaxing some of the job tasks required expands the pool of jobs, but not by much. Hourly wages for jobs with few or no requirements fall between $6.00 and $7.00 (in nominal terms of 1992 to 1994, when the data were collected), not enough to support a family and hardly enough to support an individual living alone.

Skill requirements and location are confounded with race. The policy consequence is that we cannot cleanly separate the effects of each, and policy aimed at one will be hindered by the connections among the problems. To be sure, greater policy effort is needed to invest in the skills of inner-city workers of color. This can and should be done as a combined effort of schools, firms, and training institutions. Efforts need to be made to enhance soft skills as well as hard skills. Increased access by inner-city workers to the growth of jobs in the suburbs as well as economic development efforts within the city will pay dividends. To the degree that employers act on stereotypes they hold, or statistical discrimination, the combination of more skills and better ability to communicate one's skills will be particularly effective. However, what ours and other Multi-City Study authors' research brings to light is that race not only continues to matter a lot, but that it influences employers' perceptions of skills and their perceptions of the desirability of different locations as business sites and areas from which to recruit. The effects of policies to develop the skills and mobility of workers of color will be lessened if they are not combined with innovative antidiscrimination and diversity training policies.

Possibilities for combining the stick of strategic antidiscrimination policies such as targeted audit studies that document continuing discrimination (Fix and Struyk 1993), on the one hand, with the carrot of diversity training for employers such as a "diversity management extension service" to spread best practices, on the other, may well bear significant fruit (Moss and Tilly 2000). The U.S. Equal Employment Opportunity Commission's recent announcement of a pilot audit project (U.S.

Equal Employment Opportunity Commission 1997c) and release of a re-port assessing best EEO practices in the private sector (U.S. Equal Employment Opportunity Commission 1997a) are encouraging steps toward such policies.

We gratefully acknowledge funding support from the Ford Foundation, Russell Sage Foundation, and Rockefeller Foundation. For research assistance, we thank Don Aldin, Tuck Bartholomew, Nancy Beale, Laurie Dougherty, Devon Johnson, Ivy Kennelly, Sherry Russ Lee, Michael Lichter, M. K. Park, Julie Press, Cheryl Seleski, Bob Smith, Bryan Snyder, and Susan Turner. We particularly thank Laurie Dougherty, Devon Johnson, Bob Smith, and Bryan Snyder for assistance with qualitative data. Our colleague Joleen Kirschenman shared project management with us, and contributed to earlier papers and discussions on which this chapter builds. We received very constructive comments on a previous draft from Harry Holzer, as well as other members of the Multi-City Study of Urban Inequality research team.

Notes

1. The qualitative survey only considered jobs that did not require more than a high school degree. The quantitative survey was intended to do so as well, but about 9 percent of the observations gathered information on jobs that require some college. Holzer (1996b, 38) excluded these observations from the majority of his reported results, except in a few instances when he wanted to compare jobs that require some college with those that don't. Following Holzer, we restrict our analysis to jobs that do not require college.

2. As Holzer notes, the use of computers can be quite varied and potentially ambiguous in interpretation. The range might include the very simple tasks of operating a grocery store checkout scanner or meal-ordering machine in a fast food restaurant, to word processing, to more technical computer use. (See Holzer 1996b, 46n4.)

3. As demand for and, most likely, return to skill increase, we are likely to see a supply response. To the degree they can, both white and nonwhite young people will invest in getting more skill, as they have done increasingly in the last two decades. Demand shifts tend to occur more rapidly than supply shifts, so that the labor market difficulties we attribute to increasing skill demand may continue to worsen for some time. (We thank Harry Holzer for this point.)

4. In this section and later sections, we analyze the race, ethnicity, and gender of the most recent hire in the firm. Many of the issues we raise about skill, attitudes, and screening procedures pertain as well to employer decisions *after* the point of hire. For example, decisions to train, to promote, or to fire may be affected by skills, perceptions, and procedures as well. Our data limit us to hiring outcomes.

5. Holzer notes that the geographic distribution of jobs from this survey accords with the distribution from the 1990 census, but with some exceptions that may be due to different choice of the central city-suburb border in this survey and in the census, and differential response rates across the area. In particular, the fraction of jobs in Atlanta's central city is somewhat larger for the survey than for the census. Holzer also discusses the geographic distribution of jobs broken down by industry (see Holzer 1996b, 21–25).

6. In table 10.8 we report the mean number of vacancies among the firms in each cell. In many of the cells, there was a firm that reported an unusually high value for the number of current vacancies. In almost all cells, there was only one such firm. Recognizing the possibility that the anomalous high values are either mistakes or so atypical as to distort the results, we also report a trimmed mean with the very high values deleted (a value of 200 or greater was used as the cutoff, and again there was only one such firm per cell in almost every instance). Because a large fraction of firms report no vacancies, the median number of vacancies in each cell is fairly small and ranges across the cells from a low of 2 to a high of 6.

7. This section draws heavily on and excerpts material directly from Moss and Tilly 2001.

References

Albelda, Randy, and Chris Tilly. 1997. *Glass Ceilings and Bottomless Pits: Women's Work, Women's Poverty*. Boston: South End Press.

Becker, Gary S. 1957. *The Economics of Discrimination*. Chicago: University of Chicago Press.

Bendick, Marc, Jr., Charles W. Jackson, and Victor A. Reinoso. 1994. "Measuring Employment Discrimination Through Controlled Experiments." *Review of Black Political Economy* 23 (Summer): 25–48.

Borjas, George. 1994. "The Economics of Immigration." *Journal of Economic Literature* 32(4): 1667–1717.

Bound, John, and Laura Dresser. 1999. "The Erosion of the Relative Earnings of Young African American Women During the 1980s." In *Latinas and African American Women at Work: Race, Gender and Economic Inequality*, edited by Irene Browne. New York: Russell Sage.

Bound, John, and Richard Freeman. 1992. "What Went Wrong? The Erosion of the Relative Earnings and Employment of Young Black Men in the 1980s." *Quarterly Journal of Economics* 107(1): 201–32.

Bound, John, and George Johnson. 1992. "Changes in the Structure of Wages in the 1980s: An Evaluation of Alternative Explanations." *American Economic Review* 82(3): 371–92.

Cappelli, Peter. 1993. "Are Skill Requirements Rising? Evidence from

Production and Clerical Jobs." *Industrial and Labor Relations Review* 46(3): 515–30.

Corcoran, Mary, Colleen M. Heflin, and Belinda I. Reyes. 1999. "Latino Women in the U.S.: The Economic Progress of Mexican and Puerto Rican Women." In *Latinas and African American Women at Work: Race, Gender and Economic Inequality*, edited by Irene Browne. New York: Russell Sage Foundation.

Corcoran, Mary, and Sharon Parrott. 1999. "Black Women's Economic Progress." In *Latinas and African American Women at Work: Race, Gender and Economic Inequality*, edited by Irene Browne. New York: Russell Sage Foundation.

Dipboye, Robert L. 1982. "Self-fulfilling Prophecies in the Selection-Recruitment Interview." *Academy of Management Review* 7: 579–86.

Ferguson, Ronald F. 1996. "Shifting Challenges: Fifty Years of Economic Change Toward Black-White Earnings Equality." In *An American Dilemma Revisited: Race Relations in a Changing World*, edited by Obie Clayton, Jr. New York: Russell Sage Foundation.

Fix, Michael, and Raymond Struyk. 1993. *Clear and Convincing Evidence*. Washington, D.C.: Urban Institute Press.

Holzer, Harry J. 1991. "The Spatial Mismatch Hypothesis: What Has the Evidence Shown?" *Urban Studies* 28(1): 105–22.

———. 1996a. "Employer Hiring Decisions and Antidiscrimination Policy." In *Demand-Side Strategies for Low-Wage Labor Markets*, edited by R. Freeman and P. Gottschalk. New York: Russell Sage Foundation.

———. 1996b. *What Employers Want: Job Prospects for Less-Educated Workers*. New York: Russell Sage Foundation.

———. 1996c. "Why Do Small Firms Hire Fewer Blacks than Large Ones?" Discussion Paper, Institute for Research on Poverty, University of Wisconsin at Madison.

Holzer, Harry, and David Neumark. 1999. "Are Affirmative Action Hires Less Qualified? Evidence from Employer-Employee Data on New Hires." *Journal of Labor Economics* 17(3): 534–69.

Howell, David, and Edward Wolff. 1991. "Trends in the Growth and Distribution of Skill in the U.S. Workplace, 1960–1985." *Industrial and Labor Relations Review* 44(3): 481–501.

Ihlanfeldt, Keith. 1999. "The Geography of Economic and Social Opportunity Within Metropolitan Areas." In *Governance and Opportunity in Metropolitan America*, edited by Alan A. Altshuler, William Morrill, Harold Wolman, and Faith Mitchell. Washington, D.C.: National Academy Press.

Jencks, Christopher, and Susan Mayer. 1990. "Residential Segregation, Job Proximity, and Black Job Opportunities." In *Inner-City Poverty in the United States*, edited by Laurence E. Lind and Michael McGeary. Washington, D.C.: National Academy Press.

Kain, John. 1968. "Housing Segregation, Negro Employment, and Metropolitan Decentralization." *Quarterly Journal of Economics* 82 (May): 175–97.

Kasarda, John D. 1993. "Inner-City Concentrated Poverty and Neighborhood Distress: 1970 to 1990." *Housing Policy Debate* 4(3): 253–302.

Kennelly, Ivy. 1999. "'That Single Mother Element': How White Employers Typify Black Women." *Gender and Society* 13(2): 168–92.

Kirschenman, Joleen. 1991. "Gender Within Race in the Labor Market." Paper presented at the Urban Poverty and Family Life Conference. Chicago (October 10–12, 1991).

Kirschenman, Joleen, and Kathryn M. Neckerman. 1991. "'We'd Love to Hire Them, But . . . ': The Meaning of Race for Employers." In *The Urban Underclass*, edited by Christopher Jencks and Paul E. Peterson. Washington, D.C.: Brookings Institution.

Leonard, Jonathan. 1990. "The Impact of Affirmative Action Regulation and Equal Opportunity Law on Black Employment." *Journal of Economic Perspectives*, 4(4): 47–63.

Meléndez, Edwin. 1993. "Understanding Latino Poverty." *Sage Race Relations Abstracts* 18(2): 3–43.

Moss, Philip, and Chris Tilly. 1991. *Why Black Men Are Doing Worse in the Labor Market: A Review of Supply-Side and Demand-Side Explanations*. Working Paper. New York: Social Science Research Council.

———. 1993. "A Turn for the Worse: Why Black Men's Labor Market Fortunes Have Declined in the United States." *Sage Race Relations Abstracts* 18(1): 5–45.

———. 1995. "Skills and Race in Hiring: Quantitative Findings from Face-to-Face Interviews." *Eastern Economic Journal* 21(3).

———. 1996. "'Soft' Skills and Race: An Investigation of Black Men's Employment Problems." *Work and Occupations* 23(3): 252–76.

———. 2000. *Stories Employers Tell: Race, Skills, and Hiring in America*. New York: Russell Sage Foundation.

Neal, Derek A. and William R. Johnson. 1996. "The Role of Premarket Factors in Black-White Wage Differences." *Journal of Political Economy* 104(5): 869–95.

Neckerman, Kathryn M., and Joleen Kirschenman. 1991. "Hiring Strategies, Racial Bias and Inner-City Workers." *Social Problems* 38(4): 801–15.

O'Neill, June. 1990. "The Role of Human Capital in Earnings Differences Between Black and White Men." *Journal of Economic Perspectives* 4(4): 25–46.

Osterman, Paul. 1995. "Skill, Training, and Work Organization in American Establishments." *Industrial Relations* 34(2): 125–46.

U.S. Equal Employment Opportunity Commission. 1997a. "Best Practices of Private Sector Employers: Executive Summary." Website http://www.eeoc.gov/task/prac2.html. December 22.

———. 1997b. "Budget and Staffing." Website http://www.eeoc.gov/budget.html. November 3.

———. 1997c. "EEOC Announces Pilot Projects to Test for Employment Discrimination." Website http://www.eeoc.gov/press/12-5-97.html. December 5.

———. Waldinger, Roger. 1997. "Black/Immigrant Competition Reassessed: New Evidence from Los Angeles." *Sociological Perspectives* 40(3): 365–86.

Word, Carl O., Mark P. Zanna, and Joel Cooper. 1974. "The Nonverbal Mediation of Self-Fulfilling Prophecies in Interracial Interaction." *Journal of Experimental Social Psychology* 10: 100–20.

11

ARE JOBS AVAILABLE FOR DISADVANTAGED WORKERS IN URBAN AREAS?

Harry J. Holzer and Sheldon Danziger

A RE JOBS available to everyone who wants to work? Many academic and policy debates over the nature and causes of unemployment and poverty turn on the answer to this question. For instance, William Julius Wilson (1987, 1996) has argued that the lack of jobs in inner cities has contributed to the social dislocations that have occurred there. In contrast, Lawrence Mead's arguments (1992) regarding work requirements and government paternalism implicitly (or explicitly) assume that work is available to almost anyone who seeks it.

The contentious welfare reform debate of the mid-1990s centers on the same question. The Personal Responsibility and Work Opportunity Reconciliation Act of 1996 includes work requirements and time limits on recipiency. It does not, however, require governments to provide employment of last resort, based on the assumption that most recipients can find work in regular private- or public-sector jobs (albeit at low wages).

As critical as this question is, however, the evidence either for or against the assumption of adequate job availability is not very convincing.[1] Although some (for example, Mead 1996) have interpreted recent drops in the welfare caseload and rising employment among single mothers as indicating widespread job availability, the evidence on this point to date is somewhat mixed; and the very tight labor markets of the late 1990s have certainly helped (Danziger, 1999).[2]

In this chapter, we provide new evidence on the issue of job availability. We use data from both the demand and supply sides of the labor market and calculate the degree of job availability facing specific groups of disadvantaged workers, such as blacks, high school dropouts, and welfare recipients. We compare what employers have told us about the characteristics of available jobs—their skill requirements, location, and racial composition of their firms—with what metropolitan residents have told us about their own labor market skills and experiences. We then conduct simulations in which we "match" as many workers as possible to available jobs under a variety of assumptions. The fraction of actual or potential job seekers within each group who can be "matched" determines our measure of the degree of job availability for the group.

Like any simulation exercise, our approach is limited because we cannot analyze observed market outcomes. On the other hand, we can predict the degree of job availability that those outside the labor force, such as welfare recipients, are likely to face when they enter it. Because we use actual data from the demand side of the labor market, in conjunction with labor supply data, we also generate a better prediction of the effects of various demand-side characteristics on the likely outcomes of workers than is typically derived from supply-side data sources (such as censuses or Current Population Surveys).[3] To test whether our simulations generate reasonable results, we compare predicted outcomes with those observed for workers in the labor force.

We begin by briefly reviewing the relevant labor market concepts and the previous empirical literature. We then describe our data and methodology and present results. We find that a substantial fraction of job seekers, especially among disadvantaged groups (such as high school dropouts, minorities, and welfare recipients), will face limited job availability in the short run. We close with some implications for public policy and for future research.

Labor Market Concepts and Previous Literature

Since the early 1970s, the real earnings and employment levels of less-educated workers have deteriorated both in real terms and relative to those of more-educated workers. This combination suggests that labor demand has shifted away from these workers, for reasons that include technological changes, growing international trade, and other factors (see, for example, Levy and Murnane 1992; Danziger and Gottschalk 1995).

There are, however, two possible interpretations of the declining employment rates of the less-educated, both of which are consistent with shifts in labor demand. These are illustrated in figure 11.1. The first possibility, depicted in panel A of the figure, is that the labor market is "clearing" or "in equilibrium," and less-skilled workers are simply *choosing* to work less in response to the declining wages they are

FIGURE 11.1   *Demand and Supply Shifts in Low-Wage Labor Markets*

Market in Equilibrium

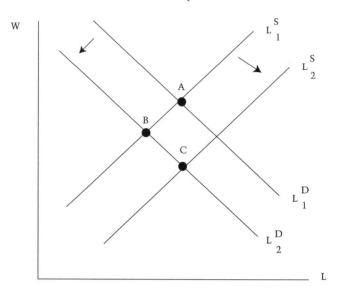

Market with Rigid Wages

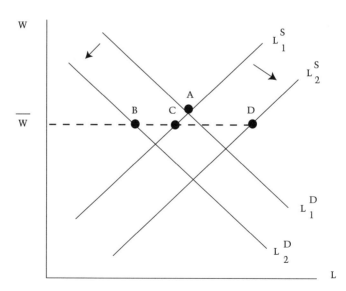

Source: Authors' compilation.
Note: "W" and "L" refer to wage and employment levels respectively, while L^S and L^D are labor supply and demand curves respectively.

offered. The market equilibrium has shifted from point A to point B, with both wages and employment declining as the labor demand curve for the less-educated shifts down along a fixed labor supply curve. Any outward shift (or increase) in the supply of such labor, such as is expected due to the legislation requiring long-term welfare recipients to search for work, will cause the labor supply curve of the less-educated to shift outward and the market equilibrium to move to point C. Though wages would then be even lower than at point B, everyone who searches for work would find a job.[4]

The alternative possibility is that the diminished demand for less-skilled labor has to do with limited job availability because of downward rigidity in wages. This is illustrated in panel B of the figure. Wages are somewhat higher than in the market-clearing case, but with employment declining even more in response to the same decline in labor demand. An excess supply of workers, measured by BC in the diagram, results when wages are downward rigid and do not fall to market-clearing levels.[5]

In this case, the labor market would not clear and would be in "disequilibrium." Unemployed workers will "queue" for available jobs, and some may experience lengthy durations of joblessness. An increase in labor supply of less-skilled workers would further add to the excess supply of labor, causing the number of unemployed workers to rise to BD, with wage rates still at $\overline{W}$. Compared to the top panel, wages are higher but employment is lower.

The type of unemployment shown for low-wage workers in the bottom panel can exist even though the labor market is tight and unemployment rates are low for other workers. In this case, the overall labor market would be characterized by "structural" or "mismatch" unemployment. This implies a deficiency in the quantity of labor demanded (relative to its supply) in some particular labor markets, even though demand is stronger in others.[6] This case is distinct from unemployment created by "deficient aggregate demand," as occurs in recessions, when limited job availability characterizes a wide range of labor markets.

Of course, less-skilled workers are not a homogeneous group. Some will no doubt find jobs at wages above the minimum; others will have trouble finding employment even at or near the minimum wage. What fractions of less-educated job seekers fit into each category? Is job availability particularly limited for disadvantaged workers, such as minorities and/or welfare recipients? Is this a problem even when the aggregate labor market is tight? We address these questions by providing evidence on the rates of "mismatch" unemployment for various groups of job seekers.

Previous Empirical Evidence

Most economic analyses of these issues have focused at the *aggregate* level and are based on estimated relationships between vacancy, unemployment, and/or inflation rates. For instance, Katherine Abraham (1983) and Harry Holzer (1989, 1996b) document that unemployment rates are generally higher than job vacancy rates during all phases of the business cycle. This suggests that, *at any moment in time*, not enough jobs are available for everyone who seeks one, and workers must queue for available jobs. The durations of unemployment for most workers, however, are fairly short—so most move through this queue rather quickly (Clark and Summers 1982).

On the other hand, a small fraction of the unemployed, especially blacks, experience lengthy durations (perhaps six months or more), even when aggregate unemployment is low. This suggests that workers at the "back of the queue" cannot gain employment within a short time. Unfortunately, aggregate unemployment and vacancy data provide little evidence on the causes of long durations and whether they reflect limited job availability and "mismatch" or supply-side factors, such as high reservation wages or low search effort among job seekers.

An alternative approach to measuring the job availability estimates a "natural rate of unemployment" or "non-accelerating inflation rate of unemployment" (NAIRU), using aggregate data on price inflation and unemployment rates. The notion here is that inflation will be stable only when the aggregate supply of and demand for labor are in balance, and that some unique rate of unemployment exists at which that appears to be true. The unemployment at that point can be "frictional" and/or "structural" in nature, but it will not represent deficiencies in aggregate demand.

Many have estimated the current NAIRU to be in the range of 5 percent. However, both theoretical and empirical questions remain (Blanchard and Katz 1997), especially because unemployment fell below 5 percent in 1997–2000 without any increase in inflation. Even if valid for the aggregate economy, NAIRU estimates provide little evidence on the extent to which particular groups (such as minorities or unskilled workers) face limited job availability, and thereby experience "structural unemployment," even when the aggregate labor market is in balance.[7]

A different approach is to conduct a *micro*level analysis of either the demand or supply side of the labor market and attempt to distinguish job availability from worker choices as determinants of unemployment (or nonemployment) among particular groups. For instance, Holzer (1986) and Petterson (1997) analyze the effects of relative labor *supply* shifts on unemployment among young blacks by estimating the effects of self-reported reservation wages on the differences in unemployment durations between young whites and blacks. Both find relatively higher reservation wages (compared to market wages) among blacks, but most of the racial difference in unemployment is not explained by these supply factors.[8]

Other recent microlevel studies focus on the *demand* side of the labor market in inner-city areas. For instance, Holzer (1996b) finds few jobs (among those that have been recently filled by employers) available to those with limited basic skills (such as reading-writing, arithmetic, computer use, and ability to interact with customers) or job-related skills (specific experience or previous training in the job). Katherine Newman and Chauncy Lennon (1995) report fourteen applicants for each job opening in a few fast food restaurants in Harlem in the early 1990s. These findings are only suggestive, however, because neither study analyzes data on both the supply and demand sides of the labor market.[9]

A few recent papers do compare both sides of the labor market, using data on the characteristics of available jobs and less-educated workers, particularly welfare recipients. Leonard Bloomquist, Leif Jensen, and Ruy Teixeira (1988) use the average educational attainment of workers in detailed occupations to determine the extent to which *vacant* jobs in those occupations might be available to welfare recipients. Paul Kleppner and Nikolas Theodore (1997) use the average skill content of jobs, as measured by the *Dictionary of Occupational Titles*, to determine the extent to which welfare recipients might face a "job gap."[10] Although our analysis is similar, our data provide better information for matching individual workers to available jobs, based on more detailed characteristics of each.

In sum, the evidence to date on the extent of job availability for unskilled workers has been plagued by the inadequacy of macrolevel models and a paucity of appropriate microlevel data.

Comparing the Demand for and Supply of Workers: Data and Methodology

We use data from both the Household and Employer Surveys in the Multi-City Study of Urban Inequality for Atlanta, Boston, Detroit, and Los Angeles. The Household Survey was administered to between 1,600 and 4,000 adults in each of the four metropolitan areas in samples that overrepresent minorities residing in low-income neighborhoods. The Employer Survey was administered by phone to 800 employers in each of the four areas. Both sets of surveys were administered between 1992 and 1994.[11]

We analyze the availability of jobs to various groups of workers, particularly the "disadvantaged." To do this, we simulate how the labor market "matches" workers to jobs along a variety of relevant dimensions. For every establishment in the employer survey, we have extensive data on its *most recently filled jobs*. A weighted sample of these jobs constitutes a fairly representative sample of the jobs that are available in local labor markets over a period of several months.[12]

The appropriate group of workers to whom these jobs should be matched is a sample of actual or potential job seekers—those who have recently sought work or who might do so in the near future. We define this sample as anyone who has searched for work within the past month, worked on the current job for a year or less, or who is currently not employed and does not self-identify as a homemaker, a student, a disabled person, or a retired worker.

The proportions of our sample of job seekers who were employed, unemployed, and out of the labor force at the time of the survey are .64, .23, and .13, respectively; thus, most of those being matched are actual rather than potential job seekers. Our sample of potential job seekers includes many welfare recipients and others who have been out of the labor force but who are widely viewed as "able to work" and may be doing so now or very soon.[13]

Our sample of job seekers constitutes about 44 percent of all respondents in the household survey who are under age sixty-five. This corresponds closely to the percentage of the labor force that loses or leaves employment and therefore seeks work in any given year.[14] Also, each job seeker appears just once in the sample, as does each job; multiple spells of each are therefore not considered here.[15]

We treat both the skill requirements of jobs and the skills of workers as predetermined; the analysis is thus in the spirit of short-run "matching" models of the labor market (for example, Davidson 1990). Wages and benefits on jobs are assumed to be fixed as well, also consistent with a short-run model. Furthermore, we assume that the aggregate labor market is in balance, as appears to have been the case in most metropolitan areas during the mid-to-late 1990s. If this is not the case (especially during recessions), our results will provide "lower-bound" estimates of the fraction of workers who will have difficulty finding jobs. We also ignore "frictional" problems—that is, the unemployment that results from the time it takes for workers and jobs to become "matched" to each other.

Thus, we focus on measuring only "structural" unemployment that might characterize disadvantaged workers even in tight labor markets. Although our model is short-run in nature, the labor market problems that limit their employability could persist for long periods of time.

Our simulations match workers and jobs along three dimensions that are considered as barriers to work for the disadvantaged: skills, race, and/or space (Wilson 1987; Holzer 1994). We do not consider the effects of individually chosen characteristics, such as reservation wages or job search methods and intensity, on the likelihood that a job seeker will gain employment.

Our simulation distributes workers and jobs across matrices based on skills, race, and/or space, allowing for interactions among a variety of dichotomous characteristics on both sides of the market.[16] We apply the simulation in two ways, each based on a different configuration of the underlying matrix; variations of each have also been explored. In each simulation, workers are matched to as many jobs as possible across the cells of the demand-side matrix. In the end, some workers go unmatched and some jobs go unfilled.

An Illustration

A simple example illustrates this method. In figure 11.2 we present a two-by-two hypothetical matrix of skills and race, where skill is defined by "high" versus "low" for both sides of the market and race by "black" versus "nonblack." Some jobs are not accessible to black workers (and are therefore considered "nonblack" only) due to reasons of space and/or discrimination. Jobs and workers are distributed as shown across the cells of each matrix. If the distributions of workers and jobs across these cells were identical, no mismatch at all would occur.

Because we assume that the labor market balances in the aggregate, we are concerned only with the *percentages* of workers and of jobs in each category, not with the raw numbers. Thus, the percentages sum to 1 in each matrix. This choice is warranted conceptually and is also consistent with data availability.[17] Furthermore, workers can flow only in the directions indicated by the arrows if they choose to, or must do so—namely, more-skilled workers can flow from higher- to lower-skill jobs, and nonblack workers can flow from jobs that are not accessible to blacks to those that are accessible, but flows cannot occur in the reverse directions.

If we assume that workers will first seek out jobs within their "own" cells, there would initially be surpluses of workers over jobs in cells 2 and 3 and shortages of workers in the others. In the absence of worker flows, 10 percent of workers would be unmatched, as would 10 percent of jobs.[18] But surplus workers in cells 2 and 3 could easily flow to excess jobs in cell 4, thereby reducing the degree of mismatch to just 5 percent of workers and jobs.

Exactly which 5 percent of workers are left without jobs in this

FIGURE 11.2   *Labor Demand, Supply, and Mismatch: An Example*

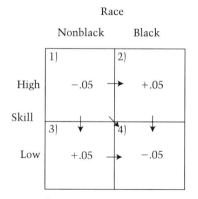

Initial Supply

Race

	Nonblack	Black
	1)	2)
High Skill	.25	.25
	3)	4)
Low	.25	.25

Initial Demand

Race

	Nonblack	Black
	1)	2)
High Skill	.30	.20
	3)	4)
Low	.20	.30

Initial Mismatch and Potential Supply Flows

Race

	Nonblack	Black
	1)	2)
High Skill	−.05	+.05
	3)	4)
Low	+.05	−.05

Source: Authors' compilation.
Note: "Mismatch" is measured at initial demand above.

hypothetical case would depend on assumptions regarding who competes effectively with whom for the remaining jobs in cell 4.[19] Furthermore, overall mismatch rates will fall if less-skilled and/or black workers can flow to unfilled higher-skill and/or white jobs, at least after the more-skilled workers have been placed. On the other hand, it is also possible that highly skilled workers who reside in one location (for example, suburbs) might initially choose jobs in other locations (say, downtown areas), thus eliminating potential jobs for those who live close to those jobs; if the latter do not, in return, have access to jobs located closer to the residences of commuters, overall mismatch rates would rise.[20]

Thus, these assumptions regarding where workers seek jobs and whom employers prefer among job candidates can have important effects on predicted rates of job availability overall and for specific groups.

Implementing the Simulations

We briefly describe our methods for simulating the "matching" process here. (A detailed description of our procedures is presented in the appendix to this chapter.) To operationalize this simulation, we specify measures of skills, race, and space that are available in our data from both sides of the labor market. For space, we specify whether or not job seekers have access to automobiles while they search, or whether they must rely on public transit; we then specify whether or not employers are located near public transit stops. For race, we specify whether job seekers are black and whether firms currently employ any blacks. Female gender or Hispanic ethnicity are not treated here as barriers to employment per se, although we calculate separate mismatch rates for these categories of workers.[21] Any disadvantages that black job seekers experience relative to other ethnic groups, especially immigrants who might benefit from stronger job search networks or preferences by employers (Kirschenman and Neckerman 1991), will be captured in our black-nonblack racial categorization.

For skills, we specify the following: the educational attainment of job seekers and the educational requirements of jobs, the occupational experience or training of job seekers and the occupational requirements of jobs, and whether job seekers have performed each of a set of basic cognitive or social tasks on a recent job and whether each task is required in newly filled jobs. Task performance and requirements are represented either as a sum across categories (in method 1) or as a set of combinations in which some tasks (such as reading-writing and arithmetic) are treated as more difficult than others (perhaps customer contact or computer use, in method 2). Either way, both "hard" and "soft" skills (Moss and Tilly 1995) are captured to some extent by these skill categories.[22]

All job seekers and newly filled jobs are allocated across the 124 cells of matrices that reflect these different characteristics. We then allocate workers to jobs through a set of "matching" algorithms that specify various job seeker and employer search patterns. The job seeker choices include where they seek work initially and where they flow if they do not get their initial choices. The employer choices include preferences across the different groups of workers who might simultaneously compete for a more limited number of jobs in a given cell.

Job seekers flow across job cells according to these search rules until they are either "matched" or have exhausted their job-matching possibilities (in which case they are "mismatched"). The percentages of job seekers (as well as jobs) in the latter situation are then calculated for the overall sample and for particular demographic subgroups. Though many simplifying assumptions are needed to keep the analysis tractable, we test the sensitivity of our results by using general algorithms that embody different assumptions about the matching process.

Results

Summary Data

We first present summary data on the characteristics of workers seeking jobs and on the jobs that are available to them. Table 11.1 presents data on the skills of workers and on whether or not car transportation is available to them. Skills are measured along three dimensions: educational attainment, occupation category of current or most recent job, and task performance on that job. The latter two are presented only for workers who are not college graduates. Tabulations on worker task performance are also presented two ways: across categories based on the numbers of tasks performed (zero to one, two, three to four) and on combinations based on performance of reading-writing and/or arithmetic. These results are presented for all job seekers in column 1, and then separately by race in columns 2, 3, and 4 and by gender in columns 5 and 6. All means are sample-weighted and sample sizes are presented in the last row. Results are pooled across the four metropolitan areas.

About 30 percent of all workers in the sample are college graduates; only 12 percent are high school dropouts. Among those who are not college graduates, more than 40 percent have performed three to four tasks on jobs, including reading-writing and arithmetic. About 20 percent have been employed in professional, managerial, or technical occupations. On the other hand, about one-fourth of these workers have performed only minimal zero to one numbers of tasks, with neither reading-writing nor arithmetic included among them, and have occupational experience only in laborer or service jobs or not at all.

Among blacks and especially Hispanics, skill levels along all dimensions are lower than among whites. There are more high school dropouts among blacks than among whites by relatively small amounts, but more among Hispanics than whites or blacks by a considerable amount

TABLE 11.1   *Worker Skills and Transportation, Total and by
Race-Gender*

Skills	By Race				By Gender	
	All	White	Black	Hispanic	Male	Female
Education						
College	.301	.363	.190	.236	.348	.252
High school or GED	.575	.563	.699	.466	.541	.611
High school dropout	.124	.074	.112	.298	.111	.137
Tasks of noncollege graduates						
Zero to one task	.283	.215	.280	.442	.318	.252
Two tasks	.282	.275	.351	.377	.263	.299
Three to four tasks	.435	.510	.370	.180	.418	.452
Reading-writing and arithmetic	.423	.484	.340	.295	.485	.367
Reading-writing only	.127	.116	.178	.179	.087	.163
Arithmetic only	.189	.212	.203	.087	.185	.193
Neither	.260	.188	.276	.439	.242	.277
Occupations of noncollege graduates						
Professional, managerial, technical	.186	.236	.126	.112	.182	.189
Clerical or sales	.310	.332	.324	.233	.154	.448
Craft or operative	.219	.192	.116	.174	.395	.063
Laborer or service	.251	.218	.356	.341	.239	.260
No occupation	.034	.022	.076	.140	.029	.040
Transportation						
Car available	.868	.937	.650	.760	.883	.856
No car available	.132	.063	.350	.240	.117	.144
Number in sample	2,547	952	927	668	1,082	1,465

Source: Multi-City Study of Urban Inequality.

(Hauser and Phang 1993). College graduation rates among both groups of minority job seekers are lower than among whites. Task performance and occupational status among blacks and Hispanics who are not college graduates are also weaker than among whites. For instance, roughly half of white job seekers without college have performed most tasks, including both reading-writing and arithmetic. Comparable rates among blacks and Hispanics are 37 and 34 percent and 18 and 30 percent, respectively. The percentages of workers with little task performance are from 19 to 22 percent among whites, but about 28 percent among blacks and 44 percent among Hispanics. Those with low (or no) occupational experience are comparably higher among the minorities.

Though not shown in the table significant variation is seen in skill attainment, both overall and by race, across the four metropolitan areas. For instance, job seekers in Atlanta and Boston are more highly educated than are those in Detroit and Los Angeles.[23] The high concentration of Hispanics and immigrants in Los Angeles reduces the overall educational attainment of the workforce there. Omitting Los Angeles observations raises the educational attainment and skills in the overall sample by a few percentage points in each category. The high concentrations of blacks in Atlanta and Detroit do not lead to similarly low levels of educational attainment, since blacks in Atlanta are more highly educated than those in Detroit.[24] These differentials in attainment across metropolitan areas affect our estimates of the relative rates of job availability and "mismatch" across these areas.

Although skill differentials across racial groups are evident, such differentials across gender groups are ambiguous. Males have somewhat higher educational attainment than females. Men are somewhat less likely to have performed large numbers of tasks, but are somewhat more likely to have performed both reading-writing and arithmetic. Women are concentrated in clerical or sales jobs, where most skills (including customer contact and computers) are used extensively, and also in the service jobs. These gender differentials in task performance also appear within each racial group (Holzer 1996b).

The data in table 11.1 show that nearly seven-eighths of all workers have access to automobiles when traveling to work. This is more true of whites than minorities, with only 6 percent of the former and 24 to 35 percent of the latter limited to public transit or other modes of transportation.

To what extent do specific groups of "disadvantaged" job seekers, such as high school dropouts and/or welfare recipients, lack these skills and transportation options? In table 11.2 we present data comparable to those that appear in table 11.1, but only for job seekers who are high school dropouts, welfare recipients (defined here as females who are receiving "public assistance"), or both. For each of these groups, we present the data for all job seekers and then separately by race.

The results of table 11.2 show that disadvantaged job seekers, especially minorities, are much more likely than others to have low skill attainment. Among all high school dropouts, 55 to 59 percent report little task performance on previous jobs, and only about 26 percent have ever been employed in a white-collar occupation. Overall, welfare recipients are somewhat more highly skilled than are dropouts; about three-fourths have graduated from high school, and just a quarter to a third

TABLE 11.2   Worker Skills and Transportation: High School Dropouts and Welfare Recipients

Skills	High School Dropouts			Welfare Recipients			Welfare Recipients Who Are High School Dropouts		
	All	White	Black-Hispanic	All	White	Black-Hispanic	All	White	Black-Hispanic
Education									
College	.000	.000	.000	.130	.131	.129	.000	.000	.000
High school or GED	.000	.000	.000	.620	.637	.613	.000	.000	.000
High school dropout	1.000	1.000	1.000	.240	.232	.258	1.000	1.000	1.000
Tasks of noncollege graduates									
Zero to one task	.548	.490	.597	.280	.129	.356	.440	.295	.449
Two tasks	.311	.307	.357	.322	.487	.334	.457	.581	.443
Three to four tasks	.141	.203	.046	.398	.382	.310	.103	.124	.108
Reading-writing and arithmetic	.193	.235	.126	.419	.429	.318	.099	.123	.104
Reading-writing only	.063	.025	.137	.142	.162	.152	.172	.167	.146
Arithmetic only	.152	.183	.097	.105	.259	.100	.156	.336	.143
Neither	.591	.557	.639	.334	.150	.430	.512	.374	.607
Occupations of noncollege graduates									
Professional, managerial, or technical	.071	.134	.027	.047	.082	.036	.004	.000	.007
Clerical or sales	.192	.251	.108	.372	.605	.280	.344	.558	.245
Craft or operative	.274	.218	.198	.085	.096	.062	.200	.210	.109
Laborer or service	.382	.372	.484	.403	.139	.508	.340	.147	.480
No occupation	.081	.026	.184	.093	.078	.116	.111	.085	.158
Transportation									
Car available	.703	.818	.485	.612	.789	.662	.339	.496	.305
No car available	.297	.182	.515	.328	.211	.338	.661	.504	.695
Number in sample	578	98	480	463	52	323	161	17	144

Source: Multi-City Study of Urban Inequality.

have little significant task performance. But minorities on welfare have much lower skill attainment than do white welfare recipients, and the skill levels observed among welfare recipients who are also dropouts are very low.[25] Their access to automobile transportation is also quite limited. Since minorities and high school dropouts on welfare are more likely to be long-term recipients, they are representative of many recipients who will be required to enter the labor market by time limits or work requirements over the next several years.[26]

How do these levels of skill attainment and access to transportation compare with those required on newly available jobs? Table 11.3 presents data similar to those in the first two tables, but for the *demand* rather than *supply* side of the labor market—that is, for characteristics and requirements of newly available jobs rather than of workers.

About one-fourth of new jobs require college degrees, and about one-fifth are available to workers without high school diplomas or GEDs. But among the jobs that do not require college, over half require the performance of three to four tasks, and about a third require both reading-writing and arithmetic on the job. About two-fifths require previous experience or training in a white-collar job. Finally, a large majority of jobs are available to those without automobiles.

In comparison with results reported on worker skills in table 11.1, those on skills demanded by employers in table 11.3 indicate that average educational requirements on jobs are lower than average educational attainment among job seekers overall. Average task and occupation-specific experience requirements on noncollege jobs, however, are somewhat higher than what we observe among noncollege job seekers. Thus, an inability to perform certain tasks and the lack of job-specific experience or training would contribute to the difficulties that some job seekers have in being matched to jobs; these difficulties will be most pronounced among disadvantaged groups such as welfare recipients and, especially, high school dropouts. Although transportation difficulties should not contribute to mismatch problems in the aggregate, they might confound the problems of unskilled or minority workers whose access to jobs is already limited by their low skill levels.

Of course, even low-skill workers who succeed in finding employment can still be plagued by other impediments, such as low wages and limited fringe benefits. Indeed, unemployment rates of unskilled workers have declined dramatically in recent years, especially relative to those in other industrial countries, but wages earned by these workers in the United States have also declined more rapidly than those earned by less-educated workers abroad (Gottschalk and Smeeding 1997).

In table 11.4 we present median starting hourly wages paid on new jobs by the employers surveyed. We also present the percentages of these

TABLE 11.3   *Skill and Transportation Requirements of Newly Filled Jobs*

Education	
College	.242
High school or GED	.539
High school dropout	.219
Tasks of noncollege graduates	
Zero to one task	.238
Two tasks	.228
Three to four tasks	.535
Reading-writing and arithmetic	.327
Reading-writing only	.263
Arithmetic only	.150
Neither	.260
Occupations of noncollege graduates	
Professional, managerial, or technical	.102
Clerical or sales	.292
Craft or operative	.156
Laborer or service	.106
No occupation	.346
Transportation	
Car required	.377
No car required	.623
Number in sample	2,598

Source: Multi-City Study of Urban Inequality.

jobs that provide health benefits. These data are for categories of jobs defined by skill or transportation, as in the previous tables.[27]

As expected, jobs requiring a college degree pay substantially more than those requiring only high school—$14.39 versus $8.40 per hour. These data are consistent with those reported in the literature on rising wage inequality (Danziger and Gottschalk 1995). Although median wages on jobs requiring high school start at $8 to $9 per hour, those that do not require high school pay just over $6. Low wages are also reported in jobs that require few tasks or little occupational experience or training. Furthermore, a significant fraction of these jobs (about 25 percent) are part-time rather than full-time, further limiting the earnings potential of those who obtain them.[28]

Finally, many low-skill jobs provide no health insurance to workers or their families. For instance, almost half of jobs for high school dropouts (or of those that do not require reading-writing or arithmetic) provide no insurance to other family members of the employee, and about one-third do not provide coverage for the workers.

TABLE 11.4   *Median Hourly Starting Wages and Availability of Health Benefits in Newly Filled Jobs*

Requirements	Median Wages	Health Benefits for Worker	Family
Education			
College	$14.39	.914	.831
High school or GED	8.40	.809	.702
High school dropout	6.31	.637	.526
Tasks of noncollege graduates			
Zero to one task	6.88	.765	.642
Two tasks	7.20	.708	.611
Three to four tasks	8.44	.778	.672
Reading-writing and arithmetic	10.87	.826	.711
Reading-writing only	8.36	.735	.641
Arithmetic only	8.49	.764	.677
Neither	6.44	.682	.558
Occupations of noncollege graduates			
Professional, managerial, or technical	10.21	.872	.722
Clerical or sales	8.36	.775	.678
Craft or operative	8.49	.814	.704
Laborer or service	.00	.760	.640
No occupation	6.20	.681	.581
Transportation			
Car required	8.15	.784	.698
No car required	8.64	.801	.694

Source: Multi-City Study of Urban Inequality.

These data confirm that, even if many unskilled workers are able to find employment, many will do so only in jobs with low wages and benefits (Blank 1995; Burtless 1995). Poverty rates among these workers will no doubt continue to be high in many cases.[29]

Mismatch Rates

In table 11.5 we present our simulated percentages of overall mismatch between workers and jobs. Results are presented for the four Metropolitan Statistical Areas (MSAs) separately and for pooled samples. Because of the unique characteristics of the labor market in Los Angeles (as already noted), the pooled results are also shown with observations from Los Angeles excluded.

We present calculations for the two different matching methods: Method 1 matches workers and jobs according to a matrix based on

TABLE 11.5   *Percentage Mismatched: Workers and Jobs*

	Method 1	Method 2
Atlanta	.072	.155
Boston	.045	.121
Detroit	.093	.195
Los Angeles	.166	.214
Average of four MSAs	.094	.171
Average, excluding Los Angeles	.070	.157

Source: Multi-City Study of Urban Inequality.

skills (the number of tasks), spatial location or transportation, and race; different tasks are treated as substitutes for one another. Method 2 replaces spatial factors and education levels below college in the matrix with an expanded set of task performance combinations.

The results of table 11.5 show overall mismatch rates of 9.4 to 17.1 percent—in other words, we expect that 9 to 17 percent of actual or potential job seekers do have difficulty finding any available job during a period of search and that employers have difficulty filling a similar percentage of jobs. If we omit Los Angeles from the pooled sample, the mismatch rate range is 7 to 16 percent. The lower estimates are obtained using method 1, where the different tasks are treated as substitutes for one another. Method 2, which assumes that reading-writing of paragraphs and arithmetic might be less easily learned on the job than computer use or customer contact, generates a greater degree of simulated mismatch.

The overall mismatch rate rises somewhat when we do not allow less-skilled workers to compete equally with more-skilled workers on jobs requiring less skill, and it also rises somewhat when we allow workers initially to seek jobs outside their race-transportation cells in proportion to where such jobs exist. But, overall, the results are relatively robust across our different assumptions of how the matching process operates. Simulated mismatch rates, using method 1 and averaged across the four metropolitan areas, are in the range of 9 to 13 percent when we incorporate these different assumptions into our algorithms.

How do these implied mismatch rates compare with observed joblessness? Can we reconcile these findings with observed aggregate unemployment rates that have been below 5 percent nationally (and in these MSAs) during much of the past three years? Our results cannot be compared directly to aggregate unemployment rates because our sample is limited to job seekers, who constitute under half of all labor force participants. We also include "potential" job seekers (13 percent of our sample) who are currently out of the labor force. If potential job seekers have much higher mismatch rates than do labor force participants, then our results are consistent with observed aggregate unemployment rates of 5 percent or less.[30]

We test this proposition by computing mismatch rates for job seekers separately by their current employment or labor force status. Since we cannot identify exactly which individuals in a cell will be mismatched at any point in time, we can only approximate mismatch rates for these different groups, and differences across groups in mismatch rates will be biased downward by measurement error.[31] Nevertheless, these approximations generate mismatch rates that look quite reasonable when using method 1.[32] Our mismatch rates (excluding Los Angeles) by labor force status are .06, .11, and .18 for the employed, the unemployed, and those out of the labor force, respectively. The average mismatch rate of .07 for those in the labor force is thus consistent with the aggregate unemployment rate.

An alternative approach compares our simulated mismatch rates with durations of unemployment and nonemployment experienced by working-age groups (especially nonstudents and males) in the population. If we assume that individuals facing high probabilities of mismatch will experience lengthy spells of unemployment (for labor market participants) or nonemployment (for those unemployed or out of the labor force), then our mismatch rates should be comparable to the percentages of the relevant groups who experience long spells without work.[33]

In fact, Murphy and Topel (1987) and Juhn, Murphy, and Topel (1991) report dramatic increases in the fractions of prime-age males with lengthy durations of nonemployment during the 1970s and 1980s, mostly concentrated among those in the bottom 10 to 20 percent of the wage distribution—including high school dropouts. Indeed, the rates and durations of nonemployment implied by Juhn, Murphy, and Topel among prime-age males are quite consistent with the results presented in table 11.5.[34]

We found large differences in mismatch rates across the different metropolitan areas. Mismatch rates in Atlanta and Boston appear relatively low, while in Detroit and especially Los Angeles they are higher, even when these markets are in aggregate balance. These differences are most likely due to the relatively higher educational attainment among workers in Atlanta and Boston than among workers in Detroit and Los Angeles. The percentage of workers who are dropouts is especially pronounced in Los Angeles, due to the higher concentration of Hispanics there. The educational attainment of blacks in Atlanta is also considerably higher than in Detroit, likely reflecting a relative out-migration of young educated blacks from Detroit and an in-migration to Atlanta over the past few decades.[35] Data from the 1990 census also indicate that racial segregation is somewhat lower in Atlanta (Frey and Farley 1993), perhaps contributing to (or reflecting) less spatial mismatch and/or racial discrimination there.

If job availability is more limited for disadvantaged workers in Detroit and Los Angeles than in Atlanta and Boston due to structural factors, relative unemployment rates in the former MSAs should be higher over an extended period of time. This is exactly what we find: throughout most of the 1980s and 1990s, annual unemployment rates in Detroit and Los Angeles exceeded those in Atlanta and Boston. Some shifts in the relative rankings of unemployment rates among the four areas occurred over this period, no doubt reflecting other factors (such as the strength of the local economy, migration rates, and so on) affecting local unemployment.[36] The high unemployment rate among Hispanics (as well as blacks) in Los Angeles is also consistent with this finding.[37]

How is any overall amount of mismatch between workers and jobs distributed across various skill, race, and transportation categories? In other words, who are the workers not placed into any jobs, and what are the jobs that are most difficult to fill? Under both methods, most workers who are mismatched are those who can do only zero to one task per job. Workers with previous experience or training in blue-collar or service jobs also account for the majority of the mismatched persons. *None of the mismatched jobs in our simulations require college degrees*, since there is an adequate supply of college-educated labor relative to jobs that require these credentials. In contrast, virtually all mismatched jobs require three to four tasks, and many require clerical or sales experience.

Mismatched workers and jobs are split fairly evenly between those having or requiring high school and those that do not, although the proportions accounted for by workers who are dropouts are significantly lower using method 1.[38] As for racial and transportation factors, a majority of mismatched workers are nonblacks with cars; of course, these are also the characteristics of the vast majority of workers. In relative terms, black workers (and/or those without cars) are most likely to be mismatched, as our results indicate.

Table 11.6 presents simulated mismatch rates for workers by race or gender, and by education and/or welfare status within each. Results presented in the first section of the table are calculated using method 1; those in the second section of the table using method 2. Results are presented separately by MSA and are pooled across samples that include or exclude Los Angeles.

Overall mismatch rates are lower among males than among females.[39] But blacks and Hispanics have much higher rates of mismatch, and thus face lower job availability, than do whites, even controlling for

TABLE 11.6   *Lack of Job Availability for Various Worker Groups: Percentage of Each Group That Is Mismatched*

	Atlanta	Boston	Detroit	Los Angeles	Total	Total, Excluding Los Angeles
Method 1						
Black-Hispanic						
Total	.114	.177	.179	.245	.179	.157
High school graduates	.144	.141	.152	.162	.150	.146
High school dropouts	.376	.354	.501	.444	.419	.410
Welfare recipients	.351	.190	.283	.237	.265	.275
White						
Total	.055	.028	.063	.066	.053	.049
High school graduates	.084	.026	.058	.082	.063	.056
High school dropouts	.181	.171	.222	.396	.242	.191
Welfare recipients	.155	.094	.091	.147	.122	.113
Male						
Total	.050	.043	.086	.166	.086	.060
High school graduates	.069	.063	.087	.137	.089	.073
High school dropouts	.187	.247	.346	.414	.299	.260
Female						
Total	.092	.047	.099	.166	.101	.079
High school graduates	.128	.026	.076	.119	.087	.077
High school dropouts	.436	.205	.308	.466	.353	.316
Welfare recipients	.297	.129	.202	.163	.196	.209
Method 2						
Black-Hispanic						
Total	.199	.369	.292	.293	.288	.287
High school graduates	.251	.379	.263	.272	.291	.298
High school dropouts	.645	.491	.636	.462	.559	.591
Welfare recipients	.495	.401	.415	.258	.392	.437
White						
Total	.120	.089	.168	.063	.110	.126
High school graduates	.193	.124	.184	.009	.150	.167

TABLE 11.6   *Continued*

	Atlanta	Boston	Detroit	Los Angeles	Total	Total, Excluding Los Angeles
High school dropouts	.298	.308	.411	.441	.365	.339
Welfare recipients	.293	.152	.161	.143	.202	.187
Male						
Total	.117	.113	.209	.208	.162	.146
High school graduates	.170	.204	.238	.228	.210	.204
High school dropouts	.210	.377	.548	.413	.387	.378
Female						
Total	.167	.132	.182	.217	.175	.160
High school graduates	.243	.125	.166	.190	.181	.178
High school dropouts	.427	.343	.466	.516	.438	.412
Welfare recipients	.433	.244	.306	.177	.290	.328

Source: Multi-City Study of Urban Inequality.

educational attainment. High school graduates are much more likely to obtain jobs than are high school dropouts. For both dropouts and welfare recipients, mismatch rates are very high, particularly among minorities. For instance, in the total sample, white welfare recipients have a mismatch rate of 12.2 percent under Method 1, and white dropouts a rate of 24.2 percent. Comparable numbers for blacks-Hispanics are 26.5 percent for welfare recipients and 41.9 percent for dropouts. Rates are substantially higher for all these groups using method 2. The omission of Los Angeles from the sample actually increases some estimates of mismatch for minorities, since blacks constitute the overwhelming majority of minorities outside Los Angeles, and they appear to have higher rates of mismatch in many cases than do Hispanics from Los Angeles.

These results suggest that a large percentage of high school dropouts or welfare recipients will have difficulty finding work. Indeed, current actual employment rates among young high school dropouts are extremely low, especially among blacks.[40] Our predictions that up to 20 percent of white and 40 percent of minority welfare recipients will not find work bear striking similarity to the roughly 30 percent of welfare recipients who permanently fail to work under a variety of different circumstances and interventions.[41]

Comparing results across the different metropolitan areas generates some additional findings. Minorities, dropouts, and welfare recipients have higher mismatch rates than whites and/or high school graduates in each metropolitan area. The variance across areas in simulated mismatch rates for whites, and for high school graduates of any racial group, is not very high; in contrast, it is the disadvantaged groups who bear the brunt of "mismatch" unemployment and who are most sensitive to variations across areas in market structure or demographics.

Blacks overall do relatively well in Atlanta, where residential segregation is somewhat less severe than in Detroit and other northern metropolitan areas (Holzer 1996a). Black dropouts and welfare recipients do very poorly in Detroit, a highly segregated metropolitan area that has experienced significant industrial job loss over the past few decades.

To what extent do the specific demand-side barriers considered (that is, skills, transportation, and race) account for the rates of mismatch? The data in tables 11.1 through 11.3 suggest that task performance and occupation-specific skills are the major contributors to mismatch problems for these groups. Indeed, analysis of the characteristics of workers actually hired into these jobs confirms this result (Holzer 1996b).

To obtain further evidence on this question, we recalculated the mismatch rates with various categories of jobs and workers "collapsed." For instance, we ran one set of simulations in which no distinct categories were used for task performance; in another set, no categories were used for occupational experience or training. Since we collapsed these categories one by one, we can compare across the calculated mismatch rates and infer the extent to which each barrier is responsible for job availability problems.

These results confirmed what was suggested by the summary data of tables 11.1 through 11.3, namely, that ability to perform tasks is the primary determinant of overall mismatch. When the task categories were collapsed, simulated mismatch rates fell by roughly three-fourths using method 1 and even more with method 2. Occupation-specific experience or training requirements accounted for much of the remaining aggregate mismatch. In contrast, educational attainment and spatial access (and even race) had little effect on simulated mismatch rates overall, although they clearly had some effect on the distribution of overall mismatch across racial-education groups. In other words, spatial factors and racial barriers generated more mismatch among black employees and less among white employees.

Discussion

It is important to acknowledge possible biases in our simulations of "mismatch" or job availability, both upward and downward. For instance, in analyzing spatial imbalances, we assume that any establishment within one-half mile of a public transit stop is accessible to anyone without a car, without considering the difficulty of getting to that transit stop or other space-related problems (relating to information, distance from central city, perceptions of hostility, and so on). We also assume that there is no discrimination against blacks in hiring at any establishment that currently employs at least some blacks in noncollege positions and there are no other employment barriers (whether caused by discrimination, child care problems, or something else) facing other minority groups or women; a GED is the equivalent of a high school diploma to employers requiring the latter; the tasks that can be performed by people who do not work are the same as those with similar demographic characteristics who do work; and most important, the overall numbers of jobs and workers are comparable when the overall market is in balance. The last assumption is clearly incorrect during recessions or any time when local labor markets have a fair amount of "slack." All these assumptions may have led to our overpredicting job availability for less-educated workers. The underrepresentation of some members of disadvantaged groups, such as young black males, in our household sample should also tend to reduce our computed mismatch rates.[42]

In contrast, other assumptions may have led us to underpredict job availability. For instance, we assume that employer skill requirements are fixed and that a credential that is "strongly preferred" is equivalent to one that is "absolutely necessary." This may not be true, especially if the willingness of employers to hire minorities or less-educated workers into jobs requiring various credentials or tasks rises in a very tight market (see, for example, Freeman 1991).[43] We may even understate the degree of market tightness that can exist at the peak of the cycle (as in 1998 to 2000) when we posit equal overall *numbers* of job seekers and jobs and look only at the distributions of each across various categories. An excess of jobs over workers in the aggregate or in major sectors might currently exist, though it is unlikely to persist for long without generating inflation.[44]

It is also possible that a higher percentage of low-skill jobs exists than we measured. For instance, our sampling procedure weighted establishments by current *employment*, rather than new hires. As noted, we counted each high-turnover job that generates several new hires per year as just one job, even though it may *temporarily* employ several low-skill workers in that year. Establishments experiencing net employment growth are also underrepresented, although this could lead to either an upward or downward bias in skill requirements. Other types of establishments are underrepresented as well. For instance, the high mismatch rates in Los Angeles, presumably attributable to the higher percentages of less-educated Hispanics and Asians there, might be upward-biased to the extent that we had difficulty including establishments from the informal and/or "ethnic" economies in our sample of employers.[45]

Perhaps most important, our measures of workers' abilities to perform tasks are based on their having done so on a previous job. Previous work may not accurately reflect current abilities, especially with regard to tasks such as computer use, where learning on the job is possible.

On the other hand, the rates of return to the performance of these skills rose substantially during the 1980s and remain high today (Murnane, Willett, and Levy 1995; Holzer 1996b); it is unclear why workers would choose to forgo these returns if they are capable of performing these tasks. Furthermore, poor cognitive skills have been observed among large proportions of disadvantaged groups, such as long-term welfare recipients (Burtless 1995; O'Neill and O'Neill 1997; Pavetti 1997), and employment rates for women with poor skills have been extremely low, regardless of whether they are on welfare.[46] Our finding that significant percentages of job seekers, especially in the disadvantaged groups, cannot perform the tasks demanded by current jobs seems quite plausible in light of these results.

Overall, we cannot measure the net effect of all the potential upward or downward biases. Relative to current aggregate unemployment rates, our simulated mismatch rates look comparable (at least using method 1, and the striking similarities between our estimates and those of nonemployment durations among less-educated workers also lead us to believe that the net bias is probably not large. Given this uncertainty, we interpret our estimates as the first results of a new analytical exercise rather than as the final word on this topic.

Conclusion

Are jobs available for all workers who seek them, especially among the disadvantaged? This question has been at the heart of many academic and public policy debates about poverty and welfare, but little solid evidence has been available to date to help answer it.

In this chapter, we compare the characteristics of actual or potential job seekers with those of available jobs in four metropolitan areas. We simulate a labor market process by which workers are "matched" to jobs on the basis of the skills, location-transportation, and racial characteristics of each. We then calculate the percentage of each that are "mismatched," which reflects the percentages of workers who have difficulty finding work and of jobs that are difficult for employers to fill.

We find that roughly 9 to 17 percent of actual and potential job seekers will have difficulty finding work in the short term. The mismatch rates vary across metropolitan areas, with Atlanta and Boston having lower rates than Detroit and Los Angeles.

Black workers, high school dropouts, and welfare recipients appear to have the greatest difficulty finding work. The mismatches are caused mostly by difficulties these workers have in gaining jobs that require large numbers of tasks or occupation-specific skills. Furthermore, our calculations suggest that up to 20 percent of white and 40 percent of minority welfare recipients face limited job availability in the short term (even without considering problems such as physical or emotional disabilities or substance abuse). Furthermore, to the extent that many less-skilled workers do find jobs, many of the jobs have high turnover rates, pay very low starting wages, and offer few benefits.

These simulations required us to make a large number of assumptions. We tested the sensitivity of our results to several and found them to be fairly robust. We also found our results to be consistent with data on nonemployment rates and durations.

Many of the workers who are "mismatched" will not face permanent unemployment, nor will the unfilled jobs be permanently vacant. Over time, new job openings will become available that should generate at least some job opportunities for these individuals. But, at a minimum, we expect lengthy durations of nonemployment for workers and vacancies for jobs in these cases.

Both workers and employers have potential ways of adjusting their behaviors in response to a lack of available jobs or workers, especially over the medium or long run. For instance, workers can (and do) migrate to local areas with tighter labor markets, or they can obtain more education or job training. Similarly, employers can reduce their hiring requirements, recruit more heavily (especially in more distant locations), provide more remedial training, or generate more jobs in response to the surplus of workers (perhaps at lower wages). Nevertheless, the costs in the short run to the workers who cannot easily find jobs might be considerable.

Are the simulated high mismatch rates for welfare recipients consistent with recent evidence of declining caseloads and rising employment in the wake of the 1996 welfare reform legislation? The dramatic drops in caseloads, especially in the context of very tight labor markets nationwide, have led to optimism about the ability of our economy to absorb these workers (see, for example, Mead 1996; *Detroit Free Press* 1997). To date, however, evidence on the actual labor market experiences of those leaving the rolls is somewhat mixed, as noted earlier. Previous evidence has indicated that unemployment rates *at any point in time* are quite high for participants in "welfare-to-work" programs, even though most gain employment eventually (Maynard 1995). Furthermore, the individuals who are hardest to employ are less likely to have entered the labor market (McMurrer, Sawhill, and Lerman 1997), and the current tightness of labor markets will certainly not last indefinitely (Holzer, 1999).

These factors are all consistent with our estimates, which suggest that most welfare recipients are potentially employable, even though a substantial minority (30 to 40 percent overall) are not. The group that will have difficulty finding work is likely larger than the 20 percent of recipients whom the new federal law allows states to exempt from five-year time limits. Our estimates are also consistent with those of other researchers who have found similar percentages of recipients to be unemployable because of personal handicaps and limitations. Those who find work will often be plagued by high turnover and/or low wages and benefits in their jobs.[47]

To the extent that welfare recipients and others lack the skills currently demanded by employers, and that these skill deficiencies are primarily responsible for the observed rates of mismatch, public policies should concentrate on improving education and job training for the disadvantaged over the long term. The unfilled jobs in our simulations do not require college degrees but instead involve basic cognitive or social task performance and/or occupational experience (primarily in clerical or sales jobs). These jobs could potentially be accessible to disadvantaged workers who receive better education or job training.

As David O'Neill and June O'Neill (1997) and others have emphasized, preventing dependency by improving the cognitive skills of disadvantaged young people is likely to be a more successful strategy than trying to dramatically raise the skills of those who have already "failed" in the classroom and job market. "School-to-work" programs that provide young people with the relevant occupational experience and training for available jobs could play an important role as well.

Our results also suggest some role for transportation and job placement assistance to deal with spatial imbalances in the labor market, and for improved enforcement of Equal Employment Opportunity (EEO) laws to overcome racial discrimination. Although these problems do not account for much of the overall mismatch, they put less-educated blacks at a disadvantage relative to comparable whites. Transportation assistance and strengthened EEO enforcement would improve the relative standing of black workers, even if they did not dramatically reduce the overall rate of structural unemployment.

Furthermore, our results suggest that many currently disadvantaged workers will likely face limited job availability in the short term. This will be particularly true in some geographic areas (that is, those with relatively high unemployment, or with large concentrations of welfare recipients and low-income minorities) and at some points in time (that is, during cyclical downturns). Thus, a need will continue for job-creation efforts by the government, either through subsidies to the private sector or through public-service employment.[48] In addition, the low wages of disadvantaged workers, and their need for services such as child care, medical care, and transportation assistance, must also be addressed.[49]

Finally, we need further research on issues of short-term job availability facing disadvantaged workers. Some can be accomplished with the types of data on workers and jobs used in this study, while other approaches will be developed as new categories of data appear (such as matched longitudinal data on employers and workers). A better understanding of how workers adjust to a lack of job availability in the long run (in terms of their migration, training, and other choices), and of employer responses to lengthy vacancy durations, is critical as well.

Appendix: Simulation Methods

The matching simulations begin by allocating workers and jobs to matrices based on the skill, spatial, and racial characteristics of each. To proxy for the racial and spatial characteristics of employers and workers, we specify whether an establishment currently employs any blacks (in its noncollege jobs), and whether it is accessible to workers without cars. Employers were asked how far their establishment is located from the nearest public transit stop. If it is within a half-mile of a stop, we assume that it is accessible by public transit.[50] On the supply side, we note whether or not workers have access to automobiles when they search or work, and whether or not they are black.

Our measures of skills focus on three characteristics: education, occupation-specific experience or training, and performance of various cognitive or social tasks. Educational requirements include whether or not the employer requires college or high school degrees. Occupation-specific requirements include whether or not the job requires previous experience in the relevant line of work or some type of skill certification from previous vocational training.[51]

For workers, we consider whether or not they have college or high school diplomas and whether or not they report any work experience or training in the relevant occupation.[52] Work experience is measured by the occupation of their current or most recent job, while training may have occurred at any time in the past. We categorize the occupations into four broad groups—professional or managerial, clerical or sales, craft or operative, and laborer or service—as well as a fifth category of jobs requiring (and people reporting) no experience or training.[53]

The cognitive or social tasks performed on jobs are: direct contact with customers (in person or over the phone), reading or writing of paragraph-length material, use of arithmetic, and use of computers. We consider whether or not each is required in jobs or used by workers on a daily basis.

We use two different simulation methods for matching workers to jobs, based on two different underlying matrices of skills-race-space. The primary difference between them is that one places less emphasis on task performance and more on educational attainment and spatial location than does the other. In the first approach (method 1), we simply sum over the number of tasks used daily (which varies from 0 to 4) and create three categories based on this sum: 0 to 1, 2, and 3 to 4. In the second (method 2), we generate twelve combinations of particular skills, with reading-writing and arithmetic given more priority than customer contact and computer use. The combinations are then ranked in terms of skills used or required.[54]

Thus, method 1 treats all tasks the same (and assumes that a person who can perform one task can perform any job that requires only one task), whereas method 2 allows for nonsubstitutability, which may be more realistic. That is, a worker who has never held a job requiring arithmetic is considered ineligible for a job that requires this task, even if he has performed two other tasks, such as customer contact or reading-writing. Because method 2 requires more task categories, we collapse other dimensions of skill, race, and space. Therefore, we do not distinguish high school graduation or dropping out and spatial location-automobile use in this method.[55]

Workers were asked about their task performance on their current or most recent job, based on the same task list used with the employers. These questions were asked only of those reporting a recent job. We therefore *predicted* task performance for each person not reporting them, based on their race, gender, education, and age. These predictions were needed for only about 7 percent of the sample.[56] Also, the task and occupation-specific requirements are specified only for people without (and jobs not requiring) college degrees; we assume that college graduates can obtain jobs that require college or professional or managerial jobs not requiring a college diploma.

Taken together, these categories yield matrices with 124 cells for each method. In method 1, we have three job tasks × five occupations ×

two educational categories (high school versus no high school) plus one cell (for college graduates without regard to tasks or occupation), thus generating thirty-one skill categories × two spatial (accessible or not accessible by public transit) × two racial (firm has or does not have black workers) categories. These are computed separately for jobs and for workers in each of the four metropolitan areas.[57] For method 2, we have the same number of cells in the matrix, with twelve task categories but none for educational attainment below college or for space or transportation.

Throughout the analysis, we assume that workers have no access to jobs that require higher skills than they have, but less-skilled and more-skilled workers compete equally for jobs where both are qualified. We also assume that, *conditional on meeting skill requirements*, nonblack workers can obtain jobs in any establishment, whereas blacks can obtain jobs only in establishments with at least some current black employees. In addition, those with cars can obtain jobs in any establishment in method 1 whereas those without cars can obtain jobs only in any establishments accessible by public transit.

In our simulations, workers initially seek employment in some subset of the jobs to which they have access; if they do not obtain these jobs, they flow to other cells with comparable skill requirements that are accessible to them, and then to those that require just a bit less skill, and so on, until they are matched to jobs. The first workers matched are thus the most skilled. For instance, in method 1 workers with college degrees are first matched to jobs requiring college. If all of them are not matched, the remaining ones flow to cells requiring only a high school degree in the professional or managerial category with three to four tasks, then to those with two tasks, and so on. A similar process then occurs for workers with only high school degrees who can do three to four tasks in each occupational category. Those people with occupational experience who do not get placed at any task level within their current occupation then flow to the category with no occupational requirements but with high school required and with the highest level of tasks that they can perform. High school graduates who are not matched to any job requiring high school then flow to the highest task jobs that they can handle in the relevant occupational category among jobs not requiring high school, until as many as possible are placed. Finally, workers without high school degrees are placed in jobs not requiring high school, following a similar pattern. Similar flows are specified in method 2 across task and occupational categories.

For each method, we have calculated mismatch rates in which we relax some of the assumptions embodied in the basic simulation. For instance, all workers initially seek employment in the cells in which they are located in the basic simulation, but in other variations we allow people to pursue jobs for which they are qualified wherever they are located.[58] We also assume initially that blacks or less-educated workers have no access at all to certain jobs, but in other cases we allow those workers to have access to the more restricted jobs once all qualified whites or more-educated workers have been placed.

Notes

1. For arguments that job availability will not be a serious problem for most welfare recipients, even though wages will be low, see Burtless 1995 and Blank 1995. For a more skeptical view, see Holzer 1996b and Bane 1997.

2. While most of those leaving the rolls gain some employment within a year, about 40 percent are not employed at the survey time (Loprest, 1999). Also, many states have only begun to place the most disadvantaged recipients in jobs (McMurrer, Sawhill, and Lerman 1997).

3. Demand-side effects on employment outcomes of individuals in supply-side data are usually estimated by the effects of proxies measured for the local geographic area (measured by Metropolitan Statistical Area or state), such as average employment growth, unemployment rates, or industrial composition. See, for instance, Freeman 1991, Hoynes 1996, and Bound and Holzer 1996. Instead, we use data from individual employers.

4. In this case, unemployment will exist only insofar as people need time to search for their most attractive job offers; in other words, only "frictional" unemployment would exist, which would presumably be short-term.

5. The causes of downward wage rigidities include minimum-wage laws and unions. But in many cases, employers choose to pay wages above the market-clearing levels (or "efficiency wages"), perhaps because it helps attract, motivate, and/or retain better workers (for example, Katz 1986; Campbell and Kamlani 1997).

6. The particular labor markets, and the mismatches that exist between them, can be based on differences across workers and firms in skills, geographic location, and so on.

7. The same would be true of other attempts to estimate "disequilibrium" components of unemployment rates using econometric techniques with aggregate data (for example, Quandt 1988; Neumark and Wascher 1995). These papers use "endogenous switching regression" models in which some markets are in equilibrium and some are not; an equation based on whether wages or prices are at

market-clearing levels is used to determine which case holds for any given year or local area.

8. Holzer (1986) finds that racial differences in reservation wages can account for 30 to 40 percent of the racial differences in unemployment durations and somewhat smaller portions of differences in unemployment rates. Stephen Petterson (1997) fails to find any relationship between these measures using updated data, although the estimated effects of reservation wages in these equations are likely to be downward-biased. Also, the notion that reservation wages for many of these workers are higher than their market wages is implicit in Chinhui Juhn's (1992) analysis of labor market withdrawals in response to declining wages, although the availability of work at these wages is assumed rather than demonstrated.

9. Holzer (1996b) does not compute the numbers of workers with very poor skills who are actually seeking these jobs, and Katherine Newman and Chauncy Lennon (1995) do not determine the number of applications filed by each job seeker, which is needed for determining the actual ratio of job seekers to jobs.

10. Both studies determine a low cutoff point (somewhat arbitrarily) for average education or skill that classifies an *entire* occupation as accessible to recipients. Leonard Bloomquist, Leif Jensen, and Ruy Teixeira (1988) then use a predicted aggregate vacancy rate (based on an aggregate relationship between unemployment and vacancies) to determine the actual number of jobs available in an occupation. Paul Kleppner and Nikolas Theodore (1997) use job hire rates by industry that are matched to occupational categories using occupation-by-industry matrices. Therefore, the numbers of jobs in the relevant occupational categories are measured quite loosely in both cases.

11. More details on sampling, response rates, and so on can be found in Holzer (1996b). Sample weights that have been generated for each data source will be used in all calculations.

12. Because some firms hire much more frequently than others, a sample of one hire per firm may underrepresent firms that hire frequently. Because the sample of employers has already been size-weighted, large firms that hire many workers are heavily represented in the sample. Establishments that hire a lot because of high turnover are not overrepresented, since we care about the underlying number of jobs that are available. Establishments that hire many workers in response to net employment growth will, however, be underrepresented here. The median length of time that elapsed between the time of the last hire and the survey date is two months, but the mean is six months. Roughly 90 percent of the jobs in the sample were filled within a year of the survey date.

13. The Household Survey was administered between 1992 and 1994. At the time of the survey, roughly 20 percent of those out of the labor force whom we include in our sample were welfare recipients, while over 60 percent reported some work experience in the preceding five years. Since that time, cuts in various benefit programs (such as welfare, food stamps, and Supplemental Security Income), as well as much tighter labor markets, have no doubt drawn many of those individuals back into the workforce. Impending work requirements and time limits on welfare and food stamp recipients will likely continue this trend over the next several years.

14. Patricia Anderson and Bruce Meyer (1994) report that 42 percent of workers in each year experience some permanent job turnover. Some of these people leave the labor force but are replaced by those entering (or reentering), therefore the percentage of people seeking work in any year should be quite similar.

15. These multiple spells should have no effects on the outcomes that we calculate since they likely "net out" across the two sides of the labor market.

16. The interactions across the different dimensions are critical, since obvious correlations exist between these characteristics (especially among workers). For instance, unskilled workers are also more likely than skilled workers to be black and to lack their own cars. To do the matching separately (and then sum across the three dimensions) would be equivalent to assuming that skill and spatial and racial characteristics are independent of one another. We suspect that this sum might dramatically overstate the extent of mismatch.

17. As noted earlier, the absolute number of jobs available at any moment need not equal the number of job seekers for the labor market to be in balance, so comparing absolute levels of jobs and people would be misleading. Data availability issues also support this choice, since we do not have data on the actual numbers of new hires in each establishment with such detailed job characteristics. Our size-weighted sample of one new hire per establishment approximates the correct sample, but is more appropriate for considering the relative composition of newly available jobs than their exact numbers.

18. By definition, the surplus of workers will always equal the absolute value of the shortage of jobs, as quantities in both sets of cells must sum to 100 percent.

19. For instance, if more-skilled and/or white workers "dominate" less-skilled or black workers even when the latter are considered "qualified," unemployment will be concentrated among the latter.

On the other hand, these groups might compete equally for jobs in which all are considered "qualified," although some are "overqualified." In the latter case, the same overall unemployment will be spread more equally across groups. In economics jargon, the question is who can be considered a "substitute" for whom.

20. Suburban workers with relatively high skills and/or access to all jobs might choose to seek employment in the inner city because wages are higher there or because the best jobs in the field happen to be located there, as might be the case with large hospitals, law firms, or other institutions in a metropolitan area.

21. These choices are made at least partly to simplify the analysis and partly because the evidence suggests greater discrimination in *employment* (as opposed to wages) against blacks (especially black men) than against other minorities or women (Holzer 1996b; Kirschenman and Neckerman 1991). To the extent that women, and especially Hispanics, face employment difficulties because of skills or spatial problems, our calculations will reflect those problems.

   The assumption that blacks face no hiring discrimination in companies where at least some blacks are currently present is also questionable; however, over 60 percent of these establishments are large (100 or more employees) and/or report using affirmative action. The evidence suggests less employment discrimination against blacks at such establishments (Holzer and Neumark 1996; Holzer 1997).

22. "Soft" skills are often described as social or verbal skills and attitudes toward work. These are partly captured through our use of customer contact as a skill requirement and by having clerical or sales jobs (where such skills are presumably quite important) as a distinct occupational category. Because "soft skills" and race appear to be highly correlated in the perceptions of employers (Moss and Tilly 1995), our racial categories should capture some of these effects as well.

23. Roughly 37 percent of job seekers in Atlanta and Boston have college degrees, while this is true of just 21 to 24 percent in Detroit and Los Angeles. High school dropouts constitute 5 to 12 percent of job seekers in each area except Los Angeles, where they account for 23 percent.

24. Thirty-one percent of black job seekers in our Atlanta sample have college degrees, while this is true of just 12 to 16 percent of job seekers in the other metropolitan areas.

25. Sample sizes are very small for whites on welfare, especially among those who are also high school dropouts. Yet the pattern of results we observe for whites versus minorities in this table is consistent across the various subsamples that we use.

26. LaDonna Pavetti (1995) notes that 63 percent of welfare recipients with at least five years on the rolls are high school dropouts, and over half are black or Hispanic.

27. Most employer interviews were administered in 1993, although some were conducted in late 1992 or early 1994. The wage results can thus be interpreted as being in 1993 dollars.

28. We define "part-time work" as anything less than thirty-five hours per week. Of course, most of those working in part-time jobs do so voluntarily, although the rates of involuntary part-time work have been rising over time among men (Blank 1997).

29. The availability of the Earned Income Tax Credit and Medicaid for low-wage workers with families will ease the hardships associated with work at these jobs.

30. If mismatch accounts for 2 to 3 percentage points of aggregate un- employment, this would be comparable to 4 to 7 percentage points among job seekers who are currently in the labor force. To generate average mismatch rates among job seekers of .07 to .16 (excluding Los Angeles), mismatch among those out of the labor force would have to be in the range of roughly 7 to 40 percent using method 1, and much higher using method 2.

31. In other words, we may know that 50 percent of the job seekers in a cell are mismatched, but not which individuals in that cell will get the jobs and which will not. Our method of approximation involves allocating different groups of individuals (for example, the employed versus the nonemployed) across cells of the matrix and then applying the mismatch rate simulated for that cell to all individuals allocated there. A weighted average of mismatch rates across the cells for each group then generates the approximate mismatch rate for that group. But by assuming the same mismatch rate for all individuals in a cell, and not taking into account unobserved differences across individ- uals in the cell that might be correlated with group membership (in this case, employment status), the approximations are likely to cause downward biases in our estimates of differences in mismatch between groups. Only when the groups in question correspond to the actual characteristics used to match workers and jobs (education, occupation, race, and so on) will the mismatch rates for these groups be measured more accurately.

32. The approximations using method 2 (which generate mismatch rates of roughly .13 for those in the labor force) are too high.

33. See Kim Clark and Lawrence Summers (1982) for a discussion of the differences between unemployment and nonemployment dura- tions.

34. Chinhui Juhn, Kevin Murphy, and Robert Topel (1991) report roughly 5.7 weeks of nonemployment per year among prime-age

males, for a rate of about 11 percent at any point in time. They also report that 69 percent of nonemployment is accounted for by those whose spells are longer than half a year. Thus, 7.6 percent of the male population is in a very long spell at any moment, and the percentage of all workers who experience such a spell in any year would be about 10 percent (as the average durations of such spells are thirty-nine weeks, or three-fourths of a year). Furthermore, wages and employment rates among the less-educated have contin-ued to deteriorate since the late 1980s (Mishel and Bernstein, 1996); and the data reported by Juhn, Murphy, and Topel also do not include those for workers below age twenty-five. Thus, the per-centage of the overall male population that currently experiences spells of more than six months could be as high as 15 percent. At least some of these lengthy spells no doubt represent supply-side factors, including physical disabilities, alternative income sources, and unwillingness to accept available low-wage jobs. If one-quarter to one-half of the total (4 to 8 percentage points) represents lack of job availability, these numbers would be quite consistent with our simulated mismatch rates (for the less than half of the population in our sample of job seekers).

35. John Bound and Harry Holzer (1996) show that young, educated blacks migrated as frequently in response to shifting local labor demand as did young, educated whites in the 1980s, and that the rate of growth in labor demand in Atlanta was considerably higher than in Detroit during that decade.

36. For most of the 1980s, the unemployment rate in Atlanta exceeded that in Boston, and unemployment in Detroit exceeded that in Los Angeles. During the 1990s, the relative rankings within each pair have been reversed, as the coastal economies weakened while the Midwest boomed and Atlanta enjoyed the economic effects of the Olympics. During the early to mid-1990s, unemployment rates av-eraged about 4 to 5 percent, 5 to 6 percent, 7 percent, and 10 per-cent in Atlanta, Boston, Detroit, and Los Angeles, respectively. Only in 1996 to 1997 did the unemployment rate in the Detroit MSA begin to approach those in Atlanta and Boston, while rates in the Midwest generally fell below those of all other regions.

37. The unemployment rates of non-Hispanic whites, blacks, and His-panics in Los Angeles in 1990 were 4.8 percent, 12 percent, and 10.1 percent, respectively.

38. These results are available in more detail from the authors.

39. Mismatch rates by gender vary somewhat within skill groups. For instance, female high school graduates are less likely than their male counterparts to be mismatched, but these females are more likely than males to be in this educational category (relative to college graduates).

40. In 1995, the labor force participation and unemployment rates of nonenrolled, sixteen- to twenty-four-year-old high school dropouts were 63.2 and 21.5 percent, respectively, implying an employment rate of just 49.6 percent (U.S. Department of Labor 1996). Among nonblacks and blacks, the employment rates are approximately 53 and 28 percent, respectively. These rates combine those for males and females, and the latter are no doubt influenced by childbearing and welfare recipiency. These data imply that the employment rates for young nonblack and black males (after adjusting for the likely differences by gender in participation rates) are approximately 60 and 40 percent, respectively.

41. For data on the employment rates over a ten-year period of anyone on welfare at the beginning of this period, see Burtless 1995; for evidence on the employment rates of recipients in fairly successful programs, such as the GAIN-Riverside program, see Maynard 1995. These figures generally do *not* include those welfare recipients who are often exempt from employment programs due to disabilities, substance abuse problems, and the like.

42. An "undercount" of black males exists in the census and in most other microlevel datasets.

43. Of the requirements listed for high school diplomas or occupational experience, roughly half are listed as "absolutely necessary," while the rest are "strongly preferred." Employers might be willing to forgo the latter in a tight market. But this is unlikely to be true in the very important area of task performance; as noted in the appendix, we count tasks as required if they are used daily.

44. Some of the "potential job seekers" we consider might not be very active searchers, even if they are counted as being in the labor force, due to the availability of unemployment insurance or other means of support (Rosenfeld 1977; Katz and Meyer 1990). Thus, an excess of available jobs over people actively seeking them could exist in the aggregate or in major sectors, although such excess demand should result in wage inflation. Furthermore, anecdotal reports of high job vacancy rates in recent years, if accurate, are just as consistent with our "mismatch" results as with an "excess labor demand" interpretation.

45. This might have occurred, because at least some of these establishments do not list phone numbers in directories, have owners or managers who do not speak English well, or have a greater distrust of answering formal questions in a survey.

46. Pavetti (1997) finds that over half of the women who have *ever* been on welfare during a ten-year period score in the bottom quartile of the Armed Forces Qualifying Test score distribution, and one-third score in the bottom decile; these numbers are no doubt higher for those currently on welfare, where those with long spells

will be overrepresented. Furthermore, roughly 60 percent of welfare recipients who have had very little labor force activity over this period (that is, who have been employed less than one-fourth of the time) fall in the bottom decile. Finally, Pavetti finds low employment rates (that is, under 50 percent) even for those who have very low test scores but have not been on welfare.

47. The greater ability of welfare recipients to find work, the greater will be the displacement of other less-skilled workers who must compete with them for jobs, causing lower wages and/or employment among the latter as well.

48. See Katz 1996 and Danziger and Gottschalk 1995 for discussions of these options.

49. In this vein, Edmund Phelps 1997 has argued for wage subsidies for disadvantaged workers, which would raise both their employment levels and their wages.

50. See Holzer and Ihlanfeldt 1996 for evidence that establishments located nearer to public transit are more likely to hire blacks. A transportation-based definition of spatial access will miss other sources of mismatch, such as the limited information that inner-city workers might have about suburban employers. Our measure of public transit captures only its proximity to employers, without capturing how difficult or time-consuming it might be for an inner-city resident to reach that employer by public transit. Nonetheless, a transportation-based measure is preferable to those based on arbitrarily drawn municipal boundaries. Furthermore, any other sources of difficulties that blacks have in gaining access to jobs will be at least partly captured by the racial composition of the firm.

51. Education, experience, or training is each considered "required" if the employer stated that it was "absolutely necessary" to be hired. A response of "strongly preferred" indicates that some candidates might be hired who lack the particular credential, especially in tight labor markets. We inquired separately about the educational attainments of workers hired into these jobs. Almost 95 percent of those hired met the stated educational requirements, and workers were much more likely to be overeducated than undereducated (relative to requirements).

52. We treated GEDs as equivalent to high school diplomas, since most employers who require a high school diploma indicated that they would hire someone with a GED. Evidence to the contrary (for example, Cameron and Heckman 1993) is based on the wages earned by workers rather than on employer willingness to hire them.

53. Given the small sample sizes in each dataset, narrower occupational definitions would generate a greater amount of mismatch that would be an artifact of the data, since many more cells on

both sides of the market would be unmatched. Our broad categories compensate for the fact that we observe only one previous job per person in defining the relevant work experience. The categories used here group together people and jobs of roughly comparable skill level, so that experience or training in one occupation suggests an individual's ability to obtain it in another occupation. Finally, the number of occupational categories had to be limited to keep the number of cells at a manageable level.

54. The twelve combinations, in order of skills required or used, are defined as follows: four broad categories are based on use of reading-writing and arithmetic, reading-writing but not arithmetic, arithmetic but not reading-writing, or neither; then within each of these categories, jobs can require (or workers can be skilled in) both computer use and customer contact, one or the other, or neither. The ranking of reading-writing and arithmetic over the others is based on the notion that computer use is frequently taught on the job to people without previous experience, while customer contact on these jobs earns workers no wage premium (Holzer 1996b) and also appears to be more easily "learnable" than the other skills.

55. Our decision to eliminate these categories in method 2 was based on empirical results from summary statistics and from simulations using method 1 indicating that these categories contribute little to overall rates of mismatch.

56. The predictions are based on regressions in which various measures of task performance are the dependent variables and the demographic variables listed here are the independent variables. These predictions are likely to be upward-biased, because nonemployed people are likely to have unobserved characteristics that are worse than those of comparable employed people. To fit the continuous predicted values into the categories used in the matrices, we round the predicted values to their nearest integers.

57. Workers cannot move easily across metropolitan areas in the short run, so we did not pool data across the four areas. We treat intermetropolitan locational differences as yet another spatial dimension, in addition to the intrametropolitan ones discussed. For evidence of the difficulties that black or less-educated workers have in relocating across metropolitan areas in response to demand shifts, see Bound and Holzer 1996.

58. This assumption generates more commuting behavior among suburban workers, of the type we observe in the data.

References

Abraham, Katherine. 1983. "Structural/Frictional vs. Demand Deficient Unemployment: Some New Evidence." *American Economic Review* 73: 708–24.

Anderson, Patricia, and Bruce Meyer. 1994. "The Extent and Consequences of Job Turnover." *Brookings Papers on Economic Activity—Microeconomics*. 177–248.

Bane, Mary Jo. 1997. "Welfare as We Might Know It." *American Prospect* 30(January–February): 47–53.

Blanchard, Olivier, and Lawrence Katz. 1997. "What We Know and Do Not Know About the Natural Rate of Unemployment." *Journal of Economic Perspectives* 11: 51–72.

Blank, Rebecca. 1995. "Outlook for the U.S. Labor Market and Prospects for Low-Wage Entry Jobs." In *The Work Alternative*, edited by Demetra Nightingale and Robert Haveman. Washington, D.C.: Urban Institute Press.

———. 1997. "Contingent Work in a Changing Labor Market." In *Demand-Side Strategies for Low-Wage Labor Markets*, edited by Richard Freeman and Peter Gottschalk. New York: Russell Sage Foundation.

Bloomquist, Leonard, Leif Jensen, and Ruy Teixeira. 1988. "Too Few Jobs for Workfare to Put Many to Work." *Rural Development Perspectives* 5: 8–12.

Bound, John, and Harry Holzer, 1996. "Demand Shifts, Population Adjustments, and Labor Market Outcomes During the 1980's." Working paper. Cambridge, Mass.: National Bureau of Economic Research.

Burtless, Gary. 1995. "The Employment Prospects of Welfare Recipients." In *The Work Alternative*, edited by Demetra Nightingale and Robert Haveman. Washington, D.C.: Urban Institute Press.

Cameron, Stephen, and James Heckman. 1993. "The Nonequivalence of High School Equivalents." *Journal of Labor Economics* 11: 1–47.

Campbell, Carl, and Kunal Kamlani. 1997. "The Reasons for Wage Rigidity: Evidence from a Survey of Firms." *Quarterly Journal of Economics* 112: 759–89.

Clark, Kim, and Lawrence Summers. 1982. "The Dynamics of Youth Unemployment." In *The Youth Labor Market Problem: Its Nature, Causes, and Consequences*, edited by Richard Freeman and David Wise. Chicago: University of Chicago Press.

Danziger, Sheldon, ed. 1999. *Economic Conditions and Welfare Reform*. Kalamazoo, Mich.: W. E. Upjohn Institute.

Danziger, Sheldon, and Peter Gottschalk. 1995. *America Unequal*. New York: Russell Sage Foundation.

Davidson, Carl. 1990. *Recent Developments in the Theory of Involuntary Unemployment*. Kalamazoo, Mich.: W. E. Upjohn Institute.

Detroit Free Press. 1997. "Welfare Rolls Slashed, Many People Find Jobs." August 12.

Freeman, Richard. 1991. "Employment and Earnings of Disadvantaged Young Men in a Labor Shortage Economy." In *The Urban Underclass*, edited by Christopher Jencks and Paul Peterson. Washington, D.C.: Brookings Institution.

Frey, William, and Reynolds Farley. 1993. "Latino, Asian and Black Segregation in Multi-Ethnic Metro Areas: Findings from the 1990

Census." Working paper. Ann Arbor: Population Studies Center, University of Michigan.

Gottschalk, Peter, and Timothy Smeeding. 1997. "Cross-national Comparisons of Earnings and Income Inequality." *Journal of Economic Literature* 35: 633–87.

Hauser, Robert, and Hanam Samuel Phang. 1993. "Trends in High School Dropout Among White, Black, and Hispanic Youth, 1973 to 1989." Discussion paper 1007-93. Madison: Institute for Research on Poverty, University of Wisconsin at Madison.

Holzer, Harry. 1986. "Reservation Wages and Their Labor Market Effects for Black and White Male Youth." *Journal of Human Resources* 21: 157–77.

———. 1989. *Unemployment, Vacancies, and Local Labor Markets.* Kalamazoo, Mich.: W. E. Upjohn Institute.

———. 1994. "Black Employment Problems: New Evidence, Old Questions." *Journal of Policy Analysis and Management* 13: 699–722.

———. 1996a. "Employer Demand, AFDC Recipients, and Labor Market Policy." Discussion Paper 1115-96. Institute for Research on Poverty, University of Wisconsin at Madison.

———. 1996b. *What Employers Want: Job Prospects for Less-Educated Workers.* New York: Russell Sage Foundation.

———. 1997. "Why Do Small Establishments Hire Fewer Blacks Than Large Ones?" Discussion paper 1119-97. Institute for Research on Poverty, University of Wisconsin at Madison.

———. 1999. "Employer Demand for Welfare Recipients and the Business Cycle." In *Economic Conditions and Welfare Reform*, edited by Sheldon Danziger. Kalamazoo, Mich.: W. E. Upjohn Institute.

Holzer, Harry, and Keith Ihlanfeldt. 1996. "Spatial Factors and the Employment of Blacks at the Firm Level." *New England Economic Review* (May/June): 65–82.

Holzer, Harry, and David Neumark. 1996. "Are Affirmative Action Hires Less Qualified? New Evidence from Employer-Employee Data." Working paper. Cambridge, Mass.: National Bureau of Economic Research.

Hoynes, Hilary. 1996. "Local Labor Markets and Welfare Spells: Do Demand Conditions Matter?" Working paper. Cambridge, Mass.: National Bureau of Economic Research.

Juhn, Chinhui. 1992. "Decline of Male Labor Market Participation: The Role of Declining Market Opportunities." *Quarterly Journal of Economics* 107: 79–121.

Juhn, Chinhui, Kevin Murphy, and Robert Topel. 1991. "Why Has the Natural Rate of Unemployment Increased over Time?" *Brookings Papers on Economic Activity*, no. 2: 75–126.

Katz, Lawrence. 1986. "Efficiency Wages: A Partial Evaluation." In *NBER Macroeconomics Annual*, vol. 1, edited by S. Fischer. Cambridge, Mass.: National Bureau of Economic Research.

———. 1996. "Wage Subsidies for the Disadvantaged." Working paper. Cambridge, Mass.: National Bureau of Economic Research.

Katz, Lawrence, and Bruce Meyer. 1990. "The Impact of the Potential Duration of Unemployment Benefits on the Duration of Unemployment." *Journal of Public Economics* 41: 45–72.

Kirschenman, Joleen, and Katherine Neckerman. 1991. " 'We'd Love to Hire Them But . . .' " In *The Urban Underclass*, edited by Christopher Jencks and Paul Peterson. Washington, D.C.: Brookings Institution.

Kleppner, Paul, and Nikolas Theodore. 1997. "Work After Welfare: Is the Midwest's Booming Economy Creating Enough Jobs?" Office for Social Policy Research, Northern Illinois University.

Levy, Frank, and Richard Murnane. 1992. "U.S. Earnings Levels and Earnings Inequality: A Review of Recent Evidence and Proposed Explanations." *Journal of Economic Literature* 30: 1333–81.

Loprest, Pamela. 1999. "How Families That Left Welfare Are Doing: A National Picture." *National Survey of America's Families*, Series B, no. B.1. Washington, D.C.: Urban Institute Press.

Maynard, Rebecca. 1995, "Subsidized Employment and Non-Labor Market Alternatives for Welfare Recipients." In *The Work Alternative*, edited by Demetra Nightingale and Robert Haveman. Washington, D.C.: Urban Institute Press.

McMurrer, Daniel, Isabel Sawhill, and Robert Lerman. 1997. "Welfare Reform and Opportunity in the Low-Wage Labor Market." Washington, D.C.: Urban Institute Press.

Mead, Lawrence. 1992. *The New Politics of Poverty: The Nonworking Poor in America*. New York: Basic Books.

———. 1996. "The Decline of Welfare in Wisconsin." *Wisconsin Policy Research Institute Report* 9(3): 1–46.

Mishel, Lawrence, and Jared Bernstein. 1996. *The State of Working America*. Armonk, N.Y.: M. E. Sharpe.

Moss, Philip, and Chris Tilly. 1995. "Soft Skills and Race." Working paper. New York: Russell Sage Foundation.

Murnane, Richard, John Willett, and Frank Levy. 1995. "The Growing Importance of Cognitive Skills in Wage Determination." Working paper. Cambridge, Mass.: National Bureau of Economic Research.

Murphy, Kevin, and Robert Topel. 1987. "The Evolution of Unemployment in the United States: 1968–1985." In *NBER Macroeconomics Annual*, vol. 2, edited by Stanley Fischer. Cambridge, Mass.: National Bureau of Economic Research.

Neumark, David, and William Wascher. 1995. "Minimum Wage Effects and Low-Wage Labor Markets: A Disequilibrium Approach." Working paper. Cambridge, Mass.: National Bureau of Economic Research.

Newman, Katherine, and Chauncy Lennon. 1995. "Finding Work in the Inner City; How Hard Is It Now? How Hard Will It Be for AFDC Recipients?" Unpublished paper. Columbia University.

O'Neill, David, and June O'Neill. 1997. *Lessons for Welfare Reform*. Kalamazoo, Mich: W. E. Upjohn Institute.

Pavetti, LaDonna. 1995. "Welfare Reform Options for Families Facing Personal or Family Challenges: Questions and Answers." Research paper. Washington, D.C.: Urban Institute Press.

———. 1997. "How Much More Can They Work? Setting Realistic Expectations for Welfare Mothers." Unpublished manuscript. Washington, D.C.: Urban Institute Press.

Petterson, Stephen. 1997. "Are Young Black Men Really Less Willing to Work?" *American Sociological Review* 62: 605–13.

Phelps, Edmund. 1997. *Rewarding Work: How to Restore Participation and Self-Support to Free Enterprise*. Cambridge, Mass.: Harvard University Press.

Quandt, Richard. 1988. *The Econometrics of Disequilibrium*. New York: Blackwell.

Rosenfeld, Carl. 1977. "Job Search of the Unemployed, May 1976." *Monthly Labor Review* 100(11): 39–43.

U.S. Department of Labor. U.S. Bureau of Labor Statistics. 1996. *Employment and Earnings*. Washington: U.S. Government Printing Office (February) 167.

Wilson, William J. 1987. *The Truly Disadvantaged: The Inner City, the Underclass, and Public Policy*. Chicago: University of Chicago Press.

———. 1996. *When Work Disappears: The World of the New Urban Poor*. New York: Knopf.

Index

Numbers in **boldface** refer to figures and tables.

Other Volumes in the Series